Of Populations

Eq. 5.2 90% confidence interval: $\overline{X} \pm 1.65\sigma_{\overline{X}}$

Eq. 5.3 95% confidence interval: $\overline{X} \pm 1.96\sigma_{\overline{X}}$

Eq. 5.4 99% confidence interval: $\overline{X} \pm 2.58\sigma_{\overline{X}}$

where $\sigma_{\overline{X}} = \dfrac{\sigma}{\sqrt{N}}$

EVALUATING DIFFERENCES

One-Sample

Eq. 6.1 $$t = \frac{\overline{X} - \mu}{\hat{\sigma}_{\overline{X}}} \quad \text{with df} = N - 1$$

where $\hat{\sigma}_{\overline{X}} = \dfrac{\hat{s}}{\sqrt{N}}$

Eq. 6.2 $$\chi^2 = \sum \frac{(f_o - f_e)^2}{f_e} \quad \text{with df} = k - 1$$

Two Independent Samples

Eq. 7.2 $$t_{\overline{X}_1 - \overline{X}_2} = \frac{(\overline{X}_1 - \overline{X}_2) - \mu_{\overline{X}_1 - \overline{X}_2}}{\hat{\sigma}_{\overline{X}_1 - \overline{X}_2}} \quad \text{with df} = N_1 + N_2 - 2$$

where $$\hat{\sigma}_{\overline{X}_1 - \overline{X}_2} = \sqrt{\left[\frac{(N_1 - 1)\hat{s}_1^2 + (N_2 - 1)\hat{s}_2^2}{N_1 + N_2 - 2}\right]\left[\frac{N_1 + N_2}{N_1 N_2}\right]}$$

Eq. 7.5 $$U = N_1 N_2 + \frac{N_1(N_1 + 1)}{2} - R_1$$

Eq. 7.7 $$\chi^2 = \sum \frac{(f_o - f_e)^2}{f_e} \quad \text{with df} = (R - 1)(C - 1)$$

(*cont.* on back endpapers)

Basic Statistics for the Social and Behaviorial Sciences

Basic Statistics for the Social and Behaviorial Sciences

George M. Diekhoff

Midwestern State University

Prentice Hall, Upper Saddle River, New Jersey 07458

Library of Congress Cataloging-in-Publication Data
DIEKHOFF, GEORGE.
Basic statistics for the social and behavioral sciences / George M. Diekhoff.
p. cm.
Includes index.
ISBN 0–02–329524–4
1. Social sciences—Statistical methods. 2. Statistics.
I. Title.
HA29.D465 1996
519.5′0243—dc20 95–18031
CIP

Acquisitions editor: Peter Janzow
Editorial/production supervision and interior design: Joan Stone
Buyer: Tricia Kenny
Cover design: Anne Bonanno Nieglos
Editorial assistant: Marilyn Coco
Copy editor: Lynne Lachenbach
Cover illustration: Michael Melford Photography

Printed in the United States of America

10 9 8 7 6 5 4 3 2 1

ISBN 0-02-329524-4

PRENTICE-HALL INTERNATIONAL (UK) LIMITED, *London*
PRENTICE-HALL OF AUSTRALIA PTY. LIMITED, *Sydney*
PRENTICE-HALL CANADA INC., *Toronto*
PRENTICE-HALL HISPANOAMERICANA, S.A., *Mexico*
PRENTICE-HALL OF INDIA PRIVATE LIMITED, *New Delhi*
PRENTICE-HALL OF JAPAN, INC., *Tokyo*
SIMON & SCHUSTER ASIA PTE. LTD., *Singapore*
EDITORA PRENTICE-HALL DO BRASIL, LTDA., *Rio de Janeiro*

For Beverly and Ben, two very good reasons for putting my work aside at the end of each day

Brief Contents

Contents

Preface

Basic Statistics provides a solid introduction to applied statistics for students in psychology, sociology, social work, and education. I have kept these students first in my mind as I have written.

After nearly 20 years of teaching statistics I can count on one hand the students who took the course as an elective! Indeed, the common denominator of students beginning their study of statistics is dread. I understand this. I haven't forgotten the confusion and frustration that I felt as I struggled through my own first course in statistics. I hope that these memories have helped me to write a friendlier book that gives a better fit to the needs of beginning statistics students.

Several helps are included in *Basic Statistics* to facilitate learning. Marginal definitions define key concepts the first time they are used in the text. Frequent comprehension checks ensure that each major idea is mastered before the next is presented. Answers and complete explanations for these comprehension checks are located at the end of each chapter. A set of review exercises, also at the end of each chapter, provides a second opportunity to strengthen understanding. Answers for review exercises appear in Appendix C at the end of the book. Examples and illustrations replace the usual proofs and derivations. Every statistical formula is followed by a step-by-step verbal description of computational mechanics. Every statistical procedure described in the book is accompanied by a complete, data-to-conclusions example. *Relevance* is the acid test applied in every decision to include or exclude material. And I have tried to sweeten the subject matter with a little humor sprinkled throughout.

The *Workbook and Computer Guide* that accompanies *Basic Statistics for the Social and Behavioral Sciences* provides even more help. This study guide provides lists of learning objectives, key concepts, important statistical formulas, more exercises, and self-tests that are useful whether or not you are working with a computer. If you are using the *SPSS/PC+ Studentware Plus* statistical software package (optional from Prentice Hall) the *Workbook and Computer Guide* illustrates how to use this software effectively.

Many people have contributed importantly to this text and the accompanying materials. My thanks go first to Dr. Ludy T. Benjamin, who has been an inspiration to me throughout my student and professional years. Many thanks also are due Christine Cardone, formerly of Macmillan Publishing Company, who encouraged me to begin this project. Pete Janzow, Executive Editor with Prentice Hall, and Marilyn Coco, Pete's assistant, have been very helpful in guiding the development of the book and its ancillaries. Thanks also go to Lynne Lachenbach, who edited my often rough prose, and to Joan Stone, who translated the manuscript into printed text. I am grateful to Lauren Ward and Diane Guarine for their work in marketing the book. Thanks go too to the artists for their work. I am also thankful for the very useful insights of the reviewers whose comments shaped this book: Bernard C. Beins, Ithaca College; Stephen W. Brown, Rockhurst College; Jane A. Halpert, DePaul University; Susan Hoernbelt, Hillsborough Community College; Stan Kary, St. Louis Community College at Florissant Valley; Linda M. Noble, Kennesaw State College; and John Pittenger, University of Arkansas Little Rock (UALR).

Finally, I am grateful to the Longman Group UK Ltd., on behalf of the Literary Executor of the late Sir Ronald A. Fisher, F.R.S., and Dr. Frank Yates, F.R.S., for permission to reprint Tables III and VII from *Statistical Tables for Biological, Agricultural and Medical Research, 6/e* (1974).

George M. Diekhoff

THE WHATS AND WHEREFORES OF STATISTICS

1

Chapter Outline

According to some recent publications in the social and behavioral sciences:

- Between 2% and 10% of students in the nation's colleges and universities register for classes late.
- The length of the average run reported by a sample of 68 joggers was 4.5 miles. On average, these joggers suffered about 1.2 running-related injuries each year.

Do these statements make sense to you? Yes? Good. Then you already understand some statistics, such as percentages and averages. Consider these excerpts:

- Late registrants who enrolled in classes in which the number of allowed absences was restricted were significantly more likely to drop the classes or be dropped than were timely registrants (χ^2 $(1, N = 122) = 4.34$, $p < .05$).
- Among recreational joggers, the number of running-related injuries was significantly correlated with type A personality ($r = .29$, $N = 66$, $p < .01$).

These statements undoubtedly made some sense to you, but probably also left you with some questions. What exactly is the meaning of the word "significantly" here? What's all the gobbledygook enclosed in parentheses?

Do you get the sense that you have more to learn about statistics? Good. This "need to know" is one of the most important elements in successful learning. And the more you read and work in the social and behavioral sciences, the more you will feel it, because statistics are everywhere in psychology, sociology, social work, and related disciplines.

Statistics are the tools of trade in the social and behavioral sciences. With these statistical tools we can sift through thousands upon thousands of otherwise meaningless bits and pieces of data to tease out meaningful trends, patterns, and relationships. We can make sense out of what would otherwise be an incomprehensible mass of numerical facts and figures. With statistics we can answer questions that would be unanswerable without these tools. Statistics enable social and behavioral scientists to bring to bear on human problems the power of mathematics.

1.1 What Are Statistics?

statistics *Procedures used to organize, condense, and analyze data.*

We have used the word "statistics" several times now. Perhaps it is time to define this term. **Statistics** are procedures used to organize, condense, and analyze data so as to answer questions about the cases represented by those data.

This definition contains two additional terms—data and cases—that we need to examine more closely. Suppose we recorded the number of errors made by each of 20 laboratory rats as they made their way from the start box to the goal box of a maze. Numbers of errors would comprise the data, and each rat would constitute a case. Consider another example. Imagine that we have recorded the number of minutes each of several toddlers sucks their thumb while viewing *Teenage Mutant Ninja Turtles* or *Barney the Friendly Dinosaur.* These numbers would now constitute the data, and each toddler would be considered a case. Finally, suppose one recorded the number of police officers per capita in each of 100 American cities. The data would now be numbers of police, and each city would be a case. Can you define the terms "data" and "case" from these examples?

Data are numerical facts and a **case** is the smallest unit of observation. You can see from these examples that social and behavioral scientists study all sorts of cases and collect all kinds of data. Statistics are the tools that we use to make sense of the data, and thus the cases that are represented by those data. Statistical analysis is not some abstract exercise in higher mathematics, divorced from the real world and pertinent only to multifunction-calculator-equipped eggheads. The numbers we work with represent living, breathing creatures, ranging from rats to toddlers to whole cities. Statistics enable us to answer potentially life-changing questions that would otherwise not be answerable.

data *Numerical facts about cases. Data can convey information about the qualitative characteristics of each case or the quantity of some attribute possessed by each case.*
case *The unit of observation about which data are recorded.*

COMPREHENSION CHECK 1.1

In each of the following examples, identify the "cases" and the "data." (a) A teacher has self-image test scores for each of her kindergarten pupils. (b) A school psychologist uses a 1–5 scale to rate the level of cooperation in each of several elementary school classrooms. (c) A researcher records the number of weapons violations reported during the last year in each of 30 school districts.

(Answer on p. 20.)

1.2 WHY DO YOU NEED STATISTICS?

Do you need to learn statistics? This is a legitimate question that all students new to statistics ask. Let me answer this question with another question. Which carpenter would you hire to build new kitchen cabinets, one whose tool box contains a hammer and saw, or one whose tools fill the back of a van? Either carpenter could build your cabinets, but what would the finished product look like? The quality of the work is limited by the quality of the tools. This is true in the social and behavioral sciences just as surely as in carpentry. The only difference is in the nature of the tools.

COMPREHENSION CHECK 1.2

In your own words, why should *you* learn about statistics? What's in it for you?

(Answer on p. 20.)

Equipped with tools for measuring, cutting, smoothing, and fastening, a carpenter can turn a pile of lumber into a cabinet, a table, or a dog house. Faced with a pile of data, the raw materials of the social and behavioral sciences, what can we do with our statistical tools? Let's sort through the statistical tool box.

1.3 Kinds of Statistics

descriptive statistics *Sometimes used as a label for statistical procedures used in the analysis of sample data. Also used as a label for statistical procedures that describe some characteristic of either a sample or a population.*
sample *A group of cases that has been examined firsthand. Samples are often viewed as a subset of a larger population and are often studied as representative of that population.*

One way to classify statistical procedures is into two categories: descriptive statistics and inferential statistics. **Descriptive statistics** are procedures used to describe a given collection of data. If we collected the scores of students in your statistics class on the first exam and computed the class average, we would be using descriptive statistics. The purpose of descriptive statistics is to describe the **sample** at hand—the collection of cases that we have examined. Whereas the original data convey information about each individual case, descriptive statistics make it possible to describe the sample as a whole. The class average, for example, tells us about the class as a whole, not about any particular student. Descriptive statistics give us a way to see the forest and not just the individual trees. We will begin our study of descriptive statistics in Chapter 2.

inferential statistics *A category of statistical procedures that enable generalizing from sample data to the larger population.*
population *The complete set of cases represented by the sample subset.*

If descriptive statistics enable us to look past the individual trees to the forest as a whole, inferential statistics enable us to look beyond a particular forest to draw conclusions about forests in general, even those that we haven't examined firsthand. **Inferential statistics** are procedures that let us generalize our findings beyond the particular sample at hand to the larger **population** represented by that sample. A developmental psychologist who assesses the impact of a children's television program on the moral development of a sample of 20 toddlers certainly cares about those 20 toddlers, but is probably even more interested in generalizing to the population of all toddlers. The family therapist who studies social interaction patterns in a sample of 20 couples in marriage counseling is interested in those couples, but probably also wants to generalize the findings to the population of all such couples. We will begin our study of inferential statistics in Chapter 5.

Comprehension Check 1.3

What do we learn from : (a) the data; (b) descriptive statistics; and (c) inferential statistics?
(Answer on p. 20.)

We have seen that descriptive statistics tell us about the sample at hand. Inferential statistics tell us about populations beyond the sample at hand. Thus the distinction between descriptive and inferential statistics is based on the target of our description: the sample or the population beyond the sample.

Another way of categorizing our statistical tools is according to *what* they tell us about that target—what the statistics *do.* A carpenter has tools that measure (measuring tape, T-square), tools that cut (saws, chisels), tools that join pieces together (hammer, clamps, screwdrivers), and tools that smooth surfaces (planes, sandpaper). So, too, statistical procedures can be grouped according to what they do, that is, what they tell us. Considered in this way, statistics can be divided into four classes: (1) descriptive statistics; (2) significant difference tests; (3) correlational statistics; and (4) regression. Let's consider each of these functions of statistics in turn.

Descriptive Statistics

One purpose of statistics is simple description. Sometimes statistics are used to describe individual cases. Percentile ranks, described in Chapter 2, describe individuals by indicating how low or high their scores are, relative to the others. The standard score or "*z* score," discussed in Chapter 4, is another statistic that is used in describing individual cases.

Other times we use statistics to describe the characteristics and attributes of a sample consisting of many individual cases. Averages, percentages, and measures of the variability of data are described in Chapters 2 and 3 and are all examples of these descriptive statistics.

Populations also need to be described, and we can use inferential statistics to describe populations on the basis of samples drawn from them. These procedures are inferential statistics in that they let us go beyond the sample at hand to the larger population. They are descriptive statistics in the sense that their purpose is to describe the population.

Let's consider an example. Suppose that a poll of 100 Rocky Bottom State University students revealed that 64% favored a four-day school week during the summer. This percentage describes the sentiment of the sample of 100 students who were polled. But what about the many other students who were not included in this sample? Can we describe the entire population of Rocky Bottom students on the basis of just this sample? The answer is yes, and the statistical procedure involved, called interval estimation, is discussed in Chapter 5. Interval estimation is considered an inferential statistic because it is used to go beyond the sample data at hand to make generalizations about some larger population. In terms of the purpose accomplished, though, interval estimation is a descriptive statistical procedure because it is used to describe the characteristics of a population.

COMPREHENSION CHECK 1.4

Explain how one statistical procedure can be considered both a descriptive statistic and an inferential statistic.
(Answer on p. 20.)

Significant Difference Tests

Other statistical procedures are used to evaluate differences—differences between a sample and a larger population, differences between two samples, before-vs.-after differences, and so on. **Significant difference tests,** discussed in Chapters 6–9, all answer this question: How large must a difference be in order for one to conclude that the difference is replicable and due to more than just chance fluctuations in the particular data at hand?

significant difference tests *A group of inferential statistical procedures that determine the likelihood that a difference seen in sample data is the result of chance fluctuations in the data. These statistics determine how big a difference must be to be considered reliable.*

Suppose that 8 toddlers viewing 30 minutes of *Teenage Mutant Ninja Turtles* cartoons sucked their thumbs an average of 6.5 minutes, compared to an average thumb-sucking time of 5.9 minutes for *Barney the Friendly Dinosaur.* Is this difference large enough that you would bet the farm on seeing it again if the study were replicated, that is, repeated with a completely new sample of toddlers? How about a difference of 8 minutes for *Turtles* and 4 minutes for *Barney*? Eighteen minutes for *Turtles* and 1 minute for *Barney*? Clearly, we need some way of determining how big a difference needs to be before we consider it reliable. This is the purpose of significant difference tests. A difference is called *significant* if it is extremely unlikely to be the product of chance fluctuations in the data. Put another way, a significant difference is a reliable difference. A significant difference is a difference seen not just in the sample data at hand, but most likely in the whole population represented by those sample data. Significant difference tests help us to determine if a difference observed in a particular sample would also be observed in the larger population from which this sample was drawn. Because significant difference tests attempt to draw conclusions beyond the sample about some larger population, they are considered inferential statistics.

COMPREHENSION CHECK 1.5

> The following research excerpt appeared at the beginning of this chapter: "Late registrants who enrolled in classes in which the number of allowed absences was restricted were *significantly* more likely to drop the course or be dropped than were timely registrants."
> What does the word "significantly" mean in this excerpt? (Answer on p. 20.)

Correlation

correlation *A relationship between variables. A variety of statistics is used to measure the strength and statistical significance (i.e., replicability) of correlations.*

Is self-concept related to academic performance? Is the number of hours spent viewing television each week associated with physical fitness? Is there any relationship between students' academic majors and their political affiliations? All of these are questions about correlation. A **correlation** is a relationship. When two characteristics, traits, or attributes are related or linked in some way, we say that they are *correlated.*

A variety of procedures is available for measuring the strength of correlations. These procedures are considered descriptive statistics when they are used to describe the strength of the correlation in the sample data at hand.

It is also possible, though, to evaluate the statistical significance of correlations, an inferential statistical process. A statistically significant correlation is one that is sufficiently strong that one would expect to see it again in a replication of the research. When a correlation is found to be statistically significant, it means that it is very likely that the correlation found in the sample at hand also exists in the larger population that the sample represents. We will study correlational procedures in Chapter 10.

COMPREHENSION CHECK 1.6

> The following research excerpt appeared at the beginning of this chapter: "Among recreational joggers, the number of running-related injuries was *significantly* correlated with type A personality."
> What does the word "significantly" mean in this excerpt? (Answer on p. 20.)

Regression

If self-concept is correlated with academic performance, if television viewing time is related to physical fitness, or if academic major is linked with political preference, it should be possible to predict one characteristic from the other. For instance, suppose we find that as television viewing time increases, physical fitness declines. Knowing this and nothing else, who would you predict would have the better level of fitness, someone who watches 20 hours of television each week or someone who limits television viewing to 5 hours per week? The answer is obvious. Even though we would not expect our predictions to be accurate all of the time, the existence of a correlation does give us some predictive power. This application of statistics, the prediction of one attribute or characteristic from another, based on a correlation between the two, is called **regression analysis.** Regression analysis enables us to make predictions beyond the data at hand, and so it falls into the category of inferential statistics. We will study regression analysis in Chapter 11.

regression analysis *Inferential statistical procedures used to predict one variable from another, based on the existence of a correlation between the variables.*

COMPREHENSION CHECK 1.7

Scores on the ACT and SAT examinations are correlated with college grade-point average (GPA), but predictions of GPA based on ACT or SAT scores are sometimes dramatically wrong. Why do you suppose this is?

(Answer on p. 20.)

1.4 MEASUREMENT IN THE SOCIAL AND BEHAVIORAL SCIENCES

Statistics are procedures used to organize, condense, and analyze data. We have examined our statistical tools and will turn now to the lumber, bricks, and mortar on which these tools operate—the data.

The data of the social and behavioral sciences are extraordinarily diverse because we study so many different variables. **Variables** are attributes or characteristics that vary from one case to the next. Age in years, academic achievement measured by grade-point average, scores on a depression inventory or intelligence test, and reaction times measured in milliseconds are just a few examples of the variables and data of the social and behavioral sciences. Though data take on many forms, all data are the result of measurement, and it is to this topic that we now turn.

variable *A variable is an attribute or characteristic that varies from one case to the next.*

Measurement is the application of rules in assigning numbers to cases so as to represent the presence or absence or quantity of an attribute possessed by each case. You are already familiar with many kinds of measurement. The rule for measuring your temperature is: Put a thermometer under your tongue for 3 minutes and then note the number at the top of the column of mercury. The rule for measuring the 3 minutes is: Count three complete revolutions of the sweep second hand of your watch.

measurement *The use of any rule to assign numbers to cases so as to represent the presence or absence or quantity of some attribute possessed by each case.*

COMPREHENSION CHECK 1.8

Describe rules that you might use in measuring: (a) employee motivation; (b) toddler aggressiveness; and (c) respect for authority among parolees.

(Answer on p. 20.)

Obviously, the rules of measurement vary depending on what is being measured. There are even more rules of measurement than there are attributes to be measured, since there is generally more than one way to measure any given attribute. Still, we find that the many rules of measurement fall into only four major categories, sometimes called "levels" or "scales" of measurement. It is important to know what scale of measurement is being used in measuring any given variable, because this will influence one's choice of statistical tools. A carpenter wouldn't use a hammer to cut a board in half, nor should we use the wrong statistical tool for the data at hand.

Nominal Scale Measurement

nominal scale *The lowest level of measurement. Involves determining for each case only the presence or absence of an attribute, not the quantity of the attribute.*

At the lowest level, **nominal scale** measurement involves determining only whether a case does or does not possess *any* of the attribute under consideration. No consideration is given to quantity, that is, *how much* of the attribute is possessed. The whole concern is with whether there is *any* or *none* of the attribute. Measurement at this level involves assigning cases to categories. These categories are often given arbitrarily chosen identifying code numbers to facilitate computerized data analysis, and these code numbers can be considered "scores" of a sort. Because nominal scale measurement focuses on identifying the *qualities* of each case and not the *quantities* of each case, nominal scale data are sometimes referred to as **qualitative data.**

qualitative data *The data resulting from nominal level measurement. Indicates the qualities possessed by each case, but provides no quantitative information.*

Consider this measurement rule for measuring gender, a common nominal scale variable: If someone says he is a male, assign a score of 1; if she says she is a female, assign a score of 0. (Don't be offended: We might as reasonably have scored males 0 and females 1!) This may not sound like measurement, but it is. By assigning cases to the gender categories of male and female and assigning each case a numerical "score" associated with its category, we are fulfilling the definition of measurement: assigning numbers to cases so as to reflect the presence or absence or quantity of an attribute possessed by each case. In this example the score tells us whether each case possesses the attribute of "maleness" or "femaleness."

Let's look at another example. A researcher studying cola taste preferences has decided to assign "scores" of 1 to taste testers who prefer Burpee Cola, 2 to those who prefer Econocola, and 3 to testers who like Old Brown. This nominal scale measurement rule again assigns arbitrarily chosen category code numbers to cases so as to reflect their taste preferences, that is, the presence or absence of a preference for each of the three test colas. The numbers assigned do not reflect *how much* preference exists, just *what kind* of preference there is.

TABLE 1.1

Cola preferences for 9 taste testers, scored 1 = Burpee Cola, 2 = Econocola, 3 = Old Brown

Taste Tester	Cola Preference
A	1
B	3
C	1
D	3
E	3
F	2
G	1
H	3
I	1

Because nominal scale measurement provides no quantitative ("how much") information, but only qualitative ("what kind") information, nominal scale variables do not lend themselves to many kinds of statistical analysis. It's hard to apply mathematics to numbers that don't represent quantity! We cannot even compute an average for a nominal scale variable. Consider the taste preference data shown in Table 1.1. This table shows the cola preferences of each of 9 taste testers measured according to the rule described previously. Add their scores and divide by 9 to compute the average and you'll get 2. Does the average taste tester really prefer Econocola? Look at the data. Only 1 of the 9 testers expressed this preference. The problem here is that by computing the average of these taste preference scores we are assuming that they convey quantitative information when, in fact, they do not. So how *are* nominal scale variables analyzed? Most often by frequency counts or percentages, that is, the number or percentage of cases in each of the categories.

COMPREHENSION CHECK 1.9

Think of two original examples of nominal scale variables pertinent to the social and behavioral sciences. Describe how you might "measure" cases on these variables. Explain why "scores" on these variables cannot be manipulated arithmetically.
(Answer on p. 20.)

Ordinal Scale Measurement

ordinal scale *The lowest level of measurement that conveys quantitative information about cases. Ordinal measurement does not use a fixed-sized unit of measure, so equal score differences do not reflect equal differences in the amount of the attribute being measured.*

quantitative data *Numerical information that conveys information about how much of some attribute each case possesses.*

Ordinal scale measurement also involves assigning numbers to cases, but unlike the "scores" associated with the categories of nominal scale variables, ordinal scale scores *do* say something about how much of the attribute is possessed by each case. Because of this, ordinal scales, as well as the interval and ratio scales of measurement to be described later, all provide **quantitative data**—that is, information about the amount of attribute that each case possesses.

The defining feature of ordinal scale measurement is that equal score differences do not necessarily reflect equal differences in the attribute being measured. This means that ordinal scale measurement is a little like measuring with a "rubber ruler," a ruler on which the distances are different between successive inch marks.

The most obvious examples of ordinal scale measurement involve rank-order data. Students ranked on the basis of academic achievement, patients ranked on severity of psychopathology, and cities ranked from most pleasant to least pleasant are all examples of ordinal scale measurement. Figure 1.1a depicts an ordinal scale measurement of statistophobia, the fear of statistics. In this figure the horizontal line represents statistophobia, and there are several statistics students located along the dimension according to the severity of their statistophobia. Laura is ranked (scored) 1 because she is least statistophobic. John is ranked 2 because he shows the second lowest level of statistophobia. Similarly, Ben is ranked 3 because he has the third lowest level, and Sean is ranked 4 because he has the worst case of statistophobia of the group. In this example, cases have been rank-ordered in ascending order. It would have been just as acceptable to rank-order them in descending order, with the highest level of statistophobia ranked 1, the second highest ranked 2, and so on. This approach would meet the requirements of the ordinal scale of measurement just as well as the approach that was taken. However, you should get used to ranking in ascending order, since this is required for some statistics that analyze ordinal scale data.

Can you see from Figure 1.1a why ordinal scales are like measuring with a rubber ruler? The differences in statistophobia between successive ranks are very different from one case to the next. The difference between the ranks for Sean and Ben ($4 - 3 = 1$) is the same as the difference between the ranks for Ben and John ($3 - 2 = 1$), even though the differences in the statistophobia levels of these pairs of cases are dramatically different.

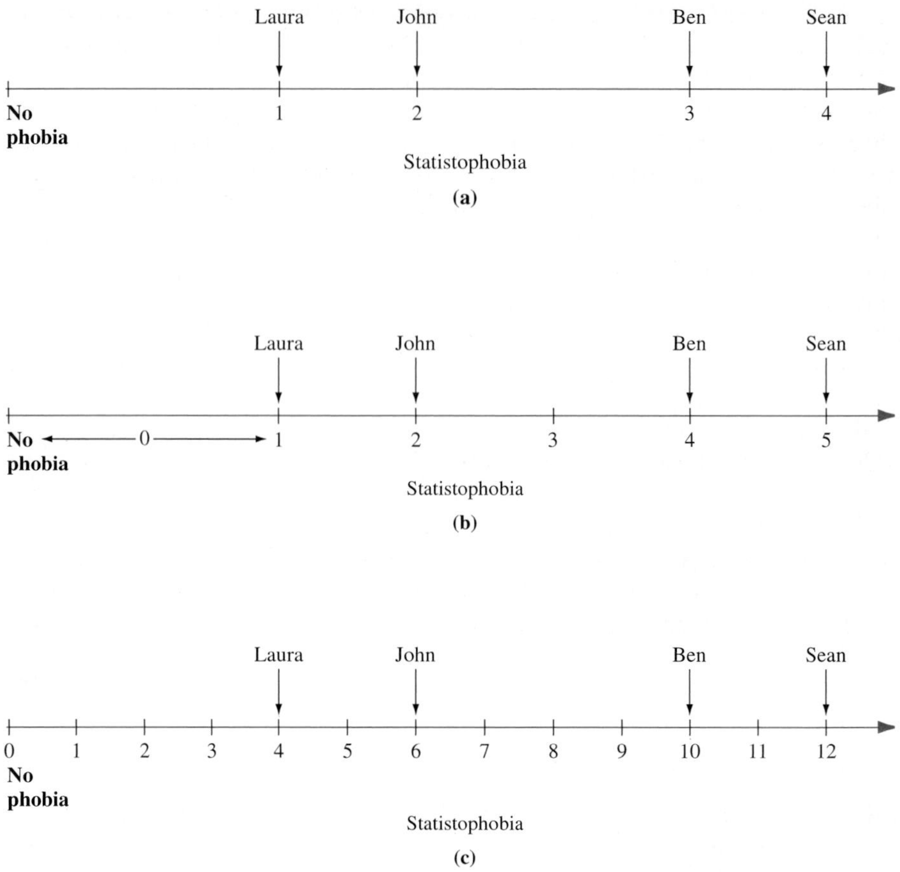

FIGURE 1.1

(a) Statistophobia measured by rank-ordering cases in ascending order. Although ranks convey quantity, equal score differences do not reflect equal differences in the attribute being measured. (b) Statistophobia measured at the interval level. Scores are based on the number of fixed-sized units of the attribute possessed by each case. Equal score differences do reflect equal differences in the attribute, but the zero point is arbitrary. (c) Statistophobia measured at the ratio level. Scores are based on the number of fixed-sized units of the attribute possessed by each case. A score of 0 represents complete absence of the attribute. Ratio statements are possible.

COMPREHENSION CHECK 1.10

Which of the following measuring rules are nominal and which are ordinal?

A. Classification in school, scored 1 = freshman, 2 = sophomore, 3 = junior, and 4 = senior

B. Religious preference, scored 1 = Protestant, 2 = Catholic, 3 = Jewish, and 4 = other

C. Political affiliation, scored 1 = Republican, 2 = Democrat, 3 = independent

D. Leadership skill, scored by rank-ordering the cases

(Answer on p. 21.)

Although rank-order data do convey something of how much attribute each case possesses, they are "just barely" quantitative. They do not convey very much quantitative information. Rank-order scores are completely relative. Suppose you know that someone ranks fourth in age in her class. How old is she? It's hard to say. For one thing, we don't know how many others were ranked. It will affect our interpretation to know if she ranks 4 out of 4 (she is the oldest in the class) or 4 out of 100 (she is one of the youngest in the class). Even with this additional information, however, rankings tell us nothing about the absolute level of the attribute. An age ranking of 4 out of 4 may not be very old at all if all four cases are preschoolers. In a college class, on the other hand, even if the first three ranked individuals are quite young, the fourth-ranked person may be very old. So, what do rank-order scores tell us? Alone, nothing. In the context of the other ranks, still very little! Even so, statisticians have developed some ingenious ways of squeezing out of rank-order data every possible bit of quantitative information that they do contain.

COMPREHENSION CHECK 1.11

What can you say about the motivational level of a student whose motivation has been given a rank-order score of 7 by a professor? What more can you say about this student if you know that the professor rank-ordered 100 students?

(Answer on p. 21.)

Interval Scale Measurement

interval scale *Quantitative measurement that bases scores for each case on the number of fixed-sized units of the attribute possessed by that case. Because the zero point is arbitrary (i.e., 0 does not necessarily indicate the absence of the attribute), ratio statements are inappropriate.*

Interval scale measurement is defined by two characteristics. First, scores on an interval scale variable are determined by the number of fixed-sized units of the attribute that each case possesses. Second, interval scales have an arbitrary zero point, meaning that a score of 0 does not necessarily indicate the complete absence of the attribute. In some instances 0 is simply one unit of measure below a score of $+1$ and one unit of measure above a score of -1. In other instances 0 represents an immeasurably low quantity of the attribute. Examples of interval scale measurement abound. When we measure temperature in either Fahrenheit or Celsius degrees, we are using interval scale measurement. On both the Fahrenheit and Celsius scales, the temperature of an object is equal to the number of fixed-sized degrees of temperature possessed by that object. One degree of temperature is equal to any other degree of temperature. Also, the zero point of both scales is arbitrary. A temperature of 0, either Fahrenheit or Celsius, does *not* indicate the *absence* of temperature. A temperature of 0 is simply one degree colder than a temperature of $+1$ and one degree warmer than a temperature of -1.

Figure 1.1b illustrates the interval scale measurement of statistophobia. We again find Laura, John, Ben, and Sean located along the statistophobia dimension, which is now marked off into fixed-sized units. Statistophobia scores are now equal to the number of fixed-sized units of statistophobia possessed by each student. Because Laura has 1 unit, her score is 1. John has 2 units, so his score is 2. Ben and Sean possess 4 and 5 units of statistophobia, respectively, thus their scores are 4 and 5. Notice, finally, that a score of 0 does not indicate the complete absence of statistophobia. Zero in this example simply means that a case's statistophobia level is immeasurably low, less than 1. Thus, the zero point of this scale is arbitrary.

Because interval scale scores are based on fixed-sized units, equal score differences will reflect equal differences in the amount of the attribute being measured. Remember that we could not say this for ordinal variables. Look again at Figure 1.1b. The difference between Sean's score of 5 and Ben's score of 4 is 1. The difference between John's score of 2 and Laura's score of 1 is also 1. Consistent with these equal score differences, we see that Laura and John differ in the severity of their statistophobia by the same amount as Ben and Sean. With an interval scale of measurement we leave behind the problems of the rubber ruler. The most powerful statistical procedures are available to us when our data are measured at the interval level.

COMPREHENSION CHECK 1.12

Identify each of the following measurement rules as nominal, ordinal, or interval.

A. Cognitive speed, scored as the number of arithmetic problems each case solves in 60 seconds

B. Educational attainment, scored 0 = no high school diploma, 1 = high school graduate, 2 = associate's degree, 3 = bachelor's degree, 4 = master's degree, 5 = doctorate

C. Attitudes toward a proposed tax, scored 0 = oppose, 1 = favor

(Answer on p. 21.)

Though it is more precise than ordinal measurement, interval scale measurement has one weakness. When working with interval scales one cannot make ratio statements like "Ben is twice as statistophobic as John." Why not? Look at Figure 1.1b again. Even though Ben's score (4) is twice as high as John's (2), Ben is *less* than twice as statistophobic as John. You can prove this to yourself by measuring the distance from the left end of the statistophobia scale to John's location and then to Ben's location. Ben is not twice as far from the no-phobia point as John, therefore, he is not twice as phobic. This limitation of interval scale variables is a result of the arbitrary placement of the zero point.

Ratio Scale Measurement

ratio scale *Quantitative measurement that bases scores for each case on the number of fixed-sized units of the attribute possessed by that case. Because the zero point is nonarbitrary (i.e., 0 indicates the absence of the attribute), ratio statements are appropriate.*

The highest, most flexible level of measurement is achieved at the **ratio scale.** Ratio scale data avail themselves to all of the most powerful statistical procedures in our tool box. Ratio scales are like interval scales in one way: Both scales of measurement base scores on the number of fixed-sized units of the attribute each case possesses. Unlike interval scales, though, ratio scales have a nonarbitrary, absolute zero point. This means simply that a ratio scale score of 0 indicates that a case possesses *none* of the attribute being measured.

We can think of many examples of ratio scale variables studied in the social and behavioral sciences. Age is measured in fixed-sized units (e.g., weeks, years) and a score of 0 means no age. Reaction time is measured in fixed-sized units (e.g., milliseconds, seconds), and 0 means no time has elapsed. Number of children, number of years of education completed, annual income, and many other variables are all measured at the ratio scale.

Figure 1.1c illustrates ratio scale measurement of statistophobia. The scale is again marked off into fixed-sized units and each student's score is based on how many units he or she possesses. The difference now is that a score of 0 falls at the no-phobia end of the dimension. Rather than reflecting an arbitrarily low statistophobia level, the ratio scale score of 0 is assigned only to cases that possess *no* statistophobia.

Because the zero point of a ratio scale is nonarbitrary, ratio statements are perfectly legitimate. Sean's statistophobia score of 12 is twice as high as John's score of 6, and we can accurately say that Sean is twice as statistophobic as John (you can confirm this by measuring from the no-phobia end of the scale).

COMPREHENSION CHECK 1.13

Identify each of the following measurement rules as ordinal, interval, or ratio:

A. Intelligence, measured by the number of IQ test items answered correctly
B. Academic performance, measured as one's ranking in the class
C. Obesity, measured as percentage of body fat

(Answer on p. 21.)

Changing Scales

A variable that can be measured at one level can always be "scaled down" and measured at lower levels as well. Table 1.2 illustrates this principle for the variable of college education. Measured at the ratio level, the college education of each of 10 students is recorded as the number of credit hours completed. Each credit hour is a fixed-sized unit, and a score of 0 means that *no* college credits have been earned. We can scale down to the interval level by measuring college education as the number of credit hours completed beyond the first 30 (though I do that here only to make the point). We are still using a fixed-sized unit of measure—credit hours—but the score of 0 is now assigned to any case with 30 or fewer credit hours. The zero point is now arbitrary. Moving down to the ordinal level, we might rank-order students

TABLE 1.2

College education measured at the ratio (number of credit hours completed), interval (number of credits beyond 30 hours), ordinal (cases rank-ordered in ascending order), and nominal (freshman = 3, sophomore = 1, junior = 4, senior = 2) levels

Student	Ratio	Interval	Ordinal	Nominal
A	15	0	3	3
B	65	35	7	4
C	110	80	10	2
D	31	1	4	1
E	10	0	2	3
F	9	0	1	3
G	55	25	5	1
H	62	32	6	4
I	75	45	8	4
J	85	55	9	4

according to the number of credit hours each has completed. Ranked in ascending order, the student with the fewest credits is ranked 1, the student with the second fewest hours is ranked 2, and so on. Finally, to measure college education at the nominal level, we can categorize students as freshmen, sophomores, juniors, and seniors, assign each category a numerical code, and use this code as the "score" for all students falling in each category. (You should notice, though, that if we used a coding scheme such as freshman = 1, sophomore = 2, junior = 3, senior = 4, we would still have an ordinal scale because the numerical scores would still reflect information about the quantity of education completed. For our categories to be truly nominal, we would have to assign numerical codes in a manner that removes even ordinal information, e.g., freshmen = 3, sophomores = 1, juniors = 4, seniors = 2.)

Although variables that are measured at one level can be scaled down and measured at lower levels, it is not possible to "scale up." Look at the nominal scale measurement of college education in Table 1.2. Given *just* this information, would you be able to work your way back up to determine exactly how many credit hours each student completed? No. Can you work up to the interval or ratio level from rank orders? No.

The lesson to be learned from all this is that it is good practice to collect data that are measured at the highest possible level in the first place. Should you wish for some reason to do so, you can always scale down to a lower level of measurement. However, data that are gathered at a lower level of measurement cannot ever be scaled up.

COMPREHENSION CHECK 1.14

In an investigation of pain sensitivity, a researcher asks subjects to immerse their arms in ice water for 60 seconds. He records: (a) number of seconds to the initial report of pain; (b) ratings of pain following 20 seconds of immersion; (c) rank orders of subjects based on the number of seconds to the first report of pain; and (d) whether subjects did or did not report pain by 10 seconds following immersion.

Of these four measurement rules, which is most clearly ratio, interval, ordinal, and nominal?

(Answer on p. 21.)

Which Scale Is It?

Despite the seemingly clear differences between ordinal, interval, and ratio scale data, it is often difficult or impossible to know exactly at what level one's variables have been measured. Consider the example of nervousness, measured as the number of eye blinks per minute.

First, let us ask if this measurement rule provides any quantitative information about nervousness. One would feel safe in answering that people who blink a lot are *generally* more nervous than those who blink less. We know, then, that eye blink rate provides *at least* an ordinal measure of nervousness—the lowest scale of measurement that assesses quantity.

But does eye blink rate give an interval scale of measurement? Does each eye blink measure a fixed-sized amount of nervousness? Can we say with any certainty that the increase *in nervousness* that we get when we move from 5 blinks per minute to 15 blinks (an increase of 10 blinks per minute) is the same as when we move from 30 to 40 blinks (also an increase of 10 blinks per minute)? There's no way to know, because we can't see nervousness independent of our measures of it. Thus, though eye blinks per minute certainly provides an ordinal measure of nervousness, this measure may or may not be interval.

Since we can't be sure whether each eye blink measures a fixed-sized amount of nervousness, we also can't determine whether eye blink rate provides a ratio scale measure of nervousness. It seems doubtful, though, since one would be hard-pressed to justify the notion that the absence of eye blinks indicates the complete absence of nervousness—the nonarbitrary zero point required by the ratio scale of measurement.

Viewed from another perspective, though, there is no doubt at all that eye blink rate is not only ordinal, but provides a fully ratio scale of measurement. Instead of thinking of eye blink rate as representing nervousness, let's look just at eye blink rate *itself.* An eye blink is an eye blink; each is the same as the next. Thus, we have fixed-sized units. Moreover, 0 eye blinks means no eye blinks. So we have a nonarbitrary zero point. Someone who blinked 20 times per minute has blinked twice as much as someone who blinked 10 times per minute. We see that we can make legitimate ratio statements. We have a ratio scale.

On the one hand, we have argued that eye blink rate is clearly ordinal, only questionably interval, and probably not ratio. On the other hand, we have made the case that eye blink rate is a fully ratio scale of measurement. It all depends on how you look at it.

Faced with this dilemma, and motivated by the desire to use the more powerful statistics appropriate to interval and ratio scale data, but not ordinal scale data, most social and behavioral scientists routinely assume that their data, unless obviously ordinal (such as rank-order data), are "close enough" to be treated as interval or ratio scales. As one psychometrician (someone who studies the measurement of things psychological) has said, "The numbers don't know where they come from."

COMPREHENSION CHECK 1.15

Explain in your own words the meaning of the last sentence above: "The numbers don't know where they come from."
(Answer on p. 21.)

1.5 RESEARCH DESIGN AND STATISTICS

Statistics and research go hand in hand. Scientists, including those in the social and behavioral sciences, use a **research design** to gather data pertinent to their questions. Statistics are then applied to these data to extract the answers.

research design *A plan for gathering data suitable to answering the research question at hand.*

Although the questions that scientists seek to answer are many and varied, they have a common theme. All scientific research aims to explain data variability. The big difference from one science to the next is in what variables are studied. A chemist might want to explain why the speed of a chemical reaction varies from one occasion to the next, sometimes faster and sometimes slower, whereas a psychologist might want to explain why some children are more aggressive than others. A meteorologist might wonder why the weather varies from day to day, sometimes cloudy and sometimes clear, whereas a sociologist might wonder why crime rate varies from one city to another. Regardless of which variables we study in the social and behavioral sciences, the goal is always the same: to explain why those variables vary. And these explanations are sought by conducting research. We will consider here the two most basic research designs—experiments and correlational research.

Experiments

experiment *A type of research used to establish cause-and-effect relationships.*

One way of explaining data variability is to identify the factors that *cause* that variability. Much of the research of the social and behavioral sciences is of this type. For example, what factors cause some children to be more aggressive than others? What factors cause some college students to be more dedicated to their studies than others? An **experiment** is used to gather the data pertinent to determining the causes of data variability, and we use statistics to make sense of those data.

To understand what experiments are and how they establish cause-and-effect relationships, picture yourself taking a walk through a field. On the ground in front of you, you find a black box with a knob on the front and a light bulb on the top. Curious, you twist the knob to the right and notice an immediate increase in the brightness of the light bulb. You twist the knob slowly to the left and discover that the light gets slowly dimmer. A quick twist to the right and then back to the left produces a rapid increase and then a decrease in the light's brightness. It wouldn't take you long to conclude that turning the knob *causes* the brightness of the light to vary. You've conducted an experiment.

independent variable *In an experiment, the independent variable is actively manipulated by the experimenter to see if it has a causal effect on a second variable, called the dependent variable.*
dependent variable *In an experiment, the dependent variable is passively observed and measured by the experimenter to see if it has been affected by manipulations of the independent variable.*

In any experiment we manipulate one factor or variable, called the **independent variable,** and we subsequently observe and measure a second variable, called the **dependent variable.** In our light bulb experiment above, the independent variable is the position of the knob—actively manipulated by the experimenter. The dependent variable is the brightness of the light bulb—passively observed and measured by the experimenter. We conclude that an independent variable exerts a causal effect on a dependent variable when we observe that changing the independent variable is followed by a change in the dependent variable.

This same principle is used in experiments in the social and behavioral sciences. To test the notion that frustration exerts a causal effect on aggression, we might conduct a simple experiment. See if you can identify the independent variable—the knob—and the dependent variable—the light bulb—in this experiment. Suppose we gave one group of children a difficult, frustrating puzzle to work on while a second group of children worked on an easy puzzle. After 15 minutes we would stop all of the children and let them play with each other while we watched and counted the number of times each child initiated some sort of aggressive interaction. In this experiment, frustration level is the independent variable—the knob on the front of the black box. The number of incidents of aggression recorded is the dependent variable—the observed brightness of the light bulb. Observing more incidents of aggressive behavior in the high-frustration group than in the low-frustration group would lead to the reasonable conclusion that frustration level is one of the causes of variability in aggression.

Identify the independent and dependent variables in the following experiments. (a) A teacher gives stickers for good behavior to students in one of her classes and uses verbal approval alone to reward good behavior in a second class. She later compares the conduct grades of students in her two classes. (b) A physiological psychologist injects one group of rats with an acetylcholine-enhancing drug and gives rats in a second group a saline injection. Four hours later he compares the maze-learning performance of the rats in the two groups, measured by number of trials to perfect performance.

(Answer on p. 21.)

Comprehension Check 1.16

So where do statistics fit in here? We need statistics to organize, condense, and analyze the data that we collect in an experiment. Table 1.3 lists data like those that might be produced in our frustration–aggression experiment: number of aggressive episodes initiated by each child in the low- and high-frustration groups. You can see that the low-frustration group seems generally less aggressive than the high-frustration group, but descriptive statistics would help to describe more precisely just how much aggression is seen in each group. And a significant difference test would be useful in determining if the difference between the groups is big enough to be considered reliable and replicable. The experiment provides the data; statistics help to make sense of those data.

Table 1.3

Number of incidents of aggression observed in children under conditions of low and high frustration

Low-Frustration Group	High-Frustration Group
0	2
1	1
0	3
2	3
0	2
0	3

Correlational Research

In addition to experiments, social and behavioral scientists often use **correlational research** to explain data variability. Correlational research explains data variability by identifying which variables are related to each other. Correlational research is often used when experiments would be impossible. Suppose, for instance, that you wanted to know if the phase of the moon affects people's mental stability. An experiment designed to answer this question would require that you manipulate the phase of the moon—the independent variable—and that you subsequently watch for changes in mental stability—the dependent variable—to see if it has been affected by your manipulation. There's just one problem here: You can't manipulate the phase of the moon. You can only watch passively as it changes.

correlational research *Research that passively measures two variables to determine if the two variables vary together—are correlated.*

An experiment cannot be used in this case. But you could use correlational research to see if mental stability and moon phase "go together." In correlational research we passively observe as two variables vary and then use statistics to determine if the variables varied together. Table 1.4 lists the kind of data that might be obtained from a correlational study of "lunar madness": the number of commitments made to a state mental hospital during each of three moon phases. You can see from the raw data that mental stability seems to vary depending on the phase of the moon. Statistical analyses, though, would answer at least two important questions. First, how strong is this linkage? Second, is the relationship strong enough to be considered reliable and replicable, or is it just a quirk of this particular data set?

Table 1.4

Number of state hospital commitments during each of three phases of the moon

Moon Phase	State Hospital Commitments
Full moon	8
Half moon	5
No moon	2

COMPREHENSION CHECK 1.17

Explain why the following research is a correlational study and not an experiment: A researcher compares scores on the verbal portion of the SAT for male and female college freshmen.
(Answer on p. 21.)

Other Issues in Research Design

Conducting research involves more than just choosing between an experimental or a correlational research design. There are a multitude of other issues to consider. In our frustration–aggression experiment, for instance, frustration was manipulated by giving some children difficult puzzles while other children worked on easy puzzles. But there might be some better approach to manipulating this independent variable. In the same experiment, aggression was measured by counting the number of aggressive incidents initiated by each child during a period of free play. Here again, though, you might think of some better way to measure the dependent variable of aggression. In any research, experimental or correlational, we have to settle on **operational definitions,** rules which define our variables and specify how they are to be manipulated or measured.

operational definitions
Definitions of variables that specify the rules by which those variables are to be manipulated or measured.

COMPREHENSION CHECK 1.18

Try your hand at operationally defining the following variables: (a) intelligence; (b) therapist empathy; and (c) racial tension.
(Answers on p. 21.)

In the lunar madness study, we examined the correlation between moon phase and state hospital commitments. There, too, research design decisions had to be made. How many phases of the moon should we study? Does the number of state hospital commitments provide a good operational definition of "mental stability?" Who should we study? Just adults? Just children? Suppose we decide to study just adults. Since we couldn't begin to study the entire population of adults, we'll have to use a sample from that population. How should we obtain this sample? Should we assess the mental stability of the same sample under each phase of the moon, or should we examine different samples in each moon phase?

These and many other questions are all issues of research design. This is not a book about research design, though. It is a book about statistics—analyzing data once they have been collected. Even so, you will learn quite a lot about research design as you learn about statistics. This is because how we collect data—the research design—is inevitably shaped and constrained by how we are able to analyze those data—our statistics. There is no point in collecting data that cannot be analyzed. It follows that the more ways we have of analyzing data, the more flexibility we will have in designing research. Though you might suppose that students of the social and behavioral sciences would take a course in research design first and follow up with a statistics course, it is more common to see these courses taken in the opposite sequence. Learning about statistics prepares one to learn about research design.

COMPREHENSION CHECK 1.19

How are research design and statistics different? How are they related?
(Answer on p. 21.)

Let me ask once again a question that I posed earlier in this chapter. Which carpenter would you hire to build new kitchen cabinets, one whose tool box contains a hammer and saw, or one whose tools fill the back of a van? Now, which social and behavioral scientist has the greatest likelihood of designing research that will change lives for the better and make a difference in the world, the one equipped with an average and a percentage, or the one with a full assortment of descriptive, significant difference, correlational, and regression statistics?

SUMMARY

Statistics are the tools of the social and behavioral sciences. Therefore, it behooves anyone who anticipates working in these areas to become conversant with statistics and their uses. Even so fundamental a task as staying current with the thinking in one's area demands reading about and understanding statistics.

With descriptive statistics we can describe samples and the populations they represent. Significant difference tests enable us to evaluate the reliability of differences observed between various groups. With correlational statistics we can discover patterns of relationship between variables and measure the strength of these relationships. And with regression analysis we can even predict the future.

Statistics organize, condense, and analyze data—the measured and numerically expressed characteristics and attributes of the cases under investigation, be they individuals or larger social units. Measurement procedures vary widely, but can be categorized as nominal, ordinal, interval, or ratio scale. Though the distinctions between these levels of measurement can be blurry, the choice of appropriate statistical procedures is affected by the level at which the variables analyzed are measured.

Statistics are the tools used to make sense of the data gathered through research. There are two basic types of research—experiments and correlational research. Experiments explain the variability of the world around us by identifying the factors that cause that variability. Correlational research does not identify causes, but it points out which variables vary together.

Learning about statistics will not only give you familiarity with the tools of the social and behavioral sciences, it will also mold your thinking about doing research. One's plan for collecting data is inevitably affected by how one plans to analyze those data. The more you know about the statistical options, the more research design options become available.

REVIEW EXERCISES

1.1. Identify the "cases" and "data" in each of the following examples: (a) a family therapist records the number of children in each of several families; (b) a psychophysiologist measures the blood pressure of each of 10 executives; (c) a sociologist records population densities for each of 15 cities.

1.2. What is the difference between descriptive statistics and inferential statistics?

1.3. Identify the purpose served (description, significant difference test, correlation, regression) by statistics in each of the following examples: (a) a teacher analyzes test scores to see if student performance early in the semester is related to performance later in the semester; (b) a personnel psychologist computes the average duration of employment for male and female production workers in a factory; (c) a sociologist predicts a city's crime rate based on the city's population density; (d) a social worker compares levels of depression seen in terminal AIDS patients and terminal cancer patients.

1.4. What does it mean to say that "subjects receiving biofeedback therapy experienced significantly fewer headaches than an untrained group of subjects"?

1.5. What does it mean to say that "a significant correlation was observed between scores on the first and second statistics tests"?

1.6. Why is a variable called a "variable"?

1.7. Describe a rule that you might use to measure your weight.

1.8. Identify the scale of measurement (nominal, ordinal, interval, or ratio) used in measuring each of the following variables: (a) family size, categorized as "small," "medium," or "large"; (b) classroom size, measured as number of pupils; (c) psychopathology, scored 1 = depression, 2 = schizophrenia, and 3 = personality disorder; (d) academic achievement, measured as number of items answered correctly on a test.

1.9. Suppose that statistics test scores were found to differ dramatically between male and female students. Why could one *not* conclude that gender has a causal impact on performance in the statistics class?

1.10. Identify the independent and dependent variables in each of the following experiments: (a) number of math problems completed in 30 minutes is compared for students who received either 50 mg or 100 mg of caffeine; (b) statistics test scores are compared for students taught using two different teaching methods.

1.11. Which of the following research designs is correlational and which is an experiment? (a) researchers compare life satisfaction scale scores of married and single 25-year-old males; (b) researchers compare the performance of athletes who were trained to use mental practice with that of athletes who were not trained this way.

1.12. Operationally define: (a) stress; (b) concentration.

1.13. What is the role of statistics in research?

ANSWERS TO COMPREHENSION CHECKS

1.1. (A) Each kindergarten pupil is a case, and their self-image test scores are the data. (B) Each classroom is a case, and ratings of cooperation are the data. (C) Each school district is a case, and numbers of weapon violations reported in each district are the data.

1.2. You should learn about statistics in order to read the literature of your discipline, stay abreast of current thinking, communicate effectively with your colleagues, and perform basic statistical analyses. Some familiarity with statistics will give you a sense of professional competence and self-assurance.

1.3. The data provide information about each case, descriptive statistics tell us about the sample as a whole, and inferential statistics enable us to draw conclusions about the entire population represented by the sample at hand.

1.4. A given statistical procedure can be considered both descriptive and inferential if it is used to describe (i.e., descriptive) a population on the basis of a study of a sample (i.e., inferential).

1.5. "Significantly" means that the difference between late and timely registrants observed in this sample of students would probably be seen again in a completely different sample of students. It means that the finding is reliable and replicable and is a characteristic of the much larger population of students from which the sample at hand was drawn.

1.6. "Significantly" means that the correlation observed in this sample of joggers would probably be seen again in a completely different sample of joggers. It means that the finding is reliable and replicable and is a characteristic of the population from which the sample at hand was drawn.

1.7. Although ACT and SAT scores are correlated with college GPA, this linkage is not perfect. That is, a few students with very low ACT/SAT scores do very well in college, and a few with very high ACT/SAT scores do very poorly. Because the correlation is not perfect, neither will be the predictions based on this correlation.

1.8. Approaches to measurement are limited only by one's imagination and creativity. What follow are only examples of the kinds of rules of measurement that might be useful here. Employee motivation might be measured by the number of times each month the employee works more than an 8-hour day. Toddler aggressiveness might be measured by a child's choice of aggressive or nonaggressive toys from a toy box. Respect for authority among parolees could be measured by the promptness with which parolees meet their parole officers.

1.9. Many examples are possible. One nominal variable is handedness, perhaps measured left-handed = 1, right-handed = 2. A second nominal variable is marital status, which could be measured single = 1, divorced = 2, married = 3, widowed = 4. Nominal scale data cannot be manipulated arithmetically because the "scores" are just code numbers that do not carry any quantitative meaning.

1.10. (A) Ordinal, because as scores increase so does the amount of education. (B) Nominal, because the scores are purely arbitrary and do not reflect the quantity of religious preference, only the type of preference. (C) Nominal, for the same reason as in B. (D) Ordinal, because rank-orders reflect the amount of leadership skill.

1.11. A rank-order of 7 means nothing by itself. Knowing that 100 students were ranked tells us that the student ranked 7th was judged to possess *relatively* little motivation. Even so, this student's motivation level may be quite high in absolute terms if all of the other 99 students are even higher.

1.12. (A) Interval, if we can assume that each arithmetic problem is equally as difficult as the others. A score of 0 would not indicate a complete lack of cognitive speed, just an immeasurably slow rate. (B) Ordinal, because as educational attainment increases, so do scores. Even so, educational attainment has not been measured using fixed-sized units. (C) Nominal, because we are concerned here with the presence or absence of opinions, not the strength of those opinions.

1.13. (A) Interval, if we can assume that each successive IQ test item measures the same additional amount of intelligence as the other items. If no questions were answered correctly, the resulting score of 0 would not indicate a complete lack of intelligence, just an immeasurably low level. (B) Ordinal, because rank-orders reflect quantity but do not provide measurement in fixed-sized units. (C) Ratio, because each percentage unit is the same as the others, and 0% means *no* body fat.

1.14. (A) Ratio, because seconds of time provide a fixed-sized unit of measure and because a score of 0 reflects immediate sensitivity to pain, with no delay. (B) Interval, if we can assume that the amount of sensitivity from one point on the rating scale to the next measures the same amount of pain. (C) Ordinal, because rank-orders do reflect quantity but do not provide measurement in fixed-sized units. (D) Nominal, because this rule measures the presence or absence of pain, not the quantity.

1.15. "The numbers don't know where they come from" is a reference to the fact that *we* have to decide whether the scores provide measurement at one level or another, and this decision depends on how we look at the measurement rule. There is nothing in the numbers themselves that can make this determination.

1.16. (a) The independent variable being actively manipulated is type of reward—stickers vs. verbal approval. The dependent variable that is passively measured is conduct, measured by students' conduct grades. (b) The independent variable is the type of injection—acetylcholine enhancer vs. saline. The dependent variable is ability to learn a maze, measured by number of trials to perfect performance.

1.17. This is not an experiment, because the researcher has no control over any of the variables—either gender or SAT scores. Both of these variables are passively measured to see if they vary together, making this correlational research.

1.18. There are many potential ways of operationally defining these variables. A few possibilities follow. (a) Intelligence is often measured by scores on an intelligence test. It is hard to imagine how one might go about actively manipulating intelligence. (b) Therapist empathy might be measured by asking clients to rate that quality on a 1–5 scale. Empathy might be manipulated by instructions to therapists on how to behave in a low-empathy vs. high-empathy manner. (c) Racial tension might be measured by scores on a racial attitude survey. Racial tension might be manipulated by providing a group with information designed to heighten or lower tensions.

1.19. Research design is the plan for gathering data. Data must be gathered before they can be analyzed with statistics. Even so, the kinds of statistics that are available for use in analyzing data will influence how one designs the research.

2 Data Distributions and Graphs

Chapter Outline

In a recent study of academic cheating,[1] an educational psychologist mailed surveys to several hundred university students. Among other questions, this survey included a 10-item questionnaire designed to measure students' attitudes toward cheating. Before you continue, take a couple of minutes to complete the 10-item Cheating Justification Questionnaire.

Cheating Justification Questionnaire

Indicate your feelings concerning each of the following statements by marking one of the following responses next to each statement:

1 = Strongly Disagree
2 = Disagree
3 = Agree
4 = Strongly Agree

When you have marked each item, add your responses to get a total score.

"Jack should not be blamed for cheating if"

______ **1.** the course material is too hard; no matter how much he studies he can't understand it.
______ **2.** he is in danger of losing his scholarship due to low grades.
______ **3.** he doesn't have time to study because he is working to pay for school.
______ **4.** the instructor doesn't seem to care if he learns the material.
______ **5.** the instructor acts like his/her course is the only one he is taking; too much material is assigned.
______ **6.** his cheating isn't hurting anyone.
______ **7.** everyone else in the room seems to be cheating.
______ **8.** the people sitting around him made no attempt to cover their papers and he could see the answers.
______ **9.** the instructor left the room to talk to someone during the test.
______ **10.** the course is required for his degree but the information seems useless. He is only interested in the grade.

______ TOTAL SCORE

Table 2.1 shows Cheating Justification Questionnaire scores for 120 of the students who responded to the survey. Just looking at the raw scores in this table, what would you say is the average or typical score? Where does

[1]LaBeff, E. E., Clark, R. E., Haines, V., and Diekhoff, G. M. (1990). Situational ethics and college student cheating. *Sociological Inquiry, 60,* 190–198.

TABLE 2.1

Cheating Justification Questionnaire scores from 120 college students

25	30	31	33	19	36
37	34	39	32	33	37
20	27	38	29	23	36
29	39	30	28	33	35
27	27	25	24	29	38
28	26	34	23	36	17
40	31	29	28	33	38
26	31	32	35	37	32
30	29	37	33	33	25
18	19	33	40	31	29
27	23	40	24	36	38
24	27	35	33	32	32
34	30	31	31	36	36
24	25	25	26	27	28
34	32	28	35	33	29
35	29	35	31	28	27
31	34	37	36	36	35
40	29	31	34	34	33
30	32	30	29	29	30
31	33	33	34	35	34

your score fall? High, low, or around the average? What would be considered an unusually low score? What would be considered an unusually high score?

Is it hard to answer these questions? Do you find it difficult to "read" the scores in Table 2.1? It isn't hard to understand why. After all, people are able to apprehend only about 7 pieces of information at one time, about the equivalent of a telephone number. Trying to sort through and make sense of a disorganized list of the 120 numbers in Table 2.1 exceeds this capacity by a fair margin!

What these data need is some organization! This is the purpose of data distributions, the topic of this chapter. Data may be organized using several kinds of distributions, each of which can be presented either as a table or as a graph. Tabular and graphic data distributions are extremely useful as we begin to make sense of what would otherwise be an incomprehensible mass of numbers. Distributions are important tools in our statistical tool box.

COMPREHENSION CHECK 2.1

What purpose is served by tabular (that is, presented in a table) and graphic data distributions?

(Answer on p. 53.)

2.1 TABULAR DATA DISTRIBUTIONS

In this chapter we will look at four kinds of data distributions: frequency, percentage, cumulative frequency, and cumulative percentage. Each of these kinds of distributions may be either grouped or ungrouped.

ungrouped frequency distribution *Indicates the frequency of occurrence of each score in a data set.*

Ungrouped Frequency Distributions

An **ungrouped frequency distribution** lists, from highest to lowest, all scores in the data set and indicates the frequency of occurrence of each of the

TABLE 2.2

Cheating Justification Questionnaire scores (X) organized as ungrouped frequency (f), percentage (%), cumulative frequency (f_c), and cumulative percentage ($\%_c$) distributions

X	f	%	f_c	$\%_c$
40	4	3.3	120	100.0
39	2	1.7	116	96.7
38	4	3.3	114	95.0
37	5	4.2	110	91.7
36	8	6.7	105	87.5
35	8	6.7	97	80.8
34	9	7.5	89	74.2
33	12	10.0	80	66.7
32	7	5.8	68	56.7
31	10	8.3	61	50.8
30	7	5.8	51	42.5
29	11	9.2	44	36.7
28	6	5.0	33	27.5
27	7	5.8	27	22.5
26	3	2.5	20	16.7
25	5	4.2	17	14.2
24	4	3.3	12	10.0
23	3	2.5	8	6.7
22	0	0.0	5	4.2
21	0	0.0	5	4.2
20	1	0.8	5	4.2
19	2	1.7	4	3.3
18	1	0.8	2	1.7
17	1	0.8	1	0.8
		$N = 120$		

scores. The first two columns of Table 2.2, labeled X (a symbol often used to represent scores on a variable) and f (for frequency), form an ungrouped frequency distribution. (We'll deal with the other columns of this table in due time.)

The first column, X, of the ungrouped frequency distribution lists the entire range of scores on the Cheating Justification Questionnaire, beginning at the top with the highest score (40) and ending at the bottom with the lowest score (17). (It is equally reasonable to list scores from lowest to highest, and some people prefer this format.) The second column, f, lists the number (frequency) of cases (students) that received each score. We see from Table 2.2, for example, that four students received scores of 40, two scored 39, four scored 38, and so on for each of the other scores. At the bottom of the frequency (f) column appears the letter N, which is the symbol commonly used to represent the total number of cases in the data set. In the present example there were 120 students, so $N = 120$. Notice that N will always be equal to the sum of the frequencies listed in the table. You can prove this to yourself by adding all of the values appearing in the frequencies column. They sum to $N = 120$.

With the data organized in the form of an ungrouped frequency distribution, we can see quickly that scores ranged from a low of 17 to a high of 40 and that scores in the upper 20s and lower 30s were more typical or average than either lower or higher scores. There is no question that Table 2.2 provides a clearer, more useful depiction of scores on the Cheating Justification Questionnaire than we got from the raw data in Table 2.1. Where does your score fall in this distribution?

COMPREHENSION CHECK 2.2

Use the scores that follow to construct an ungrouped frequency distribution.

25	24	21	23	18	19	23	19
18	21	21	19	17	22	17	15

(Answer on p. 53.)

Ungrouped Percentage Distributions

ungrouped percentage distribution *Indicates the percentage of cases that received each score in a data set.*

An **ungrouped percentage distribution** lists the percentage of cases that received each score in a set of data. In Table 2.2, the column labeled with a percent sign (%) forms an ungrouped percentage distribution. Percentages are computed according to Equation 2.1.

Equation 2.1

$$\% = \frac{f}{N} \times 100$$

where

% = the percentage of cases falling at the specified score
f = the number of cases falling at the specified score
N = the total number of cases in the distribution

In words, the percentage of cases receiving any particular score (%) is computed by: (1) dividing the number of cases that received that score (f) by the total number of cases in the data set (N), and (2) multiplying this quotient by 100.

COMPREHENSION CHECK 2.3

Use the data presented in Comprehension Check 2.2 to construct an ungrouped percentage distribution.
(Answer on p. 53.)

A percentage distribution will not tell us anything about the data that we couldn't determine from a frequency distribution. Both frequency and percentage distributions make clear the range of scores and where scores are concentrated. Percentage distributions do have one advantage over frequency distributions, though. That advantage is in comparing two or more data distributions, especially when the two distributions are of very different sizes.

Table 2.3 depicts Feetal Anxiety Inventory scores (measuring fear of one's feet) for 7,050 male and 150 female psychopodiatric patients. As always, scores are arranged from highest to lowest in the columns labeled X, the numbers of cases receiving each score are listed in the frequencies columns (f), and the percentages of cases receiving each score are listed in the columns labeled with a percent sign (%).

Look first just at the frequencies listed for the two samples. You can probably see that the two frequency distributions follow the same general pattern; both males and females show relatively few extremely low or high scores, and scores are concentrated in the 80s and 90s. In other words, the two distributions appear to be fairly similar.

Now look at the percentage distributions of the two samples. Not only are the two distributions similar, it turns out that they are identical! This example illustrates that it is easier to compare percentage distributions than frequency

Table 2.3

Feetal Anxiety Inventory scores (X) for 7,050 male and 150 female psychopodiatric patients, depicted as ungrouped frequency (f) and percentage (%) distributions

Males			Females		
X	f	%	X	f	%
100	470	6.7	100	10	6.7
90	1,410	20.0	90	30	20.0
80	2,350	33.3	80	50	33.3
70	940	13.3	70	20	13.3
60	470	6.7	60	10	6.7
50	470	6.7	50	10	6.7
40	940	13.3	40	20	13.3
	N = 7,050			N = 150	

distributions, because percentages "correct" for the influence of different sample sizes.

Comprehension Check 2.4

When is a percentage distribution more useful than a frequency distribution? When doesn't it matter?
(Answer on p. 53.)

Ungrouped Cumulative Frequency Distributions

In addition to frequency and percentage information, we can list with each score the number of cases scoring at *and below* that score, the **ungrouped cumulative frequency distribution.** This information is provided in Table 2.2 in the column labeled f_c. The cumulative frequency listed for the score of 20 is 5, because 5 cases scored at and below this score: 1 scored 20, 2 scored 19, 1 scored 18, and 1 scored 17. Similarly, a cumulative frequency of 120 is associated with the score of 40, because all 120 cases scored at or below this top value. Cumulative frequency information is of little direct value, but it is important in computing cumulative percentages, discussed next.

ungrouped cumulative frequency distribution *Indicates for each score in a data set the number of cases falling at that score and lower.*

Comprehension Check 2.5

Use the data presented in Comprehension Check 2.2 to construct an ungrouped cumulative frequency distribution.
(Answer on p. 53.)

Ungrouped Cumulative Percentage Distributions

ungrouped cumulative percentage distribution *Indicates for each score in a data set the percentage of cases falling at that score and lower. Cumulative percentages are also known as percentile ranks.*

The percentage of cases scoring at *and below* each score comprises the **ungrouped cumulative percentage distribution.** Cumulative percentages are listed in Table 2.2 under the column labeled $\%_c$. Cumulative percentages are computed according to Equation 2.2.

Equation 2.2

$$\%_c = \frac{f_c}{N} \times 100$$

where
$\%_c$ = the cumulative percentage for a specified score
f_c = the cumulative frequency associated with the specified score
N = the total number of cases in the distribution

In words, the cumulative percentage corresponding to any given score ($\%_c$) is computed by: (1) dividing the score's cumulative frequency (f_c) by the total number of cases in the data set (N); and (2) multiplying this quotient by 100.

In Table 2.2, the cumulative percentage listed for the score of 40 is 100. This is because 100% of the cases will necessarily fall at or below the highest score. For a score of 32, the cumulative percentage is 56.7, because 56.7% of the 120 cases have scored at or below the score of 32.

COMPREHENSION CHECK 2.6

Use the data presented in Comprehension Check 2.2 to construct an ungrouped cumulative percentage distribution.
(Answer on p. 54.)

Grouped Data Distributions

The data distributions that we have studied thus far have all been *ungrouped.* Frequency, percentage, cumulative frequency, and cumulative percentage information is provided for each and every score in an ungrouped distribution. Although this preserves every possible bit of information present in the original, unorganized raw scores, it sometimes preserves too much information. Ungrouped distributions can be almost as unwieldy as the unorganized raw data. Further condensation and simplification of information is sometimes called for. This is provided by grouped data distributions.

grouped data distribution *Indicates frequency, percentage, cumulative frequency, and cumulative percentage information for each of several ranges of scores or class intervals in a data set.*
class intervals *Groups or ranges of adjacent scores used in grouped data distributions.*

interval width (i) *The width of class intervals in a grouped data distribution. Interval width is equal to the difference between the upper limit and the lower limit of each interval, plus one.*

A **grouped data distribution** is constructed by organizing scores into groups called **class intervals,** then listing frequencies, percentages, cumulative frequencies, and cumulative percentages associated with each of the class intervals. Table 2.4 is a grouped data distribution for the Cheating Justification Questionnaire scores presented originally in Table 2.1. (Ignore the column headed *m.* We'll get to that in a minute.) Notice that scores have been grouped into several class intervals. In this example, each class interval spans a range of three scores (38–39–40, 35–36–37, 32–33–34, and so on). Therefore, we would say that the interval width (i) is 3 in this grouped distribution. **Interval width** refers to the number of scores that form each of the class intervals in a grouped data distribution. Notice also that the class intervals are organized by listing them from the highest (38–40), at the top of the table, to the lowest (17–19), at the bottom. Finally, notice how frequency (f), percentage (%), cumulative frequency (f_c), and cumulative percentage ($\%_c$) information is given for each class interval. This information is interpreted in pretty much the same way as in an ungrouped distribution. Entries in the frequencies column tell how many cases scored in each class interval, percentages indicate the percentage of cases that scored in each class interval, cumulative frequencies specify the number of cases that scored in and below each class interval, and cumulative percentages show the percentage of cases that scored in and below each class interval. As with ungrouped distributions, frequencies and cumulative frequencies are determined simply by counting, and percentages and cumulative percentages are computed using Equations 2.1 and 2.2.

X (i = 3)	m	f	%	f_c	$\%_c$
38–40	39	10	8.3	120	100.0
35–37	36	21	17.5	110	91.7
32–34	33	28	23.3	89	74.2
29–31	30	28	23.3	61	50.8
26–28	27	16	13.3	33	27.5
23–25	24	12	10.0	17	14.2
20–22	21	1	0.8	5	4.2
17–19	18	4	3.3	4	3.3
		N = 120			

TABLE 2.4

Cheating Justification Questionnaire scores (X) organized as grouped frequency (f), percentage (%), cumulative frequency (f_c), and cumulative percentage ($\%_c$) distributions

COMPREHENSION CHECK 2.7

Use the data provided in Comprehension Check 2.2 to complete the grouped data distribution below.

X (i = 2)	f	%	f_c	$\%_c$
24–25				
22–23				
20–21				
18–19				
16–17				
14–15				

(Answer on p. 54.)

Compare the ungrouped distribution of Table 2.2 and the grouped distribution of Table 2.4. The simplification of information that results from grouping scores into class intervals is obvious. Grouped distributions are shorter, present less information, and often are more easily read because they eliminate some of the "noise" and excessive detail that is present in ungrouped distributions.

But in statistics, as in life, there are no free lunches. We pay for the condensation and simplification that grouped distributions provide by sacrificing precision and specificity. For instance, from Table 2.2 we know precisely how many students posted scores of 26 on the Cheating Justification Questionnaire. There were 3. From Table 2.4 we see that 16 students scored in the class interval 26–28, but we no longer can tell how many scored 26. Information about individual score identity has been lost in the grouped distribution. The more we simplify and condense information, the more information we lose.

COMPREHENSION CHECK 2.8

What are the advantages of grouped data distributions over ungrouped distributions? What are the disadvantages?
(Answer on p. 54.)

apparent limits *Apparent limits are the top and bottom scores included in each of the class intervals that form a grouped data distribution.*

real limits *Real limits extend beyond the upper and lower apparent limits of each class interval by one-half the unit of measure.*

Apparent and Real Limits. The values that mark the end points of each class interval in a grouped distribution are called the **apparent limits.** For example, in Table 2.4 the apparent limits of the highest class interval are 38 and 40, the apparent limits of the second highest class interval are 35 and 37, and so on. In addition to apparent limits, each class interval also has **real limits:** the upper apparent limit plus one-half the unit of measure, and the lower apparent limit minus one-half the unit of measure. The Cheating Justification Questionnaire scores depicted in Table 2.4 are measured as whole numbers. Based on our definition of real limits, the real limits of the score intervals listed in Table 2.4 are 37.5–40.5 for the top interval, 34.5–37.5 for the second interval, 31.5–34.5 for the third interval, and so on. We will return later to the distinction between real and apparent limits.

COMPREHENSION CHECK 2.9

List the apparent and real limits of the grouped distribution in Comprehension Check 2.7.
(Answer on p. 54.)

midpoint (m) *The score falling exactly halfway between the upper and lower limits of a class interval.*

Midpoints. Sometimes it is useful to have a single score that can serve to represent all of the scores within a class interval. This single score is the midpoint. The **midpoint** of a score interval is the score that falls exactly halfway between the upper and lower limits (either real or apparent) of the interval. Midpoints are listed in Table 2.4 in the column labeled m. The midpoint of the top interval falls exactly halfway between 38 and 40—at 39, the midpoint of the second interval falls exactly halfway between 35 and 37—36, and so on. Midpoints are another idea to which we will return later. Midpoints are computed using Equation 2.3.

Equation 2.3

$$m = \frac{\text{UL} + \text{LL}}{2}$$

where

m = the midpoint of a specified class interval
UL = the upper limit of the specified class interval
LL = the lower limit of the specified class interval

In words, the midpoint of a given class interval (m) is computed by: (1) adding the upper limit of the interval (UL) to the lower limit of that interval (LL), and (2) dividing this sum by 2.

COMPREHENSION CHECK 2.10

Compute the midpoints of the class intervals of the grouped distribution in Comprehension Check 2.7.
(Answer on p. 54.)

Grouped Distributions: Some Guidelines. Perhaps it has occurred to you that the grouped distribution given in Table 2.4 is one of many that could have been constructed. This particular grouped distribution uses an interval width of 3, but there is nothing sacred about this choice. We could have used a wider or narrower class interval instead. This is our choice. Too, once an interval width is selected, we choose which scores to group together in forming the class intervals.

In constructing a grouped distribution it is important to remember our purpose—we are trying to get a clearer impression of the patterns and trends in the data set. The choices we make in deciding how to construct the grouped distribution should be made with this ultimate goal in mind. Frankly, trial and error—trying one grouping scheme and comparing it against another—is often the best way of getting the most informative grouped distribution. Still, a few guidelines can be offered that should cut down on the amount of time spent in trial and error.

In choosing an interval width, the first rule to follow—and really the only one that is critical—is that all intervals should be of the same width. Using intervals of varying widths will distort one's impression of the characteristics of the distribution. The grouped frequency distribution given in Table 2.5a uses five class intervals, each with an interval width of 10, to organize test scores from 49 statistics students. This distribution indicates that both high and low scores are relatively uncommon, with scores in the intermediate range predominating. Compare this to the impression given by Table 2.5b. This grouped distribution is based on the same scores, but uses different interval widths from one class interval to the next: 81–100 (i = 20), 77–80 (i = 4), 75–76 (i = 2), 71–74 (i = 4), and 51–70 (i = 20). A casual inspection of this grouped frequency distribution might easily lead one to conclude mistakenly that scores are concentrated at the top and bottom of the distribution, with relatively few in the middle ranges. Which table gives the more accurate impression of the actual distribution of scores? Table 2.5a does, with its equal interval widths.(See Note 1)

Comprehension Check 2.11

Redesign the interval widths of the grouped distribution in Comprehension Check 2.7 to make it appear that most cases scored high, with fewer and fewer cases scoring at lower levels.
(Answer on p. 54.)

Related to the rule to use equal interval widths is the decision about which specific scores to group together in the class intervals. One should avoid grouping scores in a way that would include impossible scores in the top and/or bottom class intervals. For example, given that the top possible score on the Cheating Justification Questionnaire is 40, which of the following groupings of scores would be more desirable?

38–40		39–41
35–37		36–38
32–34	or	33–35
.		.
.		.
.		.

TABLE 2.5

Grouped frequency distributions of statistics test scores (X). Table 2.5a uses equal interval widths (i = 10) for all class intervals, whereas Table 2.5b uses different interval widths.

(a) X	f	(b) X	(f)
91–100	5	81–100	17
81–90	12	77–80	11
71–80	20	75–76	2
61–70	10	71–74	7
51–60	2	51–70	12

Both grouping schemes use equal interval widths ($i = 3$), but the first arrangement is better because the second includes an impossible score in the top class interval—41. Because this score is impossible, the actual width of this class interval is only 2, not the intended 3.(See Note 2)

COMPREHENSION CHECK 2.12

Use the data given in Comprehension Check 2.2 and assume that the top possible score is 25. With this in mind, construct a grouped frequency distribution having an interval width of $i = 3$. Next, assume that the bottom possible score is 15 and construct a grouped frequency distribution having an interval width of $i = 3$.

(Answer on p. 54.)

We have seen that all class intervals should be equally wide, but how wide should they be? How does one select a proper interval width? Of course, the wider the class intervals, the fewer class intervals there will be and the more information will be lost. To illustrate this point, look at Table 2.6. This grouped frequency distribution groups our Cheating Justification Questionnaire scores into only three class intervals, each having a width of 10. Such a broad interval width used with these data results in an absurdly small number of class intervals, and we lose practically all information about scoring patterns and trends.

TABLE 2.6

Cheating Justification Questionnaire scores (*X*) organized as a grouped frequency distribution (*f*) with an interval width (*i*) of 10

X ($i = 10$)	*f*
31–40	69
21–30	46
11–20	5
	$N = 120$

At the same time, we don't want to use too narrow an interval width. The narrower the class intervals, the more class intervals there will be, and the more information will be retained. If this extra information includes unimportant details and "noise," the whole purpose of a grouped distribution has been defeated. Choose an interval width narrow enough to retain as much *useful* information as possible and broad enough to eliminate *superfluous* information.

Class intervals should be sufficiently broad that there are few, if any, that contain no cases, that is, frequencies of 0. Class intervals should be sufficiently narrow that the distribution provides a clear indication of the typical or average score in the data set. It is generally recommended that one choose an interval width that will yield around 10 class intervals across the range of scores with which one is working, but this is only a guideline and a starting point. Remember that there is no "wrong" interval width. Each interval width simply provides a different perspective on the data.

COMPREHENSION CHECK 2.13

Use the introductory psychology test scores listed below to construct grouped frequency distributions having interval widths of $i = 2$, $i = 5$, and $i = 10$. What are the advantages and disadvantages of each interval width?

88, 91, 63, 88, 68, 76, 100, 81, 71, 63, 83, 61, 100, 71, 83, 66, 91, 71, 86, 56

(Answer on p. 54.)

Distributions of Ordinal and Nominal Variables

In addition to organizing interval and ratio scale data like those we have examined thus far in this chapter, data distributions can be used to organize nominal scale data and some kinds of ordinal scale data as well.

Nominal Scale Distributions. Table 2.7 gives frequency and percentage distributions for the nominal scale variable of religious preference for 60 survey respondents. You should note two things about Table 2.7. First, categories of religious preference are not listed in any particular order. In the distributions we have worked with up to this point, scores were listed in order, from highest to lowest. Nominal scale data, though, have no "highest" or "lowest" categories. The categories are qualitatively, but not quantitatively, different from one to the next, so it doesn't matter in what order they are listed.

The second point to note is that Table 2.7 does not include either cumulative frequency or cumulative percentage information. A moment's reflection will reveal why this is so. Cumulative frequency and cumulative percentage distributions deal with the numbers and percentages of cases that score at *and below* a given score. Since no nominal scale category is "below" another category, cumulative frequency and percentage distributions would be meaningless.

For the same reason, there is no such thing as a grouped distribution for nominal scale data. The class intervals in a grouped distribution consist of ranges of scores that are adjacent along a continuous scale. When working with the discrete, discontinuous categories of a nominal scale variable, though, it makes no sense to form ranges of categories.(See Note 3)

Ordinal Scale Distributions. Some ordinal scale variables are easily organized using data distributions and others are not. Table 2.8 presents frequency, percentage, cumulative frequency, and cumulative percentage distributions for the academic ranks of 6,907 psychology professors.[2] Notice that academic ranks have been ordered from highest (professor) to lowest (instructor/lecturer). Notice too that cumulative frequency and cumulative percentage distributions make sense in the context of these ordinal data because some ranks *are* higher and others are lower. Finally, notice that it would be acceptable to form a grouped distribution of these data, because the academic ranks form a continuum.

[2]Wicherski, M., and Kohout, J. (1993, May). *1992–93 faculty salaries in graduate departments of psychology.* Washington, DC: American Psychological Association.

TABLE 2.7

Religious preferences of 60 survey respondants organized as frequency (f) and percentage (%) distributions

Religious Preference	f	%
Lutheran	9	15.0
Baptist	15	25.0
Catholic	11	18.3
Jewish	6	10.0
Other	19	31.7
	$N = 60$	

TABLE 2.8

Frequency (f), percentage (%), cumulative frequency (f_c), and cumulative percentage ($\%_c$) distributions of academic ranks for 6,907 psychology professors

Academic Rank	f	%	f_c	$\%_c$
Full professor	3,419	49.50	6,907	100.00
Associate professor	1,849	26.77	3,488	50.50
Assistant professor	1,564	22.64	1,639	23.73
Lecturer/instructor	75	1.09	75	1.09
	$N = 6{,}907$			

Rank-order data (not to be confused with the academic ranks of the preceding example), though also ordinal, are not appropriate for analysis with data distributions. An example will show why this is so. Suppose a psychotherapist rank-ordered 20 clients from least functional to most functional. Scores (ranks) would range from 1 to 20 and, assuming there were no ties, there would be one case (client) for each rank order. A data distribution could be constructed for these rank-order data, but it would point out only that each of the rank-order scores from 1 to 20 occurred once. This is not the kind of insight that one hopes to get from a data distribution.

COMPREHENSION CHECK 2.14

For each of the variables listed below, indicate if: (a) the ordering of scores or categories in the frequency distribution is important; (b) cumulative frequency and cumulative percentage distributions are appropriate; (c) a grouped distribution might be reasonable.

intelligence test scores
movie ratings (G, PG, etc.)
political preferences

(Answer on p. 55.)

2.2 PERCENTILE RANKS, PERCENTILES, AND QUARTILES

Percentile Ranks

percentile rank *Synonymous with cumulative percentage, percentile rank refers to the percentage of cases in a data set that score at and below a given score or class interval.*

We have already studied cumulative percentages in both ungrouped and grouped data distributions. Another name for cumulative percentage is **percentile rank.** The two terms mean the same thing; both refer to the percentage of cases scoring at and below a given point.

Percentile ranks give us information that is not present in the original raw scores. Specifically, percentile ranks locate scores in the distribution and convey information about how good or how bad, how high or how low any given score is. Suppose your friend tells you that his score on the Phrenological Aptitude Test is 450. Is this good, bad, or average? Suppose that you also know that your friend's score has a percentile rank of 80. Now you know that 80% of the people who took the test scored at or below your friend; only 20% scored higher. This is a pretty respectable score.

Or is it? What if everybody who took the test scored horribly on it? In this case, your friend's score at the 80th percentile is better than most, but it's still bad! The point is that percentile ranks provide purely relative information. They tell us whether a given score is high or low *relative to the other scores in the distribution.*

Finding Percentile Ranks. Finding the percentile rank for any given score in an ungrouped distribution is simply a matter of locating the score and determining its cumulative percentage. Look at Table 2.2, for instance. You can see that a score of 32 has a cumulative percentage of 56.7. This is also the percentile rank for that score.

Use Table 2.2 to determine the percentile rank of your score on the Cheating Justification Questionnaire. Interpret the meaning of this percentile rank.

(Answer on p. 55.)

COMPREHENSION CHECK 2.15

It is a little trickier to find percentile ranks when the data are in the form of a grouped distribution. Look at Table 2.4, for instance. How would we determine the percentile rank of a score of 32 in this grouped distribution? There is no cumulative percentage listed specifically for that score. When working with grouped distributions, we can only estimate percentile ranks. Equation 2.4 can be used for this purpose.

Equation 2.4

$$PR = \%_{c_B} + \left[\left(\frac{X - LRL}{i}\right)\%\right]$$

where

PR = the percentile rank for the specified score
$\%_{c_B}$ = cumulative percentage ($\%_c$) recorded for the class interval *below* the critical interval
X = the specified score
LRL = the lower real limit of the critical interval
i = interval width
% = percentage of cases in the critical interval

In words, we compute the estimated percentile rank for a given raw score (PR) by first identifying the class interval that contains that score, that is, the *critical interval.* We then proceed by: (1) subtracting from the raw score (X) the lower real limit of the critical interval (LRL); (2) dividing the result of step 1 by the interval width (i); (3) multiplying the result of step 2 by the percentage of cases in the critical interval (%); and (4) adding to step 3 the cumulative percentage listed for the class interval just below the critical interval ($\%_{c_B}$).

Equation 2.4 estimates the percentile rank of a score X by finding the percentile rank of the highest score in the next lower interval and then adding on a few additional percentage points based on how far into the next higher interval X is located. The closer X is to the bottom of its class interval, the fewer percentage points will be added; the closer X is to the top of its class interval, the more percentage points will be added. It is assumed in adding on these percentage points that scores are evenly distributed throughout each class interval. Estimated percentile ranks will be in error to the degree that this assumption is violated.(Note 4)

Use Equation 2.4 to estimate the percentile rank of a score of 21 in the grouped distribution in Comprehension Check 2.7.

(Answer on p. 55.)

COMPREHENSION CHECK 2.16

Example 2.1 provides a step-by-step illustration of the use of Equation 2.4 in estimating percentile ranks in grouped distributions. You will see from this example that the estimated percentile rank for a score of 32 in Table 2.4 is 54.68. We saw earlier that the *true* percentile rank of the score of 32 is 56.7. These percentile ranks differ because one is actual and the other is estimated.

EXAMPLE 2.1

Estimating Percentile Ranks in Grouped Distributions

Equation 2.4 provides a way of estimating the percentile rank of any specified score in a grouped distribution. We will work through an example here by estimating the percentile rank for a score of 32 in the grouped distribution depicted in Table 2.4, a portion of which is reproduced below.

X (*i* = 3)	*f*	%	f_c	$\%_c$	
.	.	.	.	.	
.	.	.	.	.	
.	.	.	.	.	
35–37	21	17.5	110	91.7	
32–34	28	23.3	89	74.2	critical interval
29–31	28	23.3	61	50.8	
.	.	.	.	.	
.	.	.	.	.	
.	.	.	.	.	

We begin by identifying the class interval that contains the specified score of 32, the so-called critical interval. It is the interval 32–34. Then we use Equation 2.4 to estimate the percentile rank for this score.

$$\text{PR} = \%_{c_B} + \left[\left(\frac{X - \text{LRL}}{i}\right)\%\right]$$

where

$\%_{c_B}$ = the cumulative percentage listed for the class interval just *below* the critical interval = 50.8
X = the specified score = 32
LRL = the lower real limit of the critical interval, that is, the lower apparent limit minus one-half the unit of measure: 32 − 0.5 = 31.5
i = the interval width of the grouped distribution = 3
% = the percentage of cases falling in the critical interval = 23.3

Substituting these numerical values into Equation 2.4, we have

$$\text{PR} = 50.8 + \left[\left(\frac{32 - 31.5}{3}\right)23.3\right]$$
$$= 54.68$$

The estimated percentile rank for a score of 32 in the grouped distribution depicted in Table 2.4 is 54.68. Approximately 55% of the cases scored at and below this value, with approximately 45% scoring higher.

Percentiles and Quartiles

percentile *Refers to the raw score having a specified percentile rank. For instance, the 50th percentile is the score that has a percentile rank of 50.*

Whereas the term *percentile rank* is used to refer to a raw score's cumulative percentage, the term **percentile** is used to refer to the raw score corresponding to a specified percentile rank. For instance, we saw in Table 2.2 that a Cheating Justification Questionnaire score of 32 has a cumulative percentage, that is, a *percentile rank* of 56.7. Thus, we can say that the 56.7th *percentile* is 32. The percentile rank refers to the cumulative percentage; the percentile refers to the raw score at that cumulative percentage.

The 25th, 50th, and 75th percentiles divide the cases into four equal groups, each consisting of one-quarter of the cases. These landmarks in a distribution are called **quartiles.** The first quartile falls at the 25th percentile, the second quartile is at the 50th percentile, and the third quartile is at the 75th percentile.

quartiles *The first quartile has a percentile rank of 25, the second quartile has a percentile rank of 50, and the third quartile has a percentile rank of 75.*

Finding Percentiles. Sometimes we need to find scores at specified percentile ranks, that is, percentiles. For instance, in order to compare the ages, gender composition, or other characteristics of low and high scorers on the Cheating Justification Questionnaire, we might want to determine which scores fall at the 25th and 75th percentiles. Students scoring above the 75th percentile would constitute our high-scoring group, and students scoring below the 25th percentile would form the low-scoring group.

Finding percentiles in an ungrouped distribution is a straightforward process. First, find the desired percentile rank (cumulative percentage) and see what score (percentile) is listed for this percentile rank. When, as often happens, the percentile rank we are interested in is not listed, we find the next higher percentile rank and use the score associated with it as the desired percentile. Let's use this procedure to find the 40th percentile in Table 2.2. There is no cumulative percentage of 40% listed, so we'll use the next higher value that is listed—42.5%. The score of 30 corresponding to this percentile rank is used as the 40th percentile.

COMPREHENSION CHECK 2.17

What scores mark the first, second, and third quartiles in Table 2.2? (Answer on p. 55.)

Things again get a bit more complicated when we are working with grouped distributions. We used Equation 2.4 to estimate percentile ranks from raw scores in grouped distributions. We should be able to use this same equation, in rearranged form, to estimate raw scores (percentiles) from specified percentile ranks. Equation 2.5 describes this procedure.

Equation 2.5

$$X = \frac{(\text{PR} - \%_{c_B})i}{\%} + \text{LRL}$$

where

X = the percentile (score) for the specified percentile rank
PR = the specified percentile rank
$\%_{c_B}$ = the cumulative percentage ($\%_c$) recorded for the class interval *below* the critical interval
i = interval width
% = the percentage of cases in the critical interval
LRL = the lower real limit of the critical interval

In words, to estimate the percentile corresponding to a specified percentile rank (X), we first identify the critical class interval—the interval that contains the percentile we seek. This critical interval is the one that lists a cumulative percentage equal to or just higher than the specified percentile rank. Once this critical interval is identified, we proceed by: (1) subtracting the cumulative percentage of the class interval below the critical interval ($\%_{c_B}$) from the specified percentile rank (PR); (2) multiplying the result of step 1 by the interval width (i); (3) dividing the result of step 2 by the percentage of cases in the critical interval (%); and (4) adding the lower real limit (LRL) of the critical interval to the result of step 3.

Example 2.2 shows how to use Equation 2.5 to estimate percentiles in grouped distributions. You will see from this example that the estimated percentile corresponding to a percentile rank of 10 in Table 2.4 is 24.24. This estimate compares closely with the actual percentile found in Table 2.2—24.0.

EXAMPLE 2.2

Estimating Percentiles in Grouped Distributions

Just as we can estimate the percentile rank of a score in a grouped distribution (Example 2.1), we can also begin with the percentile rank and work backward to estimate its corresponding score, called the *percentile.* We will use Equation 2.5 here to estimate the score having a percentile rank of 10 (that is, the score at the 10th percentile) in Table 2.4, a portion of which is reproduced below.

X ($i = 3$)	f	%	f_c	$\%_c$	
.	.	.	.	.	
.	.	.	.	.	
.	.	.	.	.	
26–28	16	13.3	33	27.5	
23–25	12	10.0	17	14.2	critical interval
20–22	1	.8	5	4.2	
.	.	.	.	.	
.	.	.	.	.	
.	.	.	.	.	

We begin by identifying the class interval that captures the score at the 10th percentile—the critical interval. The critical interval is the class interval that lists a cumulative percentage equal to or just higher than the specified percentile rank. It *is not* the interval 20–22, because only 4.2% of the cases fall at and below this interval. It *is* the interval 23–25, because 14.2% of the cases fall at and below this point, thus including the score at the 10th percentile. Then we use Equation 2.5 to estimate the score at the 10th percentile.

$$X = \frac{(\text{PR} - \%_{c_B})i}{\%} + \text{LRL}$$

where

PR $=$ the specified percentile rank $= 10$
$\%_{c_B}$ $=$ the cumulative percentage recorded for the class interval just *below* the critical interval $= 4.2$
i $=$ the interval width of the grouped distribution $= 3$
% $=$ the percentage of cases falling in the critical interval $= 10$
LRL $=$ the lower real limit of the critical interval, that is, the lower apparent limit minus one-half the unit of measure: $23 - 0.5 = 22.5$

Substituting these numerical values into Equation 2.5, we have

$$X = \frac{(10 - 4.2)3}{10} + 22.5$$
$$= 24.24$$

The score estimated to mark the 10th percentile in Table 2.4 is 24.24. Approximately 10% of the cases scored at and below this value and approximately 90% scored higher.

COMPREHENSION CHECK 2.18

Use Equation 2.5 to estimate the 50th percentile in the grouped distribution in Comprehension Check 2.7.
(Answer on p. 55.)

2.3 METHODS OF GRAPHING DATA

If one picture is worth a thousand words, one graph is certainly worth a thousand tables. (Well, not quite, but you get the idea.) Tabular data distributions do an excellent job of preserving the particulars of a data set, but they are not always effective in revealing the characteristics of the whole distribution. Tabular distributions show us the details but may not give a good impression of the overall theme. Graphs provide a remedy. A graph merges the many elements of a tabular distribution into a single image.

We will explore only the most common, basic approaches to graphing distributions in this chapter: bar graphs, histograms, and frequency curves.

Bar Graphs

A **bar graph** is commonly used to display frequency or percentage distributions of nominal scale data. Figure 2.1 is a bar graph depicting the frequency distribution of religious preferences presented earlier as Table 2.7. Categories of the nominal scale variable are shown along the horizontal axis, called the ***X* axis** or **abscissa.** These categories are listed in no particular order because nominal scale categories possess no ordinal characteristics. Frequencies are represented along the vertical axis, called the ***Y* axis** or **ordinate.** Directly above each of the nominal categories, a bar rises vertically to an altitude that indicates the number (frequency) of cases in that category. Consistent with the discrete, discontinuous nature of the categories of nominal scales variables, the bars of a bar graph are visually separated and discontinuous.

bar graph *A type of graph used with nominal scale data to depict frequency or percentage distributions. The altitude of the bars on the ordinate represents the frequency or percentage of each nominal scale category on the abscissa.*

X axis or abscissa *Synonyms that refer to the horizontal axis of a graph. In graphed data distributions, scores, class intervals, or nominal scale categories are represented along the X axis or abscissa.*

Y axis or ordinate *Synonyms that refer to the vertical axis of a graph. In graphed data distributions, frequencies, percentages, cumulative frequencies, or cumulative percentages are represented along the Y axis or ordinate.*

COMPREHENSION CHECK 2.19

Use the tabular frequency distribution shown below to draw a bar graph.

Academic Major	*f*
Psychology	197
Sociology	57
Social work	93

(Answer on p. 56.)

FIGURE 2.1

A bar graph depicting the frequency distribution of religious preferences.

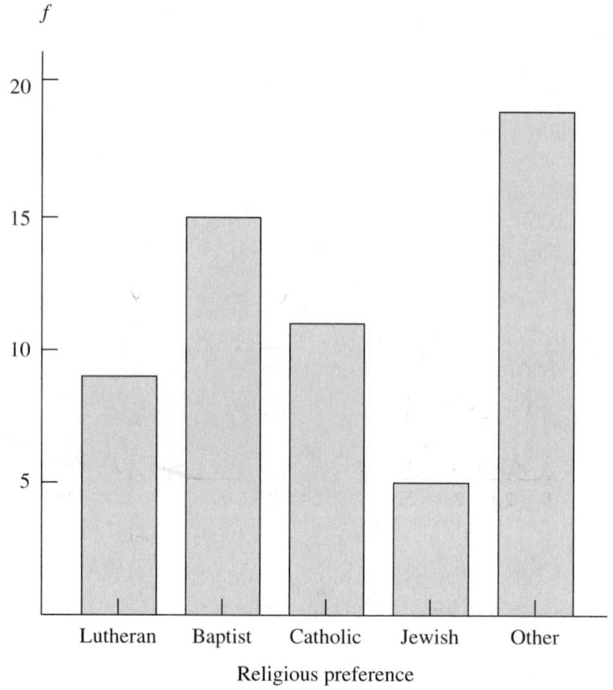

Histograms

histogram *A type of graph similar to a bar graph, except that there is no separation between the bars. Histograms are used to depict distributions of ordinal, interval, and ratio scale data.*

A **histogram** is similar to a bar graph, but it is used to depict frequency or percentage distributions of ordinal, interval, or ratio scale data. Figure 2.2a depicts the ungrouped frequency distribution given earlier in tabular form as Table 2.2. Figure 2.2b is a histogram based on the grouped frequency distribution given as Table 2.4.

Histograms are constructed just like bar graphs, with scores or class intervals represented on the abscissa and frequencies represented on the ordinate. Also like bar graphs, histograms use vertically rising columns to mark the frequencies associated with each score or class interval.

Because histograms are used with continuous ordinal, interval, and ratio scale variables, they differ from bar graphs in two important respects. First, scores are listed on the abscissa from lowest on the left to highest on the right. Second, the vertical bars of the histogram are pushed together so that they touch each other. The visual continuity that this provides echoes the quantitative continuity of the variables that histograms are used to describe.

COMPREHENSION CHECK 2.20

Use the grouped frequency distribution in Comprehension Check 2.7 to construct a histogram.

(Answer on p. 56.)

Frequency Polygons and Curves

frequency polygon *A type of graph used to depict distributions of continuous variables. The connected points forming the polygon depict frequencies or percentages (on the ordinate) for each score or class interval (on the abscissa).*

Figure 2.3 shows two **frequency polygons** based on the ungrouped (Figure 2.3a) and grouped (Figure 2.3b) frequency distributions of Cheating Justification Questionnaire scores (Tables 2.2 and 2.4). A frequency polygon represents scores or class intervals from left to right in ascending order along

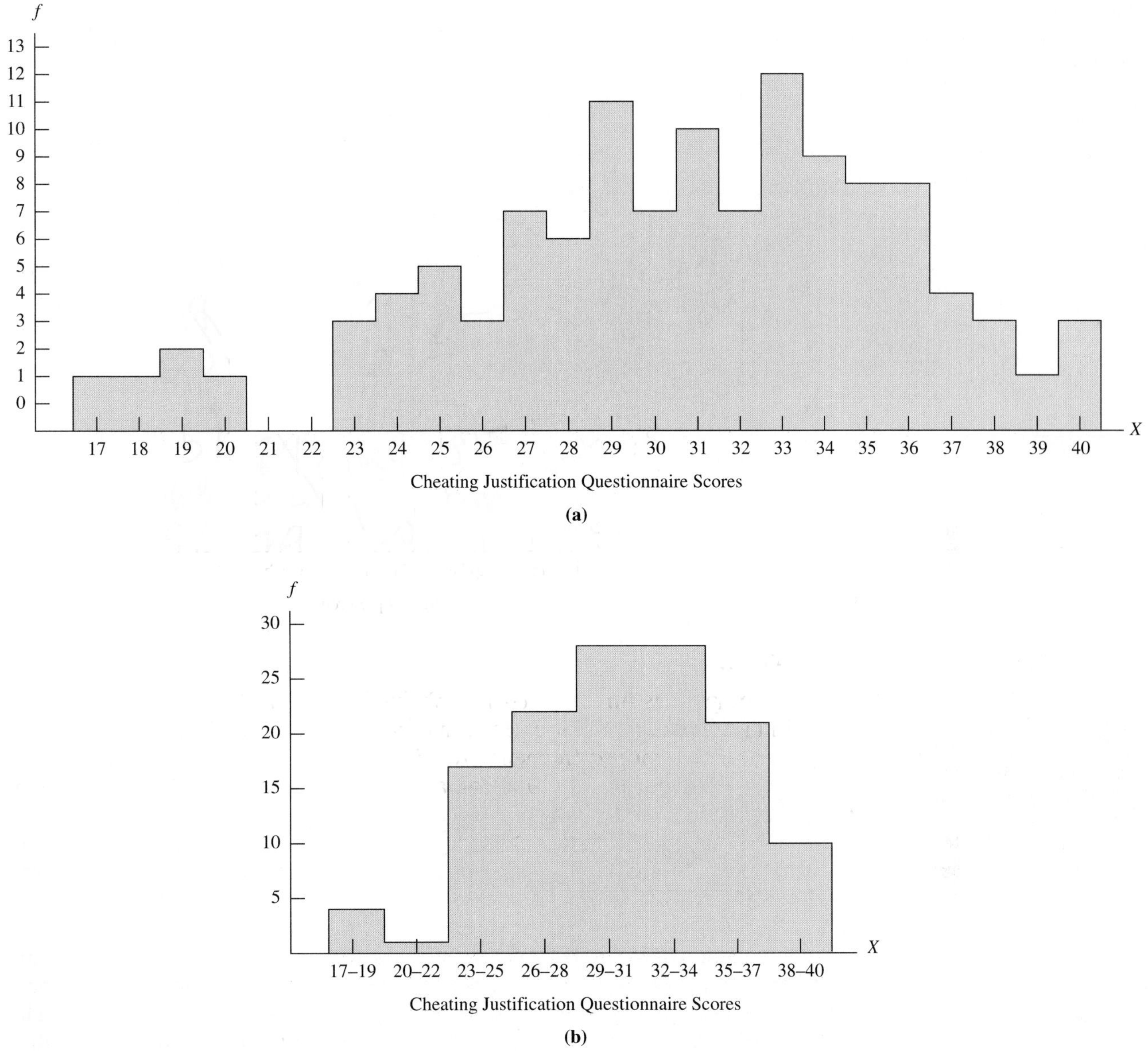

FIGURE 2.2

Two histograms depicting the distribution of scores on the Cheating Justification Questionnaire. (a) is an ungrouped distribution; (b) is a grouped distribution.

the abscissa and frequencies along the ordinate. The number of cases falling at each score or within each class interval is indicated by the altitude of a point above that score or class interval. Finally, the points are connected with straight lines.

COMPREHENSION CHECK 2.21

Use the ungrouped frequency distribution in Comprehension Check 2.2 to construct a frequency polygon.
(Answer on p. 56).

FIGURE 2.3

Two frequency polygons depicting the distribution of scores on the Cheating Justification Questionnaire. (a) is an ungrouped distribution; (b) is a grouped distribution.

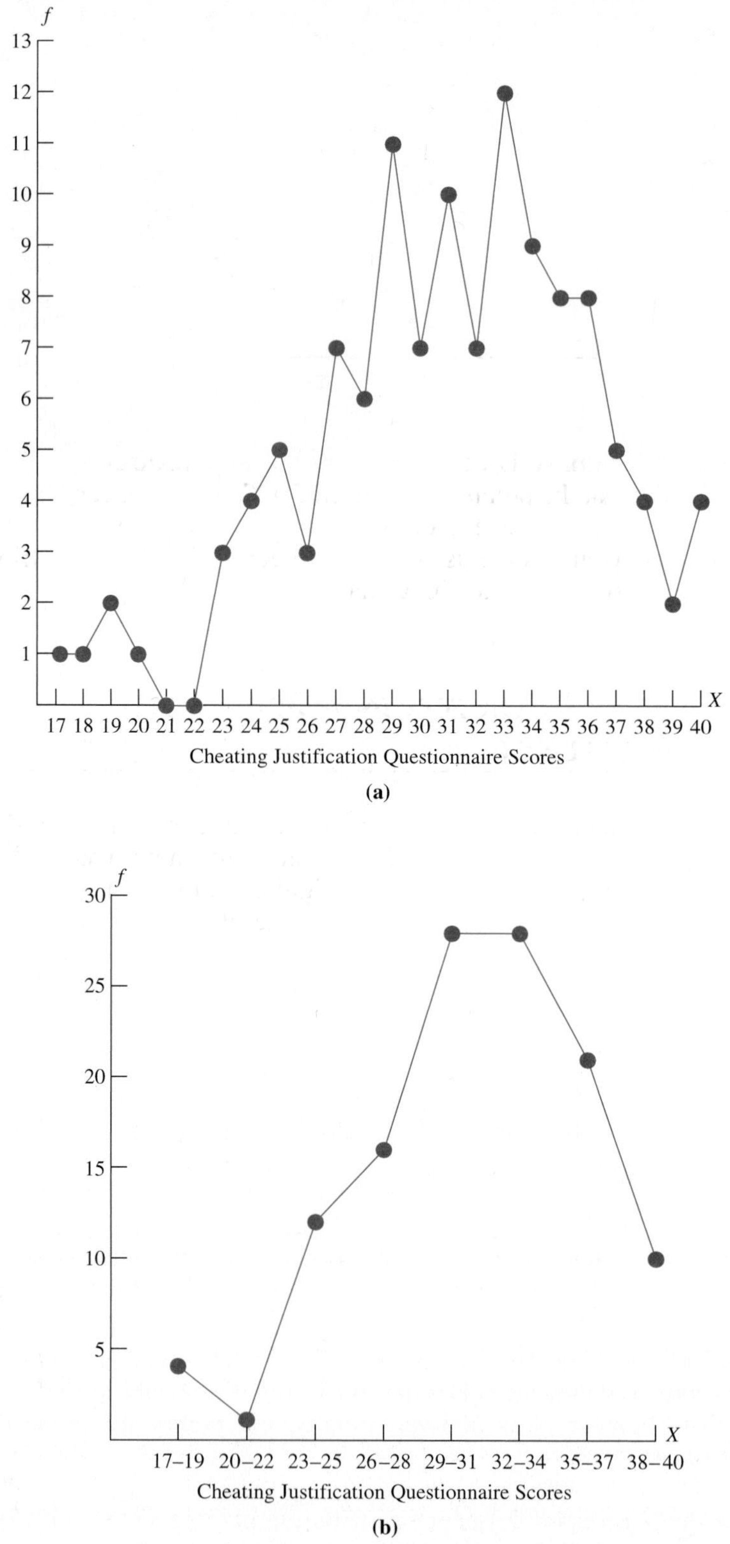

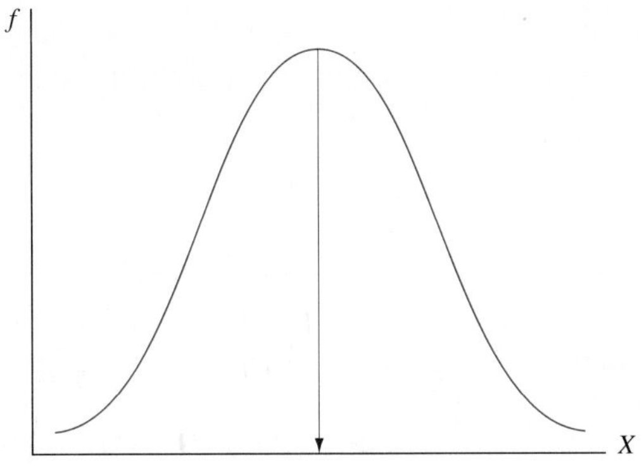

FIGURE 2.4
The central tendency of a distribution is often found toward the center of the frequency distribution.

A **frequency curve** is constructed in the same manner as a frequency polygon except that the points are connected with a smooth curve rather than with straight lines. Look ahead to Figure 2.4 for an example of a frequency curve. Frequency curves are usually used to depict theoretical distributions; frequency polygons are used with actual data.

frequency curve *Similar to the frequency polygon except that the lines connecting the points are replaced with a smooth curve.*

2.4 WHAT TO LOOK FOR IN A FREQUENCY DISTRIBUTION

Have you ever looked at an X-ray? To the untrained eye an X-ray looks unreadably blurry and shadowy. To those trained to know what to look for, though, each wisp, streak, shadow, and highlight carries an important message. Reading frequency distributions is a little like reading X-rays. In both cases you have to know what to look for. We will explore in this section just what we are looking for in graphed frequency distributions.

Central Tendency

Once we turn from the scores of individuals to consider the sample distribution as a whole, one of the first questions we ask concerns the typical or average score. This is called **central tendency.** When we read that recreational joggers suffer an average of 1.2 running-related injuries per year or that the average life expectancy of a woman of age 75 is 10 years, we are dealing with central tendency. Some joggers will suffer fewer than 1.2 injuries each year and some will suffer more, but most will suffer around 1.2 injuries. Some women aged 75 years will live fewer than 10 more years and some will live longer, but the typical or average 75-year-old woman will live 10 more years. Central tendency gives us a way, when we need it, to ignore the variability of individuals within a group and to concentrate on describing the group as a whole. Central tendency is called *central* tendency because the typical or average score very often (though not always) falls toward the center of the distribution. As seen in Figure 2.4, the central tendency of a distribution is marked by a noticeable frequency peak located over the scores or class intervals that are typical or average.

central tendency *Refers to the average or typical score in a distribution.*

COMPREHENSION CHECK 2.22

> Looking at the histogram you constructed in Comprehension Check 2.20, describe the central tendency of the distribution.
> (Answer on p. 56.)

Variability

variability *Refers to the degree to which scores in a distribution are dispersed across a broad range.*

Central tendency describes the group as a whole, but in doing so ignores differences from one individual case to the next, that is, **variability.** Sometimes, though, we are more interested in this variability than in the average or typical score. Wouldn't a physician feel more comfortable prescribing a medication that affects everyone in just about the same way over one that has very different effects? Before enrolling your child in a preschool program, wouldn't you like to know not just how the average child reacts to the program's curriculum, but something about the variability of children's reactions?

Data variability is represented very clearly by the breadth of graphed frequency distributions. Figure 2.5 shows that highly variable data form a broad frequency distribution. A narrower frequency distribution indicates a less variable distribution.

COMPREHENSION CHECK 2.23

> Looking at the histogram you constructed in Comprehension Check 2.20, describe the variability of the distribution.
> (Answer on p. 56.)

Normal Distributions and Deviations from Normality

normal distribution *A bell-shaped, symmetrical distribution often found in nature. Most scores are moderate, with fewer and fewer scores found as one moves above and below the center of the distribution.*

Figure 2.6 is a symmetrical, bell-shaped, **normal distribution.** In a normal distribution, most cases score toward the center of the range of scores and there are fewer and fewer cases as we move in either direction away from this central point. Many of the variables that are studied by social and behavioral scientists are normally distributed. Intelligence, personality and aptitude test scores, age, level of psychopathology, and many other variables are normally distributed. Many of the statistics that we use are based on the assumption that our data are normally distributed. Because of this, it is important to know if the data at hand really *are* normally distributed. Though "real-life" data are seldom if ever exactly normally distributed, some data sets come closer to the normal model than do others. The fastest way to determine if the data at hand

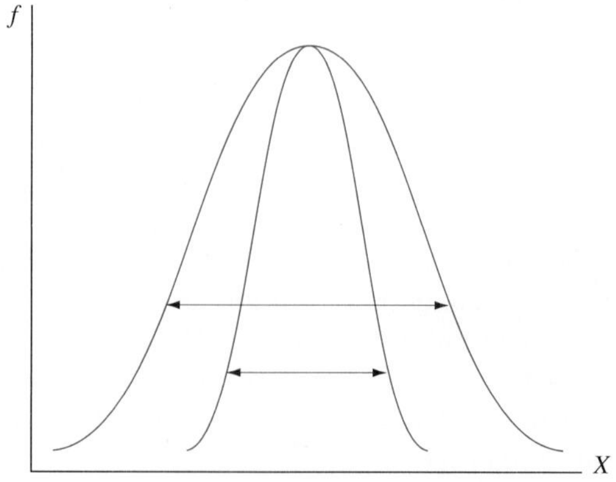

FIGURE 2.5
The variability of a distribution is reflected in the width of the frequency distribution. The narrow distribution indicates low variability; the wider distribution indicates greater variability of scores.

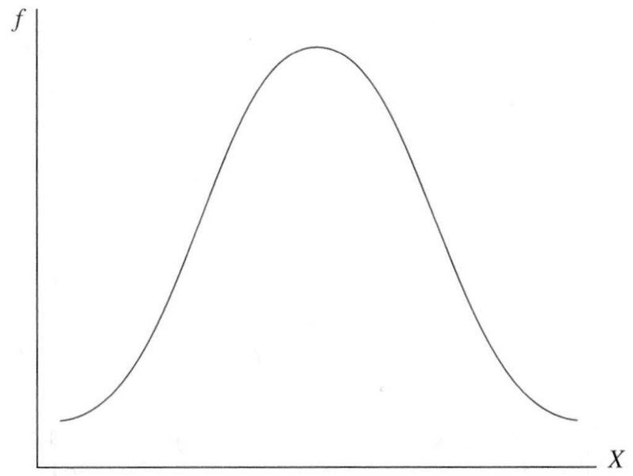

FIGURE 2.6

The normal distribution is bell-shaped and symmetrical.

provide a close approximation to the normal distribution is to look at the frequency distribution for signs of various deviations from normality.

Skew. One common deviation from the symmetry of the normal distribution is the asymmetrical or skewed distribution. Figure 2.7a shows a **negatively skewed** distribution. Most cases in this distribution show relatively high scores, with a few low-scoring **outliers**—cases whose scores fall out away from the majority of cases. The distribution of students' grades provides one common example of a negatively skewed distribution. Because of the attrition of low-performing students during the semester, there tend to be more high grades than low grades by the end of the semester.

negative skew *Refers to an asymmetrical distribution in which most scores are relatively high but there are a handful of low-scoring outliers.*

outliers *Cases whose scores fall out away from the majority of cases.*

positive skew *Refers to an asymmetrical distribution in which most scores are relatively low but there are a handful of high-scoring outliers.*

Figure 2.7b illustrates **positive skew.** Here we see relatively few high-scoring outliers with most cases scoring toward the low end of the distribution. Annual income in the United States is positively skewed, with only a relative handful of high-income outliers earning above $100,000 annually.

Skewness in either "direction," that is, negative or positive, is important to identify. For one thing, strongly skewed data may not be appropriately analyzed using statistical procedures that assume a normal distribution. We will see in the next chapter, for example, that even so simple a statistic as the mean is distorted by skewed data. Skewed data also limit our ability to draw unequivocal conclusions. The outliers in a skewed distribution are exceptions to whatever rule characterizes the other cases in the distribution. Because of the outliers in a skewed distribution, we must qualify our statements: "Most students did quite well in the course, *but there were a handful of Fs.*" "Most Americans earn between $20,000 and $50,000, *but a handful can expect to earn much more than this.*" Outliers are unusual by definition and can make

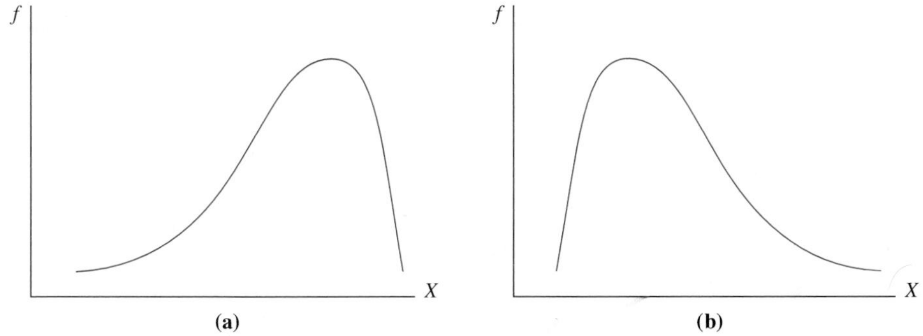

FIGURE 2.7

Skewed distributions. (a) shows a negatively shewed distribution; (b) shows a positively skewed distribution.

for an interesting study in and of themselves, but first we must identify them. A graphed frequency distribution is often the easiest way of accomplishing this.

COMPREHENSION CHECK 2.24

Think of your own examples of distributions that would probably be positively skewed or negatively skewed.
(Answer on p. 56.)

mesokurtic *Refers to a distribution that is of moderate peakedness. A normal distribution is mesokurtic.*
leptokurtic *Refers to a distribution that is more peaked or steeper than a normal distribution.*
platykurtic *Refers to a distribution that is flatter than a normal distribution.*

Kurtosis. The *kurtosis* of a distribution refers to the peakedness or flatness of the distribution. A normal distribution is said to be **mesokurtic.** A distribution that is steeper than the normal distribution is called **leptokurtic.** A distribution that is flatter than the normal distribution is called **platykurtic.** Figure 2.8 gives examples of mesokurtic (Figure 2.8a), leptokurtic (Figure 2.8b), and platykurtic (Figure 2.8c) frequency distributions.

COMPREHENSION CHECK 2.25

How are kurtosis and variability related?
(Answer on p. 56.)

unimodal *Refers to a distribution that shows one clear frequency peak.*
bimodal *Refers to a distribution that shows two clear frequency peaks. A bimodal distribution suggests the presence of two distinct subgroups within the data set.*
multimodal *Refers to a distribution that shows three or more clear frequency peaks. Multimodal distributions suggest the presence of multiple distinct subgroups within the data set.*

Modality Characteristics. All of the distributions we have looked at so far have had one frequency peak and are called **unimodal.** This single frequency peak is centered in the normal distribution and is off-center in skewed distributions. Some distributions, though, have two or more frequency peaks. Those with two clearly defined frequency peaks are called **bimodal** distributions; those with three or more peaks are called **multimodal** distributions.

Figure 2.9a shows the distribution of annual salaries of 3,553 psychology professors teaching in doctoral programs in the United States.[3] The distribution is bimodal, showing two clear frequency peaks, one over the salary interval \$35,000–\$44,999, and the other over the interval \$55,000–\$64,999.

Bimodal and multimodal distributions alert us to the presence of two or more distinctly different homogeneous subgroups within the larger distribution, with each frequency peak representing one of those subgroups. The bimodal nature of Figure 2.9a is the result of combining the rather different

[3]Ibid.

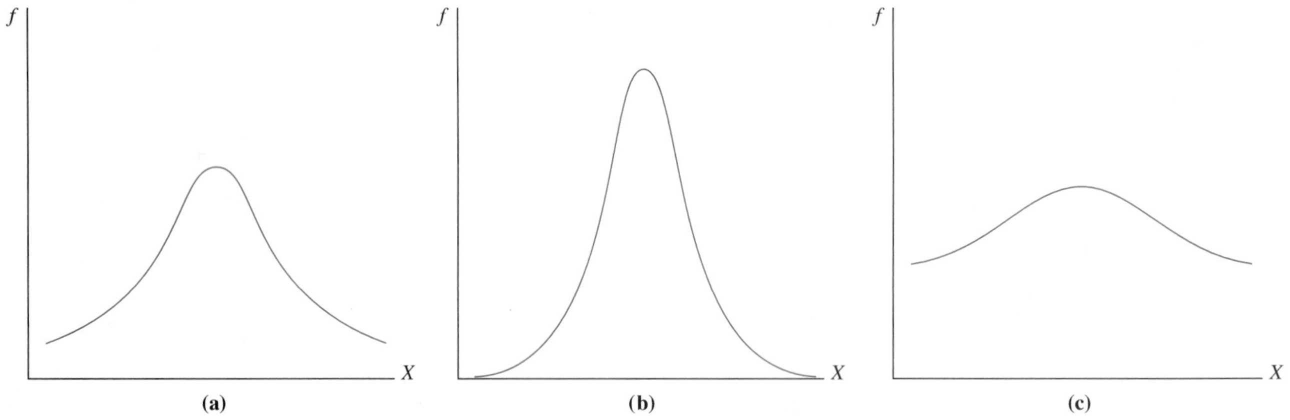

FIGURE 2.8
Frequency distributions displaying various forms of kurtosis. (a) is mesokurtic, (b) is leptokurtic, and (c) is platykurtic.

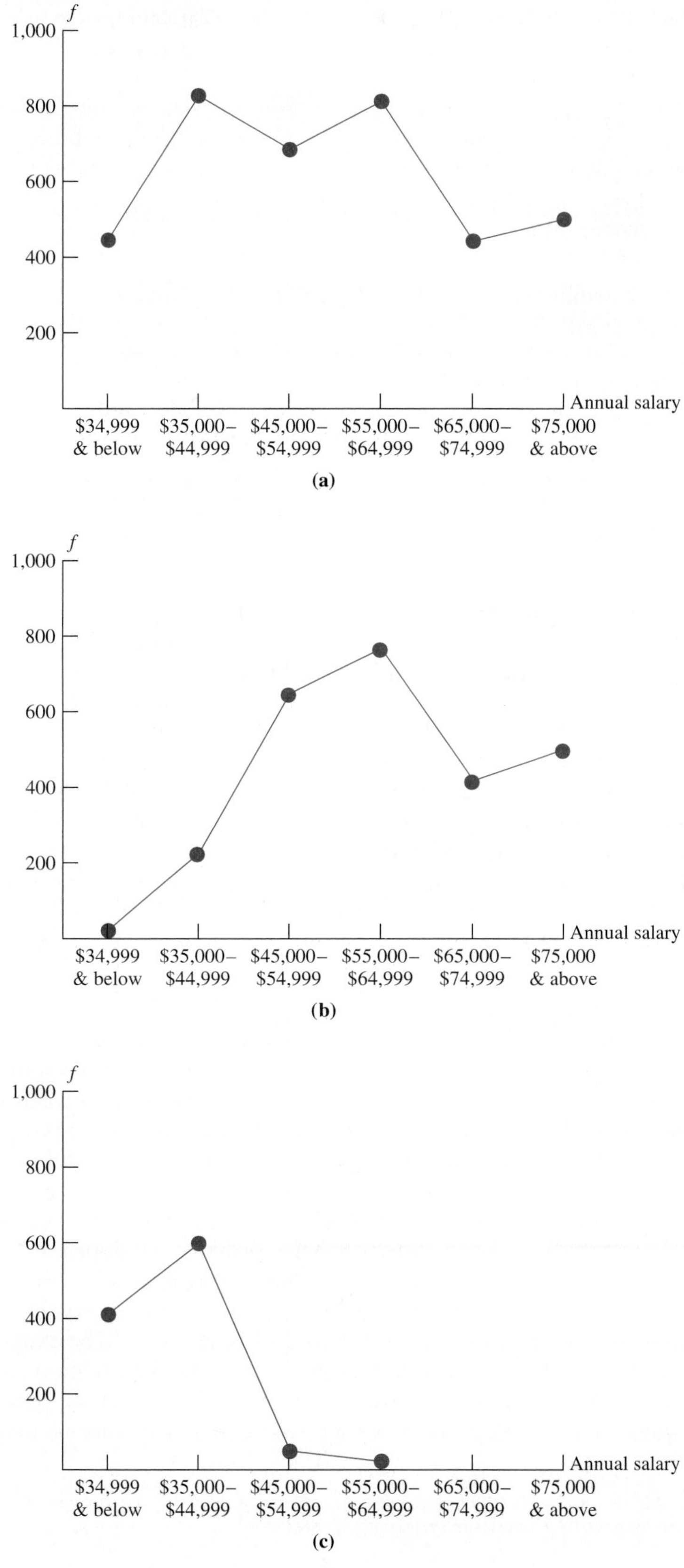

FIGURE 2.9

The bimodal distribution of salaries of psychology professors seen in (a) results from combining salary data from full professors (b) and assistant professors (c).

salary data from full professors (Figure 2.9b) and assistant professors (Figure 2.9c).

COMPREHENSION CHECK 2.26

Early in freshman-level courses it is common to see a bimodal distribution of grades. By semester's end, grades usually have taken on a unimodal appearance. Can you offer any explanation for this observation?

(Answer on p. 56.)

rectangular distribution *Refers to a distribution that has no noticeable frequency peak; all scores occur with approximately equal frequency.*

Some distributions, called **rectangular distributions,** show no frequency peak at all. Figure 2.10 illustrates the general form of this type of distribution. A rectangular distribution results when all scores occur with approximately equal frequency.

FIGURE 2.10

A rectangular distribution exists when all scores occur with approximately equal frequency.

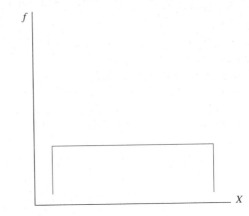

2.5 MISTAKES TO AVOID IN GRAPHING DATA DISTRIBUTIONS

Contrary to popular belief, statistics do not lie. Even so, statistics sure can fool the statistically naive! But communication, not confusion, is the appropriate goal of statistical analysis. We need to make every effort not to use statistics improperly. Graphed data distributions can provide a powerful tool to help in understanding the characteristics of the cases represented by a collection of data. When misused, though, they can be equally powerful in painting a distorted picture.

Some distortions result from using an abscissa that is too short or too long. It is generally recommended that the ordinate be approximately the same length as the abscissa. When the ordinate is too short, differences in frequencies or percentages from one category, score, or score interval to the next will be hidden. When the ordinate is too long, differences will be exaggerated. Figures 2.11a and 2.11b illustrate this principle with data from a survey of psychology doctoral training programs.[4] Both graphs depict the percentages of U.S. doctoral psychology students who are enrolled in various major sub-

[4]Wicherski, M., and Kohut, J. (1992, Sept.). *Characteristics of graduate departments of psychology: 1990–91.* Washington, DC: American Psychological Association.

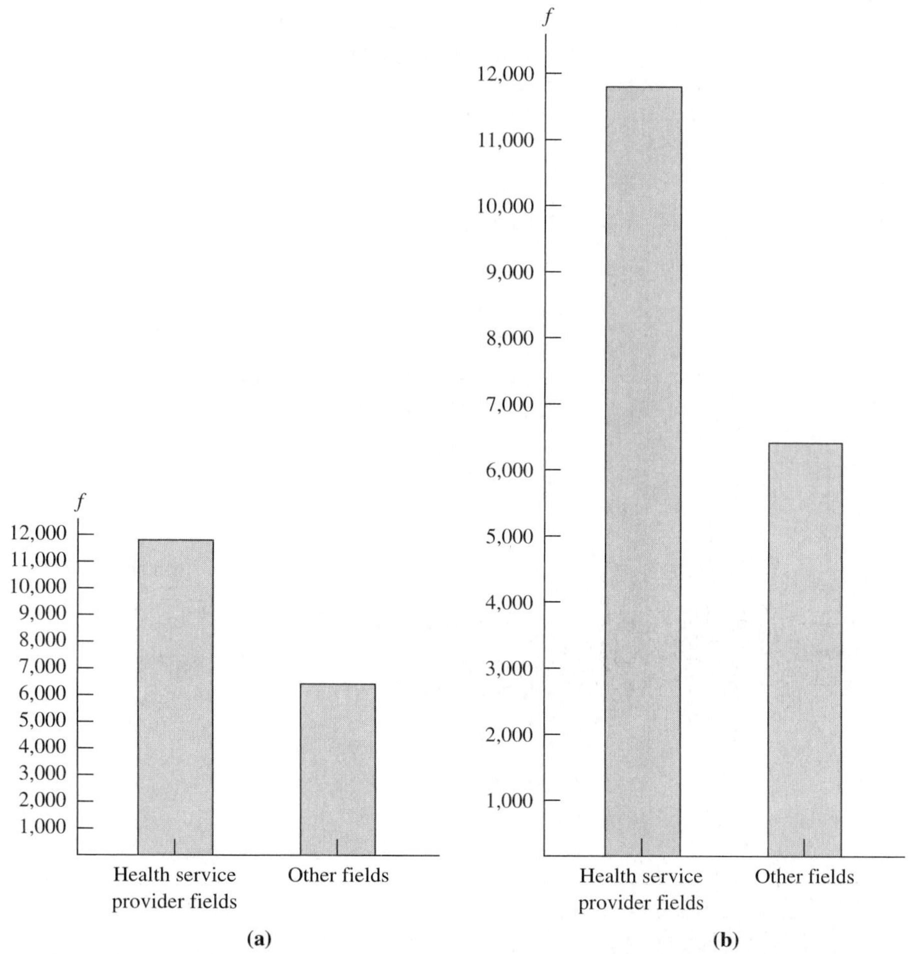

FIGURE 2.11

Numbers of psychology doctoral students enrolled in health service provider and "other" training programs. When the ordinate is too short (a), differences are obscured. When the ordinate is too long (b), differences are exaggerated.

field areas, but the graphs create rather different impressions because of the way they are constructed. Figure 2.11a uses an excessively short ordinate that gives the impression of little difference in levels of enrollment in the categories of psychological training. Figure 2.11b uses an excessively long ordinate that amplifies the difference.

Another distortion in graphed frequency and percentage distributions results when the frequency or percentage scale on the ordinate omits the zero point and starts at an above-zero level. Figure 2.12 illustrates this kind of distortion with the same doctoral training data we examined just above. In Figure 2.12a the graph is constructed properly. Compare Figure 2.12b, where the ordinate lists frequencies beginning with 7,000. One can easily get a mistakenly low impression of the number of students enrolled in "other fields" from this graph.

The practice of employing different interval widths in constructing grouped distributions was criticized earlier. Figure 2.13a is a grouped frequency distribution of scores on a statistics test. This well-designed frequency polygon uses equal interval widths for all class intervals. Figure 2.13b is based on the same data, but uses different interval widths from one class interval to the next. The distortion that results is obvious.

One of my statistics students once complained that "You can say anything you want with statistics!" This is a common perception that deserves

FIGURE 2.12

Numbers of psychology doctoral students enrolled in health service provider and "other" training programs. Starting the ordinate at an above-zero frequency (b) distorts the proper picture provided by (a).

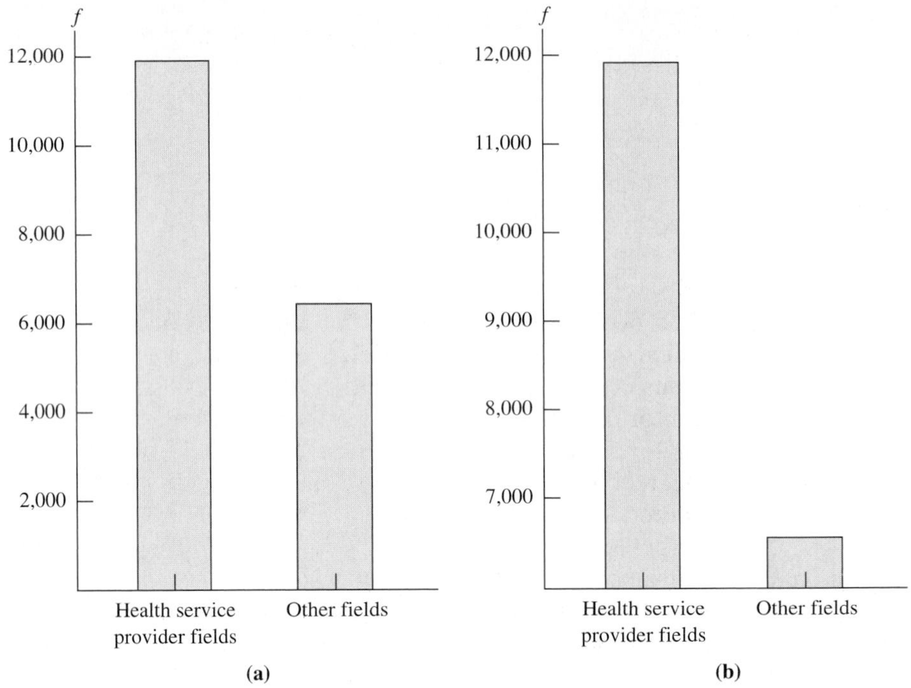

FIGURE 2.13

Grouped frequency distributions of statistics test scores. (a) correctly uses equal interval widths for all class intervals. (b) presents a distorted picture of the same data by using unequal interval widths.

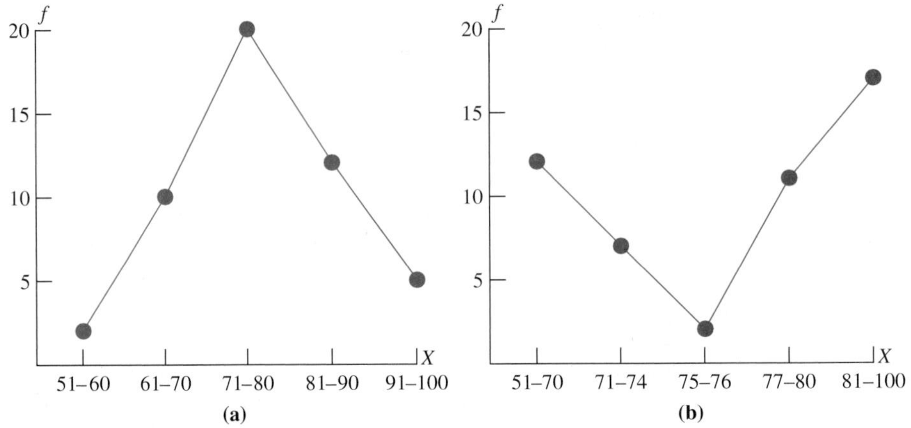

comment, especially in light of the examples we've just seen. It is important to remember that you *can't* "say anything you want with statistics." None of the graphs we have looked at in this section "lie" or present any false information. Every graph presents an accurate, albeit different, picture of the data. The problem is not with the statistics, but with the failure of the consumer of the statistics to know how to interpret them.

Ironically, statistical presentations in the professional literature of the social and behavioral sciences are less likely to invite misinterpretation than those found in the popular press. Professionals in the social and behavioral sciences know how to use statistics to avoid misinterpretations. This expertise is not always as evident in the popular press. Because of this, we are in the odd position of needing less statistical expertise to interpret statistics presented in the professional literature than in the popular press!

Look through a recent issue of a newsmagazine for examples of the misuse of graphs described in this section.
(Answer on p. 56.)

COMPREHENSION CHECK 2.27

SUMMARY

This chapter describes how distributions are used to organize and condense numerical data. Data distributions help us to see trends and patterns in the data and to understand better the cases represented by those data.

Data distributions can be either ungrouped or grouped. Ungrouped distributions provide information about each and every score in the data set: the number of cases that received each score (frequency distributions), the percentage of cases that received each score (percentage distributions), the number of cases that scored at and below each score (cumulative frequency distributions), and the percentage of cases that scored at and below each score (cumulative percentage or percentile rank distributions).

Grouped distributions give us the same kinds of information, but for ranges of scores called class intervals, rather than for every score. Grouped distributions condense and simplify the data, but at the cost of lost specificity of information.

Cumulative percentages are also called percentile ranks and provide valuable information about the positioning of scores in a distribution. Percentile ranks tell us, in relative terms, how high or low, how good or bad any given score is.

Related to percentile ranks are percentiles. A percentile is the score that falls at a specified percentile rank. For instance, the 50th percentile is the score that has a percentile rank of 50.

Data distributions can be presented either as tables or as graphs. Although tables are good at conveying the details of a distribution, graphs are better at depicting general trends and characteristics. Several types of graphs are described in this chapter, including bar graphs, useful in graphing nominal scale distributions; and histograms and frequency polygons, used in graphing data possessing at least ordinal characteristics.

In examining graphed distributions, one looks for indications of: central tendency—the typical or average score; variability—how broadly the scores range; skew—asymmetry in the arrangement of scores; kurtosis—unusual flatness or peakedness of the distribution; and modality characteristics indicating the presence of homogeneous subgroups within the data set.

Used properly, graphs can yield valuable insights into the characteristics of the cases represented by the data. Used improperly, graphs can obscure these characteristics.

NOTES

1. The rule that all class intervals should be of the same width is occasionally violated by leaving the top and/or bottom class intervals open-ended. This is an appropriate practice when there are relatively few high and/or

low scores and these are spread out over a broad range. For example, in presenting annual income information in the form of a grouped distribution, one might reasonably use open-ended top and bottom class intervals like these:

$100,000 and above
$90,000–$99,999
.
.
.
$20,000–$29,999
$19,999 and below

2. To avoid intervals that include impossible scores, make sure that interval width (i) is chosen so that:

$$\frac{\text{highest possible score} - \text{lowest possible score} + 1}{i} = \text{a whole number}$$

3. Although it makes no sense to group the discontinuous categories of a nominal scale variable to form a grouped distribution, the categories can be combined on the basis of semantics. In Table 2.7, for example, Baptists and Lutherans could be combined to form a category of Protestants. As another example, the political preference categories of Republicans and Democrats could be combined to form a category of "Traditional Political Affiliations" and Independents and Libertarians could be combined to form a category of "Nontraditional Political Affiliations."
4. Another method of estimating percentile ranks uses the cumulative percentage of a class interval as the estimated percentile rank for all scores falling within that interval. Using this method, we would estimate the percentile rank for a Cheating Justification Questionnaire score of 32 as 74.2—the cumulative percentage for the class interval 32–34. You can see that this estimate deviates considerably from both the actual percentile rank—56.7—and the estimated percentile rank computed using Equation 3.3—54.7. Though easy, this method of estimating percentile ranks is error-prone, another example of getting what you pay for in statistics.

REVIEW EXERCISES

2.1. Use the statistics test scores that follow to construct tabular frequency, percentage, cumulative frequency, and cumulative percentage distributions.

88, 84, 89, 81, 50, 98, 72, 79, 68, 81,
85, 86, 80, 84, 57, 71, 60, 86, 81, 71,
84, 60, 85, 85, 84

2.2. Shown below are frequency and percentage distributions for the nominal scale variable of academic major at two colleges. Compare the two frequency distributions. Now compare the two percentage distributions. Which provides the clearer comparison?

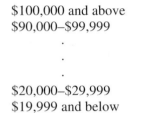

College A			College B		
Major	*f*	%	*Major*	*f*	%
Psychology	230	58.97	Psychology	520	57.91
Sociology	50	12.82	Sociology	120	13.36
Social work	110	28.21	Social work	258	28.73

2.3. Use the statistics test scores presented in Review Exercise 2.1 to construct two tabular grouped frequency, percentage, cumulative frequency, and cumulative percentage distributions, one with an interval width of $i = 5$, and the second with an interval width of $i = 10$. (Assume that the top possible score is 100.)

2.4. Compute midpoints for each of the class intervals you constructed in Review Exercise 2.3.

2.5. Use the ungrouped distribution you constructed in Review Exercise 2.1 to identify the percentile ranks of scores of 60 and 88.

2.6. Estimate the percentile ranks of scores of 60 and 88 in the grouped distribution ($i = 10$) you constructed in Review Exercise 2.3.

2.7. Use the ungrouped distribution you constructed in Review Exercise 2.1 to identify the scores marking the 20th and 75th percentiles.

2.8. Estimate the scores marking the 20th and 75th percentiles in the grouped distribution ($i = 5$) you constructed in Review Exercise 2.3.

2.9. Use a bar graph to depict the frequency distribution of academic majors at College A in Review Exercise 2.2.

2.10. Use a histogram to depict the grouped frequency distribution ($i = 10$) you constructed in Review Exercise 2.3.

2.11. Use a frequency polygon to depict the grouped frequency distribution ($i = 10$) you constructed in Review Exercise 2.3.

2.12. Look at the frequency polygon you constructed in Review Exercise 2.11 and describe: central tendency, variability, skew, kurtosis, and modality characteristics.

2.13. Suppose that an extremely easy test was given in an introductory psychology class. Draw and describe the kind of frequency distribution of scores that might likely result.

2.14. Suppose that an extremely difficult test was given in an introductory psychology class. Draw and describe the kind of frequency distribution of scores that might likely result.

2.15. Draw graphs that: (a) create the false impression of a bimodal grouped distribution of the scores presented in Review Exercise 2.1; and (b) minimize the differences between students majoring in psychology, sociology, and social work in Review Exercise 2.2.

Answers to Comprehension Checks

2.1. Data distributions take unorganized raw data and impose an organization on it. They condense a large quantity of numerical information into a smaller, more manageable quantity.

2.2. An ungrouped frequency distribution is constructed by listing scores from highest to lowest, counting the number of times (frequency) each score occurred, and recording this value next to each listed score.

X	f
25	1
24	1
23	2
22	1
21	3
20	0
19	3
18	2
17	2
16	0
15	1
	$N = 16$

2.3. Equation 2.1 is used to convert each frequency to a percentage. The percentage corresponding to a score of 25 is computed below:

$$\% = \frac{f}{N} \times 100$$

$$= \frac{1}{16} \times 100$$

$$= 6.25$$

Percentages for the other scores are shown below:

X	%
25	6.25
24	6.25
23	12.50
22	6.25
21	18.75
20	0.00
19	18.75
18	12.50
17	12.50
16	0.00
15	6.25

2.4. A percentage distribution is better than a frequency distribution when: (a) one seeks to compare two or more distributions; and (b) these distributions are based on different sample sizes (N). It does not matter whether one uses a frequency or percentage distribution if: (a) there is only one distribution (i.e., no comparison is planned); or (b) the distributions are of approximately equal size (N).

2.5. An ungrouped cumulative frequency distribution is constructed by determining for each score how many people scored at that point *or lower.*

X	f_c
25	16
24	15
23	14
22	12
21	11
20	8
19	8
18	5
17	3
16	1
15	1

2.6. Equation 2.2 is used to convert each score's cumulative frequency to a cumulative percentage. The cumulative percentage corresponding to a score of 21 is computed below:

$$\%_c = \frac{f_c}{N} \times 100$$

$$= \frac{11}{16} \times 100$$

$$= 68.75$$

Cumulative percentages for the other scores are shown below:

X	$\%_c$
25	100.00
24	93.75
23	87.50
22	75.00
21	68.75
20	50.00
19	50.00
18	31.25
17	18.75
16	6.25
15	6.25

2.7.

X ($i = 2$)	f	%	f_c	$\%_c$
24–25	2	12.50	16	100.00
22–23	3	18.75	14	87.50
20–21	3	18.75	11	68.75
18–19	5	31.25	8	50.00
16–17	2	12.50	3	18.75
14–15	1	6.25	1	6.25
	$N = 16$			

2.8. Grouped distributions have the advantage of providing greater condensation and simplification of data. The disadvantage is that specific information about each score is lost in a grouped distribution.

2.9. Apparent limits list the actual scores that are included in each class interval of a grouped distribution. The upper real limit is equal to the upper apparent limit plus one-half the unit of measure. The lower real limit is equal to the lower apparent limit minus one-half the unit of measure.

Apparent Limits	Real Limits
24–25	23.5–25.5
22–23	21.5–23.5
20–21	19.5–21.5
18–19	17.5–19.5
16–17	15.5–17.5
14–15	13.5–15.5

2.10. Equation 2.3 is used to compute midpoints of class intervals. The midpoint of the interval 20–21 is computed below:

$$m = \frac{UL + LL}{2}$$

$$= \frac{21 + 20}{2} \quad \text{or} \quad \frac{21.5 + 19.5}{2}$$

$$= 20.5$$

2.11. There are several possibilities for redesigning the distribution, one of which is shown below:

X	f
20–25	8
18–19	5
16–17	2
14–15	1

2.12.

X ($i = 3$)	f	X ($i = 3$)	f
23–25	4	24–26	2
20–22	4	21–23	6
17–19	7	18–20	5
14–16	1	15–17	3

2.13. Narrow class intervals have the advantage of preserving as much information as possible from the original raw data. The disadvantage is that too much useless detail may be preserved. Broad class intervals have the advantage of providing for the greatest possible condensation and simplification of information. The disadvantage is that useful details may be lost.

X (i = 2)	f	X (i = 5)	f	X (i = 10)	f
99–100	2	96–100	2	91–100	4
97–98	0	91–95	2	81–90	6
95–96	0	86–90	3	71–80	4
93–94	0	81–85	3	61–70	5
91–92	2	76–80	1	51–60	1
89–90	0	71–75	3		
87–88	2	66–70	2		
85–86	1	61–65	3		
83–84	2	56–60	1		
81–82	1				
79–80	0				
77–78	0				
75–76	1				
73–74	0				
71–72	3				
69–70	0				
67–68	1				
65–66	1				
63–64	2				
61–62	1				
59–60	0				
57–58	0				
55–56	1				

2.14. *Intelligence test scores:* (a) ordering of scores is important because this is a continuous (interval scale) variable; (b) cumulative distributions are appropriate because we can reasonably talk about scores at a certain point *and below;* (c) a grouped distribution is reasonable because the scores fall along a continuous scale.

Movie ratings: (a) ordering of movie ratings is important because they do possess ordinal properties; (b) cumulative distributions are appropriate because we can reasonably talk about movies at a certain age-acceptability level *and lower;* (c) a grouped distribution is reasonable because movie ratings fall along a continuum.

Political preferences: (a) ordering of political preferences is unimportant because they possess no ordinal properties; (b) cumulative distributions are inappropriate because we cannot reasonably talk about how many cases fall at one political preference *and lower;* (c) a grouped distribution is not reasonable because political affiliations do not fall along a continuum.

2.15. To determine your percentile rank, look up your score in Table 2.2 and find its associated cumulative percentage. This cumulative percentage or percentile rank indicates the percentage of students in the academic cheating study who scored at and below your score.

2.16. First we find the critical interval that captures the raw score of 21. This score falls in the interval 20–21.

X (i = 2)	f	%	f_c	$\%_c$
.	.	.	.	.
.	.	.	.	.
.	.	.	.	.
22–23	3	18.75	14	87.50
20–21	3	18.75	11	68.75 critical interval
18–19	5	31.25	8	50.00
.	.	.	.	.
.	.	.	.	.
.	.	.	.	.

Then we use Equation 2.4 to estimate the percentile rank for this score:

$$\text{PR} = \%_{c_B} + \left[\left(\frac{X - \text{LRL}}{i}\right)\%\right]$$

$$= 50 + \left[\left(\frac{21 - 19.5}{2}\right)18.75\right]$$

$$= 64.06$$

2.17. The first quartile is the score at the 25th percentile. The second quartile falls at the 50th percentile. The third quartile falls at the 75th percentile. To find these scores we look up the specified percentile ranks and see what score is associated with each. When the exact percentile ranks we seek are not listed (as is the case in this example), we use the next higher listed percentile rank. In this example, these percentile ranks and the corresponding scores are:

Percentile	Listed percentile rank	Score
25th	27.5	28
50th	50.8	31
75th	80.8	35

2.18. First we find the critical interval that includes the score at the 50th percentile. The 50th percentile falls in the interval 18–19.

X (i = 2)	f	%	f_c	$\%_c$
.	.	.	.	.
.	.	.	.	.
.	.	.	.	.
20–21	3	18.75	11	68.75
18–19	5	31.25	8	50.00 critical interval
16–17	2	12.50	3	18.75
.	.	.	.	.
.	.	.	.	.
.	.	.	.	.

Then we use Equation 2.5 to estimate the score at the 50th percentile:

$$X = \frac{(\text{PR} - \%_c)i}{\%} + \text{LRL}$$

$$= \frac{(50 - 18.75)2}{31.25} + 17.5$$

$$= 19.5$$

2.19.

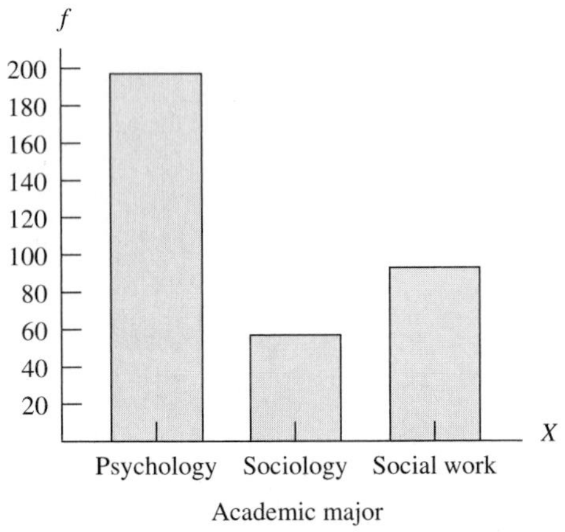

2.20.

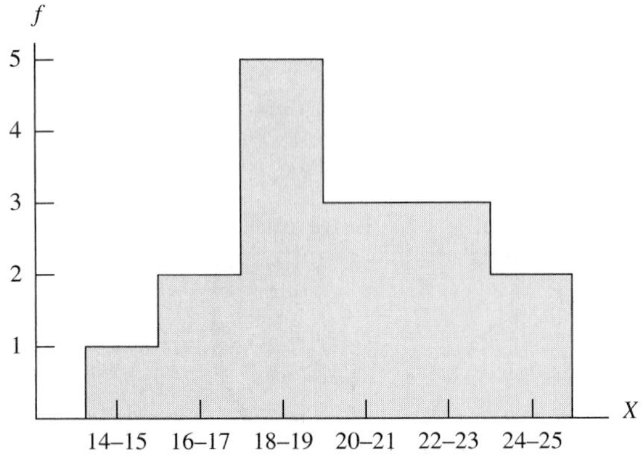

2.21.

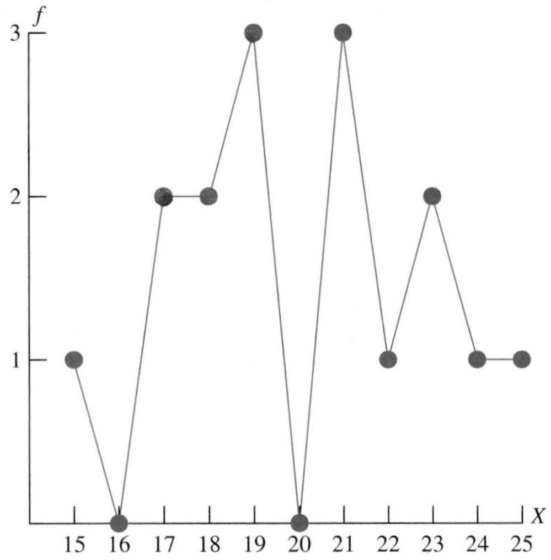

2.22. The frequency peak is over the class interval 18–19, but more scores fall higher than this. We can estimate that the average or typical score is around 20-21.

2.23. We can see that scores varied from a lowest class interval of 14–15 to a highest class interval of 24–25. Other than noting this, little more can be said. A broader distribution would have indicated greater variability; a narrower distribution would have indicated less variability.

2.24. It can be hard to think of examples of skewed distributions. This is because so many variables in the world are normally distributed—not skewed. One example of a positively skewed distribution is the cost of construction of new homes. Most are moderately priced, with a relatively small number of very high-priced outliers. An example of a negatively skewed distribution is the age of residents in nursing/convalescent homes. Most are quite old, but there are a handful of relatively young outliers.

2.25. Platykurtic distributions are very broad, indicating high variability. Leptokurtic distributions are very narrow, indicating low variability.

2.26. The bimodal grade distribution early in the semester points to two distinct subgroups of students—those who are serious, motivated, and capable, and those who are not. The bimodal distribution usually disappears by the end of the semester and grades take on a unimodal distribution as the first group either drops out or gets serious about academics.

2.27. A variety of misuses may be seen, including unequal interval widths, *Y* axes that are too short or too long, and beginning the ordinate at an above-zero frequency.

Descriptive Statistics

3

Chapter Outline

Thirty statistics students ask, "How did we do?" on the last exam. A neuropsychologist evaluating a new medication for Parkinson's disease wants to know, "How are my patients responding?" to the new treatment. A sociologist thumbing through the latest census figures wonders, "At what age are American women having their first children?" None of these are questions about individual students, patients, or American women. They are questions about whole groups.

We learned in the preceding chapter that organizing data into distributions is one way of studying group characteristics. Graphed frequency and percentage distributions are especially useful in this regard. These graphs let us leap-frog over the myriad individual details to get a more general, global impression of the entire distribution. The graphs contain important clues to the central tendency, variability, and other characteristics of our data and the cases that are represented by those data. Even so, the information conveyed by data distributions is approximate and imprecise. We may learn from looking at a frequency polygon or histogram, for instance, that statistics test scores are "narrowly distributed" with an average in the "middle to upper 70s," that Parkinson's patients show "highly variable" reactions to a new medication, or that the average first child is born to a woman in her "early 20s," but there are occasions that call for greater exactitude than this.

Tabular and graphic data distributions are useful *first* tools for the statistical craftsman. With data distributions we can knock our numerical lumber into a rough approximation of the final product, but precision calls for some finishing tools. This is where descriptive statistics come in. **Descriptive statistics** are numbers computed from data that serve to describe those data. Descriptive statistics are available to describe central tendency, variability, and various aspects of the shape of a distribution. We'll learn about descriptive statistics in this chapter.

descriptive statistics *Numbers computed from the data that serve to describe some characteristic of the cases represented by those data.*

COMPREHENSION CHECK 3.1

Why are tabular and graphic frequency distributions alone insufficient to describe group characteristics? What advantages do descriptive statistics have over frequency distributions?

(Answer on p. 88.)

3.1 MEASURES OF CENTRAL TENDENCY

One important characteristic of a distribution that we learned about in the preceding chapter is central tendency—the average or typical case in a distribution. Three descriptive statistics of central tendency are used commonly: the mean, the median, and the mode. All three of these descriptive statistics distill the many scores that comprise a distribution into a single value that we can use to describe the data as a whole, but each defines the typical or average score from a different perspective. Each measure of central tendency has its own strengths, weaknesses, and applications.

Mean

The most commonly used measure of central tendency is the **mean.** There are two good reasons for the mean's popularity. First, the mean is easy to compute. Second, the mean is used as a component in many other statistical procedures, making it a building-block statistic. We will use the symbol $\overline{X}$ (pronounced "X bar") to represent the mean of a sample and the symbol μ (pronounced "mu") to represent the mean of a population. Subscripts can be used to refer to the means of specific samples or populations. For instance, $\overline{X}_1$ is the mean of group 1, μ_2 is the mean of population 2, and so on.

mean ($\overline{X}$, μ) *The arithmetic balancing point in the distribution. The mean is the most common measure of central tendency.*

COMPREHENSION CHECK 3.2

What is the meaning of each of the following symbols?

$$\overline{X}, \overline{X}_2, \mu, \mu_1$$

(Answer on p. 88.)

Procedures for computing the mean from raw data, ungrouped frequency distributions, and grouped frequency distributions will be described next. Example 3.1 illustrates these computational procedures.

Computing the Mean from Raw Scores. The mean of a set of raw scores is computed according to Equation 3.1.

Equation 3.1

$$\overline{X} = \frac{\Sigma X}{N}$$

where

$\overline{X}$ = the mean
X = scores on the variable X
N = the number of cases

In words, the mean ($\overline{X}$) of a set of raw scores (X) is computed by: (1) adding the values of X, and (2) dividing this sum by the number of cases in the sample (N).

COMPREHENSION CHECK 3.3

Compute the mean of the following scores:

23, 46, 27, 50

(Answer on p. 88.)

Computing the Mean of an Ungrouped Frequency Distribution. Equation 3.2 is used to compute the mean of an ungrouped frequency distribution.

Equation 3.2

$$\overline{X} = \frac{\Sigma fX}{N}$$

where

$\overline{X}$ = the mean
X = scores on the variable X
f = frequencies listed for each value of the variable X
N = the number of cases

In words, the mean ($\overline{X}$) of an ungrouped frequency distribution is computed by: (1) multiplying each score (X) by its corresponding frequency (f); (2) adding these products; and (3) dividing this sum by the number of cases in the sample (N).

COMPREHENSION CHECK 3.4

Compute the mean of the following ungrouped frequency distribution:

X	f
5	2
4	1
3	3
2	2
1	1

(Answer on p. 88.)

Estimating the Mean of a Grouped Frequency Distribution. When the data are in the form of a grouped frequency distribution, it is not possible to compute the mean exactly. This is because in grouping scores into class intervals we lose information about individual scores that is necessary to determine the mean exactly. However, we can estimate the mean of a grouped frequency distribution using Equation 3.3. This equation assumes that every score within a given class interval falls exactly at the midpoint of that interval.

Equation 3.3

$$\overline{X} = \frac{\Sigma fm}{N}$$

where

$\overline{X}$ = the mean (estimated)
m = midpoints of each class interval
f = frequencies listed for each class interval
N = the number of cases

In words, we estimate the mean of a grouped frequency distribution ($\overline{X}$) by: (1) multiplying the midpoint (m) of each class interval by its corresponding frequency (f); (2) adding these products; and (3) dividing this sum by the number of cases in the sample (N).

COMPREHENSION CHECK 3.5

Estimate the mean of the following grouped distribution. Why is the mean computed according to Equation 3.3 seldom exactly correct?

X	f
91–100	4
81–90	7
71–80	3
61–70	1

(Answer on p. 88.)

EXAMPLE 3.1

Computing the Mean

Equations 3.1–3.3 describe the computation of the mean for raw scores, ungrouped frequency distributions, and grouped frequency distributions, respectively. Each of these procedures will be illustrated here.

Computing the Mean for Raw Scores

Data from the Cheating Justification Questionnaire were presented first in Table 2.1 in Chapter 2. The mean of these 120 scores is computed here according to Equation 3.1:

$$\begin{aligned}\overline{X} &= \frac{\Sigma X}{N}\\ &= \frac{25 + 37 + 20 + \cdots + 33 + 30 + 34}{120}\\ &= 28.81\end{aligned}$$

This value presents one perspective on the typical or average score in the distribution. Compared to the graphed frequency distribution of Cheating Justification Questionnaire scores depicted in Figure 2.2a, a mean of $\overline{X} =$ 28.81 appears to fall slightly to the left of the center of the distribution. This is the result of the distribution's slight negative skew. The mean has been pulled in the direction of the low-scoring outliers.

Computing the Mean for an Ungrouped Distribution

Table 2.2 in Chapter 2 presents scores on the Cheating Justification Questionnaire in the form of an ungrouped frequency distribution. Equation 3.2 is used to compute the mean for this ungrouped frequency distribution:

$$\begin{aligned}\overline{X} &= \frac{\Sigma fX}{N}\\ &= \frac{(4 \times 40) + (2 \times 39) + \cdots + (1 \times 18) + (1 \times 17)}{120}\\ &= 28.81\end{aligned}$$

Ungrouped frequency distributions do not lose any information about specific scores. Because of this, the value of the mean will always be the same, whether it is computed from raw scores or from an ungrouped frequency distribution.

Estimating the Mean from a Grouped Distribution

Table 2.4 in Chapter 2 presents scores on the Cheating Justification Questionnaire in the form of a grouped frequency distribution. Equation 3.3 is used to estimate the mean for this grouped frequency distribution:

$$\begin{aligned}\overline{X} &= \frac{\Sigma fm}{N} \\ &= \frac{(10 \times 39) + (21 \times 36) + \cdots + (1 \times 21) + (4 \times 18)}{120} \\ &= 31.03\end{aligned}$$

This is only an estimated mean. An exact mean cannot be computed from an ungrouped frequency distribution because information about the frequency of specific scores is lost when scores are grouped into class intervals. Because of this, the value computed here, $\overline{X} = 31.03$, differs somewhat from the actual mean of $\overline{X} = 28.81$ computed above.

Characteristics of the Mean. The mean is the arithmetic balancing point in the distribution. In other words, scores that are higher than the mean are balanced exactly in magnitude by scores that fall lower than the mean. It is in this sense that the mean points to the typical or average score, the central tendency of a distribution.

The concept of the mean as a balancing point is illustrated in Figure 3.1, which depicts the distribution of nine IQ scores. Positioned where it is, the mean of this distribution, $\overline{X} = 100$, provides a fulcrum or balancing point for the distribution.

FIGURE 3.1

The mean acts as a balancing point in the distribution. Scores that deviate above the mean are balanced by scores that deviate below the mean.

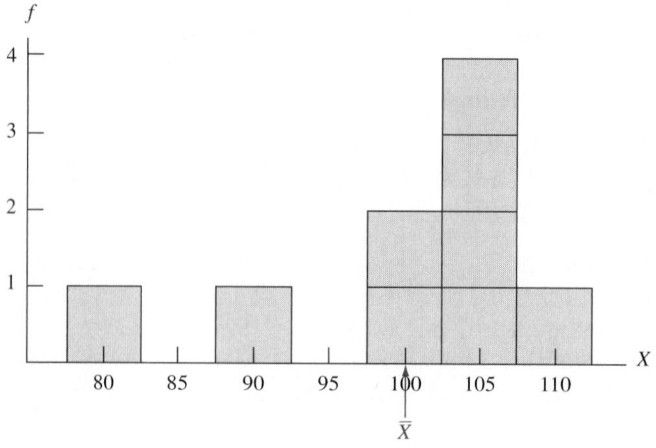

Comprehension Check 3.6

Think of the histogram below as a seesaw and each block as one score. Without computing the mean, locate a fulcrum to represent the mean in a position that balances the seesaw. Next, compute the mean and see how accurate you were in positioning the fulcrum.

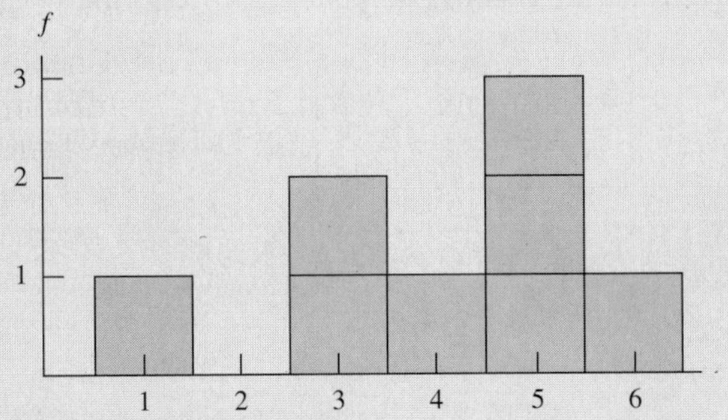

(Answer on p. 88.)

This description of the mean as a balancing point can be expressed in more mathematical terms: The mean is the point in a distribution around which the deviations (differences between scores and the mean) sum to zero. Table 3.1 lists all nine IQ scores depicted in Figure 3.1 along with their deviations from the mean. Scores below the mean show negative deviations, scores falling exactly at the mean show deviations of zero, and scores above the mean show positive deviations. The sum of the deviations around the mean is zero. Or, expressed in summation notation: $\Sigma(X - \overline{X}) = 0$.

Comprehension Check 3.7

Compute $\Sigma(X - \overline{X})$ for the data depicted in Comprehension Check 3.6.

(Answer on p. 88.)

A second characteristic of the mean, perhaps its most important feature from a practical standpoint, is the reactivity of the mean to extreme scores—outliers. The mean is pulled excessively in the direction of outliers. Because of this, the mean gives a distorted indication of the typical or average score whenever outliers are present, that is, in skewed distributions.

Figure 3.2 illustrates the disproportionate influence of outliers on the mean. Here we see the negatively skewed distribution of Feetal Anxiety Inventory scores of 35 of Dr. Claude Hopper's psychopodiatric patients. Most of Dr. Hopper's patients are in pretty bad shape—over half score in the highest three class intervals—but Dr. Hopper treats a few low-scoring outliers as well. The estimated mean of this grouped distribution, computed using Equation 3.3, does not fall in the 70s, 80s, or 90s, though: It is 68.99. The mean has been pulled in the direction of the outlying low scores and gives a mistakenly low impression of the typical score in the distribution. Stated generally, the mean will fall below the true typical score in a negatively skewed distribution and will fall above the true typical score in a positively skewed distribution.

TABLE 3.1

The sum of the deviations around the mean will always be zero

Scores (X)	Deviations Around the Mean $(X - X)$	
80	$80 - 100 = -20$	deviations below the mean
90	$90 - 100 = -10$	
100	$100 - 100 = 0$	
100	$100 - 100 = 0$	
105	$105 - 100 = +5$	deviations above the mean
105	$105 - 100 = +5$	
105	$105 - 100 = +5$	
105	$105 - 100 = +5$	
110	$110 - 100 = +10$	
	$\Sigma(X - \overline{X}) = 0$	

FIGURE 3.2

The mean of this negatively skewed distribution of Feetal Anxiety Inventory scores is pulled in the direction of the low-scoring outliers.

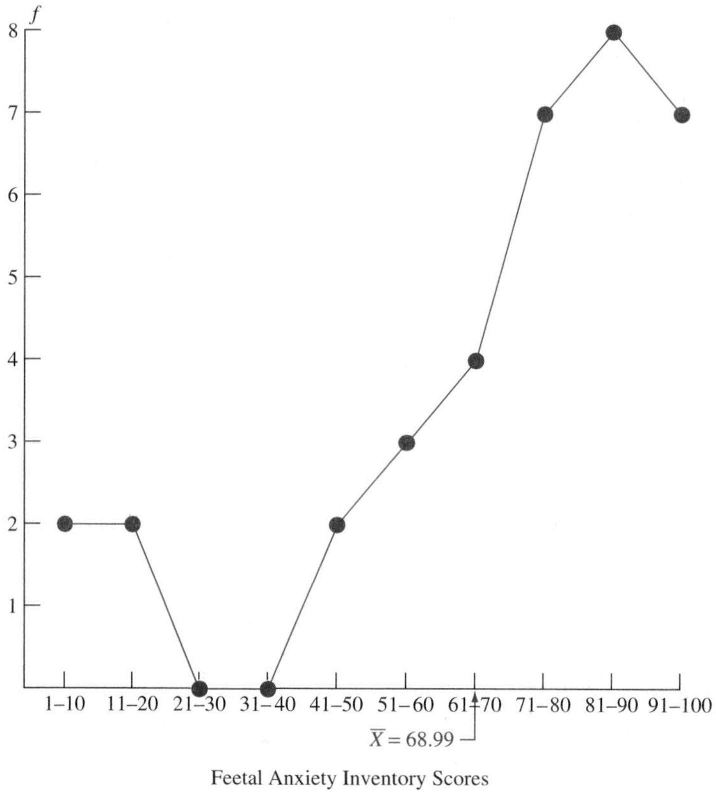

COMPREHENSION CHECK 3.8

Sketch a positively skewed frequency distribution and indicate: (a) the approximate position of the typical score; (b) the location of the mean.

(Answer on p. 88.)

median (Md) *A measure of central tendency above and below which an equal number of cases score: the middle score in a distribution.*

Median

The median, abbreviated Md, provides a different perspective on the central tendency of a distribution. The **median** is that point in a distribution above and below which an equal number of cases fall.

Computation of the median from raw data, ungrouped frequency distributions, and grouped frequency distributions will be described next. Example 2.2 illustrates these computational procedures.

Computing the Median from Raw Scores. The median of a set of raw scores is identified using Equation 3.4.

Equation 3.4

$$\text{Md} = \left(\frac{N+1}{2}\right)\text{th score in an ordered array}$$

where

Md = the median
N = the number of cases

In words, we identify the median (Md) of a set of raw scores by first arranging the scores in either ascending or descending order, that is, as an **ordered array.** This first step can be quite tedious when there are many scores, perhaps explaining the greater popularity of the mean. Once scores are ordered, we find the position of the middle score, the median, by: (1) adding 1 to the number of scores in the distribution (N), and (2) dividing this sum by 2. The median occupies the $[(N + 1)/2]$th position ("the N plus one over two-th position") in an ordered array of raw scores.

ordered array *A set of scores arranged in either ascending or descending order.*

COMPREHENSION CHECK 3.9

Compute the medians of the following scores:

(a) 27, 86, 32, 97, 41
(b) 16, 32, 16, 41, 90
(c) 32, 15, 20, 18

(Answer on pp. 88–89.)

Computing the Median of an Ungrouped Frequency Distribution. Equation 3.4 presented above as the raw score formula for the median is also used to identify the median of an ungrouped frequency distribution. The median is the value that occupies the $[(N + 1)/2]$th position in the ungrouped frequency distribution, counting frequencies either down from the top or up from the bottom of the distribution.

COMPREHENSION CHECK 3.10

Compute the median of the following ungrouped frequency distribution:

X	f
10	3
9	1
8	4
7	3
6	2

(Answer on p. 89.)

Estimating the Median of a Grouped Frequency Distribution. Just as we can only estimate the mean of a grouped distribution, we can only estimate the median of a grouped distribution. Equation 3.5 is used for this purpose.

Equation 3.5

$$\text{Md} = \text{LRL} + \left[\frac{(N/2) - f_{c_B}}{f}\right]i$$

where

Md = the median (estimated)
LRL = the lower real limit of the critical interval
N = the number of cases
f_{c_B} = the cumulative frequency of the class interval just below the critical interval
f = the frequency listed for the critical interval
i = the interval width of the grouped distribution

In words, the median of a grouped distribution (Md) is estimated by first identifying the class interval that contains the $[(N + 1)/2]$th score. Once this critical interval is identified, we proceed by: (1) dividing N by 2; (2) subtracting the cumulative frequency of the interval *below* the critical interval (f_{c_B}) from the result of step 1; (3) dividing the result of step 2 by the frequency listed for the critical interval (f); (4) multiplying the result of step 4 by the interval width of the grouped distribution (i); and (5) adding the lower real limit of the critical interval (LRL) to the result of step 4.

Comprehension Check 3.11

Estimate the median of the following grouped frequency distribution:

X	f
91–100	3
81–90	2
71–80	7
61–70	5
51–60	1

(Answer on p. 89.)

Example 3.2

Computing the Median

The median is that value above and below which an equal number of cases have scored. Equation 3.4 describes how to find the median of a set of raw scores or an ungrouped distribution. Equation 3.5 describes how to estimate the median of a grouped distribution.

Computing the Median of Raw Scores

You are probably less familiar with the median than with the mean, so we'll consider several examples of the median. Let's begin by computing the median of the following IQ scores:

$$97, \quad 102, \quad 100, \quad 110, \quad 99$$

The first step in computing the median is to arrange the scores into an ordered array, that is, in either ascending or descending order. The IQ scores listed above are presented next as an ordered array:

$$97, \quad 99, \quad 100, \quad 102, \quad 110$$

The median is defined by Equation 3.4 as:

$$\text{Md} = \left(\frac{N + 1}{2}\right)\text{th score in an ordered array}$$

Because there are five scores, $N = 5$, and the $[(N + 1)/2]$th score is the $[(5 + 1)/2]$th score, that is, the third score. The third score in this ordered array, counting either from the top or the bottom, is 100, and this is the median. Notice that the median is *not* 3. The median is in the third *position.*

Let's look at another example using the following IQ scores:

$$98, \quad 98, \quad 102, \quad 103, \quad 110$$

The median of this ordered array of scores is again the score in the $[(N + 1)/2]$th position. Because N is again 5, the median is again in the third position—102. The important thing to notice in this example is that there are two scores of 98 and that each was counted in finding the median.

Consider another example, this time involving an even number of IQ scores:

$$97, \quad 103, \quad 106, \quad 110$$

The median of these scores, as always, is in the $[(N + 1)/2]$th position. Because N here is 4, this would be the $[(4 + 1)/2]$th or 2.5th score. What score is this? It is the value that is exactly halfway between the scores in the second and third positions. The score in the second position (counting from lowest to highest) is 103. The score in the third position (again counting from lowest to highest) is 106. The value exactly halfway between 103 and 106 is 104.5—the median. (Just add the two values together and divide by 2.) The point to notice here is that the median need not always be a score that actually appears in the distribution.

Computing the Median of an Ungrouped Distribution

Look at the ungrouped distribution of Cheating Justification Questionnaire scores in Table 2.2 in Chapter 2. Finding the median of an ungrouped distribution like this one is made easier by virtue of the fact that the scores are already arranged in order. All we have to do to find the median is count.

The median is always the $[(N + 1)/2]$th score in an ordered array. Table 2.2 represents 120 cases, so $N = 120$. Thus, the median of this distribution is the value located in the $[(120 + 1)/2]$th position in the distribution. This is the 60.5th score. The 60.5th score is located exactly halfway between the 60th score and the 61st score. Counting up from the bottom score (17), the score in the 60th position is 31: 17 is in the first position, 18 is second, there are two scores of 19 that fall in the third and fourth positions, 20 is in the fifth position, 23 occurs three times in the sixth, seventh, and eighth positions, and so on. Counting from the bottom score, the score in the 61st position is also 31.

The value exactly halfway between 31 and 31, the 60.5th score, is 31, and this is the median of the distribution of scores on the Cheating Justification Questionnaire.

Estimating the Median of a Grouped Distribution. Equation 3.5 describes the procedure for estimating the median of a grouped distribution. We will use the grouped distribution of 120 Cheating Justification Questionnaire scores presented in Table 2.4 in Chapter 2 to illustrate this procedure. A portion of this table is reproduced below.

X ($i = 3$)	f	%	f_c	$\%_c$	
.	.	.	.	.	
.	.	.	.	.	
.	.	.	.	.	
32–34	28	23.3	89	74.2	
29–31	28	23.3	61	50.8	critical interval
26–28	16	13.3	33	27.5	
.	.	.	.	.	
.	.	.	.	.	
.	.	.	.	.	

We begin by identifying the critical interval, that is, the class interval that contains the $[(N + 1)/2]$th score—the median. With 120 cases ($N = 120$), this is the 60.5th score and it is found in the class interval 29–31. Do you see why? Count scores (frequencies) beginning either at the top or the bottom of the distribution and you will find that both the 60th and 61st scores fall in the interval 29–31. Next, we use Equation 3.5 to estimate the median of this grouped distribution:

$$\text{Md} = \text{LRL} + \left[\frac{(N/2) - f_{c_B}}{f}\right]i$$

where

LRL	= the lower real limit of the critical class interval, that is, the lower apparent limit minus one-half the unit of measure $(29 - 0.5)$	= 28.5
N	= the number of cases in the distribution	= 120
f_{c_B}	= the cumulative frequency of the class interval just *below* the critical interval	= 33
f	= the frequency corresponding to the critical interval	= 28
i	= the interval width of the distribution	= 3

Substituting these numerical values into Equation 3.5, we have:

$$\text{Md} = 28.5 + \left[\frac{(120/2) - 33}{28}\right]3$$

$$= 31.39$$

Remember that this value is only an estimate. This explains why it differs slightly from the actual median computed above (Md = 31).

Characteristic of the Median. The median, like the mean, is a type of balancing point in the distribution. The difference is that the median balances on the basis of *how many* cases fall on each side of the fulcrum, whereas the mean balances on the basis of *how far* the cases fall on each side.

This difference can be seen by comparing Figures 3.1 and 3.3. Figure 3.1 shows that the mean balances scores based on how far they fall from the mean. Figure 3.3 shows that the median (Md = 105) balances the distribution by locating an equal number of cases (four) above and below the median.

Because the median uses only information about how many scores there are and not how extreme they are, the median resists the influence of outliers. Thus, the median, unlike the mean, is not distorted by the presence of outliers and is suitable for use in describing the central tendency of both skewed and unskewed distributions.

Figure 3.4 illustrates this important property of the median in the grouped distribution of Feetal Anxiety Inventory scores examined previously. The mean of this distribution ($\overline{X} = 68.99$) was drawn excessively in the direction of the low outliers. The median, estimated using Equation 3.5, is 76.93, almost eight points higher than the mean. This value more accurately reflects the average feetal anxiety level seen among Dr. Hopper's patients.

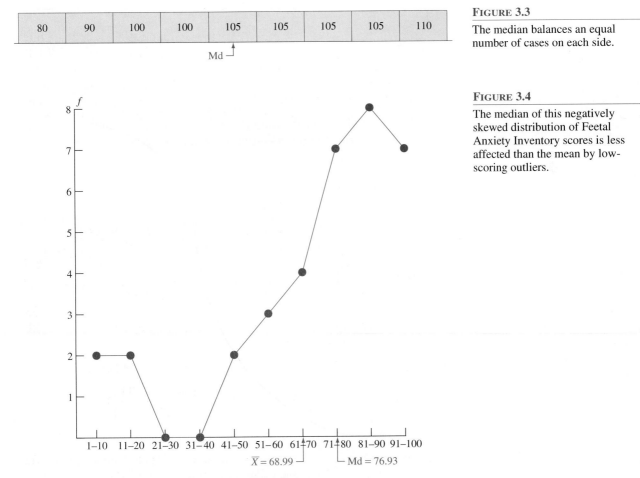

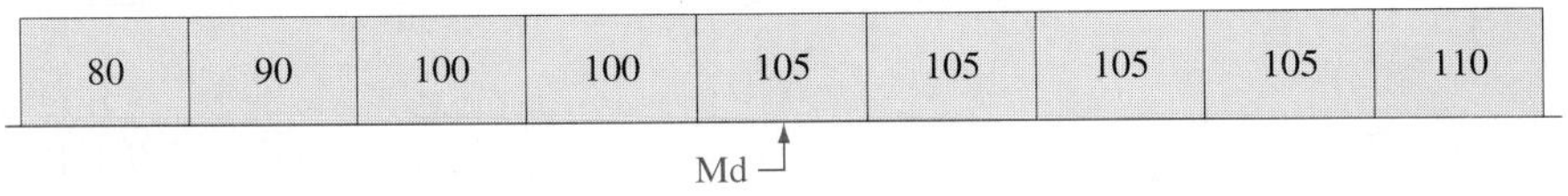

FIGURE 3.3
The median balances an equal number of cases on each side.

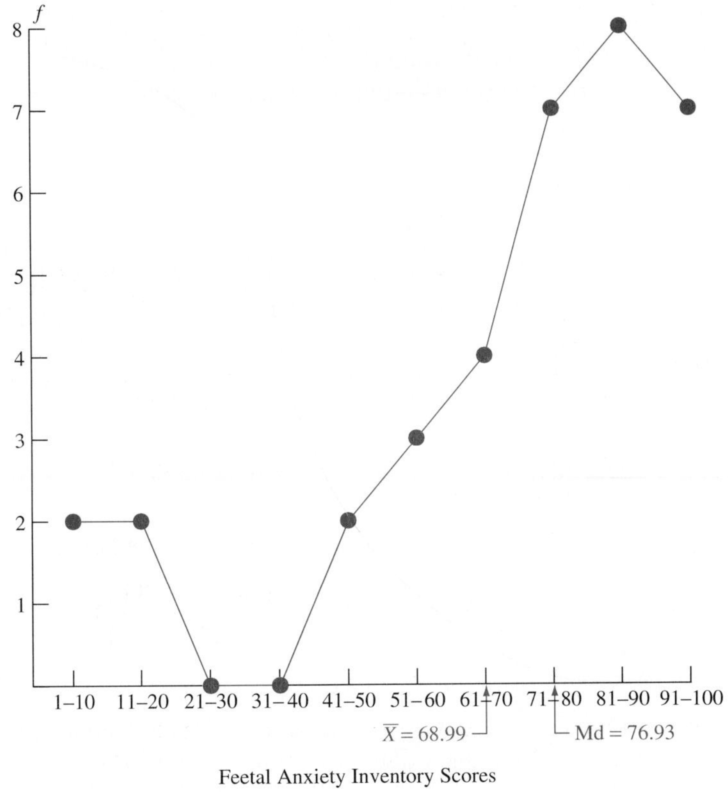

FIGURE 3.4
The median of this negatively skewed distribution of Feetal Anxiety Inventory scores is less affected than the mean by low-scoring outliers.

COMPREHENSION CHECK 3.12

Think of the histogram below as a seesaw and each block as one score. Locate the mean as a fulcrum at the balancing point. Now locate the median. Explain why the locations of the mean and median differ.

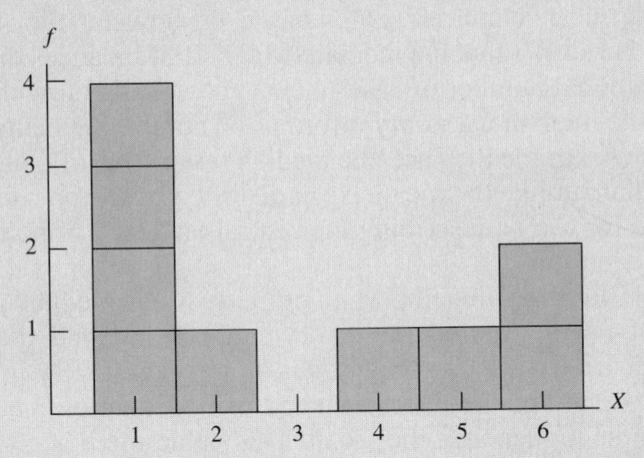

(Answer on p. 89.)

Mode

mode *A measure of central tendency defined as the most frequently occurring score(s), class interval(s), or nominal scale category or categories.*

The **mode** is defined as the most frequently occurring score, class interval, or nominal scale category in a distribution. The mode identifies the average or typical score as the most common score in the distribution.

There can be more than one mode in a distribution if more than one score, class interval, or nominal scale category occurs with equally high frequency. It is also possible for a distribution to have no mode if no single score occurs more frequently than the others—that is, when all scores occur with exactly the same frequency.

Computing the Mode. The mode of a distribution is not so much computed as it is identified. There is no "formula" or "equation" that describes the computation of the mode. The mode is determined simply by identifying which score, class interval, or nominal scale category occurs most often. This is easily determined in a tabular frequency distribution by examining the frequencies listed for each score or class interval. In a graphed frequency distribution the mode is the score or midpoint corresponding to the frequency peak. In Figure 3.1, for instance, the mode is 105.

COMPREHENSION CHECK 3.13

Identify the mode(s) for each of the following data sets:

(a) 21, 16, 16, 2, 3

(b)

X	f
5	3
4	5
3	2
2	5
1	1

(cont.)

(c)

Class	f
Senior	1,750
Junior	1,802
Sophomore	1,894
Freshman	2,033

(Answer on p. 89.)

When to Use the Mode. Two occasions call for the use of the mode as a measure of central tendency. First, when a distribution is bimodal or multimodal, information about the modes can give more information about the typical or average score than either the mean or the median. Figure 3.5 depicts a bimodal distribution of introductory sociology test scores. The mean ($\overline{X}$ = 73.48) and median (Md = 74.5) both give a misleading impression of the typical or average score in this distribution. It is more useful to note that the distribution is bimodal, with most students scoring quite low (56–60) or quite high (81–85) and relatively few scoring in the middle of the distribution.

If you've been reading carefully, you probably noticed that the distribution depicted in Figure 3.5 doesn't meet the *technical* definition of a bimodal distribution. Strictly speaking, this is a unimodal distribution, since one class interval (56–60) occurs more frequently than any other. It is common practice, though, to refer to any noticeable frequency peak as a mode. It is this convention that leads us to consider Figure 3.5 a bimodal distribution.

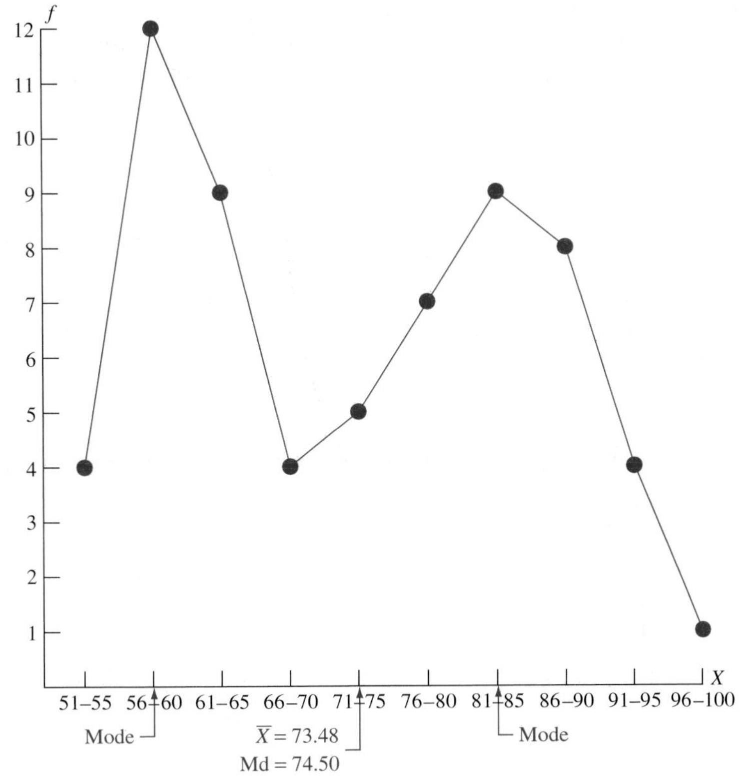

FIGURE 3.5

In this bimodal distribution of sociology test scores, neither the mean nor the median gives a good indication of the typical or average score. The modes are a more useful indicator.

COMPREHENSION CHECK 3.14

What might explain the bimodal shape of the distribution of scores depicted in Figure 3.5?

(Answer on p. 89.)

A second occasion calling for the use of the mode to describe the typical or average case occurs when data are measured on a multicategory nominal scale variable. The phrase "modal category" is used in such instances to indicate the category showing the highest frequency of occurrence. In Figure 3.6, for example, the modal religious preference is "Other."

COMPREHENSION CHECK 3.15

Describe the central tendency of the following frequency distribution of preferred fast-food restaurants:

Restaurant	*f*
Wendy's	40
McDonald's	47
Burger King	16
Jack-in-the-Box	15

(Answer on p. 89.)

FIGURE 3.6

The modal category in this distribution of religious preferences is "Other."

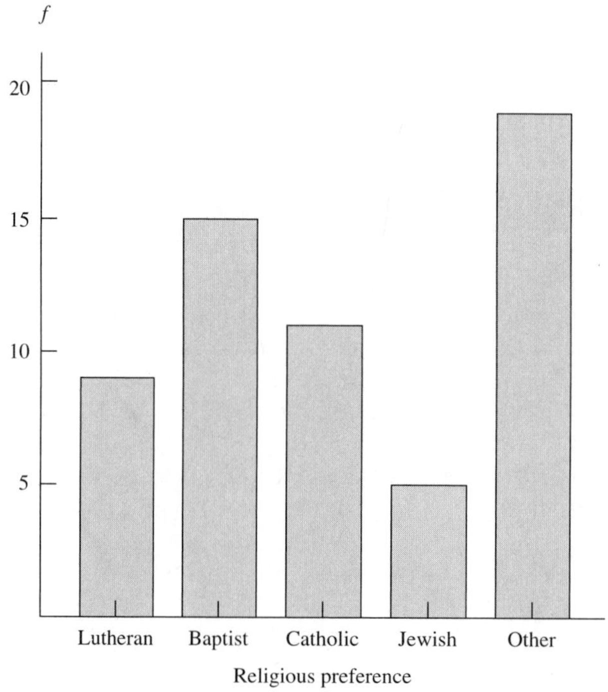

3.2 Measures of Variability

Central tendency statistics use a single number to describe an entire distribution of cases: the average IQ is 100; the mean life expectancy for American males at birth is 77; the median annual income of American families is \$34,000. The mean, median, and mode give the impression that all the cases are pretty much the same. In fact, though, cases may be quite variable from one to the next.

The variability of scores limits the degree to which we can characterize the whole distribution in terms of the mean, median, or mode. Measuring this diversity gives a more complete impression of our data: IQ scores range broadly, with 95% falling between 70 and 130; the life spans of American males born today will range from less than an hour to over 100 years; annual family incomes vary widely, with about 95% falling between \$5,000 and \$100,000. Information about score variability is just as important as information about central tendency.

Comprehension Check 3.16

Describe the relationship between the variability of a distribution and the degree to which the scores of the cases represented by that distribution are predictable.

(Answer on p. 89.)

The most common measures of variability are the range, the interquartile range, the variance, the sum of squares, and the standard deviation. Just as each measure of central tendency presents a slightly different picture of the typical or average score in a distribution, so too each measure of variability gives a slightly different perspective on data variability.

Range

range *A measure of variability equal to the highest score minus the lowest score in the distribution.*

The **range** is defined by Equation 3.6 as the difference between the highest score and the lowest score in a distribution.

Equation 3.6

$$\text{Range} = \text{highest score} - \text{lowest score}$$

In words, we compute the range of a distribution by subtracting the lowest score in the distribution from the highest score in the distribution.

Consider the three distributions of IQ scores depicted in Figure 3.7. All seven scores in Figure 3.7a are the same. Consistent with this lack of variability, the range is computed according to Equation 3.6 as $100 - 100 = 0$. The distribution shown in Figure 3.7b is slightly more variable. This increased variability is reflected in a larger range: $105 - 95 = 10$. And Figure 3.7c shows even more variability and an even larger computed range: $110 - 90 = 20$.

In sum, the range is a number computed from the data that serves to describe the variability of those data—a descriptive statistic of variability. As variability increases, so does the range. As variability decreases, so does the range.

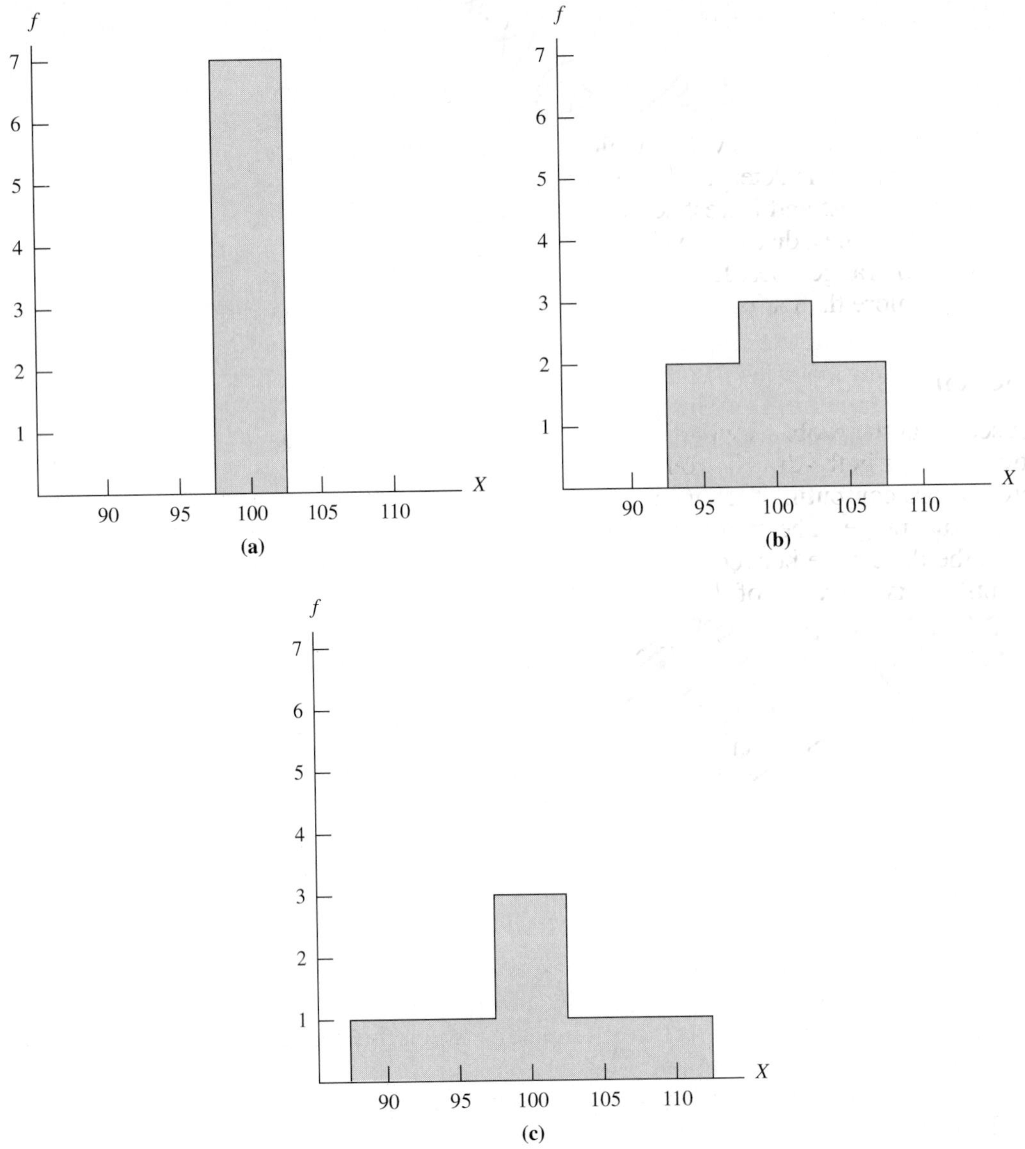

FIGURE 3.7

Three frequency distributions depicting IQ scores. (a) shows no variability; (b) is more variable; (c) shows the greatest variability of scores.

COMPREHENSION CHECK 3.17

Compute the range of these scores: 47, 92, 92, 87, 75, 80.
(Answer on p. 89.)

Often the range is not computed, but is presented indirectly, in a narrative fashion: "Scores *ranged* from a low of *x* to a high of *y*." Following this convention in describing the variability of the IQ scores seen in Figure 3.7c, for instance, we would say: "Scores ranged from a low of 90 to a high of 110." This manner of expression provides information not only about the range, but clearly specifies minimum and maximum score values as well.

COMPREHENSION CHECK 3.18

Describe the range of scores in Comprehension Check 3.17 in terms of minimum and maximum values.

(Answer on p. 89.)

The problem with the range is its vulnerability to outliers. The range is not just influenced by outliers, it is determined completely by them. The range is based entirely on the highest and lowest scores in the distribution. It doesn't make much sense to describe a distribution in terms of its two weirdest scores, but that is just what the range does. It is for this reason that the range is seldom used to provide more than a rough estimate of data variability.

Interquartile Range

We have just seen that the problem with the range is that it is determined by the most extreme scores in the distribution. One solution is to eliminate these extreme scores before computing the range. This is what is done in computing the interquartile range. The **interquartile range** (IQR) is defined by Equation 3.7 as the difference between the scores at the 75th percentile and the 25th percentile. It is the range of the middle 50% of the scores.

interquartile range (IQR) *A measure of variability equal to the difference between the scores at the 75th and 25th percentiles.*

Equation 3.7

$$IQR = X_{75} - X_{25}$$

where

IQR = interquartile range
X_{75} = score at the 75th percentile
X_{25} = score at the 25th percentile

In words, to compute the interquartile range we: (1) find the score at the 75th percentile (X_{75}); (2) find the score at the 25th percentile (X_{25}); and (3) subtract the 25th percentile from the 75th percentile.

As an example of the computation of the interquartile range, look back at Table 2.2, the distribution of Cheating Justification Questionnaire scores we studied in Chapter 2. The 75th percentile is 35 (remember, if we don't find the exact percentile rank we want, we use the next higher value), and the 25th percentile is 28. Computed according to Equation 3.7, then, the interquartile range is $35 - 28 = 7$.

COMPREHENSION CHECK 3.19

Compute the interquartile range of the distribution that follows:

X	f
10	2
9	13
8	10
7	12
6	13
5	15
4	10
3	12
2	8
1	5

(Answer on p. 89.)

The interquartile range has the advantage over the range of eliminating the most extreme scores (approximately the top and bottom 25%) before the range is computed. Even so, the interquartile range is used infrequently and is not a component in other statistical procedures.

Variance

The variance is one of the two most frequently used measures of data variability, the other being the standard deviation. Both of these descriptors of variability are important components in other statistical procedures, and the computation of each is illustrated in Example 3.3.

variance (s^2, σ^2) *A measure of variability equal to the average squared deviation of scores around the mean.*

The **variance** measures the variability of a distribution as the average squared deviation of scores around the mean. Look back at Figure 3.7. In Figure 3.7a, scores show no variability at all. In this distribution, all scores fall exactly at the mean ($\overline{X} = 100$). Because none of the scores deviates (differs) from the mean, the average *squared* deviation (difference), the variance, is 0. In Figure 3.7b there is greater variability of scores. Now some of the scores *do* deviate from the mean. Specifically, two scores of 95 deviate 5 points below the mean, and two scores of 105 deviate 5 points above the mean. Computed according to Equation 3.8, presented in the next section, the average *squared* deviation of scores around the mean in Figure 3.7b, the variance, is 14.29. Even more variability is depicted in Figure 3.7c. The greater dispersion of scores around the mean seen here is reflected in an even higher variance: 35.71.

There is nothing mysterious about the variance. It, like all other descriptive statistics of variability, is just a number computed from the data that serves to measure score variability. When there is no variability, that is, when all scores are identical, the variance will be 0. As score variability increases, so will the value of the variance.

COMPREHENSION CHECK 3.20

What does it mean to say that the variance of a set of IQ scores is 225? What does it mean to say that the variance is 100?

(Answer on p. 89.)

The symbol used to represent the variance of a sample is s^2. The symbol for the variance of a population is σ^2 (σ is the lowercase Greek letter sigma). Subscripts are used to specify *which* variance one is referring to if there are several samples, populations, or variables. For instance, s_2^2 represents the variance of sample 2, σ_1^2 refers to the variance of population 1, and s_Y^2 is the sample variance of variable *Y*.

COMPREHENSION CHECK 3.21

Identify each of the following symbols:

$$s_X^2,\ s_1^2,\ \sigma^2,\ \sigma_Y^2$$

(Answer on p. 89.)

Computing the Variance from Raw Scores. The variance of a set of raw scores is computed according to Equation 3.8:(See Note 1)

$$s^2 = \frac{\Sigma(X - \overline{X})^2}{N}$$

Equation 3.8

where

s^2 = the sample variance
X = scores on the variable X
$\overline{X}$ = the mean
N = the number of cases

In words, the variance (s^2) of a set of raw scores (X) is computed by: (1) subtracting the mean ($\overline{X}$) from each score; (2) squaring each of these differences; (3) summing the values from step 2; and (4) dividing the result of step 3 by the number of cases in the sample (N).

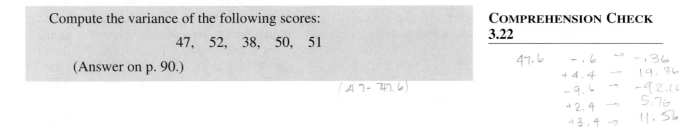

COMPREHENSION CHECK 3.22

Compute the variance of the following scores:

47, 52, 38, 50, 51

(Answer on p. 90.)

Computing the Variance of an Ungrouped Frequency Distribution. Equation 3.9 is used to compute the variance of an ungrouped frequency distribution.

$$s^2 = \frac{\Sigma f(X - \overline{X})^2}{N}$$

Equation 3.9

where

s^2 = the sample variance
X = values on the variable X
$\overline{X}$ = the mean
f = frequencies listed for each value of the variable X
N = the number of cases

In words, the variance (s^2) of an ungrouped frequency distribution is computed by: (1) subtracting the mean ($\overline{X}$) from each raw score (X); (2) squaring each of these differences; (3) multiplying each of the squared differences from step 2 by its corresponding frequency (f); (4) summing the values from step 3; and (5) dividing the result of step 4 by the number of cases in the sample (N).

COMPREHENSION CHECK 3.23

Compute the variance of the following ungrouped frequency distribution:

X	f
110	1
105	4
100	2
95	0
90	1
85	0
80	1

(Answer on p. 90.)

Estimating the Variance of a Grouped Frequency Distribution. We can only estimate the variance of a grouped frequency distribution, because information about specific scores is lost when scores are combined into class intervals. Equation 3.10 estimates the variance of grouped data by assuming that all scores in a given class interval fall exactly at the midpoint.

Equation 3.10

$$s^2 = \frac{\Sigma f(m - \overline{X})^2}{N}$$

where

s^2 = the sample variance (estimated)
m = midpoints of each class interval
$\overline{X}$ = the mean
f = frequencies listed for each class interval
N = the number of cases

In words, the variance (s^2) of a grouped frequency distribution is estimated by: (1) subtracting the mean ($\overline{X}$) from each class interval midpoint (m); (2) squaring each of these differences; (3) multiplying each of the squared differences from step 2 by its corresponding frequency (f); (4) summing the values from step 3; and (5) dividing the result of step 4 by the number of cases in the sample (N).

COMPREHENSION CHECK 3.24

Estimate the variance of the following grouped frequency distribution:

X	f
91–100	3
81–90	4
71–80	5
61–70	3
51–60	2

(Answer on p. 90.)

Estimating the Population Variance. Equations 3.8–3.10 are used to compute the variance of a sample. Often, though, one is more interested in knowing the variance of the population from which the sample was drawn. You might suppose that we could simply use the sample variance as the best available estimate of the population variance. The flaw in this strategy is that the variance of a population is typically somewhat greater than the variance of any given sample drawn from that population. Statisticians say that the sample variance gives a "biased" estimate of the population variance. It is predictably too low. The reason is that any given sample will consist of far fewer cases than comprise the population. Because a sample contains relatively few cases, it is unlikely that it will include the unusual low and high scores that are found in the population. These extreme scores boost the variance of the population, but because they aren't included in most samples, the sample variance is usually lower than the population variance.

COMPREHENSION CHECK 3.25

Compute the variance (σ^2) of this small population of scores:

20, 30, 30, 30, 40, 40, 40, 40, 50, 50, 50, 60

Now draw a sample of three scores at random from the population and compute their variance (s^2).

Compare these two values. Which is larger? Why is σ^2 generally larger than s^2?

(Answer on p. 90.)

corrected sample variance ($\hat{s}^2$) *Computed from sample data, the corrected sample variance provides an estimate of the population variance.*

The sample variance underestimates the variance of the population, but it can be adjusted to provide a better estimate. The **corrected sample variance** used to estimate the variance of a population is represented by the symbol $\hat{s}^2$ and is computed using Equation 3.11:(See Note 2)

Equation 3.11

$$\hat{s}^2 = \frac{\Sigma(X - \overline{X})^2}{N - 1}$$

where

$\hat{s}^2$ = corrected sample variance
X = scores on the variable X
$\overline{X}$ = the mean
N = the number of cases

In words, the corrected sample variance ($\hat{s}^2$) is computed by: (1) subtracting the mean ($\overline{X}$) from each raw score (X); (2) squaring each of these differences; (3) summing the values from step 2; and (4) dividing the result of step 3 by one less than the number of cases in the sample ($N - 1$).

Compare Equations 3.8 and 3.11. Notice that the only difference is in the denominator of the equations. In computing the corrected sample variance we divide by $N - 1$ rather than N. Lowering the denominator by 1 has the effect of increasing slightly the computed value of the variance. The amount of boost given the variance by using $N - 1$ in the denominator will depend on how large the sample is. When N is small, the boost will be substantial. When N is large, the boost will be minimal. This is as it should be, because a large sample has a greater likelihood than a small sample of including the unusually high and low scores that elevate population variance. To illustrate, the sample variance for the 120 Cheating Justification Questionnaire scores presented in Table 2.1 is $s^2 = 24.38$. The corrected sample variance is only slightly larger: $\hat{s}^2 = 24.59$. This is an increase of less than 1%. In contrast, the sample variance of the nine IQ scores depicted in Figure 3.7c is $s^2 = 35.71$. The corrected sample variance of these same nine scores is $\hat{s}^2 = 41.67$. This is an increase of over 16%. Because most research in the social and behavioral sciences is based on relatively large sample sizes, the difference between s^2 and $\hat{s}^2$ is often scarcely noticeable. In fact, many computerized statistical packages and statistical calculators compute only the corrected variance.

COMPREHENSION CHECK 3.26

Compute the corrected sample variance ($\hat{s}^2$) for the three scores forming your sample in Comprehension Check 3.25. Compare this to s^2 and σ^2. Is s^2 or $\hat{s}^2$ closer to σ^2?

(Answer on p. 90.)

Sum of Squares

sum of squares (SS) *A measure of variability equal to the sum of squared deviations of scores around the mean.*

A fourth measure of data variability is called the **sum of squares** (SS), and is equal to the sum of the squared deviations of scores around the mean. In other words, the sum of squares is the numerator of the variance formula:

$$\Sigma(X - \overline{X})^2$$

Like the other measures of variability we've examined, the sum of squares increases as data variability increases. When all scores are identical, so that there is no variability, the sum of squares is equal to 0.

The sum of squares is seldom used to measure data variability outside the context of a family of statistical procedures called analysis of variance. We will return to the sum of squares in Chapters 8 and 9 when we learn about these procedures.

Standard Deviation

If your statistics professor told you that a "squared error" of 16 points was made in computing your last test score, what would you do first? No, you wouldn't point and make donkey noises! You'd find the square root of 16 to determine that the error was 4 points, and attribute your professor's rather unusual manner of expression to too many years spent teaching statistics. If a waiter at a restaurant told you that your bill came to 64 "squared dollars," what would you do? Certainly, before figuring the tip, you'd determine that the square root of 64 squared dollars is $8. Just as your professor described an error in terms of "squared points" and the waiter gave you a bill expressed in "squared dollars," the variance describes score variability as the average "squared deviation" of scores around the mean. Although the variance has important statistical applications, it is a little awkward to think about score variability in terms of squared deviations from the mean.

standard deviation (s, σ) *A measure of variability equal to the square root of the variance. Approximately equal to the average absolute deviation of scores around the mean.*

A more directly interpretable alternative to the variance is its square root, called the **standard deviation.** As the square root of the variance, the standard deviation can be thought of as approximately (though not exactly) equal to the average absolute deviation of scores around the mean.(See Note 3) Thus, the scores depicted in Figure 3.7a show a variance of 0 and a standard deviation of $\sqrt{0} = 0$. The average distance of scores from the mean in this distribution is 0 points. In Figure 3.7b the variance is 14.29, so the standard deviation must be $\sqrt{14.29} = 3.78$. We know from this that the scores in the distribution deviate around the mean by an average of about 3.78 points. Finally, the variance of Figure 3.7c is 35.71, which makes the standard deviation $\sqrt{35.71} = 5.98$. This tells us that the average distance of scores from the mean in this distribution is about 5.98 points.

COMPREHENSION CHECK 3.27

What does it mean to say that the standard deviation of a set of IQ scores is 15? What would it mean if the standard deviation were 10?
(Answer on p. 90.)

The symbol used to represent the standard deviation of a sample is s, the standard deviation of a population is σ (the lowercase Greek letter sigma), and the **corrected sample standard deviation,** which estimates the population standard deviation, is symbolized $\hat{s}$. As with the variance, subscripts can be used to specify which standard deviation one is referring to. Equations 3.12 and 3.13 show that the standard deviation is computed easily enough once one knows the variance.

corrected sample standard deviation ($\hat{s}$) *Computed from sample data, the corrected sample standard deviation provides an estimate of the population standard deviation.*

Equation 3.12

$$s = \sqrt{s^2}$$

where

s = the sample standard deviation
s^2 = the sample variance

Equation 3.13

$$\hat{s} = \sqrt{\hat{s}^2}$$

where

$\hat{s}$ = the corrected sample standard deviation
$\hat{s}^2$ = the corrected sample variance

In words, the standard deviation of a sample is computed by finding the square root of the sample standard deviation. The corrected sample standard deviation is the square root of the corrected sample variance.

COMPREHENSION CHECK 3.28

Compute s and $\hat{s}$ for the data given in Comprehension Checks 3.22, 3.23, and 3.24.
(Answer on p. 90.)

EXAMPLE 3.3

Computing the Variance and Standard Deviation

Psychologists at Bubba's Mental Health Emporium and Laundromat want to compare two approaches used in treating depression. Scores on the Gloomy Gus Depression Inventory are shown below for clients treated using cognitive behavior modification (clients put buckets on their heads several times each day and shout "Every day in every way, I'm getting better and better!") and implosion therapy (clients are encouraged to wallow in self-pity in the hope that they'll soon get tired of feeling so lousy).

Cognitive Behavior Modification	Implosion Therapy
29	29
26	29
28	28
28	28
30	29
28	28
27	27
25	28
27	28
29	27
31	27

Although the two treatments are equally effective *on average* ($\overline{X} = 28$ for both groups), casual inspection shows that scores are more variable for clients receiving cognitive behavior modification than for clients receiving implosion therapy. The variance and standard deviation will be computed here in order to quantify the variability of these two sets of scores.

Computing the Sample Variance

Equation 3.8 is used to compute the variance of each treatment group. First, for cognitive behavior modification:

$$\begin{aligned} s^2 &= \frac{\Sigma(X - \overline{X})^2}{N} \\ &= \frac{(29 - 28)^2 + (26 - 28)^2 + \cdots + (29 - 28)^2 + (31 - 28)^2}{11} \\ &= \frac{30}{11} \\ &= 2.73 \end{aligned}$$

Next, for implosion therapy:

$$\begin{aligned} s^2 &= \frac{\Sigma(X - \overline{X})^2}{N} \\ &= \frac{(29 - 28)^2 + (29 - 28)^2 + \cdots + (27 - 28)^2 + (27 - 28)^2}{11} \\ &= \frac{6}{11} \\ &= 0.55 \end{aligned}$$

The average squared deviation of scores around the mean (variance) is 2.73 for clients treated with cognitive behavior modification and only 0.55 for clients treated with implosion therapy. We can conclude that although the two treatments show equal *average* effectiveness, outcomes associated with cognitive behavior modification are considerably more variable, that is, less predictable.

Computing the Corrected Sample Variance

Equation 3.11 describes the computation of the corrected sample variance. This corrected variance is used to estimate the variance of a population based on sample data. It inflates the sample variance slightly so as to provide an estimate of the population variance. The corrected sample variance for the cognitive-behavior modification treatment group is

$$\hat{s}^2 = \frac{\Sigma(X - \overline{X})^2}{N - 1}$$

$$= \frac{30}{11 - 1}$$

$$= 3.0$$

Next, for implosion therapy,

$$\hat{s}^2 = \frac{\Sigma(X - \overline{X})^2}{N - 1}$$

$$= \frac{6}{11 - 1}$$

$$= 0.60$$

Each of these corrected sample variances is based on a sample of only 11 clients. Each provides an estimate of the variability that would be seen in the hypothetical populations of *all* persons treated as these samples have been treated. Notice that both corrected sample variances are larger than their corresponding sample variance values.

Computing the Standard Deviation

The sample standard deviation is computed using Equation 3.12. The sample standard deviation is the square root of the sample variance. For the data being analyzed in this example, these sample standard deviations are

Cognitive Behavior Modification	Implosion Therapy
$s = \sqrt{s^2}$	$s = \sqrt{s^2}$
$= \sqrt{2.73}$	$= \sqrt{0.55}$
$= 1.65$	$= 0.74$

These standard deviation values can be interpreted as roughly equal to the average absolute deviation of scores around the mean. The average distance of scores around the mean for those receiving cognitive behavior modification was about 1.65 points. For those in implosion therapy, the average distance of scores around the mean was about 0.74 points.

Computing the Corrected Sample Standard Deviation

Corrected sample standard deviations are computed using Equation 3.13. For the data at hand, these corrected sample standard deviations are

Cognitive Behavior Modification	Implosion Therapy
$\hat{s} = \sqrt{\hat{s}^2}$	$\hat{s} = \sqrt{\hat{s}^2}$
$= \sqrt{3.00}$	$= \sqrt{0.60}$
$= 1.73$	$= 0.77$

These corrected sample standard deviations provide an estimate of the standard deviations of the hypothetical populations of all people treated as these samples have been treated.

3.3 Measuring Skew

Skew refers to the lopsidedness of a distribution of scores. Positively skewed distributions contain a few high-scoring outliers; negatively skewed distributions contain a few low-scoring outliers. One quick and simple measure of skew is given by Equation 3.14.

Equation 3.14

$$\text{Sk} = \overline{X} - \text{Md}$$

where

Sk = a measure of skew
$\overline{X}$ = the mean
Md = the median

In words, the skewness (Sk) of a distribution is computed by subtracting the median (Md) from the mean ($\overline{X}$).

Comprehension Check 3.29

Use Equation 3.14 to compute the skew of the data depicted in Figure 3.1.

(Answer on p. 90.)

Equation 3.14 is based on the relationship between the mean and median in skewed and unskewed distributions as illustrated in Figure 3.8. In a positively skewed distribution (Figure 3.8a), the mean will be larger than the median, making the difference between the mean and median positive. In a negatively skewed distribution (Figure 3.8b), the mean is smaller than the median, and the difference is negative. When the distribution is unskewed (Figure 3.8c), the mean and median are equal, and the difference between the two will be zero. Thus, the sign of the difference between mean and median reflects the direction of skew—positive or negative. The relative size of the difference reflects the magnitude of the skew. To illustrate the use of Equation 3.14, look back at Figure 3.2, the negatively skewed distribution of Feetal Anxiety Inventory scores. The mean of this distribution was estimated previously to be $\overline{X} = 68.99$. The median was estimated to be Md = 76.93. Skew, measured using Equation 3.14, is $68.99 - 76.93 = -7.94$. The negative value of Sk is consistent with the negative skew apparent in Figure 3.2; the size of the computed value of Sk gives a relative indication of the magnitude of the skew.

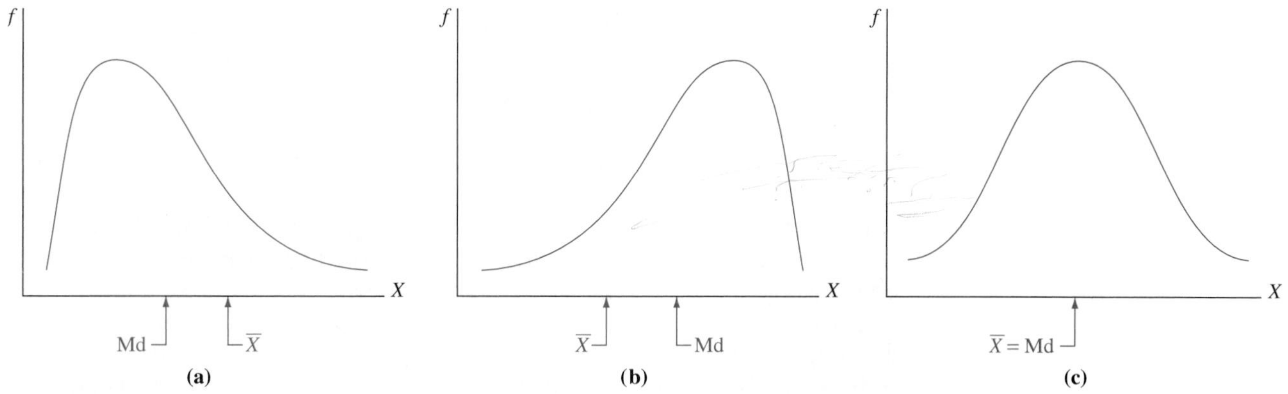

FIGURE 3.8

The relationship between the mean and median indicates the nature of the skew of a distribution. In a positively skewed distribution (a), the mean is higher than the median. In a negatively skewed distribution (b), the mean is lower. In a symmetrical distribution (c), the mean and the median are equal.

Although Equation 3.14 gives a quick measure of skew, more widely used is Equation 3.15, developed by E. S. Pearson.

Equation 3.15

$$\text{Sk} = \frac{3(\overline{X} - Md)}{s}$$

where

Sk = Pearson's measure of skew
$\overline{X}$ = the mean
Md = the median
s = the standard deviation

In words, skewness (Sk) is computed by: (1) subtracting the median (Md) from the mean ($\overline{X}$); (2) multiplying this difference by 3; and (3) dividing the result of step 2 by the standard deviation of the distribution (s).

The sign of Pearson's measure of skew indicates the direction of the skew, if any. The size of Pearson's Sk reflects the magnitude of the skew. Values of Sk more extreme than −.50 and +.50 indicate sufficient skew that one should be cautious in choosing statistical procedures. Applied to the data depicted in Figure 3.2, Pearson's measure of skew is computed as

$$\text{Sk} = \frac{3(68.99 - 76.93)}{25.57}$$

$$= -.93$$

The negative sign of Pearson's Sk shows that the distribution is negatively skewed. The magnitude of the value of Sk indicates that these data are sufficiently skewed that data analysis is likely to be affected by the skew. Indeed, we have seen previously that the mean of these scores gave a misleading impression of the typical or average score.

COMPREHENSION CHECK 3.30

Use Equation 3.15 to compute the skew of the data depicted in Figure 3.1.

(Answer on p. 90.)

SUMMARY

Tabular and graphic frequency distributions give us a useful first look at our data, but the impressions gained are often imprecise. The descriptive statistics discussed in this chapter provide greater precision in describing our data. Descriptive statistics are numbers computed from the data that describe the central tendency, variability, skew, and other characteristics of those data.

Central tendency, the typical or average score in a distribution, is most often measured using the mean. Although the mean is widely used, it is distorted by outliers. For this reason, the mean is not recommended when the data are skewed. The median, the middle score in the distribution, is less affected by outliers and is useful with skewed data. The mode, the most frequently occurring score(s) in the distribution, is used most often to describe nominal scale variables or when the distribution is bimodal or multimodal.

Measures of data variability include the range, the difference between the highest and lowest scores. Related to the range is the interquartile range, computed as the difference between the scores at the 75th and 25th percentiles. The range is determined by the two most extreme scores in the distribution. The interquartile range, in contrast, is based on just the middle 50% of the scores. The variance, defined as the average squared deviation of scores around the mean, is widely useful as a measure of variability. Closely related to the variance is the sum of squares, the sum of squared deviations of scores around the mean. Finally, the standard deviation is defined technically as the square root of the variance, but can be thought of as approximately equal to the average absolute deviation of scores around the mean.

Measures of skew are based on the fact that the mean is greater than the median in positively skewed distributions and less than the median in negatively skewed distributions.

NOTES

1. A computationally more convenient formula for use in computing the variance from raw scores is

$$s^2 = \frac{N\Sigma X^2 - (\Sigma X)^2}{N^2}$$

2. A computationally more convenient formula for use in computing the corrected sample variance from raw scores is

$$\hat{s}^2 = \frac{N\Sigma X^2 - (\Sigma X)^2}{N(N - 1)}$$

3. The standard deviation will usually be 10–20% larger than the average absolute deviation of scores around the mean.

REVIEW EXERCISES

3.1. Listed below are scores on the quantitative subtest of the Graduate Record Examination (GRE) for 10 students. Compute the mean.

500, 520, 440, 450, 500,
560, 560, 510, 590, 520

3.2. The GRE scores listed in Review Exercise 3.1 are organized into an ungrouped frequency distribution below. Compute the mean of this distribution.

X	f
590	1
560	2
520	2
510	1
500	2
450	1
440	1

3.3. Listed below as a grouped frequency distribution are ages at which a sample of 86 women had their first children. Estimate the mean of this grouped distribution.

X ($i = 5$)	f
41–45	2
36–40	8
31–35	10
26–30	23
21–25	25
16–20	18

3.4. Plot and describe the grouped distribution given in Review Exercise 3.3. Is there anything about this distribution that would affect the usefulness of the mean as a measure of central tendency?

3.5. Compute the median of the 10 GRE scores listed in Review Exercise 3.1.

3.6. Compute the median of the ungrouped frequency distribution given in Review Exercise 3.2.

3.7. Estimate the median of the grouped frequency distribution given in Review Exercise 3.3.

3.8. Which provides the better indication of central tendency for the grouped frequency distribution given in Review Exercise 3.3, the mean or the median?

3.9. What is the mode of the 10 GRE scores listed in Review Exercise 3.1?

3.10. What is the mode of the ungrouped frequency distribution given in Review Exercise 3.2?

3.11. Estimate the mode of the grouped distribution given in Review Exercise 3.3.

3.12. Describe the central tendency of the following distribution of scores on the nominal scale variable of color preference:

Color	f
Red	8
Orange	2
Yellow	4
Green	5
Blue	5

3.13. Compute the range of the 10 GRE scores listed in Review Exercise 3.1.

3.14. Compute the interquartile range of the data that follow:

X	f
50	5
40	6
30	4
20	3
10	2

3.15. Compute the variance of the 10 GRE scores listed in Review Exercise 3.1.

3.16. Compute the variance of the ungrouped distribution given in Review Exercise 3.2.

3.17. Estimate the variance of the grouped frequency distribution given in Review Exercise 3.3.

3.18. Compute the corrected sample variance for the 10 GRE scores listed in Review Exercise 3.1. Compare this to the value of the sample variance computed in Review Exercise 3.15.

3.19. Compute the standard deviation and corrected sample standard deviation for the 10 GRE scores listed in Review Exercise 3.1. Compare these values.

3.20. Compute a measure of skew for the 10 GRE scores listed in Review Exercise 3.1. Estimate a measure of skew for the grouped frequency distribution given in Review Exercise 3.3.

Answers to Comprehension Checks

3.1. Although frequency distributions tell us about central tendency, variability, modality characteristics, skew, and kurtosis in a single glance, this information is imprecise. Descriptive statistics give a more precise measure of these features of a distribution.

3.2. These symbols represent the sample mean, the mean of sample 2, the population mean, and the mean of population 1.

3.3. The mean of raw scores is computed according to Equation 3.1:

$$\overline{X} = \frac{\Sigma X}{N}$$

$$= \frac{23 + 46 + 27 + 50}{4}$$

$$= 36.50$$

3.4. The mean of an ungrouped distribution is computed according to Equation 3.2:

$$\overline{X} = \frac{\Sigma fX}{N}$$

$$= \frac{(2 \times 5) + (1 \times 4) + (3 \times 3) + (2 \times 2) + (1 \times 1)}{9}$$

$$= 3.11$$

3.5. The mean of a grouped distribution is computed according to Equation 3.3:

$$\overline{X} = \frac{\Sigma fm}{N}$$

$$= \frac{(4 \times 95.5) + (7 \times 85.5) + (3 \times 75.5) + (1 \times 65.5)}{15}$$

$$= 84.83$$

The mean estimated using Equation 3.3 is based on the assumption that all scores in a given class interval fall exactly at the midpoint of that interval. Because this assumption is unlikely to be met, the estimated mean is often slightly in error.

3.6. The mean is located at a score of 4. Scores deviate above and below this mean by an equal amount.

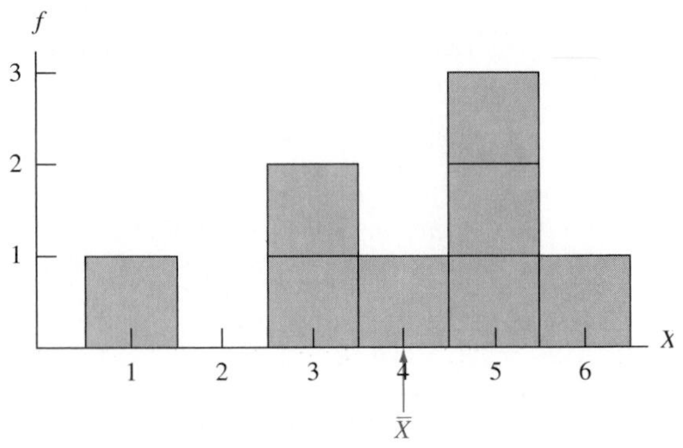

3.7. The sum of the deviations around the mean will always be zero:

X	$(X - \overline{X})$
1	$1 - 4 = -3$
3	$3 - 4 = -1$
3	$3 - 4 = -1$
4	$4 - 4 = 0$
5	$5 - 4 = +1$
5	$5 - 4 = +1$
5	$5 - 4 = +1$
6	$6 - 4 = +2$
	$\Sigma(X - \overline{X}) = 0$

3.8.

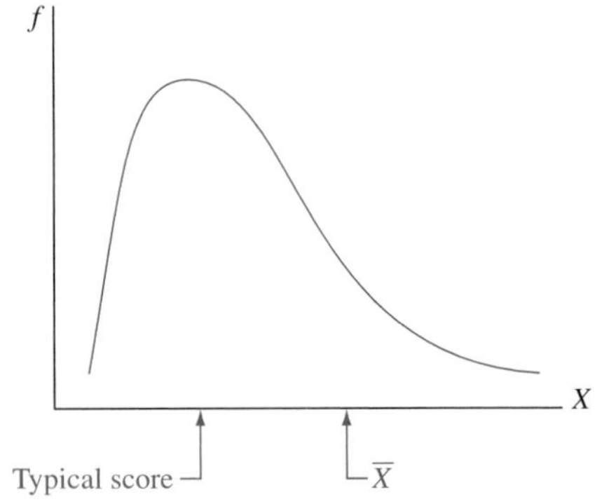

3.9. The first step in computing the median of a set of raw scores is to arrange the scores in order:
a. 27 32 41 86 97
b. 16 16 32 41 90
c. 15 18 20 32
Then, the median is computed according to Equation 3.4:

$$\text{Md} = \left(\frac{N + 1}{2}\right)\text{th score in an ordered array}$$

For the first data set,

$$\text{Md} = \left(\frac{5+1}{2}\right)\text{th score} = \text{the third score, which is 41.}$$

For the second data set,

$$\text{Md} = \left(\frac{5+1}{2}\right)\text{th score} = \text{the third score, which is 32.}$$

For the third data set,

$$\text{Md} = \left(\frac{4+1}{2}\right)\text{th score} = \text{2.5th score, which is halfway between 18 and 20, that is, 19.}$$

3.10. The median of an ungrouped frequency distribution is computed according to Equation 3.4:

$$\text{Md} = \left(\frac{N+1}{2}\right)\text{th score in an ordered array}$$

Since $N = 13$ in this distribution, Md $= (13 + 1)/2$th score, which is the seventh score. Counting from the bottom, the seventh score, the median, is 8.

3.11. The first step in estimating the median of a grouped distribution is to identify the critical interval that contains the $[(N + 1)/2]$th score. In this example, $N = 18$, so the $[(N + 1)/2]$th score is the 9.5th score. Counting from the bottom of the distribution, the 9th and 10th scores are both in the interval 71–80.

X	f	f_c	
91–100	3	18	
81–90	2	15	
71–80	7	13	critical interval
61–70	5	6	
51–60	1	1	

Next, the median is estimated according to Equation 3.5:

$$\text{Md} = \text{LRL} + \left[\frac{(N/2) - f_{c_B}}{f}\right]i$$

$$= 70.5 + \left[\frac{(18/2) - 6}{7}\right]10$$

$$= 74.79$$

3.12. The mean and median balance the distribution in different ways. The mean balances so that the magnitude of deviations is equal on each side. The median balances so that the number of scores is equal on each side.

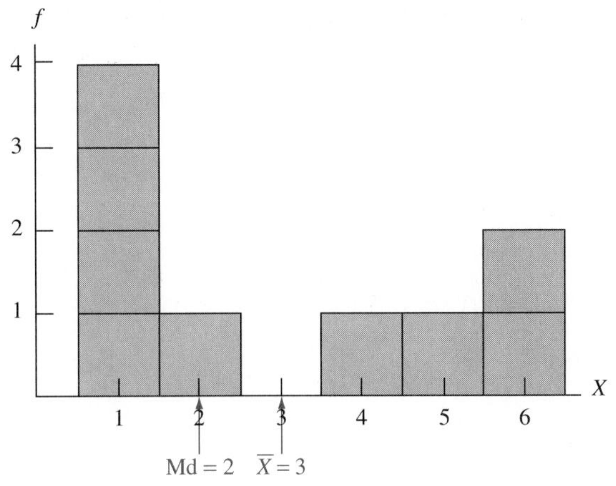

3.13. The mode is the most frequently occurring score, class interval, or nominal scale category. The modes in these examples are (a) 16; (b) 2 and 4; and (c) freshmen.

3.14. The bimodal distribution of test scores indicates the presence of two relatively homogenous subgroups within the sample. One of these subgroups performed at a relatively low level; the other performed at a relatively high level.

3.15. This distribution could best be described as bimodal, with two fast-food restaurants preferred over the others: Wendy's and McDonald's.

3.16. If scores show little variability from one case to the next, it is easy to predict accurately the score of any given individual. However, the more variable the scores are, the less predictable they become.

3.17. The range is computed according to Equation 3.6:

$$\text{Range} = \text{highest score} - \text{lowest score}$$

$$= 92 - 47$$

$$= 45$$

3.18. "Scores ranged from a low of 47 to a high of 92."

3.19. The interquartile range is computed according to Equation 3.7 as the difference between the scores at the 75th and 25th percentiles:

$$\text{IQR} = X_{75} - X_{25}$$

$$= 7 - 3$$

$$= 4$$

3.20. A variance 225 means that some scores deviate by more than 225 squared points from the mean, some deviate by fewer squared points than this, but on average, scores deviate by 225 squared points from the mean. The variance of 100 is interpreted similarly, but represents less variability.

3.21. These symbols stand for the sample variance of the variable *X*, the variance of sample 1, the variance of the population, and the population variance on the variable *Y*.

3.22. The variance is computed according to Equation 3.8:

$$s^2 = \frac{\Sigma(X - \overline{X})^2}{N}$$

$$= \frac{(47 - 47.6)^2 + (52 - 47.6)^2 + \cdots + (51 - 47.6)^2}{5}$$

$$= 25.84$$

3.23. The variance of an ungrouped frequency distribution is computed according to Equation 3.9:

$$s^2 = \frac{\Sigma f(X - \overline{X})^2}{N}$$

$$= \frac{1(110 - 100)^2 + 4(105 - 100)^2 + \cdots + 1(80 - 100)^2}{9}$$

$$= 77.78$$

3.24. The variance of a grouped frequency distribution is computed according to Equation 3.10:

$$s^2 = \frac{\Sigma f(m - \overline{X})^2}{N}$$

$$= \frac{3(95.5 - 77.26)^2 + \cdots + 2(55.5 - 77.26)^2}{17}$$

$$= 155.71$$

3.25. Both the population and sample variances are computed according to Equation 3.8, but each has its own symbol. The population variance, σ^2, is equal to 116.67. One sample drawn from this population consists of the three scores 50, 40, and 30. The variance of this sample, s^2, is 66.67.

It is usually the case that a sample will show lower variance than the population. The population variance reflects all scores, even extreme scores. The sample may not include these rare extreme scores, and so the sample variance will be lower.

3.26. The corrected sample variance is computed in the same manner as the sample variance (Equations 3.8–3.10) except that the denominator changes to $N - 1$. The corrected sample variance for a sample consisting of 50, 40, and 30 is

$$\hat{s}^2 = \frac{\Sigma(X - \overline{X})^2}{N - 1}$$

$$= \frac{(50 - 40)^2 + (40 - 40)^2 + (30 - 40)^2}{3 - 1}$$

$$= 100.00$$

The variance of the population from which this sample was drawn was $\sigma^2 = 116.67$. The sample variance of the three scores was $s^2 = 66.67$. The corrected sample variance, $\hat{s}^2 = 100.00$, provides a better estimate of the population variance than does the sample variance.

3.27. A standard deviation of 15 indicates that although some scores deviate from the mean by more than 15 points and some deviate by less than this, the average deviation of scores from the mean is about 15 points. A standard deviation of 10 is interpreted similarly, but indicates less variability.

3.28. Equations 3.12 and 3.13 show that standard deviations are computed as the square root of the variance. The standard deviations and corrected sample standard deviations for the data given in Comprehension Checks 3.22–3.24 are

$$3.22{:}\ s = \sqrt{25.84} = 5.08;\ \hat{s} = \sqrt{32.30} = 5.68$$

$$3.23{:}\ s = \sqrt{77.78} = 8.2;\ \hat{s} = \sqrt{87.50} = 9.35$$

$$3.24{:}\ s = \sqrt{155.71} = 12.48;\ \hat{s} = \sqrt{165.44} = 12.86$$

3.29. A simple measure of skew is computed according to Equation 3.14:

$$\text{Sk} = \overline{X} - \text{Md}$$

$$= 100 - 105$$

$$= -5$$

3.30. Pearson's measure of skew is computed according to Equation 3.15:

$$\text{Sk} = \frac{3(\overline{X} - Md)}{s}$$

$$= \frac{3(100 - 105)}{8.82}$$

$$= -1.70$$

The negative value of Pearson's Sk indicates a negatively skewed distribution. The absolute magnitude of the value exceeds .50, so the distribution can be considered sufficiently skewed to call for caution in interpreting other statistics.

Probability and the Normal Distribution

4

Chapter Outline

Scores on the subscales of the Scholastic Aptitude Test (SAT) are computed in such a way that the distribution will have a mean of 500 and a standard deviation of 100. Knowing this and nothing more, how would a college admissions officer who wants to identify and recruit "hot" prospects determine the SAT score at the 90th percentile? A superintendent of schools is planning the budget for the next school year. Students whose IQs are 130 or higher qualify for special "gifted and talented" classes. If the mean IQ of all school-aged children is 100 and the standard deviation is 15, what percentage of the students in the superintendent's district will qualify for these classes? A neuropsychologist is considering using biofeedback to treat patients who suffer from frequent, severe migraine headaches. She knows from the research literature that patients like hers still average 3.2 migraines per month even following biofeedback treatment. Some have more headaches than this, though, and some have fewer, with a standard deviation of .75. Before beginning a biofeedback treatment program, she wants to know the probability that a patient who is trained to use biofeedback will experience two or fewer migraines per month.

Answers to these kinds of questions change lives. They determine who will be recruited by a prestigious university, they affect public school budgeting decisions, and they influence selection of treatment options.

The focus of this chapter is the normal distribution. You will learn that questions like those posed above can be answered, *provided* one is able to assume that the data are normally distributed. Because so many variables that are of interest to social and behavioral scientists are normally distributed, the statistical procedures described in this chapter are extremely useful.

COMPREHENSION CHECK 4.1

Before you read any further, try to guess the answers to the questions posed in the first paragraph of this chapter. What SAT score marks the 90th percentile? What percentage of school children have IQs of 130 or higher? What is the probability that a patient treated for migraines with biofeedback will experience two or fewer migraines per month?

(Answer on p. 116.)

4.1 The Normal Distribution

We first encountered the normal distribution in Chapter 2. As shown again in Figure 4.1, there are several characteristics of the normal distribution that we will consider next.

The Normal Distribution as a Theoretical Distribution

empirical distribution *A distribution of actual scores. Empirical distributions describe real data.*

First, the normal distribution is a theoretical distribution, not an empirical distribution. An **empirical distribution** is a distribution of real, observed (thus the word "empirical") scores. The distribution of scores on the first test in your statistics course, the distribution of scores on the Cheating Justification Questionnaire (Figure 2.2 in Chapter 2), and the distribution of SAT scores obtained from this year's cohort of graduating American high school seniors

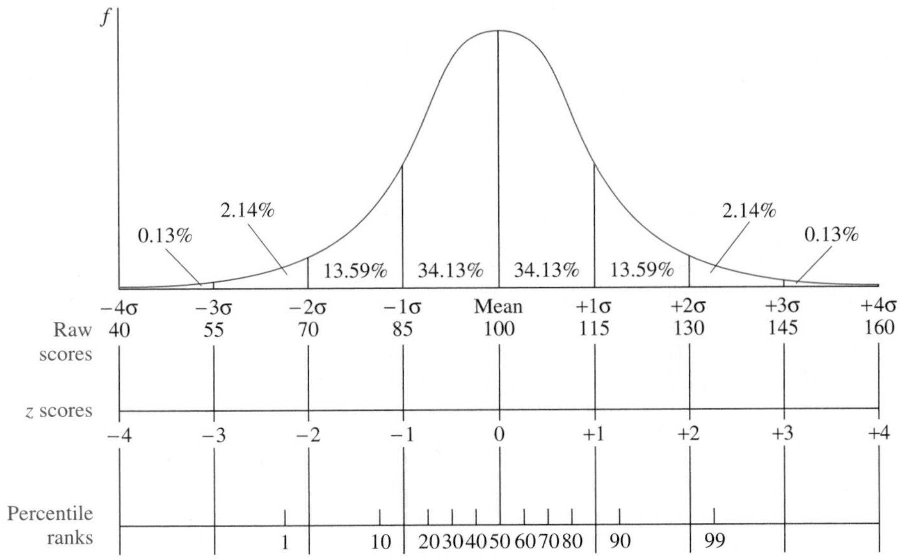

FIGURE 4.1

The normal distribution is bell-shaped and symmetrical. In this particular normal distribution, the mean is 100 and the standard deviation is 15. The shape of the normal distribution is defined by the percentages of cases that fall between specified scores. Also shown in this figure are *z* scores and percentile ranks.

are all examples of empirical distributions. A **theoretical distribution,** in contrast, is an ideal distribution, one that we can imagine and one that may be *approximated* by an empirical distribution, but one that does not actually exist.

theoretical distribution *An ideal, imaginary distribution of scores that exists only in theory, not in reality.*

COMPREHENSION CHECK 4.2

Give an original example of an empirical distribution. Explain why it is not a theoretical distribution.
(Answer on p. 116.)

The normal distribution is a theoretical distribution because it can never be obtained with actual data. For one thing, the scores that form the normal distribution are completely continuous; between any two scores there is another score. This isn't true of any of the variables we work with in the real world of the social and behavioral sciences. Because of limitations in our ability to measure things, there are always gaps between scores. For instance, one can have an IQ of 100 or 101, but not 100.5. A rat can make 7 or 8 errors in getting through a maze, but not 7.5 errors.

A second reason we never achieve a perfectly normal distribution in the real world is that the normal distribution is based on a sample size of infinity. Most researchers in the social and behavioral sciences are not so optimistic as to try to tackle data sets this large!

Third, the tails of the normal distribution extend infinitely outward in both directions, never reaching the bottom of the ordinate. In other words, there are no bottom or top scores in the normal distribution. Minimum and maximum scores *are* a part of reality and empirical distributions.

Even though the normal distribution is a purely theoretical, ideal entity, it is closely approximated by many of the variables with which we work in the social and behavioral sciences. Intelligence, personality traits, political opinions, and a multitude of other variables all conform closely, though not exactly, to the normal distribution. Other important distributions called "sampling distributions," which we will study in subsequent chapters, can also take on the shape of the normal distribution.

COMPREHENSION CHECK 4.3

Why should we care about the normal distribution if it doesn't exist in the real world?

(Answer on p. 116.)

The Shape of the Normal Distribution

We've seen that the normal distribution is a theoretical distribution that is often approximated in nature. A second way of describing the normal distribution is to note its shape. The normal distribution is bell-shaped and symmetrical. But not all bell-shaped, symmetrical distributions are normal distributions. The normal distribution is defined by the percentages of cases that fall between specified points in the normal distribution. You can see from Figure 4.1 that 34.13% of the cases fall between the mean and the score located one standard deviation above the mean, 13.59% score between 1 and 2 standard deviations above the mean, 2.14% are found between 2 and 3 standard deviations above the mean, 0.13% appear between 3 and 4 standard deviations above the mean, and a tiny fraction of the cases score higher than this. Because the normal distribution is symmetrical, the same percentages are found below the mean: 34.13% of the cases score between the mean and 1 standard deviation below the mean, 13.59% fall between 1 and 2 standard deviations below the mean, and so on.

You may have noticed in reading the preceding paragraph that we are now using the standard deviation in a manner that is different from what you're used to. The standard deviation was presented in Chapter 3 as a measure of the variability of scores in a distribution. We are now using it as a yardstick for measuring distances in a distribution. The standard deviation is used in both of these ways.

Figure 4.1 shows a normal distribution of IQ scores with a standard deviation of 15. The standard deviation of this distribution tells us something about the variability of the IQ scores—the average absolute deviation of scores around the mean is about 15 points. But we can also use the standard deviation to measure distances between scores in the distribution. Thus, an IQ score of 115 falls 15 points above the mean, or, measured using the standard deviation as our yardstick, the score falls 1 standard deviation above the mean. Similarly, an IQ of 70 falls 30 points or 2 standard deviations below the mean. In a like manner, there are 4 standard deviations (60 IQ points) between an IQ of 70 and an IQ of 130. We will return later in this chapter to the idea of using the standard deviation as a way of measuring distances in a distribution.

COMPREHENSION CHECK 4.4

Scores on a statistics test are approximately normally distributed with $\overline{X} = 75$ and $s = 10$. What score falls: (a) one standard deviation above the mean? (b) two standard deviations below the mean?

How many standard deviations separate scores of: (c) 70 and 80? (d) 65 and 85?

(Answer on p. 116.)

Area Under the Curve and Probability

The percentages that define the shape of the normal distribution can be thought of in three ways. First, we've seen already that they tell us what percentages of cases fall within specified score ranges in a normal distribution. Second, they measure areas under the normal curve. Thus, when we say that 34.13% of the cases score between the mean and 1 standard deviation above the mean in a normal distribution, it is the same thing as saying that 34.13% of the total area under the normal curve falls in this range. Third, the percentages that define the shape of the normal distribution reflect probabilities. When we say that 34.13% of the cases or area under the normal curve fall between the mean and 1 standard deviation above the mean, it is equivalent to saying that the probability is 34.13% (or, expressed as a decimal, .3413) that any one case drawn at random from the distribution will fall in this score range. Similarly, we know that 13.59% of the cases or area under the normal curve are found between the scores that fall at 1 and 2 standard deviations above the mean. Therefore, the probability of drawing a score at random that falls in this range of scores is 13.59% or .1359. To summarize, statements about percentages of cases, percentages of area under the curve, and probabilities are equivalent.

COMPREHENSION CHECK 4.5

In an approximately normal distribution of statistics test scores with $\overline{X} = 75$ and $s = 10$, what percentage of students score between 75 and 85? What is the probability of a student scoring between 75 and 85? What percentage falls between 55 and 65? What is the probability of finding a score in this range?

(Answer on p. 116.)

4.2 RULES OF PROBABILITY

When you turn the key in your automobile ignition, your car almost always starts. The car starting is a high-probability event because it is something that happens almost every time you try. When you enter the lottery, you almost never win. Winning the lottery is a low-probability event because it is an event that almost never happens even in a large number of tries. Stated generally, the **probability** of an outcome, represented by the letter p, refers to that outcome's relative frequency of occurrence, that is, how often the outcome occurs relative to the total number of various possible outcomes. This relative frequency definition of probability is expressed more formally in Equation 4.1.

probability *The probability of an outcome, its likelihood of occurrence, is determined by the relative frequency of that outcome—how often that outcome occurs relative to the total number of possible outcomes.*

Equation 4.1

$$p(A) = \frac{f(A)}{N}$$

where

$p(A)$ = the probability of outcome A
$f(A)$ = the frequency of occurrence of outcome A
N = the total number of possible outcomes

In words, the probability of observing outcome A is equal to the number of times outcome A has occurred, $f(A)$, divided by the total number of *possible* outcomes (N).

As an example, suppose that there are 12 males and 18 females in a class of 30 students. The probability of picking a male at random from the class is determined according to Equation 4.1:

$$p(\text{male}) = \frac{f(male)}{N} = \frac{12}{30} = .40$$

In other words, the probability of drawing a male from the class is .40 or 40%. The probability of an outcome is determined by the relative frequency of occurrence of that outcome. The more times some outcome occurs in any set of observations, the more probable is that outcome. The fewer times some outcome occurs in any set of observations, the less probable is that outcome.

Comprehension Check 4.6

In a class of 37 statistics students there are 10 freshmen, 14 sophomores, 8 juniors, and 5 seniors. What is the probability that a student chosen at random from the class will be a: (a) freshman; (b) sophomore; (c) junior; (d) senior?

(Answer on p. 116.)

The relative frequency definition of probability also applies to finding the probabilities of scores in a distribution. Look back at Figure 4.1 and answer this question. What is more likely, drawing a case from the normal distribution whose score is between the mean and 1 standard deviation above the mean, or drawing a case from this distribution whose score falls between 2 and 3 standard deviations above the mean? Far more scores fall in the first of these two score ranges than in the second. Obviously, it is more likely that a case drawn at random from the distribution will fall between the mean and 1 standard deviation above the mean (p = .3413) than it is that the case will score between 2 and 3 standard deviations above the mean (p = .0214). The point is that the probability of finding any given score in a distribution is determined by the frequency of that score relative to the total number of scores. This relative frequency, or probability, is reflected by the area under the normal curve. The greater the area, the greater the relative frequency, and the greater will be the probability.

Comprehension Check 4.7

In the normal distribution of IQ scores shown in Figure 4.1, which is more probable, drawing a score between 70 and 85 or drawing a score between 130 and 145? Explain why.

(Answer on p. 117.)

mutually exclusive events *Two or more events or outcomes are considered mutually exclusive if only one of the outcomes can occur on any single observation.*

Mutually Exclusive and Independent Outcomes

Two outcomes are said to be **mutually exclusive events** if either one *or* the other can occur, but not both. In a coin toss, for instance, heads and tails are mutually exclusive outcomes, because one or the other can occur, but not both. Similarly, a student can get any one score between 0 and 100 on a statistics test, but *only* one score. Each score is mutually exclusive to the others. In a like manner, any given individual's age can range from 0 years to over 100 years, but each person has only one age at any one time. Scores on the variable of age are mutually exclusive.

COMPREHENSION CHECK 4.8

Which of the following are mutually exclusive and why?: (a) having blond hair and being 13 years old; (b) being depressed and being female; (c) being Protestant and being Catholic; (d) being 13 years old and being a lawyer.
(Answer on p. 117.)

Two outcomes are said to be **independent events** if the occurrence of one in no way affects the occurrence of the other. In two tosses of a coin, for instance, the outcome of one toss in no way affects the outcome of the other toss. Even if you've flipped a coin 100 times and it's come up heads every time, the next toss of the coin is an independent event, with a probability of .5 for heads and .5 for tails. In a similar manner, when two students take a statistics test, their scores are independent. How one student scores in no way affects the score of the other.

independent events *Two or more events or outcomes are considered independent if the occurrence of one outcome in no way affects the probability of the occurrence of the other outcome(s).*

COMPREHENSION CHECK 4.9

Which of the following are independent outcomes and why?: (a) winning the lottery and having an IQ of 105; (b) your spouse catching a cold and you catching a cold; (c) you voting Republican and your spouse voting Democrat; (d) getting an A in statistics and having blond hair.
(Answer on p. 117.)

The Converse Rule

When outcomes are mutually exclusive, the probability that outcome A *will* occur, $p(A)$, is related to the probability that outcome A *will not* occur, $p(\bar{A})$. The **converse rule** of probability that describes this relationship is expressed in Equation 4.2.

converse rule *A rule of probability that states that the probability that an event will not occur is equal to 1 minus the probability that the event will occur.*

Equation 4.2

$$p(\bar{A}) = 1 - p(A)$$

where

$p(\bar{A})$ = the probability that outcome A will *not* occur
$p(A)$ = the probability that outcome A *will* occur

In words, the probability that outcome A will not occur, $p(\bar{A})$, is equal to 1 minus the probability that outcome A will occur, $p(A)$.

To illustrate, suppose that the probability of winning the lottery, p(winning), is .000001 (1 in 1 million). If this is so, the converse rule tells us that the probability of *not* winning, $p(\overline{\text{winning}})$, is 999,999 in 1 million:

$$p(\overline{\text{winning}}) = 1 - p(\text{winning})$$
$$= 1 - .000001$$
$$= .999999$$

COMPREHENSION CHECK 4.10

Use the converse rule to determine the probability that you will not catch a cold from your spouse if the probability is .3 that you will. Use the converse rule to determine the probability that you will get an A in statistics if the probability of being blond is .25.
(Answer on p. 117.)

The converse rule also applies to finding the probabilities of scores in frequency distributions. The probability that a score drawn at random from a normal distribution will fall between the mean and 1 standard deviation above the mean is .3413. According to the converse rule, the probability that the score will *not* fall within this range is $1 - .3413 = .6587$.

COMPREHENSION CHECK 4.11

Based on Figure 4.1 and the converse rule, what is the probability of obtaining an IQ in some range other than 130–160?
(Answer on p. 117.)

addition rule *A rule of probability that states that the probability of observing one or another of a set of mutually exclusive events is equal to the sum of the separate probabilities of those outcomes.*

The Addition Rule

Another rule helps us to determine the probability of observing any one of a set of mutually exclusive possible outcomes. The **addition rule,** sometimes called the *or rule,* is expressed in Equation 4.3.

Equation 4.3

$$p(A \text{ or } B \text{ or } C) = p(A) + p(B) + p(C)$$

where

$p(A \text{ or } B \text{ or } C)$ = the probability of observing outcome A or B or C in a single observation
$p(A)$ = the probability of outcome A
$p(B)$ = the probability of outcome B
$p(C)$ = the probability of outcome C

In words, the probability of observing outcome A or B or C in a single observation, $p(A \text{ or } B \text{ or } C)$, is equal to the sum of the separate probabilities of outcome A, $p(A)$, outcome B, $p(B)$, and outcome C, $p(C)$.

Imagine, for example, a jar containing 10 coins: 5 pennies, 3 nickels, and 2 dimes. According to our relative frequency definition of probability (Equation 4.1), the probability of drawing a penny from the jar is $5/10 = .5$. The probability of drawing a nickel is $3/10 = .3$. And the probability of drawing a dime is $2/10 = .2$. The addition rule tells us that the probability of drawing a penny *or* a nickel on a single trial is found by summing the separate probabilities of these outcomes:

$$p(\text{penny or nickel}) = p(\text{penny}) + p(\text{nickel})$$
$$= .5 + .3$$
$$= .8$$

As another example, the probability of drawing a nickel or a dime is also found by summing their separate probabilities:

$$p(\text{nickel or dime}) = p(\text{nickel}) + p(\text{dime})$$
$$= .5 + .2$$
$$= .7$$

COMPREHENSION CHECK 4.12

If the probability of catching a cold from your spouse is .3 and the probability of catching a cold from a co-worker is .1, what is the probability of catching a cold from either your spouse or the co-worker?

(Answer on p. 117.)

The addition rule is also useful in working with distributions of scores. For instance, the probability of drawing a score from a normal distribution that falls *either* between the mean and 1 standard deviation above the mean *or* between 2 and 3 standard deviations below the mean is equal to the sum of the separate probabilities of these outcomes: .3413 + .0214 = .3627.

COMPREHENSION CHECK 4.13

The probability of obtaining an IQ score above 130 is .02. The probability of obtaining an IQ score below 70 is also .02. What is the probability that a score drawn at random from the distribution of IQ scores will be either higher than 130 or lower than 70?

(Answer on p. 117.)

The Multiplication Rule

The addition rule deals with the probability of observing any one of several outcomes on a single observation. Sometimes we want to know the probability of observing some *combination* of two or more mutually exclusive, independent outcomes in a series of observations. The **multiplication rule,** sometimes called the *and rule,* is expressed in Equation 4.4 and describes how this probability is determined.

multiplication rule *A rule of probability that states that the probability of observing a combination of two or more mutually exclusive, independent events is equal to the product of the separate probabilities of those outcomes.*

Equation 4.4

$$p(A \text{ and } B \text{ and } C) = p(A) \times p(B) \times p(C)$$

where

$p(A \text{ and } B \text{ and } C)$ = the probability of observing outcomes A and B and C
$p(A)$ = the probability of outcome A
$p(B)$ = the probability of outcome B
$p(C)$ = the probability of outcome C

In words, the probability of observing the combination of outcomes *A* and *B* and *C*, *p*(*A* and *B* and *C*), is equal to the product of the separate probabilities of these outcomes.

For example, what is the probability of rolling a die three times and getting 3, 1, and 6? The probability of each of these individual outcomes is 1/6 or .17. Therefore, the multiplication rule gives us the probability of the combination of the outcomes as the product of their separate probabilities:

$$\begin{aligned} p(3 \text{ and } 1 \text{ and } 6) &= p(3) \times p(1) \times p(6) \\ &= .17 \times .17 \times .17 \\ &= .005 \end{aligned}$$

COMPREHENSION CHECK 4.14

In six flips of a coin, what is the probability of each of the following sequences of outcomes, where H=heads and T=tails? (a) HHHHHH; (b) HTHTHT; (c) TTTTTT.

(Answer on p. 117.)

The multiplication rule is also useful in working with distributions of scores. We can use the multiplication rule to determine the probability of observing any given combination of scores. Suppose, for instance, that two cases are drawn at random from a normal distribution. What is the probability that one will score between 2 and 3 standard deviations above the mean *and* that the second will fall between 1 and 2 standard deviations below the mean? According to the multiplication rule, the probability of observing this combination of events is equal to the product of their separate probabilities: $.0214 \times .1359 = .003$.

COMPREHENSION CHECK 4.15

Adult male heights are normally distributed with $\overline{X} = 69$ inches and $s = 3$. What is the probability that two men drawn at random from this distribution will both be 72 inches or taller?

(Answer on p. 117.)

4.3 STANDARD SCORES

In learning about the normal distribution we discovered that the standard deviation is more than just a measure of score variability. It is also a yardstick used in measuring distances in a distribution. In the distribution of IQ scores depicted in Figure 4.1, the mean is 100 and the standard deviation is 15. Thus, an IQ score of 115 falls 15 points, or 1 standard deviation, above the mean. As another example, in a distribution of ages having a mean of 37 years and a standard deviation of 13, the individual who is 11 years old falls 26 years, or 2 standard deviations, below the mean.

standard scores or *z* scores *Represented by the lower-case letter z, a standard score or z score measures the difference between a raw score and the mean of the distribution using the standard deviation of the distribution as the unit of measure.*

When scores are expressed in terms of how many standard deviations they fall from the mean of a distribution, they are called **standard scores.** Because the lower-case letter z is the symbol used to represent standard scores, they are often called *z scores.* Equation 4.5 describes how raw scores are transformed to z scores.

$$z_X = \frac{X - \overline{X}}{s}$$

Equation 4.5

where

z_X = the standard score or z score corresponding to raw score X
X = a raw score
$\overline{X}$ = the mean of the distribution of raw scores
s = the standard deviation of the distribution of raw scores

In words, the z score corresponding to a raw score of X (z_X) is computed by: (1) subtracting the mean of the distribution ($\overline{X}$) from the raw score (X), and (2) dividing this difference by the standard deviation of the distribution (s).

Consider some examples. An IQ score of 115 in a distribution having a mean of 100 and a standard deviation of 15 falls 1 standard deviation above the mean so, by Equation 4.5, its z score equivalent is

$$z_X = \frac{X - \overline{X}}{s} = \frac{115 - 100}{15} = +1$$

The positive sign of the z score indicates that the score falls above the mean. The absolute magnitude of the z score, 1, tells us how far the score falls from the mean measured in standard deviations: 1 standard deviation.

As another example, in a distribution of ages having a mean of 37 and a standard deviation of 13, the standard score corresponding to an age of 11 years is

$$z_X = \frac{X - \overline{X}}{s} = \frac{11 - 37}{13} = -2$$

The negative sign of this z score indicates that this age falls below the mean. The absolute size of the z score, 2, tells us how far the score falls from the mean: 2 standard deviations.

Standard scores are not limited to whole numbers. Fractional values are also interpretable. In a distribution of statistics test scores having a mean of 75 and a standard deviation of 10, the individual scoring 78 has a z score of

$$z_X = \frac{X - \overline{X}}{s} = \frac{78 - 75}{10} = +.3$$

This student's score falls .3 standard deviation above the mean. Similarly, the student whose score was 60 has a z score of

$$z_X = \frac{X - \overline{X}}{s}$$
$$= \frac{60 - 75}{10}$$
$$= -1.5$$

This is a score 1.5 standard deviations below the mean.

COMPREHENSION CHECK 4.16

In the distribution of IQ scores, $\overline{X} = 100$ and $s = 15$. Compute z scores for IQs of: (a) 100; (b) 73; and (c) 107.
(Answers on p. 117–118.)

Characteristics of Standard Scores

Suppose that you transformed an entire distribution of raw scores into z scores using Equation 4.5. The resulting distribution of z scores would have three characteristics.

First, the distribution of z scores would have exactly the same shape as the original distribution of raw scores. Transforming raw scores into z scores has no effect at all on the shape of the distribution. Only the scores change—from raw score form to z-score form. If the raw scores are normally distributed, the z scores will be normally distributed as well. If the raw scores are skewed, the z scores will be skewed.

Second, the mean of any distribution of z scores will always equal 0. It's easy to see why this is so. Each z score is an expression of a score's deviation from the mean. Remember from Chapter 3 that the sum of the deviations of scores around the mean is always 0. Since z scores also reflect deviations around the mean, their sum will also be 0. And since the sum of a distribution of z scores will always be 0, the mean of the z scores will be 0 too. See Note 1 at the end of this chapter if you want a more formal proof that the mean of a distribution of z scores will always equal 0.

The third feature of any distribution of standard scores is that the variance of the z scores will always equal 1. And since the standard deviation is just the square root of the variance, the standard deviation of a distribution of z scores will also equal 1. The proof of this characteristic is more complicated and not particularly important, but see Note 2 at the end of this chapter if you're curious.

COMPREHENSION CHECK 4.17

For the raw scores listed below:

(a) Plot the frequency distribution of these raw scores.
(b) Transform the raw scores to standard scores.
(c) Plot the frequency distribution of the z scores.
(d) Describe the distribution of z scores in terms of mean, standard deviation, and shape.

$$X = 3,\ 1,\ 4,\ 2,\ 3,\ 3,\ 4,\ 5,\ 2$$

(Answer on p. 118.)

Some Uses of Standard Scores

At this point you're probably wondering, "What's all the brouhaha over z scores? We *can* transform raw scores to z scores, but why would anyone *want* to?" A more complete answer to this question will come later in this chapter, but we are ready here to consider two useful applications of z scores.

Locating Scores in a Distribution. Standard scores, like percentile ranks, are useful in helping us to locate any given score in the distribution. A percentile rank locates a score by giving the percentage of cases that fall at and below that score. A standard score locates a score by telling us how far and in what direction the score falls from the mean.

Percentile ranks and standard scores both locate scores in the distribution, but standard scores have an advantage over percentile ranks. Percentile ranks provide only an ordinal scale of measurement, whereas z scores give us a more useful interval scale of measurement. This advantage can be seen in Figure 4.1. Notice how the percentile ranks are spaced unevenly along the scale of scores. Equally distant raw scores do not always have equally distant percentile ranks. For instance, Figure 4.1 shows that to move 10 percentile ranks from 1 to 10, we must jump about 15 raw score points, from 65 to 80. To move the same 10 percentile ranks from 40 to 50, we need to move only about 5 raw score points, from 95 to 100. Ordinal scale measurement was described in Chapter 1 as being like a "rubber ruler." The uneven spacing of percentile ranks in Figure 4.1 illustrates this idea.

Now look at the z scores listed in Figure 4.1. Unlike percentile ranks, z scores are spaced at equal intervals all along the scale of scores. They provide an interval scale of measurement. Equally distant raw scores have equally distant z scores.

Still, z scores aren't perfect. Many people find it easier to interpret percentile rank information than z scores. It takes a little experience working with z scores to begin to get a sense of exactly what constitutes a "high" z score and what is "low."

COMPREHENSION CHECK 4.18

What does a percentile rank tell you that a z score does not? What does a z score provide that a percentile rank does not?
(Answer on p. 118.)

Comparing Scores on Different Variables. Standard scores have a second valuable application. They enable us to compare scores on different variables. Which reflects the greater scholastic aptitude, an ACT composite score of 20 or an SAT total score of 900? Which is more extreme, an oral temperature of 99.3 degrees Fahrenheit or an adult height of 72 inches? With z scores we can answer questions like these that seem at first to be like comparing apples and oranges. By converting raw scores to z scores, we locate them in their distributions and so can judge which is higher and which is lower. Standard scores give us a standard way of expressing scores on different variables so that we can compare scores on those variables. Example 4.1 illustrates this application of z scores.

EXAMPLE 4.1

Using Standard Scores to Compare Scores on Different Variables

Here's something to think about: Is Dirty Harry dirtier or hairier? We'll use standard scores to settle this question. One hundred adult men, including Dirty Harry, were measured for body hair by counting the number of hairs per square inch on each of their backs. The average man showed 8.3 hairs per square inch, with a standard deviation of 2.6. Dirty Harry's back yielded 11 hairs per square inch. Dirtiness was assessed in the same group of men by weighing each man before and after bathing. On average, the men lost 1.7 grams of dirt, with a standard deviation of .5 grams. Dirty Harry lost 3.1 grams of dirt in the process of bathing.

We know how dirty Dirty Harry is (3.1 grams of dirt) and how hairy he is (11 hairs per square inch), but these values cannot be compared directly. They are different variables and are expressed in different units of measure. But let's convert both of Harry's raw scores to z-score form. Using Equation 4.5 to transform his score on hairiness, we get

$$z_X = \frac{X - \overline{X}}{s} = \frac{11 - 8.3}{2.6} = +1.04$$

His raw score on dirtiness can also be converted to z score form using Equation 4.5:

$$z_X = \frac{X - \overline{X}}{s} = \frac{3.1 - 1.7}{.5} = +2.80$$

We can see from these positive z scores that Dirty Harry is both hairier and dirtier than the average man. However, he is only slightly over 1 standard deviation above the mean in hairiness ($z = +1.04$) and is 2.8 standard deviations above the mean in dirtiness ($z = +2.80$). On this basis, we can conclude that Dirty Harry is dirtier than he is hairy.

COMPREHENSION CHECK 4.19

IQ scores have a mean of 100 and a standard deviation of 15. SAT scores have a mean of 500 and a standard deviation of 100. Which score is higher, an SAT of 580 or an IQ of 108?

(Answer on p. 118.)

4.4 THE STANDARD NORMAL DISTRIBUTION

standard normal distribution *A normal distribution of standard scores, having a mean of 0, a variance and standard deviation of 1, and a normal shape.*

We have now studied the normal distribution and standard scores. Let's put these two concepts together. If we converted a normal distribution of raw scores to standard scores, we would have a normal distribution of standard scores. This is called the **standard normal distribution.**

Characteristics of the Standard Normal Distribution

Because the standard normal distribution is a distribution of standard scores, all of the usual characteristics of standard scores apply to this distribution: The mean is equal to 0 and the variance and the standard deviation are equal to 1. Because the standard normal distribution has a normal shape, scores are distributed according to the percentages depicted in Figure 4.1. Thus, 34.13% of the cases score between 0 (the z score at the mean) and +1 (the z score 1 standard deviation above the mean), 13.59% score between z scores of +1 and +2, and so on.

Proportions of area under the standard normal distribution are listed in Table 1 of Appendix B, "Table of Areas Under the Standard Normal Distribution." Find this table in the back of your textbook before you read any further. The table of areas is laid out in three columns. Column A lists z scores, column B lists the proportion of area under the curve between each z score and the mean, and column C indicates the proportion of area located "beyond" each z score. For positive z scores, "beyond" means to the right (higher); for negative z scores, "beyond" means to the left (lower). Although the table lists only positive z scores, the standard normal distribution is perfectly symmetrical, so the table can also be used to find proportions associated with negative z scores. These areas are shown in Figure 4.2.

A few examples will help you learn to read the table of areas. Find a z score of +.75 in column A. Listed in column B is the value .2734. This is the proportion of cases in the distribution that score between $z = +.75$ (three-quarters of a standard deviation above the mean) and $z = 0$ (the mean). Expressed as a percentage, this is 27.34% of the cases. Remembering that areas under the curve also represent probabilities, we can also say that the probability is .2734 that a single case drawn at random from a normal distribution will score between z scores of 0 and +.75. The value listed in column C for a z score of +.75 is .2266. This is the proportion of cases that score at and above a z score of +.75 and also tells us the probability of finding a score three-quarters of a standard deviation or more above the mean.

Take as another example the z score −.80. Although no negative z score values are listed in the table, we can find the positive value, +.80, in column A. Listed in column B is .2881. This is the proportion of cases falling between $z = -.80$ and $z = 0$, the mean. It is also the probability of drawing a score at random from within that range of values. Column C lists the value .2119.

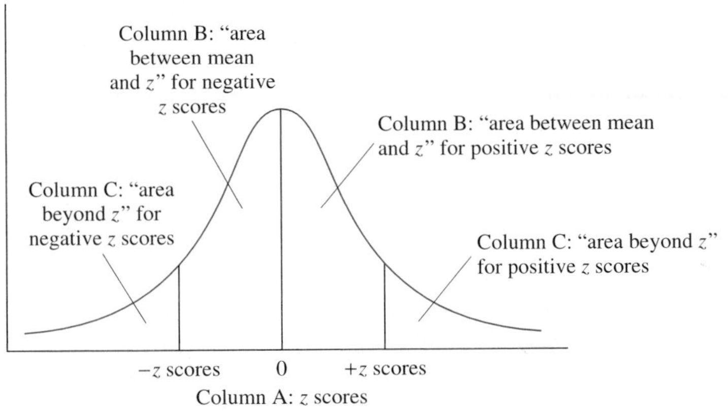

FIGURE 4.2

The table of areas under the standard normal distribution lists z scores (column A), proportions of area between the z score and the mean (column B), and proportions of area beyond the z score (column C).

Remembering that column C lists proportions "beyond" the z score and that "beyond" means *lower* for negative z scores, the listing of .2119 tells us the proportion of cases in the distribution that score .8 standard deviation or more below the mean. It is also the probability of finding a z score of $-.80$ or lower in the normal distribution.

COMPREHENSION CHECK 4.20

Scores on a statistics test are normally distributed with $\overline{X} = 75$ and $s = 10$. Find the following proportions using the table of areas under the normal curve. (*Hint:* Remember that this table is set up to use z scores, so you'll have to begin by converting all raw scores to z scores.)

(a) Proportion of cases between 75 and 85
(b) Proportion of cases higher than 85
(c) Proportion of cases between 55 and 75
(b) Proportion of cases lower than 55

(Answer on p. 118.)

Other proportions that are not listed in the table of areas can be determined quite easily. For instance, what proportion of the cases in a normal distribution falls below $z = +1.20$? This proportion is represented by the shaded area under the curve in Figure 4.3a. We first find the z score of 1.20 in column A. From column B we get the proportion of cases falling between $z = +1.20$ and $z = 0$, that is, the mean: .3849. But what proportion of the cases score even lower than this? Obviously, one-half do, or .5. The total proportion below a z score of $+1.20$ is therefore $.3849 + .5 = .8849$ or 88.49%.

Look at another example illustrated in Figure 4.3b. Suppose we want to know the proportion of cases scoring above $z = -1.5$. We first find $z = 1.5$ in column A. Column B gives the proportion of cases between this z score and the mean: .4332. An additional half of the area under the curve falls above the mean: .5. Adding these values gives us the total area above $z = -1.5$: $.4332 + .5 = .9332$.

Figure 4.3c illustrates one more situation. We want the proportion of cases between $z = +.20$ and $z = +.40$. Looking up $z = .20$, we find that the area beyond this z score (column C) is .4207. This includes the shaded region but also includes the area beyond $z = +.40$ that isn't shaded. Looking up $z = .40$, we find from column C that the area beyond this z score is .3446. To find the proportion of area that is shaded between $z = +.20$ and $z = +.40$, we subtract: $.4207 - .3446 = .0761$.

COMPREHENSION CHECK 4.21

Heights of American adult males are normally distributed with $\overline{X} = 69$ inches and $s = 3$. Find the following proportions: (a) proportion of men shorter than 72 inches; (b) proportion of men taller than 62 inches; (c) proportion of men between 62 and 72 inches.

(Answer on p. 118.)

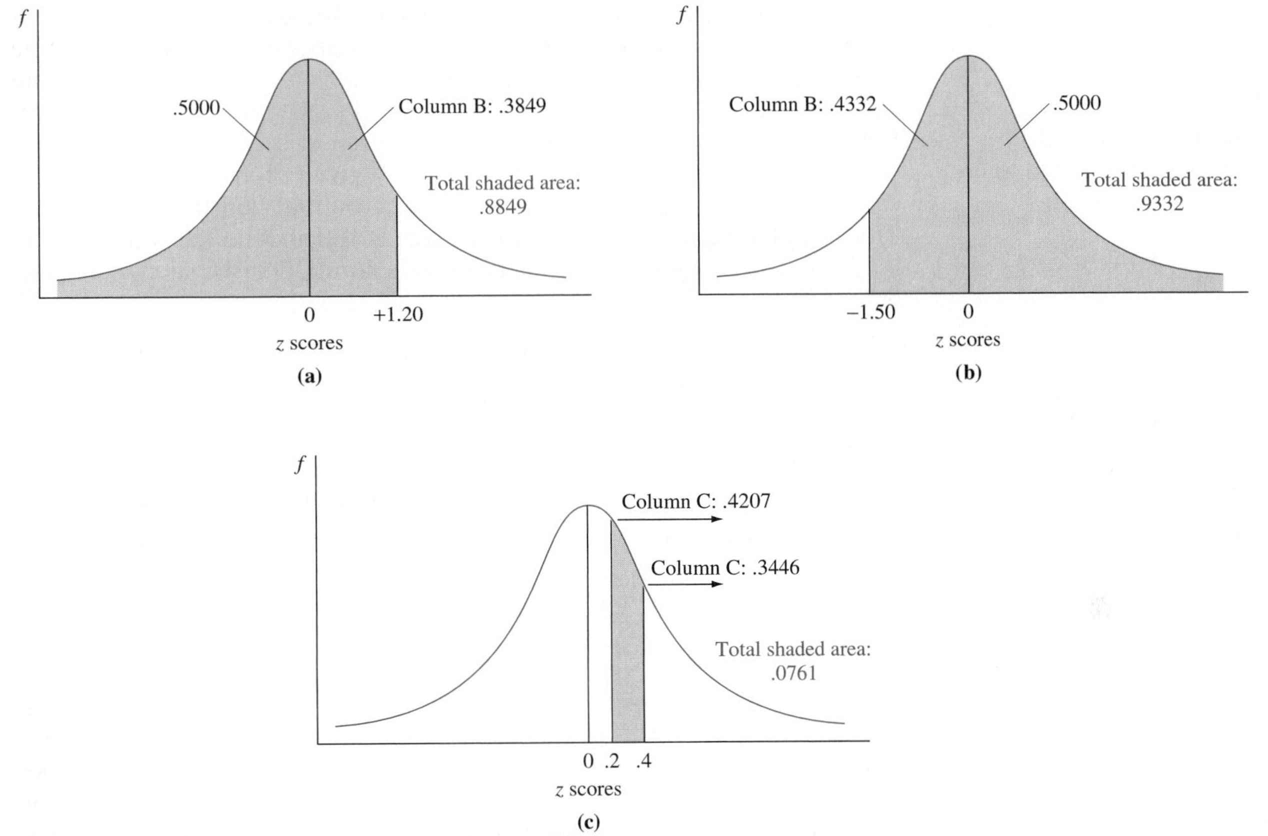

FIGURE 4.3

How to find areas that are not listed in the table of areas under the normal curve.

Some Uses of the Standard Normal Distribution

Assuming that two planks are made of a soft wood, a carpenter may choose a hammer and nails to join them. If the planks are made of a hardwood, though, nails may split the wood. Carpenters choose their tools based on assumptions about the materials with which they will be working. In a like manner, our choice of statistical procedures depends on what assumptions we make about our raw materials—the data. We will see in the remainder of this chapter that *if one's data can be assumed to approximate a normal distribution,* the standard normal distribution is a useful tool to use in answering questions about those data.

Estimating Percentages Below Specified Scores: Percentile Ranks. One application of the standard normal distribution is in estimating the percentage of cases that fall at and below a specified score. You may remember from Chapter 2 that this is the definition of a score's percentile rank. If we have the complete set of scores, we can determine the exact percentile rank for any given score by simply counting: The percentile rank for a score is equal to the cumulative frequency of the score divided by *N,* multiplied by 100 (Equation 2.2). If we don't have the scores but can assume that the distribution is approximately normal, we can estimate the percentage of cases falling at and below any given score by using the standard normal distribution. Example 4.2 illustrates this application of the standard normal distribution.

EXAMPLE 4.2

Using the Standard Normal Distribution to Estimate Percentile Ranks

Even without a complete frequency distribution of scores to work with, we can still estimate the percentile rank for any given score, provided the data can be assumed to approximate a normal distribution. Consider this example. The mean IQ of elementary school children is 100 and the standard deviation is 15. We will assume that the distribution is normally distributed as depicted below:

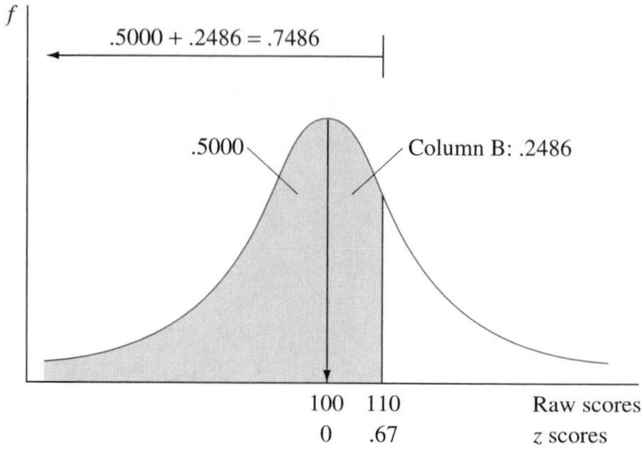

Given this information and nothing more, what is the percentile rank of an IQ of 110?

The shaded area to the left of 110 in the diagram represents the percentage of cases scoring at and below 110. This percentage is the percentile rank that we seek. The table of areas under the normal curve (Table 1 in Appendix B) lists percentages like the one we're looking for, but only for z scores, not raw scores. So the first thing we must do is transform the raw score of 110 to a z score. This is done with Equation 4.5:

$$z_X = \frac{X - \overline{X}}{s}$$

$$= \frac{110 - 100}{15}$$

$$= .67$$

Now that we have expressed the raw score as a z score, we can use the table of areas to find the percentage of area, that is, the percentage of cases, scoring at and below this point. The proportion of area between the mean and $z = .67$ is .2486. This is *part* of the shaded area, but not all of it. What remains is half the distribution, or, expressed as a proportion, .5. The sum of these two values, $.2486 + .5 = .7486$, tells us the proportion of area at and below the z score of .67. To express this as a percentage, we multiply by 100: 74.86%. This is the percentage of cases at and below a z score of .67 (or a raw IQ score of 110) and is the percentile rank that we sought.

Maybe this isn't how you would have approached solving this problem. There are other ways. For example, beginning with the z score of .67, we could look in column C of the table of areas for the "area beyond" this z score: .2514. This is the area represented by the unshaded portion of our diagram. If we subtract this value from 1, the whole area, we will have the proportion that is shaded: $1 - .2514 = .7486$. Or, expressed as a percentage, 74.86%. The point you should notice is that there is no one "right" way to solve problems like this one. Draw a diagram, shade the area that corresponds to the portion you want to determine, and let the diagram help you figure out how to find that area.

COMPREHENSION CHECK 4.22

A problem was presented in the first paragraph of this chapter that you are now prepared to answer. If severe migraine sufferers who receive biofeedback treatment have a mean of 3.2 migraines per month with $s = .75$, what is the probability that any given migraine patient receiving biofeedback will have 2 or fewer migraines per month? (*Hint:* Remember that proportions of area under the normal curve correspond to probabilities.)

(Answer on p. 119.)

Estimating Percentiles. If we can use the standard normal distribution to estimate the percentile rank of any specified score, we should be able to work backward and estimate the score that falls at any specified percentile rank. Using the standard normal distribution to estimate percentiles is illustrated in Example 4.3.

EXAMPLE 4.3

Using the Standard Normal Distribution to Estimate Percentiles

The Department of Cheese Technology at Rocky Bottom State University wants to consider only those applicants to their graduate studies program whose GRE scores are at the 75th percentile or higher. Dr. Johnny B. Gouda, Head Cheese of the department, is responsible for screening applicants to the program and needs to know what score this is. How high does an applicant have to score on the GRE to "make the cut"? This problem is depicted in the following diagram:

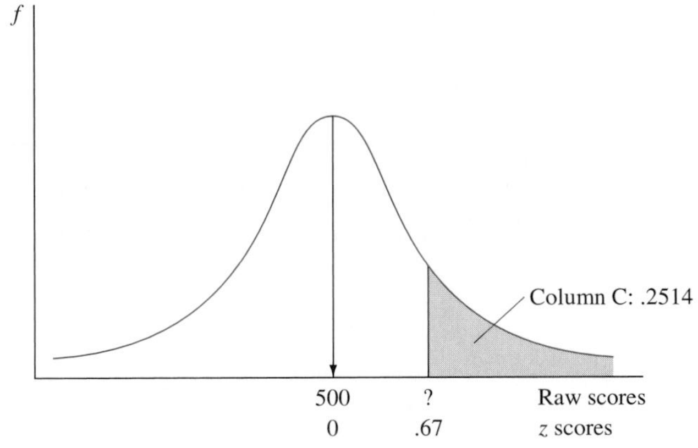

GRE scores are computed in such a manner that the mean is 500, the standard deviation is 100, and the scores are normally distributed. The shaded region in the diagram marks the 25% of the cases that fall at and above the cutoff score. Dr. Gouda wants to know what this cutoff score is.

Let's begin by finding the z score at the 75th percentile. The shaded area of our diagram would be considered an "area beyond" in the table of areas (column C). Scan down column C of this table for a listing of .25. The closest value listed in column C is .2514. The z score corresponding to this area is .67. This is the standard score at the cutoff point, but how do we find the raw score?

We have used Equation 4.5 previously to compute z scores from raw scores. With a little basic algebra we can also use it to compute raw scores (X) from z scores:

$$z_X = \frac{X - \overline{X}}{s} \qquad \text{(from Equation 4.5)}$$

$$.67 = \frac{X - 500}{100} \qquad \text{(by substitution)}$$

$$X - 500 = 67 \qquad \text{(cross-multiplying)}$$

$$X = 567 \qquad \text{(adding 500 to both sides)}$$

We can conclude that the raw score marking the 75th percentile, that is, the top 25% of the GRE scores, is 567.

Notice that a somewhat different approach could have been taken to solving this problem. Instead of finding the z score at the cutoff point by looking for an "area beyond" of .25, we could have scanned column B for an "area between the mean and z" of .25. The closest value listed in column B is .2486, which again points to a z score of .67. The point again is that there is more than one way to solve these problems.

COMPREHENSION CHECK 4.23

A problem was presented in the first paragraph of this chapter that you are now prepared to solve. A college admissions officer wants to recruit students with high scholastic ability. If SAT scores are normally distributed with a mean of 500 and a standard deviation of 100, what score marks the 90th percentile?

(Answer on p. 119.)

Estimating Percentages Above Specified Scores. Sometimes we are more interested in the percentage of cases that fall above a score than in the percentage below that score. Using the standard normal distribution to determine percentages above specified scores is a straightforward extension of the preceding applications. First, identify the location of the z score. Then, use the table of areas to determine the proportion of area that falls above that point.

COMPREHENSION CHECK 4.24

A problem was described in the first paragraph of this chapter that you are now prepared to answer. A superintendent of schools needs to know what percentage of the children have IQ scores of 130 or

(cont.)

higher so that "gifted and talented" programs can be made available to them. If IQs are normally distributed with $\overline{X} = 100$ and $s = 15$, what is the answer? If there are 12,300 students in the school district, about how *many* students will require "gifted and talented" programs?
(Answer on p. 119.)

Estimating Percentages Between Specified Scores. The standard normal distribution also enables us to estimate proportions or percentages of cases that fall *between* any two specified scores. This application is illustrated in Example 4.4.

EXAMPLE 4.4

Using the Standard Normal Distribution to Estimate the Percentage of Cases Between Two Specified Scores

Wegotchu Corporation is considering marketing a two-seat sports convertible in the United States. Males in mid-life crisis are considered the most likely buyers of the automobile. The car has sold well in Asian markets, but there is some concern that its somewhat restricted dimensions may not be compatible with the size requirements of taller American consumers. Human factors psychologists at Wegotchu have determined that the car's dimensions will comfortably accommodate drivers between 62 and 70 inches tall. They want to know what percentage of American males will find the car comfortable.

The height of adult American males is normally distributed with a mean of 69 inches and a standard deviation of 3 inches. The diagram below depicts this distribution. The shaded area represents the percentage of cases who fall between 62 and 70 inches in height. We need to determine the percentage of the total area under the curve that is shaded.

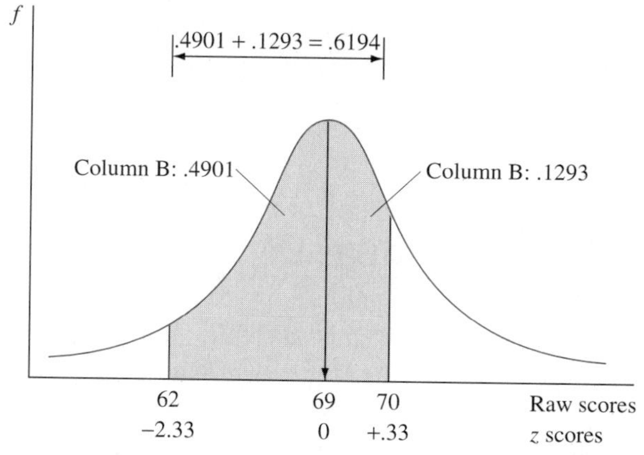

The table of areas provides percentages like these, but only for z scores. The first step, then, is to convert to z scores the heights that mark off the shaded area. Using Equation 4.5, we find the z score corresponding to a height of 62 inches:

$$z_X = \frac{X - \overline{X}}{s}$$

$$= \frac{62 - 69}{3}$$

$$= -2.33$$

Similarly, the z score corresponding to a height of 70 inches is computed as

$$z_X = \frac{X - \overline{X}}{s}$$

$$= \frac{70 - 69}{3}$$

$$= +.33$$

We can now use the table of areas to find the percentage of cases that are found between these two z-score values. Column B gives us the proportion of cases between $z = -2.33$ and the mean: .4901. Column B also tells the proportion of cases between $z = +.33$ and the mean: .1293. The total shaded area is the sum of these two values: .4901 + .1293 = .6194. About 62% of adult American males would be comfortable in the cockpit of Wegotchu's sports car.

Once again let's consider an alternative approach to solving this problem. Instead of identifying the shaded area in our diagram, we could have focused on the unshaded area. The proportion of area to the left of $z = -2.33$ is found from column C ("area beyond") to be .0099. Column C also gives the proportion of area to the right of $z = +.33$: .3707. Together this totals .0099 + .3707 = .3806. This is the proportion of adult American males who would *not* find the car comfortable. Subtracting this proportion from 1, we get the proportion that *would* fit in the car: 1 − .3806 = .6194, or 62%—the same answer we obtained above.

COMPREHENSION CHECK 4.25

If statistics test scores are normally distributed with $\overline{X} = 75$ and $s = 10$, what is the probability that any given student will score between 60 and 65?

(Answer on p. 119.)

4.5 WHAT IF THE DISTRIBUTION IS NOT NORMALLY DISTRIBUTED?

The carpenter who hammers a nail into oak, thinking it is pine, may be disappointed when the lumber splits. The statistician who uses the standard normal distribution when the data are not normally distributed may also be disappointed. The accuracy and adequacy of statistical procedures are limited by the degree to which the data meet the assumptions on which those procedures are based.

In this chapter we have used the standard normal distribution to estimate percentages of cases below, above, and between specified scores. All of these procedures are based on the assumption that the data are normally distributed. But what if the scores are *not* normally distributed? This is not just a possibility, it is a certainty. As we learned previously, the normal distribution is a theoretical distribution that is often approximated in nature but is never matched exactly. Because of this, estimates based on the standard normal distribution will be in error to the degree that the data deviate from the normal shape.

To illustrate, look at Table 4.1. This is a portion of the distribution of the Cheating Justification Questionnaire scores first presented as Table 2.2 in

X	z	f	f_c	$\%_c$	Estimated Percentile Rank
40	2.27	4	120	100.0	99.84
39	2.06	2	116	96.7	98.03
38	1.86	4	114	95.0	96.86
37	1.66	5	110	91.7	95.15
.	.	.	.	.	.
.	.	.	.	.	.
.	.	.	.	.	.
20	−1.78	1	5	4.2	3.75
19	−1.99	2	4	3.3	2.33
18	−2.19	1	2	1.7	1.43
17	−2.39	1	1	.8	.84

TABLE 4.1

Cheating Justification Questionnaire raw scores (X), standard scores (z), frequencies (f), cumulative frequencies (f_c), cumulative percentages ($\%_c$), and estimated percentile ranks. Because the distribution is not exactly normal, percentile ranks estimated using the standard normal distribution do not match exactly with the actual percentile ranks (cumulative percentages).

Chapter 2. These scores do not deviate radically from the normal distribution (see Figure 2.2 in Chapter 2), but the distribution is not exactly normal. Thus, estimates based on the assumption of normality will show some errors. The mean of this distribution is 28.81 and the standard deviation is 4.94. Standard scores are listed in Table 4.1 for each raw score, and percentile ranks have been estimated using these z scores. Notice the discrepancies between these *estimated* percentile ranks and the *true* percentile ranks (cumulative percentages).

Even relatively minor deviations from the normal distribution result in noticeable errors when we use statistical procedures that are based on the assumption of normally distributed data. Keep this in mind in future chapters when we study the many other statistical methods that assume normally distributed data.

COMPREHENSION CHECK 4.26

Explain in your own words why we cannot use the standard normal distribution to estimate percentile ranks or other percentages for data that deviate strongly from the normal distribution.
(Answer on p. 119.)

SUMMARY

The normal distribution is a theoretical, bell-shaped, symmetrical distribution that is often approximated by empirical distributions. To the degree that data approximate the normal distribution, we can use the normal distribution as a model to answer questions about those data.

Some of these questions have to do with the probability of observing various scores or other outcomes. The probability of an outcome is defined by its relative frequency of occurrence. Outcomes that occur quite frequently are by definition more probable than are outcomes that occur less frequently. The converse rule, the addition rule, and the multiplication rule are useful in solving many probability problems, including determining the probability of observing scores in various ranges of normally distributed variables.

Standard scores, also called z scores, are transformed raw scores that measure the deviation between a raw score and the mean of the distribution using the standard deviation of the distribution as a yardstick. Standard scores are useful in locating scores in a distribution and also enable us to compare scores that are measured using different units of measure.

When we transform a normal distribution of raw scores to standard score form, we create a standard normal distribution. This is a very useful distribution, because the table of areas under the normal curve gives detailed information about the proportions of cases that fall between specified z scores in the standard normal distribution. Using the standard normal distribution, we can estimate the percentage of cases scoring at and below a specified score (percentile rank), the percentage scoring at and above a specified score, and the percentage falling between any two specified scores. However, these estimates will be in error if the data are not normally distributed.

NOTES

1. Proof that the mean of a distribution of standard scores will always equal 0:

$$\bar{X}_z = \frac{\Sigma z}{N} \quad \text{by definition of the mean}$$

$$= \frac{\Sigma[X - \bar{X}/s]}{N} \quad \text{by substitution}$$

$$= \frac{0}{N} \quad \text{because } \Sigma(X - \bar{X}) = 0$$

$$= 0$$

2. Proof that the variance and standard deviation of a distribution of standard scores will always equal 1:

$$s_z^2 = \frac{\Sigma(z - \bar{X}_z)^2}{N} \quad \text{by definition of the variance}$$

$$= \frac{\Sigma(z - 0)^2}{N} \quad \text{because } \bar{X}_z = 0$$

$$= \frac{\Sigma z^2}{N} \quad \text{because subtracting 0 from } z \text{ leaves } z$$

$$= \frac{\Sigma[X - \bar{X}/s]^2}{N} \quad \text{because } z = \frac{X - \bar{X}}{s}$$

$$= \frac{\Sigma(X - \bar{X})^2/s^2}{N} \quad \text{by rearrangement}$$

$$= \frac{\Sigma(1/s^2)\,(X - \bar{X})^2}{N} \quad \text{by rearrangement}$$

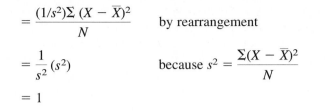

$$= \frac{(1/s^2)\Sigma\,(X - \overline{X})^2}{N} \quad \text{by rearrangement}$$

$$= \frac{1}{s^2}(s^2) \quad \text{because } s^2 = \frac{\Sigma(X - \overline{X})^2}{N}$$

$$= 1$$

Review Exercises

4.1. Statistics test scores show a mean of $\overline{X} = 79$ and a standard deviation of $s = 9$. How many standard deviations fall between the mean and a test score of 90? What score falls 1.5 standard deviations below the mean?

4.2. In a normal distribution of IQ scores, with $\overline{X} = 100$ and $s = 15$:
(a) What proportion of the area under the curve falls between scores of 115 and 130?
(b) What percentage of the cases have scores between 115 and 130?
(c) What is the probability that a case drawn at random will score between 115 and 130?

4.3. If 8 of 46 students got As on an exam, what is the probability of getting an A?

4.4. Approximately 20% of the population will suffer from clinically significant depression. In a group of 136 people, how many would you expect to develop depression?

4.5. Shown below is the distribution of grades in an introductory social work class. Determine probabilities associated with each grade. What is the probability of *not* getting each grade?

Grade	f
A	26
B	42
C	89
D	37
F	14

4.6. Using the grade distribution given in Review Exercise 4.5, what is the probability of getting:
(a) Either an A or a B?
(b) Either a D or an F?
(c) An A or C or F?

4.7. In the grade distribution given in Review Exercise 4.5, what is the probability that two students drawn at random from the class will:
(a) Both have grades of A?
(b) Have grades of A and F, respectively?
(c) Both have grades of C?

4.8. If the probability of developing schizophrenia is .03 and the probability of being hit by lightning is .000001, what is the probability that a person will develop schizophrenia and then be hit by lightning?

4.9. In a distribution of test scores showing a mean of $\overline{X} = 75$ and a standard deviation of $s = 10$, compute z scores corresponding to raw scores of 95, 60, and 90.

4.10. In a distribution of test scores showing a mean of $\overline{X} = 75$ and a standard deviation of $s = 10$, what raw scores correspond to z scores of -1.2, 1.6, and 0?

4.11. Convert the raw scores listed below to z scores and plot the frequency distribution of these z scores. What does transforming to z score form do to the shape of the distribution?

Raw scores:	1	5	3	3	4	1	4	3	3	1
	2	5	3	4	3	3	1	2	3	

4.12. Compute the mean, variance, and standard deviation of the z scores you computed in Review Exercise 4.11.

4.13. On one measure of scholastic aptitude, having a mean of $\overline{X} = 20$ and a standard deviation of $s = 5$, student A has a score of 27. On a different test, having a mean of $\overline{X} = 600$ and a standard deviation of $s = 150$, student B has a score of 675. Which student has the higher scholastic aptitude?

4.14. Use the table of areas under the normal curve to find the proportion of cases:
(a) Between the mean and $z = 1.07$
(b) Between the mean and $z = -1.07$
(c) Between $z = -1.0$ and $z = 1.0$
(d) Between $z = -1.30$ and $z = 1.50$
(e) Beyond $z = 1.50$
(f) Beyond $z = -1.75$
(g) Beyond $z = 0$
(h) Between $z = -1$ and $z = -2$
(i) Between $z = 1.3$ and $z = 1.8$

4.15. In a normal distribution of IQ scores having a mean of $\overline{X} = 100$ and a standard deviation of $s = 15$, what proportion of the cases score:
(a) Between 100 and 120?
(b) Between 100 and 90?
(c) Higher than 108?
(d) Lower than 96?

(e) Between 105 and 110?
(f) Between 90 and 95?
(g) Lower than 110?
(h) Higher than 90?

4.16. In a normal distribution of ages, with $\overline{X} = 40$ and $s = 14$, what is the percentile rank of an age of 45?

4.17. If IQs of 286 cases are normally distributed with $\overline{X} = 100$ and $s = 15$, how many cases would you expect to find with scores:
(a) At 115 or higher?
(b) At 85 or lower?
(c) Between 100 and 115?

4.18. Complete the $\%_c$ column for the following distribution:

X	f	$\%_c$
5	4	
4	6	
3	10	
2	12	
1	3	

Now, use z scores to estimate percentile ranks for each score in the distribution. How do you explain the differences between $\%_c$ values and estimated percentile ranks?

Answers to Comprehension Checks

4.1. You know that the 90th percentile on the SAT will be considerably higher than the mean of 500, but that's about all you have to go on. Similarly, you know that an IQ of 130 is considerably higher than the mean IQ of 100, so relatively few children can be expected to have an IQ this high. Finally, you know that patients receiving biofeedback treatment show an average of 3.2 headaches per month, so there is less than a 50% chance that any given patient who receives this treatment will have 2 or fewer migraines per month. By the time you've reached the end of this chapter, you will be able to provide much more precise answers to these questions.

4.2. An empirical distribution is any distribution of real, observed scores: scores on a statistics test, heights of 23 men, ages of the students at a university, and so on. Theoretical distributions, in contrast, are imaginary distributions. Although we can envision what these theoretical distributions look like, they don't actually exist.

4.3. Although the normal distribution is a theoretical entity and is never found in the real world, it is still useful to us. Most of this chapter is devoted to explaining *how* the theoretical normal distribution can be put to work in answering questions about the real world. Briefly, to the degree that data *approximate* the normal distribution, everything we know about the normal distribution also applies to our data.

4.4. (a) $\overline{X} + 1(s) = 75 + 1(10) = 85$
(b) $\overline{X} - 2(s) = 75 - 2(10) = 55$
(c) 70 vs. 80 = 10 points = 1 standard deviation
(d) 65 vs. 85 = 20 points = 2 standard deviations

4.5. The score of 75 falls at the mean of the distribution and 85 is 1 standard deviation above the mean. In a normal distribution, 34.13% of the cases fall between the mean and the score 1 standard deviation above the mean. Expressed as a proportion, this gives us the probability of finding a score in this range: .3413.

The score of 55 falls 2 standard deviations (20 points) below the mean and 65 falls 1 standard deviation (10 points) below the mean. In any normal distribution, 13.59% of the cases fall between 1 and 2 standard deviations below the mean. Expressed as a proportion, this gives us the probability of finding a score in this range: .1359.

4.6. The relative frequency definition of probability given by Equation 4.1 enables us to determine these probabilities:

$$p(\text{freshman}) = \frac{f(\text{freshman})}{N} = \frac{10}{37} = .27$$

$$p(\text{sophomore}) = \frac{f(\text{sophomore})}{N} = \frac{14}{37} = .38$$

$$p(\text{junior}) = \frac{f(\text{junior})}{N} = \frac{8}{37} = .22$$

$$p(\text{senior}) = \frac{f(\text{senior})}{N} = \frac{5}{37} = .14$$

4.7. It is more likely that a score would be drawn from the range 70–85 ($p = .1359$) than from the range 130–145 ($p = .0214$) because scores in the first range occur more frequently. The probability of an event is equal to its relative frequency of occurrence.

4.8. **(a)** Not mutually exclusive, because one can be both blond and 13
(b) Not mutually exclusive, because one can be both depressed and female
(c) Mutually exclusive, because one cannot be both Protestant and Catholic at the same time
(d) Mutually exclusive, because state laws prohibit 13-year-olds from being lawyers

4.9. **(a)** Independent, because IQ is unrelated to whether or not a person will win the lottery
(b) Not independent, because if one's spouse has a cold, one's own chance of catching the cold increases
(c) Not independent, because one's political views are affected by those of one's spouse
(d) Independent, because hair color is unrelated to performance in statistics

4.10. Equation 4.2, the converse rule, can be used to determine the probability of not catching a cold because catching the cold and not catching the cold are mutually exclusive events.

$$p(\overline{\text{catch cold}}) = 1 - p(\text{catch cold})$$
$$= 1 - .3$$
$$= .7$$

The converse rule cannot be used to determine the probability of not getting an A in statistics if one is blond, because being blond and getting an A are not mutually exclusive events of the sort to which this rule applies.

4.11. Figure 4.1 shows that $p = .0227$ that a score will fall in the range 130–160. To find the probability that a score will *not* fall in this range, we can use Equation 4.2, the converse rule.

$$p(\overline{\text{score in range 130–160}}) = 1 - p(\text{score in range 130–160})$$
$$= 1 - .0227$$
$$= .9773$$

4.12. Equation 4.3, the addition rule, can be applied to finding the probability of occurrence of one of these mutually exclusive events.

$$p(\text{cold from spouse } or \text{ cold from co-worker}) = p(\text{cold from spouse}) + p(\text{cold from co-worker})$$
$$= .3 + .1$$
$$= .4$$

4.13. Equation 4.3, the addition rule, can be applied to finding the probability of drawing a score from one range or another of a distribution. The separate probabilities can be obtained from Figure 4.1.

$$p(\text{score above 130 } or \text{ score below 70}) = p(\text{score above 130}) + p(\text{score below 70})$$
$$= .0227 + .0227$$
$$= .0454$$

4.14. Equation 4.4, the multiplication rule, can be applied to finding each sequence of independent, mutually exclusive outcomes.

$$p(\text{HHHHHH}) = p(\text{H}) \times p(\text{H}) \times p(\text{H}) \times p(\text{H}) \times p(\text{H}) \times p(\text{H})$$
$$= .5 \times .5 \times .5 \times .5 \times .5 \times .5$$
$$= .0156$$
$$p(\text{HTHTHT}) = p(\text{H}) \times p(\text{T}) \times p(\text{H}) \times p(\text{T}) \times p(\text{H}) \times p(\text{T})$$
$$= .5 \times .5 \times .5 \times .5 \times .5 \times .5$$
$$= .0156$$
$$p(\text{TTTTTT}) = p(\text{T}) \times p(\text{T}) \times p(\text{T}) \times p(\text{T}) \times p(\text{T}) \times p(\text{T})$$
$$= .5 \times .5 \times .5 \times .5 \times .5 \times .5$$
$$= .0156$$

4.15. Notice that 71 inches falls 1 standard deviation (3 inches) above the mean. In a normal distribution like this one, 15.87% of the cases fall at or above the score located 1 standard deviation above the mean. Expressed as a proportion, this is the probability of finding *one* man 71 inches or taller. The multiplication rule tells us the probability of finding *two* men this tall:

$$p(71+ \text{ in. and } 71+ \text{ in.}) = p(71+ \text{ in.}) \times p(71+ \text{ in.})$$
$$= .1587 \times .1587$$
$$= .0252$$

4.16. Equation 4.5 is used to transform raw scores to z scores:

(a) $$z_X = \frac{X - \overline{X}}{s}$$

$$z_{100} = \frac{100 - 100}{15}$$
$$= 0$$

(b) $$z_{73} = \frac{73 - 100}{15}$$
$$= -1.8$$

(c) $z_{107} = \dfrac{107 - 100}{15}$

$= .47$

4.17. (a)

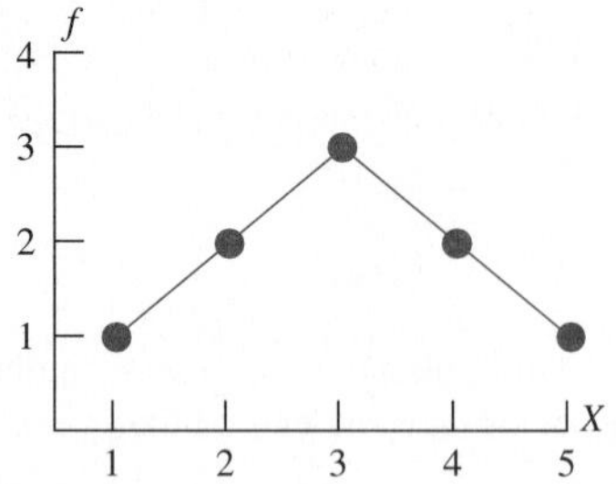

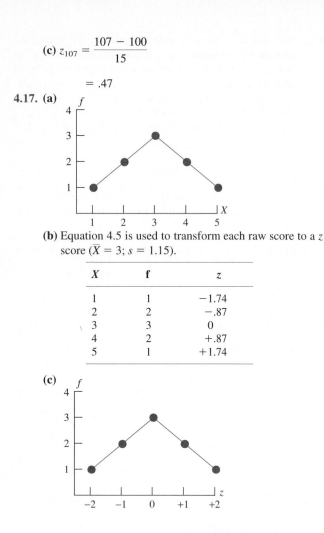

(b) Equation 4.5 is used to transform each raw score to a z score ($\bar{X} = 3$; $s = 1.15$).

X	f	z
1	1	−1.74
2	2	−.87
3	3	0
4	2	+.87
5	1	+1.74

(c)

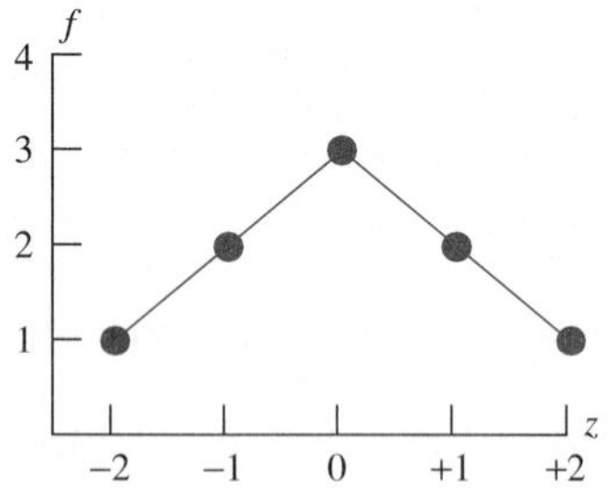

(d) The distributions of raw scores and standard scores are identical in shape. Transforming to standard score form does not alter the shape of the distribution. However, the mean and standard deviation of the z scores is different. The mean is 0 (allowing for rounding error) and the standard deviation is 1 (also allowing for rounding error).

4.18. Both z scores and percentile ranks locate scores in the distribution, but they convey different information. Percentile ranks tell one *directly* the percentage of cases falling at and below the specified score. But percentile ranks provide only an ordinal scale of measurement. Standard scores do not locate scores in as understandable a manner as percentile ranks, but z scores do maintain an interval scale of measurement.

4.19. Equation 4.5 is used to convert both raw scores to z-score form so that they can be compared directly:

$$z_{SAT=580} = \frac{580 - 500}{100}$$

$$= +.80$$

$$z_{IQ=108} = \frac{108 - 100}{15}$$

$$= +.53$$

We can conclude that the SAT of 580 falls slightly higher in its distribution than does the IQ of 108 in its distribution. If both distributions are based on the same cases or cases that are equivalent, we can conclude that the SAT of 580 implies greater cognitive capability.

4.20. The table of areas under the normal curve provides the kinds of percentages we are looking for here, but only for standard scores. Our first step, then, must be to convert all the raw scores in this problem to z scores using Equation 4.5. The diagram below includes both raw scores and z scores and shows in which columns of the table of areas one can find the specified percentages.

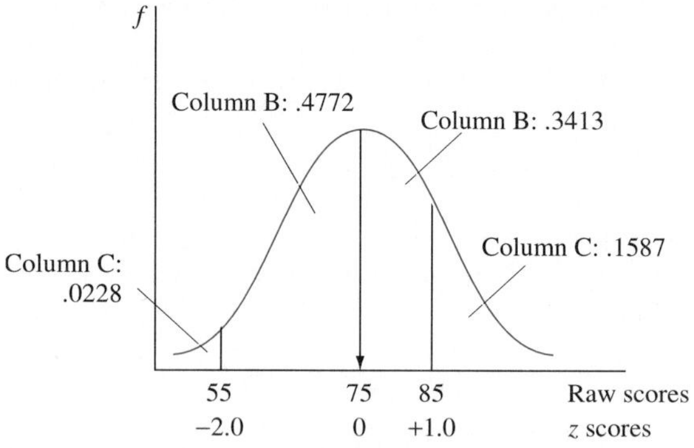

4.21. This problem is diagrammed below. We begin again by converting all raw scores to z scores so that we can find the areas we need in the table of areas under the normal curve. The diagram below includes raw scores, z scores, and the proportions specified.

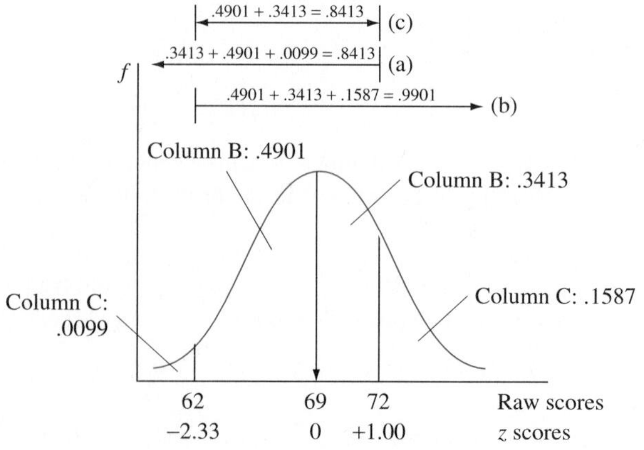

4.22. This problem is diagrammed below. We begin by assuming that the number of migraines is normally distributed. The shaded area represents the proportion of patients who suffer 2 or fewer migraines per month. A raw score of 2 is equivalent to a z score of -1.60. The table of areas under the normal curve (column C) tells us the proportion of cases that score at and below this point: .0548. This value is also the probability that any given patient will suffer 2 or fewer migraines per month.

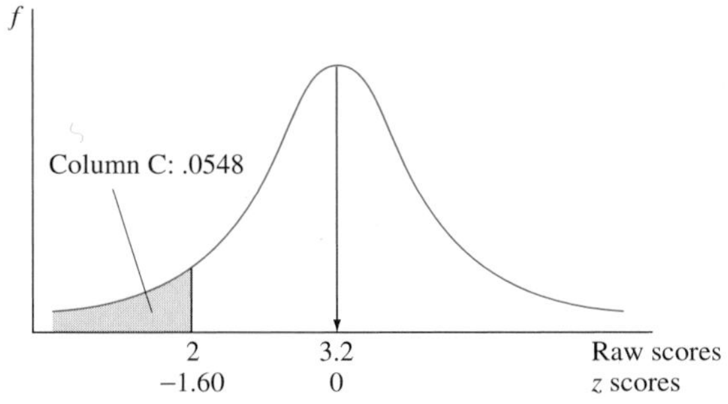

4.23. This problem is diagrammed below. The 90th percentile is that score at and below which 90% of the cases fall. That means that 10% score higher—the unshaded region of the diagram). This unshaded region is an "area beyond" (column C) in the table of areas under the normal curve. Scanning down column C, the closest match we find to .1000 (10%) is .1003, which corresponds to a z score of 1.28. We can now use Equation 4.5 and a little algebra to transform this z score back into a raw score:

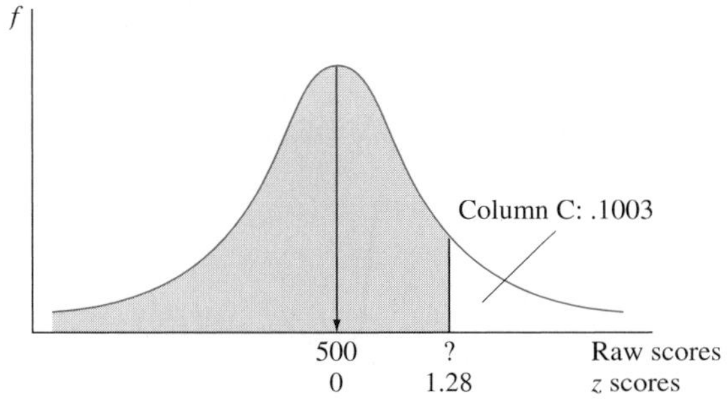

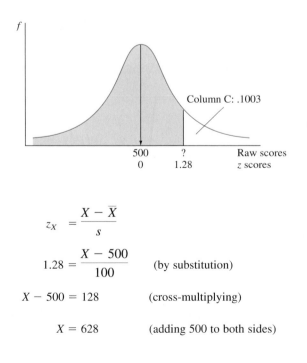

$$z_X = \frac{X - \overline{X}}{s}$$

$$1.28 = \frac{X - 500}{100} \quad \text{(by substitution)}$$

$$X - 500 = 128 \quad \text{(cross-multiplying)}$$

$$X = 628 \quad \text{(adding 500 to both sides)}$$

4.24. This problem is diagrammed below. The shaded area represents the proportion of students with IQs of 130 ($z = 2.0$) or higher in the normal distribution of IQ scores. The table of areas under the normal curve (column C) gives us the proportion of area that is shaded: .0228, or 2.28% of the students. With 12,300 students, this amounts to $.0228 \times 12{,}300 = 280$ students that qualify for "gifted and talented" programs.

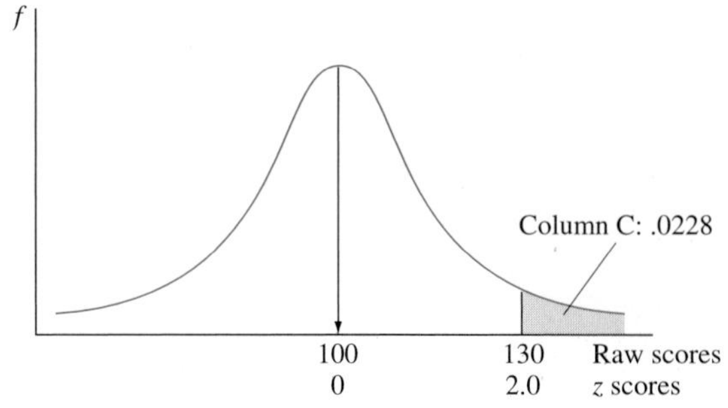

4.25. This problem is diagrammed below, showing both raw scores and z scores. The shaded area represents the proportion of area between 60 ($z = -1.5$) and 65 ($z = -1.0$). The proportion beyond 65 is .1587; the proportion beyond 60 is .0668. Subtracting gives us the proportion between these two scores: $.1587 - .0668 = .0919$. This is the probability that any given student will score between 60 and 65.

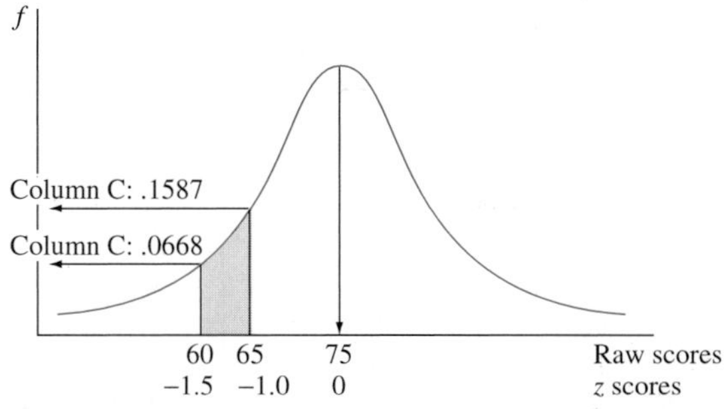

4.26. We cannot use the standard normal distribution to estimate percentages for nonnormal data, because these estimates will be as inaccurate as the data are nonnormal.

5 Sampling Distributions and Interval Estimation

Chapter Outline

It is reported on the evening news that a telephone survey of 1,000 households has revealed that the President's overall approval rating has slipped to 48%. But there are millions of households in America. Can we draw any reliable conclusions about millions of Americans based on just 1,000?

A researcher has surveyed 500 adults and found that the average age at which they took their first drink of an alcoholic beverage was 14.8 years. How confident can we be that this average accurately depicts the age of first exposure to alcohol for the entire population?

Although research data are often gathered from relatively small samples, the questions we seek to answer most often go beyond those samples. We study samples, but we usually want to be able to draw conclusions about entire populations. Chapter 1 introduced the concept of inferential statistics, procedures that enable us to generalize beyond our samples to the populations represented by those samples. Much of the remainder of this book examines one type of statistical inference or another. In this chapter we will set the stage for our study of inferential statistics by looking at the concept of sampling distributions. Sampling distributions are the foundation on which all inferential statistics are built. In this chapter we will also examine one specific inferential statistical tool, interval estimation, which is useful in answering the kinds of questions that introduced this chapter.

COMPREHENSION CHECK 5.1

Why must we be cautious when drawing conclusions about populations on the basis of sample data?
(Answer on p. 146.)

5.1 SAMPLING DISTRIBUTIONS

Suppose that you drew all possible samples of size $N = 5$ from your statistics class, computed the mean height of the students in each sample, and graphed the frequency of occurrence of the various means obtained from one sample to the next. What would you have? It would be called the sampling distribution of the mean. Suppose instead that you drew all possible samples of size $N = 12$ from the class, computed the proportion of students in each sample who support a limitation on handgun sales, and graphed the frequency of occurrence of the various proportions obtained from one sample to the next. What would this frequency distribution be called? It is the sampling distribution of the proportion.

Sampling distributions come in many shapes, sizes, and varieties. We will first study sampling distributions in general terms, then we'll look at two sampling distributions that are especially useful in analyzing the data of the social and behavioral sciences: the sampling distribution of the mean and the sampling distribution of the proportion.

A **sampling distribution** may be defined as a theoretical distribution that depicts the frequency of occurrence of values of some statistic computed for all possible samples of size *N* drawn from some population. Let's analyze the components of this definition in reverse order.

sampling distribution *A theoretical distribution showing the frequency of occurrence of values of some statistic computed for all possible samples of size* N *sampled with replacement from a population.*

First, sampling distributions are a little different from the distributions you're used to. The distributions you've worked with up to now have described *single samples.* Sampling distributions, in contrast, are based on *all possible samples* of some fixed size (N) drawn from a population. A sample distribution gives information about just one sample from a population. A sampling distribution gives information about every sample of size N that can be drawn from the population.

Second, the distributions we've worked with up to now have depicted how many *cases* received each of the various *scores* on some variable. Sampling distributions do not convey information about the scores of individual cases. Instead, they depict how many *samples* drawn from a population received each of the various values of some *statistic* computed for each sample. Which statistic? Sometimes the mean, sometimes the proportion or percentage of cases that possess some characteristic, and sometimes statistics with which you are not yet familiar. Many different statistics can be computed from one sample to the next, so there are many different kinds of sampling distributions.

Third, sampling distributions are frequency distributions. They depict *how often* various values of some statistic occur as that statistic is computed from one sample to the next. Recall from Chapter 4 that frequency distributions also convey information about probability. The more frequently a score occurs in a distribution, the more probable is that score. This relative frequency definition of probability applies to sampling distributions as well. Values of the statistic that occur more often are more probable than are values that occur less often.

Finally, sampling distributions are *theoretical distributions.* Theoretical distributions were described in Chapter 4 as imaginary or ideal entities. Sampling distributions are theoretical distributions in the sense that we normally never see one; we just think about them. Actually constructing a sampling distribution would require an enormous amount of effort. One would literally have to study each and every one of the multitude of possible samples of size N within a population. Not only would this be an awful lot of work, it would be senseless work because (1) if we are able to study every sample drawn from a population, we could have more simply just studied the population itself—we wouldn't need the sampling distribution to help us in our inferential leapfrog from sample to population; and (2) statisticians have studied sampling distributions sufficiently that we don't actually have to construct them to know all of their essential characteristics. We saw in Chapter 4 that even though theoretical distributions usually exist only in our imaginations, they are useful because what we know about them applies as well to any empirical distribution that approximates the theoretical distribution. In the same way, even though sampling distributions are theoretical entities, what we know about them enables us to answer important questions about real data.

COMPREHENSION CHECK 5.2

Several distributions are described below. Which of these are sampling distributions? Which are not? Explain why.

(a) A distribution showing the frequency of occurrence of IQ scores for 100 college freshmen

(cont.)

(b) A distribution showing the frequency of occurrence of mean IQ scores computed for all possible samples of size $N = 75$ drawn from the entire freshman class

(c) A distribution depicting the proportions of people in a sample of 25 who favor and who do not favor a school bond issue

(d) A distribution depicting the frequency of occurrence of various sample proportions for all possible samples of size $N = 30$ drawn from an entire population

(Answer on p. 146.)

As suggested above, there are many different sampling distributions. They can be distinguished by which statistic is used to describe each sample drawn from the population. In this chapter we will consider two related sampling distributions, the sampling distribution of the mean and the sampling distribution of the proportion.

The Sampling Distribution of the Mean

The **sampling distribution of the mean** is constructed by drawing all possible samples of size *N* from a population, computing the mean for each sample, and plotting the frequency of occurrence of the various values that are obtained from one sample mean to the next. Although this is not done in actual practice, it may be instructive to construct a sampling distribution of the mean here just to clarify what they are.

sampling distribution of the mean *A theoretical distribution showing the frequency of occurrence of values of the mean computed for all possible samples of size* N *sampled with replacement from a population.*

Figure 5.1 illustrates the construction of the sampling distribution of the mean. We begin with IQ scores for a population of five cases as shown in Figure 5.1a. The size of this population is artificially small to keep the task

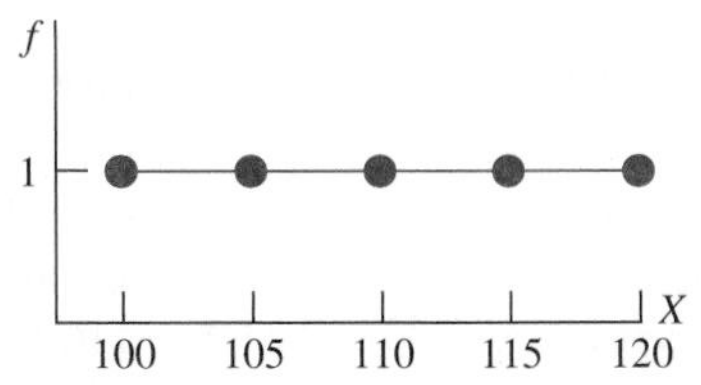

(a)

Samples ($N = 2$)		$\overline{X}$
100	100	100
100	105	102.5
100	110	105
100	115	107.5
100	120	110
105	105	105
105	110	107.5
105	115	110
105	120	112.5
110	110	110
110	115	112.5
110	120	115
115	115	115
115	120	117.5
120	120	120

(b)

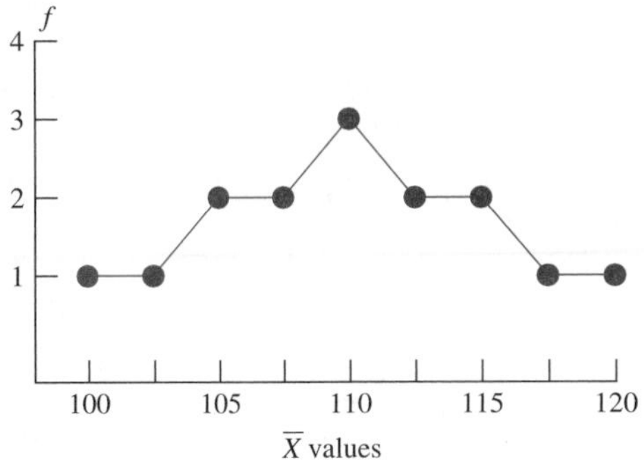

(c)

FIGURE 5.1

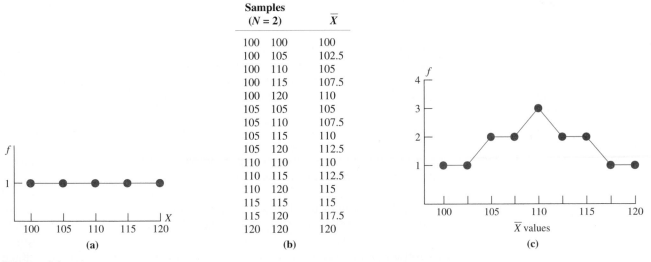

The process of forming the sampling distribution of the mean for samples of size $N = 2$. (a) shows a rectangular population distribution. (b) lists all possible samples of size $N = 2$ drawn with replacement from the population, along with their means. (c) plots the sample means, forming the sampling distribution of the mean.

manageable. You can see that the population's rectangular distribution is a far cry from the normal distribution described in Chapter 4.

Figure 5.1b lists the IQ scores that comprise all possible samples of size $N = 2$ drawn from the population. Notice that in some of these samples the same score is listed twice, for example: 100, 100; 105, 105; etc. This is because sampling distributions are formed using **sampling with replacement.** That is, each time a case is drawn from the population for inclusion in the sample, it is replaced and becomes eligible to be drawn again for inclusion in the same sample. Sampling with replacement can be contrasted with **sampling without replacement,** in which, once a case is drawn from the population for inclusion in a sample, it is *not* replaced until that sample has been completed, and so it cannot be included in any one sample more than once.(See Note 1) Listed with each sample in Figure 5.1b is the sample mean. Notice that these means vary somewhat from one sample to the next.

sampling with replacement *A sampling procedure in which each case, after being drawn for inclusion in a sample, is replaced into the population and becomes eligible for inclusion again in that same sample.*

sampling without replacement *A sampling procedure in which each case, once drawn for inclusion in a sample, is not replaced into the population and therefore cannot be included more than once in any given sample.*

Figure 5.1c depicts the variability of sample means by graphing the frequency of occurrence of values of $\overline{X}$ computed for all possible samples of size $N = 2$ drawn from the specified population. This is the sampling distribution of the mean.

COMPREHENSION CHECK 5.3

Listed below are IQ scores for five cases that constitute a small population. Construct and graph the sampling distributions of the mean for samples of size $N = 2$ and $N = 3$.

Population data: 100, 105, 110, 115

(Answer on pp. 146–147.)

Characteristics of the Sampling Distribution of the Mean. We constructed a sampling distribution of the mean in Figure 5.1, but we could do so only because the population was extraordinarily small. Real populations—all males, all Americans, all white rats, and so on—are typically very large, even innumerable. It would not be possible to draw the many samples from these large populations that are required to construct the sampling distribution of the mean. As stated previously, though, we don't have to, because we know all of the important characteristics of the sampling distribution of the mean even without actually constructing it.

The **central limit theorem** describes three key features of the sampling distribution of the mean: its shape, its mean, and its standard deviation. We will consider each of these features in turn.

central limit theorem *A theorem that describes the sampling distribution of the mean (and related sampling distributions). This theorem states that when* $N \geq 50$: *(1) the sampling distribution will be normally distributed; (2)* $\mu_{\overline{X}} = \mu$; *and (3)* $\sigma_{\overline{X}} = \sigma/\sqrt{N}$.

First, if the samples drawn from a population are relatively large, the sampling distribution of the mean will have a normal shape, regardless of the shape of the population distribution. Compare Figures 5.1a, the population distribution, and 5.1c, the sampling distribution of the mean. In this example our samples were extremely small ($N = 2$), and the population distribution was decidedly nonnormal. Despite this, the sampling distribution of the mean is already beginning to resemble the unimodal, symmetrical, bell-shaped normal distribution. How large do the samples have to be before the sampling distribution of the mean becomes completely normal? It depends on the shape of the population distribution. If the population is normally distributed, sample sizes as low as $N = 1$ will produce a normally distributed sampling distribution of the mean. As the population distribution deviates more and more from the normal shape, the sample size required to produce a normal sampling distribution of the mean increases. The usual rule of thumb is that samples of size 50 or larger will produce a fairly normal sampling distribution of the mean, regardless of the shape of the population distribution.

The fact that the sampling distribution of the mean can be assumed to be normally distributed is enormously useful. Everything that you learned in the last chapter about the normal distribution applies as well to the normally distributed sampling distribution of the mean. This is an idea to which we will return later in this chapter.

COMPREHENSION CHECK 5.4

Compare the shapes of the sampling distributions you graphed in Comprehension Check 5.3 with the shape of the population distribution. How do they compare? What changes in the shape of the sampling distribution of the mean do you notice as the sample size increases?

(Answer on p. 147.)

The central limit theorem also tells us that the mean of the sampling distribution of the mean (symbolized $\mu_{\overline{X}}$) will equal the mean of the population from which the samples were drawn:

$$\mu_{\overline{X}} = \mu$$

This is true regardless of the shape of the population distribution and regardless of the sample size. Figure 5.1 provides an example. The mean of that population is $\mu = 110$. The mean of the sampling distribution of the mean is also $\mu_{\overline{X}} = 110$. In other words, we can speak interchangeably of μ and $\mu_{\overline{X}}$, because they always have the same value.

COMPREHENSION CHECK 5.5

Compute the mean (μ) of the population given in Comprehension Check 5.3. Also compute the means ($\mu_{\overline{x}}$) of the sampling distributions of the mean constructed in that comprehension check. How do they compare?

(Answer on p. 147.)

The third thing that the central limit theorem tells us about the sampling distribution of the mean concerns its variability. From one sample to the next drawn from a population, the means will vary somewhat. As you can see from Figure 5.1, the *single* most likely outcome is that $\overline{X}$ will equal μ. But some sample means are higher than μ, and some are lower. This chance variability of sample means from one to the next is said to be due to **sampling error.** Because most of the samples drawn from a population differ somewhat from the population as a whole, it can be said that they give an "erroneous" view of the population. This difference between a sample and the population from which it came can be thought of as an "error." This is the source of the term sampling error.

sampling error *Refers to the discrepancies that exist between the characteristics of a population and characteristics of samples drawn from that population.*

standard error of the mean ($\sigma_{\overline{X}}$) *The standard deviation of the sampling distribution of the mean. Approximately equal to the average absolute difference between the sample means and the mean of the population from which the samples were drawn.*

The most useful measure of the variability of the sampling distribution of the mean is its standard deviation. But "the standard deviation of the sampling distribution of the mean" is too big a mouthful even for statisticians, so it's been dubbed the **standard error of the mean,** symbolized $\sigma_{\overline{X}}$. Like any standard deviation, $\sigma_{\overline{X}}$ is roughly equal to the average absolute deviation of sample means around $\mu_{\overline{X}}$. The central limit theorem tells us to compute the standard error of the mean according to Equation 5.1:

Equation 5.1

$$\sigma_{\overline{X}} = \frac{\sigma}{\sqrt{N}}$$

where

$\sigma_{\overline{X}}$ = standard error of the mean
σ = population standard deviation
N = sample size

In words, the standard error of the mean ($\sigma_{\overline{X}}$) is computed by dividing the population standard deviation (σ) by the square root of the size of the samples being drawn from the population (N).

To illustrate, let's compute the standard error of the mean for the sampling distribution of the mean for samples of size $N = 50$ drawn from the population of all SAT scores. SAT scores are computed in such a way that the standard deviation of the scores (σ) will equal 100. According to Equation 5.1:

$$\sigma_{\overline{X}} = \frac{\sigma}{\sqrt{N}}$$

$$= \frac{100}{\sqrt{50}}$$

$$= 14.14$$

This value, $\sigma_{\overline{X}} = 14.14$, is simply an index of how variable the sample means are from one to the next in the sampling distribution of the mean. The average difference between the sample means and the population mean is about 14.14 points.

COMPREHENSION CHECK 5.6

Use Equation 5.1 to compute the standard error of the mean when $\sigma = 10$ and $N = 100$. Explain what this value tells you about the sampling distribution of the mean.
(Answer on p. 147.)

Notice from Equation 5.1 that as N increases, $\sigma_{\overline{X}}$ decreases. That is, the larger the samples drawn from the population, the more closely their means will cluster around the population mean. The smaller the samples, the more diverse their means will be. This makes some intuitive sense. Small samples can often include just the most extreme scores from the population, making those sample means extreme as well. Large samples provide more opportunity for a few extreme scores to be balanced by more moderate scores. The means of large samples are less subject to wild fluctuations from one sample to the next.

You can also see from Equation 5.1 that as σ increases, $\sigma_{\overline{X}}$ will also increase. This also makes sense if you stop to think that samples simply mirror the population from which they are drawn. As the variability of scores in a population (σ) increases, one would expect the samples drawn from that population to become more variable as well ($\sigma_{\overline{X}}$).

COMPREHENSION CHECK 5.7

Suppose you have drawn a sample from some large population and have computed the sample's mean. Under which of the following circumstances would the sample mean be most likely to fall close to the population mean? Under which circumstances would the sample mean be most likely to show a large deviation from the population mean?

(a) Small sample size; low data variability
(b) Large sample size; low data variability
(c) Small sample size; high data variability
(d) Large sample size; high data variability

(Answer on p. 147.)

The Sampling Distribution of the Proportion

In the population of all registered American voters, some proportion believes that the President is doing a "good job." Let's use the symbol p_U to represent this population proportion, where the p stands for "proportion" and the subscript U stands for "universe," synonymous with population. Suppose now that we drew all possible samples of size N from this population and identified the proportion in each sample that gave the President a favorable evaluation. Each of these sample proportions can be represented with the symbol p. From one sample to the next, we would expect to see the sample proportions varying somewhat. Why? This is the same chance fluctuation we labeled "sampling error" before. If we plotted how many times the various sample proportions occurred from one sample to the next, we would have the **sampling distribution of the proportion.** Just as the sampling distribution of the mean is used to help us make inferences about a population mean on the basis of the study of a single sample, so too will the sampling distribution of the proportion help us to generalize from sample to population proportion.

sampling distribution of the proportion *A theoretical distribution showing the frequency of occurrence of values of the proportion computed for all possible samples of size* N *sampled with replacement from a population.*

The sampling distribution of the proportion, like the sampling distribution of the mean, is normally a theoretical entity that exists only in our minds. Even so, it may make it easier to understand this sampling distribution if we actually construct one. This process is illustrated in Figure 5.2. The entire population of the little town of Gopher Gulch consists of only four residents. Each resident has an opinion about the President's performance, coded 0 to represent dissatisfaction with the President and 1 to represent satisfaction. These data are listed in Figure 5.2a and are graphed to show that the town is evenly divided on this issue, with half approving of the President's performance ($p_U = .5$) and half disapproving.

Figure 5.2b lists the opinion data for all possible samples of size $N = 3$ drawn (with replacement) from the population. Listed with each of these samples is the proportion that approves of the President's performance (p). Notice that the sample proportions vary somewhat from one sample to the next, a result of sampling error.

Figure 5.2c graphs the frequency of occurrence of the sample proportions (p) computed for all possible samples of size $N = 3$ drawn from the specified population. This is the sampling distribution of the proportion.

Population data:

Resident	Opinions
A	0
B	1
C	1
D	0

0 = dissatisfied
1 = satisfied

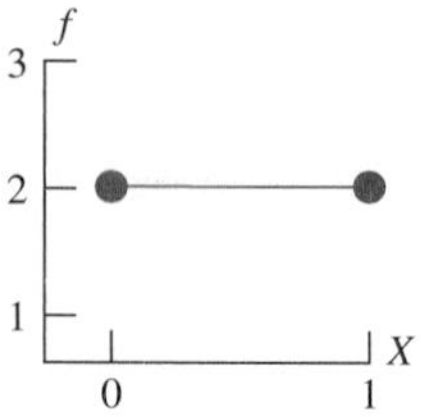

(a)

Samples ($N = 3$)	Opinions	Proportion Satisfied
A, A, A	0 0 0	0
A, A, B	0 0 1	.33
A, A, C	0 0 1	.33
A, A, D	0 0 1	.33
A, B, B	0 1 1	.67
A, B, C	0 1 1	.67
A, B, D	0 1 0	.33
A, C, C	0 1 1	.67
A, C, D	0 1 0	.33
A, D, D	0 0 0	0
B, B, B	1 1 1	1
B, B, C	1 1 1	1
B, B, D	1 1 0	.67
B, C, C	1 1 1	1
B, C, D	1 1 0	.67
B, D, D	1 0 0	.33
C, C, C	1 1 1	1
C, C ,D	1 1 0	.67
C, D, D	1 1 0	.67
D, D, D	0 0 0	0

(b)

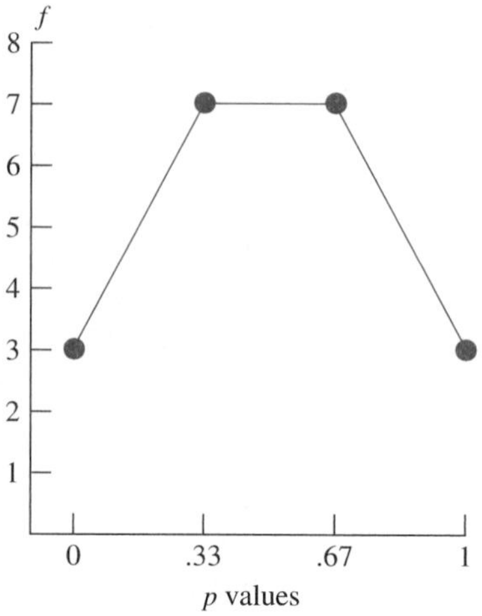

(c)

FIGURE 5.2

The process of forming the sampling distribution of the proportion for samples of size $N = 3$. (a) shows a rectangular population distribution. (b) lists all possible samples of size $N = 3$ drawn with replacement from the population, along with their proportions expressing satisfaction. (c) plots the sample proportions, forming the sampling distribution of the proportion.

COMPREHENSION CHECK 5.8

In the following small population, each case is "scored" 0 if female and 1 if male. Draw all possible samples of size $N = 2$, compute the proportion of males in each sample, and draw a graph to show the frequency of occurrence of the various sample proportions that occur from one sample to the next—the sampling distribution of the proportion.

population data: 0, 1, 1, 0, 0

(Answer on p. 147.)

Characteristics of the Sampling Distribution of the Proportion. You know more about the sampling distribution of the proportion than you think. As we will see next, a proportion is really just a mean. Because of that, the sampling distribution of the proportion is really the same thing as the sampling distribution of the mean. And all of the characteristics of the sampling distribution of the mean apply equally well to the sampling distribution of the proportion.

Look back at Figure 5.2b, where opinion data are listed for all the samples drawn from the population of Gopher Gulch. Compute the mean and variance of the first sample: 0, 0, 0. The mean is 0. That is also the proportion of cases in the sample who evaluate the President favorably. The variance is 0, accurately reflecting the absence of variability from one case to the next in this sample. Now compute the mean and variance of the second sample: 0, 0, 1. The mean is .33, which is also the proportion of cases who are satisfied with the President's performance. The variance of this sample is .22, accurately indicating the presence of some variability of the scores. In general, when cases are scored 0 to reflect the absence of some characteristic (such as disapproval of the President) and 1 to represent the presence of that characteristic (such as approval of the President), the mean gives us the proportion of cases that possesses the characteristic. The variance and standard deviation are also interpretable, indicating how much variability exists from one case to the next.(See Note 2)

COMPREHENSION CHECK 5.9

In each of the following data sets, cases are scored 1 if they favor a school bond issue and 0 if they do not. For each data set, compute: the proportion who favor the school bond issue; the mean; and the variance. Compare the proportions and means. Interpret the variances.

(a) 1, 1, 1, 1, 1, 0
(b) 1, 0, 1, 0, 1, 0
(c) 1, 1, 1, 1, 1, 1

(Answer on pp.147–148.)

Since proportions and means are the same thing, the sampling distribution of the proportion is the same as the sampling distribution of the mean. And it follows that the central limit theorem, which describes the sampling distribution of the mean, also describes the sampling distribution of the proportion. Perhaps it would be simplest if we just forgot that we ever heard of the sampling distribution of the proportion! Let's do that, and just think of proportions as means.

5.2 Interval Estimation

Having laid our theoretical foundations, it's time to put sampling distributions to work. In this section of the chapter we will see how the sampling distribution of the mean (and proportion) can be used to estimate population means (or proportions) based on a sample mean (or proportion) using a procedure known as interval estimation.

Interval estimation is an inferential statistical procedure that uses sample data to compute a range of values having a known probability (or *confidence*) of capturing some population parameter of interest, usually the population mean or proportion. This range of values is called the **confidence interval.** When Dan Blather reports on the evening news that "A telephone survey of 1,000 households has shown that the President's approval rating has slipped to 48%, with a margin of error of plus or minus 3 percentage points," he is citing a confidence interval. Implied in his statement, but not stated explicitly, is the fact that this sample-based confidence interval has some known probability—mostly likely 95% or 99%—of accurately capturing the sentiment of the entire population of Americans. Let's see how confidence intervals are constructed.

interval estimation *An inferential statistical procedure used in estimating population parameters from sample data through the construction of confidence intervals.*

confidence interval *A range of values computed from sample data that has a known probability of capturing some population parameter of interest.*

COMPREHENSION CHECK 5.10

What kinds of research questions call for the use of interval estimation? What is the purpose of constructing a confidence interval?
(Answer on p. 148.)

Confidence Interval for the Population Mean

confidence interval for the population mean *A range of values computed from sample data that has a known probability of capturing the population mean.*

The **confidence interval for the population mean** is a range of values having a known probability of capturing the population mean. To understand how this confidence interval is constructed, let's use our imaginations and a few pictures.

Imagine some very large population. Now imagine that you've drawn every possible sample of some fixed size of at least 50 cases each from that population, and that you've computed the sample mean for each of these many samples. Finally, imagine plotting the frequency of occurrence of the various means observed from one sample to the next. This would give you the sampling distribution of the mean shown in Figure 5.3a. The central limit theorem tells us that this sampling distribution has a normal shape, regardless of how

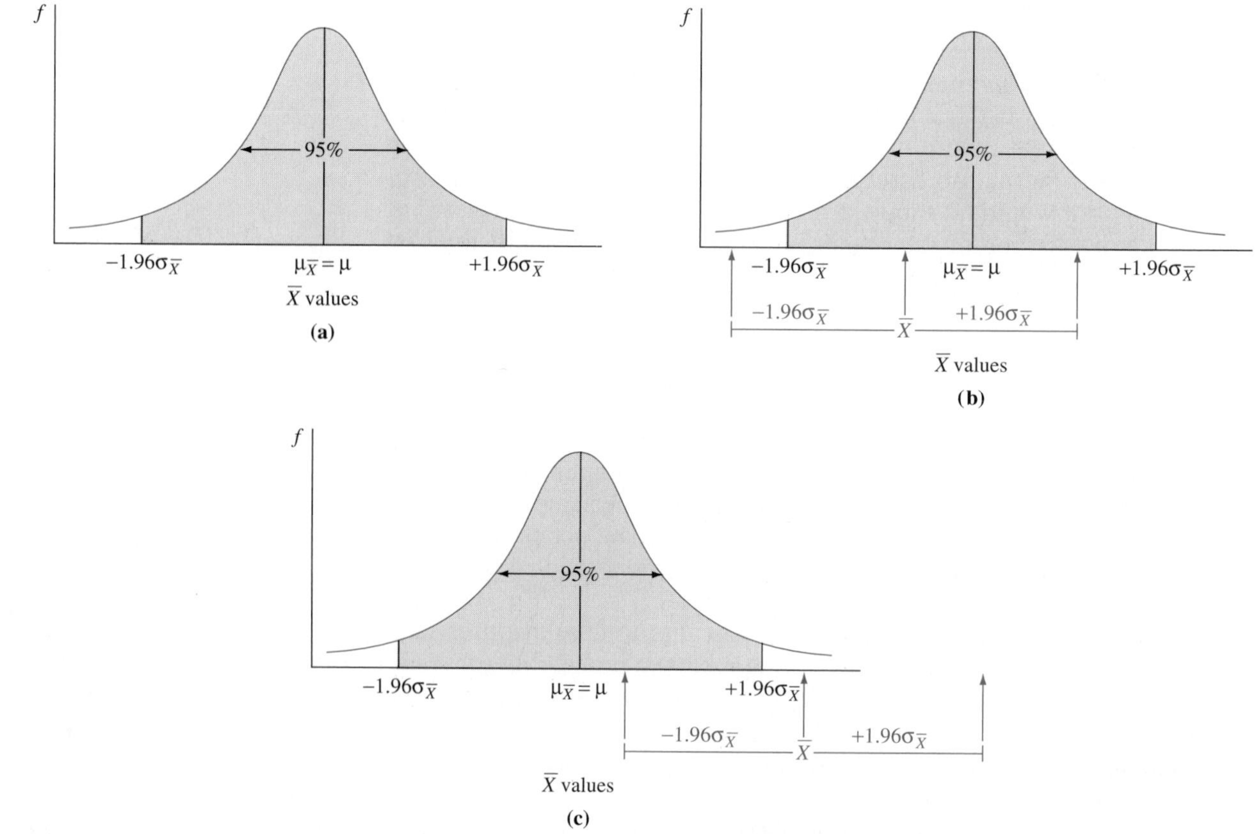

FIGURE 5.3

The 95% confidence interval for the population mean. (a) shows the sampling distribution of the mean, normally distributed, with 95% of the $\overline{X}$ values falling between $\pm 1.96\sigma_{\overline{X}}$. In (b), a sample mean that falls within this shaded region is surrounded on each side by $1.96\sigma_{\overline{X}}$, creating a range of values that captures μ. In (c), a sample mean that falls outside the shaded region is surrounded on each side by $1.96\sigma_{\overline{X}}$, creating a range of values that fails to capture μ.

the population is distributed. We also know from the central limit theorem that the mean of the sampling distribution of the mean is equal to the mean of the population from which the samples were drawn: $\mu_{\overline{X}} = \mu$. Finally, the central limit theorem tells us how to compute the standard error of the mean:

$$\sigma_{\overline{X}} = \frac{\sigma}{\sqrt{N}}$$

Given that the sampling distribution is normally distributed, how many standard errors of the mean (that is, standard deviations) must we travel from the center of the distribution in order to capture, say, 95% of all the $\overline{X}$ values? The table of areas under the normal curve (Table 1 in Appendix B) says that 95% of the area under a normal curve is contained between ± 1.96 standard deviations from the mean. This area is shaded in Figure 5.3a. To translate to the present situation, 95% of the sample means drawn from a population will fall within $\pm 1.96\sigma_{\overline{X}}$ from the center of the sampling distribution of the mean. Remember that this center point is equal to the population mean.

In other words, the probability is 95% (or .95) that any one sample drawn from the population will fall within the shaded portion of Figure 5.3a. If a sample mean falls *anywhere* inside this shaded area, such as the sample mean depicted in Figure 5.3b, it is no farther than 1.96 standard errors of the mean from $\mu_{\overline{X}} = \mu$. Therefore, surrounding that sample mean on each side by 1.96 standard errors of the mean ($\overline{X} \pm 1.96\sigma_{\overline{X}}$) will give a range of values that includes or captures the population mean. This range of values, shown in Figure 5.3b, is called the 95% confidence interval, because the probability is 95% or .95 that it captures the population mean.

COMPREHENSION CHECK 5.11

In a normally distributed sampling distribution of the mean, how many $\sigma_{\overline{X}}$ units must one go on each side of the centerpoint to capture 80% of the sample means? What percentage of the samples drawn from a population will have means between $2.10\sigma_{\overline{X}}$ above and $2.10\sigma_{\overline{X}}$ below the center point?

(Answer on p. 148.)

Ninety-five percent of the time, a sample mean will fall close enough to the center of the sampling distribution of the mean that surrounding it by $\pm 1.96\sigma_{\overline{X}}$ will capture μ. But this also means that 5% of the time a sample drawn from some population will yield a mean that falls farther away from the center point than this. Figure 5.3c depicts this situation. Surrounding this sample mean on each side with 1.96 standard errors of the mean ($\overline{X} \pm 1.96\sigma_{\overline{X}}$) produces a range of values that fails to capture the population mean.

To summarize, because the sampling distribution of the mean is normally distributed, the probability is 95% that any given sample mean will fall within $\pm 1.96\sigma_{\overline{X}}$ of $\mu_{\overline{X}} = \mu$. Thus the range of values defined by $\overline{X} \pm 1.96\sigma_{\overline{X}}$ has a 95% likelihood of capturing μ. But there is a 5% probability that any given sample mean will fall farther from $\mu_{\overline{X}} = \mu$ than $\pm 1.96\sigma_{\overline{X}}$. Thus the range of values defined by $\overline{X} \pm 1.96\sigma_{\overline{X}}$ will fail to capture μ 5% of the time.

When we draw a sample and use its mean to estimate the mean of a population, we do not know which one of the many possible sample means we have. Is it one of the sample means that lies close to the center of the sampling distribution of the mean? Is it one of the means that falls out in one of the tails? We don't know for sure, but we do know the probabilities. We're not *certain* that the confidence interval surrounding any given sample mean captures μ, but we do have some known *level of confidence* that it does.

COMPREHENSION CHECK 5.12

The confidence interval defined by $\overline{X} \pm 1.28\sigma_{\overline{X}}$ will capture μ in what percentage of the samples drawn from a population? In what percentage of the samples will this confidence interval fail to capture μ? What about the confidence interval defined by $\overline{X} \pm 2.10\sigma_{\overline{X}}$?

(Answer on p. 148.)

The 95% confidence interval is only one of many possible confidence intervals. We can use the table of areas under the normal curve to define confidence intervals having any desired probability of capturing the population mean. The most commonly used confidence intervals are 90%, 95%, and 99%. The table of areas tells us that 90% of all the sample means in a normally distributed sampling distribution of the mean will fall within $\pm 1.65\sigma_{\overline{X}}$ of $\mu_{\overline{X}} = \mu$. Any single sample drawn from the population, then, has a 90% chance of falling within this region. If it does fall within this region, we can be 90% confident that surrounding the sample mean on each side by $1.65\sigma_{\overline{X}}$ will give a range of values that captures μ.

The same logic applies to the 99% confidence interval. Ninety-nine percent of the samples drawn from a population will produce means that are within $\pm 2.58\sigma_{\overline{X}}$ from $\mu_{\overline{X}} = \mu$. The probability is therefore 99% that any one sample drawn from the population will fall within this region. If it does, surrounding it on each side by $2.58\sigma_{\overline{X}}$ will capture μ.

Equations 5.2 through 5.4 define the 90%, 95%, and 99% confidence intervals.

Equation 5.2

$$\overline{X} \pm 1.65\sigma_{\overline{X}}$$

Equation 5.3

$$\overline{X} \pm 1.96\sigma_{\overline{X}}$$

Equation 5.4

$$\overline{X} \pm 2.58\sigma_{\overline{X}}$$

where

$\overline{X}$ = sample mean
$\sigma_{\overline{X}}$ = standard error of the mean

In words, we compute a confidence interval for the population mean by: (1) computing the sample mean ($\overline{X}$); (2) computing the standard error of the mean ($\sigma_{\overline{X}}$) according to Equation 5.1; (3) multiplying the result of step 2 by 1.65 (for the 90% confidence interval), or 1.96 (for the 95% interval), or 2.58 (for the 99% confidence interval); and (4) subtracting and adding the result of step 3 from the sample mean computed in step 1. Example 5.1 provides a concrete example of the construction of the confidence interval for the population mean.

EXAMPLE 5.1

Confidence Interval for the Population Mean

Organizational psychologists at Coma Products (best known for their bored games Monotony and Conjugation) are concerned about excessive turnover among production employees. Before pursuing a remedy, though, they want to gather more information. Data from the personnel files of a sample of 50 employees will be used to construct a 95% confidence interval to estimate the mean duration of employment for the entire population of production employees.

In this sample, the mean duration of employment was $\overline{X} = 24.2$ months. Based on the sample data, the researchers felt confident in estimating the population standard deviation at $\sigma = 9$ months.

The sample at hand is one of many possible samples that could have been drawn from the population of production employees. And the mean of this sample is one of the many possible sample means that might have been obtained. The mean of this sample is one of the means that constitute the following sampling distribution of the mean:

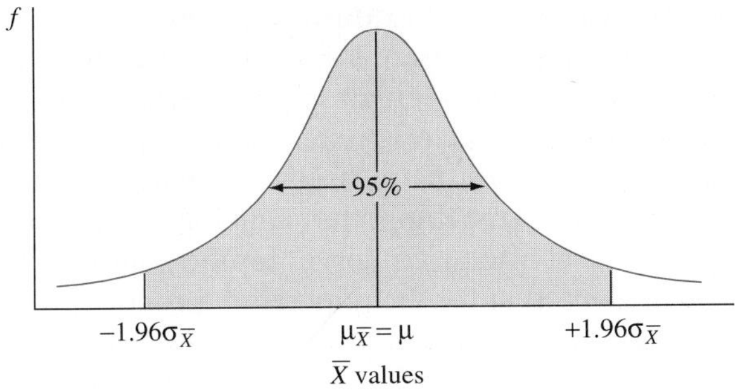

The central limit theorem tells us several things about this sampling distribution of the mean:

1. $\mu_{\overline{X}} = \mu$
2. $\sigma_{\overline{X}} = \dfrac{\sigma}{\sqrt{N}}$

   $= \dfrac{9}{\sqrt{50}}$

   $= 1.27$
3. The sampling distribution of the mean is normally distributed.

Because the sampling distribution of the mean is normally distributed, we know that 95% of the sample means are located between 1.96 standard deviations (standard errors of the mean) below the mean of the sampling distribution and 1.96 standard deviations (standard errors of the mean) above the mean of the sampling distribution. This 95% area is shaded in the diagram.

If the sample mean, $\overline{X} = 24.2$, falls within this shaded range, it lies no farther than $1.96\sigma_{\overline{X}}$ from $\mu_{\overline{X}} = \mu$. Thus, if we surround $\overline{X}$ on each side by $1.96\sigma_{\overline{X}}$, we will have a range of values that has a 95% certainty of capturing μ. According to Equation 5.3,

$$\text{95\% confidence interval:} \quad \overline{X} \pm 1.96\sigma_{\overline{X}}$$

$$24.2 \pm 1.96(1.27)$$

$$24.2 \pm 2.49$$

In other words, the researchers can be 95% certain that the average production employee will remain with Coma Products for between 21.71 and 26.69

months before quitting. There is a 5% chance, though, that the sample mean has fallen outside the 95% shaded region of the sampling distribution. If this is the case, the confidence interval will not capture the true population mean.

Comprehension Check 5.13

Use Equations 5.2–5.4 to compute the 90%, 95%, and 99% confidence intervals for the population mean when $N = 50$, $\sigma = 15$, and $\overline{X} = 100$.

(Answer on p. 148.)

Confidence Interval for the Population Proportion

confidence interval for the population proportion *A range of values computed from sample data that has a known probability of capturing the population proportion.*

The **confidence interval for the population proportion** is a range of values computed from sample data that has a known probability of capturing the population proportion. We have seen already that when cases are scored 0 if they do not possess some characteristic and 1 if they do, the mean score is equal to the proportion of cases that possess the characteristic. Because proportions and means are the same thing, the same logic and computational procedures that apply to the confidence interval for the population mean apply as well to the confidence interval for the population proportion. Example 5.2 illustrates the procedure for constructing the confidence interval for the population proportion.

Example 5.2

Confidence Interval for the Population Proportion

Congress has just approved funding for research to develop and evaluate treatments for cranial calcification ("bonehead") syndrome, a disorder in which many legislators have a personal interest. In the belief that bonehead syndrome is best treated early, one researcher wants to target junior high school students. Before she embarks on research with this group, though, she wants to have a better sense of what proportion of this population suffers from the syndrome by constructing a 99% confidence interval for the population proportion (p_U).

A sample of 100 junior high school students is examined, and each student is scored 0 if there is no evidence of the syndrome and 1 if the syndrome is diagnosed. The mean of these scores is $\overline{X} = .17$, which is also the proportion of students in the sample (p) who show signs of the syndrome. It is estimated that for the entire population of junior high school students, the standard deviation is $\sigma = .38$. The sample mean (proportion) obtained is one of the many means (proportions) that comprise the sampling distribution of the mean (proportion) depicted below. The central limit theorem tells us several things about this sampling distribution of the mean (proportion):

1. $\mu_{\overline{X}} = \mu = p_U$
2. $\sigma_{\overline{X}} = \dfrac{\sigma}{\sqrt{N}}$

   $= \dfrac{.38}{10}$

   $= .038$
3. The sampling distribution of the mean (proportion) is normally distributed.

Because the sampling distribution of the mean (proportion) is normally distributed, we know that 99% of the sample means (proportions) are located between 2.58 standard deviations (standard errors of the mean) below the center of the sampling distribution (where $\mu_{\overline{X}} = \mu = p_U$) and 2.58 standard deviations (standard errors of the mean) above the center. This 99% area is shaded in the following diagram.

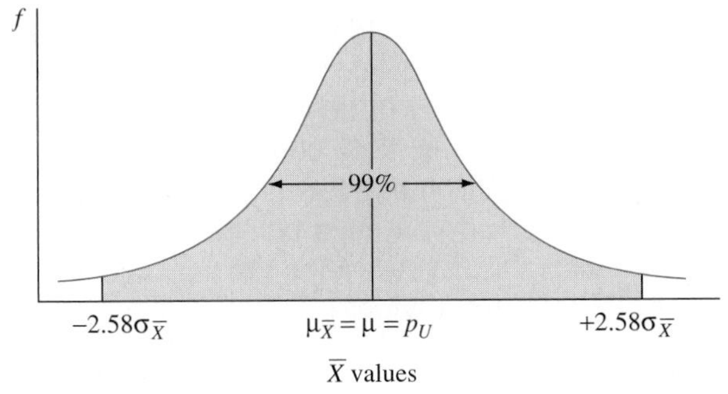

If the sample mean (proportion), $\overline{X} = .17$, falls within this shaded region, it lies no farther than $2.58\sigma_{\overline{X}}$ from $\mu_{\overline{X}} = \mu = p_U$. Thus, if we surround $\overline{X}$ on each side by $2.58\sigma_{\overline{X}}$, we will have a range of values that has a 99% certainty of capturing the population proportion. According to Equation 5.4,

$$\text{99\% confidence interval:} \quad \overline{X} \pm 2.58\sigma_{\overline{X}}$$
$$.17 \pm 2.58(.038)$$
$$.17 \pm .098$$

In other words, we are 99% certain that the proportion of junior high school students who are boneheads is between .07 and .27. There is a 1% chance that the sample mean (proportion) has fallen outside the 99% shaded region of the sampling distribution. In this case the confidence interval will not capture p_U.

COMPREHENSION CHECK 5.14

Use Equations 5.2–5.4 to construct the 90%, 95%, and 99% confidence intervals for the population proportion when $N = 50$, $\sigma = .25$, and $p = .5$.
(Answer on p. 148.)

The Width of Confidence Intervals

Not all confidence intervals are created equal. Some are wider and some are narrower. All things considered, we would rather have a narrow confidence interval than a wide one. For instance, it is preferable to say

> We are 95% certain that between 45% and 51% of Americans approve of the President's performance.

than it is to say

> We are 95% certain that between 18% and 78% of Americans approve of the President's performance.

The first confidence interval is better because it is only 6 percentage points wide. The second, in contrast, is 60 percentage points wide. The broader the confidence interval, the less it really tells us about the population.

Three factors influence the width of confidence intervals: level of confidence, data variability, and sample size. We will consider each of these factors in the sections that follow.

Level of Confidence. All other things being equal, the greater the level of confidence, the wider the confidence interval is. Thus, for a given set of data, the 99% confidence interval will be wider than the 95% confidence interval, which will be wider than the 90% confidence interval. This is just another example of getting what you pay for in statistics. You can have a nice, narrow confidence interval, but you must be willing to pay for it with a reduced level of confidence. Or, if you want a greater level of confidence, you must pay for that by settling for a wider confidence interval.

Two confidence intervals are constructed below that illustrate this relationship between level of confidence and interval width. Both confidence intervals are based on the same data ($N = 100$ and $\sigma = 15$ for both). They differ only in that one is a 90% and the other a 99% confidence interval.

The 90% confidence interval is defined by Equation 5.2 as

$$\overline{X} \pm 1.65\sigma_{\overline{X}} \qquad \left(\text{where } \sigma_{\overline{X}} = \frac{\sigma}{\sqrt{N}}\right)$$

$$100 \pm 1.65\left(\frac{15}{\sqrt{100}}\right)$$

$$100 \pm 2.475$$

This interval has a width of 4.95 points. Compare this width with that of the 99% confidence interval for the same data. The 99% confidence interval is defined by Equation 5.4 as

$$\overline{X} \pm 2.58\sigma_{\overline{X}} \qquad \left(\text{where } \sigma_{\overline{X}} = \frac{\sigma}{\sqrt{N}}\right)$$

$$100 \pm 2.58\left(\frac{15}{\sqrt{100}}\right)$$

$$100 \pm 3.87$$

This interval has a width of 7.74 points, which is 2.79 points wider than the 90% confidence interval for the same data. As the level of confidence increases, so does the width of the confidence interval.

The general relationship between level of confidence and the width of the confidence interval is diagrammed in Figure 5.4a. The relationship is nonlinear: As the level of confidence increases, the width of the confidence interval increases at an accelerating rate. Thus, one pays more dearly in terms of increased interval width to increase from the 95% to the 99% confidence level than to increase from the 90% to the 95% confidence level.

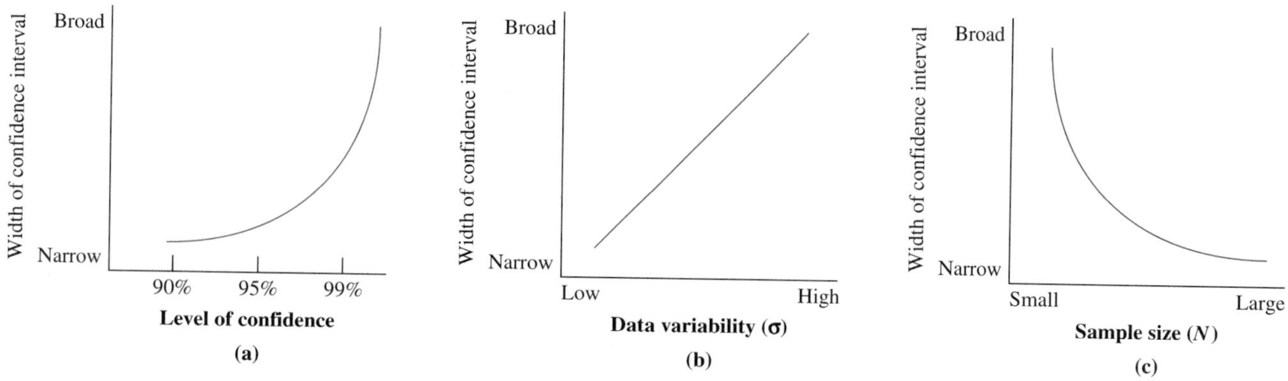

FIGURE 5.4
The width of a confidence interval varies as a function of level of confidence (a), data variability (b), and sample size (c).

COMPREHENSION CHECK 5.15

In Comprehension Checks 5.13 and 5.14 you constructed 90%, 95%, and 99% confidence intervals for the population mean and proportion, respectively. How do the widths of these confidence intervals compare?

(Answer on p. 148.)

Data Variability. The second factor that influences confidence interval width is data variability. All other things being equal, the more variable the data, the wider is the confidence interval.

Except for differences in data variability, the two 95% confidence intervals that follow are based on identical data ($N = 100$ and $\overline{X} = 100$). For the first confidence interval, $\sigma = 15$; for the second, $\sigma = 30$.

The 95% confidence interval is defined by Equation 5.3 as

$$\overline{X} \pm 1.96\sigma_{\overline{X}} \qquad \left(\text{where } \sigma_{\overline{X}} = \frac{\sigma}{\sqrt{N}}\right)$$

$$100 \pm 1.96\left(\frac{15}{\sqrt{100}}\right)$$

$$100 \pm 2.94$$

This interval has a width of 5.88 points. Compare this width with that of the confidence interval that results when $\sigma = 30$:

$$\overline{X} \pm 1.96\sigma_{\overline{X}} \qquad \left(\text{where } \sigma_{\overline{X}} = \frac{\sigma}{\sqrt{N}}\right)$$

$$\overline{X} \pm 1.96\left(\frac{30}{\sqrt{100}}\right)$$

$$\overline{X} \pm 5.88$$

This interval has a width of 11.76, twice that of the first. The general relationship between interval width and data variability, measured by σ, is linear, as shown in Figure 5.4b.

In order to keep confidence intervals as narrow as possible, we would like our data to show as little variability as possible. But the data will vary, and legitimately so. Still, efforts made to reduce *random* variability in the data—the "noise" associated with unreliable measuring instruments and procedures—will translate into narrower confidence intervals.

COMPREHENSION CHECK 5.16

Compare the widths of the 95% confidence intervals to estimate the population mean when $N = 50$, $\overline{X} = 100$, and

(a) $\sigma = 10$

(b) $\sigma = 100$

(Answer on p. 148.)

Sample Size. Sample size and confidence interval width are inversely related: As N increases, width decreases. Thus, you can buy a narrower confidence interval by expending the greater effort required to study a larger sample.

The two confidence intervals that follow illustrate this relationship between sample size and interval width. Both confidence intervals are based on the same data ($\overline{X} = 100$, $\sigma = 15$), except that $N = 50$ for the first confidence interval and $N = 100$ for the second.

The 95% confidence interval is defined by Equation 5.2 as

$$\overline{X} \pm 1.96\sigma_{\overline{X}} \qquad \left(\text{where } \sigma_{\overline{X}} = \frac{\sigma}{\sqrt{N}}\right)$$

$$100 \pm 1.96\left(\frac{15}{\sqrt{50}}\right)$$

$$100 \pm 4.16$$

This interval has a width of 8.32 points. Compare this width with that of the confidence interval based on $N = 100$:

$$\overline{X} \pm 1.96\sigma_{\overline{X}} \qquad \left(\text{where } \sigma_{\overline{X}} = \frac{\sigma}{\sqrt{N}}\right)$$

$$100 \pm 1.96\left(\frac{15}{\sqrt{100}}\right)$$

$$100 \pm 2.94$$

This interval has a width of 5.88 points, which is 2.44 points narrower than the confidence interval for $N = 50$ computed above.

The general relationship between sample size and interval width is depicted in Figure 5.4c. As N increases, width decreases, but at a decelerating rate. Even a modest increase in a small sample size results in an appreciable decrease in confidence interval width. However, a very large increase in a large sample is required to have a noticeable effect on the width of the confidence interval.

Comprehension Check 5.17

Compare the widths of the 95% confidence intervals to estimate the population proportion when $p = .5$, $\sigma = .25$, and

(a) $N = 50$
(b) $N = 500$

(Answer on p. 148.)

Selecting an Appropriate Sample Size

One of the most basic questions that faces anyone who intends to conduct research is: "How big a sample should I study?" The answer to this question depends on what kind of research is to be done and what sorts of statistical procedures are to be used. If the intent is to estimate a population's mean or proportion and the statistical procedure is interval estimation, the relationships described above among interval width, level of confidence, data variability, and sample size can be used to choose a sample of an appropriate size.

If $1 + 2 + 3 + X = 10$, what is X? Of course, X is 4. We can solve for X because it is the only unknown value in this equation. In pretty much the same way, if we can specify the desired level of confidence and the width of the confidence interval, and we can estimate data variability, then we can determine how big a sample we need. This is illustrated in Example 5.3.

Example 5.3

Determining Sample Size in Interval Estimation

Given any desired level of confidence, the desired width of the confidence interval, and a good estimate of data variability, it is possible to estimate the necessary sample size. In Example 5.1 we constructed a 95% confidence interval to estimate the mean duration of employment in the population of Coma Products production employees. What sample size should we study if: (a) we want a 99% confidence interval; (b) we want the confidence interval to be only 3 months wide (that is, $\overline{X} \pm 1.5$ months); and (c) we are confident that the population standard deviation will be approximately $\sigma = 9$ months? Recall first the form of the 99% confidence interval as given in Equation 5.4:

$$\overline{X} \pm 2.58\sigma_{\overline{X}}$$

If the confidence interval is to be 3 points wide, the sample mean must be surrounded on each side by 1.5 points. Thus, the confidence interval will look like this:

$$\overline{X} \pm 1.5$$

It follows that these two expressions are equivalent:

$$\overline{X} \pm 2.58\sigma_{\overline{X}} = \overline{X} \pm 1.5$$

We can therefore eliminate $\overline{X} \pm$ from both sides of the equation:

$$2.58\sigma_{\overline{X}} = 1.5$$

By definition of $\sigma_{\overline{X}}$,

$$2.58\left(\frac{\sigma}{\sqrt{N}}\right) = 1.5$$

By substitution,

$$2.58\left(\frac{9}{\sqrt{N}}\right) = 1.5$$

Dividing both sides by 2.58,

$$\frac{9}{\sqrt{N}} = \frac{1.5}{2.58} = \frac{.58}{1}$$

Cross-multiplying,

$$.58\sqrt{N} = 9$$

Dividing both sides by .58,

$$\sqrt{N} = \frac{9}{.58} = 15.52$$

Squaring both sides of the equation,

$$N = 15.52^2 = 240.87$$

Thus, it would be necessary to examine a sample of about 241 cases in order to construct a 99% confidence interval having a width of 3 months, provided that the population standard deviation has been estimated correctly at $\sigma = 9$.

COMPREHENSION CHECK 5.18

Suppose you want to construct a 99% confidence interval to estimate the proportion of people who favor stricter gun control. You want this confidence interval to be 6 percentage points wide (that is, $\pm .03$) and have estimated that the population standard deviation may be as high as $\sigma = .25$. How large a sample will you need in order to construct this confidence interval?

(Answer on p. 149.)

When σ Is Unknown or N Is Small

In the foregoing discussion of interval estimation it has been assumed that: (1) we know the standard deviation of the population (σ); and (2) we are dealing with relatively large sample sizes ($N \geq 50$). The first assumption is necessary in order to compute the standard error of the mean (look at the numerator of Equation 5.1). The second assumption is necessary in order for us to be assured by the central limit theorem that the sampling distribution of the mean will take on a normal shape. But what if we don't know σ? Or what if we are working with a small sample? Confidence intervals can still be constructed under these circumstances, but the procedure is a little different.

When σ Is Unknown. Equation 5.1 indicates that we need to know σ in order to compute $\sigma_{\overline{X}}$. In many situations this is no problem. Some variables, such as IQ scores or SAT scores, are computed in such a manner that the population standard deviation is very predictable. Sometimes previous research gives us sufficient familiarity with a variable that we can be confident in our ability to estimate accurately the population standard deviation. But most of the time we don't have much information about the population, including information about the population's standard deviation.

How can we construct confidence intervals when we don't know σ? One solution that springs to mind is to estimate the population standard deviation from sample data. In Chapter 3 we learned that the sample variance (Equation 3.8) and sample standard deviation (Equation 3.12) tend to be lower than the corresponding population values. That is what we mean when we say that these sample statistics provide a "biased" estimate of the population parameters. We also learned in Chapter 3, though, that the *corrected* sample variance ($\hat{s}^2$) and *corrected* sample standard deviation ($\hat{s}$) (Equations 3.11 and 3.13) are slightly larger in value than the uncorrected statistics and therefore provide better estimates of the population values. When we do not know σ, we have no choice but to estimate $\hat{\sigma}_{\overline{X}}$ (notice the change in symbol) using $\hat{s}$ in the numerator as shown in Equation 5.5:

Equation 5.5

$$\hat{\sigma}_{\overline{X}} = \frac{\hat{s}}{\sqrt{N}}$$

where

$\hat{\sigma}_{\overline{X}}$ = estimated standard error of the mean
$\hat{s}$ = corrected sample standard deviation
N = sample size

In words, the estimated standard error of the mean ($\hat{\sigma}_{\overline{X}}$) is computed by dividing the corrected sample standard deviation ($\hat{s}$) by the square root of the sample size (N).

This would be a great solution if $\hat{s}$ provided an accurate estimate of σ, but it doesn't. Particularly when sample sizes are small, $\hat{s}$ underestimates σ more than half the time. You can see from Equation 5.5 that if $\hat{s}$ is too low, then $\hat{\sigma}_{\overline{X}}$ will also be too low.

Let's see what effect this has on a confidence interval that uses $\hat{\sigma}_{\overline{X}}$ in place of $\sigma_{\overline{X}}$. Consider the 95% confidence interval as an example. Equation 5.3 defines the 95% confidence interval as

$$\overline{X} \pm 1.96\sigma_{\overline{X}}$$

However, if the value of $\sigma_{\overline{X}}$ that we have estimated is too small, this confidence interval will not be quite wide enough. It will actually take slightly more than 1.96 of our too-small estimated standard errors of the mean on each side of $\overline{X}$ to provide a confidence interval that is wide enough to capture μ 95% of the time. The next question is how many of these too-small estimated standard errors of the mean *are* required? That depends on our sample size. Remember that the underestimate of $\sigma_{\overline{X}}$ by $\hat{\sigma}_{\overline{X}}$ becomes increasingly severe as N becomes smaller.

Fortunately, statisticians have worked out all of these details. Table 2 in Appendix B, "Critical Values of t," tells us, for any given value of N, how many $\hat{\sigma}_{\overline{X}}$ units must surround $\overline{X}$ on each side in order to capture μ with any specified level of confidence. We will become more familiar with the t statistic and the table of critical values of t in the next chapter, but let's see here how this table is used in constructing confidence intervals.

Turn to the table of critical values of t. In order to enter the table one must know two things: (1) the number of degrees of freedom (abbreviated df); and

(2) the desired level of confidence. In the context of interval estimation, "number of degrees of freedom" is practically synonymous with sample size, because df $= N - 1$, where N is the number of cases in the sample. For example, if one is constructing a confidence interval based on a sample of $N = 20$ cases, df $= N - 1 = 20 - 1 = 19$. For a sample of $N = 10$, df $= N - 1 = 10 - 1 = 9$. Degrees of freedom are listed down the left side of the table of critical values of t. Notice that once we get to 30 degrees of freedom, the table jumps to 40, then to 60, and then to 120. What if the sample is of size $N = 51$, such that df $= 50$? The convention in such situations is to use the next *lower* listed df value, in this case 40.

Levels of confidence are not listed directly in the table. Instead, we use the columns labeled "Level of significance for two-tail test." (The values that label the columns in the table refer to the proportions of area under the curve that is found in the tails. We will see in the next chapter what is meant by "one-tail" and "two-tail.") For a 90% confidence interval, we use the column headed .10; for a 95% confidence interval, we use the column headed .05; for a 99% confidence interval, we use the column headed .01.

As an example, suppose you wanted to construct a 95% confidence interval using sample data from $N = 61$ cases, but you don't know σ and so must estimate $\hat{\sigma}_{\overline{X}}$. First, compute df $= N - 1 = 60$ and find that row in the table. Next, find the correct column of the table. For the 95% confidence level that would be the .05 column listed under "Level of significance for two-tailed test." Now find the intersection of the row and column you have identified. The value listed there, $t = 2.000$, tells you how many $\hat{\sigma}_{\overline{X}}$ units must surround each side of $\overline{X}$ in order to produce the 95% confidence interval:

$$\overline{X} \pm 2.000\hat{\sigma}_{\overline{X}}$$

When *N* Is Small. The central limit theorem guarantees a normally distributed sampling distribution of the mean only when samples are fairly large ($N \geq 50$). What if you are working with a sample that is smaller than this? If the population is normally distributed, the sampling distribution of the mean will also be normally distributed, no matter how small the samples are. But what if you don't know if the population is normally distributed? Or what if you have reason to believe that it's not normal? When the population is nonnormal, small samples will produce a nonnormal sampling distribution of the mean. Under these circumstances we again need some help to figure out how many $\hat{\sigma}_{\overline{X}}$ units we must go on each side of the center of the sampling distribution of the mean in order to capture 95% (or 90% or 99%) of the means.

Again, the table of critical values of t comes to the rescue. The table is used here in the same manner as described in the preceding section. We first compute the number of degrees of freedom (df $= N - 1$) and find the corresponding row in the table. We next find the column in the table that corresponds to the desired level of confidence: Using the listings under "Level of significance for two-tail test," .10 is used for the 90% confidence interval, .05 is used for the 95% interval, and .01 is used for the 99% interval. Finally, the value listed in the body of the table at the intersection of the selected row and column tells us how many $\hat{\sigma}_{\overline{X}}$ units we must go on each side of the center of the sampling distribution in order to capture the desired percentage of sample means.

As an example, suppose you want to construct a 95% confidence interval using a small sample—say, of size $N = 10$ cases. First, compute df $= N - 1 = 10 - 1 = 9$ and find that row in the table. Next, find the correct column of the table. For the 95% confidence level that would be the .05 column under "Level of significance for two-tailed test." Now find the intersection of the row and column you've identified. The value listed there, $t = 2.262$, tells you how many $\hat{\sigma}_{\overline{X}}$ units must surround each side of $\overline{X}$ in order to produce the 95% confidence interval:

$$\overline{X} \pm 1.262\hat{\sigma}_{\overline{X}}$$

Equations 5.6 to 5.8 summarize the computation of the 90%, 95%, and 99% confidence intervals when σ is unknown and/or N is small.

$$\overline{X} \pm t_{(\mathrm{df} = N - 1;\ .10)}\hat{\sigma}_{\overline{X}}$$

Equation 5.6

$$\overline{X} \pm t_{(\mathrm{df} = N - 1;\ .05)}\hat{\sigma}_{\overline{X}}$$

Equation 5.7

$$\overline{X} \pm t_{(\mathrm{df} = N - 1;\ .01)}\hat{\sigma}_{\overline{X}}$$

Equation 5.8

where

$\overline{X}$ = sample mean
t = critical value of t listed for df $= N - 1$ and specified two-tail significance level
N = sample size
$\hat{\sigma}_{\overline{X}}$ = estimated standard of the mean

In words, we compute a confidence interval for the population mean or proportion by: (1) computing the sample mean or proportion ($\overline{X}$); (2) identifying the critical value of t for df $= N - 1$ and the appropriate confidence level; (3) estimating the standard error of the mean ($\hat{\sigma}_{\overline{X}}$) according to Equation 5.5; (4) multiplying the result of step 3 by the critical value of t identified in step 2; and (5) subtracting and adding the result of step 4 from the sample mean or proportion computed in step 1.

COMPREHENSION CHECK 5.19

Use the distribution of t to construct the 95% confidence interval for the population mean for the following data: $N = 15$, $\overline{X} = 50$, $\hat{s} = 10$. Use the distribution of t to construct the 99% confidence interval for the population proportion for the following data: $N = 20$, $p = .5$, $\hat{s} = .58$.

(Answer on p. 149.)

How Important Is This? Much can be made of the distinction between confidence intervals constructed using the table of areas under the normal distribution (Equations 5.2 to 5.5) and those constructed using the table of critical values of t (Equations 5.6 to 5.8), but in actual practice these procedures typically do not produce very different results.

In order to keep confidence intervals narrow enough to be useful, researchers doing interval estimation must keep sample sizes quite large ($N \geq 50$). This means that one can count on the central limit theorem to be in effect. In addition, even though σ is often unknown, the large sample sizes used in most interval estimation research mean that $\hat{s}$ will provide a close approximation to σ, and there will be little difference between $\sigma_{\overline{X}}$ and $\hat{\sigma}_{\overline{X}}$.

Consider this example comparing the two interval estimation procedures. A researcher wanted to estimate the proportion of college students who preregister late for classes. She gathered data from a sample of $N = 50$ students and found $p = .50$ and $\hat{s} = .53$. The estimated standard error of the mean computed according to Equation 5.5 is

$$\hat{\sigma}_{\overline{X}} = \frac{\hat{s}}{\sqrt{N}}$$

$$= \frac{.53}{7.07}$$

$$= .075$$

The 95% confidence interval based on the normal distribution is defined by Equation 5.3:

$$\overline{X} \pm 1.96\sigma_{\overline{X}}$$

$$.50 \pm 1.96(.075)$$

$$.50 \pm .147$$

The 95% confidence interval based on the t distribution is defined by Equation 5.7:

$$\overline{X} \pm t_{(\text{df} = N - 1; .05)}\hat{\sigma}_{\overline{X}}$$

$$.50 \pm 2.00(.075)$$

$$.50 \pm .150$$

You can see that the difference between these confidence intervals is inconsequential, amounting to only three-tenths of a percentage point. In general, if the sample is of size 50 or greater, it is safe to base confidence intervals on values in the table of areas under the normal curve.

SUMMARY

Sampling distributions are fundamental to all inferential statistics—procedures that involve generalizing from sample data to whole populations. This chapter describes two sampling distributions, the sampling distribution of the mean and the sampling distribution of the proportion. The sampling distribution of the mean is formed by drawing all possible samples of size N from a population, computing the mean for each, and plotting the frequency of occurrence of the various mean values obtained in this way. The sampling distribution of the proportion is constructed in a like manner, except that the statistic computed for each sample is a proportion rather than a mean. The central limit theorem describes the essential characteristics of both of these sampling distributions.

This chapter describes how sampling distributions are used in interval estimation—the construction of confidence intervals. A confidence interval is a range of values computed from sample data that has a known probability of capturing a population parameter of interest, usually the population mean or proportion.

All other things being equal, narrow confidence intervals are preferable to broad confidence intervals. Narrow confidence intervals can be "purchased" by accepting a lower level of confidence, exercising the extra rigor necessary to eliminating random data variability, and expending the effort to study larger samples. Because confidence interval width, level of confidence, data variability, and sample size are interrelated, it is possible to determine the sample size necessary to construct a confidence interval of any desired confidence level and width if one can estimate data variability.

When the population standard deviation is unknown and/or the sample size is small, special procedures may be used to construct confidence intervals.

NOTES

1. It is interesting to note that the sampling distributions on which so many statistical procedures are based are formed using sampling *with* replacement, but sampling *without* replacement is used when one actually draws a sample for purposes of research. If research were done using sampling with replacement, it is conceivable that one could end up with a sample consisting of the same case drawn over and over! This would be acceptable from the theoretical perspective, but it wouldn't make much practical sense. Although statistical theory assumes sampling with replacement and real-world research is done using sampling without replacement, this statistical violation is a minor one that has little or no effect on the accuracy of our conclusions.
2. The variance of a variable on which scores are either 0 or 1 can range from a low of 0 (when all scores are 0 or all are 1) to a high of .25 (when there are an equal number of 0s and 1s). The standard deviation, which is the square root of the variance, can range from a low of 0 to a high of .50. Although the variance of a dichotomously scored variable can be computed using the usual formula (Equation 3.8), it is often more convenient to use the following computational formula:

$$s^2 = pq$$

where

s^2 = the variance
p = the proportion of cases with scores of 1
q = the proportion of cases with scores of 0

REVIEW EXERCISES

5.1. Listed below are ages of the entire population of a small town in Texas. Construct a sampling distribution of the mean for samples of size $N = 2$ drawn from this population.

ages = 10 30 50 70 90

5.2. Plot the frequency distribution of the population data given in Review Exercise 5.1. Also plot the sampling distribution of the mean constructed in Review Exercise 5.1. Compare these distributions.

5.3. Compute the mean of the population data given in Review Exercise 5.1. Also compute the mean of the sampling distribution of the mean constructed in Review Exercise 5.1. Compare these values.

5.4. Compute the standard deviation of the sample means forming the sampling distribution of the mean constructed in Review Exercise 5.1. Also use Equation 5.1 to compute the standard error of the mean for this sampling distribution. Why do these values differ?

5.5. In the population data listed below, each case is scored 0 if female and 1 if male. Construct a sampling distribution of the proportion for samples of size $N = 2$ drawn from this population.

genders = 0 1 1 0 1

5.6. Construct 90%, 95%, and 99% confidence intervals to estimate the population mean based on the following data:

$$\overline{X} = 100$$

$$N = 50$$

$$\sigma = 15$$

5.7. Compute a 75% confidence interval to estimate the population mean based on the data given in Review Exercise 5.6.

5.8. Compute 90%, 95%, and 99% confidence intervals for the population proportion based on the following data:

$$p = \overline{X} = .8$$

$$N = 100$$

$$\sigma = .42$$

5.9. Compute an 80% confidence interval for the population proportion based on the data given in Review Exercise 5.8.

5.10. Explain how the level of confidence affects the width of the confidence interval.

5.11. Explain how data variability affects the width of the confidence interval.

5.12. Explain how sample size affects the width of the confidence interval.

5.13. Suppose you wanted to construct a 95% confidence interval for the population mean. This confidence interval is to have a total width of 6 points, and the population standard deviation is estimated to be $\sigma = 12$. How large a sample do you need?

5.14. Suppose you wanted to construct a 99% confidence interval for the population proportion. This confidence interval is to have a width of $\pm .03$, and the population standard deviation is estimated to be $\sigma = .50$. How large a sample do you need?

5.15. Using the sample ages below, construct a 90% confidence interval for the population mean.

21, 18, 19, 25, 21, 20, 24, 27, 29

5.16. In the sample data shown below, political preference (Democrat or Republican) is shown for each of 10 cases. Construct a 95% confidence interval to estimate the proportion of Republicans in the population.

Republican	Republican
Democrat	Democrat
Democrat	Republican
Republican	Republican
Democrat	Republican

ANSWERS TO COMPREHENSION CHECKS

5.1. We must be cautious when drawing conclusions about populations based on sample data because no one sample drawn from a population is likely to provide a perfect reflection of the population.

5.2. Distributions (a) and (c) are not sampling distributions. They are sample distributions that describe the distribution of scores in single samples. Distributions (b) and (d) are sampling distributions. They describe the frequency of occurrence of a sample statistic [the mean in (b) and the proportion in (d)] for all possible samples drawn from some population.

5.3. Sampling with replacement all possible samples of size $N = 2$ gives the samples shown to the right. Also shown are sample means for each sample.

Scores		$\overline{X}$
100	100	100
100	105	102.5
100	110	105
100	115	107.5
105	105	105
105	110	107.5
105	115	110
110	110	110
110	115	112.5
115	115	115

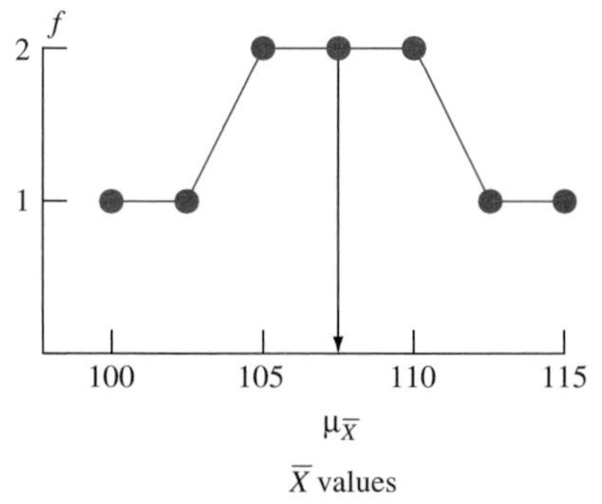

Shown next are all possible samples of size $N = 3$ and their means.

Scores			$\overline{X}$
100	100	100	100
100	100	105	101.7
100	100	110	103.3
100	100	115	105
100	105	105	103.3
100	105	110	105
100	105	115	106.7
100	110	110	106.7
100	110	115	108.3
100	115	115	110
105	105	105	105
105	105	110	106.7
105	105	115	108.3
105	110	110	108.3
105	110	115	110
105	115	115	111.7
110	110	110	110
110	110	115	111.7
110	115	115	113.3
115	115	115	115

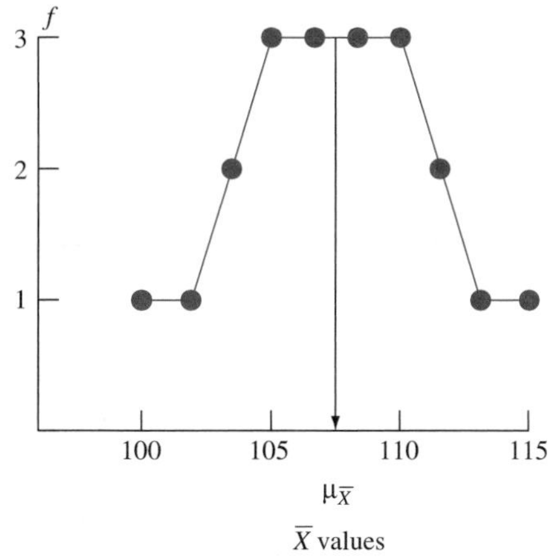

5.4. The population shows a rectangular distribution. Both sampling distributions are symmetrical, unimodal distributions. As sample size increases, the sampling distribution of the mean becomes a closer approximation to the normal distribution.

5.5. The population mean is $\mu = 107.5$. Both sampling distributions also have means of $\mu_{\overline{X}} = 107.5$. It is always true that $\mu = \mu_{\overline{X}}$.

5.6. According to Equation 5.1,

$$\sigma_{\overline{X}} = \frac{\sigma}{\sqrt{N}}$$

$$= \frac{10}{\sqrt{100}}$$

$$= 1.00$$

This is the standard deviation of the sampling distribution of the mean. A value of 1 means that the average absolute deviation of sample means around the population mean is about 1 point.

5.7. The least variability of sample means (standard error of the mean) occurs when sample size is large and data variability is low. It is under these circumstances (b) that any given sample mean would be most likely to fall close to the population mean. The greatest variability of sample means occurs when sample size is low and data variability is high. It is under these circumstances (c) that any given sample mean would be most likely to deviate substantially from the population mean.

5.8. Sampling with replacement all possible samples of size $N = 2$ gives the samples shown below. Also shown are sample proportions.

Scores		p
0	0	0
0	1	.5
0	1	.5
0	0	0
0	0	0
1	1	1
1	1	1
1	0	.5
1	0	.5
1	1	1
1	0	.5
1	0	.5
0	0	0
0	0	0
0	0	0

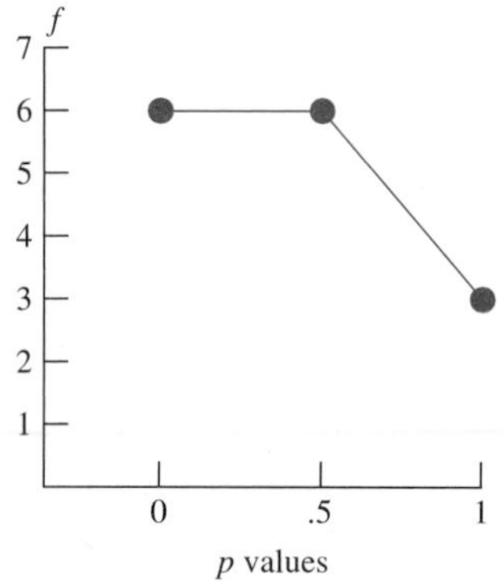

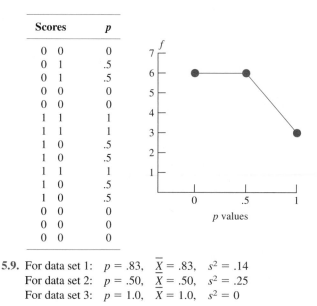

5.9. For data set 1: $p = .83$, $\overline{X} = .83$, $s^2 = .14$
For data set 2: $p = .50$, $\overline{X} = .50$, $s^2 = .25$
For data set 3: $p = 1.0$, $\overline{X} = 1.0$, $s^2 = 0$

When cases are scored dichotomously—either 0 or 1—the mean will equal the proportion of cases that scored 1. The variance of these scores is also interpretable. The last data set shows no variability (all cases scored 1), and the variance is 0. The second data set shows the greatest possible variability (with half scoring 0 and half scoring 1), and the variance of this data set is as high as it can be for dichotomous data. The first data set shows just a little variability (all but one case score 1), and the variance for these data is just a little more than 0.

5.10. Interval estimation is used when one wishes to estimate a population parameter (such as the mean or proportion) based on sample data. A confidence interval provides a range of values that has a known probability of capturing the population parameter.

5.11. Eighty percent of the sample means in a normally distributed sampling distribution are found within $\pm 1.28\sigma_{\overline{X}}$ of the center point. And 96.42% of the sample means in a normally distributed sampling distribution are found within $\pm 2.10\sigma_{\overline{X}}$ of the center point.

5.12. Provided that sample sizes are $N \geq 50$, about 80% of the samples drawn from a population will have means that fall within $\pm 1.28\sigma_{\overline{X}}$ of μ. All of these means are within $1.28\sigma_{\overline{X}}$ units of μ, and so surrounding any one of them by $\pm 1.28\sigma_{\overline{X}}$ will capture μ. About 20% of the samples will produce confidence intervals that fail to capture μ.

About 96% of the sample means would fall within $\pm 2.10\sigma_{\overline{X}}$ of μ. Surrounding any of these means with $\pm 2.10\sigma_{\overline{X}}$ would therefore capture μ. About 4% of the sample means would fall beyond $\pm 2.10\sigma_{\overline{X}}$ from μ.

5.13. When $N = 50$ and $\sigma = 15$, $\sigma_{\overline{X}} = 15/\sqrt{50} = 2.12$. Equation 5.2 defines the 90% confidence interval as

$$\overline{X} \pm 1.65\sigma_{\overline{X}}$$

$$100 \pm 1.65(2.12)$$

$$100 \pm 3.50$$

Equation 5.3 defines the 95% confidence interval as

$$\overline{X} \pm 1.96\sigma_{\overline{X}}$$

$$100 \pm 1.96(2.12)$$

$$100 \pm 4.16$$

Equation 5.4 defines the 99% confidence interval as

$$\overline{X} \pm 2.58\sigma_{\overline{X}}$$

$$100 \pm 2.58(2.12)$$

$$100 \pm 5.47$$

5.14. When $N = 50$ and $\sigma = .25$, $\sigma_{\overline{X}} = .035$. Remembering that a proportion is the same thing as a mean, we can substitute the sample proportion given ($p = .5$) for $\overline{X}$ in Equations 5.2 to 5.4. Equation 5.2 defines the 90% confidence interval as

$$\overline{X} \pm 1.65\sigma_{\overline{X}}$$

$$.5 \pm 1.65(.035)$$

$$.5 \pm .058$$

Equation 5.3 defines the 95% confidence interval as

$$\overline{X} \pm 1.96\sigma_{\overline{X}}$$

$$.5 \pm 1.96(.035)$$

$$.5 \pm .069$$

Equation 5.4 defines the 99% confidence interval as

$$\overline{X} \pm 2.58\sigma_{\overline{X}}$$

$$.5 \pm 2.58(.035)$$

$$.5 \pm .090$$

5.15. As the confidence level increases, the width of the confidence interval increases. The increase in width from the 95% to the 99% confidence interval is substantially greater than the increase from the 90% to the 95% confidence interval.

5.16. For $\sigma = 10$ and $N = 50$, $\sigma_{\overline{X}} = 1.41$. Equation 5.3 defines the 95% confidence interval as

$$\overline{X} \pm 1.96\sigma_{\overline{X}}$$

$$\overline{X} \pm 1.96(1.41)$$

$$\overline{X} \pm 2.76$$

For $\sigma = 100$ and $N = 50$, $\sigma_{\overline{X}} = 14.14$. Equation 5.3 defines the 95% confidence interval as

$$\overline{X} \pm 1.96\sigma_{\overline{X}}$$

$$\overline{X} \pm 1.96(14.14)$$

$$\overline{X} \pm 27.71$$

As data variability (σ) increases, so does the width of the confidence interval.

5.17. For $N = 50$, $\sigma_{\overline{X}} = .035$. Equation 5.3 defines the 95% confidence interval as:

$$\overline{X} \pm 1.96\sigma_{\overline{X}}$$

$$.5 \pm 1.96(.035)$$

$$.5 \pm .069$$

For $N = 500$, $\sigma_{\overline{X}} = .011$. Equation 5.3 defines the 95% confidence interval as

$$\overline{X} \pm 1.96\sigma_{\overline{X}}$$

$$.5 \pm 1.96(.011)$$

$$.5 \pm .022$$

As N increases, the width of the confidence interval decreases.

5.18. Equation 5.4 defines the 99% confidence interval as

$$\overline{X} \pm 2.58\sigma_{\overline{X}}$$

If this confidence interval is to have a width of .06, the sample mean (actually, a proportion in this case) must be surrounded on each side by .03 points: $\overline{X} \pm .03$. It follows that these two expressions are equivalent:

$$\overline{X} \pm 2.58\sigma_{\overline{X}} = \overline{X} \pm .03$$

We can eliminate the expression "$\overline{X}\pm$" from both sides of the equation:

$$2.58\sigma_{\overline{X}} = .03$$

By definition of $\sigma_{\overline{X}}$,

$$2.58\left(\frac{\sigma}{\sqrt{N}}\right) = .03$$

By substitution,

$$2.58\left(\frac{.25}{\sqrt{N}}\right) = .03$$

Dividing both sides of the equation by 2.58,

$$\frac{.25}{\sqrt{N}} = .012$$

Cross-multiplying,

$$.012\sqrt{N} = .25$$

Dividing both sides of the equation by .012,

$$\sqrt{N} = 20.83$$

Squaring both sides of the equation,

$$N = 433.89$$

5.19. For $N = 15$ and $\hat{s} = 10$, $\hat{\sigma}_{\overline{X}} = 2.58$. Equation 5.7 defines the 95% confidence interval as

$$\overline{X} \pm t_{(\text{df} = N = 1;\ .05)}\hat{\sigma}_{\overline{X}}$$

$$\overline{X} \pm t_{(\text{df} = 14;\ .05)}\hat{\sigma}_{\overline{X}}$$

$$\overline{X} \pm 2.145(2.58)$$

$$\overline{X} \pm 5.53$$

For $N = 20$ and $\hat{s} = .58$, $\hat{\sigma}_{\overline{X}} = .130$. Equation 5.8 defines the 99% confidence interval as

$$\overline{X} \pm t_{(\text{df} = N - 1;\ .01)}\hat{\sigma}_{\overline{X}}$$

Remembering that proportions are means,

$$.5 \pm t_{(\text{df} = 19;\ .01)}\hat{\sigma}_{\overline{X}}$$

$$.5 \pm 2.093(.130)$$

$$.5 \pm .272$$

6 One-Sample Significant Difference Tests

Chapter Outline

Data from the Cheating Justification Questionnaire were presented previously (see Chapter 2, Table 2.1). Scores on this questionnaire measure the tendency to justify or rationalize cheating (for instance, "Jack should not be blamed for cheating if everyone else in the room seems to be cheating"). These data, along with information about student classification (freshman, sophomore, junior, senior), age, gender, and a host of other variables, were gathered from a sample of 120 students attending a university of 6,000.

Of immediate concern to the researchers was the representativeness of the sample. Are the 120 students who responded to this survey like the student body as a whole? Can conclusions drawn from a study of volunteer respondents be extended to the entire student population? There are some indications that this sample was somewhat different than the university population. Freshmen and sophomores were overrepresented in the sample (84% of the sample versus 60% of the university population). Females were also overrepresented (62% of the sample versus 55% of the university population). And the mean age of the sample was 22.7 years, versus 25.7 for the university as a whole. Are these differences small enough to attribute to the sampling error that makes most samples slightly different from their parent populations? Or are the differences so great that we must conclude that volunteer survey respondents like those making up this sample differ systematically from the university student body? How great must the difference be between a sample and a population before we conclude that the sample is unrepresentative of that population?

Now consider this related problem. Among their other findings, the researchers reported that the mean Cheating Justification Questionnaire score was 32.92 for students who admitted to cheating in school during the preceding year. Among those who had not cheated, the mean score was 29.18. This is a difference of 3.74 points, with dishonest students showing a greater tendency to justify cheating than honest students. But maybe this difference is unique to this particular sample. If we repeated the study with a completely new sample of students, would we get the same pattern of results? How great must the difference be between two (or more) groups before we conclude that the difference is reliable, and not just a fluke of the specific samples we have examined?

Finally, consider this problem. The researchers reported that age showed a correlation of −.34 with scores on the Cheating Justification Questionnaire. We will study correlation in Chapter 10, but briefly, a correlation of −.34 signals a moderately strong inverse relationship between age and justification of cheating: As age increases, justification of cheating tends to decrease; and as age decreases, justification of cheating tends to increase. Again, though, the reliability of this finding can be questioned. This correlation was observed in the particular sample investigated. But would it be seen again if the study were repeated with an entirely new sample? Or would it disappear? How strong must a correlation be before we trust that it is reliable and replicable, and not just idiosyncratic to the sample at hand?

It seems that we have as many questions as answers here, questions pertaining to the replicability or reliability of the results obtained when we study samples. How great must the difference be between a sample and a population before we conclude that the sample is *really* unrepresentative of the population?

How big must the difference be between two or more samples before we trust that difference to be *reliable*? How strong must a correlation be before we count on it to be *replicable*? These are all issues of *statistical significance*.

COMPREHENSION CHECK 6.1

In your own words, what does it mean to say that a difference or a correlation is "statistically significant"?
(Answer on p. 182.)

6.1 WHAT IS STATISTICAL SIGNIFICANCE?

statistically significant *A statistically significant finding is a sample finding that most probably is true of the theoretical population of cases treated like the sample. A significant finding is a reliable, replicable finding.*

The meaning of statistical significance may be dawning on you from the preceding examples, but here is a formal definition. A **statistically significant** finding, be it a difference observed between a sample and population, a difference observed between two or more samples, or a correlation seen in sample data, is a reliable finding. It is a finding that would most probably be seen again in a replication involving completely new samples. A statistically significant finding is one that is probably not sample-specific, occurring in just one sample. It is a finding that would be seen again and again, in sample after sample. A statistically significant finding is reliable from one sample to the next because it describes the reality of the population from which the many samples are drawn.

COMPREHENSION CHECK 6.2

A sample of 20 couples who completed premarital counseling showed a divorce rate significantly lower than the national average after 10 years of marriage. What does the statistical significance of this finding tell us?
(Answer on p. 182.)

significance tests *Inferential statistical procedures that determine which differences are large enough and which correlations are strong enough to be considered statistically significant.*

We will begin our study of statistical significance tests in this chapter. **Significance tests** are inferential statistical procedures that help us to decide when we can generalize what we've seen in our samples to entire populations. Significance tests tell us which sample findings we can trust and which are questionable. The results of significance tests change the ways we live and do business. They affect the way we treat whole populations of people based on what we've seen in relatively small samples. Consider these examples.

- When a new Alzheimer's drug was found to produce statistically significant memory improvements in a sample of a few hundred Alzheimer's patients, the pharmaceutical company that produced the drug committed hundreds of thousands of dollars to develop it for the entire population of Alzheimer's sufferers.
- When a sample of a few dozen teenagers in a summer program for at-risk youth showed a statistically significant improvement in grades the next school year, the program sponsors redirected scarce resources to expand the program to reach even more youths the next summer.
- When personnel psychologists employed by a large corporation found a statistically significant correlation between scores on an aptitude test and

job performance in a sample of employees, the test was quickly adopted for use in screening all new hires.

Significance tests are the power tools in our statistical tool box. Indeed, phrases such as "statistically significant difference" or "significant correlation" are everywhere in the professional literature of the social and behavioral sciences. Whether one intends to become a statistical practitioner or simply a consumer of statistics, it is important to understand what statistical significance means and what it does not mean.

Comprehension Check 6.3

What do you think statistical significance *does not* mean?
(Answer on p. 182.)

6.2 Types of Significant Difference Tests

One of the differences between a good carpenter and a great carpenter lies in having (and using) the right tools for the job. This is true as well in the social and behavioral sciences, where it is important to know which significance test to use in each particular situation. All significant difference tests are used to evaluate the reliability of an observed difference, but there are some important differences from one of these procedures to the next.

Tests for significant differences vary with regard to how many samples are being compared. **One-sample significant difference tests,** like those examined in this chapter, evaluate the difference between a single sample and a population. For instance, is the cheating study sample of 120 students significantly different than the population of 6,000 university students from which the sample was drawn? This is a problem to which we would apply a one-sample difference test.

one-sample significant difference tests *Procedures used to evaluate the significance of differences observed between a sample and a larger population.*

Two-sample significant difference tests are used in comparing two samples. Is the difference between honest and dishonest students' Cheating Justification Questionnaire scores a statistically significant difference? We need a two-sample difference test to answer this question.

two-sample significant difference tests *Procedures used to evaluate the significance of differences observed between two samples.*

We can also compare three or more samples. These comparisons usually call for one of the family of statistical procedures known as **analysis of variance,** to which we turn in Chapters 8 and 9.

analysis of variance *A family of procedures used to evaluate the significance of differences observed between two or more samples.*

Comprehension Check 6.4

Indicate whether each of the following scenarios calls for a one-sample, two-sample, or analysis of variance test:

(a) A teacher wants to compare average test scores for males and females.

(b) A social worker wants to compare recidivism rates for parolees in three different rehabilitation programs.

(c) A program administrator wants to compare the average IQ of a sample of adult functional illiterates against the national average IQ.

(Answer on p. 182.)

Another way we can distinguish among the various significant difference tests is by counting how many ways the samples differ. That is, how many different independent variables define the samples? In comparing scores of males and females on the Cheating Justification Questionnaire, the samples differ on only one independent variable—gender. What if we compared dishonest males, honest males, dishonest females, and honest females? These four samples are defined by two independent variables: honesty (honest vs. dishonest) and gender (male vs. female). When two or more independent variables define the samples, a group of procedures known as **factorial analysis of variance** is useful. We will examine these procedures in Chapter 9.

factorial analysis of variance *A family of procedures used to evaluate the significance of differences between samples that are defined by two or more independent variables.*

Comprehension Check 6.5

How many independent variables define these groups?

rural male, rural female, suburban male, suburban female, urban male, urban female

(Answer on p. 182.)

Significant difference tests can also be categorized as parametric or nonparametric procedures. **Parametric tests** are based on certain assumptions about the nature of the data being analyzed. Certain data characteristics or *parameters* must be present in order for these tests to be used appropriately. Parametric tests generally assume that data have been obtained on an interval or ratio scale, distributions are normal, and variances are similar in the samples being compared. **Nonparametric tests** relax these assumptions about the parameters of the data.

parametric tests *Significance tests that assume that the data being analyzed meet certain characteristics or parameters.*

nonparametric tests *Significance tests that relax some of the assumptions associated with parametric tests.*

Finally, we can distinguish one significant difference test from another by asking what kind of difference is being evaluated. Are we looking at a difference between means? A difference between variances? A difference between distribution shapes? Each type of comparison calls for the appropriate statistical procedure.

Comprehension Check 6.6

What do you suppose happens if you use the wrong statistical significance test for the data at hand?

(Answer on p. 182.)

6.3 Uses of One-Sample Significant Difference Tests

One-sample significant difference tests are used when we want to compare the characteristics of a sample against those of a population. Two situations most commonly call for this type of comparison. First, one-sample tests are often used to determine whether or not a given sample can be considered representative of some larger population. This question normally arises in research when we need to know if the study of a particular sample will produce results that may be generalized to some larger population. In the academic cheating study, for instance, it is important to know whether the sample of 120 students is representative of the larger population of 6,000 students before sample findings are generalized to the population. It would not be a good idea, for example, to assume that the entire student body's attitude toward cheating is like that of the sample if the sample is known to differ significantly from the population on age, gender, student classification, or other variables. On the other hand, the absence of significant differences between the sample and population would clear the way for making these kinds of generalizations.

COMPREHENSION CHECK 6.7

Suppose the academic cheating study sample *does* differ significantly from the university student body as a whole. How would that limit conclusions drawn from the survey?
(Answer on p. 182.)

We can also use a one-sample significant difference test when we want to evaluate the effect of some treatment that is unique to the sample. The term **treatment** is used loosely here. A treatment may occur within the context of an experiment. We saw in Chapter 1 that an experiment always involves some kind of experimenter-controlled manipulation or handling. For example, an experimenter who gives an experimental drug to a sample of subjects might evaluate that treatment by comparing the treated sample against some larger population of untreated cases. However, in our broad use of the term, a treatment need not always be controlled or administered by the researcher. Suppose, for instance, that one wished to compare the average IQ of 100 blond females against the average IQ of the entire American adult population. The "treatment" in this **ex-post-facto** research (a type of correlational research as discussed in Chapter 1) consists of being blond and female, even though neither hair color nor gender is controlled or administered by an experimenter.

treatment *A term used loosely to refer to either: (1) an experimenter-administered manipulation or handling of some sample; or (2) some unique characteristic associated with a sample that is not under the control of the experimenter.*

ex-post-facto research *A form of research involving a comparison of preexisting groups. The treatment in this research is not under the control of an experimenter, but is a characteristic of one of the preexisting groups.*

COMPREHENSION CHECK 6.8

Identify the "treatment" in each item that follows.

(a) A sample of 100 callers to a radio talk show are significantly more politically conservative than the population of adults in the United States.
(b) The spouses of a sample of 20 Alzheimer's patients are significantly more likely to suffer depression than are those in the general population.
(c) A sample of 30 freshmen who completed a freshman orientation course are significantly more satisfied with their freshman year than are freshmen in general.

(Answer on p. 182.)

Having considered the kinds of problems that are addressed by one-sample significant difference tests, let's look at the two most commonly used tests of this type: the one-sample *t* test and the chi-square goodness-of-fit test.

6.4 THE ONE-SAMPLE *t* TEST

The **one-sample *t* test** is used to evaluate the significance of a difference observed between a sample mean and a population mean. The one-sample *t* test

one-sample *t* test *A parametric significant difference test used to evaluate the difference between a sample mean and a population mean.*

is one of several parametric statistics that we will examine in this book. As you learned previously, this means that the t test is valid only if the data being analyzed conform to certain parameters or characteristics. Specifically, the one-sample t test assumes that the dependent variable being analyzed is continuous—measured at the interval or ratio scale—and that the population from which the sample has been drawn is normally distributed. How important are these assumptions? It is generally concluded that the t test is quite **robust** to minor violations of the assumption of a normal distribution, especially as sample size increases ($N \geq 50$). In other words, the conclusions drawn from the t test aren't altered appreciably by nonnormal data, as long as one is working with a sample that is of size 50 or larger.

robustness *A statistical procedure is robust to the degree that the accuracy of its conclusions are unaffected by deviations of the data from the parametric assumptions of the procedure.*

COMPREHENSION CHECK 6.9

Which of the assumptions of the one-sample t test is the most critical?

(Answer on p. 182.)

Logic of the *t* Test

The logic of the one-sample t test—how the procedure works—will be presented in this section. This is an important section, because many of the ideas presented here apply as well to other significance tests. Some of this material is a bit abstract, but Example 6.1 provides a concrete illustration that should help you stay anchored in reality.

Null and Alternative Hypotheses. Suppose that a difference is observed between a sample mean ($\overline{X}$) and the mean of some specified population (μ). How can we explain it? One explanation for the difference, called the **null hypothesis** (symbolized H_0), is that the difference between the sample and the population can be attributed to sampling error. H_0 explains away an observed difference between $\overline{X}$ and μ by proposing that the difference is small enough to be expected in samples drawn from the specified population. It is a sample that one would see quite routinely when sampling from that population. H_0 therefore suggests that the sample at hand can be considered representative of the specified population, even though it differs somewhat from that population. H_0 concludes that there is no compelling evidence that the sample has been treated in any manner different than the specified population. In the shorthand of statistics, the null hypothesis labels the observed difference between $\overline{X}$ and μ "nonsignificant."

null hypothesis ***(H_0)*** H_0 *is an explanation of an observed difference that attributes the difference to sampling error.*

The **alternative hypothesis** (symbolized H_1) offers a completely different explanation for an observed difference between $\overline{X}$ and μ. H_1 proposes that the difference between the sample and population is too large to be expected purely on the basis of sampling error. Samples this different from the specified population are rarely seen in samples drawn from that population. Because the obtained difference between $\overline{X}$ and μ is so large as to exceed what might reasonably be expected on the basis of sampling error, the difference must be explained in some other way. H_1 concludes that the sample has been treated in some manner that makes it different than the comparison population. The sample does not represent the specified population, but represents some other population instead. Which population? The theoretical population of all cases treated just like the sample at hand. Put succinctly, the

alternative hypothesis **(H_1)** H_1 *is an explanation of an observed difference that attributes the difference to the operation of something more than sampling error—a treatment effect.*

alternative hypothesis labels the observed difference between $\overline{X}$ and μ "statistically significant."

Under what circumstances would a researcher hope to attribute a difference to H_0? When would H_1 be a more welcome explanation?
(Answer on p. 182.)

COMPREHENSION CHECK 6.10

The Test Statistic. These two explanations for the observed difference between $\overline{X}$ and μ are mutually exclusive, and one or the other must be true. We need some way to choose between them. This is accomplished using a **test statistic.** A test statistic is a statistic (that is, a number computed from the data) that varies in value as a function of the size of the difference being tested for significance. A test statistic gives us a standardized way of measuring the difference that we are testing for significance. We don't evaluate the difference between $\overline{X}$ and μ directly. We evaluate the difference indirectly, using a test statistic that reflects this difference. In the case of the one-sample t test, the test statistic is t, computed according to Equation 6.1.

test statistic *A number computed from data (i.e., a statistic) which varies in value as a function of the size of the difference (or correlation) being tested for significance.*

Equation 6.1

$$t = \frac{\overline{X} - \mu}{\hat{\sigma}_{\overline{X}}}$$

where

t = the one-sample test statistic t
$\overline{X}$ = the sample mean
μ = the population mean
$\hat{\sigma}_{\overline{X}}$ = the estimated standard error of the mean (from Equation 5.5)

In words, the one-sample t statistic (t) is computed by: (1) subtracting the population mean (μ) from the sample mean ($\overline{X}$); and (2) dividing this difference by the estimated standard error of the mean ($\hat{\sigma}_{\overline{X}}$), computed using Equation 5.5.

The 120 students who responded to the academic cheating survey showed a mean age of $\overline{X} = 22.7$ and a standard deviation of $\hat{s} = 15.2$. The mean age of the student body population was 25.7. Use Equation 6.1 to compute the test statistic t for these data.
(Answer on p. 182.)

COMPREHENSION CHECK 6.11

You can see from the numerator of Equation 6.1 that the t statistic directly reflects the $\overline{X} - \mu$ difference being tested for significance. You can see from the denominator of the equation that this $\overline{X} - \mu$ difference is measured using $\hat{\sigma}_{\overline{X}}$ as a yardstick. We will look more later at the role played by $\hat{\sigma}_{\overline{X}}$ in the t statistic, but for now notice simply that as the $\overline{X} - \mu$ difference increases, so does the absolute value of t. If $\overline{X} = \mu$, t will be 0. If $\overline{X} > \mu$, t will be positive. And if $\overline{X} < \mu$, t will be negative.

The Sampling Distribution of *t*. The test statistic t provides a way of measuring the difference between $\overline{X}$ and μ. Next, we need to determine whether or not this difference, as represented by t, is likely (H_0) or unlikely (H_1) to be the simple result of sampling error. This is made possible by the sampling distribution of t, to which we will now turn.

sampling distribution of ***t*** *The theoretical distribution of values of the* t *statistic obtained when all possible samples of size* N *are drawn from a population and the* t *statistic is computed for each sample.*

Imagine drawing all possible samples of size N from some specified population and computing t for each sample according to Equation 6.1. Because all of these samples have come from the same specified population, we know that they have all been treated exactly like that population. Even so, the values of t obtained from one sample to the next will vary somewhat just because of sampling error. The resulting distribution of t values is called the **sampling distribution of** t and is shown in Figure 6.1. The single most frequently occurring value of t is 0, which occurs in samples in which $\overline{X} = \mu$. It makes sense that t should equal 0 more often than any other single value, because the single most likely outcome when sampling from a population is that $\overline{X}$ will equal μ. Figure 6.1 shows relatively few very large absolute values of t. That is because these large values of t depend on large $\overline{X} - \mu$ differences. Such large differences can and do occur when one samples from a population, but they occur very infrequently.

COMPREHENSION CHECK 6.12

Fill in the blanks: The __________ distribution of t depicts the relative __________ of occurrence of values of the ______ statistic computed for ______ __________ samples of size N drawn from a specified __________.

(Answer on p. 182.)

Figure 6.1 also shows that the shape of the sampling distribution of t changes depending on sample size. When samples are small, the sampling distribution is flatter than a normal distribution. As sample sizes increase, the sampling distribution of t comes closer and closer to approximating the normal distribution. That the t distribution changes shape depending on N shouldn't come as a complete surprise if you remember from Chapter 5 that the sampling distribution of the mean also changes shape as sample sizes change.

The shape of the t distribution depends on the shape of the population from which samples are drawn as well as on sample size. Especially when samples are small, the sampling distribution of t will echo any deviations from normality that are present in the population distribution.

With the shape of the sampling distribution of t varying both with sample size and with the shape of the population distribution, keeping track of the

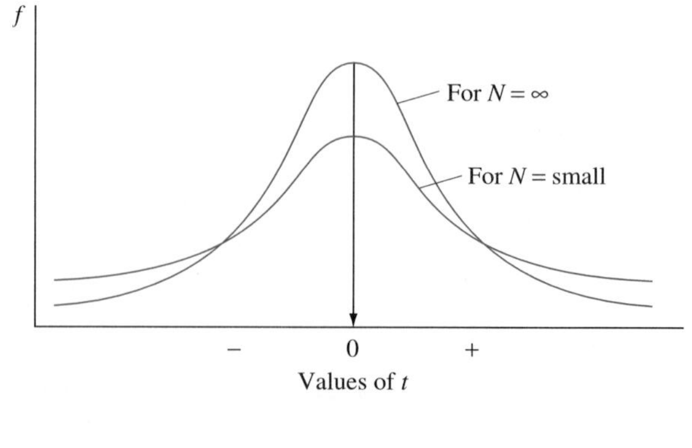

FIGURE 6.1

The sampling distribution of t is the theoretical distribution of values of the t statistic for all possible samples of size N drawn from some population. The shape of the t distribution varies with sample size.

shape of the t distribution can get complicated. It is for this reason that we assume a normal population distribution when we use the one-sample t test. That way we only have to keep track of sample size.

Table 2 in Appendix B, "Critical values of the t statistic," describes how the sampling distribution of t varies with sample size. Take a look at this table. The values listed in the main body of the table are the **critical values** of t that mark off the upper and lower tails of the sampling distribution of t, the so-called **critical regions** shaded in Figure 6.2, below. The proportions of samples with values of t located in these tails (and thus the probabilities of obtaining these samples from a population) are given by the columns headed "Level of significance." The column labeled "df" refers to degrees of freedom, a term that means essentially the same thing as sample size here, because df $= N - 1$ for the one-sample t-test.(See Note 1)

critical values *Values of a test statistic that mark the extreme tail(s) of the sampling distribution of that test statistic. Values exceeding the critical values are considered "unlikely" to occur as a result of sampling error alone.*

critical regions *The extreme tail(s) of the sampling distribution of a test statistic. Values falling within the critical regions are considered "unlikely" to occur as a result of sampling error alone.*

An example will clarify how the table of critical values of t is used. Figure 6.2a depicts the sampling distribution of t that results when all possible samples of size $N = 20$ (df $= N - 1 = 19$) are drawn from a specified population and the t statistic is computed for each sample. To find the critical value of t that marks off the upper 5% of the distribution (or .05, expressed as a proportion), first find df $= 19$ in the left-hand column of the table. Next, find the value .05 in the column labeled "Level of significance for one-tail test." Scan down that column until you reach the row marked by df $= 19$. There you will find the critical value of t: 1.729. This is the value of t that marks off the upper 5% tail of the distribution. Only 5% of the samples drawn from a population produce values of t this large or larger. Thus the probability that a sample drawn from a specified population will produce a value of t greater than or equal to 1.729 is less than 5%. Or, as this is commonly abbreviated, $p < .05$.

What about the other end of the distribution? What is the critical value of t that marks the lower 5% tail? Because the t distribution is symmetrical (assuming a normal population distribution), the critical value of t for df $= 19$ and a .05 level of significance is -1.729. And again, the probability is less than 5% ($p < .05$) that a sample drawn from a specified population will produce a value of t this negative or more strongly negative.

COMPREHENSION CHECK 6.13

Using the data presented in Comprehension Check 6.11, find the critical values of t that mark: (a) the upper 5% tail of the sampling distribution of t; (b) the lower 1% tail of the sampling distribution of t.
(Answer on p. 182.)

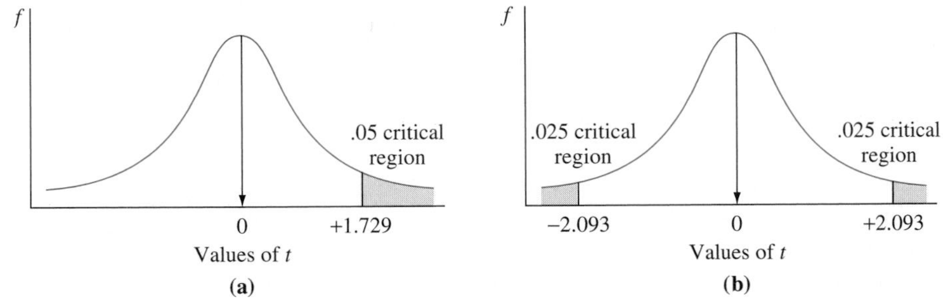

FIGURE 6.2

The sampling distribution of t for $N = 20$ (df $= 19$). (a) shows the critical value of $t = 1.729$ that marks the upper .05 critical region. (b) shows the critical values of $t = \pm 2.093$ that mark the two regions that *together* capture 5% of the values of t.

There is one additional feature of the table of critical values of t to consider here, the difference between one-tail and two-tail significance levels. We have just seen that the values of t listed under the columns labeled "Levels of significance for one-tail test" mark off critical regions at one end *or* the other end of the distribution (thus the phrase "one-tail significance"). In contrast, values of t listed under the columns labeled "Level of significance for two-tail test" mark off critical regions at *both* ends of the distribution, which *combine* to capture a specified total percentage of the samples. Consider Figure 6.2b. What values of t mark off the upper and lower tails that *together* contain 5% of the samples? As before, find df = 19. Now, find the .05 level of significance for two-tail tests. Scan down that column until you get to the row marked by df = 19. There you will find the critical value of t: 2.093. This is the absolute value of t that marks off the two critical regions that together capture 5% of the samples—2.5% in the upper tail and 2.5% in the lower tail. We will have more to say later about one- vs. two-tail significance tests.

COMPREHENSION CHECK 6.14

Using the data presented in Comprehension Check 6.11, find the absolute value of t that marks off the upper and lower critical regions that *together* capture: (a) 5% of the samples; (b) 1% of the samples. (Answer on p. 182.)

Choosing Between the Null and Alternative Hypotheses. To review quickly, the one-sample t test begins with the observation that there is a difference between $\overline{X}$ and μ. H_0 attributes this difference to sampling error and says that a difference of this size is quite likely to occur in a sample drawn from the specified population. H_1 says that a difference of this size is too big to be due just to sampling error. The sample is unrepresentative of the specified population, and better represents some other population. The test statistic t is used to provide a standardized way of measuring the obtained $\overline{X} - \mu$ difference. The sampling distribution of t is the distribution of values of t obtained when all possible samples of size N are drawn from a population and t is computed for each sample.

In the final step of the significance testing process, we choose between the null and alternative hypotheses by comparing the obtained value of t against the sampling distribution of t. This comparison enables determining the likelihood that the obtained t is a result of simple sampling error (H_0) or the result of something more than sampling error (H_1).

COMPREHENSION CHECK 6.15

Suppose a sample produces a value of t that falls within the 5% critical region of the sampling distribution of t. Is this a sample that is likely or unlikely to have been drawn from the specified population? Is this a value of t that is more likely to be explained by H_0 or H_1? (Answer on p. 182.)

What if the obtained value of t is rarely seen in samples drawn from the specified population, that is, in the sampling distribution of t? (By "rarely," it is commonly meant 5% or less of the time. Obtained test statistic values that meet or exceed the critical values listed for the .05 level of significance meet this definition of "rarely.") Under these circumstances we conclude that the sample that produced the obtained t value is quite unlikely to have been drawn from the specified population. Sampling error alone is unlikely ($p < .05$) to produce a $\overline{X} - \mu$ difference and corresponding t this large. The sample is unrepresentative of the specified population and is therefore more representative of some other population—specifically, the theoretical population of all cases treated like the sample at hand. In coming to this conclusion we have rejected H_0, and the $\overline{X} - \mu$ difference is declared "statistically significant."

COMPREHENSION CHECK 6.16

Suppose a sample produces a value of t that falls in the middle portion of the sampling distribution of t, outside the critical regions. Is this a sample that is likely or unlikely to have been drawn from the specified population? Is this a value of t that is more likely to be explained by H_0 or H_1?
(Answer on p. 182.)

On the other hand, what if the obtained value of t *is* seen commonly in samples drawn from the specified population? (The generally agreed-upon standard defining what is "common" is 95%. Thus, any value of the test statistic that fails to meet or exceed the critical values listed for the .05 level of significance would be considered a "common" value.) Under these circumstances we would conclude that the sample that yielded this t value is quite likely to have been drawn from the specified population. The sample is representative of that population and differs by no more than can be explained through the action of sampling error. Here we accept H_0 as a reasonable explanation for the observed $\overline{X} - \mu$ difference, and the difference is declared nonsignificant.

One-Tail vs. Two-Tail *t* Tests

One-tail vs. two-tail significance levels were mentioned briefly above. Let us consider now which circumstances call for using one-tail values and which call for two-tail values.

one-tail significance test *A one-tail* t *test is used when one has predicted the direction of the difference in advance.*

One-tail significance tests are used when the researcher has predicted in advance of collecting data the direction of the difference being tested for significance. Consider this example. Psychopodiatrist Dr. Claude Hopper treats feetal anxiety with implosion therapy. He locks his patients barefooted in a room for 24 hours on the theory that they will discover that they have nothing to fear from their feet. To evaluate this innovative treatment, Dr. Hopper intends to compare the mean feetal anxiety of his treatment sample against the mean of the much larger population of feetal anxiety patients who have received more conventional therapies elsewhere. Dr. Hopper has predicted that the mean feetal anxiety of his sample ($\overline{X}$) will be lower than the population's mean (μ). This is a directional prediction. Confirmation of Dr. Hopper's prediction depends on his obtaining a t value within the critical region on the negative side of the sampling distribution of t. This is the only critical region of the sampling distribution of t in which Dr. Hopper is interested. The one-tail critical value of t that marks this one tail is listed under "One-tail significance levels." In sum, we use one-tail significance tests when we have predicted in advance the direction of the difference.

Consider now an example of a situation that calls for a two-tail test. The American Feetal Anxiety Foundation ("A foot is a terrible thing to waste") is also interested in evaluating Dr. Hopper's implosion technique. Somewhat less optimistic than Dr. Hopper, though, foundation researchers suspect that implosion therapy may be as likely to exacerbate as alleviate feetal anxiety. A difference between Dr. Hopper's sample and the population in *either* direction is important in their evaluation of Dr. Hopper's treatment. Thus, either a positive or negative value of t is relevant and needs to be evaluated. Both tails of the sampling distribution of t must be considered. Anytime we believe that there may be a difference between a sample and the population as a whole, but we are unable to predict in advance the direction of that difference, either a large positive or large negative t value would be of interest to us, and a **two-tail significance test** is appropriate.

two-tail significance test *A two-tail* t *test is used when one has not predicted the direction of the difference in advance.*

COMPREHENSION CHECK 6.17

Does the significance test for the data presented in Comprehension Check 6.11 call for a one-sample or two-sample t test? Find the appropriate critical values of t for the .05 level of significance. Is there a significant difference between the mean age of the academic cheating sample and the general student population?

(Answer on p. 182.)

EXAMPLE 6.1

One-Sample t Test

Administrators at Red Rum State Psychiatric Center believe that they have developed the most inefficient admissions procedure in the entire state hospital system. In the last 100 admissions at Red Rum, the average number of separate forms requiring completion was $\overline{X} = 34$. Some patients required slightly more, and some less, with a corrected sample standard deviation of $\hat{s} = 6$.

Believing that they may have a shot at winning the Inter-Agency Red Tape Competition this year, the administrators at Red Rum want to see if their admissions process is significantly more cumbersome than the state average of 28 forms per admission. A one-sample t test is used for this purpose.

Null and Alternative Hypotheses

H_0: The difference between the sample mean ($\overline{X} = 34$) and the population mean ($\mu = 28$) is a consequence of sampling error. A sample drawn from the specified population would be likely to deviate by the amount observed here. Therefore, there is no evidence that the difference should be attributed to the different admissions process used at Red Rum.

H_1: The difference between the sample and population is too large to be attributed reasonably to sampling error alone. A sample drawn from the specified population of state hospitals and treated like the other samples in that population would be very unlikely to deviate by the amount seen here. The Red Rum sample, therefore, is unrepresentative of the state hospital population. Instead, it represents a different population, the theoretical population of hospitals using the Red Rum admissions process.

Test Statistic

The one-sample t statistic is computed according to Equation 6.1:

$$t = \frac{\overline{X} - \mu}{\hat{\sigma}_{\overline{X}}} \quad \text{where} \quad \hat{\sigma}_{\overline{X}} = \frac{\hat{s}}{\sqrt{N}}$$

$$= \frac{34 - 28}{.6} \qquad = \frac{6}{\sqrt{100}}$$

$$= 10.0 \qquad = .6$$

Choosing Between H_0 and H_1

The obtained t statistic is compared against the sampling distribution of t to determine if it is likely (H_0) or unlikely (H_1) to occur in samples drawn from the specified population. The table of critical values of t (Table 2 in Appendix B) provides details about this sampling distribution. For df $= N - 1 = 100 - 1 = 99$, the critical value of t marking the .0005 critical region is 3.460. (Note: Because there is no listing in the table for 99 degrees of freedom, we use the next lower listing, df = 60. A one-tail significance level is used for this test because the administrators at Red Rum predicted in advance that their procedure would involve more paperwork than the state average.) This sampling distribution of t is depicted below.

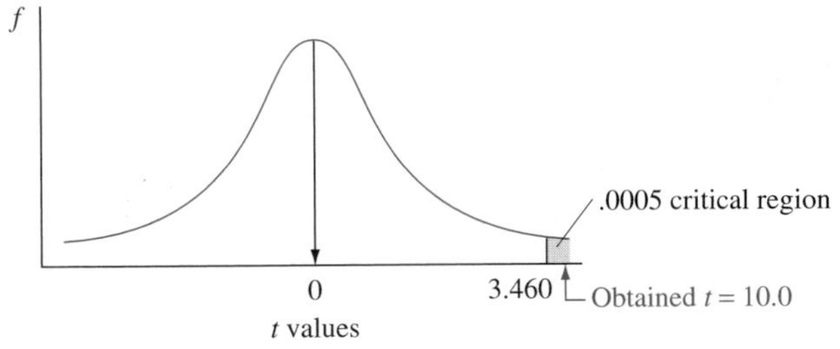

The obtained value of $t = 10.0$ falls well within the .0005 critical region. We can conclude that this value, and the difference it represents, occurs very infrequently in samples drawn from the specified population of state hospitals. The difference cannot be attributed reasonably to simple sampling error. Instead, it is a likely result of the different admissions process used at Red Rum. The difference is declared statistically significant—H_1. Although Red Rum may not win the Red Tape award this year, it won't be for lack of inefficiency.

6.5 The Chi-Square Goodness-of-Fit Test

The one-sample t test is very useful in evaluating the difference between a sample mean and a population mean, but samples and populations can differ in ways that don't involve central tendency. Figure 6.3 illustrates several examples of this. In none of these situations would a t test be useful, because all of the distributions have identical means. Clearly, though, the distributions differ dramatically in their other characteristics.

COMPREHENSION CHECK 6.18

Figure 6.3 does not exhaust all the ways in which two distributions can have identical means, yet differ in shape. Can you think of any other possibilities?

(Answer on p. 182.)

chi-square goodness-of-fit test *A nonparametric significant difference test used to compare an entire sample distribution against a population distribution.*

We need something other than a *t* test to assess differences that involve whole distributions—the **chi-square goodness-of-fit test.** The chi-square test (symbolized χ^2) is an example of a nonparametric statistic. Nonparametric statistics relax some of the assumptions of the parametric statistics. Where the *t* test assumes that the population distribution is normal, the χ^2 goodness-of-fit test makes no such assumption. Where the *t* test assumes continuous data, the χ^2 test can be used to compare sample and population distributions on discontinuous (nominal scale) variables.

With all this flexibility working for the χ^2 test, you might wonder why anyone ever uses the *t* test. Why not just always use χ^2? The answer is simple. When the assumptions of the *t* test are met, it provides a much more powerful test of the difference between sample and population central tendencies than does χ^2. To put this another way, a given difference between sample and population means is more likely to be found statistically significant with the *t* test than with the χ^2 test.

COMPREHENSION CHECK 6.19

Indicate for each scenario below whether the *t* test or the χ^2 test would be more suitable.

(a) A teacher wants to know if the distribution of male scores on a statistics test is more variable than the distribution of female scores.

(b) A teacher wants to know if the mean male score on a statistics test differs from the mean female score.

(Answer on p. 182.)

Logic of the Chi-Square Test

The logic of the chi-square goodness-of-fit test is much the same as for the *t* test. Only the test statistic and sampling distribution change. Example 6.2 at

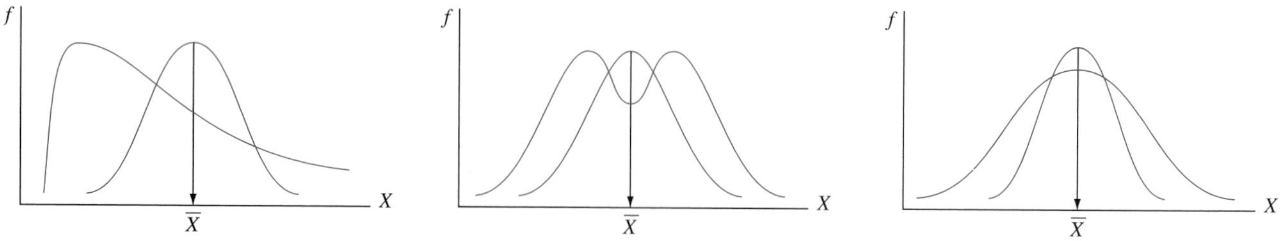

FIGURE 6.3

Distributions that show equal means can still be quite different in their other characteristics.

the end of this section provides a concrete example of the χ^2 goodness-of-fit test.

Null and Alternative Hypotheses. The χ^2 goodness-of-fit test begins with the observation that there is some difference between a sample distribution and a population distribution. As an example, the distribution of student classifications in the academic cheating study sample showed a disproportionately large number of freshmen and sophomores and a disproportionately small number of juniors and seniors in comparison to the student population. How are we to explain this difference?

The null hypothesis, as always, attributes the difference between sample and population distributions to sampling error. According to this explanation, a sample drawn from the specified population would likely show a distribution as deviant as that observed. The sample can still be considered representative of the population, though, and the difference is nonsignificant.

The alternative hypothesis, as always, describes the difference between sample and population distributions as being greater than can reasonably be attributed to sampling error alone. It is improbable that a sample drawn from the specified population would have a distribution so deviant from the population. The sample is unrepresentative of the specified population, and is therefore more representative of some other population. The difference is statistically significant.

COMPREHENSION CHECK 6.20

Do you suppose that researchers analyzing the academic cheating study data would be happier to attribute the observed difference between their sample and the student population to H_0 or H_1?

(Answer on p. 183.)

The χ^2 Test Statistic. Next we need a test statistic: a number computed from the data that varies in value as a function of the size of the difference being tested for significance. The test statistic for the goodness-of-fit test is χ^2. χ^2 takes on a value of 0 when the sample and population distributions are identical and increases in value as the distributions become increasingly discrepant.

It will be helpful in learning how to compute χ^2 to use an example. Table 6.1 presents the population and sample distributions of student classification from the academic cheating study. Values listed under "Population %"

TABLE 6.1

Student classification distributions for the study of student cheating. Population % figures describe the student population as a whole. Observed frequencies (f_o) describe the sample. Expected frequencies (f_e) indicate numbers of students one would expect to see in each student classification category if the sample and population were distributed identically.

		Sample	
Student Classification	**Population %**	f_o	f_e
Freshmen/Sophomores	60%	101	72
Juniors/Seniors	40%	19	48
		$N = 120$	

describe the distribution of students in the entire university population: 60% were freshmen and sophomores; 40% were juniors and seniors. Listed under "Sample" are two columns: observed frequencies, symbolized f_o, and expected frequencies, symbolized f_e. Observed frequencies are the numbers of cases that were observed in each of the student classification categories: There were 101 freshmen and sophomores and 19 juniors and seniors in the academic cheating study sample, for a total of $N = 120$ cases. Expected frequencies are the numbers of cases that one would expect to see in each student classification category *if the sample were distributed exactly like the population.* Let's see how these expected frequencies are determined. We know that 60% of the population consisted of freshmen and sophomores. If the sample were distributed exactly like the population, what percentage of the sample should be freshmen and sophomores? Right—60%. But *how many* students is this? Sixty percent of 120 cases gives us an expected frequency of 72 ($.60 \times 120 = 72$). The expected frequency for the category of juniors and seniors is determined in the same manner. We know that 40% of the population consists of juniors and seniors. If the sample were distributed exactly like the population, we would expect to see 40% of the sample consisting of juniors and seniors as well. Forty percent of 120 cases gives us an expected frequency of 48 ($.40 \times 120 = 48$).

COMPREHENSION CHECK 6.21

The following table summarizes the percentages of cases found in specified z-score intervals in a normal distribution. In a sample of 260 cases, how many cases would one expect to see in each score interval if the sample were normally distributed?

Population Normal Distribution		**Sample**	
z scores	%	f_o	f_e
−3 to −2	2.14	18	
−2 to −1	13.59	40	
−1 to 0	34.13	85	
0 to +1	34.13	90	
+1 to +2	13.59	25	
+2 to +3	2.14	2	
		$N = 260$	

(Answer on p. 183.)

Compare the observed and expected frequencies in Table 6.1. The expected frequencies tell us how many people we should see in each student classification category if the sample and population were distributed identically. However, you can see in Table 6.1 that the expected frequencies are not exactly equal to the observed frequencies. This tells us that the sample is distributed somewhat differently than the population. The χ^2 statistic, computed according to Equation 6.2, enables us to quantify the magnitude of this difference.

Equation 6.2

$$\chi^2 = \Sigma\frac{(f_o - f_e)^2}{f_e}$$

where

χ^2 = the chi-square test statistic
f_o = the frequency observed in each category of the dependent variable
f_e = the frequency expected in each category of the dependent variable if the sample and population were distributed identically

In words, the χ^2 statistic is computed by: (1) subtracting each category's expected frequency (f_e) from that category's observed frequency (f_o); (2) squaring each of these differences; (3) dividing each of the values obtained in step 2 by that category's expected frequency; and (4) summing the values obtained in step 3.

COMPREHENSION CHECK 6.22

Use Equation 6.2 to compute χ^2 for the data presented in Comprehension Check 6.21.
Use Equation 6.2 to compute χ^2 for the data presented in Table 6.1.
(Answer on p. 183.)

The χ^2 statistic measures the overall amount of deviation between the sample and population distributions accumulated across all of the categories of the dependent variable. When there is no difference between the sample and population distributions, such that all f_o and f_e values are the same, χ^2 will equal 0. As the sample and population become more discrepant, such that the f_o and f_e values become more divergent, χ^2 will grow increasingly large. Thus, the χ^2 statistic meets our definition of a test statistic: a value computed from the data that varies as a function of the size of the difference being tested for significance.

The Sampling Distribution of χ^2. We saw previously that the sampling distribution of the *t* statistic enables us to determine the likelihood that any given sample's *t* value would occur in samples drawn from a specified population. The **sampling distribution of χ^2** serves this same purpose for the χ^2 statistic.

sampling distribution of χ^2 *The theoretical distribution of values of the χ^2 statistic obtained when all possible samples of size* N *are drawn from a population and the χ^2 statistic is computed for each sample.*

Imagine some large population. Now imagine drawing all possible samples of size *N* from that population and computing the χ^2 statistic for each sample according to Equation 6.2. From one sample to the next we would expect the χ^2 value to vary somewhat, simply because of sampling error. Most of the sample distributions would provide a fairly good fit to the population distribution. These samples would produce fairly low χ^2 values. A few samples would show distributions quite different than the population distribution. These samples would produce larger χ^2 values. A plot of the frequency of occurrence of these χ^2 values gives us the sampling distribution of χ^2 as depicted in Figure 6.4. The most frequently occurring values in the χ^2 sampling distribution are relatively low, because most samples drawn from a population will

FIGURE 6.4

The sampling distribution of χ^2 is the theoretical distribution of values of the χ^2 statistic for all possible samples of size N drawn from some population. The shape of the χ^2 distribution varies with degrees of freedom (df = $k - 1$, where k = the number of categories of the dependent variable).

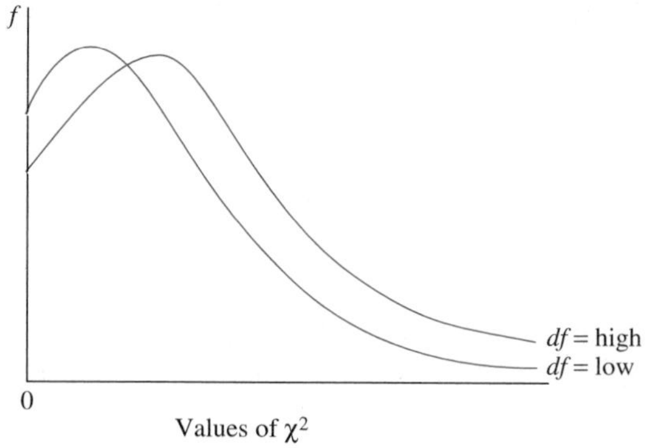

not deviate very much from that population and will produce low values of χ^2. Higher χ^2 values occur less and less frequently because these values occur only in those relatively few samples whose distributions deviate strongly from the population distribution.

Figure 6.4 also shows that the shape of the sampling distribution of χ^2 changes shape depending on degrees of freedom (df). You should be comfortable by now with the idea that sampling distributions are shape changers, varying with the number of degrees of freedom. In the case of the χ^2 distribution, degrees of freedom are computed as df $= k - 1$, where k = the number of categories of the dependent variable. Table 3 in Appendix B provides more information about the χ^2 sampling distribution. The table of critical values of χ^2 lists the critical values of χ^2 that mark off selected critical regions in the tail of the χ^2 distribution. Unlike the t statistic, there are no negative values of χ^2, because each $f_o - f_e$ difference is squared in computing χ^2. Thus, all of the tabled values refer to the right-hand tail of the χ^2 distribution. The χ^2 table is used pretty much like the table of critical values of t. Degrees of freedom (df) are listed in the left-hand column of the table, significance levels are listed across the top of the table, and the critical value of χ^2 is found in the main body of the table at the intersection of the appropriate df and significance level values.

COMPREHENSION CHECK 6.23

Find the critical values of χ^2 for the .05 and .01 significance levels for the data presented in Comprehension Check 6.21.
Find the same critical values for the academic cheating study data presented in Table 6.1.
(Answer on p. 183.)

Choosing Between the Null and Alternative Hypotheses. To review, the χ^2 goodness-of-fit test begins with the observation that there is a difference between a sample distribution and a specified population distribution. H_0 attributes this difference to sampling error and says that a difference of the magnitude observed is quite likely to occur in a sample drawn from the specified population. H_1 says that a difference of the observed size is too big to be due just to sampling error. A sample this different is unlikely to have been drawn from the specified population and is more representative of some different population. The test statistic χ^2 is used to measure the observed difference between the sample and population distributions. The sampling distribution of χ^2 is the distribution of values of χ^2 obtained when all possible samples of size N are drawn from the specified population and χ^2 is computed for each sample.

In the final step of the significance testing process, we choose between the null and alternative hypotheses by comparing the obtained value of χ^2 against the sampling distribution of χ^2. This comparison enables determining the likelihood that the obtained χ^2 is a result of simple sampling error (H_0) or the result of something more than sampling error (H_1).

If the obtained value of χ^2 is seen commonly in samples drawn from the specified population (that is, χ^2 falls outside the critical region), it follows that the sample that yielded this χ^2 value is representative of the population. We accept H_0 and conclude that any difference between the sample and population distributions is attributable to sampling error. The difference is nonsignificant.

On the other hand, if the obtained χ^2 is seldom obtained from samples drawn from the specified population (that is, χ^2 falls within the critical region), it tells us that the sample that yielded this χ^2 value is unrepresentative of the population. The difference between this sample and the population is too great to be a likely result of sampling error alone. Something more must be at work, perhaps some treatment unique to the sample. We reject H_0, accept H_1, and declare the difference to be statistically significant.

Comprehension Check 6.24

Is there a significant difference between the sample distribution and normal population distribution in Comprehension Check 6.21?
Is there a significant difference between the student classification distributions presented in Table 6.1? What implication does this have for interpreting the results of the academic cheating survey?
(Answer on p. 183.)

Small Expected Frequencies

The χ^2 statistic has one annoying feature. It doesn't work at all well when the data produce low expected frequencies. Suppose you were comparing a sample and population on a dependent variable consisting of $k = 6$ categories. Suppose further that in one of these categories $f_o = 5$ and $f_e = 1$. Based on this information alone, we already know that χ^2 is statistically significant. Let's compute χ^2:

$$\chi^2 = \Sigma\frac{(f_o - f_e)^2}{f_e}$$

$$= \frac{(5 - 1)^2}{1} + \frac{(?)}{?} + \frac{(?)}{?} + \frac{(?)}{?} + \frac{(?)}{?} + \frac{(?)}{?}$$

$$= 16 + ?$$

Without knowing anything about the observed or expected frequencies for the other five categories, we already know that χ^2 will be at least 16. For df $= k - 1 = 5$, the critical value of χ^2 for the .05 significance level is 11.07.

Regardless of what data appear in the unknown categories of the variable, the outcome of the χ^2 test has been determined. Worse yet, χ^2 is statistically significant because of a difference of only 4 cases between observed and expected frequencies. When expected frequencies are small, even a slight difference between distributions can generate a significant χ^2 value.

Because of this, it is recommended that when $k = 2$, both expected frequencies should be 5 or larger. When $k > 2$, the χ^2 goodness-of-fit test should not be used if more than 20% of the expected frequencies are less than 5 or if any expected frequency is less than 1. When expected frequencies are small, it is sometimes possible to combine or eliminate categories of the dependent variable to obtain expected frequencies that are sufficiently large. As an alternative, one may add data from more cases to increase the sizes of expected frequencies.

COMPREHENSION CHECK 6.25

The column of the table below labeled "Population" describes the distribution of letter grades for all sections of an introductory sociology class. The column labeled "Sample f_e" lists expected frequencies for a sample of size $N = 20$.

Grades	Population	Sample f_e ($N = 20$)
A	15%	3
B	25%	5
C	29%	5.8
D	20%	4
F	11%	2.2

(a) Combine grade categories to eliminate expected frequencies lower than 5.

(b) Keep the original grade categories, but determine how large a sample you must have to eliminate expected frequencies lower than 5.

(Answer on p. 183.)

EXAMPLE 6.2

Chi-Square Goodness-of-Fit Test

The marketing firm of Conum, Dupum, and Lie has been hired to market a new cola, Burpee. Their consumer psychologists have recruited a sample of 80 taste testers to try Burpee and give their reactions. In order to make sure that the sample of taste testers is representative of the cola-drinking population, though, the researchers want to compare their sample's distribution of cola preferences against that of the U.S. population.

The population percentages shown below reflect cola preferences in the United States, based on market share. Also shown below are the numbers of taste testers in the sample who reported favoring each cola variety (f_o).

		Sample	
Cola	**Population %**	f_o	f_e
Same Old Soda	25%	18	20.0
Old Brown	20%	12	16.0
Sweet One	14%	13	11.2
Econocola	10%	15	8.0
Tickle	9%	6	7.2
Zippy	7%	8	5.6
Other	15%	8	12.0

Since two entire distributions are to be compared, the chi-square goodness-of-fit test is appropriate.

Null and Alternative Hypotheses

H_0: The difference between the sample and population distributions is a consequence of sampling error. A sample drawn from the specified population of cola drinkers would be likely to deviate by the amount observed here. Therefore, the sample can be considered representative of the population.

H_1: The difference between the sample and population distributions is too large to be attributed to sampling error alone. A sample drawn from the specified population of U.S. cola drinkers would be very unlikely to deviate by the amount observed here. Therefore the sample does not represent the specified population, but rather some other, different population.

Test Statistic

We need observed frequencies (f_o) and expected frequencies (f_e) to compute the χ^2 test statistic. Observed frequencies are provided above. These are the numbers of taste testers who expressed a preference for each listed cola. Expected frequencies are the numbers of cases we would expect to express a preference for each cola *if the sample and population distributions were identical.* Because 25% of the population prefers Same Old Soda, we would expect this same percentage of the sample to prefer that cola: $.25 \times 80 = 20.0$. Similarly, because 20% of the population prefers Old Brown, we would expect this same percentage of the sample to prefer that cola: $.20 \times 80 = 16.0$. The remaining expected frequencies were computed in a similar manner and are listed above.

The χ^2 statistic is computed according to Equation 6.2:

$$\chi^2 = \Sigma \frac{(f_o - f_e)^2}{f_e}$$

$$= \frac{(18 - 20)^2}{20} + \frac{(12 - 16)^2}{16} + \ldots + \frac{(8 - 12)^2}{12}$$

$$= 10.18$$

Choosing Between H_0 *and* H_1

The obtained χ^2 statistic is compared against the sampling distribution of χ^2 to determine if it is likely (H_0) or unlikely (H_1) to occur in samples drawn from the specified population. The table of critical values of χ^2 (Table 3 in Appendix B) provides details about this sampling distribution. For df $= k - 1 = 7 - 1 = 6$ (where $k =$ the number of categories in the dependent variable), the critical value of χ^2 marking the .05 critical region is 12.592. This sampling distribution of χ^2 is depicted below.

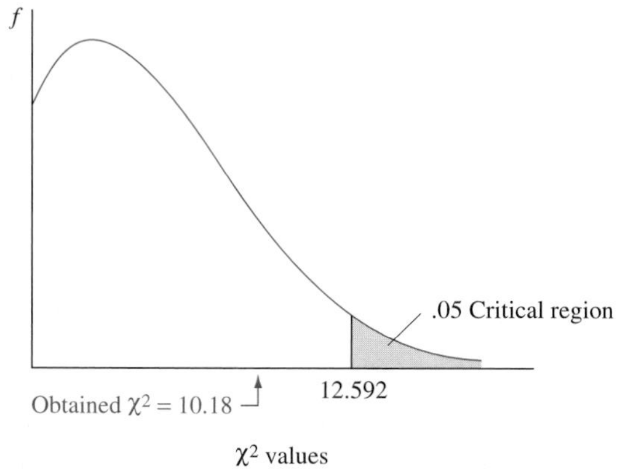

Because the obtained value of $\chi^2 = 10.18$ falls outside the critical region, we can conclude that this value, and the difference it represents, occurs rather frequently in samples drawn from the specified population. The sample of taste testers is representative of the cola-drinking population. H_0 provides a reasonable explanation for the observed difference, and the difference is declared nonsignificant. The researchers may proceed with the study of this sample, secure in the knowledge that it is representative of the population of U.S. cola drinkers, at least with regard to cola preferences.

6.6 Type I and Type II Errors

Whenever we make a decision on the basis of probabilities, there is some chance that our decision will be wrong. Knowing that a particular surgical procedure has a 99% survival rate, you may feel pretty confident about proceeding with the operation. Still, you may not survive. Aware that the chance of winning the lottery is infinitesimally small, you may decide against purchasing a ticket. But you might have won.

In a similar way, statistical significance tests lead us to make decisions on the basis of probabilities, and these decisions are not always correct. We may conclude from a significance test that a difference between a sample and a population is so great as to be *unlikely* due to simple sampling error. But it *might* be due just to sampling error. Or we may conclude from a significance test that a difference between a sample and a population is so small as to be the *probable* result of sampling error alone. But it is *possible* that the difference is a result of something more than sampling error, something unique to that sample that made it different than the population. It is to these kinds of statistical decision errors, called Type I and Type II errors, that we will turn next.

COMPREHENSION CHECK 6.26

If statistical significance tests can lead to wrong conclusions, why do we bother with them?
(Answer on p. 183.)

Type I Errors

Table 6.2 summarizes what can happen when we compute a significant difference test. Sometimes the reality of the situation is that a sample differs from a population only because of sampling error. The sample has not been treated any differently than the population, at least not in a way that made a difference. This is the null hypothesis, H_0. Given this reality, a significance test can lead us to either of two conclusions. If we choose H_0 as the most likely explanation of the difference, and declare the difference to be nonsignificant, we have called the situation correctly (cell 1).

But there are a few samples in any population that are very deviant from the population just because of sampling error. If our sample is one of these, we may wrongly conclude that the sample differs from the population for reasons beyond simple sampling error, H_1. This is called a **Type I error** (cell 2). A Type I error occurs when a difference that is really due just to sampling error is so large as to be unlikely due to sampling error and we conclude incorrectly that there must be more than sampling error at work to produce the difference. Although very large differences and the extreme test statistic values they generate are *unlikely* to result from sampling error alone, they *can* result from sampling error alone.

Type I error *A Type I error occurs when a difference that is really due to sampling error is falsely attributed to a treatment effect—the null hypothesis is falsely rejected.*

The probability of making a Type I error is always equal to one's chosen level of significance. A researcher may decide that a difference will be declared significant only if the test statistic that reflects that difference has a probability of less than .05 of occurring in samples drawn from the population. This means, though, that 5% of the samples drawn from the population—samples that are not treated any differently than the population as a whole—will generate test statistic values extreme enough to be declared significant. Adopting a more stringent significance level, say, .01, reduces the likelihood of making a Type I error, but doesn't eliminate it. Using the .01 significance level means that 1% of the samples drawn from a population—

TABLE 6.2

Two kinds of errors can occur in conjunction with significance tests. A Type I error occurs when a difference that is really due to sampling error is falsely attributed to a treatment effect. A Type II error occurs when a difference that is really due to a treatment effect is falsely attributed to sampling error.

	Reality: H_0: *No Treatment Effect*	Reality: H_1: *Treatment Effect*
Decision H_0: *No Treatment Effect*	1 Correct	3 Type II error
Decision H_1: *Treatment Effect*	2 Type I error	4 Correct

samples that haven't been treated any differently than the population—will generate test statistic values extreme enough to be declared falsely significant.

Comprehension Check 6.27

How do we *know* when we have made a Type I error? (Answer on p. 183.)

Type II Errors

Another possible reality shown in Table 6.2 is that a sample differs from a specified population because it has been treated differently than that population. It represents some different population. This is the situation described by H_1. Under these circumstances, a significance test will sometimes accurately find the difference between sample and population too great to be a likely result of sampling error alone. We choose H_1, and the difference is correctly declared to be significant (cell 4).

Other times, though, a sample that really is treated differently than the specified population shows a spuriously small reaction to that unique treatment. The result is a difference that is small enough to be a likely result of sampling error alone. When this happens, we wrongly choose H_0 and erroneously conclude that the difference is a nonsignificant consequence of sampling error alone. This is called a Type II error (cell 3). A **Type II error** occurs when we attribute a difference to sampling error alone when, in fact, the difference is the result of some unique treatment received by the sample. Although small differences and the low and moderate test statistic values they generate are *probably* the result of sampling error, they *can* occur even when there is a treatment effect.

Type II error *A Type II error occurs when a difference that is really due to a treatment effect is falsely attributed to sampling error—the null hypothesis is falsely accepted.*

Determining the probability of occurrence of a Type II error is not as easy as finding the probability of a Type I error, but the following generalization is true: Anything that makes it easier to find a difference statistically significant will lower the probability of a Type II error. It is easy to understand why this is true. If a difference is declared to be *significant,* no Type II error can occur, because a Type II error means erroneously declaring a difference to be *nonsignificant.* Let's look next at the factors that affect statistical significance.

Comprehension Check 6.28

How do we *know* when we have made a Type II error? (Answer on p. 183.)

6.7 Factors Affecting Statistical Significance

It is obvious that the larger the difference, the greater is the likelihood that it will be found statistically significant. In addition to the size of the difference being tested for significance, four factors determine the **power** of significance tests, that is, their ability to identify a given difference as statistically significant: one's choice of significance level, using a one- or two-tail significance test, the size of the sample, and data variability. The influence of each will be considered in the paragraphs that follow.

power *The power of a significant difference test refers to its resistance to Type II errors. A powerful test is resistant to Type II errors because its great sensitivity enables finding even relatively small differences statistically significant.*

COMPREHENSION CHECK 6.29

Remembering the two usual purposes of one-sample significant difference tests (evaluating the representativeness of a sample and assessing a treatment effect), why do we want our one-sample tests to be as powerful as possible?

(Answer on p. 183.)

Choice of Significance Level

Our choice of significance levels is one factor that determines whether a given difference will or will not be found statistically significant. When we adopt a less stringent significance level, such as .05, rather than a more stringent significance level, such as .01, we make it easier to find a difference significant. Suppose, for example, that a given $\overline{X} - \mu$ difference is reflected by a t-statistic value of 2.00. With df = 10 and using a one-tail test at the .01 level of significance, this is nonsignificant. It does reach significance, though, at the .05 level. You should notice, however, that although adopting a less stringent significance level makes it easier to find a difference significant and reduces the likelihood of Type II error, it is at the expense of increasing the likelihood of a Type I error. When we change significance levels, we're just swapping one type of error for another. In statistics, as in life, there are no free lunches.

COMPREHENSION CHECK 6.30

In 100 significance tests using the .05 level of significance, how many would you expect to produce Type I errors? Type II errors?

(Answer on p. 183.)

One- vs. Two-Tail Tests

A difference of a given size is more likely to be found significant if it is tested with a one-tail significance test than if it is tested with a two-tail test. Consider the example just cited, of an obtained value of $t = 2.00$ with df = 10. The one-tail critical value of t at the .05 level of significance is 1.812. The obtained t exceeds this critical value, and the one-tail t test is significant. What happens, though, if we use a two-tail test? The critical value of t for a two-tail t test at the .05 level of significance is 2.228. Our obtained t falls short of this value, and the two-tail test is nonsignificant.

We use one-tail tests when we know enough about a situation in advance of collecting the data to be able to predict the direction of the difference. Two-tail tests are used when we're fumbling around in ignorance, looking for differences in either direction. You can think of it this way: The knowledge needed to make directional predictions in research is a kind of statistical currency with which we can buy the extra power of the one-tail test.

COMPREHENSION CHECK 6.31

Suppose a researcher predicted a positive t value before collecting data and so decided to use a one-tail significance test. When the data are collected, the obtained t is actually strongly negative, enough so to be significant had the researcher only predicted in the opposite direction. How should the researcher handle this turn of events?

(Answer on p. 183.)

Sample Size

A difference of a given size is more likely to be found significant if it is based on a large sample than a small sample. This makes some intuitive sense if you remember that significance tests are really tests of the reliability or replicability of findings. They tell us if things we see in samples are or are not likely to be true in populations as well. If we were to see a difference of a given size in a study of a small sample of cases, we probably wouldn't be surprised to see this difference disappear in an attempted replication of the study. On the other hand, if the difference was observed in a study involving a very large sample, we would be more confident of its reliability. Findings based on small samples tend to be a little idiosyncratic; findings based on large samples are more likely to be trustworthy.

If this explanation misses the mark, perhaps some examples will help. Let's consider first the effects of sample size (N) on the one-sample t test. Look at the one-sample t tests summarized in Table 6.3. The $\bar{X} - \mu$ difference is the same in both t tests: $17 - 15 = 2$. Data variability is also the same in both tests: $\hat{s} = 5$. The only difference between the t tests is in N: $N = 10$ in the first test and $N = 20$ in the second.

Notice first how N affects the size of the obtained value of t. In the first t test, $t = 1.27$. In the second t test, $t = 1.79$. As N increases, $\hat{\sigma}_{\bar{X}}$ decreases (see Equation 5.5), and as $\hat{\sigma}_{\bar{X}}$ decreases, the absolute value of t increases (see Equation 6.1).

Notice next how N affects degrees of freedom (df) and the critical value of t. In the first t test, df $= 9$ and the critical value of t for a one-tail test at the .05 significance level is 1.833. The obtained value of $t = 1.27$ fails to reach this critical value and we would conclude that the 2-point difference between $\bar{X}$ and μ is nonsignificant. In the second t test, df $= 19$ and the critical value of t for a one-tail test at the .05 significance level is reduced to 1.729. The obtained value of $t = 1.79$ exceeds this critical value and the difference now becomes statistically significant. As N increases, df increases and the critical value of t decreases.

Let's look next at the effect of sample size on the χ^2 goodness-of-fit test. Consider the χ^2 tests summarized in Table 6.4. The data for these two χ^2 tests are identical except that the first is based on a sample of $N = 50$ and the second is based on a sample of $N = 100$. Notice how sample size affects the size of the obtained χ^2. In the first test, $\chi^2 = 5.13$. For df $= k - 1 = 4$, the critical value of χ^2 for the .05 level of significance is 9.488. Thus, we would con-

TABLE 6.3

Sample size (N) affects the t test in two ways: (a) As N increases, $\hat{\sigma}_{\bar{X}}$ decreases and t increases; (b) as N increases, *df* increases and the critical value of t decreases

$N = 10$		$N = 20$	
$\bar{X} = 17$	$\mu = 15$	$\bar{X} = 17$	$\mu = 15$
$\hat{s} = 5$		$\hat{s} = 5$	
$t = \frac{\bar{X} - \mu}{\hat{\sigma}_{\bar{X}}}$	$\hat{\sigma}_{\bar{X}} = \frac{\hat{s}}{\sqrt{N}}$	$t = \frac{\bar{X} - \mu}{\hat{\sigma}_{\bar{X}}}$	$\hat{\sigma}_{X} = \frac{\hat{s}}{\sqrt{N}}$
$= \frac{17 - 15}{1.58}$	$= \frac{5}{\sqrt{10}}$	$= \frac{17 - 15}{1.12}$	$= \frac{5}{\sqrt{20}}$
$= 1.27$	$= 1.58$	$= 1.79$	$= 1.12$
critical $t_{(.05,\ df=N-1=9)} = 1.833$		critical $t_{(.05,\ df=N-1=19)} = 1.729$	
The t statistic is nonsignificant.		The t statistic is statistically significant.	

clude that the first χ^2 test is nonsignificant. In the second test, with a larger sample, χ^2 is increased to 10.26. Neither degrees of freedom nor the critical value of χ^2 is changed in this test: df $= k - 1 = 4$, and the critical value of χ^2 is still 9.488. Because the obtained value of χ^2 is higher, though, this test is significant at the .05 level.

Sample size affects the χ^2 test by acting on the computed value of χ^2. As N increases, the values of f_o and f_e also increase, producing an increase in χ^2 (see Equation 6.2). Thus, a given difference between a sample distribution and a population distribution is more likely to be found significant when N is large than when N is small.

It is true of all significance tests—t tests, χ^2 tests, and others—that the extra effort expended in studying large samples will buy increased statistical power. A difference of a given size will be more likely to be found statistically significant in large-sample research than in small-sample research.

COMPREHENSION CHECK 6.32

Remembering the two usual uses of the one-sample significant difference tests (evaluating the representativeness of samples and assessing a treatment), for which purpose would a cautious researcher choose a small sample size, and for which would a large sample size give the more cautious results?

(Answer on p. 184.)

Data Variability

Data variability is the fourth factor that affects statistical power. Table 6.5 illustrates this principle with two one-sample t tests. The data for these two tests are identical except for data variability. In the first t test, using highly variable data ($\hat{s} = 15$), the obtained value of t is 1.05. With df $= 9$, this obtained t is nonsignificant at the one-tail .05 level of significance. The second t test is based on less variable data ($\hat{s} = 5$) and produces a higher obtained

TABLE 6.4

Sample size (N) affects the χ^2 test by influencing the values of f_o and f_e. As N increases, the differences between f_o and f_e values increase, and χ^2 increases.

$N = 50$				$N = 100$			
Dependent Variable Category	*Population %*	*Sample* f_o	*Sample* f_e	*Dependent Variable Category*	*Population %*	*Sample* f_o	*Sample* f_e
A	15	5	7.5	A	15	10	15
B	20	9	10.0	B	20	18	20
C	30	22	15.0	C	30	44	30
D	20	9	10.0	D	20	18	20
E	15	5	7.5	E	10	10	15

$N = 50$:

$$\chi^2 = \Sigma\frac{(f_o - f_e)^2}{f_e}$$
$$= \frac{(15 - 7.5)^2}{7.5} + \cdots + \frac{(5 - 7.5)^2}{7.5}$$
$$= 5.13$$

critical $\chi^2_{(.05,\ df=k-1=4)} = 9.488$

The χ^2 statistic is nonsignificant.

$N = 100$:

$$\chi^2 = \Sigma\frac{(f_o - f_e)^2}{f_e}$$
$$= \frac{(10 - 15)^2}{15} + \cdots + \frac{(10 - 15)^2}{15}$$
$$= 10.26$$

critical $\chi^2_{(.05,\ df=k-1=4)} = 9.488$

The χ^2 statistic is statistically significant.

value of $t = 3.16$. This t test is statistically significant. As data variability decreases, $\hat{\sigma}_{\overline{X}}$ decreases, and as $\hat{\sigma}_{\overline{X}}$ decreases, the obtained value of t increases and becomes more likely to reach significance.

Table 6.6 illustrates the effect of data variability on the χ^2 goodness-of-fit test. Two χ^2 tests are presented here. In the first test the data are highly variable—the population is evenly split between the two categories of the dependent variable. In the second test, the data are less variable—90% of the cases comprising the population fall in one category of the variable. Notice that the difference between sample and population distributions is the same in both χ^2 tests. In both tests, f_o for the first category is 6 cases lower than f_e, and f_o for the second category is 6 cases higher than f_e. But this is where the similarities stop. The obtained χ^2 for the first test is 1.44. With df $= k - 1 = 1$, this obtained χ^2 fails to reach the critical value of $\chi^2 = 3.841$ for the .05 level of significance and we would conclude that the difference is nonsignificant. The second χ^2, though, based on less variable data, is considerably higher: $\chi^2 = 4.0$. This χ^2 is significant at the .05 level. As data variability decreases, the obtained value of χ^2 increases and a difference of a given size between a sample distribution and a population distribution is more likely to reach statistical significance.

Stated in general terms, the less variable the data, the more likely it is that a difference of a given magnitude will reach significance. Unfortunately,

TABLE 6.5

Data variability ($\hat{s}$) affects the t test by influencing $\hat{\sigma}_{\overline{X}}$. As $\hat{s}$ decreases, $\hat{\sigma}_{\overline{X}}$ decreases, and t increases

$\hat{s} = 15$

$\overline{X} = 25$ $\quad \mu = 20$
$N = 10$

$$t = \frac{\overline{X} - \mu}{\hat{\sigma}_{\overline{X}}} = \frac{25 - 20}{4.74} = 1.05 \qquad \hat{\sigma}_{\overline{X}} = \frac{\hat{s}}{\sqrt{N}} = \frac{5}{\sqrt{10}} = 4.74$$

critical $t_{(.05,\ df=N-1=9)} = 1.833$

The t statistic is nonsignificant.

$\hat{s} = 5$

$\overline{X} = 25$ $\quad \mu = 20$
$N = 10$

$$t = \frac{\overline{X} - \mu}{\hat{\sigma}_{\overline{X}}} = \frac{25 - 20}{1.58} = 3.16 \qquad \hat{\sigma}_{\overline{X}} = \frac{\hat{s}}{\sqrt{N}} = \frac{5}{\sqrt{10}} = 1.58$$

critical $t_{(.05,\ df=N-1=9)} = 1.833$

The t statistic is significant.

TABLE 6.6

Data variability affects the χ^2 test by influencing the computed value of χ^2. As variability decreases, χ^2 increases

High Variability

Dependent Variable Category	*Population %*	*Sample* f_o	*Sample* f_e
A	50	44	50
B	50	56	50
		$N = 100$	

$$\chi^2 = \Sigma\frac{(f_o - f_e)^2}{f_e} = \frac{(44 - 50)^2}{50} + \frac{(56 - 50)^2}{50} = 1.44$$

critical $\chi^2_{(.05,\ df=k-1=1)} = 3.841$

The χ^2 statistic is nonsignificant.

Low Variability

Dependent Variable Category	*Population %*	*Sample* f_o	*Sample* f_e
A	90	84	90
B	10	16	10
		$N = 100$	

$$\chi^2 = \Sigma\frac{(f_o - f_e)^2}{f_e} = \frac{(84 - 90)^2}{90} + \frac{(16 - 10)^2}{10} = 4.00$$

critical $\chi^2_{(.05,\ df=k-1=1)} = 3.841$

The χ^2 statistic is statistically significant.

there is relatively little that one can do to control data variability except to eliminate as much random measurement error as possible. Using reliable measuring instruments and procedures, measuring under well-controlled, standardized conditions, and exercising good experimental rigor will buy improved statistical power by lowering random data variability.

COMPREHENSION CHECK 6.33

Give an example of "exercising good experimental rigor" in collecting IQ scores from a sample of college students.
(Answer on p. 184.)

6.8 STATISTICAL VS. PRACTICAL SIGNIFICANCE

You've learned in this chapter what a statistically significant difference is. A statistically significant difference is a difference that is larger than can reasonably be attributed to random, chance fluctuations in the sample data. It is a difference that is reliable and replicable.

It's now time to learn what a statistically significant difference *is not.* A statistically significant difference is not necessarily an important difference. A significant difference may or may not be a difference that makes a difference. Statistical and practical significance are separate issues.

Suppose a "wonder drug" was developed to increase intelligence. In the population at large, the mean IQ is 100 with a standard deviation of 15. In a comparison sample of 1,000 cases who received the drug, the mean IQ is 101. Let's compute a one-sample t test to evaluate this difference:

$$t = \frac{\overline{X} - \mu}{\hat{\sigma}_{\overline{X}}}$$

$$= \frac{101 - 100}{.47}$$

$$= 2.13$$

With $N - 1 = 999$ degrees of freedom, this obtained value of t exceeds the critical value marking the upper .025 tail of the sampling distribution of t. It is extremely unlikely ($p < .025$) that a sample drawn from the general population and treated like the general population would differ from the population by as much as this sample does. The difference observed is greater than can reasonably be attributed to sampling error. It is more likely that it is due to the drug treatment. The difference is statistically significant.

But does a difference of 1 IQ point *make* a difference? No. Is this a drug that will change anyone's life? No. Would you pay a dollar a pill or more to take it? I hope not! What we have here is a significant difference that doesn't make a difference. The difference is reliably unimportant!

As this example has shown, even a very small difference can be found to be statistically significant if the sample is large enough. Statistical significance alone, though, does not define a difference as practically significant. This being the case, you may wonder at this point why we bother with significance tests at all. The answer is simple. If a difference is statistically nonsignificant, it is almost *certainly* unimportant. If it is statistically significant, it *may* be important. Significance tests tell us which findings warrant our further scrutiny. After that, common sense provides the best test of which differences matter and which don't.

Comprehension Check 6.34

Why is a statistically nonsignificant finding "almost certainly unimportant"?

(Answer on p. 184.)

Summary

Statistical significance tests evaluate the replicability of sample findings. This chapter examines one family of significance tests, the one-sample significant difference tests. The one-sample *t* test and the chi-square goodness-of-fit test both test the significance of a difference between a sample and some larger population. The *t* test is sensitive to differences between $\overline{X}$ and μ, and the χ^2 test compares entire distributions.

The logic of both tests is the same. The test begins with the observation that a difference exists between a sample and some specified population. The null hypothesis (H_0) attributes this difference to sampling error: A difference of the observed size is likely in samples drawn from the specified population. The alternative hypothesis (H_1) attributes the difference to something more than sampling error: A difference of the observed size is unlikely in samples drawn from the specified population and, therefore, the sample must represent some different population. A test statistic (either t or χ^2) is computed that varies in value as a function of the size of the difference being tested for significance. The computed test statistic is then compared against the sampling distribution of that test statistic. This sampling distribution depicts the relative frequency of occurrence of values of the test statistic for all possible samples drawn from the specified population. From this comparison it can be concluded either that the observed test statistic value (and the difference it represents) would be likely (H_0) or would not be likely (H_1) to occur in samples drawn from the specified population.

Because the choice between the null and alternative hypotheses is based on probabilities, there is always some chance of error. Type I errors occur when a difference that is declared statistically significant (H_1) was, in reality, a consequence of sampling error alone. Type II errors occur when a difference that was declared statistically nonsignificant (H_0) was, in reality, the consequence of a treatment unique to the sample.

Several factors combine to determine whether or not a given difference will be found statistically significant, including the size of the difference, one's choice of significance levels, the use of one- or two-tail significance tests, sample size, and data variability. It is important to remember, though, that statistical significance may or may not translate to practical significance. A significant difference is merely a reliable difference; it may or may not make a difference.

Note

1. Technically, degrees of freedom refers to the number of values that are free to vary once we have placed certain restrictions on the data. In the case of the one-sample t test, the restriction is that the scores must show a mean equal to $\overline{X}$. With this restriction in place, $N - 1$ values of X can take on any value—that is, they are free to vary—but the Nth value of X must be such that $\Sigma X/N = \overline{X}$.

Review Exercises

6.1. Which of the following research questions is most suited to a one-sample significant difference test?

(a) An industrial/organizational psychologist wants to compare the productivity of male and female employees.

(b) A sociologist wants to compare the educational achievements of three different racial groups.

(c) A clinical social worker wants to compare the average age of a group of sex offenders with the average age of the population of convicts in a prison.

6.2. Identify the independent variable and the dependent variable in each of the research questions listed in Review Exercise 6.1.

6.3. Is the sample of 10 students whose ages are listed below representative of a population with a mean age of 27?

25, 28, 24, 21, 18, 19, 35, 19, 20, 21

6.4. Listed below are ages in months at which 8 toddlers were successfully toilet trained. Does the average age of toilet training in this sample differ significantly from the national average of 28 months?

19, 30, 28, 24, 29, 27, 28, 22

6.5. Is the distribution of academic majors in the sample below representative of the distribution of majors in the population?

Population		**Sample**	
Majors	*f*	*Majors*	*f*
Psychology	210	Psychology	25
Sociology	80	Sociology	15
Social work	150	Social work	20

6.6. Does the sample's distribution of IQ scores listed below differ significantly from the population distribution?

Population		**Sample**	
Scores	%	*Scores*	f
70–85	13%	70–85	8
86–100	34%	86–100	24
101–115	34%	101–115	32
116–130	13%	116–130	20

6.7. Using the distribution of IQ scores given in Review Exercise 6.6, how large a sample must be studied to avoid expected frequencies lower than 5?

6.8. Describe what one can do in each of the areas listed below to enhance the likelihood of finding a difference statistically significant.

(a) Level of significance

(b) One- vs. two-tail test

(c) Sample size

(d) Data variability

Answers to Comprehension Checks

6.1. When a sample finding is statistically significant, it means that whatever was found in that sample will also most likely be seen in the theoretical population of all cases treated exactly like that sample. Because of this, a significant sample finding is a reliable, replicable finding.

6.2. The significance of this finding indicates that the finding is reliable and replicable, and not just a fluke of the sample at hand. The lower divorce rate of this sample would most likely be seen again in other samples that received the same counseling.

6.3. A statistically significant finding is reliable, but it may or may not be important from a practical perspective.

6.4. (a) two-sample; (b) analysis of variance; (c) one-sample

6.5. Two independent variables define the samples: place of residence (rural, suburban, or urban), and gender (male, female).

6.6. The old saying, "Garbage in, garbage out," pretty much sums up the situation in which one uses the wrong statistic for the data at hand. The results will be misleading or uninterpretable.

6.7. A significant difference between the academic cheating study sample and the university student population would suggest that the sample is unlike the population and that any findings pertaining to cheating behavior and attitudes seen in the sample might not generalize to the student body as a whole.

6.8. (a) The "treatment" here is not under the control of a researcher. Instead, it is defined by the characteristics of the sample: people who listen to the talk show, heard the invitation to call, and decided to respond. The question in this scenario is whether people like this differ from the general population in political attitudes. (b) This is another "treatment" outside the control of a researcher. It consists of being the spouse of an Alzheimer's patient. (c) The treatment here consists of the freshman orientation course.

6.9. The most important assumption of the one-sample t test is that the data be measured at a level at which the mean is interpretable—interval or ratio. It would not make sense, for instance, to use a t test in analyzing data on a multicategory, nominal scale dependent variable, because the mean of such a variable would be meaningless.

6.10. A researcher who is evaluating the representativeness of a sample generally hopes to find no significant difference between that sample and the population to which generalizations are to be made. A researcher who is evaluating the effect of some treatment unique to the sample generally does hope to find that the sample differs significantly from some larger population that has not received the treatment.

6.11. Equation 6.1 is used to compute the one-sample t statistic:

$$t = \frac{\overline{X} - \mu}{\hat{\sigma}_{\overline{X}}} \qquad \text{where} \qquad \hat{\sigma}_{\overline{X}} = \frac{\hat{s}}{\sqrt{N}}$$

$$= \frac{22.7 - 25.7}{1.39} \qquad\qquad = \frac{15.2}{\sqrt{120}}$$

$$= -2.16 \qquad\qquad = 1.39$$

6.12. The *sampling* distribution of t depicts the relative *frequency (or probability)* of occurrence of values of the t statistic computed for *all possible* samples of size N drawn from a specified *population.*

6.13. For these data, df $= N - 1 = 119$. The critical values of t that mark the upper 5% and lower 1% tails are $+1.671$ and -2.390, respectively. Note: The table fails to list the exact df value, so we use the next lower value, df $= 60$.

6.14. For these data, df $= N - 1 = 119$. The two-tail absolute critical values of t for the .05 and .01 levels of significance are 2.000 and 2.660, respectively.

6.15. This is a sample that is relatively unlikely ($p < .05$) to be drawn from the specified population. This value of t, and the difference it represents, is unlikely to be due to sampling error alone (H_0). Therefore, H_1 provides the more likely explanation for the observed difference.

6.16. This is a value of t that occurs quite frequently in samples drawn from the specified population. This is consistent with the null hypothesis (H_0) that attributes the difference to sampling error.

6.17. A two-tail test would be appropriate here, because a significant difference in either direction would make the sample unrepresentative of the population and no directional prediction was made in advance. The appropriate two-tail critical value of t for df $= 119$ at the .05 significance level is 2.000. The obtained value, computed in Comprehension Check 6.11, was $t = -2.16$. This obtained value exceeds the critical value of t, and we conclude that the sample is significantly younger than the university student body as a whole.

6.18. There are many possibilities, one of which is shown below.

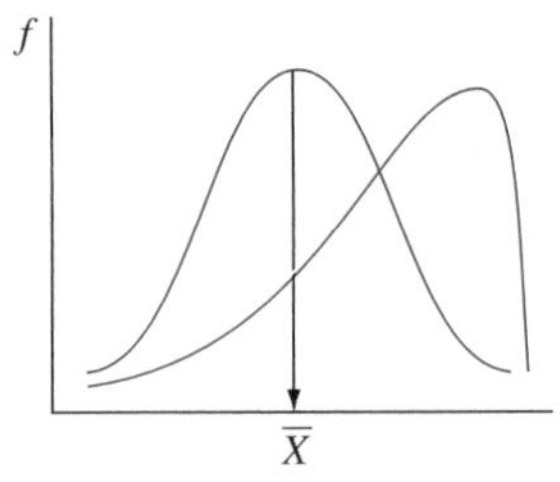

6.19. (a) This calls for a χ^2 test, because the difference being tested does not involve central tendency, but the breadth (variability) of the distributions. (b) This calls for the t test, because the difference being tested does involve central tendency.

6.20. The researchers would undoubtedly prefer to attribute differences between their sample and the population to sampling error (H_0), because finding significant differences (H_1) would limit the justification for generalizing sample findings pertaining to academic cheating to the student body population.

6.21. The expected frequency for each category is the number of cases that one would expect to see in that category if the sample and population were distributed identically. These are determined by multiplying each category's population percentage by the sample size: $.0214 \times 260 = 5.56$; $.1359 \times 260 = 35.33$; $.3413 \times 260 = 88.74$; $.3413 \times 260 = 88.74$; $.1359 \times 260 = 35.23$; $.0214 \times 260 = 5.56$.

6.22. Equation 6.2 is used to compute χ^2 as shown for the data presented in Comprehension Check 6.21:

$$\chi^2 = \Sigma\frac{(f_o - f_e)^2}{f_e}$$

$$= \frac{(18 - 5.56)^2}{5.56} + \frac{(40 - 35.33)^2}{35.33} + \dots + \frac{(2 - 5.56)^2}{5.56}$$

$$= 33.93$$

Equation 6.2 is used to compute χ^2 as shown for the data presented in Table 6.1:

$$\chi^2 = \Sigma\frac{(f_o - f_e)^2}{f_e}$$

$$= \frac{(101 - 72)^2}{72} + \frac{(19 - 48)^2}{48}$$

$$= 29.20$$

6.23. The .05 and .01 critical values of χ^2 for the data presented in Comprehension Check 6.21 are found for $df = k - 1 = 6 - 1 = 5$: 11.070 and 15.086, respectively.

The critical values of χ^2 for the data presented in Table 6.1 are found for $df = k - 1 = 1$: 3.841 and 6.635, respectively.

6.24. The obtained χ^2 value of 33.93 exceeds the critical χ^2 value of 15.086 for significance at the .01 level. This is a value that would seldom be seen in samples drawn from the specified normal population. The difference in distributions is significant. This sample is not normally distributed.

The obtained χ^2 value of 29.20 exceeds the critical χ^2 value of 6.635 for significance at the .01 level. This is a value that would seldom be seen in samples drawn from the specified population. The difference in student classification distributions seen between the academic cheating study sample and the student population is significant. Because the sample is unlike the student body as a whole, we must limit generalizations from the sample to just that theoretical population of cases that are like the sample.

6.25. **(a)** By combining grade categories A, B and D, F, we get the following expected frequencies:

A/B	$.40 \times 20 = 8$
C	$.29 \times 20 = 5.8$
D/F	$.31 \times 20 = 6.2$

(b) If the sample size is increased to $N = 46$, none of the expected frequencies will be lower than 5:

A	$.15 \times 46 = 6.9$
B	$.25 \times 46 = 11.5$
C	$.29 \times 46 = 13.34$
D	$.20 \times 46 = 9.2$
F	$.11 \times 46 = 5.06$

6.26. We use anesthesia during routine dental surgery even though a small number of people will suffer bad reactions. We do this because anesthesia works most of the time for most of the people. We put roofs on our houses even though roofs occasionally spring a leak. We do this because roofs usually keep the rain out. We use statistical significance tests because there is no better way to make decisions of the sort that are addressed by these tests.

6.27. Short of studying the entire theoretical population of interest in the significance test, we can never know if we have made a Type I error. Repeated failures to replicate a statistically significant finding, though, indicate that that significance was likely a Type I error.

6.28. Short of studying the entire theoretical population of interest in the significance test, we can never know if we have made a Type II error. However, if the research that was originally nonsignificant is repeated and is found to be significant, it may indicate that the original nonsignificance was a Type II error.

6.29. A powerful significance test ensures that even a relatively small difference between a sample and population will be found significant. This will prevent us from generalizing from a sample to an inappropriate population. It also ensures that we will not fail to spot a treatment effect in research aimed at evaluating a treatment unique to some sample.

6.30. When using the .05 significance level, we would expect about 5 tests out of 100 to yield Type I errors: 5% of the samples drawn from a population will produce test statistic values extreme enough to fall into the .05 critical region. Even more Type II errors will likely occur.

6.31. A hard-nosed statistician might argue that the difference must be labeled "nonsignificant" because it falls outside the specified critical region. It would be more realistic and helpful, though, to report the finding exactly as described: The direction was exactly opposite to that predicted, and significantly so.

6.32. A conservative researcher would prefer a small sample when evaluating the effect of a treatment unique to a sample. With a small sample, only a fairly strong effect would be detected as statistically significant. A conservative researcher would prefer a large sample when evaluating the representativeness of a sample to some population. With a large sample, even a small difference between the sample and population would be detected as significant.

6.33. "Good experimental rigor" would include standardizing the instructions given to test takers, testing at the same time of day, perhaps on the same day of the week, using the same test administrator, keeping the temperature of the room constant, etc.

6.34. A statistically nonsignificant finding is almost always unimportant because it cannot be trusted. It is a finding that may well be a fluke of the specific sample at hand.

TWO-SAMPLE SIGNIFICANT DIFFERENCE TESTS

7

Chapter Outline

In the study of academic cheating we've been following, researchers identified several variables on which professed cheaters and noncheaters differed. Sample means for cheaters and noncheaters are summarized below on the variables of age, grade-point average, and the Cheating Justification Questionnaire.

Variable	**Cheaters (*N* = 65)**	**Noncheaters (*N* = 55)**
Age	20.3	25.6
Grade-point average	2.5	2.8
Cheating Justification Questionnaire	32.9	29.2

You can see that cheaters and noncheaters differed on all three variables, but these are just samples, and sample data can be quirky. Can we trust these sample findings to be replicable? Do these sample findings describe the entire *populations* of college cheaters and noncheaters?

Consider another, related problem. In their recent survey of American graduate psychology departments,[1] the American Psychological Association received responses from a sample of 412 departments. The surveys that were returned revealed that white faculty members were generally employed at higher faculty ranks than were minority faculty members. Percentages of white and minority faculty members at each faculty rank are summarized below.

Faculty Rank	**White (*N* = 6,627)**	**Minorities (*N* = 421)**
Full professor	50%	25%
Associate professor	26%	30%
Assistant professor	21%	41%
Lecturer/Instructor	1%	2%
Other	2%	2%

But these are also sample findings. Is what we see in these samples true in the larger populations of *all* white and minority academic psychologists? Or are these findings sample-specific, and not characteristic of the larger populations?

You may recognize that these are questions of statistical significance. When we wonder if a difference observed between two samples is replicable and reflects the reality of larger populations, we are asking if the difference between those samples is statistically significant. Two-sample significant difference tests are used to answer this question.

COMPREHENSION CHECK 7.1

What does it mean to say that two samples differ significantly? What does it mean to say that the difference between two samples is statistically nonsignificant?

(Answer on p. 221.)

[1]Wicherski, M., and Kahout, J. (1992). *Characteristics of graduate departments of psychology: 1990–1991*. Washington, DC: American Psychological Association.

7.1 Uses of Two-Sample Significant Difference Tests

In this chapter we will study significance tests used in several sorts of two-sample comparisons. Sometimes the independent variable that defines the two samples is manipulated by the researcher within the context of a true experiment. A study comparing anxiety levels of subjects randomly assigned to either a drug-treatment group or a placebo control group illustrates this kind of application. At other times, in ex-post-facto research, the independent variable is not controlled by the researcher, but varies naturally. A comparison of male vs. female anxiety levels is an example of this kind of research. Two-sample significant difference tests are also available for comparing samples on a variety of dependent variables. There are significance tests for nominal, ordinal, interval, and ratio scales of measurement. Finally, two-sample procedures can be used either to compare the same cases measured twice (for example, anxiety before vs. after receiving an experimental drug) or two separate sets of cases (for example, subjects who receive an experimental drug vs. subjects who do not).

Comprehension Check 7.2

A variety of research situations call for two-sample significant difference tests. List three ways in which these situations differ from one to the next.

(Answer on p. 221.)

These differences notwithstanding, all two-sample significant difference tests answer the same fundamental question: How big must the difference be between two samples before we decide that the difference is reliable and replicable, reflects the reality of the populations represented by those samples, and is not just sample-specific?

7.2 The Independent-Samples *t* Test

The **independent-samples *t* test** is used to compare the means of two samples to determine if those means differ significantly. The phrase "independent-samples" means that the cases that comprise one sample are independent from, unrelated to, and in no way influenced by the cases that comprise the other sample. The procedure is called a *t* test because it uses *t* as the test statistic. The independent-samples *t* test uses the *t* statistic to measure and evaluate the statistical significance of the difference between the means of two unrelated samples.

independent-samples *t* test *A parametric significant difference test that uses the* t *statistic to compare the means of two independent samples.*

The *t* test is a parametric procedure, which means that certain characteristics or parameters are assumed to be true of the data being analyzed. First, the *t* test is useful only when the dependent variable is measured on an interval or ratio scale. Second, it is assumed that the populations represented by the two samples are normally distributed. Finally, it is assumed that the variances of the populations represented by the two samples are approximately equal. However, the *t* test is extremely robust to violations of the normality and variance assumptions, especially if only one or the other assumption is violated, and when both samples are relatively large ($N \geq 25$) and approximately equal in size.

COMPREHENSION CHECK 7.3

To which one of the following scenarios would the independent-samples t test be most appropriate? Why?

(a) A personnel psychologist is curious to know if male and female salespersons differ in productivity, measured by rank orders.
(b) A clinical psychologist wants to know if traditional and nontraditional students seeking treatment at the university clinic differ in depression as measured by the Beck Depression Inventory.
(c) State hospital patients are ranked from least compliant to most compliant before and after completing an assertiveness training program. The program administrator wants to know if the program affects compliance level.
(d) A sociologist needs to know if there is a difference between minority and white teenage drug abusers in drug of choice.
(e) A marriage counselor wants to compare the scores of husbands and their wives on the Zuckerman Sensation Seeking Scale.

(Answer on p. 221.)

Like all significance tests, the independent-samples t test is based on a sampling distribution. We will examine now the characteristics of that distribution, called the sampling distribution of the difference between means.

The Sampling Distribution of the Difference Between Means

Imagine some very large population of cases, all of whom have been treated identically. (Here, as in the preceding chapter, the term "treatment" will be used in the broad sense.) Now imagine drawing from this population all possible *pairs* of samples of sizes N_1 and N_2. Here, N_1 refers to the size of the first sample in each pair and N_2 refers to the size of the second sample in each pair. The samples can be of the same size ($N_1 = N_2$) or different sizes ($N_1 \neq N_2$), but N_1 and N_2 will remain constant across the many pairs of samples.

sampling distribution of the difference between means *The theoretical distribution formed by drawing all possible pairs of samples from a population of identically treated cases, computing the difference between the means of the samples in each pair, and plotting the frequency of occurrence of the $\overline{X}_1 - \overline{X}_2$ differences.*

Each sample in each pair will have a mean ($\overline{X}_1$ and $\overline{X}_2$, respectively), and we can anticipate that the difference between these two means ($\overline{X}_1 - \overline{X}_2$) will vary somewhat from one pair of samples to the next because of sampling error. If we plot the frequency of occurrence of the various $\overline{X}_1 - \overline{X}_2$ differences obtained from one pair of samples to the next, we have the **sampling distribution of the difference between means.** To save ink, let's just call this the sampling distribution of the difference; it is shown in Figure 7.1.

COMPREHENSION CHECK 7.4

For the population data listed below, construct the sampling distribution of the difference between means for samples of sizes $N_1 = 2$ and $N_2 = 2$. (Remember to sample with replacement.)

Population: 1, 2, 3

(Answer on p. 221.)

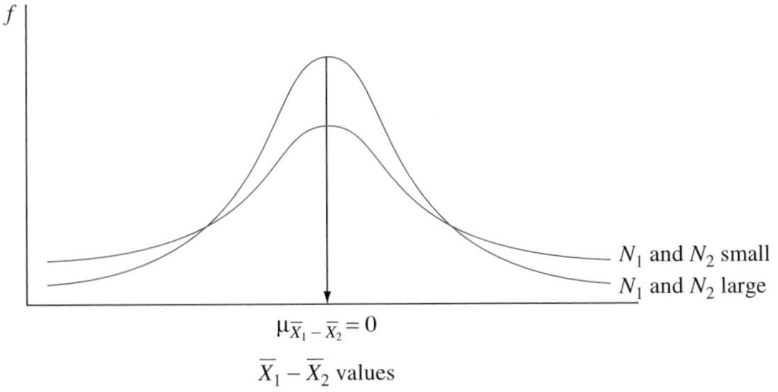

FIGURE 7.1

The sampling distribution of the difference between means is the theoretical distribution of $\overline{X}_1 - \overline{X}_2$ values for all possible pairs of samples of sizes N_1 and N_2 drawn from a population of identically treated cases. The shape of the sampling distribution of the difference varies with sample size.

The sampling distribution of the difference displays three predictable characteristics. First, the mean of this sampling distribution ($\mu_{\overline{X}_1 - \overline{X}_2}$), which is also the single most likely value of $\overline{X}_1 - \overline{X}_2$, will always equal zero. This makes sense: Because every case in the population has been treated identically, and every pair of samples is drawn from this population, it follows that the two samples in each pair have been treated identically. It is not surprising that two samples treated identically will frequently have identical means.

COMPREHENSION CHECK 7.5

Identify the mean of the sampling distribution of the difference ($\mu_{\overline{X}_1 - \overline{X}_2}$) constructed in Comprehension Check 7.4.
(Answer on p. 221.)

Second, the sampling distribution of the difference shows some variability. Sampling error alone will produce some pairs of samples in which $\overline{X}_1 > \overline{X}_2$, so that $\overline{X}_1 - \overline{X}_2$ is positive. Too, in some pairs of samples $\overline{X}_1 < \overline{X}_2$, so that $\overline{X}_1 - \overline{X}_2$ is negative. We have already seen that the single most likely $\overline{X}_1 - \overline{X}_2$ difference is zero. The variability of $\overline{X}_1 - \overline{X}_2$ values seen from one pair of samples to the next in the sampling distribution of the difference is measured by the standard deviation of the sampling distribution of the difference, called the **standard error of the difference.** Equation 7.1 describes how we can estimate this variability based on sample data.(See Note 1)

standard error of the difference ($\hat{\sigma}_{\overline{X}_1 - \overline{X}_2}$) *The standard deviation of the sampling distribution of the difference between means.*

Equation 7.1

$$\hat{\sigma}_{\overline{X}_1 - \overline{X}_2} = \sqrt{\left[\frac{(N_1 - 1)\hat{s}_1^2 + (N_2 - 1)\hat{s}_2^2}{N_1 + N_2 - 2}\right]\left[\frac{N_1 + N_2}{N_1 N_2}\right]}$$

where

$\hat{\sigma}_{\overline{X}_1 - \overline{X}_2}$ = the standard error of the difference
N_1 = the size of the first sample
N_2 = the size of the second sample
$\hat{s}_1^2$ = the corrected variance of the first sample
$\hat{s}_2^2$ = the corrected variance of the second sample

In words, the standard error of the difference ($\hat{\sigma}_{\overline{X}_1 - \overline{X}_2}$) is estimated by: (1) multiplying the corrected variance of the first sample ($\hat{s}_1^2$) by one less than the size of the first sample ($N_1 - 1$); (2) multiplying the corrected variance of the second sample ($\hat{s}_2^2$) by one less than the size of the second sample ($N_2 - 1$); (3) subtracting 2 from the sum of N_1 and N_2 ($N_1 + N_2 - 2$);

(4) dividing the sum of N_1 and N_2 ($N_1 + N_2$) by the product of N_1 and N_2 (N_1N_2); (5) adding the results of steps 1 and 2; (6) dividing the result of step 5 by the result of step 3; (7) multiplying the result of step 6 by the result of step 4; and (8) finding the square root of the result of step 7.

COMPREHENSION CHECK 7.6

Use Equation 7.1 to compute $\hat{\sigma}_{\overline{X}_1 - \overline{X}_2}$ based on the following sample data:

$$N_1 = 10 \qquad N_2 = 10$$

$$\hat{s}_1^2 = 8.5 \qquad \hat{s}_2^2 = 7.2$$

(Answer on p. 221.)

The third characteristic of the sampling distribution of the difference seen in Figure 7.1 pertains to its shape. If sample sizes are relatively large, the sampling distribution of the difference will approximate a normal distribution. As sample sizes decrease, however, the sampling distribution of the difference becomes increasingly flat (platykurtic).

The Test Statistic $t_{\overline{X}_1 - \overline{X}_2}$

The statistic $t_{\overline{X}_1 - \overline{X}_2}$, computed according to Equation 7.2, serves as the test statistic in the independent-samples t test.

Equation 7.2

$$t_{\overline{X}_1 - \overline{X}_2} = \frac{(\overline{X}_1 - \overline{X}_2) - \mu_{\overline{X}_1 - \overline{X}_2}}{\hat{\sigma}_{\overline{X}_1 - \overline{X}_2}}$$

where

$t_{\overline{X}_1 - \overline{X}_2}$ = the independent-samples t statistic
$\overline{X}_1$ = the mean of the first sample
$\overline{X}_2$ = the mean of the second sample
$\mu_{\overline{X}_1 - \overline{X}_2}$ = the mean of the sampling distribution of the difference between independent sample means (equal to 0)
$\hat{\sigma}_{\overline{X}_1 - \overline{X}_2}$ = the standard error of the difference (Equation 7.1)

In words, $t_{\overline{X}_1 - \overline{X}_2}$ is computed by: (1) computing the difference between the two sample means ($\overline{X}_1 - \overline{X}_2$); (2) subtracting the mean of the sampling distribution of the difference between means ($\mu_{\overline{X}_1 - \overline{X}_2} = 0$) from the result of step 1; and (3) dividing the result of step 2 by the standard error of the difference ($\hat{\sigma}_{\overline{X}_1 - \overline{X}_2}$) computed according to Equation 7.1.(See Note 2)

COMPREHENSION CHECK 7.7

Use Equation 7.2 to compare the means of cheaters and noncheaters on the Cheating Justification Questionnaire presented at the beginning of this chapter:

(cont.)

Cheaters	Noncheaters
$N_1 = 65$	$N_2 = 55$
$\overline{X}_1 = 32.90$	$\overline{X}_2 = 29.20$
$\hat{s}_1^2 = 29.27$	$\hat{s}_2^2 = 36.12$

(Answer on p. 222.)

Let's examine this statistic. First, notice that $t_{\overline{X}_1 - \overline{X}_2}$ measures how far the obtained difference between two sample means ($\overline{X}_1 - \overline{X}_2$) falls from the difference that is most likely to be seen if both samples were drawn from a population of identically treated cases ($\mu_{\overline{X}_1 - \overline{X}_2}$). The yardstick used to measure this distance is $\hat{\sigma}_{\overline{X}_1 - \overline{X}_2}$. To put this another way, $t_{\overline{X}_1 - \overline{X}_2}$ tells how many standard errors of the difference the obtained $\overline{X}_1 - \overline{X}_2$ difference falls from the value that would be most likely if the two samples were treated identically.

Second, notice that $t_{\overline{X}_1 - \overline{X}_2}$ will equal 0 if there is no difference between the sample means. It will take on a negative value if $\overline{X}_1 < \overline{X}_2$, and will take on a positive value if $\overline{X}_1 > \overline{X}_2$.

Finally, notice that $t_{\overline{X}_1 - \overline{X}_2}$ meets our definition of a test statistic: a number computed from data that varies in value as a function of the size of the difference being tested for significance. As the difference between $\overline{X}_1$ and $\overline{X}_2$ grows in the numerator of Equation 7.2, so does the absolute value of $t_{\overline{X}_1 - \overline{X}_2}$. We will examine the role of $\hat{\sigma}_{\overline{X}_1 - \overline{X}_2}$ in $t_{\overline{X}_1 - \overline{X}_2}$ in a later section of this chapter.

COMPREHENSION CHECK 7.8

What does the value of $t_{\overline{X}_1 - \overline{X}_2}$ computed in Comprehension Check 7.7 tell us about the difference between the mean Cheating Justification Questionnaire scores of cheaters and noncheaters?

(Answer on p. 222.)

The Logic of the Independent-Samples *t* Test

Having now laid the conceptual foundation of the independent-samples *t* test, we're ready to examine the logic of this statistical procedure. Example 7.1 will provide a concrete example to illustrate the general discussion that follows.

Null and Alternative Hypotheses. When two sample means are observed to differ, there are two mutually exclusive explanations for the observed difference. The null hypothesis (H_0) attributes the difference to sampling error. H_0 proposes that two samples drawn from a population of identically treated cases will be quite likely to differ by the amount observed. This being the case, both samples can be considered representative of the same population. Put simply, the difference is statistically nonsignificant.

The alternative hypothesis (H_1) proposes that the observed difference is too great to be a likely result of sampling error alone. This explanation suggests that two samples drawn from a population of identically treated cases will be very unlikely to differ by the amount observed. Therefore, it is more likely that the two samples do *not* represent the same population, but *different* populations that differ from each other on the dependent variable under consideration. Which populations? The theoretical populations of all cases that are like the cases that form the samples at hand. Put simply, the difference is statistically significant.

COMPREHENSION CHECK 7.9

> State the null and alternative hypotheses in words that are specific to the difference between mean Cheating Justification Questionnaire scores of cheaters ($\overline{X}_1 = 32.9$) and noncheaters ($\overline{X}_2 = 29.2$).
> (Answer on p. 222.)

The Test Statistic. In order to choose the more likely explanation of the observed $\overline{X}_1 - \overline{X}_2$ difference, we next compute the test statistic $t_{\overline{X}_1 - \overline{X}_2}$ according to Equation 7.2. This statistic reflects the size of the $\overline{X}_1 - \overline{X}_2$ difference being tested for significance by measuring the deviation between the observed difference and the difference that would be most likely had the samples been treated identically ($\mu_{\overline{X}_1 - \overline{X}_2} = 0$).

The Sampling Distribution of the Difference. The sampling distribution of the difference enables us to determine the relative probability that any given $\overline{X}_1 - \overline{X}_2$ difference will be seen in two samples drawn from a population of identically treated cases. Look back at Figure 7.1. An observed $\overline{X}_1 - \overline{X}_2$ difference falling toward the middle of the sampling distribution is a relatively likely result of sampling error (H_0). The rather small $\overline{X}_1 - \overline{X}_2$ values that fall in this middle portion of the sampling distribution of the difference are seen frequently in pairs of samples drawn from a population of identically treated cases. Thus, when a difference of this magnitude is observed, it is reasonable to conclude that the samples that produced it were drawn from and represent the same population. The difference is described as statistically nonsignificant.

On the other hand, an observed $\overline{X}_1 - \overline{X}_2$ difference that falls within either tail of the sampling distribution of the difference is unlikely to result from sampling error alone (H_1). The large $\overline{X}_1 - \overline{X}_2$ differences found in the tails of the sampling distribution of the difference occur only rarely in pairs of samples drawn from a population of identically treated cases. Thus, when a difference is observed that is large enough to fall into one of these critical regions, we can conclude that the samples that produced that difference probably did not come from a single population. Instead, the samples more probably represent two different populations, and the difference is said to be statistically significant.

But how can we locate any given $\overline{X}_1 - \overline{X}_2$ difference in the sampling distribution of the difference? How do we know if an observed $\overline{X}_1 - \overline{X}_2$ difference falls toward the middle of the sampling distribution of the difference or in one of the tails? This is where the $t_{\overline{X}_1 - \overline{X}_2}$ statistic comes in. The $t_{\overline{X}_1 - \overline{X}_2}$ statistic locates any given $\overline{X}_1 - \overline{X}_2$ difference in the sampling distribution of the difference by telling us how many standard errors of the difference that $\overline{X}_1 - \overline{X}_2$ value falls from the center of the sampling distribution.

The table of critical values of t (Table 2 in Appendix B) lists values of the $t_{\overline{X}_1 - \overline{X}_2}$ statistic that mark various critical regions of the sampling distribution of the difference. This table provides us with information about the relative probabilities of observing various $\overline{X}_1 - \overline{X}_2$ differences in pairs of samples drawn from a population of identically treated cases.

Procedures for using the table of critical values of t were explained in Chapter 6. The only change for the independent-samples t test is in the computation of degrees of freedom (df) used to enter the table. For the independent-samples t test, df $= N_1 + N_2 - 2$. One-tail significance levels are used if the direction of the $\overline{X}_1 - \overline{X}_2$ difference was predicted in advance; two-tail significance levels are used if the direction of the difference was not specified.

COMPREHENSION CHECK 7.10

Draw a diagram of the sampling distribution of the difference like the one shown in Figure 7.1 and locate the $\overline{X}_1 - \overline{X}_2$ difference between cheaters ($\overline{X}_1 = 32.9$) and noncheaters ($\overline{X}_2 = 29.2$) using the $t_{\overline{X}_1 - \overline{X}_2}$ statistic you computed in Comprehension Check 7.7.

(Answer on p. 222.)

Choosing Between the Null and Alternative Hypotheses. Once we know from the $t_{\overline{X}_1 - \overline{X}_2}$ statistic the relative likelihood that an obtained $\overline{X}_1 - \overline{X}_2$ difference would be seen in a pair of samples from a population of identically treated cases, we are prepared to choose between H_0 and H_1. If the $\overline{X}_1 - \overline{X}_2$ difference (and the $t_{\overline{X}_1 - \overline{X}_2}$ value that represents it) is likely, we conclude that the difference is of a size that can reasonably be attributed to sampling error—H_0. If the $\overline{X}_1 - \overline{X}_2$ difference (and its associated $t_{\overline{X}_1 - \overline{X}_2}$ value) is unlikely, we conclude that the samples probably do not represent a single population, but instead, two different populations—H_1.

COMPREHENSION CHECK 7.11

Based on your work in Comprehension Check 7.10, which is the more likely explanation of the observed difference between mean Cheating Justification Questionnaire scores of cheaters and noncheaters: H_0 or H_1?

(Answer on p. 222.)

EXAMPLE 7.1

Independent-Samples *t* Test

Sam and Ella, proprietors of Sam 'n Ella's Diner and long-time students of human behavior, have noticed that some patrons seem to linger excessively long over their meals. They are interested in conducting an experiment to see if they can move patrons through the diner more rapidly by playing snappy tunes on the radio.

To get a baseline, Sam records how many minutes patrons take to finish their lunches on Monday, without the radio on. On Tuesday, Ella turns on her favorite "oldies" station and records eating times. Their data are shown below, along with descriptive statistics. An independent-samples t test follows on the next page.

Null and Alternative Hypotheses

H_0: The difference between the means is a consequence of sampling error. Two samples drawn from a population of identically treated cases would be likely to differ by the amount observed here. Therefore, there is no evidence that the observed difference should be attributed to the different musical conditions to which the groups were exposed.

H_1: The difference between the means is too large to be attributed to sampling error alone. Two samples drawn from a population of identically treated cases would be very unlikely to differ by the amount observed here.

No Music	Music
25	21
12	15
33	29
35	30
43	38
17	22
29	23
37	30
29	24
23	23
19	22
35	29
35	27
28	31
24	19
27	32
$\overline{X}_1 = 28.19$	$\overline{X}_2 = 25.94$
$\hat{s}_1^2 = 65.90$	$\hat{s}_2^2 = 33.60$
$N_1 = 16$	$N_2 = 16$

Therefore, these two samples probably do not represent such a population. Instead, they represent two different populations, the theoretical populations of all patrons exposed to music and all patrons not exposed to music.

Test Statistic

The independent-samples t test is computed according to Equation 7.1, using $\hat{\sigma}_{\overline{X}_1-\overline{X}_2}$ computed according to Equation 7.2:

$$t_{\overline{X}_1-\overline{X}_2} = \frac{(\overline{X}_1 - \overline{X}_2) - \mu_{\overline{X}_1-\overline{X}_2}}{\hat{\sigma}_{\overline{X}_1-\overline{X}_2}}$$

$$= \frac{(28.19 - 25.94) - 0}{2.49}$$

$$= .90$$

where

$$\hat{\sigma}_{\overline{X}_1-\overline{X}_2} = \sqrt{\left[\frac{(N_1 - 1)\hat{s}_1^2 + (N_2 - 1)\hat{s}_2^2}{N_1 + N_2 - 2}\right]\left[\frac{N_1 + N_2}{N_1 N_2}\right]}$$

$$= \sqrt{\left[\frac{(16 - 1)65.90 + (16 - 1)33.66}{16 + 16 - 2}\right]\left[\frac{16 + 16}{16(16)}\right]}$$

$$= 2.49$$

Choosing Between H_0 and H_1

The test statistic $t_{\overline{X}_1-\overline{X}_2} = .90$ indicates that the obtained difference ($\overline{X}_1 - \overline{X}_2 = 2.25$) falls .90 standard error of the difference from the value most likely (0) in pairs of samples drawn from a population in which all cases are treated identically. For df $= N_1 + N_2 - 2 = 30$ degrees of freedom, the table of critical values of t (Table 2 in Appendix B) shows a critical value of $t = 1.697$ marking the .05 critical region. (Note that a one-tail significance test is used because it was predicted in advance that music would decrease time spent eating.)

As shown in the sampling distribution of the difference depicted below, the obtained $\overline{X}_1 - \overline{X}_2$ difference (and the $t_{\overline{X}_1-\overline{X}_2}$ value that represents it) falls short of the .05 critical region. We can conclude that the obtained $\overline{X}_1 - \overline{X}_2$ difference is one that occurs quite often in pairs of samples drawn from a population of identically treated cases. The two samples differ by no more than would be expected on the basis of sampling error. There is no evidence that the samples represent different populations. We accept the null hypothesis (H_0) as a reasonably likely explanation of the observed difference between the samples at hand, and declare the difference to be statistically nonsignificant.

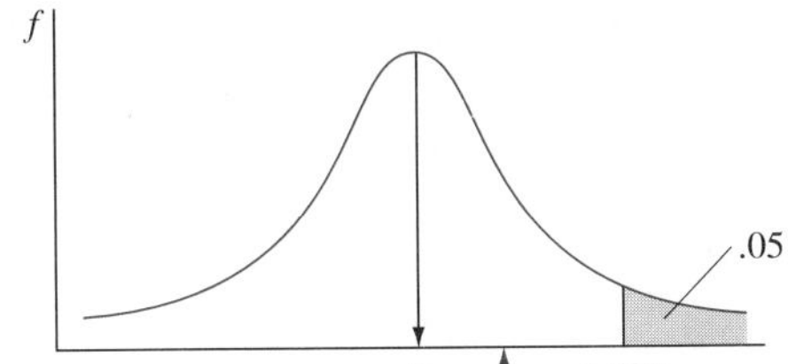

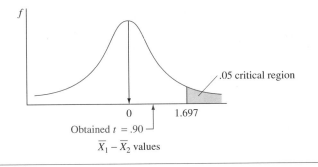

7.3 The Dependent-Samples *t* Test

The independent-samples *t* test discussed in the preceding section is used to compare the means of two separate and unrelated samples, that is, independent samples. In this *t* test, which cases comprise one sample are in no way affected by which cases comprise the other sample. We might use the independent-samples *t* test, for instance, to compare the mean weight of a sample of cases who completed an eating behavior-modification program with the mean weight of a waiting-list control group.

There are some research situations, though, in which the samples being compared are not independent, but dependent. In these research designs, the composition of one sample is very much affected by the composition of the other sample. In **repeated-measures** (or pretest–posttest) **research designs**, for instance, the same cases are measured twice, before receiving some experimental treatment and again after treatment. As an example, a researcher might compare the mean weight of a sample of cases before they begin and again after they complete an eating behavior-modification program. Here, of course, the cases comprising one sample very much affect which cases comprise the other sample: They are the same. In another kind of research design, the **matched-samples research design**, the cases that comprise the second sample are different from those in the first sample, but are selected so as to match or mirror in one or more ways the cases that comprise the first sample. As an example of a matched-samples design, a researcher wanting to evaluate an eating behavior-modification program might form two groups. Cases assigned to receive the experimental treatment would be selected at random, but cases selected to form the waiting-list control group would not be selected randomly. Instead, each case selected for inclusion in the control group would be selected because he or she matched in one or more ways—age, gender,

repeated-measures research design
A research design in which the same cases are measured twice—before treatment and again after treatment—and then compared. Also known as a pretest–posttest design.

matched-samples research design
A research design in which the cases that comprise one sample are selected specifically so as to match the characteristics of cases comprising a second sample.

marital status, and the like—one of the cases in the experimental group. Here again the samples are not independent. The characteristics of cases in one sample very much influence the characteristics of cases in the second sample.

dependent-samples *t* test *A parametric significant difference test that uses the* t *statistic to compare the means of two dependent samples, usually in the context of a repeated-measures or matched-samples research design.*

When two samples are dependent like this, the **dependent-samples *t* test** is commonly used to compare their means. As we will discover, the dependent-samples *t* test offers the statistical advantage of greater power than the independent-samples *t* test. This means that, all other things being equal, the dependent-samples *t* test will identify as statistically significant a smaller difference than is required to reach significance with an independent-samples *t* test. Let's see why.

COMPREHENSION CHECK 7.12

To which of the scenarios listed in Comprehension Check 7.3 would the dependent-samples *t* test be most appropriate?

(Answer on p. 222.)

The *t* Test in the Repeated-Measures Design

To understand how the dependent-samples *t* test achieves its power advantage over the independent-samples *t* test, we need to return to the sampling distribution of the difference. When all possible pairs of independent samples are drawn from a population of identically treated cases, values of the $\bar{X}_1 - \bar{X}_2$ difference vary from one pair of samples to the next. This variability is measured by $\hat{\sigma}_{\bar{X}_1-\bar{X}_2}$ and results from sampling error. Looking back at Equation 7.2, you can see that $\hat{\sigma}_{\bar{X}_1-\bar{X}_2}$ is the enemy in our effort to find any given $\bar{X}_1 - \bar{X}_2$ difference significant, because the higher the value of $\hat{\sigma}_{\bar{X}_1-\bar{X}_2}$, the lower the value of $t_{\bar{X}_1-\bar{X}_2}$, and the less likely it is that that $t_{\bar{X}_1-\bar{X}_2}$ value will reach significance. It follows that anything we can do to reduce $\hat{\sigma}_{\bar{X}_1-\bar{X}_2}$ will raise $t_{\bar{X}_1-\bar{X}_2}$ and increase the likelihood that a given $\bar{X}_1 - \bar{X}_2$ difference will be found statistically significant. If we can figure out what causes sampling error, we may be able to reduce it, and thereby lower $\hat{\sigma}_{\bar{X}_1-\bar{X}_2}$.

measurement error *Inaccuracy in measurement that introduces variability into scores, and ultimately, into sampling distributions.*

Measurement error, simple inaccuracy in measuring individual cases, causes some of the variability in the sampling distribution of the difference. Suppose you weighed yourself on a bathroom scale 10 times in a row. Do you think you'd get exactly the same weight all 10 times? Probably not, simply because no scale, whether it measures weight, intelligence, or anything else, is perfectly accurate. This same inaccuracy contributes to the standard error of the difference. In a population of identically treated cases, some of the variability in scores from one case to the next is due to measurement error. Because the scores of the individual cases vary, so will the means of samples drawn from the population. And this means that the $\bar{X}_1 - \bar{X}_2$ differences seen from one pair of samples to the next drawn from this population will vary somewhat. In short, measurement error produces some of the variability in the sampling distribution of the difference that is reflected in $\hat{\sigma}_{\bar{X}_1-\bar{X}_2}$.

COMPREHENSION CHECK 7.13

Shown below are nine lines of varying lengths. Write down estimates of the length in millimeters of each of the lines. *Without looking at these first estimates,* do it again. Do your first and second estimates match exactly? If not, why?

(a) ___ (d) _ (g) _____

(b) ____ (e) _____________ (h) _____________

(c) _______ (f) ____ (i) _______

(Answer on p. 222.)

Individual difference characteristics are a second source of variability in the sampling distribution of the difference, a more important source for purposes of this discussion. When the cases that form a population are treated identically, they do not react identically to that treatment. This is because of their individual difference characteristics. To continue our previous example, consider the entire theoretical population of people who have completed an eating behavior-modification program. Even though everyone gets the same treatment, would you expect that they would all weigh the same when they finished the program? Of course not. Individual difference characteristics such as differences in starting weight, age, metabolic rate, and a myriad of other characteristics would produce variability in weights from case to case. As a result, the means of samples drawn from the population of identically treated cases would vary somewhat from one sample to the next. And that means that the $\overline{X}_1 - \overline{X}_2$ values seen from one pair of samples to the next drawn from this population would vary. It is in this way that individual differences contribute to the variability seen in the sampling distribution of the difference—$\hat{\sigma}_{\overline{X}_1-\overline{X}_2}$.

individual difference characteristics *Differences in the characteristics from one case to the next that introduce variability into scores, and ultimately, into sampling distributions.*

In forming the sampling distribution of the difference, we have randomly drawn all possible pairs of independent samples from a population of identically treated cases. For one pair of samples, the $\overline{X}_1 - \overline{X}_2$ difference may be rather small because the two samples forming that pair just happen to be quite similar in their individual difference characteristics. In the next pair, though, the $\overline{X}_1 - \overline{X}_2$ difference may be quite large because the two samples forming that pair just happen to be quite different in their individual difference characteristics. When we draw all possible pairs of independent samples from a population, this makes for lots of variability in $\overline{X}_1 - \overline{X}_2$ values and a large $\hat{\sigma}_{\overline{X}_1-\overline{X}_2}$.

Now imagine a slightly different scenario. We begin, as always, with a population of identically treated cases. Now, instead of computing $\overline{X}_1 - \overline{X}_2$ for all possible pairs of *independent* samples, suppose we compute $\overline{X}_1 - \overline{X}_2$ for all possible *single* samples, *each measured twice,* that is, using a repeated measures procedure. We draw the first sample, measure it once and compute $\overline{X}_1$, then measure the same sample again and compute $\overline{X}_2$, and then compute the $\overline{X}_1 - \overline{X}_2$ difference. We then draw the next sample, measure it twice and compute the next $\overline{X}_1 - \overline{X}_2$ difference, and so on until we have drawn all possible samples and measured each twice. Will the two means in each of these pairs probably be the same? No, because measurement error will still introduce some variability into the scores. But we have eliminated individual difference characteristics as a source of variability in the sampling distribution of the difference. The first sample in each pair now consists of exactly the same cases as the second sample in each pair, so the individual difference characteristics of the two samples are identical and the means of the two samples will not differ because of individual difference characteristics.

By using a repeated-measures procedure we can reduce some of the variability seen in the sampling distribution of the difference. This means that $\hat{\sigma}_{\overline{X}_1-\overline{X}_2}$ will be lower, and that in turn means that any given $\overline{X}_1 - \overline{X}_2$ difference will produce a higher value of $t_{\overline{X}_1-\overline{X}_2}$—one more likely to reach significance.

COMPREHENSION CHECK 7.14

In Comprehension Check 7.4 you constructed the sampling distribution of the difference for independent samples of sizes $N_1 = 2$ and $N_2 = 2$ drawn from a population of three cases. Now use a repeated-

(cont.)

FIGURE 7.2

Sampling distributions of the difference for independent samples (broader distribution) and repeated measures (narrower distribution). The independent-samples distribution requires a larger $X_1 - X_2$ difference in order to be significant. A smaller $X_1 - X_2$ difference will be significant in the repeated-measures distribution.

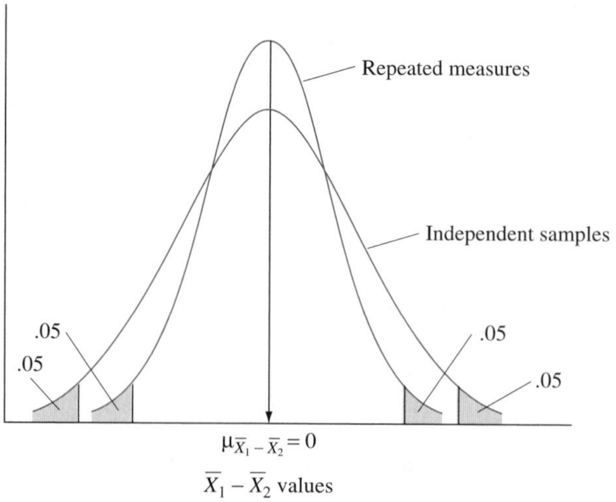

measures procedure to construct the sampling distribution of the difference for samples of size $N = 2$. Compare the two sampling distributions. (Answer on p. 222.)

Figure 7.2 compares the sampling distributions of the difference for independent samples and repeated-measures samples. Independent sampling results in more variability—the broader sampling distribution. Repeated-measures sampling results in less variability—the narrower sampling distribution. Notice how an $\bar{X}_1 - \bar{X}_2$ difference that is very rare in the narrower sampling distribution (and thus is statistically significant) might well fall short of the critical region in the more variable sampling distribution. Any given $\bar{X}_1 - \bar{X}_2$ difference is more likely to be found statistically significant in a sampling distribution of the difference based on repeated-measures sampling than in a sampling distribution based on independent samples.

The *t* Test in the Matched-Samples Design

The repeated-measures procedure lowers the variability of the sampling distribution of the difference by ensuring that the individual difference characteristics of the two samples in each pair will be identical. Measuring the same cases twice is not the only way of accomplishing this, though. We can also use a matched-samples procedure.

In a matched-samples research design, similarity between the samples that make up each pair is ensured by selecting cases for the second sample that match cases in the first sample in one or more ways. The similarity between samples probably will not be as great as if the same sample were measured twice, but it will be greater than if the two samples in each pair were selected independently.

In using a matched-samples research design we must decide which individual difference characteristic(s) will provide the basis for matching. Should we match subjects on the basis of age? Race? Socioeconomic status? Selecting matching variables is a matter of identifying the individual difference characteristics that are most likely to contribute to variability in scores on whatever dependent variable is the focus of the research. If our dependent variable is body weight, metabolic rate might be an appropriate matching variable, but religious preference probably would not be. If the dependent variable is attitude toward abortion, religious preference would be an important matching variable, but metabolic rate would be irrelevant.

Once the matching variables have been selected, the matching process is quite straightforward. Say, for example, that we have decided to match samples on the basis of age. If the first case in the first group is 25 years old, we should select as the first case in the second group another individual who is 25. If the second case in the first group is 33 years old, the second case in the second group should also be 33, and so on.

COMPREHENSION CHECK 7.15

A developmental psychologist wants to use a matched-samples design to compare the stress reactions of preschoolers exposed to 30-minute episodes of either *Teenage Mutant Ninja Turtles* or *Barney the Friendly Dinosaur.* Reasoning that gender and age may influence stress reactions, these have been chosen as matching variables. Select from the following list subjects to comprise two groups, each of size $N = 8$, to be assigned to watch *Turtles* or *Barney.*

Case No.	Gender	Age (months)
1	M	27
2	M	36
3	F	21
4	M	48
5	M	50
6	F	32
7	M	26
8	F	38
9	M	51
10	M	48
11	F	32
12	M	52
13	M	48
14	F	20
15	F	39
16	M	36

(Answer on pp. 222–223.)

Computations for the Dependent-Samples *t* Test

Although the sampling procedures are different for repeated-measures and matched-samples research designs, the same computational procedures are used in analyzing the data from both designs. Example 7.2 provides a computational example of the dependent-samples *t* test.

Recall that both dependent-samples designs (repeated measures and matched samples) lead to reduced variability of the sampling distribution of the difference. Equation 7.3 describes the computation of the estimated standard error of the difference for dependent-samples data, symbolized $\hat{\sigma}_{\overline{D}}$.

Equation 7.3

$$\hat{\sigma}_{\overline{D}} = \frac{\sqrt{\Sigma(D - \overline{D})^2/(N - 1)}}{\sqrt{N}}$$

where

$\hat{\sigma}_{\overline{D}}$ = the standard error of the difference for dependent samples
D = the differences between corresponding values of the first and second samples
N = the number of pairs of scores

In words, we estimate the standard error of the difference for dependent samples ($\hat{\sigma}_{\overline{D}}$) by: (1) computing differences between corresponding scores in the first and second samples (D) and the mean of these differences ($\overline{D}$); (2) subtracting $\overline{D}$ from each value of D, squaring each difference, and summing the squared differences; (3) dividing the result of step 2 by one less than the number of pairs of scores ($N - 1$); (4) finding the square root of step 3; and (5) dividing the result of step 4 by the square root of the number of pairs of scores (N).

Comprehension Check 7.16

Times spent in thumb-sucking behavior, rounded to the nearest minute, are listed below for matched samples who viewed 30-minute episodes of either *Teenage Mutant Ninja Turtles* or *Barney*. Use Equation 7.3 to compute $\hat{\sigma}_{\overline{D}}$.

Turtles				**Barney**			
Case	*Gender*	*Age*	*Time*	*Case*	*Gender*	*Age*	*Time*
1	M	27	12	7	M	26	10
14	F	20	8	3	F	21	18
2	M	36	8	16	M	36	2
8	F	38	5	15	F	39	4
4	M	48	3	13	M	48	0
12	M	52	0	9	M	51	0
10	M	48	4	5	M	50	7
6	F	32	12	11	F	32	6

(Answer on p. 223.)

Once we have the estimated standard error of the difference for dependent samples, $t_{\overline{X}_1 - \overline{X}_2}$ is computed as before, substituting $\hat{\sigma}_{\overline{D}}$ for $\hat{\sigma}_{\overline{X}_1 - \overline{X}_2}$ as shown in Equation 7.4.

Equation 7.4

$$t_{\overline{X}_1 - \overline{X}_2} = \frac{(\overline{X}_1 - \overline{X}_2) - \mu_{\overline{X}_1 - \overline{X}_2}}{\hat{\sigma}_{\overline{D}}}$$

where

$t_{\overline{X}_1 - \overline{X}_2}$ = the dependent-samples t statistic
$\overline{X}_1$ = the mean of the first sample

(cont.)

$\overline{X}_2$ = the mean of the second sample

$\mu_{\overline{X}_1-\overline{X}_2}$ = the mean of the sampling distribution of the difference between dependent sample means (equal to zero)

$\hat{\sigma}_{\overline{D}}$ = the standard error of the difference for dependent samples (Equation 7.3)

In words, the dependent-samples $t_{\overline{X}_1-\overline{X}_2}$ statistic is computed by: (1) computing the difference between the two sample means ($\overline{X}_1 - \overline{X}_2$); (2) subtracting the mean of the sampling distribution of the difference between means ($\mu_{\overline{X}_1-\overline{X}_2} = 0$) from the result of step 1; and (3) dividing the result of step 2 by the standard error of the difference for dependent samples ($\hat{\sigma}_{\overline{D}}$) computed according to Equation 7.3.

There is another computational difference between the independent-samples and dependent-samples t tests. In the dependent-samples t test, degrees of freedom used to enter the table of critical values of t are computed as df = $N - 1$, where N = the number of pairs of scores.

Comprehension Check 7.17

Use Equation 7.4 to compute the dependent-samples $t_{\overline{X}_1-\overline{X}_2}$ statistic for the matched-samples data given in Comprehension Check 7.16. Evaluate the statistical significance of the difference between the mean thumb-sucking times of the two groups of preschoolers.

(Answer on p. 223.)

Example 7.2

Dependent-Samples t Test

An independent-samples t test was used in Example 7.1 to evaluate the difference between mean eating times of patrons who listened to music while they ate and patrons who ate in silence. The difference was found to be nonsignificant. For purposes of this example, which illustrates the increased power of the dependent-samples t test, let's suppose that the same data were collected using a repeated-measures design.

Since many of the patrons of Sam 'n Ella's Diner are "regulars," it was possible to observe the same patrons on both Monday, the no-music day, and Tuesday, the music day, and to record eating times on both days. Data and descriptive statistics are presented on the next page from this repeated-measures design. Notice that these times and descriptive statistics are identical to those given in Example 7.1, except that there were 32 cases in Example 7.1 (N_1 = 16 and N_2 = 16) and there are only 16 cases here, each measured twice. Also included in this data table are values of D, the difference between corresponding values of the dependent variable. These values are used in computing the dependent-samples t test.

Null and Alternative Hypotheses

H_0: The difference between the means is a consequence of sampling error. In a population of cases measured twice under identical conditions, one would be quite likely to observe a sample showing a difference of the size observed here. Therefore, the sample at hand probably represents such a population. There is no evidence that the difference should be attributed to the different musical conditions to which the sample was exposed.

No Music	Music	D
25	21	4
12	15	−3
33	29	4
35	30	5
43	38	5
17	22	−5
29	23	6
37	30	7
29	24	5
23	23	0
19	22	−3
35	29	6
35	27	8
28	31	−3
24	19	5
27	32	−5
$\overline{X}_1 = 28.19$	$\overline{X}_2 = 25.94$	$\overline{D} = 2.25$
$\hat{s}_1^2 = 65.90$	$\hat{s}_2^2 = 33.66$	
	$N = 16$	

H_1: The difference between the means is too large to be attributed to sampling error alone. In a population of cases measured twice under identical conditions, one would be quite unlikely to observe a sample showing a difference as great as the one observed here. Therefore, this sample probably does not represent such a population. Instead, it represents a population in which each measure is taken under different conditions. The difference observed here should be attributed to the different musical conditions to which the sample was exposed.

Test Statistic

The dependent-samples t test is computed according to Equation 7.4, using $\hat{\sigma}_{\overline{X}_1-\overline{X}_2}$ computed according to Equation 7.3.

$$t = \frac{(\overline{X}_1 - \overline{X}_2) - \mu_{\overline{X}_1-\overline{X}_2}}{\hat{\sigma}_{\overline{D}}}$$

$$= \frac{(28.19 - 25.94) - 0}{1.14}$$

$$= 1.97$$

where

$$\hat{\sigma}_{\overline{D}} = \frac{\sqrt{\Sigma(D - \overline{D})^2/(N - 1)}}{\sqrt{N}}$$

$$= \frac{\sqrt{313/(16 - 1)}}{\sqrt{16}}$$

$$= 1.14$$

Choosing Between H_0 and H_1

The test statistic $t_{\overline{X}_1-\overline{X}_2} = 1.97$ indicates that the obtained difference $(\overline{X}_1 - \overline{X}_2 = 2.25)$ falls 1.97 standard errors of the difference from the value most likely (0) in pairs of samples drawn from a population in which cases are measured twice under identical conditions. For df = $N - 1 = 15$ degrees of freedom, the table of critical values of t (Table 2 in Appendix B) shows a critical value of $t = 1.753$ marking the .05 critical region. (We have again used a one-tail significance test because it was predicted in advance that music would decrease time spent eating.)

As shown in the sampling distribution of the difference depicted below, the obtained $\overline{X}_1 - \overline{X}_2$ difference falls within the .05 critical region of the sampling distribution of the difference. We can conclude that this $\overline{X}_1 - \overline{X}_2$ difference (and the $t_{\overline{X}_1 - \overline{X}_2}$ value that represents it) would occur relatively infrequently in pairs of samples drawn from a population of cases measured twice under identical conditions. Therefore, the two samples at hand probably do not represent such a population, but instead represent a population in which the cases were measured twice under different conditions—music and no music. The alternative hypothesis (H_1) provides a more likely explanation than the null hypothesis (H_0) for the observed difference, and we declare this difference to be statistically significant.

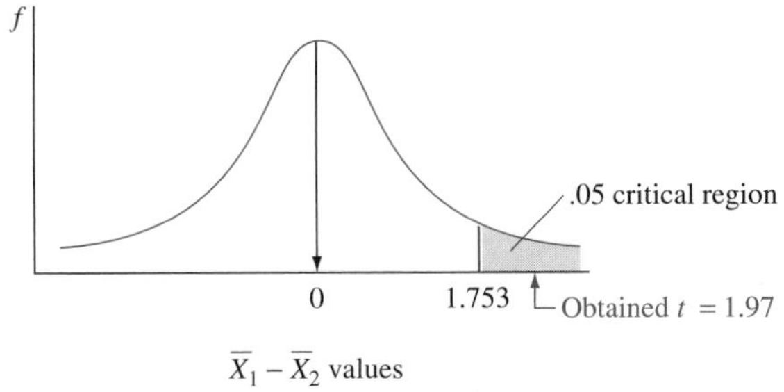

7.4 The Mann-Whitney U

Both independent- and dependent-samples t tests make some parametric assumptions: approximately normal population distributions, approximately equal population variances, and a dependent variable measured at the interval or ratio scale. The **Mann-Whitney U** is a nonparametric alternative to the independent-samples t test that relaxes all of these assumptions. Consistent with the principle that you get what you pay for, the Mann-Whitney U is a less powerful statistical procedure than the t test, but where the parametric assumptions of the t test are strongly violated, the Mann-Whitney U provides a useful alternative method of evaluating differences between two independent samples.

Mann-Whitney U *A nonparametric alternative to the independent-samples* t *test. Evaluates the statistical significance of the difference between rank-order scores of two independent samples.*

Data for the Mann-Whitney U

The Mann-Whitney U analyzes rank-order data. The data may already come in this form, or interval or ratio scale data may be converted to rank orders. In ranking the data for the Mann-Whitney U, the data from both groups are first combined; the groups are not ranked separately. Next, the scores are ranked from lowest to highest (that is, the lowest score is ranked 1, the next higher score is ranked 2, and so on). Finally, when two or more scores are tied, all of the tied scores receive the same rank, equal to the average of the positions of those scores in an ordered array. For example, look at the following statistics test scores, their positions in the ordered array, and their ranks:

Raw Scores	Positions	Ranks
67	1	1
72	2	2.5
72	3	2.5
75	4	4
87	5	6
87	6	6
87	7	6
93	8	8

Notice that scores are ranked from lowest to highest. Notice too that each score's rank is equal to its position in the ordered array except when several scores are tied. Then, each tied score receives a rank equal to the mean of the positions of the tied scores. In this example there are two scores of 72, in positions 2 and 3. Each receives a rank equal to the mean of 2 and 3: $(2 + 3)/2 = 2.5$. Similarly, there are three scores of 87, in positions 5, 6, and 7. Each receives a rank equal to the mean of 5, 6, and 7: $(5 + 6 + 7)/3 = 6$.

COMPREHENSION CHECK 7.18

To which of the scenarios listed in Comprehension Check 7.3 would the Mann-Whitney *U* test be most appropriate?
(Answer on p. 223.)

The Test Statistic *U*

When scores from two same-sized groups ($N_1 = N_2$) are combined and rank-ordered, the sum of ranks for one group will differ from the sum of ranks for the other group to the degree that those groups differ on the dependent variable. Of course, if one group contains more cases than the other, the groups' sums of ranks can no longer be compared directly, because these sums will reflect not only differences between the groups on the dependent variable but also differences in sample sizes.

Some adjustment must be made to the sums of ranks to correct for the effects of sample sizes. The Mann-Whitney *U* is a test statistic that reflects the difference between two groups' sums of ranks corrected for the influence of sample sizes. The *U* statistic is computed according to Equation 7.5.

Equation 7.5

$$U = N_1N_2 + \frac{N_1(N_1 + 1)}{2} - R_1$$

where

U = the Mann-Whitney U statistic
N_1 = the size of the first sample
N_2 = the size of the second sample
R_1 = the sum of ranks for the first sample

In words, we compute U by: (1) multiplying the size of the first group by the size of the second group (N_1N_2); (2) adding 1 to the size of the first group ($N_1 + 1$) and multiplying this sum by the size of the first group (N_1); (3) dividing the result of step 2 by 2; (4) summing the ranks of the first group (R_1); (5) adding the results of steps 1 and 3; and (6) subtracting the result of step 4 from the result of step 5.

COMPREHENSION CHECK 7.19

Use Equation 7.5 to compute the Mann-Whitney U statistic to compare the following test scores of male and female statistics students. Why would the Mann-Whitney U test be more appropriate here than the independent-samples t test?

Males:	98	47	82	97	93	84	88	92
Females:	70	86	89	89	84	84	86	

(Answer on p. 223.)

You may wonder how U can reflect the difference in the sums of ranks of two groups when only the first group's sum of ranks (R_1) appears in Equation 7.5. Where is R_2? It's there, you just can't see it. Realize first that the sum of ranks for the entire set of scores will be limited by the total number of cases ($N_1 + N_2$). Suppose, for example, that there are 10 cases in all. The smallest rank will be 1, the largest rank will be 10, and the sum of all the ranks will be $1 + 2 + \cdots + 10 = 55$. If we know the sum of ranks for one group (R_1), the sum of ranks for the second group (R_2) can be determined. To continue the example begun above, if $R_1 = 25$, R_2 must be

55	(the sum of all the ranks)
−25	(the sum of ranks of the first group)
30	(the sum of ranks of the second group)

Thus, although R_2 does not actually appear in Equation 7.5, it is represented by its relationship to values that do appear: N_1, N_2, and R_1.

The test statistic U reflects the size of the difference between the sums of ranks of two groups by becoming either increasingly larger, if the second group's ranks are higher than those of the first group; or becoming smaller, if the first group's ranks are higher than those of the second group. The U statistic will take on intermediate values when the two groups' sums of ranks are approximately equal. Thus either a very small or very large value of U signals a large difference between groups.

The Sampling Distribution of U

The **sampling distribution of *U*** is the theoretical distribution of values of U that are obtained when all possible pairs of samples of sizes N_1 and N_2 are drawn from a population of identically treated cases and U is computed for each pair. Because the samples in most pairs will be quite similar, most values of U will take on intermediate values. Very large and very small values of U will occur relatively infrequently, because these values occur only when the samples are substantially different. The exact shape of the sampling distribution of U depends on N_1 and N_2, with critical values of U for

sampling distribution of *U* *The theoretical distribution of values of the Mann-Whitney* U *statistic obtained when all possible independent pairs of samples are drawn from a population of identically treated cases and the* U *statistic is computed for each pair.*

one- and two-tail significance tests listed in the table of critical values of U (Table 4 in Appendix B). In order for a given value of U to be found statistically significant, it must fall outside (that is, higher or lower than) the critical boundary values listed in the table.(See Note 3) Example 7.3 illustrates the use of the Mann-Whitney U in comparing two independent samples.

COMPREHENSION CHECK 7.20

Evaluate the statistical significance of the Mann-Whitney U statistic you computed in Comprehension Check 7.19.
(Answer on p. 223.)

EXAMPLE 7.3

Mann-Whitney *U*

Example 7.1 illustrated the use of the independent-samples t test to compare the mean eating times of cases in two groups: those who ate in silence and those who ate while listening to music. The Mann-Whitney U is a nonparametric alternative to the independent-samples t test, which is used here in an analysis of the same data.

Rank-Ordering the Data

The Mann-Whitney U test analyzes rank-order data. Sometimes the data are already in this form, but we must begin this example by ranking the data. Data from the two samples are first combined and then ranked from lowest to highest, with tied scores assigned a rank equal to the average position of those scores in an ordered array. Raw scores and ranks are given below.

No Music		Music	
Raw Scores	*Ranks*	*Raw Scores*	*Ranks*
25	14	21	6
12	1	15	2
33	26	29	19.5
35	28	30	22.5
43	32	38	31
17	3	22	7.5
29	19.5	23	10
37	30	30	22.5
29	19.5	24	12.5
23	10	23	10
19	4.5	22	7.5
35	28	29	19.5
35	28	27	15.5
28	17	31	24
24	12.5	19	4.5
27	15.5	32	25

Null and Alternative Hypotheses

H_0: The difference between the ranks of the two samples (the mean rank for the no-music group is 18.03, compared to 14.97 for the music group) is a consequence of sampling error. Two samples drawn from a population of identically treated cases would be likely to differ by the amount seen here. Therefore there is no evidence that the difference should be attributed to the different musical conditions to which the groups were exposed.

H_1: The difference between the ranks of the two groups is too large to attribute to sampling error alone. Two samples drawn from a population of identically treated cases would be very unlikely to differ by as much as is observed here. Therefore these two samples probably do not represent such a population. Rather, they represent two different populations, the theoretical populations of all patrons not exposed to music and all patrons who are exposed to music.

Test Statistic

The Mann-Whitney U statistic is computed according to Equation 7.5.

$$U = N_1N_2 + \frac{N_1(N_1 + 1)}{2} - R_1$$

$$= 16(16) + \frac{16(16 + 1)}{2} - 288.5$$

$$= 103.5$$

Choosing Between H_0 *and* H_1

Extremely large and small values of U occur when the ranks of two samples differ substantially. Intermediate values of U reflect smaller differences between groups. The table of critical values of U (Table 4 in Appendix B) defines "large" and "small" values of U for various sample sizes. For a one-tail test at the .05 level of significance, with $N_1 = 16$ and $N_2 = 16$, the critical boundary values of U are 83 and 173. The obtained $U = 103.5$ falls within these boundary values and can therefore be considered an "intermediate" value. This is a value of U that occurs quite frequently in pairs of samples drawn from a population of identically treated cases. We conclude that the observed difference can be attributed reasonably to sampling error (H_0) and is nonsignificant.

7.5 The Wilcoxon *T* Test

The **Wilcoxon *T* test** provides a nonparametric alternative to the dependent-samples t test. Although it is less powerful than the t test when the parametric assumptions of the t test are met (normal population distributions, approximately equal variances, and an interval or ratio scale dependent variable), the Wilcoxon procedure is useful in comparing two dependent samples when the assumptions of the t test are seriously violated.

Wilcoxon *T* test *A nonparametric alternative to the dependent-samples* t *test. Evaluates the statistical significance of the difference between rank-order scores of two dependent samples.*

Comprehension Check 7.21

To which of the scenarios listed in Comprehension Check 7.3 would the Wilcoxon T test be most appropriate?
(Answer on p. 223.)

The Wilcoxon T Statistic

The Wilcoxon T statistic is computed by calculating a difference score for each case or pair of matched cases: $D = X_1 - X_2$. Next, ignoring the signs of the difference scores, they are rank-ordered from smallest to largest on the basis of absolute size, except for difference scores of zero, which are ignored. Then, each of the ranks is given a positive or negative sign to reflect the sign of the corresponding difference score. Finally, T is computed according to Equation 7.6.

Equation 7.6

T = the smaller of: (1) the absolute sum of the positive ranks, or (2) the absolute sum of the negative ranks

where

T = the Wilcoxon T statistic

In words, the Wilcoxon T is computed by: (1) summing the absolute values of the positive ranks; (2) summing the absolute values of the negative ranks; and (3) choosing the smaller of the results of steps 1 and 2 as T.

When two sets of scores are equal, the sum of the positive ranks and the sum of the negative ranks will be equal. As the two sets of scores become more disparate, these two sums will also become increasingly different. If scores in the first set are higher than scores in the second set, the sum of positive ranks will exceed the sum of negative ranks. If scores in the first set are lower than those in the second set, the sum of negative ranks will exceed the sum of positive ranks. Because the statistic T is equal to the smaller of these two sums, T will vary inversely with the magnitude of the difference between the two sets of scores. That is, T will become larger as the difference between samples becomes smaller, and smaller as the difference between samples becomes larger.

COMPREHENSION CHECK 7.22

Use Equation 7.6 to compute the Wilcoxon T statistic for the thumb-sucking data presented in Comprehension Check 7.16.
(Answer on p. 223.)

The Sampling Distribution of the Wilcoxon T

sampling distribution of T *The theoretical distribution of values of the Wilcoxon* T *statistic obtained when all possible dependent pairs of samples are drawn from a population of identically treated cases and the* T *statistic is computed for each pair.*

The **sampling distribution of** T is the distribution of values of T computed for all possible pairs of dependent samples drawn from a population of identically treated cases. Critical values of T for one- and two-tail significance tests are listed in the table of critical values of T (Table 5 in Appendix B).(See Note 4) This table is entered using N, the number of *ranked* pairs of scores. Thus, any pair of scores showing a difference of zero (which would not have been ranked) does not contribute to N. In order to be considered significant, the obtained value of T must be less than or equal to the tabled critical value. Example 7.4 demonstrates the use of the Wilcoxon T test in comparing two dependent samples.

Evaluate the statistical significance of the Wilcoxon T statistic computed in Comprehension Check 7.22.
(Answer on pp. 223–224.)

COMPREHENSION CHECK 7.23

EXAMPLE 7.4

Wilcoxon T

Example 7.2 illustrated the use of the dependent-samples t test to compare mean eating times under music and no-music conditions in a repeated-measures design. The Wilcoxon T test is a nonparametric alternative to the dependent-samples t test and is used here in an analysis of the same data.

Null and Alternative Hypotheses

H_0: The difference between the two sets of scores can be attributed reasonably to sampling error alone. A sample drawn from a population of cases measured twice under identical conditions would be likely to produce scores that differ by as much as is seen here.

H_1: The difference between the two sets of scores is too large to be a likely result of sampling error alone. A sample drawn from a population of cases measured twice under identical conditions would be very unlikely to produce two sets of scores that differ by as much as is seen here. Instead, this sample represents a population in which each measure is taken under different conditions. The difference observed here should be attributed to the different musical conditions to which the sample was exposed.

Test Statistic

We begin the Wilcoxon T test by computing differences (D) between corresponding values of the dependent variable. These differences are then rank-ordered from smallest to largest on the basis of absolute size, except for differences of 0, which are left unranked. Next, each of the ranks is given a sign corresponding to the sign of its corresponding difference (D) score. Finally, T is computed according to Equation 7.6. The data for this analysis are shown below.

No Music	Music	D	Signed Ranks
25	21	4	+ 4.5
12	15	−3	− 2
33	29	4	+ 4.5
35	30	5	+ 8.5
43	38	5	+ 8.5
17	22	−5	− 8.5
29	23	6	+12.5
37	30	7	+14
29	24	5	+ 8.5
23	23	0	Unranked
19	22	−3	− 2
35	29	6	+12.5
35	27	8	+15
28	31	−3	− 2
24	19	5	+ 8.5
27	32	−5	− 8.5

The test statistic T is equal to the smaller of: (1) the absolute sum of the positive ranks (97 here), or (2) the absolute sum of the negative ranks (23 here). Therefore, $T = 23$ in this example.

Choosing Between H_0 *and* H_1

The test statistic $T = 23$ is evaluated by comparing it to the sampling distribution of T described in Table 5 of Appendix B. For a one-tail test at the .05 level of significance and $N = 15$ (the number of *ranked* pairs of scores), this table of critical values of T lists a critical value of $T = 30$. The obtained value of $T = 23$ is smaller than this critical value and is therefore considered statistically significant. (Note that, unlike most test statistics, which must *meet or exceed* the tabled critical value, the Wilcoxon T must be *less than or equal to* the tabled value to be considered statistically significant.)

We can conclude that it is unlikely that a sample drawn from a population of cases measured twice under identical conditions would produce scores that differ by as much as is seen here. It is therefore more likely that the sample represents a population in which cases are observed under different conditions—music and no music. The alternative hypothesis (H_1) offers a more likely explanation for the observed difference than does the null hypothesis (H_0).

7.6 The Chi-Square Test for Two Independent Samples

chi-square test for two independent samples *A nonparametric significant difference test used to compare the entire distributions of two independent samples.*

The chi-square goodness-of-fit test was described in the preceding chapter as a procedure that is useful in comparing the distributions of a sample and a population. The **chi-square test for two independent samples** is used to compare the distributions of two independent samples. The dependent variable in these comparisons can be measured on a nominal scale, or a continuous variable can be scaled down to the nominal level and analyzed using the chi-square procedure. The chi-square test is a nonparametric procedure that makes no assumptions about distribution shapes, variances, or levels of measurement.

Comprehension Check 7.24

To which of the scenarios listed in Comprehension Check 7.3 would the chi-square test for two independent samples be most appropriate? (Answer on p. 224.)

Organizing the Data

contingency table *A table used to organize the data analyzed using the chi-square test for two independent samples. Columns represent the samples being compared; rows represent categories of the dependent variable.*

The chi-square test for two independent samples analyzes data organized into a **contingency table** like the one shown in Example 7.5. The columns of the contingency table represent the samples being compared, and each row represents one of the categories of the dependent variable. Recorded in each cell of the contingency table are: (1) observed frequencies (f_o), the number of cases in each sample that falls into each category of the dependent variable; and (2) expected frequencies (f_e), the number of cases in each sample that would be expected in each dependent variable category *if the two samples* *were distributed identically.* Any differences between observed and expected frequencies in the contingency table, then, give evidence that the distributions are different. The computation of expected frequencies is best explained through example. See Example 7.5 for an illustration of this process.

The Chi-Square Test Statistic

The chi-square test statistic (χ^2) for two independent samples is computed using Equation 7.7 just as it was for the goodness-of-fit test.

Equation 7.7

$$\chi^2 = \sum\frac{(f_o - f_e)^2}{f_e}$$

where

χ^2 = the chi-square test statistic
f_o = the frequency observed in each cell of the contingency table
f_e = the frequency expected in each cell of the contingency table if there were no difference between the groups' distributions

In words, the χ^2 test statistic is computed by: (1) subtracting each cell's expected frequency (f_e) from that cell's observed frequency (f_o); (2) squaring each of these differences; (3) dividing each of the values obtained in step 2 by the corresponding cell's expected frequency; and (4) summing the values obtained in step 3.

When distributions of two samples are identical, so that $f_o = f_e$ in every cell of the contingency table, χ^2 will equal zero. As the two distributions become increasingly disparate, the value of χ^2 increases as well.

COMPREHENSION CHECK 7.25

Use Equation 7.7 to compute the χ^2 statistic to compare the following introductory sociology grade distributions of traditional and nontraditional students.

Grade	*Traditional*	*Nontraditional*
A	7	16
B	10	24
C	23	15
D	8	6
F	2	1

(Answer on p. 224.)

The Sampling Distribution of χ^2

sampling distribution of χ^2 *The theoretical distribution of values of the χ^2 statistic obtained when all possible pairs of independent samples are drawn from a population of identically treated cases and the χ^2 statistic is computed for each pair.*

The **sampling distribution of** χ^2 is the distribution of values of χ^2 computed for all possible pairs of independent samples drawn from a population of identically treated cases. The lowest possible value of χ^2 is 0, which occurs when both samples in a pair are identical. Because most pairs of samples drawn from a population of identically treated cases will be quite similar, low values of χ^2 occur relatively frequently in this sampling distribution. Higher values occur less frequently. The exact shape of the sampling distribution of χ^2 varies as a function of degrees of freedom, equal to $(R - 1)(C - 1)$, where R = the number of rows in the contingency table and C = the number of columns in the table. Critical values of χ^2 that mark critical regions of the χ^2 sampling distribution are listed in the table of critical values of χ^2 (Table 3 in Appendix B). Example 7.5 illustrates the use of the χ^2 test in comparing the distributions of two independent samples.

COMPREHENSION CHECK 7.26

Evaluate the statistical significance of the χ^2 statistic you computed in Comprehension Check 7.25.
(Answer on p. 224.)

Small Expected Frequencies

We learned in Chapter 6 that the χ^2 statistic is affected strongly by small expected frequencies. This is true for both the χ^2 goodness-of-fit test and the χ^2 test for two independent samples.

To illustrate, suppose you have a contingency table with two rows and two columns. Suppose, too, that the observed frequency in one cell of this table is $f_o = 3$, and the expected frequency in this cell is $f_e = 1$. Without knowing anything about the rest of the table, we can already say that the difference is significant. The contribution of the known cell to χ^2 is

$$\frac{(3 - 1)^2}{1} = 4$$

Even if observed and expected frequencies match perfectly in all of the other cells of the table, χ^2 will be at least 4. For df $= (R - 1)(C - 1) = (2 - 1)(2 - 1) = 1$, the critical value of χ^2 at the .05 level of significance is 3.841. In this example, χ^2 is statistically significant because of a difference of only two cases between observed and expected frequencies in only one cell of the contingency table.

Because χ^2 is so sensitive to the effects of small expected frequencies, the χ^2 test for two independent samples should be used only when all expected frequencies in a 2 × 2 contingency table are at least 5. For larger tables, at least 80% of the cells should contain expected frequencies of 5 or greater, and no cell should contain an expected frequency of less than 1. When expected frequencies are too small, we may sometimes combine categories of the dependent variable and/or increase sample size to boost expected frequencies to an acceptable level.

Yates's correction *An adjustment used in computing the χ^2 statistic when a 2 × 2 contingency table contains expected frequencies less than 5.*

Another alternative, useful only with 2 × 2 contingency tables, is to compute χ^2 using **Yates's correction**, as shown in Equation 7.8. (See Note 5)

Equation 7.8

$$\chi^{2'} = \sum \frac{[(|f_o - f_e|) - .5]^2}{f_e}$$

where

$\chi^{2'}$ = the corrected value of chi squared
f_o = the frequency observed in each cell of the contingency table
f_e = the frequency expected in each cell of the contingency table if there were no difference between the groups' distributions

In words, we compute χ^2 with Yates's correction ($\chi^{2'}$) by: (1) finding the absolute difference in each cell between that cell's observed frequency and the cell's expected frequency ($|f_o - f_e|$); (2) subtracting .5 from each of these absolute differences; (3) squaring each of these differences; (4) dividing each of the values obtained in step 3 by that cell's expected frequency; and (5) summing the values obtained in step 4.

If Yates's correction were applied to the preceding data, $\chi^{2'}$ would not be significant, at least not by virtue of the data in just one cell of the contingency table:

$$\frac{[(|3 - 1|) - .5]^2}{1} = 2.25$$

Comprehension Check 7.27

Compute χ^2 using Yates's correction (Equation 7.8) to compare the numbers of traditional and nontraditional students who passed (grades A to D) and failed (F) introductory sociology (see the data in Comprehension Check 7.25). Evaluate the statistical significance of this statistic.

(Answer on pp. 224–225.)

Example 7.5

Chi-Square Test for Two Independent Samples

Data were presented at the beginning of this chapter summarizing the percentages of white and minority psychologists employed at the academic ranks of full professor, associate professor, assistant professor, lecturer/instructor, and other. In these sample data, whites are more often employed at higher academic ranks than are minorities. We must ask, however, whether this finding is sample-specific and peculiar to the sample at hand, or whether the entire populations of white and minority academic psychologists show the same difference in rank of employment seen in these samples. This is a question of statistical significance that can be addressed by the chi-square test for two independent samples.

The data are shown again in the contingency table below. This table provides observed frequencies (f_o) for each group in each academic rank. Also shown in the contingency table are column totals, row totals, and row percentages (the percentage of the total number of cases found in each row of the table). Finally, the contingency table includes expected frequencies (f_e) in parentheses for each group in each academic rank. These are the frequencies of white and minority academic psychologists that one would expect to see employed at each rank *if there are no differences in employment patterns between white and minority psychologists.*

These expected frequencies are crucial to computing the χ^2 statistic, so let's see how they were determined. First, for full professors, because 48% of the total sample is employed at the rank of full professor, we expect this percentage to apply equally to white and minority psychologists if there are no differences between these groups. Forty-eight percent of 6,627 white psychologists is 3,181 ($.48 \times 6{,}627 = 3{,}181$). Forty-eight percent of 421 minority psychologists is 202 ($.48 \times 421 = 202$). Next, for associate professors, because 26% of the total sample is employed at the rank of associate professor, we expect this percentage to apply equally to white and minority psychologists if there are no differences between these groups. Twenty-six percent of 6,627 white psychologists is 1,723 ($.26 \times 6{,}627 = 1{,}723$). Twenty-six percent of 421 minority psychologists is 109 ($.26 \times 421 = 109$). Expected frequencies for each of the other cells of the contingency table are computed in a similar manner, that is, by multiplying row percentages (expressed as proportions) by column totals. You may notice that one of the cells in this table includes an expected frequency of less than 5. This falls within the accepted limit that no more than 20% of the cells of the contingency table show expected frequencies lower than 5.

	White (*N = 6,627*)	*Minorities* (*N = 421*)	**Row totals**	**Row percentages**
Full professor	3,314 3,181	105 (202)	3,419	48%
Associate professor	1,723 (1,723)	126 (109)	1,849	26%
Assistant professor	1,392 (1,458)	173 (93)	1,565	22%
Instructor/lecturer	66 (66)	8 (4)	74	1%
Other	132 (133)	9 (8)	141	2%
Column totals	6,627	421	$N = 7{,}048$	

Null and Alternative Hypotheses

H_0: The employment distributions of white and minority academic psychologists differ by no more than would be expected in two samples drawn from a population of identically treated cases. The difference observed can be attributed to sampling error. There is no evidence that whites and minorities are treated differently.

H_1: The difference in employment distributions of white and minority psychologists is too large to be a likely consequence of sampling error alone. Two samples drawn from a population of identically treated cases would be very unlikely to show distributions as different as these. Therefore, these two samples probably do not represent a population of identically treated cases, but instead, two populations—white and minority—that are treated differently.

Test Statistic

The chi-square statistic is computed according to Equation 7.7.

$$\chi^2 = \sum \frac{(f_o - f_e)^2}{f_e}$$

$$= \frac{(3{,}314 - 3{,}181)^2}{3{,}181} + \frac{(105 - 202)^2}{202} + \cdots + \frac{(9 - 8)^2}{8}$$

$$= 130.73$$

***Choosing Between* H_0 *and* H_1**

The test statistic $\chi^2 = 130.73$ is evaluated by comparing it to the sampling distribution of χ^2. For df $= (R - 1)(C - 1) = (5 - 1)(2 - 1) = 4$, the table of critical values of χ^2 gives 13.277 as the value marking the .01 tail of the distribution. As shown in the sampling distribution of χ^2 depicted below, the obtained χ^2 value far surpasses this critical value. We can conclude that the obtained value of χ^2, and the difference between white and minority employment distributions that it represents, is extremely unlikely to be produced by two samples drawn from a population of identically treated cases. Therefore, the samples at hand probably do not represent such a population. It is more likely that these samples represent different populations—white and minority academic psychologists—and that these populations differ in patterns of employment. The difference is statistically significant.

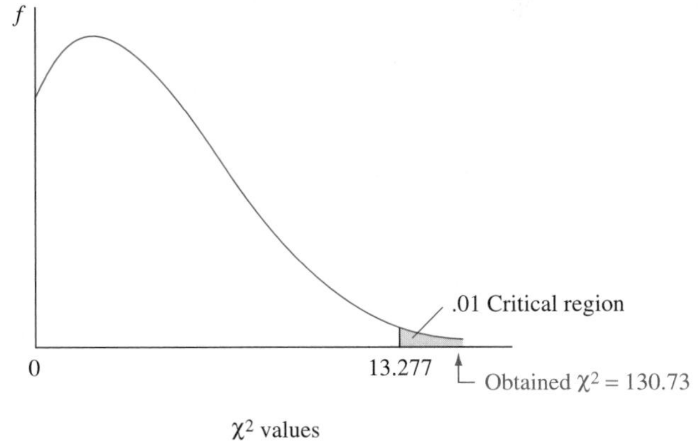

7.7 Type I and Type II Errors

Two-sample significant difference tests enable us to choose which explanation for an observed difference between two samples is most likely—H_0 or H_1. If the difference between two samples (and the test statistic that represents this difference) is unlikely to be seen in pairs of samples drawn from a population of identically treated cases, it follows that the samples at hand probably do not represent such a population. It is more likely that they represent two different populations. If the difference (and its associated test statistic) is likely to be seen in pairs of samples drawn from a population of identically treated cases, it follows that the samples at hand probably represent such a population. We learned in Chapter 6, though, that "probably" doesn't mean "certainly," and "likely" doesn't mean "definitely." When we base conclusions on statistical probabilities, there will be some probability that our conclusions are wrong. This principle applies as much to two-sample significant difference tests as to one-sample tests.

In the context of two-sample tests, a Type I error occurs when the difference between two samples is declared significant when, in fact, the populations represented by the two samples are really identical. A Type II error occurs when the difference between two samples is declared nonsignificant when, in fact, the populations represented by the two samples are really different.

The same forces that affect statistical decision making in the context of one-sample significant difference tests are also at work in two-sample tests: level of significance, choice of one-tail vs. two-tail tests, sample size, and data variability. We can reduce Type I errors by (1) adopting a more stringent significance level; and (2) using two-tail tests rather than one-tail tests. Type II errors rates are reduced by (1) adopting a less stringent significance level; (2) using one-tail tests rather than two-tail tests; (3) studying larger samples rather than smaller samples; and (4) reducing random data variability.

COMPREHENSION CHECK 7.28

Example 7.1 found no significant difference between eating times of diners who listened to music and those who ate in silence. Which type of error might have been committed here, Type I or Type II? Example 7.5 found a statistically significant difference between the employment patterns of white and minority academic psychologists. Which type of error might have been committed here, Type I or Type II?

(Answer on p. 225.)

7.8 STATISTICAL VS. PRACTICAL SIGNIFICANCE

Another principle learned in the context of one-sample significant difference tests applies as well to two-sample tests: A statistically significant difference is not necessarily a practically important difference. Particularly when sample sizes are very large, some very unimportant differences can turn out to be statistically significant. Consequently, it is important to use common sense in evaluating the meaning of a statistically significant difference between two groups.

Knowing that two samples differ significantly tells us only that the difference observed in the samples at hand is most likely also true in the populations represented by those samples. It is a difference that can be counted on to be reliable and replicable. Knowing this, we can proceed to ask if the difference is one that makes a difference.

measures of association strength *Statistics that are used in conjunction with significant difference tests to measure the strength of association between independent and dependent variables.*

Measures of association strength are useful tools in helping to answer this question. Knowing that a difference between two samples is statistically significant tells us that there is a reliable relationship (or *association*) between the independent variable and the dependent variable. For instance, if older students are significantly less likely than younger students to justify cheating in college, we know that the variables age and attitude toward cheating are related. A measure of association strength can tell us how strong that reliable relationship is. Two measures of association strength are presented here: omega-square and Cramer's *V.*

Omega-Square

The statistic **omega-square,** symbolized ω^2, quantifies the strength of the relationship between the independent and dependent variables in a two-sample *t* test. This measure of association is computed according to Equation 7.9.

omega-square (ω^2) *A measure of association strength used with the* t *test.*

Equation 7.9

$$\omega^2 = \frac{t^2 - 1}{t^2 + df + 1}$$

where

ω^2 = omega-square
t = the value of the two-sample *t* statistic
df = the degrees of freedom in the two-sample *t* test

In words, we compute omega-square (ω^2) by: (1) subtracting 1 from the squared value of t ($t^2 - 1$); (2) summing the squared value of *t,* the degrees of freedom in the problem (df $= N_1 + N_2 - 2$ for independent-samples *t* tests or df $= N - 1$ for dependent-samples *t* tests), and 1 ($t^2 +$ df $+ 1$); and (3) dividing the result of step 1 by the result of step 2.

Omega-square provides a standardized measure of relationship strength that ranges in value from 0 to 1. When $\omega^2 = 1$, it means that we can predict without error which group any given case belongs to if we know that case's score on the dependent variable. As the strength of association between the independent and dependent variable declines, ω^2 will approach 0.(See Note 6) When $\omega^2 = 0$, we have lost all ability to predict a case's group membership based on the dependent variable.

COMPREHENSION CHECK 7.29

Use Equation 7.9 to compute omega-square for the *t* tests you computed in Comprehension Check 7.7 and 7.17. Interpret these values. (Answer on p. 225.)

Cramer's V

Cramer's *V* is useful in evaluating the practical significance of a statistically significant two-sample χ^2 test. Cramer's *V* ranges from 0, when there is no difference between the two groups' distributions, to 1, when one can predict without error a case's group membership based on his or her dependent variable category. Cramer's *V* is computed according to Equation 7.10.

Cramer's *V* (*V*) *A measure of association strength used with the* χ^2 *test.*

Equation 7.10

$$V = \sqrt{\frac{\chi^2}{N(n - 1)}}$$

where

V = Cramer's V statistic
χ^2 = the chi-square statistic
N = the total sample size
n = the number of rows or columns in the contingency table, whichever is smaller

In words, we compute Cramer's V by: (1) subtracting 1 from the number of rows or columns in the contingency table, whichever is smaller $(n - 1)$; (2) multiplying the result of step 1 by the total number of cases (N); (3) dividing χ^2 by the result of step 2; and (4) finding the square root of the result of step 3.

COMPREHENSION CHECK 7.30

Use Equation 7.10 to compute Cramer's V statistic for the χ^2 test you computed in Comprehension Check 7.25. Interpret this value. (Answer on p. 225.)

SUMMARY

Two-sample significant difference tests tell us how big the difference must be between two samples before we can be confident that the sample difference reflects a difference between the populations represented by those samples. When two samples differ significantly, we can be fairly certain that the difference is not just a fluke of the particular samples at hand, but would be seen again and again, in replication after replication.

This chapter describes a variety of two-sample significant difference tests. The independent-samples t test is used to compare the means of two unrelated samples. This t test is used when the dependent variable is measured on an interval or ratio scale and it can be assumed that the populations represented by the samples are normally distributed and show approximately equal variances.

The dependent-samples t test is based on the same assumptions as the independent-samples t test, but is used when the two samples being compared are not independent. Repeated-measures research designs, where the same cases are measured twice and the two sets of measurements are compared, is one common application of the dependent-samples t test. Matched-samples research designs, where the cases comprising one group are selected so as to match cases in the other group on some characteristic(s), are a second application of this t test. The dependent-samples t test has the advantage over the independent-samples t test of greater power.

A variety of nonparametric two-sample significant difference tests are also available that relax some of the assumptions of the t tests. The Mann-Whitney U is a nonparametric alternative to the independent-samples t test that compares the rank-order data of cases in two independent samples. The Wilcoxon T test is a nonparametric alternative to the dependent-samples t test that compares the rank-order data of two dependent samples. The chi-square test for two independent samples compares the entire distributions of two independent samples.

Two statistics are introduced in this chapter that are useful in evaluating the practical significance of statistically significant differences. The omega-square statistic provides a measure of the strength of association between independent and dependent variables in situations in which the t test is used. Cramer's V statistic offers a similar measure of association strength for use in conjunction with the chi-square test.

NOTES

1. When samples sizes are equal ($N_1 = N_2$), the standard error of the difference is more simply computed as

$$\hat{\sigma}_{\overline{X}_1-\overline{X}_2} = \sqrt{\frac{\hat{s}_1^2}{N_1} + \frac{\hat{s}_2^2}{N_2}}$$

where

$\hat{s}_1^2$ = the corrected variance of the first sample
$\hat{s}_2^2$ = the corrected variance of the second sample
N_1 = the size of the first sample
N_2 = the size of the second sample

2. Because $\mu_{\overline{X}_1-\overline{X}_2} = 0$, Equation 7.2 can be simplified to

$$t_{\overline{X}_1-\overline{X}_2} = \frac{\overline{X}_1 - \overline{X}_2}{\hat{\sigma}_{\overline{X}_1-\overline{X}_2}}$$

3. The table of critical values of U (Table 4 in Appendix B) provides critical values only for samples up to size N = 20. For larger samples, U can be transformed to z_U and the table of areas under the normal curve (Table 1 in Appendix B) can be used in assessing significance:

$$z_U = \frac{U - (N_1N_2/2)}{\sqrt{[N_1N_2(N_1 + N_2 + 1)]/12}}$$

4. The table of critical values of T (Table 5 in Appendix B) provides critical values only for samples up to size $N = 50$. For larger samples, T can be transformed to z_T, and the table of areas under the standard normal curve (Table 1 in Appendix B) can be used in assessing significance.

$$z_T = \frac{T - [N(N + 1)/4]}{\sqrt{[N(N + 1)(2N + 1)]/24}}$$

(Note: Remember that N refers to the number of *ranked* pairs.)

5. Although Yates's correction has been widely used in the past, use of the procedure is declining because it results in an overly conservative test.
6. If t is less than 1, the value of ω^2 computed using Equation 7.9 will be negative. Because this is meaningless, when $t < 1$, ω^2 is set at zero.

Review Exercises

Review Exercises 7.1 through 7.5 describe a variety of research questions. Select for each the most appropriate statistical procedure from the following list: (a) independent-samples t test; (b) dependent-samples t test; (c) Mann-Whitney U *test; (d) Wilcoxon* T *test; and (e) chi-square test for two independent samples.*

7.1. A researcher wants to evaluate women's self-esteem 6 months before and again 6 months after the birth of their first child.

7.2. A sociologist has rank-ordered the populations of 10 cities for civic pride both before and again after the eruption of riots in those cities. She now wishes to compare those rankings to evaluate the effect of the riots.

7.3. An industrial/organizational psychologist has rank-ordered the stress hardiness of 10 managers and 10 manager-trainees and wants to compare those two groups.

7.4. A researcher wants to compare depression inventory scores of a sample of women in treatment for infertility with a sample of women who are fertile.

7.5. A sociologist wants to compare the distributions of religious preference for a group of prisoners and a group of prison guards.

7.6. Use an independent-samples t test to compare the Beck Depression Inventory scores of six healthy males and six male cardiac patients listed below:

Healthy	Cardiac
20	40
42	48
11	30
15	15
50	25
10	36

7.7. Vocabulary test scores follow for 10 children who were tested at 6 and 10 years of age. Use a dependent-samples t test to determine if there has been a significant improvement in the scores.

6 Years	10 Years
14	28
25	32
10	15
8	12
16	30
22	28
25	27
21	38
28	42
10	15

7.8. Use a Mann-Whitney U test to analyze the Beck Depression Inventory scores given in Review Exercise 7.6.

7.9. Use a Wilcoxon T test to analyze the vocabulary test scores given in Review Exercise 7.7.

7.10. Shown below are grade frequency distributions for two sections of an undergraduate statistics class. Use a chi-square test to see if these distributions differ significantly.

Grade	*Section 1*	*Section 2*
A	10	8
B	13	15
C	24	27
D	15	10
F	3	0

7.11. Shown below are distributions of political affiliation for samples of traditional and nontraditional college students. Use a chi-square test to see if these distributions differ significantly.

	Traditional	*Nontraditional*
Republican	4	5
Democrat	9	3

7.12. Compute and interpret ω^2 for the independent-samples and dependent-samples t tests you performed in Review Exercises 7.6 and 7.7.

7.13. Compute and interpret Cramer's V for the chi-square tests you performed in Review Exercises 7.10 and 7.11.

7.1. A significant difference between two samples indicates that the samples probably differ because they were drawn from two differing populations. A significant difference is a replicable difference because if the populations differ, most samples drawn from those populations—one sample from one population and the other sample from the other population—will also differ. Statistical nonsignificance means that the two samples differ by no more than would be likely in two samples drawn from a single population of identically treated cases.

7.2. (a) true experiments vs. ex-post-facto comparisons; (b) scale of measurement of the dependent variable; (c) comparisons of two separate sets of cases vs. repeated measures of a single set

7.3. Scenario (b) is most appropriate to the independent-samples *t* test, because it involves a comparison of two unrelated samples on an interval-scale dependent variable.

7.4. Population Data: 1, 2, 3

All possible samples of size $N_1 = 2$ for first sample in each pair:

1,1
1,2
1,3
2,2
2,3
3,3

All possible samples of size $N_2 = 2$ for second sample in each pair:

1,1
1,2
1,3
2,2
2,3
3,3

All possible pairs of samples of sizes $N_1 = 2$ and $N_2 = 2$, along with sample means and differences between sample means:

First Sample	$\bar{X}_1$	Second Sample	$\bar{X}_2$	$\bar{X}_1 - \bar{X}_2$
1,1	1	1,1	1	0
1,1	1	1,2	1.5	−.5
1,1	1	1,3	2	−1
1,1	1	2,2	2	−1
1,1	1	2,3	2.5	−1.5
1,1	1	3,3	3	−2
1,2	1.5	1,1	1	.5
1,2	1.5	1,2	1.5	0
1,2	1.5	1,3	2	−.5
1,2	1.5	2,2	2	−.5
1,2	1.5	2,3	2.5	−1

(cont.)

First Sample	$\bar{X}_1$	Second Sample	$\bar{X}_2$	$\bar{X}_1 - \bar{X}_2$
1,2	1.5	3,3	3	−1.5
1,3	2	1,1	1	1
1,3	2	1,2	1.5	.5
1,3	2	1,3	2	0
1,3	2	2,2	2	0
1,3	2	2,3	2.5	−.5
1,3	2	3,3	3	−1
2,2	2	1,1	1	1
2,2	2	1,2	1.5	.5
2,2	2	1,3	2	0
2,2	2	2,2	2	0
2,2	2	2,3	2.5	−.5
2,2	2	3,3	3	−1
2,3	2.5	1,1	1	1.5
2,3	2.5	1,2	1.5	1
2,3	2.5	1,3	2	.5
2,3	2.5	2,2	2	.5
2,3	2.5	2,3	2.5	0
2,3	2.5	3,3	3	−.5
3,3	3	1,1	1	2
3,3	3	1,2	1.5	1.5
3,3	3	1,3	2	1
3,3	3	2,2	2	1
3,3	3	2,3	2.5	.5
3,3	3	3,3	3	0

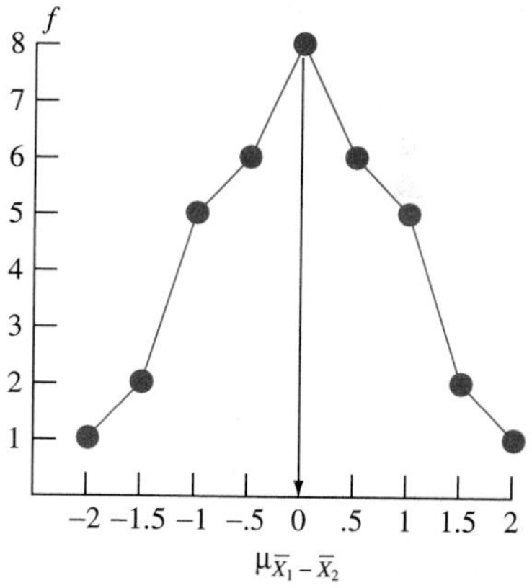

$\bar{X}_1 - \bar{X}_2$ values for all possible pairs of samples of sizes $N_1 = 2$ and $N_2 = 2$

7.5. In all sampling distributions of the difference, $\mu_{\bar{X}_1 - \bar{X}_2} = 0$.

7.6. Equation 7.1 is used to compute $\hat{\sigma}_{\bar{X}_1 - \bar{X}_2}$.

$$\hat{\sigma}_{\bar{X}_1 - \bar{X}_2} = \sqrt{\left[\frac{(N_1 - 1)\hat{s}_1^2 + (N_2 - 1)\hat{s}_2^2}{N_1 + N_2 - 2}\right]\left(\frac{N_1 + N_2}{N_1 N_2}\right)}$$

$$= \sqrt{\left[\frac{(10 - 1)8.5 + (10 - 1)7.2}{10 + 10 - 2}\right]\left(\frac{10 + 10}{10(10)}\right)}$$

$$= 1.25$$

7.7. Equation 7.2 is used to compute the independent-samples $t_{\bar{X}_1-\bar{X}_2}$ statistic.

$$t_{\bar{X}_1-\bar{X}_2} = \frac{(\bar{X}_1 - \bar{X}_2) - \mu_{\bar{X}_1-\bar{X}_2}}{\hat{\sigma}_{\bar{X}_1-\bar{X}_2}}$$

$$= \frac{(32.90 - 29.20) - 0}{1.04}$$

$$= 3.56$$

where

$$\hat{\sigma}_{\bar{X}_1-\bar{X}_2} = \sqrt{\left[\frac{(N_1 - 1)\hat{s}_1^2 + (N_2 - 1)\hat{s}_2^2}{N_1 + N_2 - 2}\right]\left(\frac{N_1 + N_2}{N_1 N_2}\right)}$$

$$= \sqrt{\left[\frac{(65 - 1)29.27 + (55 - 1)36.12}{65 + 55 - 2}\right]\left(\frac{65 + 55}{65(55)}\right)}$$

$$= 1.04$$

7.8. Because $t_{\bar{X}_1-\bar{X}_2} = 3.56$, we know that this is how many standard deviations the observed difference ($\bar{X}_1 - \bar{X}_2 = 3.7$) falls above the value in the sampling distribution of the difference that would be most likely if the two samples were drawn from a population of identically treated cases ($\mu_{\bar{X}_1-\bar{X}_2} = 0$). Although the sampling distribution of the difference is not exactly normally distributed, we know from our work with the normal distribution that 3.56 standard deviations is quite a substantial distance.

7.9. H_0: The difference between mean Cheating Justification Questionnaire scores of cheaters and noncheaters is no greater than would be expected of two samples drawn from a population of identically treated cases. Therefore, these two samples probably represent such a population.

H_1: The difference between mean Cheating Justification Questionnaire scores of cheaters and noncheaters is too great to be a likely result of sampling error alone. Two samples drawn from a population of identically treated cases would not be likely to differ this much. Therefore, these samples probably do not represent such a population but, instead, two populations—cheaters and noncheaters—that differ in their attitudes toward cheating as measured by this questionnaire.

7.10. We know that the observed difference ($\bar{X}_1 - \bar{X}_2 = 3.7$) falls to the right of $\mu_{\bar{X}_1-\bar{X}_2} = 0$ because it is positive. We know from the value of $t_{\bar{X}_1-\bar{X}_2} = 3.56$ that it falls quite a great distance to the right of $\mu_{\bar{X}_1-\bar{X}_2} = 0$.

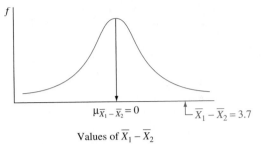

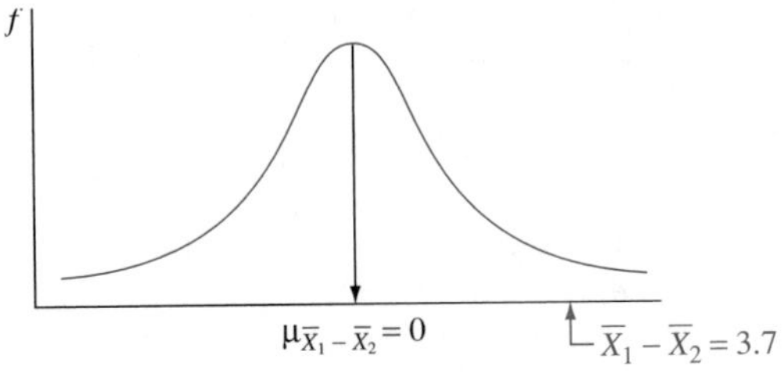

7.11. The observed difference ($\bar{X}_1 - \bar{X}_2 = 3.7$) appears to occur very infrequently in pairs of samples drawn from a population of identically treated cases. Therefore, it is relatively more likely that these samples represent populations that differ: H_1.

7.12. Scenario (e) is most appropriate to the dependent-samples *t* test. These samples of husbands and wives are not independent, because the wives that form the second sample are not just *any* wives; they are the wives of the husbands that form the first sample. The dependent variable is a continuous one (interval scale) appropriate to the *t* test.

7.13. Your first and second estimates of line length probably do not match because of measurement error: variation in measurements that result from errors in the way those measurements are obtained.

7.14. All possible samples of size $N = 2$:

1,1
1,2
1,3
2,2
2,3
3,3

All possible pairs of samples, each measured twice:

First Sample	$\bar{X}_1$	Second Sample	$\bar{X}_2$	$\bar{X}_1 - \bar{X}_2$
1,1	1	1,1	1	0
1,2	1.5	1,2	1.5	0
1,3	2	1,3	2	0
2,2	2	2,2	2	0
2,3	2.5	2,3	2.5	0
3,3	3	3,3	3	0

A repeated-measures procedure ensures that individual difference characteristics will not contribute to the variability of the sampling distribution of the difference. The absence of measurement error in this example eliminates the other source of variability in this sampling distribution.

7.15. In a matched-samples procedure, we try to make sure that the characteristics of each case in the first sample are matched as closely as possible by similar characteristics of corresponding cases in the second sample:

First Sample			Second Sample		
Case no.	*Gender*	*Age*	*Case no.*	*Gender*	*Age*
1	M	27	7	M	26
14	F	20	3	F	21
2	M	36	16	M	36
8	F	38	15	F	39
4	M	48	13	M	48
12	M	52	9	M	51
10	M	48	5	M	50
6	F	32	11	F	32

7.16. $\hat{\sigma}_{\overline{D}}$ is computed using Equation 7.3.

$$\hat{\sigma}_{\overline{D}} = \frac{\sqrt{\Sigma(D - \overline{D})^2/(N-1)}}{\sqrt{N}}$$

$$= \frac{\sqrt{(2 - .63)^2 + (-10 - .63)^2 + \cdots + (6 - .63)^2/(8-1)}}{\sqrt{8}}$$

$$= 1.85$$

7.17. The dependent-samples $t_{\overline{X}_1-\overline{X}_2}$ statistic is computed using Equation 7.4.

$$t_{\overline{X}_1-\overline{X}_2} = \frac{(\overline{X}_1 - \overline{X}_2) - \mu_{\overline{X}_1-\overline{X}_2}}{\hat{\sigma}_{\overline{D}}}$$

$$= \frac{(6.5 - 5.88) - 0}{1.85}$$

$$= .34$$

With df $= N - 1 = 7$, the one-tail critical value of t marking the .05 critical region is 1.895. The obtained value of $t_{\overline{X}_1-\overline{X}_2}$ falls short of this critical value. We can conclude that the observed difference occurs fairly frequently in pairs of samples drawn from a population of identically treated cases. There is no significant difference.

7.18. Scenario (a) is most appropriate to the Mann-Whitney *U*. There are two independent groups in this scenario—males and females—and they are to be compared on a dependent variable measured at the ordinal scale.

7.19. We begin the computations for the Mann-Whitney *U* test by combining the data from both groups and rank-ordering scores from lowest to highest. Ties are assigned a rank equal to the average position of the tied scores in the ordered array:

Scores:	47 70 82 84 84 84 86 86 88 89 89 92 93 97 98
Ranks:	1 2 3 5 5 5 7.5 7.5 9 10.5 10.5 12 13 14 15

The rank-order scores are reassigned to their original groups:

Males:	15	1	3	14	13	5	9	12
Females:	2	7.5	10.5	10.5	5	5	7.5	

Equation 7.5 is used to compute the Mann-Whitney *U* statistic.

$$U = N_1N_2 + \frac{N_1(N_1 + 1)}{2} - R_1$$

$$= 8(7) + \frac{8(8+1)}{2} - 72$$

$$= 20$$

The Mann-Whitney *U* is more appropriate to these data than the independent-samples *t* test because the groups show very different variances ($\hat{s}_1^2 = 269.85$; $\hat{s}_2^2 = 42.33$) and the data show a pronounced negative skew. The *t* test assumes that the populations represented by the groups being compared show approximately equal variances and that the data are normally distributed.

7.20. For $N_1 = 8$ and $N_2 = 7$, the table of critical values of *U* (Table 4 in Appendix B) lists critical boundary values of 10 and 46 for a two-tail test at the .05 significance level. (A two-tail test is used because there was no prediction in advance of the direction of the difference.) The obtained value of $U = 20$ falls within these boundary values and is therefore statistically nonsignificant. The observed difference between males and females is small enough to be seen regularly in two samples treated identically.

7.21. Scenario (c) is most appropriate to the Wilcoxon *T* test. This is a repeated-measures design that compares samples on an ordinal scale dependent variable.

7.22. Computation of the Wilcoxon *T* statistic begins by calculating difference scores for corresponding values in the two samples. Next, ignoring the signs of the difference scores, they are rank-ordered from lowest to highest, except for difference scores of 0, which are ignored. Then, each rank is given a positive or negative sign to reflect the sign of the corresponding difference score. Data are shown at the top of p. 224.
Next, the Wilcoxon *T* statistic is computed using Equation 7.3.

$T =$ the smaller of: (1) the absolute sum of the positive ranks, or (2) the absolute sum of the negative ranks.

The absolute sum of the positive ranks = 17.5. The absolute of the negative ranks = 10.5. Therefore, $T = 10.5$.

7.23. The table of critical values of the Wilcoxon *T* statistic (Table 5 in Appendix B) for $N = 7$ (the number of ranked pairs of scores) at the one-tail .05 level of significance is 3. The obtained value, $T = 10.5$, is greater than this critical value and is therefore not statistically significant. The observed difference in thumb-sucking times between children exposed to *Teenage Mutant Ninja Turtles* and *Barney* is attributable to sampling error.

Turtles				Barney					
Case	*Gender*	*Age*	*Time*	*Case*	*Gender*	*Age*	*Time*	*D*	*Signed Ranks*
1	M	27	12	7	M	26	10	2	+2
14	F	20	8	3	F	21	18	−10	−7
2	M	36	8	16	M	36	2	6	+5.5
8	F	38	5	15	F	39	4	1	+1
4	M	48	3	13	M	48	0	3	+3.5
12	M	52	0	9	M	51	0	0	
10	M	48	4	5	M	50	7	− 3	−3.5
6	F	32	12	11	F	32	6	6	+5.5

7.24. Scenario (d) is most appropriate to the chi-square test for two independent samples. Minority and white drug-abusing teenagers constitute independent samples, and the comparison is being made on the nominal scale variable of drug of choice.

7.25. The chi-square test for two independent samples begins with the computation of expected frequencies—numbers that one would expect to see in each cell of the contingency table if there were no difference in the grade distributions of traditional and nontraditional students. These f_e values are shown in parentheses below:

Letter grades	*Traditional*	*Nontraditional*	**Row Totals**	**Row Percentages**
A	7 (10.3)	16 (12.7)	23	20.5%
B	10 (15.2)	24 (18.8)	34	30.4%
C	23 (17.0)	15 (21.0)	38	33.9%
D	8 (6.3)	6 (7.8)	14	12.5%
F	2 (1.4)	1 (1.7)	3	2.7%
Column Totals	50	62	$N = 112$	

Expected frequencies are computed as follows. In the first row we see that 20.5% (.205) of the entire sample ($N = 112$) earned a grade of A. If there were no difference between the grades of traditional and nontraditional students, we would expect 20.5% of the traditional students ($.205 \times 50 = 10.3$) and 20.5% of the nontraditional students ($.205 \times 62 = 12.7$) to earn As. In the second row we see that 30.4% of the entire sample earned a grade of B. If there were no difference between traditional and nontraditional students, this percentage should apply to each: $.304 \times 50 = 15.2$ and $.304 \times 62 = 18.8$. Expected frequencies in the remaining cells of the contingency table are computed similarly, that is, by multiplying each column total by each row proportion.

Once expected frequencies have been computed, Equation 7.7 is used to compute the χ^2 statistic.

$$\chi^2 = \Sigma\frac{(f_o - f_e)^2}{f_e}$$

$$= \frac{(7 - 10.3)^2}{10.3} + \frac{(16 - 12.7)^2}{12.7} + \cdots + \frac{(1 - 1.7)^2}{1.7}$$

$$= 10.15$$

7.26. For df $= (R - 1)(C - 1) = (5 - 1)(2 - 1) = 4$, the table of critical values of chi-square (Table 3 in Appendix B) lists a critical value of χ^2 of 9.488 as marking the .05 critical region of the sampling distribution of χ^2. The obtained value of $\chi^2 = 10.15$ falls within this critical region and is defined as a value that is unlikely to be seen in pairs of samples drawn from a population of identically treated cases. It is therefore more likely that the two samples that produced this χ^2 value represent different populations with different grade distributions. The difference is statistically significant. Looking at the observed frequencies, we see a trend for nontraditional students to perform at somewhat higher levels than traditional students.

7.27. The data are presented below in a contingency table. Expected frequencies are shown in parentheses.

Grades	*Traditional*	*Nontraditional*	**Row Totals**	**Row Percentages**
Pass	48 (48.7)	61 (60.3)	109	97.3%
Fail	2 (1.4)	1 (1.7)	3	2.7%
Column Totals	50	62	$N = 112$	

Since two of the cells in this 2×2 contingency table show expected frequencies less than 5, we use Yates's correction to compute χ^2 (Equation 7.8).

$$\chi^{2'} = \Sigma\frac{[(|f_o - f_e|) - .5]^2}{f_e}$$

$$= \frac{[(|48 - 48.7|) - .5]^2}{48.7} + \cdots + \frac{[(|1 - 1.7|) - .5]^2}{1.7}$$

$$= .03$$

With df = $(R - 1)(C - 1) = 1$, the critical value of χ^2 listed for the .05 level of significance is 3.841. The obtained value falls short of this value and is therefore statistically nonsignificant.

7.28. Because the difference in Example 7.1 was nonsignificant, a Type I error could not have occurred. Type I errors occur when samples are found to differ significantly when their populations do not differ. This could be a Type II error, though, where a difference between samples is found to be nonsignificant when the populations actually do differ.

Because the difference in Example 7.5 was significant, a Type II error could not have occurred. Type II errors occur when populations that are really different produce samples that are not different enough for the difference to be statistically significant. This could be a Type I error, though, where sampling error alone has produced an unusually large difference between the samples.

7.29. For the data in Comprehension Check 7.7,

$$\omega^2 = \frac{t^2 - 1}{t^2 + df + 1}$$

$$= \frac{3.56^2 - 1}{3.56^2 + 118 + 1}$$

$$= .09$$

Omega-square ranges in value from 0 to 1. An ω^2 value of .09 is very low, indicating that the relationship between group membership (cheaters vs. noncheaters) and scores on the Cheating Justification Questionnaire, though statistically significant, is very weak.

For the data in Comprehension Check 7.17,

$$\omega^2 = \frac{t^2 - 1}{t^2 + df + 1}$$

$$= \frac{.34^2 - 1}{.34^2 + 7 + 1}$$

$$= -.11$$

When t is less than 1, as it is in this example, the value of ω^2 is negative. Because this is meaningless, ω^2 is set at 0, indicating essentially no relationship between group membership (viewing *Turtles* vs. *Barney*) and time spent thumb sucking.

7.30. Equation 7.10 is used to compute Cramer's *V*.

$$V = \sqrt{\frac{\chi^2}{N(n - 1)}}$$

$$= \sqrt{\frac{10.46}{112(2 - 1)}}$$

$$= .31$$

Cramer's *V* ranges in value from 0 to 1. On this scale a value of $V = .31$ represents an association between racial status and academic rank of moderate strength.

8

MULTIPLE-SAMPLE SIGNIFICANT DIFFERENCE TESTS

Chapter Outline

Are there reliable differences in the efficacy of three medications used in treating depression? Do the residents of urban, suburban, and rural areas hold differing opinions concerning the development of natural resources? Do teenagers from lower-, middle-, and upper-class families differ in their levels of sexual knowledge?

Comparisons of three or more samples are common in the social and behavioral sciences. The question in these comparisons, as always, is this: Are the differences observed among samples sufficiently large to conclude that they are the product of something more than chance? Would we probably see similar differences in a replication of the research? Do the differences seen among the samples reflect a similar pattern of differences in the populations that these samples represent? As we saw in Chapter 7, these questions are really all just variations on the same theme, statistical significance.

There are a variety of multiple-sample significant difference tests designed for various data types and research designs. When the dependent variable is continuous, measured at the interval or ratio scale, the most widely used comparison procedure is analysis of variance. Different forms of analysis of variance are available for use in comparing independent and dependent samples. When the dependent variable is ordinal, various nonparametric statistical procedures are available, including the Kruskal-Wallis analysis of variance by ranks.

Comprehension Check 8.1

What do we mean when we say that three samples differ "significantly"?

(Answer on p. 263.)

8.1 Introduction to One-Way Analysis of Variance

One-way analysis of variance (often abbreviated with the acronym ANOVA) enables us to evaluate the statistical significance of differences between two or more sample means. The term "one-way" comes from the fact that the samples being compared are defined by a single ("one") independent variable. The samples may differ, for example, in type of medication received (brand X, Y, or Z), location of residence (urban, suburban, or rural), or socioeconomic status (lower-, middle-, or upper-class). The independent variable, sometimes called a **factor** in the parlance of ANOVA, can either be manipulated in an experiment (for instance, type of medication) or can involve preexisting groups (such as location or residence or socioeconomic status) in ex-post-facto research. The phrase "analysis of variance" reflects the fact that differences among sample means are evaluated by examining variances. You will learn in this chapter how that can be.

one-way analysis of variance (ANOVA) *Procedures used to evaluate the significance of differences between two or more sample means.*

factor *In the terminology of analysis of variance, a factor is the same thing as an independent variable.*

Comprehension Check 8.2

What is the intended purpose of the one-way ANOVA? Why is it called "one-way"? Why is it called analysis of "variance"?

(Answer on p. 263.)

The Data for One-Way ANOVA

One-way ANOVA is used in evaluating the statistical significance of differences between two or more sample means. To use ANOVA, three criteria must be met. First, the data should be measured on an interval or ratio scale. Second, the samples should come from populations that are normally distributed. Third, the samples being compared should have approximately equal variances. You should notice that these are the same assumptions on which the t test (Chapter 7) is based. Violations of these assumptions will distort the shape of the sampling distribution of the F statistic, the test statistic in one-way ANOVA. Even so, experience tells us that the F test, like the t test, is very robust with respect to small to moderate violations of the assumptions of normal distributions and equal variances, especially if sample sizes are approximately equal and contain 15 or more cases per sample. When the assumptions of one-way ANOVA are seriously violated, nonparametric alternatives are available. We will look at one of these later, the Kruskal-Wallis test. See Siegel and Castellan (1988)[1] for more information about these nonparametric methods.

COMPREHENSION CHECK 8.3

What are the three assumptions of one-way ANOVA? How can we evaluate our data to see if they meet these assumptions?
(Answer on p. 263.)

completely randomized ANOVA *An ANOVA that compares two or more independent samples.*

randomized-block ANOVA *An ANOVA that compares two or more dependent samples.*

There are two major variants of one-way ANOVA. The first of these is called **completely randomized ANOVA.** This ANOVA is like an extension of the independent-samples t test in that the completely randomized ANOVA requires that the cases comprising each sample be independent and unrelated. The second major form of one-way ANOVA is called **randomized-block ANOVA.** This ANOVA is like an extension of the dependent-samples t test and is used with repeated-measures and matched-samples research designs. Provided it makes sense to use matching or repeated measures, randomized-block ANOVA gives a more powerful test of significance than does completely randomized ANOVA. Our examination of one-way ANOVAs will emphasize completely randomized ANOVA. This will provide the conceptual foundation for understanding all ANOVAs. Only computational changes required for the randomized-block ANOVA will be presented.

COMPREHENSION CHECK 8.4

Describe the differences between the completely randomized and randomized-block one-way ANOVAs.
(Answer on p. 263.)

One-Way ANOVA vs. Multiple *t* Tests

You may wonder why we even *need* the one-way ANOVA. In situations in which there are several sample means—say, $\overline{X}_1$, $\overline{X}_2$, $\overline{X}_3$, and $\overline{X}_4$, couldn't we simply perform several t tests?

[1]Siegel, S., & Castellan, N. J., Jr. (1988). *Nonparametric statistics for the behavioral sciences.* New York: McGraw-Hill.

$$\overline{X}_1 \text{ vs. } \overline{X}_2$$
$$\overline{X}_2 \text{ vs. } \overline{X}_3$$
$$\overline{X}_1 \text{ vs. } \overline{X}_4$$
$$\overline{X}_2 \text{ vs. } \overline{X}_3$$
$$\overline{X}_2 \text{ vs. } \overline{X}_4$$
$$\overline{X}_3 \text{ vs. } \overline{X}_4$$

The short answer is yes. However, there are two clear disadvantages to using multiple *t* tests in comparing several sample means.

First, given a set of *k* means, there will be $(k^2 - k)/2$ possible pairwise comparisons (that is, comparisons between two samples). Thus, with $k = 5$ sample means, we have $(5^2 - 5)/2 = 10$ comparisons. With $k = 10$ means, we have $(10^2 - 10)/2 = 45$ comparisons. With $k = 15$ means, there are $(15^2 - 15)/2 = 105$ comparisons. As you can see, the number of comparisons increases at an accelerating rate as the number of samples increases. Laziness alone should send us scrambling for an alternative to computing all these *t* tests!

COMPREHENSION CHECK 8.5

How many pairwise comparisons are possible given eight sample means?

(Answer on p. 263.)

Second, remember that each significance test carries a chance of Type I and Type II error, so the more *t* tests we compute, the more Type I and Type II errors will occur. Using the .05 level of significance, we would expect that 5 of every 100 *t* tests would yield a Type I error. Particularly when samples are of relatively small size, Type II errors are even more common than Type I errors, so we would not be surprised to see even more Type II errors in a group of 100 comparisons. The use of multiple *t* tests results in unacceptably large numbers of Type I and Type II errors.

COMPREHENSION CHECK 8.6

In pairwise comparisons of eight sample means, how many Type I errors would one expect to occur when using the .05 level of significance?

(Answer on p. 263.)

The one-way ANOVA gives us a way around these difficulties. This procedure provides a *single* test of significance no matter how many sample means are being compared. With only one significance test, we can rest assured that the probability of Type I error is equal to the selected level of significance. As we've seen before, though, there are no free statistical lunches. What we gain in computational ease and control over error rates using the one-way ANOVA is purchased through loss of analytic specificity. A significant one-way ANOVA tells us only that there is a significant difference *somewhere* among the means. It does not tell us *where* that difference lies. Further analysis, using **post-hoc comparison** procedures, is necessary to identify where the significance is coming from. The problem is that these post-hoc comparison procedures suffer from relatively low power. Post-hoc comparisons are discussed later in this chapter.

post-hoc comparisons
Comparisons between sample means that follow a significant F *in the ANOVA. Used to identify the source(s) of the significant* F.

COMPREHENSION CHECK 8.7

How does the one-way ANOVA overcome the disadvantages of multiple *t* tests? What is the disadvantage of the ANOVA?

(Answer on p. 263.)

8.2 COMPLETELY RANDOMIZED ONE-WAY ANOVA

within-group variance *Variability of scores within each treatment condition.*
between-group variance *Variability seen among the means of different treatment conditions.*

Figure 8.1 depicts the kind of data that are analyzed using one-way ANOVA. Shown are three sample distributions, each with its own mean and range of scores. Two kinds of variance can be seen in this figure. First, we see that the scores within each of the three groups vary. This is called **within-group variance.** Second, the group means vary from one to the next. This is called **between-group variance.** One-way ANOVA involves comparing these two kinds of variance, so it is important that we understand each.

COMPREHENSION CHECK 8.8

What are two kinds of variability seen in the data from two or more groups?

(Answer on p. 263.)

Within-Group Variance

Within-group variance is the variability in scores that occurs from one case to the next within each sample. Let's consider what would cause the scores within a group to vary. First, even though all cases within a given group have been treated the same (again, using the term "treatment" broadly), individual differences will cause the cases to react differently to that treatment. As an example, suppose that three groups of migraine sufferers are evaluated for headache pain following ingestion of 10, 20, or 30 milligrams of an experimental pain medication. We would expect to see some variability in pain scores within each of these groups simply because of individual difference characteristics of the group members. Body weight, pretreatment pain levels,

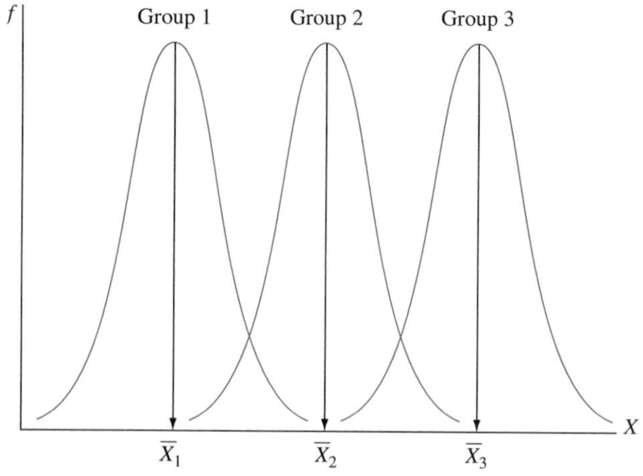

FIGURE 8.1
These three frequency distributions show two kinds of variability. Within-group variability is seen within each of the distributions. Between-group variability refers to the variability of the group means.

and a host of physiological variables would be expected to affect response to treatment.

Measurement error also contributes to within-group variability. Measurement error, you will recall, refers to imprecision in measurement of the dependent variable. Measurement error introduces random variability into the scores that does not reflect true variability among cases. Two migraine sufferers experiencing precisely the same level of pain might well show somewhat different headache pain scores. This is measurement error.

In sum, a variety of individual difference characteristics produce differences from case to case on the dependent variable being measured. And measurement error contributes further random variability to the scores. Within-group variance is the result of these two sources of variability.

COMPREHENSION CHECK 8.9

Name two things that cause scores to vary within a treatment group.
(Answer on p. 263.)

Between-Group Variance

Between-group variance is also visible in Figure 8.1. Between-group variance refers to the variability seen among sample means.

Let us consider now what causes between-group variance. For one thing, the same individual differences that cause scores within a group to vary will also cause group means to vary. In our hypothetical study of migraine patients, it is unlikely that all three dosage groups would display exactly the same average body weight, pretreatment pain level, and other physiological characteristics. Chance differences between the groups on these and other individual difference variables would result in some between-group variability in levels of posttreatment pain.

Measurement error also affects between-group variance. Just as measurement error causes random variation of scores from one case to the next, it also causes random variation of means from one group to the next.

Over and above individual differences and measurement error, however, between-group variance is affected by **treatment effects.** Group means may differ because the groups were treated differently. Groups of migraine patients given 10, 20, or 30 milligrams of an experimental pain medication who subsequently report high, medium, and low levels of pain, respectively, may very well be displaying a treatment effect.

treatment effects *Between-group differences on the dependent variable that are associated with the different levels of the independent variable. Treatment effects affect between-group variance but not within-group variance.*

In sum, differences among group means can result from individual differences, measurement error, and treatment effects. Differences among group means over and above those that can be attributed to individual differences and measurement error are due to treatment effects.

COMPREHENSION CHECK 8.10

What are three sources of between-group variance? Which of these affects between-group variance that does not affect within-group variance?
(Answer on p. 263.)

Treatment Effects and Within- and Between-Group Variance

We have just seen that between-group variance reflects the influence of (1) individual differences, (2) measurement error, and (3) treatment effects. Within-group variance, in contrast, reflects the influence of (1) individual differences and (2) measurement error. It follows that if there is no treatment effect, between-group and within-group variance will be approximately equal, both having been determined by the same two things—individual differences and measurement error. On the other hand, as a treatment effect grows stronger, between-group variance will grow larger than within-group variance, because between-group variance, but not within-group variance, is affected by treatment effects.

As an example of this, let us return to our hypothetical study of migraine sufferers. Suppose that the medication received by the three dosage groups is, in actuality, completely ineffective. Samples of migraine sufferers given 10, 20, and 30 milligrams of the medication would undoubtedly show small differences in mean levels of pain following treatment, but this between-group variance would be no greater than the within-group variance seen within each of the groups. This scenario is depicted in Figure 8.2a. Notice how scores within each group show about the same range as is seen between the lowest and highest group means. Between-group variability and within-group variability are approximately equal, because both are affected only by individual differences and measurement error. There is no treatment effect to boost between-group variability.

On the other hand, what would happen if the medication provided very effective treatment for migraine pain? Means of the 10-, 20-, and 30-milligram samples would show much larger differences. This scenario is depicted in Figure 8.2b. Notice how the range from the lowest mean to the highest mean is now substantially greater than the range within any one group. Here, between-group variability exceeds within-group variability because the strong treatment effect has boosted between-group variability. In general, as a treatment effect becomes stronger, sample means become more and more diverse, and this diversity is reflected in increasing between-group variance. At the same time, within-group variance is unaffected by treatment effects, so the difference between between-group variance and within-group variance provides a clue to the strength of the treatment effect.

Comprehension Check 8.11

How does the presence of a treatment effect affect between-group and within-group variance?

(Answer on p. 263.)

The *F* Statistic and Treatment Effects

***F* statistic** *The ratio of between-group variance to within-group variance.* F *reflects the size of the treatment effect and is the test statistic in the ANOVA.*

The ***F* statistic** is the test statistic in one-way ANOVA. Like any test statistic, *F* is computed from sample data and varies in value as a function of the size of the difference being tested for significance. The difference being tested for significance in one-way ANOVA is the difference between between-group variance and within-group variance. *F* is computed as the ratio of between-group variance to within-group variance:

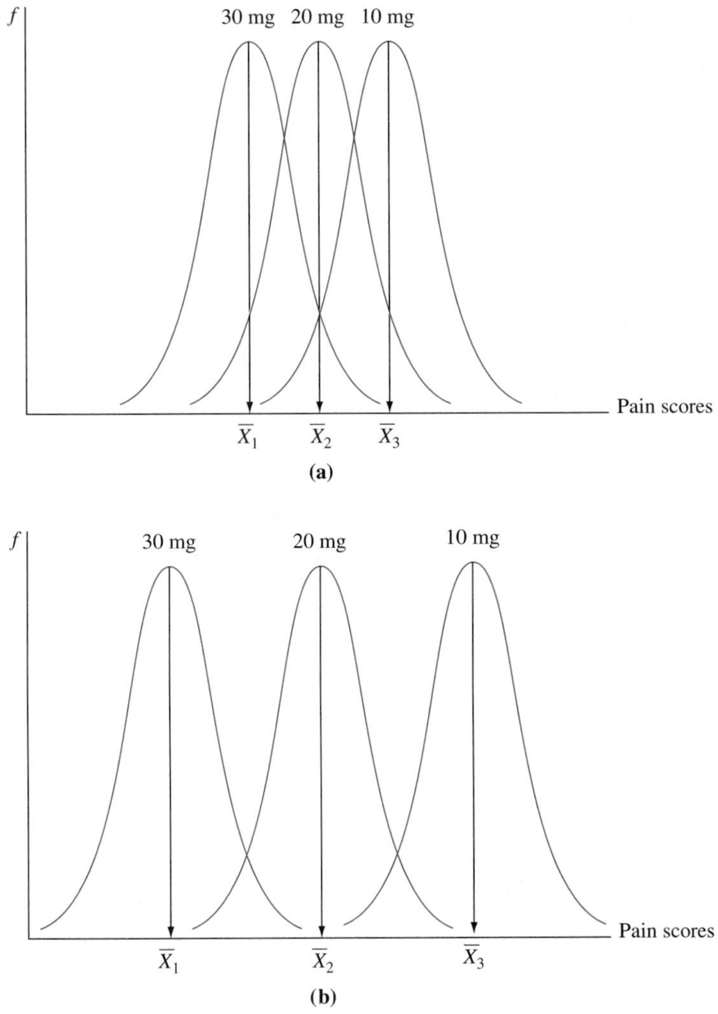

FIGURE 8.2

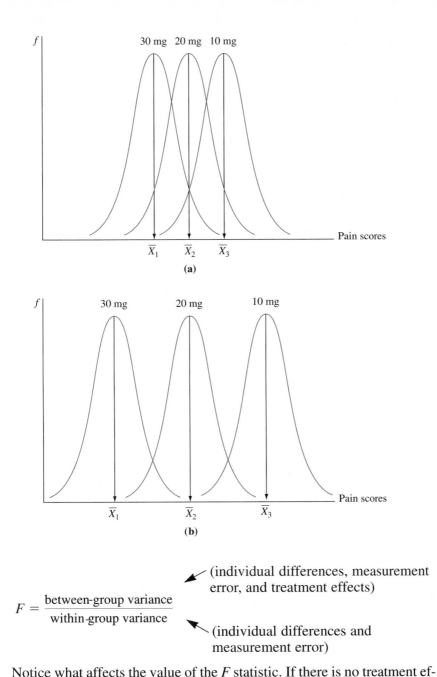

The stronger the treatment effect, the greater is the between-group variance. (a) depicts a weak treatment effect, where between-group and within-group variance are approximately equal. (b) depicts a stronger treatment effect, where between-group variance is considerably greater than within-group variance.

$$F = \frac{\text{between-group variance}}{\text{within-group variance}}$$

Numerator: (individual differences, measurement error, and treatment effects)

Denominator: (individual differences and measurement error)

Notice what affects the value of the F statistic. If there is no treatment effect, such that the differences among means are small, between-group variance and within-group variance will both be determined by the same two factors—individual differences and measurement error. Being affected by the same two factors, between-group and within-group variance will be equal, and F will equal 1. If there is a strong treatment effect, such that the differences among means are large, between-group variance will be larger than within-group variance, and F will be greater than 1. Stated simply, as treatment effects become stronger, (1) the differences among sample means become greater, (2) between-group variance becomes larger than within-group variance, and (3) the value of the F statistic increases. Thus, we see that the

F statistic reflects the size of the differences among the sample means by comparing between-group variance and within-group variance.

COMPREHENSION CHECK 8.12

Explain why the *F* statistic is defined as a "test statistic."
(Answer on p. 263.)

The Sampling Distribution of F

sampling distribution of *F* *The theoretical distribution of values of* F *obtained when all possible sets of samples of size* N *are drawn from a population of identically treated cases and* F *is computed for each set of samples.*

We've seen how the *F* statistic measures the size of the differences among a set of sample means. What we need now is some way to determine the likelihood that any given value of *F* would be seen in a set of samples drawn from a population of identically treated cases. The **sampling distribution of *F*** accomplishes this.

Let us consider now this sampling distribution. Imagine a population in which all cases have been treated identically. Next, imagine drawing all possible sets of, say, three samples, each of size *N,* from this population. Now, in each of these sets of samples there will be some within-group variability and some between-group variability. We could therefore compute *F* for each set of samples as the ratio of between-group variance to within-group variance. Because all the cases in our imaginary population were treated identically (that is, there is no treatment effect), in most of the sets that we draw, the samples will have means that are quite similar. In these sets of samples, the value of *F* will be fairly small, around 1. In a few sets of samples, there may actually be no differences at all between means. The absence of any between-group variance in these sets of samples means that *F* will equal 0. And, simply because of sampling error, samples in some of the sets will show fairly large differences in means, leading to large values of *F.* If we plot the frequency of occurrence of the values of *F* obtained from one set of samples to the next, we have the sampling distribution of *F,* as depicted in Figure 8.3.

The lowest possible value of *F* is 0. This value occurs when the means in a set of samples are exactly equal, such that between-group variance = 0. The single most frequently occurring value of *F* is 1.0. This is because the samples in each set have been drawn from a population in which there are no treatment effects (remember, all the cases in the population have been treated identically), so between-group and within-group variance are equal and *F* is 1. Also, there are fewer and fewer high values of *F,* because large values of *F*

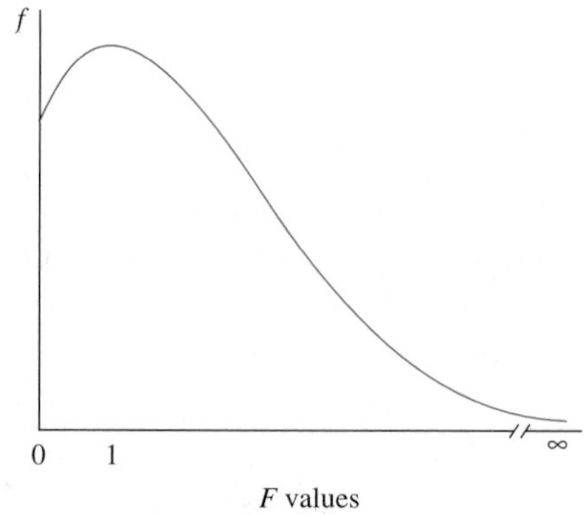

FIGURE 8.3

The sampling distribution of *F* depicts values of the *F* statistic obtained when *F* is computed for all possible sets of samples of size *N* drawn from a population of identically treated cases. The lowest possible value is 0. The single most frequently occurring value is 1.

require large differences between sample means, something that *can* occur by sampling error, but that occurs relatively infrequently.

COMPREHENSION CHECK 8.13

Explain why the lowest possible value of F is 0, why 1 is the single most frequently occurring value in the sampling distribution of F, and why larger values of F occur less and less frequently in the sampling distribution of F.

(Answer on p. 263.)

In the preceding discussion we have imagined the sampling distribution of F formed when all possible sets of three samples were drawn from a population of identically treated cases. Figure 8.3 shows the general characteristics of this sampling distribution of F. However, the exact shape of the sampling distribution of F varies somewhat depending on how many samples are included in each set (we could have imagined drawing all possible sets of four samples or five samples, etc.) and the total number of cases that are examined. More will be said about this later.

Computations for the Completely Randomized One-Way ANOVA

We have seen that the F statistic varies in value as a function of the size of the difference between two or more sample means. It is equal to the ratio of between-group variance to within-group variance. But how do we compute between-group and within-group variance? We will turn now to the computational aspects of the completely randomized one-way ANOVA. Recall that this analysis assumes that the cases comprising each group are different and independent.

Sums of Squares. The first step in computing F is to compute values called sums of squares. These are of two sorts: between-groups and within-groups.

sum of squares between groups ($SS_{Between}$) *Based on the sum of squared deviations of sample means around the grand mean, $SS_{Between}$ reflects between-group variability.*

The **sum of squares between groups** ($SS_{Between}$) reflects between-group variability and is computed according to Equation 8.1.

Equation 8.1

$$SS_{Between} = (\overline{X}_1 - \overline{X}_G)^2 (N_1) + (\overline{X}_2 - \overline{X}_G)^2 (N_2) + \cdots + (\overline{X}_k - \overline{X}_G)^2 (N_k)$$

where

$\overline{X}_1$ to $\overline{X}_k$ = the means of groups 1 to k
k = the number of groups
N_1 to N_k = sample sizes of the k groups
$\overline{X}_G$ = the grand mean (the mean of all the scores)

In words, $SS_{Between}$ is computed by: (1) subtracting the grand mean ($\overline{X}_G$) from each sample mean ($\overline{X}_1$, $\overline{X}_2$, etc.); (2) squaring each of these differences; (3) multiplying the values obtained in step 2 by their corresponding sample sizes (N_1, N_2, etc.); and (4) summing the values obtained in step 3.

Comprehension Check 8.14

Given the following data, compute $SS_{Between}$.

Group 1	Group 2	Group 3
4	5	9
3	7	8
1		7
		10

(Answer on pp. 263–264.)

sum of squares within groups (SS_{Within}) *The sum of squared deviations of scores around the sample means, SS_{Within} reflects within-group variability.*

Next we compute the **sum of squares within groups** (SS_{Within}) which reflects within-group variability. Equation 8.2 is used in computing within-group sum of squares.

Equation 8.2

$$SS_{Within} = \sum_{i=1}^{N_1}(X_i - \overline{X}_1)^2 + \sum_{i=1}^{N_2}(X_i - \overline{X}_2)^2 + \cdots + \sum_{i=1}^{N_k}(X_i - \overline{X}_k)^2$$

where

$\overline{X}_1$ to $\overline{X}_k$ = the means of the k groups
k = the number of groups
N_1 to N_k = sample sizes of the k groups

In words, SS_{Within} is computed by: (1) subtracting the sample mean ($\overline{X}_1$, $\overline{X}_2$, etc.) from each score in that sample; (2) squaring these differences; (3) summing the values obtained in step 2 for each sample; and (4) summing the values obtained in step 3 across the samples.

Comprehension Check 8.15

Given the data in Comprehension Check 8.14, compute SS_{Within}. (Answer on p. 264.)

total sum of squares (SS_{Total}) *The total of $SS_{Between} + SS_{Within}$, SS_{Total} is the sum of squared deviations of scores around the grand mean and reflects the total variability seen in the data.*

There are only two kinds or "sources" of variability in the data of a completely randomized one-way ANOVA: between-group variability, reflected in $SS_{Between}$, and within-group variability, reflected in SS_{Within}. The sum or "total" of these two sums of squares is called the **total sum of squares.** Although SS_{Total} is not used directly in the calculations of the completely randomized one-way ANOVA, it provides a useful check on the computational accuracy of $SS_{Between}$ and SS_{Within}. Check to see that SS_{Total}, computed according to Equation 8.3, is equal to $SS_{Between} + SS_{Within}$.

Equation 8.3

$$SS_{Total} = \sum_{i=1}^{N}(X_i - \overline{X}_G)^2 = SS_{Between} + SS_{Within}$$

where

N = the total number of cases in the analysis
$\overline{X}_G$ = the grand mean (the mean of all the scores)

In words, SS_{Total} is computed by: (1) subtracting the grand mean ($\overline{X}_G$) from each score (X) in the analysis: (2) squaring each of these differences; and (3) adding these squared values. The value of SS_{Total} obtained in this way should equal the sum of $SS_{Between} + SS_{Within}$.

Given the data in Comprehension Check 8.14, compute SS_{Total} using Equation 8.3. Show that $SS_{Total} = SS_{Between} + SS_{Within}$.
(Answer on p. 264.)

COMPREHENSION CHECK 8.16

Mean Squares. We first encountered the sum of squares in Chapter 3, where it was introduced as a measure of data variability in single samples. It was noted there that although the sum of squares does reflect data variability, it is also affected by how many scores are used in computing it. The more scores, the larger the sum of squares will be. We also learned that the variance removes the influence of number of scores from the sum of squares by averaging (i.e., dividing) the sum of squares by one fewer than the number of scores in the sample:

$$\hat{s}^2 = \frac{\Sigma(X - \overline{X})^2}{N - 1} = \frac{SS}{N - 1}$$

Likewise, $SS_{Between}$ and SS_{Within} reflect between-group and within-group variability, respectively, but are also affected by the number of groups and the number of cases within each group. To get purer measures of variability, we need to average these sums of squares.

To obtain a measure of between-group variance, we divide $SS_{Between}$ by one fewer than the number of sample means (k) whose varying values make up between-group variance. The value $k - 1$ is called the **degrees of freedom between groups** ($df_{Between}$). The **mean squares between groups** ($MS_{Between}$), our measure of between-group variance, is computed according to Equation 8.4.

degrees of freedom between groups ($df_{Between}$) *In completely randomized one-way ANOVA, equal to $k - 1$, where k = the number of groups.*

mean squares between groups ($MS_{Between}$) *The measure of between-group variance used as the numerator in the F statistic in the completely randomized one-way ANOVA.*

Equation 8.4

$$MS_{Between} = \frac{SS_{Between}}{df_{Between}}$$

In words, $MS_{Between}$ is computed by dividing $SS_{Between}$ by $df_{Between}$.

Given the data in Comprehension Check 8.14, compute $df_{Between}$ and $MS_{Between}$.
(Answer on p. 264.)

COMPREHENSION CHECK 8.17

We also need a measure of within-group variability that is free from the influence of sample sizes. This measure is called the **mean squares within groups** (MS_{Within}). To compute MS_{Within} we must average each sample's sum of squares by one fewer than the number of cases in that sample:

mean squares within groups (MS_{Within}) *The measure of within-group variance used as the denominator in the F statistic in the completely randomized one-way ANOVA.*

$$MS_{Within} = \frac{\sum_{i=1}^{N_1}(X_i - \overline{X}_1)^2}{N_1 - 1} + \frac{\sum_{i=1}^{N_2}(X_i - \overline{X}_2)^2}{N_2 - 1} + \cdots + \frac{\sum_{i=k}^{N_k}(X_i - \overline{X}_k)^2}{N_k - 1}$$

This is equivalent to dividing SS_{Within} by $N - k$, which is called **degrees of freedom within groups,** as shown in Equation 8.5.

Equation 8.5

$$MS_{Within} = \frac{SS_{Within}}{df_{Within}}$$

degrees of freedom within groups (df_{Within}) *In one-way ANOVA, equal to* N − k, *where* N = *the total number of cases in the analysis and* k = *the number of groups.*

In words, MS_{Within} is computed by dividing SS_{Within} by df_{Within} and measures within-group variance.

COMPREHENSION CHECK 8.18

Given the data in Comprehension Check 8.14, compute df_{Within} and MS_{Within}.
(Answer on p. 264.)

The *F* Statistic. Having seen now how we compute $MS_{Between}$ (Equation 8.4) and MS_{Within} (Equation 8.5), we are ready to compute the value of *F* as given in Equation 8.6.

Equation 8.6

$$F = \frac{MS_{Between}}{MS_{Within}}$$

In words, *F* is equal to $MS_{Between}$, our measure of between-group variance, divided by MS_{Within}, our measure of within-group variance.

COMPREHENSION CHECK 8.19

Given the data in Comprehension Check 8.14, compute the value of the *F* statistic.
(Answer on p. 264.)

The ANOVA Summary Table. Although the computations involved in the one-way ANOVA are not particularly difficult, there are quite a few of them and it is useful to have a way of presenting the results of the analysis in a standardized form. This is provided by the **ANOVA summary table.** Table 8.1 gives an example of an ANOVA summary table in which the necessary computational equations for the completely randomized one-way ANOVA have been summarized. Normally this table displays the outcomes of these computations, not the equations. The column heading "Source" refers to the kind of variability under consideration—between groups or within groups. The headings SS, df, and MS stand for sums of squares, degrees of freedom, and mean squares, respectively. Finally, the column heading *F* indicates the value of the *F* statistic.

ANOVA summary table *Used to summarize the results of the ANOVA in a standardized format.*

COMPREHENSION CHECK 8.20

Construct an ANOVA summary table summarizing the results of your computations in Comprehension Checks 8.14 to 8.19.
(Answer on p. 264.)

The Logic of the One-Way ANOVA

The logic of the one-way ANOVA as a test of the significance of differences among two or more sample means can be broken down into the same four elements we encountered with the *t* test: (1) null and alternative hypotheses are

TABLE 8.1

The ANOVA summary table provides a standardized format within which the results of the ANOVA are presented. The equations of the one-way ANOVA are summarized in this table.

Source	SS	df	MS	*F*
Between groups	$(\overline{X}_1 - \overline{X}_G)^2(N_1) + (\overline{X}_2 - \overline{X}_G)^2(N_2) + \cdots + (\overline{X}_k - \overline{X}_G)^2(N_k)$	$k - 1$	$\frac{SS_{Between}}{df_{Between}}$	$\frac{MS_{Between}}{MS_{Within}}$
Within groups	$\sum_{i=1}^{N_1}(X_i - \overline{X}_1)^2 + \sum_{i=1}^{N_2}(X_i - \overline{X}_2)^2 + \cdots + \sum_{i=1}^{N_k}(X_i - \overline{X}_k)^2$	$N - k$	$\frac{SS_{Within}}{df_{Within}}$	
Total	$\sum_{i=1}^{N}(\overline{X}_i - \overline{X}_G)^2$	$N - 1$		

formed to explain differences among sample means; (2) a test statistic is computed that measures the size of the differences among the means; (3) the obtained value of the test statistic is compared against its sampling distribution to determine its probability under conditions of the null hypothesis; and (4) we choose between H_0 and H_1 the explanation of the observed difference that is most likely. Example 8.1 provides a concrete example of the completely randomized one-way ANOVA to illustrate the general discussion that follows. Refer to this example as you read the next several sections.

The Null and Alternative Hypotheses. We begin the one-way ANOVA when we see that there are differences among two or more group means and wish to determine the most likely explanation for the observed differences. The null hypothesis (H_0) states that the observed differences can be attributed to sampling error. Samples drawn from a population of identically treated cases would likely display means as different as those observed. There is insufficient evidence to conclude that any treatment effect is at work.

The alternative hypothesis (H_1) states that the observed differences cannot easily be attributed to sampling error. A set of samples drawn from a population of identically treated cases would be very unlikely to display means as different as those observed. It is more likely, then, that the cases do not represent such a population. Instead, they probably represent different populations. There probably is a treatment effect at work.

COMPREHENSION CHECK 8.21

To what do the null and alternative hypotheses attribute differences seen between sample means in the one-way ANOVA?
(Answer on p. 264.)

The Test Statistic. The *F* statistic, computed according to Equations 8.1 to 8.6, is the test statistic in the completely randomized one-way ANOVA. We have seen that the value of *F* increases as the differences among group means increase. The *F* statistic provides a measure of the strength of the treatment effect.

The Sampling Distribution of *F*. The probability of obtaining a given value of F if all cases have been treated identically is found by comparing the computed value of F against the sampling distribution of F as described by Table 6 in Appendix B, "Critical values of *F*." This table lists values of F that mark the upper 5% (in light type) and 1% (in boldface type) critical regions of the sampling distribution of F as depicted in Figure 8.4. As noted previously, the exact shape of the sampling distribution of F depends on how many samples are being compared, as reflected in $df_{Between} = k - 1$, and the number of cases being examined, as reflected in $df_{Within} = N - k$. Thus, we enter the table of critical values of F using $df_{Between}$ (for $df_{Numerator}$ in the table) and df_{Within} (for $df_{Denominator}$ in the table).(See Note 1) The tabled values of F listed at the intersection of these two df values are the critical values of F for the .05 and .01 levels of significance.

COMPREHENSION CHECK 8.22

If $df_{Between} = 2$ and $df_{Within} = 6$, what are the critical values of F for the .05 and .01 significance levels?
(Answer on p. 264.)

Choosing Between the Null and Alternative Hypotheses. If the computed value of F meets or exceeds either of the critical values in the table, we know that the computed F has a probability of less than .05 (or .01 if F meets or exceeds the boldface value) of occurring in a set of samples drawn from a population of identically treated cases. A value of F this large reflects differences among sample means that are unlikely to occur by virtue of sampling error alone. Instead, the samples probably represent populations that differ on the dependent variable under consideration. Under these circumstances, we reject the null hypothesis and accept the alternative hypothesis. The means are significantly different.

On the other hand, if the computed value of F is smaller than the critical value in the table, we know that the computed F has a fairly high probability of occurring (greater than .05 or .01, depending on which significance level is being used) in samples that are drawn from a population of identically treated cases. Thus, the samples that yielded this small F value may very likely represent such a population. Under these circumstances, the null hy-

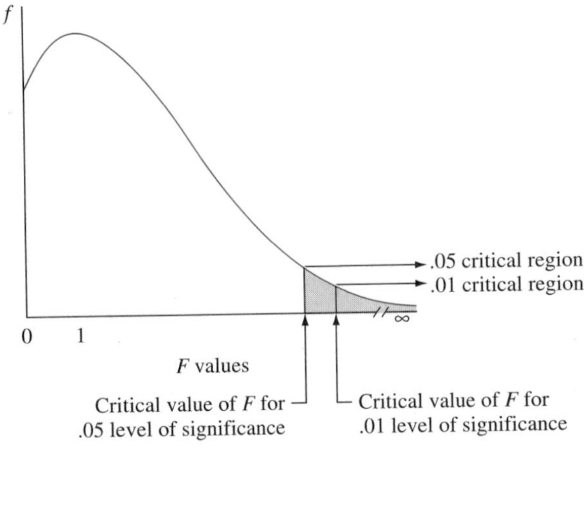

FIGURE 8.4
Table 6 in Appendix B provides critical values of F that mark off the .05 and .01 critical regions for specified values of $df_{Between}$ and df_{Within}.

pothesis provides a reasonable explanation of the observed between-group differences. There is no evidence of a treatment effect. The differences among means are nonsignificant.

COMPREHENSION CHECK 8.23

Based on the results summarized in Comprehension Check 8.20, where $df_{Between} = 2$, $df_{Within} = 6$, and $F = 14.94$, is the difference between sample means statistically significant? If so, at what level of significance? Does the null or the alternative hypothesis provide the more acceptable explanation for the differences observed between the means?

(Answer on p. 264.)

EXAMPLE 8.1

Completely Randomized One-Way ANOVA

Neighbors of the Home for Retired Statisticians have been complaining lately. It seems that the retirees have taken to shouting obscenities at passersby. Dr. Jerry Atric, Chief Psychologist and Custodian at the home, has decided to try a system of fines—taking away computer time—to control these outbursts.

Retirees involved in the experiment were randomly assigned to be fined 0, 10, or 20 minutes of computer time for each outburst. Dr. Atric recorded the number of obscene outbursts from each subject during the week following the initiation of this program. These data appear below, along with descriptive statistics.

Treatment Groups		
No Fine	*10 min*	*20 min*
21	15	5
16	20	10
25	14	2
10	10	15
20	19	8
18	11	9
19	15	
	16	
$N_1 = 7$	$N_2 = 8$	$N_3 = 6$
$\overline{X}_1 = 18.43$	$\overline{X}_2 = 15.00$	$\overline{X}_3 = 8.17$
$\hat{s}_1^2 = 21.62$	$\hat{s}_2^2 = 11.97$	$\hat{s}_3^2 = 19.77$
	$N = 21$	
	$\overline{X}_G = 14.19$	

The dependent variable, number of obscene outbursts, clearly meets the ANOVA assumption of interval- or ratio-scale data. It is impossible to determine from so few cases if the data are normally distributed, but there is no a-priori reason to assume that this variable would deviate wildly from normality. Finally, the corrected sample variances are similar, so it is safe to assume that the populations represented by these samples have fairly homogeneous variances. All in all, these data appear to be appropriate for analysis using one-way ANOVA.

Null and Alternative Hypotheses

H_0: Differences between the sample means are small enough to be attributed to sampling error. That is, samples treated identically would often display means that differ by the amount seen here.

H_1: Differences between the sample means are too large to be attributed to sampling error. That is, samples treated identically would very seldom display means that differ by the amount seen here. It is more likely that the sample means differ because of the action of a treatment effect, in this situation, lost computer time.

Test Statistic

The test statistic F is computed according to Equations 8.1 to 8.6.

According to Equation 8.1,

$$\begin{aligned} SS_{Between} &= (\overline{X}_1 - \overline{X}_G)^2 (N_1) + (\overline{X}_2 - \overline{X}_G)^2 (N_2) + \cdots + (\overline{X}_k - \overline{X}_G)^2 (N_k) \\ &= (18.43 - 14.19)^2(7) + (15.00 - 14.19)^2(8) + (8.17 - 14.19)^2(6) \\ &= 348.69 \end{aligned}$$

According to Equation 8.2,

$$\begin{aligned} SS_{Within} &= \Sigma(X_i - \overline{X}_1)^2 + \Sigma(X_i - \overline{X}_2)^2 + \cdots + \Sigma(X_i - \overline{X}_k)^2 \\ &= (21 - 18.43)^2 + (16 - 18.43)^2 + \cdots + (15 - 15.00)^2 + \\ &\quad (20 - 15.00)^2 + \cdots + (5 - 8.17)^2 + \cdots + (9 - 8.17)^2 \\ &= 312.55 \end{aligned}$$

According to Equation 8.3,

$$\begin{aligned} SS_{Total} &= \Sigma(X_i - \overline{X}_G)^2 \\ &= (21 - 14.19)^2 + (16 - 14.19)^2 + \cdots + (9 - 14.19)^2 \\ &= 661.24 \end{aligned}$$

According to Equation 8.4,

$$\begin{aligned} MS_{Between} &= \frac{SS_{Between}}{df_{Between}} \\ &= \frac{348.69}{3 - 1} \\ &= 174.35 \end{aligned}$$

According to Equation 8.5,

$$\begin{aligned} MS_{Within} &= \frac{SS_{Within}}{df_{Within}} \\ &= \frac{312.55}{21 - 3} \\ &= 17.36 \end{aligned}$$

According to Equation 8.6,

$$F = \frac{MS_{Between}}{MS_{Within}}$$

$$= \frac{174.35}{17.36}$$

$$= 10.04$$

These results are summarized in the ANOVA summary table that follows:

Source	SS	df	MS	*F*
Between groups	348.69	2	174.35	10.04
Within groups	312.55	18	17.36	
Total	661.24	20		

Choosing Between H_0 *and* H_1

Finally, we compare the obtained value of $F = 10.04$ to the sampling distribution of *F*. The general shape of this sampling distribution is shown below. Critical values of *F* marking the .05 and .01 critical regions for $df_{Between} = 2$ (for $df_{Numerator}$) and $df_{Within} = 18$ (for $df_{Denominator}$) are found in Table 6 in Appendix B.

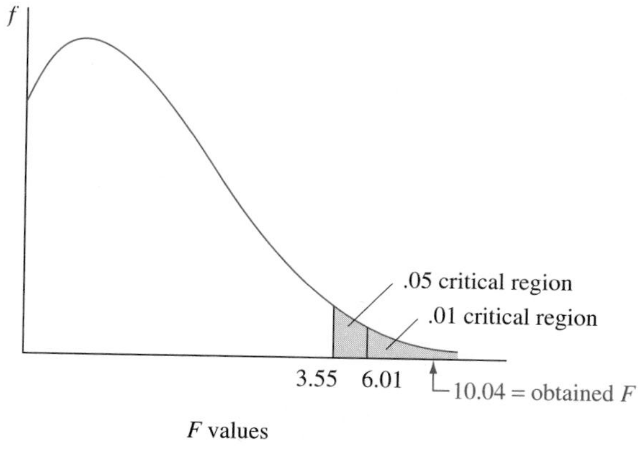

We see that the obtained value of $F = 10.04$ occurs only infrequently in sets of identically treated samples. Our $F = 10.04$ exceeds the critical value of $F = 6.01$ for the .01 level of significance. It is therefore unlikely that such a large *F* would result from sampling error alone. Instead, it is probably the result of a treatment effect. We can conclude that the system of fines had a significant effect in reducing the number of obscene outbursts.

8.3 Randomized-Block One-Way ANOVA

You read in Chapter 7 that repeated-measures and matched-samples research designs offer greater power in statistical comparisons than is available from an independent-samples design. This advantage is not limited to two-sample comparisons; it extends as well to multiple-sample designs. When the same cases are measured repeatedly, under two or more treatment conditions, or when the cases that comprise two or more samples are matched on some individual difference characteristic(s), the randomized-block one-way ANOVA offers greater power than the completely randomized ANOVA to identify significant differences among sample means. Only the computational aspects of the randomized-block ANOVA will be presented here. Readers who are interested in more conceptual details should refer to Hinkle, Wiersma, and Jurs (1988),[2] or Shavelson (1988).[3]

Because the summation notation associated with the randomized-block ANOVA is rather complicated, it will be simpler to describe the necessary calculations verbally. Refer to Example 8.2 as you read about the computations of the randomized-block ANOVA.

Preliminary Calculations

Begin by organizing the data into a table like the one shown in Example 8.2. Then calculate the following preliminary components:

1. Compute row and column sums.
2. Square each row sum and divide by the number of treatment conditions.
3. Square each column sum and divide by the number of cases in that column.
4. Sum all of the scores in the data table.
5. Square the result of step 4 and divide this by the total number of scores in the data table.
6. Sum the values computed in step 2.
7. Sum the values computed in step 3.
8. Square each score in the data table and sum these squared values.

sum of squares for subjects ($SS_{Subjects}$) *Reflects data variability due to individual differences among subjects in the randomized-block ANOVA.*

sum of squares for treatments ($SS_{Treatments}$) *Reflects variability in means from one treatment condition to the next that is due to different treatments in the randomized-block ANOVA.*

residual sum of squares ($SS_{Residual}$) *Reflects data variability due to measurement error and individual differences in the randomized-block ANOVA.*

Calculating Sums of Squares

The total sum of squares (SS_{Total}) in the randomized-block ANOVA is broken down into three components: $\mathbf{SS_{Subjects}}$ (variability due to individual differences); $\mathbf{SS_{Treatments}}$ (variability due to treatment conditions); and $\mathbf{SS_{Residual}}$ (variability that is left over). Sums of squares for the randomized-block one-way ANOVA are computed according to Equations 8.7 to 8.10 using the preliminary components described above.

Equation 8.7

$$SS_{Total} = \text{step 8} - \text{step 5}$$

Equation 8.8

$$SS_{Subjects} = \text{step 6} - \text{step 5}$$

Equation 8.9

$$SS_{Treatments} = \text{step 7} - \text{step 5}$$

Equation 8.10

$$SS_{Residual} = SS_{Total} - SS_{Subjects} - SS_{Treatments}$$

[2]Hinkle, D. E., Wiersma, W., & Jurs, S. G. (1988). *Applied statistics for the behavioral sciences.* Boston: Houghton Mifflin.

[3]Shavelson, R. J. (1988). *Statistical reasoning for the behavioral sciences.* Boston: Allyn & Bacon.

Calculating Mean Squares

Mean squares for the randomized-block one-way ANOVA are computed according to Equations 8.11 to 8.13 by dividing the sums of squares by their corresponding degrees of freedom.

$$MS_{\text{Subjects}} = \frac{SS_{\text{Subjects}}}{df_{\text{Subjects}}}$$

Equation 8.11

$$MS_{\text{Treatments}} = \frac{SS_{\text{Treatments}}}{df_{\text{Treatments}}}$$

Equation 8.12

$$MS_{\text{Residual}} = \frac{SS_{\text{Residual}}}{df_{\text{Residual}}}$$

Equation 8.13

where

$df_{\text{Subjects}} = N - 1$ (where N = the number of cases in each treatment group)
$df_{\text{Treatments}} = k - 1$ (where k = the number of treatment groups)
$df_{\text{Residual}} = (k - 1)(N - 1)$

The *F* Statistic in the Randomized-Block One-Way ANOVA

The *F* statistic for the randomized-block one-way ANOVA is computed according to Equation 8.14.(See Note 2)

$$F = \frac{MS_{\text{Treatments}}}{MS_{\text{Residual}}}$$

Equation 8.14

This *F* statistic is evaluated for significance by comparing it to the critical value of *F* (Table 6 in Appendix B) for $df_{\text{Treatments}}$ (for $df_{\text{Numerator}}$) and df_{Residual} (for $df_{\text{Denominator}}$).

COMPREHENSION CHECK 8.24

Perform a randomized-block one-way ANOVA for the following data.

Sample 1	Sample 2	Sample 3
6	2	9
8	3	10
7	1	9
6	1	8

(Answer on pp. 264–265.)

EXAMPLE 8.2

Randomized-Block One-Way ANOVA

Kids ask the darndest questions! Dr. Joyce Bothers has collected questions from 2-, 3-, and 4-year-olds, like these:

> "Mommy put cheese in the toilet. What're you going to do to her?" (2 years old)
>
> "How can cows be naughty if they don't have hands?" (3 years old)
>
> "Have you ever cut fish with a comb?" (4 years old)

Dr. Bothers believes that children's questions are sometimes hard for adults to answer because of the mismatch between their levels of cognitive development. According to this theory, questions from older children should be easier for adults to answer than questions from younger children.

To test her theory, Dr. Bothers asked six adults a series of questions like those listed above, from 2-, 3-, and 4-year-olds, and recorded their response latencies (that is, the time taken to begin answering) in seconds. Her repeated-measures data, organized in the data table below, show differences among mean response latencies that are consistent with her prediction: Adults respond faster to the questions of older children than to those of younger children. The statistical significance of these differences are evaluated here using a randomized-block one-way ANOVA.

	Treatment conditions		
Subjects	*2-Year-Olds' Questions*	*3-Year-Olds' Questions*	*4-Year-Olds' Questions*
1	5.3	5.0	5.1
2	2.7	3.0	2.1
3	3.1	3.0	2.8
4	4.4	3.8	3.2
5	3.9	3.4	3.0
6	4.9	4.0	3.8
$\overline{X}$	4.05	3.70	3.33
$\hat{s}^2$	1.03	.57	1.05

Preliminary Calculations

1. Sum the rows: 15.4 7.8 8.9 11.4 10.3 12.7
   Sum the columns: 24.3 22.2 20.0
2. Square the row sums and divide by the number of treatment conditions:

$$\frac{15.4^2}{3} = 79.05$$

$$\frac{7.8^2}{3} = 20.28$$

$$\frac{8.9^2}{3} = 26.40$$

$$\frac{11.4^2}{3} = 43.32$$

$$\frac{10.3^2}{3} = 35.36$$

$$\frac{12.7^2}{3} = 53.76$$

3. Square the column sums and divide by the number of subjects:

$$\frac{24.3^2}{6} = 98.42$$

$$\frac{22.2^2}{6} = 82.14$$

$$\frac{20.0^2}{6} = 66.67$$

4. Sum all scores in the data table:

$$66.5$$

5. Square step 4 and divide by the total number of scores:

$$\frac{66.5^2}{18} = 245.68$$

6. Sum the values computed in step 2:

$$79.05 + 20.28 + \cdots + 53.76 = 258.17$$

7. Sum the values computed in step 3:

$$98.42 + 82.14 + 66.67 = 247.23$$

8. Square each score in the data table and sum:

$$5.3^2 + 2.7^2 + \cdots + 3.8^2 = 260.51$$

Sums of Squares

Sums of squares for the randomized-block one-way ANOVA are computed according to Equations 8.7 to 8.10.

According to Equation 8.7,

$$\begin{aligned} SS_{\text{Total}} &= \text{step } 8 - \text{step } 5 \\ &= 260.51 - 245.68 \\ &= 14.83 \end{aligned}$$

According to Equation 8.8,

$$\begin{aligned} SS_{\text{Subjects}} &= \text{step } 6 - \text{step } 5 \\ &= 258.17 - 245.68 \\ &= 12.49 \end{aligned}$$

According to Equation 8.9,

$$\begin{aligned} SS_{\text{Treatments}} &= \text{step 7} - \text{step 5} \\ &= 247.23 - 245.68 \\ &= 1.55 \end{aligned}$$

According to Equation 8.10,

$$\begin{aligned} SS_{\text{Residual}} &= SS_{\text{Total}} - SS_{\text{Subjects}} - SS_{\text{Treatments}} \\ &= 14.83 - 12.49 - 1.55 \\ &= .79 \end{aligned}$$

Mean Squares

Mean squares for the randomized-block one-way ANOVA are computed by dividing the sums of squares by their respective degrees of freedom according to Equations 8.11 to 8.13.

According to Equation 8.11,

$$\begin{aligned} MS_{\text{Subjects}} &= \frac{SS_{\text{Subjects}}}{(N - 1)} \\ &= \frac{12.49}{6 - 1} \\ &= 2.50 \end{aligned}$$

According to Equation 8.12,

$$\begin{aligned} MS_{\text{Treatments}} &= \frac{SS_{\text{Treatment}}}{k - 1} \\ &= \frac{1.55}{3 - 1} \\ &= .78 \end{aligned}$$

According to Equation 8.13,

$$\begin{aligned} MS_{\text{Residual}} &= \frac{SS_{\text{Residual}}}{(k - 1)(N - 1)} \\ &= \frac{.79}{(3 - 1)(6 - 1)} \\ &= .08 \end{aligned}$$

The F *Statistic*

The F test for the treatment effect is computed according to Equation 8.14.

$$F = \frac{MS_{Treatments}}{MS_{Residual}}$$

$$= \frac{.78}{.08}$$

$$= 9.75$$

The results of the analysis are summarized in the ANOVA summary table that follows.

Source	SS	df	MS	*F*
Subjects	12.49	5	2.50	
Treatments	1.55	2	.78	9.75
Residual	.79	10	.08	
Total	14.83	17		

Choosing Between H_0 *and* H_1

The obtained value of $F = 9.75$ is compared to the sampling distribution of the F statistic for $df_{Treatment} = 2$ (for $df_{Numerator}$) and $df_{Residual} = 10$ (for $df_{Denominator}$). The critical value of F at the .01 level is 7.56. The obtained value exceeds this critical value. We conclude that a value of F this large, and the differences among means it reflects, is very unlikely to be produced by sampling error alone: We reject the null hypothesis and accept the alternative hypothesis as the more likely explanation of the observed differences. Dr. Bother's hypothesis is confirmed: As the ages of children increase from 2 to 4 years, adults show a statistically significant decrease in time taken to answer their questions.

8.4 Post-Hoc Data Snooping in One-Way ANOVA

We saw earlier in this chapter that the chief advantage of one-way ANOVA over multiple pairwise t tests is the control over error rates that the one-way ANOVA provides. Using multiple t tests to compare all the various pairs of sample means guarantees that, as more tests are performed, more Type I and Type II errors will occur. The ANOVA, in contrast, provides a single significance test, the F test, that determines if there is a significant difference *anywhere* among the sample means. With just one significance test we know that the probability of a Type I error is equal to our chosen level of significance and there is similarly only one opportunity for a Type II error to occur.

We also saw earlier, though, that the chief *dis*advantage of the one-way ANOVA is that it does not locate the source of a significant F test. Given a significant F, we know that there is a difference somewhere among the means, but we do not know which means differ.

Once the one-way ANOVA has yielded a significant F test, we will usually want to do some data snooping to determine the source of the significant F. This is accomplished using post-hoc comparisons. Very popular among these is **Tukey's HSD** ("honestly significant difference") test. The Tukey HSD procedure tells how large the difference must be between any two sample means in order for that difference to be considered statistically ("honestly") significant.

Tukey's HSD *Tukey's "honestly significant difference" test is a post-hoc procedure used to perform pairwise comparisons of sample means.*

COMPREHENSION CHECK 8.25

Explain the purpose of the Tukey HSD test and describe how it works.

(Answer on p. 265.)

Computations for the Tukey HSD are slightly different for the completely randomized ANOVA (Equation 8.15) and the randomized-block ANOVA (Equation 8.16).

Equation 8.15

$$\text{HSD} = q_{(\alpha,\ \text{df}_{\text{Within}},\ k)} \sqrt{\frac{\text{MS}_{\text{Within}}}{n}}$$

Equation 8.16

$$\text{HSD} = q_{(\alpha,\ \text{df}_{\text{Residual}},\ k)} \sqrt{\frac{\text{MS}_{\text{Residual}}}{n}}$$

where

q = the value obtained from Table 7 in Appendix B (percentage points of the Studentized range statistic)
α = the desired level of significance
$\text{df}_{\text{Within}}$ = $\text{df}_{\text{Within}}$ from the completely randomized ANOVA
$\text{df}_{\text{Residual}}$ = $\text{df}_{\text{Residual}}$ from the randomized-block ANOVA
k = the number of treatment conditions
n = the sample size of the smallest treatment condition in the ANOVA

In words, to compute HSD, we: (1) find the value of q in Table 7 in Appendix B for the desired level of significance (.05 or .01), the value of $\text{df}_{\text{Within}}$ (for the completely randomized ANOVA) or $\text{df}_{\text{Residual}}$ (for the randomized-block ANOVA), and k, the number of treatment conditions in the ANOVA; (2) divide $\text{MS}_{\text{Within}}$ (for the completely randomized ANOVA) or $\text{MS}_{\text{Residual}}$ (for the randomized-block ANOVA) by n, the number of cases in the smallest sample in the ANOVA; (3) find the square root of the result of step 2; and (4) multiply the result of step 3 by the value of q found in step 1.

The computation and interpretation of Tukey's HSD procedure is illustrated in Example 8.3.

COMPREHENSION CHECK 8.26

Sample means for the data presented in Comprehension Check 8.14 are: $\overline{X}_1 = 2.67$, $\overline{X}_2 = 6.00$, and $\overline{X}_3 = 8.50$. Sample sizes are $N_1 = 3$,

(*cont.*)

$N_2 = 2$, and $N_3 = 4$. Use the Tukey HSD procedure and results summarized in Comprehension Check 8.20 ($df_{Within} = 6$, $k = 3$, $MS_{Within} = 1.95$) to determine which means differ significantly (.05 level). Sample means for the data presented in Comprehension Check 8.24 are $\overline{X}_1 = 6.75$, $\overline{X}_2 = 1.75$, and $\overline{X}_3 = 9.00$. Sample size is $N = 4$. Use the Tukey HSD procedure and the results of Comprehension Check 8.24 ($df_{Residual} = 6$, $k = 3$, and $MS_{Residual} = .20$) to determine which means differ significantly (.01 level).

(Answer on pp. 265–266.)

In light of the warnings given earlier about multiple pairwise comparisons, you may wonder if it is legitimate to use Tukey's HSD procedure to compare all the means from a one-way ANOVA. The answer to this question lies in the way in which Tukey's HSD is computed. We have already seen that as the number of samples (k) increases, the number of possible comparisons increases at an accelerating rate. The value q in Equations 8.15 and 8.16 also increases as k increases. And as q increases, so does the size of the difference required for significance (HSD). Put simply, Tukey's HSD is a significance test that adjusts itself to counteract increases in Type I errors that would otherwise accompany increases in the number of pairwise comparisons. Tukey's HSD procedure sets the probability of a Type I error at the chosen level for the *entire set* of comparisons. The more comparisons, the more conservative Tukey's HSD test becomes. This can occasionally create the perplexing situation in which the F test in an ANOVA indicates the presence of a significant difference among sample means, but none of the differences is large enough to be found significant using Tukey's HSD. Under these circumstances, the most that one can say is that the largest of the pairwise differences is significant.

COMPREHENSION CHECK 8.27

How does the Tukey HSD procedure avoid the increased Type I error rate that accompanies multiple t tests?

(Answer on p. 266.)

EXAMPLE 8.3

Tukey HSD Post-Hoc Comparisons

The significant F ratios in Examples 8.1 and 8.2 pointed to the presence of significant differences among sample means. The problem that remains is to determine which sample means differ. The Tukey HSD, illustrated in this example, is used in post-hoc pairwise comparisons of sample means following a significant F.

Post-Hoc Comparisons for the Completely Randomized ANOVA

The sample means from Example 8.1 are presented below along with differences among these means.

No Fine	10 min	20 min
$\overline{X}_1 = 18.43$	$\overline{X}_2 = 15.00$	$\overline{X}_3 = 8.17$
$N_1 = 7$	$N_2 = 8$	$N_3 = 6$
	$\overline{X}_1 - \overline{X}_2 = 3.43$	
	$\overline{X}_1 - \overline{X}_3 = 10.26$	
	$\overline{X}_2 - \overline{X}_3 = 6.83$	

Next, Tukey's HSD is computed according to Equation 8.15.

$$\text{HSD} = q_{(\alpha,\ \text{df}_{\text{Within}},\ k)} \sqrt{\frac{\text{MS}_{\text{Within}}}{n}}$$

$$= q_{(.01,\ 18,\ 3)} \sqrt{\frac{17.36}{6}}$$

$$= 4.70 \sqrt{\frac{17.36}{6}}$$

$$= 7.99$$

The value of q in this equation was found in Table 7 in Appendix B by entering the table with the values of α (the desired significance level) $= .01$, $\text{df}_{\text{Within}}$ from the significant ANOVA $= 18$, and k (the number of groups in the analysis) $= 3$.

Any between-group difference that meets or exceeds Tukey's HSD = 7.99 can be considered to be significant at the .01 level. Only one of our comparisons, $\overline{X}_1$ vs. $\overline{X}_3$, meets this standard. We conclude that retired statisticians who are fined 20 minutes of computer time for each obscene outburst show significantly fewer outbursts than do those who receive no fine. Other differences are too small to be considered reliable.

Post-Hoc Comparisons for the Randomized-Block ANOVA

The sample means from Example 8.2 are shown below along with differences among the means.

2-Year-Olds' Questions	3-Year-Olds' Questions	4-Year-Olds' Questions
$\overline{X}_1 = 4.05$	$\overline{X}_2 = 3.70$	$\overline{X}_3 = 3.33$
	$\overline{X}_1 - \overline{X}_2 = .35$	
	$\overline{X}_1 - \overline{X}_3 = .72$	
	$\overline{X}_2 - \overline{X}_3 = .37$	

Next, Tukey's HSD is computed according to Equation 8.16.

$$HSD = q_{(\alpha,\ df_{Residual},\ k)} \sqrt{\frac{MS_{Residual}}{n}}$$

$$= q_{(.01,\ 10,\ 3)} \sqrt{\frac{.08}{6}}$$

$$= 5.27 \sqrt{\frac{.08}{6}}$$

$$= .61$$

Any difference between means that meets or exceeds Tukey's HSD = .61 can be considered significant at the .01 level. Only one, the largest ($\overline{X}_1 - \overline{X}_2 = .72$), can be considered significant by this standard.

8.5 Measuring Association Strength in One-Way ANOVA

We discovered in Chapter 7 that a statistically significant difference between two samples may or may not be an important difference. This is just as true in the context of one-way ANOVA. Statistical significance means only that the observed difference is greater than one would expect on the basis of sampling error alone. It is a reliable difference that one would expect to see again in a replication. If sample sizes are large, however, even a very small and unimportant difference between samples can be found to be statistically significant.

The statistic omega-square (ω^2) was introduced in Chapter 7 as being useful in evaluating the practical importance of a statistically significant *t* test. Omega-square is also used with the one-way ANOVA. This measure of association strength is computed a little differently for the completely randomized and randomized-block ANOVAs, as shown in Equations 8.17 and 8.18.

$$\omega^2 = \frac{SS_{Between} - (k - 1)MS_{Within}}{SS_{Total} + MS_{Within}}$$

Equation 8.17

$$\omega^2 = \frac{SS_{Treatments} - (k - 1)MS_{Residual}}{SS_{Total} + MS_{Residual}}$$

Equation 8.18

where

$SS_{Between}$ = $SS_{Between}$ from the completely randomized ANOVA
$SS_{Treatments}$ = $SS_{Treatments}$ from the randomized-block ANOVA
k = the number of treatment conditions
MS_{Within} = MS_{Within} from the completely randomized ANOVA
$MS_{Residual}$ = $MS_{Residual}$ from the randomized-block ANOVA
SS_{Total} = SS_{Total} from the ANOVA

In words, omega-square is computed by: (1) multiplying MS_{Within} (for the completely randomized ANOVA) or $MS_{Residual}$ (for the randomized-block ANOVA) by $k - 1$ (where k = the number of samples in the ANOVA); (2) subtracting the result of step 1 from $SS_{Between}$ (for the completely randomized ANOVA) or $SS_{Treatments}$ (for the randomized-block ANOVA); (3) summing $SS_{Total} + MS_{Within}$ (for the completely randomized ANOVA) or $SS_{Total} + MS_{Residual}$ (for the randomized-block ANOVA); and (4) dividing the result of step 2 by the result of step 3.

Omega-square measures the strength of the treatment effect in the ANOVA in a manner that is more interpretable than the F statistic. There is no upper limit on how large F can become; this depends on score magnitude, sample sizes, and the number of samples being compared. Because of this, the value of F tells us only whether or not the differences among sample means are significant. The greater interpretability of ω^2 comes from the fact that it ranges only from 0 to 1.(See Note 3)

A strong treatment effect, indicated by a ω^2 value approaching 1, means that the independent and dependent variables are strongly associated. When ω^2 is large like this, we can predict quite accurately any given case's group membership if we know that case's score on the dependent variable. As the strength of the treatment effect declines, ω^2 also grows smaller, and our ability to predict group membership from the dependent variable score declines. The use of ω^2 is illustrated in Example 8.4.

COMPREHENSION CHECK 8.28

Compute and interpret ω^2 based on the ANOVA results summarized in Comprehension Check 8.20, where $SS_{Between} = 58.27$, $SS_{Within} = 11.67$, $MS_{Within} = 1.95$, and $k = 3$.
Compute and interpret ω^2 based on the ANOVA results from Comprehension Check 8.24, where $SS_{Treatments} = 110.17$, $SS_{Residual} = 1.17$, $MS_{Residual} = .20$, and $k = 3$.
(Answer on p. 266.)

EXAMPLE 8.4

Using Omega-Square to Measure Association Strength in One-Way ANOVA

We found in Example 8.1 that fining retired statisticians 20 minutes of computer time for each obscene outburst was significantly more effective than a no-fine condition in reducing the frequency of obscene outbursts. Example 8.2 demonstrated a significant difference in the times taken by adults to answer questions posed by 2- and 4-year-olds. Here, we will compute the statistic omega-square (ω^2) to measure the strength of the relationship between the independent and dependent variables in these two examples.

ω^2 for the Completely Randomized ANOVA

Omega-square is computed for the completely randomized ANOVA according to Equation 8.17.

$$\omega^2 = \frac{SS_{Between} - (k - 1)MS_{Within}}{SS_{Total} + MS_{Within}}$$

$$= \frac{348.69 - (3 - 1)17.36}{661.24 + 17.36}$$

$$= .46$$

Since ω^2 ranges only from 0 to 1, $\omega^2 = .46$ represents a moderate relationship between frequency of outbursts and level of fine.

ω^2 for the Randomized-Block ANOVA

Omega-square is computed for the randomized-block ANOVA according to Equation 8.18.

$$\omega^2 = \frac{SS_{Treatments} - (k - 1)MS_{Residual}}{SS_{Total} + MS_{Residual}}$$

$$= \frac{1.55 - (3 - 1).08}{14.83 + .08}$$

$$= .09$$

Since ω^2 ranges in value only from 0 to 1, $\omega^2 = .09$ represents a weak relationship between adults' response latencies in answering questions posed by children and the age of the children.

8.6 Kruskal-Wallis One-Way Analysis of Variance by Ranks

The **Kruskal-Wallis one-way analysis of variance by ranks** is a commonly used nonparametric alternative to the completely randomized one-way ANOVA. The Kruskal-Wallis test is used when: (1) each case appears in only one sample (no repeated-measures or matched samples); (2) the samples consist of at least 6 cases each and represent different levels of a single independent variable; (3) the populations represented by the samples have symmetrical distributions or are at least of similar shapes; and (4) the dependent variable is measured at the ordinal level. Thus, the procedure is particularly useful when only a rough, rank-order measure of the dependent variable is available.

Kruskal-Wallis one-way analysis of variance by ranks *A nonparametric alternative to the completely randomized one-way ANOVA that allows for the analysis of an ordinal-scale dependent variable.*

The Kruskal-Wallis test can be used to compare two or more samples, though, like one-way ANOVA, it is traditionally used when there are three or more samples. The Mann-Whitney *U*, presented in Chapter 7, is commonly used to handle two-sample rank-order comparisons.

Comprehension Check 8.29

How are the completely randomized one-way ANOVA and Kruskal-Wallis tests similar? How are they different?
(Answer on p. 266.)

The Null and Alternative Hypotheses

The Kruskal-Wallis test compares the average ranks of the samples against the average ranks that would be expected if the samples were drawn from a population of identically treated cases. These "expected" average ranks, of course, would be equal. When the groups being compared are identical, their average ranks will be equal and so they will match exactly with the expected average ranks. As the groups become more disparate, their average ranks will differ increasingly from each other and from the expected average ranks.

The null hypothesis for the Kruskal-Wallis test attributes differences between observed average ranks and expected average ranks to sampling error. That is, samples drawn from a population of identically treated cases would likely show a disparity of the observed size. The alternative hypothesis attributes the differences between observed and expected average ranks to a treatment effect: Because differences of the observed size would be unlikely in the absence of a treatment effect, they are more likely to be the result of a treatment effect.

COMPREHENSION CHECK 8.30

As group differences increase, what happens to the average group ranks? What happens to the expected average group ranks?
(Answer on p. 266.)

The Test Statistic *H*

***H* statistic** *The test statistic in the Kruskal-Wallis procedure. The value of* H *reflects the differences among observed group mean ranks and mean ranks that would be expected in the absence of any treatment effect.*

The test statistic for the Kruskal-Wallis procedure is called *H*. The ***H* statistic** varies in value as a function of the size of the disparity between observed average ranks and average ranks that would be expected if there were no treatment effect. As such, *H* reflects differences between the average ranks of the groups.

Unless the dependent variable already consists of rank orders, the first step in computing *H* is to rank-order the entire collection of scores from lowest (rank = 1) to highest (rank = *N*). Ties are treated as described in Chapter 7, with the tied scores each receiving a rank equal to the average of their positions in an ordered array.

Once the scores are ranked, *H* is computed according to Equation 8.19.(See Note 4)

Equation 8.19

$$H = \frac{12}{N(N+1)}\left[\Sigma\frac{(\Sigma R)^2}{n}\right] - 3(N+1)$$

where

H = the Kruskal-Wallis test statistic
N = the total number of cases in the analysis
R = the ranks of the cases
n = the sample sizes of each of the groups

In words, *H* is computed by: (1) dividing 12 by *N* times *N* + 1; (2) summing the ranks in each group; (3) squaring each of these sums of ranks; (4) dividing each of the values obtained in step 3 by its corresponding sample size; (5) summing the values obtained in step 5; (6) multiplying *N* + 1 times 3; (7) multiplying the result of step 1 by the result of step 5; and (8) subtracting the result of step 6 from the result of step 7.

When the groups are identical, the test statistic *H* will have a value of 0. As the groups become more disparate, the value of *H* will become greater.

COMPREHENSION CHECK 8.31

Use Equation 8.19 to compute the H statistic for following ranks.

Group 1	Group 2	Group 3
8.5	12	2
15	7	6
16.5	8.5	1
11	10	5
14	13	3.5
18	16.5	3.5

(Answer on p. 266.)

Choosing Between the Null and Alternative Hypotheses

The probability of obtaining a given value of H if all samples were treated the same is obtained by comparing the obtained H against the sampling distribution of chi-square (χ^2) for $k - 1$ degrees of freedom, where $k =$ the number of groups. You may wonder why there is no sampling distribution for the H statistic. The reason is that there is no need for one. This distribution would look just like the χ^2 distribution. This may make more sense to you if you recall that we used the χ^2 statistic in Chapter 6 and 7 to compare observed frequencies against expected frequencies across several categories of a variable. In the Kruskal-Wallis procedure we are doing much the same thing: We are comparing observed average ranks against expected average ranks across several samples.

If the computed value of H meets or exceeds the critical value of χ^2 for $\text{df} = k - 1$ at the selected significance level, we know that the obtained H has a small probability of occurring in the absence of a treatment effect. Under these circumstances, we conclude that there probably *is* a treatment effect, or, in other words, that the groups differ significantly.

COMPREHENSION CHECK 8.32

Evaluate the statistical significance of the value of H you computed in Comprehension Check 8.31.

(Answer on p. 266.)

Post-Hoc Data Snooping

Finding a significant H is like finding a significant F in the one-way ANOVA. It means only that there is a difference *somewhere* among the groups. Finding the source(s) of the significant H is the next step.

The Tukey HSD test is used to perform post-hoc pairwise comparisons following a significant Kruskal-Wallis test. We use the Tukey test to compare the mean ranks of the groups. The difference between two groups' mean ranks is statistically significant if it exceeds Tukey's HSD computed according to Equation 8.20.

Equation 8.20

$$\text{HSD} = \frac{q_{(\alpha, k, \infty)}}{\sqrt{2}} \sqrt{\frac{N(N+1)}{6n}}$$

where

q = the value obtained from Table 7 in Appendix B ("percentage points of the Studentized range statistic")
k = the number of samples
α = the desired significance level for the comparisons
∞ = the df_{error} value in Table 7
N = the total sample size
n = the size of the smallest sample in the analysis

In words, to compute HSD, we: (1) find the value of q in Table 7 of Appendix B for the desired level of significance (.05 or .01), k (the number of groups), and "error df" = infinity; (2) divide this value of q by the square root of 2; (3) multiply N by $N + 1$ and divide by 6 times the smallest sample size (n); (4) find the square root of step 3; and (5) multiply the result of step 4 by the result of step 2.

The Kruskal-Wallis procedure and Tukey HSD post-hoc comparisons are illustrated in Example 8.5.

Comprehension Check 8.33

Use the Tukey HSD procedure to compare the mean ranks of the data presented in Comprehension Check 8.31.
(Answer on p. 266.)

Example 8.5

Kruskal-Wallis One-Way Analysis of Variance by Ranks

To illustrate the Kruskal-Wallis one-way analysis of variance by ranks and subsequent post-hoc comparison procedures, let's reanalyze the data presented in Example 8.1 using this procedure.

The analysis begins with a rank-ordering of the original scores. Data from all groups are combined and the scores are ranked from lowest to highest. These ranked scores follow, along with average ranks for each group.

Treatment Groups		
No Fine	*10 min*	*20 min*
20	11	2
13.5	18.5	6
21	9	1
6	6	11
18.5	16.5	3
15	8	4
16.5	11	
	13.5	
$\bar{R}_1 = 15.79$	$\bar{R}_2 = 11.69$	$\bar{R}_3 = 4.50$

Null and Alternative Hypotheses

H_0: Differences between the mean group ranks can be attributed to sampling error. That is, samples treated identically would be quite likely to display differences of the size seen here.

H_2: Differences between the samples are too large to attribute to sampling error. Samples treated identically would be unlikely to differ by as much as is seen here. It is more likely that the groups differ because of the action of a treatment effect, in this situation, fine level.

Test Statistic

The test statistic H is computed according to Equation 8.19.

$$H = \frac{12}{N(N+1)}\left[\Sigma\frac{(\Sigma R)^2}{n}\right] - 3(N+1)$$

$$= \frac{12}{21(21+1)}\left[\frac{(20+\cdots+16.5)^2}{7} + \frac{(11+\cdots+13.5)^2}{8} + \frac{(2+\cdots+4)^2}{6}\right]$$

$$- 3(21-1)$$

$$= .03(2958.60) - 60$$

$$= 28.76$$

Choosing Between $\mathbf{H_0}$ *and* $\mathbf{H_1}$

To determine the probability of the obtained value of H under conditions of the null hypothesis, we compare the obtained value of $H = 28.76$ against the sampling distribution of χ^2 for $k - 1 = 3 - 1 = 2$ degrees of freedom. The general shape of this sampling distribution is shown below. Critical values of χ^2 are found in Table 3 in Appendix B, "Critical Values of χ^2."

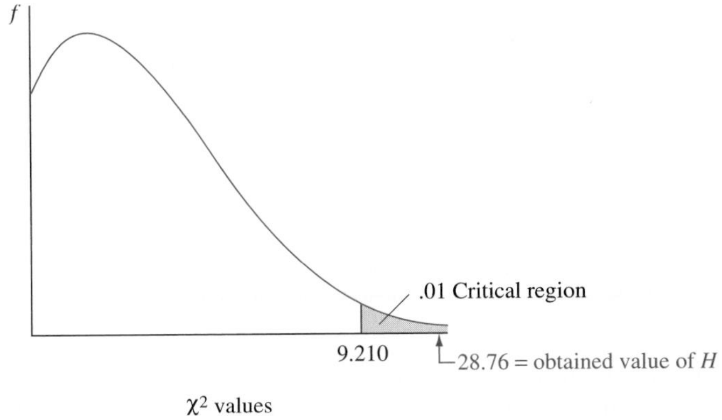

We see that the obtained value of $H = 28.76$ occurs quite infrequently when samples are treated identically. Our H exceeds the critical value of χ^2 for the .01 level of significance for $k - 1 = 3 - 1 = 2$ degrees of freedom ($\chi^2 = 9.210$). Consistent with our findings in Example 8.1, we conclude that the mean group ranks deviate significantly from the ranks that would be expected in the absence of a treatment effect.

Post-Hoc Comparisons

Having determined that there is a significant difference somewhere among the samples, the Tukey HSD post-hoc comparison procedure will be used to identify which groups differ.

The sample mean ranks were presented above with the data. Differences between these mean ranks are

$$\bar{R}_1 \text{ vs. } \bar{R}_2 = 4.10$$

$$\bar{R}_1 \text{ vs. } \bar{R}_3 = 11.29$$

$$\bar{R}_2 \text{ vs. } \bar{R}_3 = 7.19$$

Tukey's HSD is computed according to Equation 8.20.

$$\text{HDS} = \frac{q_{(\alpha, k, \infty)}}{\sqrt{2}} \sqrt{\frac{N(N + 1)}{6n}}$$

$$= \frac{q_{(.01, 3, \infty)}}{\sqrt{2}} \sqrt{\frac{21(21 + 1)}{6(6)}}$$

$$= \frac{4.12}{\sqrt{2}} \sqrt{\frac{462}{36}}$$

$$= 10.44$$

The value of q in this equation was found in Table 7 in Appendix B, "Percentage points of the Studentized range statistic," by entering the table with the values of α (the desired significance level) = .01, $df_{\text{Error}} = \infty$, and k (the number of groups in the analysis) = 3.

Any difference between group mean ranks that meets or exceeds Tukey's HSD = 10.44 can be considered to be significant at the .01 level. Only one of the differences meets this standard: $\bar{R}_1 - \bar{R}_3 = 11.29$. We can conclude that this greatest pairwise difference is statistically significant. Retirees fined 20 minutes of computer time displayed significantly fewer obscene outbursts than did those receiving no fine.

SUMMARY

This chapter describes procedures used in performing multiple-group comparisons. The completely randomized one-way analysis of variance (ANOVA) extends the independent-samples t test (Chapter 7) to comparisons of two *or more* groups. The randomized-block one-way ANOVA similarly extends the dependent-samples t test (Chapter 7) to cover multiple-sample situations. The Kruskal-Wallis test is a nonparametric procedure that relaxes some of the assumptions of the completely randomized one-way ANOVA.

The Kruskal-Wallis procedure allows one to analyze dependent variables measured at the ordinal level.

The test statistic of the one-way ANOVA is *F*. This statistic reflects differences among sample means. By comparing an obtained value of *F* against the sampling distribution of *F*, we can determine the probability that the *F*, and the differences among means that it represents, would have occurred in samples drawn from a population of identically treated cases.

A statistically significant *F* statistic tells us only that there is a difference *somewhere* among the group means that is too large to be a likely result of sampling error alone. We use post-hoc comparisons such as the Tukey HSD procedure to find *which* means differ.

The strength of the treatment effect is reflected only imperfectly in the test statistic *F*. More useful as a measure of the strength of association between the independent variable and dependent variable in one-way ANOVA is ω^2.

The Kruskal-Wallis procedure uses the test statistic *H* to compare independent samples' average ranks against the average ranks that would be expected if the samples were treated identically. An obtained value of *H* is compared against the χ^2 sampling distribution to determine the probability that the obtained *H* would occur as a result of sampling error alone. A significant *H* test can be followed with Tukey HSD post-hoc comparisons to determine the source(s) of the significance.

NOTES

1. Notice in Table 6 that not all degrees of freedom are listed. In the listing of $df_{Numerator}$ across the top of the table, we jump from 12 to 14, from 14 to 16, from 16 to 20, and so on. In the listing of $df_{Denominator}$ down the side of the table, we jump from 30 to 32, 32 to 34, 34 to 36, and so on. If the correct degrees of freedom for a particular *F* test are not listed in the table, the recommended practice is to use the next *lower* values that *are* listed. For instance if $df_{Between} = 18$ and $df_{Within} = 130$, one would use the next lower listed values: $df_{Between} = 16$ (for $df_{Numerator}$) and $df_{Within} = 125$ (for $df_{Denominator}$).
2. There is a second *F* test in the randomized-block one-way ANOVA. The ratio $MS_{Subjects}/MS_{Residual}$ provides for a test of the significance between subjects, called the *subject effect.* The critical value of *F* for this test is found in the table of critical values of *F* for $df_{Subjects}$ (for $df_{Numerator}$) and $df_{Residual}$ (for $df_{Denominator}$).
3. If *F* is less than 1, ω^2 can become negative. This is meaningless because there is no such thing as less than no association between an independent variable and dependent variable. Therefore, when *F* is less than 1, the value of ω^2 is set at 0.
4. The numbers 12 and 3 in Equation 8.19 are constants, not variables.

REVIEW EXERCISES

Review Exercises 8.1–8.5 describe a variety of research questions. Select for each the most appropriate statistical procedure from the following list: (a) completely randomized one-way ANOVA; (b) randomized-block one-way ANOVA; (c) Tukey HSD procedure; (d) omega-square; (e) Kruskal-Wallis one-way analysis of variance by ranks.

8.1. A researcher has found a significant F statistic in a one-way ANOVA comparing mean absences of college freshmen, sophomores, juniors, and seniors. How can he determine which specific groups differ?

8.2. The researcher described in Review Exercise 8.1 also wants to evaluate the strength of the association between academic class and absenteeism. What statistic can he use to do this?

8.3. An industrial/organizational psychologist wants to compare the productivity (measured in number of units produced each hour) of production workers paid \$15, \$20, and \$25 per hour.

8.4. Clients seeking treatment for the depression associated with seasonal affective disorder are exposed to bright red, yellow, blue, and white lights on four successive days. After each day's treatment, the clients complete the Beck Depression Inventory. How can differences between the four treatments be evaluated?

8.5. A social worker has rank-ordered the parenting effectiveness of fathers in treatment for alcoholism, cocaine addiction, and a control group of fathers who are not involved in any kind of treatment. How can differences between these groups be evaluated?

8.6. Shown below are statistics test scores for three groups of students who were taught using three different teaching methods. Evaluate these data to see if they are suitable to a completely randomized one-way ANOVA.

Group 1	Group 2	Group 3
87	52	78
86	98	75
92	86	72
75	67	74
78	78	79
72	92	76
75	54	76
73	68	75
74	72	72

8.7. Numbers of absences accumulated in a semester-long introductory psychology course are recorded below for freshmen, sophomores, juniors, and seniors. Use a completely randomized one-way ANOVA to evaluate differences among the groups. Present your results in an ANOVA summary table.

Freshmen	Sophomores	Juniors	Seniors
2	2	1	1
3	3	0	0
1	2	1	0
4	3	2	1
3	1	0	2
2	4	1	1
3	3	2	2
	2	2	1
		1	1

8.8. Use the Tukey HSD procedure to identify the source(s) of the significant F test obtained in Review Exercise 8.7.

8.9. Compute the ω^2 statistic to measure the strength of association between academic class (i.e., freshman–senior) and absenteeism.

8.10. Ten students were instructed to solve as many math problems as possible under each of three conditions: (a) working in a quiet room; (b) working while listening to rock music; and (c) working while listening to classical music. The number of problems solved correctly by each student under each condition is shown below. Use a randomized-block one-way ANOVA to determine if there are any significant differences among the means. Present your results in an ANOVA summary table.

Quiet	Rock	Classical
10	6	9
8	5	7
7	7	7
8	8	8
6	7	10
7	9	9
11	6	10
9	5	8
8	8	7
7	7	6

8.11. Although the F test computed in Review Exercise 8.10 is nonsignificant, compute Tukey's HSD for those data.

8.12. Using the data in Review Exercise 8.10, compute ω^2 to measure the strength of association between working condition (i.e., quiet, rock music, classical music) and mathematics performance.

8.13. Reaction-time data are shown below for drivers who have consumed no alcohol, two glasses of wine, or four glasses of wine. Why are these data most appropriately analyzed using the Kruskal-Wallis one-way ANOVA by ranks?

0 Glasses	2 Glasses	4 Glasses
.1	.1	.1
.2	.4	.6
.2	.4	.6
.2	.4	.6
.2	.4	.6
.3	.5	.6
.3	.5	.7
.4	.6	.7
.4	.7	.9

8.14. Use the Kruskal-Wallis one-way ANOVA by ranks to analyze the data given in Review Exercise 8.13.

8.15. Use the Tukey HSD procedure to determine the source(s) of the significant H statistic computed in Review Exercise 8.14.

Answers to Comprehension Checks

8.1. Samples differ "significantly" if they differ by more than can be reasonably attributed to sampling error. The difference seen is more likely due to some treatment effect of the independent variable.

8.2. The one-way ANOVA is traditionally used to evaluate the significance of differences between three or more group means. It is called "one-way" because the groups differ in their levels on just one independent variable. It is called "analysis of variance" because the procedure evaluates differences between means by analyzing variances.

8.3. The one-way ANOVA assumes: (1) an interval- or ratio-scale dependent variable; (2) the samples represent populations that have approximately normal distributions; and (3) the samples represent populations with approximately equal variances. We evaluate these assumptions by examining the sample data, because we do not have the population data.

8.4. The completely randomized ANOVA compares two or more groups that each consist of different cases. The randomized-block ANOVA is used to analyze data from repeated-measures or matched-samples designs. The randomized-block ANOVA is more powerful than the completely randomized ANOVA.

8.5. The number of pairwise comparisons is equal to $(k^2 - k)/2$, where k = the number of samples. If $k = 8$, the number of pairwise comparisons is

$$\frac{8^2 - 8}{2} = 28$$

8.6. If using the .05 significance level, of 28 pairwise comparisons, one would expect $.05(28) = 1.4$ Type I errors.

8.7. One-way ANOVA has the advantage of requiring only one significance test, thereby: (1) reducing the number of computations that must be performed; (2) reducing the number of Type I and Type II errors; and (3) keeping the probability of Type I error set at the chosen level of significance. The disadvantage of the one-way ANOVA is that the F test indicates only that there is a significant difference *somewhere* among the means; it does not tell us which means differ.

8.8. Data from multiple groups show two kinds of variability: (1) within-group variability; and (2) between-group variability.

8.9. Within-group variance is caused by (1) individual differences and (2) measurement error.

8.10. Between-group variance is caused by (1) individual differences, (2) measurement error, and (3) treatment effects. Of these, the first two affect both between-group and within-group variance. Treatment effects affect only between-group variance.

8.11. A treatment effect will cause an increase in between-group variance and will have no effect on within-group variance.

8.12. F is called a "test statistic" because it is a statistic computed from sample data that varies in value as a function of the size of the difference being tested for significance. In the case of one-way ANOVA, as differences among sample means increase, the value of F increases.

8.13. When there are no differences among sample means, the means do not vary, so between-group variance is 0 and $F = 0$. The single most frequently occurring value of F in the sampling distribution of F is 1. This is because $F = 1$ when between-group and within-group variance are equal, that is, there is no treatment effect. The sampling distribution of F is based on drawing sets of samples from a population in which there is no treatment effect. Values of F larger than 1 occur less and less frequently in the sampling distribution of F because these larger values occur only when between-group variance exceeds within-group variance. In the absence of a treatment effect, large between-group variance is relatively uncommon.

8.14. Equation 8.1 defines $SS_{Between}$ as

$$SS_{Between} = (\overline{X}_1 - \overline{X}_G)^2 (N_1) + (\overline{X}_2 - \overline{X}_G)^2 (N_2) + \cdots + (\overline{X}_k - \overline{X}_G)^2 (N_k)$$

For the data given

$\overline{X}_1 = 2.67 \quad \overline{X}_2 = 6.00 \quad \overline{X}_3 = 8.50 \quad \overline{X}_G = 6.00$

$N_1 = 3 \quad N_2 = 2 \quad N_3 = 4 \quad N = 9$

Therefore we compute SS_{Between} as

$$(2.67 - 6.00)^2\,(3) + (6.00 - 6.00)^2\,(2) + (8.50 - 6.00)^2\,(4) = 58.27$$

8.15. Equation 8.2 defines SS_{Within} as

$$SS_{\text{Within}} = \Sigma(X_i - \overline{X}_1)^2 + \Sigma(X_i - \overline{X}_2)^2 + \cdots + \Sigma(X_i - \overline{X}_k)^2$$

For the data given,

$\overline{X}_1 = 2.67 \quad \overline{X}_2 = 6.00 \quad \overline{X}_3 = 8.50$

Therefore we compute SS_{Within} as

$$(4 - 2.67)^2 + (3 - 2.67)^2 + (1 - 2.67)^2 + (5 - 6.00)^2 + (7 - 6.00)^2 + (9 - 8.50)^2 + (8 - 8.50)^2 + (7 - 8.50)^2 + (10 - 8.50)^2 = 11.67$$

8.16. Equation 8.3 defines SS_{Total} as

$$SS_{\text{Total}} = \Sigma(X_i - \overline{X}_G)^2$$

For the data given,

$$\overline{X}_G = 6.00$$

Therefore we compute SS_{Total} as

$$(4 - 6.00)^2 + (3 - 6.00)^2 + \cdots + (10 - 6.00)^2 = 70.00$$

This is within rounding error of SS_{Total}, computed as

$$SS_{\text{Total}} = SS_{\text{Between}} + SS_{\text{Within}} = 58.27 + 11.67 = 69.94$$

8.17. Equation 8.4 defines MS_{Between} as

$$MS_{\text{Between}} = \frac{SS_{\text{Between}}}{df_{\text{Between}}}$$

For the data given,

$$df_{\text{Between}} = k - 1 = 3 - 1 = 2$$

$$SS_{\text{Between}} = 58.27$$

Therefore we compute MS_{Between} as

$$\frac{58.27}{2} = 29.14$$

8.18. Equation 8.5 defines MS_{Within} as

$$MS_{\text{Within}} = \frac{SS_{\text{Within}}}{df_{\text{Within}}}$$

For the data given,

$$df_{\text{Within}} = N - k = 9 - 3 = 6$$

$$SS_{\text{Within}} = 11.67$$

Therefore we compute MS_{Within} as

$$\frac{11.67}{6} = 1.95$$

8.19. Equation 8.6 defines F as

$$F = \frac{MS_{\text{Between}}}{MS_{\text{Within}}}$$

For the data given

$$MS_{\text{Between}} = 29.14$$

$$MS_{\text{Within}} = 1.95$$

Therefore we compute F as

$$\frac{29.14}{1.95} = 14.94$$

8.20. The ANOVA summary table follows.

Source	**SS**	**df**	**MS**	***F***
Between groups	58.27	2	29.14	14.94
Within groups	11.67	6	1.95	
Total	70.00			

8.21. The null hypothesis attributes differences between sample means to sampling error. The alternative hypothesis attributes the differences to a treatment effect.

8.22. For $df_{\text{Between}} = 2$ and $df_{\text{Within}} = 6$, the critical values of F are 5.14 (for the .05 level of significance) and 10.92 (for the .01 level of significance).

8.23. For $df_{\text{Between}} = 2$ and $df_{\text{Within}} = 6$, the critical values of F are 5.14 (.05 level of significance) and 10.92 (.01 level of significance). The obtained value of $F = 14.94$ exceeds both of these values and can be considered significant at the .01 level. We would reject the null hypothesis and accept the alternative hypothesis: The differences among sample means cannot reasonably be attributed to sampling error, but more likely reflect the presence of a treatment effect.

8.24. *Preliminary calculations:*

Step 1. Compute row and column sums.

Row sums: 17 21 17 15

Column sums: 27 7 36

Step 2. Square each row sum and divide by the number of treatment conditions.

$$\frac{17^2}{3} = 96.33$$

$$\frac{21^2}{3} = 147.00$$

$$\frac{17^2}{3} = 96.33$$

$$\frac{15^2}{3} = 75.00$$

Step 3. Square each column sum and divide by the number of cases in that column.

$$\frac{27^2}{4} = 182.25$$

$$\frac{7^2}{4} = 12.25$$

$$\frac{36^2}{4} = 324.00$$

Step 4. Sum all of the scores in the data table.

$$70$$

Step 5. Square the result of step 4 and divide this by the total number of scores in the data table:

$$\frac{70^2}{12} = 408.33$$

Step 6. Sum the values computed in step 2.

$$96.33 + \cdots + 75.00 = 414.66$$

Step 7. Sum the values computed in step 3.

$$182.25 + 12.25 + 324.00 = 518.50$$

Step 8. Square each score in the data table and sum these squared values.

$$6^2 + 8^2 + \cdots + 8^2 = 526$$

Sums of squares:
Compute SS_{Total} according to Equation 8.7.

$$SS_{Total} = \text{step } 8 - \text{step } 5 = 117.67$$

Compute $SS_{Subjects}$ according to Equation 8.8.

$$SS_{Subjects} = \text{step } 6 - \text{step } 5 = 6.33$$

Compute $SS_{Treatments}$ according to Equation 8.9.

$$SS_{Treatments} = \text{step } 7 - \text{step } 5 = 110.17$$

Compute $SS_{Residual}$ according to Equation 8.10.

$$SS_{Residual} = SS_{Total} - SS_{Subjects} - SS_{Treatments} = 1.17$$

Mean squares:
Compute $MS_{Subjects}$ according to Equation 8.11.

$$MS_{Subjects} = \frac{SS_{Subjects}}{N - 1} = 2.11$$

Compute $MS_{Treatments}$ according to Equation 8.12.

$$MS_{Treatments} = \frac{SS_{Treatments}}{k - 1} = 55.09$$

Compute $MS_{Residual}$ according to Equation 8.13.

$$MS_{Residual} = \frac{SS_{Residual}}{(k - 1)(N - 1)} = .20$$

F statistic:
Compute F according to Equation 8.14.

$$F = \frac{MS_{Treatment}}{MS_{Residual}} = 275.45$$

Evaluate F for Significance: The obtained value of F is evaluated for significance by comparing it against the sampling distribution of F. For $df_{Treatments} = 2$ (for $df_{Numerator}$) and $df_{Residual} = 6$ (for $df_{Denominator}$), the critical value of F marking the .01 critical region is 10.92. The obtained value of F exceeds this, indicating that the means differ by more than one would expect on the basis of sampling error alone.

8.25. The Tukey HSD test is used to perform pairwise comparisons between sample means to locate the difference(s) that are responsible for the significant F test in the ANOVA. Tukey's HSD indicates how large the difference must be between two sample means in order to be considered statistically significant.

8.26. *Post-hoc comparisons for Comprehension Check 8.14:*

Equation 8.15 defines Tukey's HSD for the completely randomized ANOVA as

$$HSD = q_{(\alpha,\, df_{Within},\, k)} \sqrt{\frac{MS_{Within}}{n}}$$

We find the value of q from Table 7 in Appendix B for $\alpha = .05$, $df_{Within} = 6$, and $k = 3$:

$$q = 4.34$$

For the data at hand, $MS_{Within} = 1.95$ and $n = 2$. Therefore we compute HSD as

$$4.34 \sqrt{\frac{1.95}{2}} = 4.29$$

Absolute differences among the three means for data given in Comprehension Check 8.14 are

$$\overline{X}_1 - \overline{X}_2 = 3.33 \qquad \overline{X}_1 - \overline{X}_3 = 5.83 \qquad \overline{X}_2 - \overline{X}_3 = 2.50$$

Only one of these differences ($\overline{X}_1$ vs. $\overline{X}_3 = 5.83$) meets or exceeds Tukey's HSD of 4.29. Only this difference can be considered statistically significant at the .05 level.

Post-hoc comparisons for Comprehension Check 8.24:

Equation 8.16 defines Tukey's HSD for the randomized-block ANOVA as

$$\text{HSD} = q_{(\alpha,\, \text{df}_{\text{Residual}},\, k)} \sqrt{\frac{\text{MS}_{\text{Residual}}}{n}}$$

We find the value of q from Table 7 in Appendix B for $\alpha = .01$, $\text{df}_{\text{Residual}} = 6$, and $k = 3$:

$$q = 6.33$$

For the data at hand, $\text{MS}_{\text{Residual}} = .20$ and $n = 4$. Therefore we compute HSD as

$$6.33 \sqrt{\frac{.20}{4}} = 1.42$$

Absolute differences among the three means for data given in Comprehension Check 8.24 are

$\overline{X}_1 - \overline{X}_2 = 5.00$ $\quad\overline{X}_1 - \overline{X}_3 = 2.25$ $\quad\overline{X}_2 - \overline{X}_3 = 7.25$

All of these differences meet or exceed Tukey's HSD of 1.42 and can be considered statistically significant.

8.27. The Tukey HSD procedure sets the probability of Type I error at the chosen level for the entire set of comparisons.

8.28. *ω^2 for Comprehension Check 8.20:*
Equation 8.17 defines ω^2 for the completely randomized ANOVA as

$$\omega^2 = \frac{\text{SS}_{\text{Between}} - (k-1)\text{MS}_{\text{Within}}}{\text{SS}_{\text{Total}} + \text{MS}_{\text{Within}}}$$

$$= \frac{58.27 - (3-1)1.95}{70.00 + 1.95}$$

$$= .76$$

Because values of ω^2 range only from 0 to 1, $\omega^2 = .76$ represents a fairly strong relationship.

ω^2 for Comprehension Check 8.24:
Equation 8.18 defines ω^2 for the randomized-block ANOVA as

$$\omega^2 = \frac{\text{SS}_{\text{Treatments}} - (k-1)\text{MS}_{\text{Residual}}}{\text{SS}_{\text{Total}} + \text{MS}_{\text{Residual}}}$$

$$= \frac{110.17 - (3-1).20}{117.67 + .20}$$

$$= .93$$

Because values of ω^2 range only from 0 to 1, $\omega^2 = .93$ represents a very strong relationship.

8.29. Both the one-way ANOVA and the Kruskal-Wallis test are used to compare three or more groups that differ on one independent variable. The procedures differ primarily in that the ANOVA assumes an interval- or ratio-scale dependent variable and the Kruskal-Wallis test allows for ordinal-scale dependent variables.

8.30. As group differences increase, the average group ranks become more divergent. Because expected average group ranks are those that would be expected if there were no treatment effect, these expected average ranks are always equal from one group to the next, regardless of actual differences between the groups.

8.31. Equation 8.19 defines H as

$$H = \frac{12}{N(N+1)}\left[\Sigma\frac{(\Sigma R)^2}{n}\right] - 3\,(N+1)$$

$$= \frac{12}{18(18+1)}\left[\frac{(8.5 + \cdots + 18)^2}{6} + \frac{(12 + \cdots + 16.5)^2}{6}\right.$$

$$\left. + \frac{(2 + \cdots + 3.5)^2}{6}\right] - 3(18+1)$$

$$= .035\left(\frac{83^2}{6} + \frac{67^2}{6} + \frac{21^2}{6}\right) - 57$$

$$= 11.94$$

8.32. For $k - 1 = 3 - 1 = 2$ degrees of freedom, the critical value of χ^2 at the .01 level of significance is 9.21. The obtained value of $H = 11.94$ exceeds this critical value. We conclude that the probability that the groups would differ by the amount observed in the absence of a treatment effect is less than .01.

8.33. Equation 8.20 defines the Tukey HSD for the Kruskal-Wallis ANOVA as

$$\text{HSD} = \frac{q_{(\alpha,\, k,\, \infty)}}{\sqrt{2}} \sqrt{\frac{N(N+1)}{6n}}$$

We find the value of q from Table 7 in Appendix B for $\alpha = .05$, $\text{df}_{\text{error}} = \infty$, and $k = 3$:

$$q = 3.31$$

For the data at hand, $N = 18$ and n (the smallest sample) $= 6$. Therefore we compute HSD as

$$\text{HSD} = \frac{3.31}{\sqrt{2}} \sqrt{\frac{18(18+1)}{6(6)}}$$

$$= 7.21$$

Two of the differences between mean ranks meet or exceed this value and are significant:

$$\overline{R}_2 - \overline{R}_3 = 7.67$$

$$\overline{R}_1 - \overline{R}_3 = 10.33$$

Factorial Analysis of Variance

9

Chapter Outline

Researchers in the social and behavioral sciences have reported that:

- College students who register late for classes are absent from classes more often than timely registrants, but only in classes that do not place limits on absences, not in classes with restrictive attendance policies.
- Speed of mathematical problem solving increases as one's level of physiological arousal increases, but only for simple problems, not for complex problems.
- Paying children for earning good grades reduces their intrinsic scholastic motivation, but only for children who are interested in school in the first place, not for those who are less interested in school.

Did you notice that each of these examples included more than one independent variable (or "factor")? Indeed, there are two factors in each study. The first explored the influence of both timeliness of registration (late vs. timely) and attendance policy (restrictive vs. nonrestrictive) on absenteeism. The second study examined the effects of both physiological arousal level (low, medium, and high) and problem complexity (simple vs. complex) on problem-solving speed. And the third study investigated how both reward condition (reward vs. no reward) and initial level of interest (interested vs. disinterested) affect children's intrinsic scholastic motivation.

Did you notice the qualifying phrases in the examples? The classroom attendance of late registrants is not the same under all circumstances; it depends on the attendance policy. Physiological arousal does not always have the same effect on problem-solving performance; it depends on how difficult the problems are. Paying children for earning good grades does not affect everyone's intrinsic motivation in the same way; it depends on the child's initial level of scholastic interest.

factorial analysis of variance *A family of ANOVA procedures that examines the separate and combined effects of two or more independent variables (factors) within the context of a single study.*
main effect *The effect of a single factor on the dependent variable.*
interaction effect *The effect on the dependent variable of the various combinations of levels of two or more factors. An interaction effect exists when the effect of one factor is influenced by the level of another factor.*

These are examples of the kinds of research results that are produced by factorial analysis of variance. **Factorial analysis of variance** is used to examine the separate and combined effects of two or more independent variables ("factors") within the context of a single study. Factorial ANOVA enables us to determine if each factor considered singly has an effect on the dependent variable. These are called **main effects.** In addition, factorial ANOVA identifies **interaction effects,** the conditional effects illustrated by the examples that introduced this chapter. An interaction effect exists when the effect of one factor depends on the level of some other factor.

Is biofeedback effective in treating migraine headache? Is it equally effective for stress-related and hormone-related migraines? Do statistics students give higher evaluation ratings to male or to female statistics instructors? Does it depend on the gender of the student? Is behavioral therapy or psychodynamic therapy more effective in alleviating depression? Does the client's intelligence affect this relationship? These are all examples of the kinds of research questions that beg to be answered through factorial ANOVA. In each we are interested in the effects of two factors as well as the interaction between the factors.

COMPREHENSION CHECK 9.1

Identify the factors in each of the three sample research questions posed in the preceding paragraph. Identify the dependent variable in each.

(Answer on p. 298.)

9.1 Types of Factorial ANOVA

Factorial ANOVA is actually a whole family of statistical procedures. One way of designating a factorial ANOVA is according to how many factors are being investigated and how many levels are included in each factor. A factorial ANOVA that examines two factors is called a **two-way ANOVA;** a **three-way ANOVA** is one that includes three factors; and so on.

two-way ANOVA *A factorial ANOVA that includes two factors.*
three-way ANOVA *A factorial ANOVA that includes three factors.*

Factorial ANOVAs are also labeled according to the number of levels within each factor. For example, a factorial study of the effects of arousal level (low, moderate, or high) and problem complexity (simple vs. difficult) could be described as a two-way ANOVA or a 2×3 ("two by three") factorial ANOVA because there are two factors, the first containing two levels and the second containing three levels. A study of the effects of instructor gender (male vs. female) and student gender (male vs. female) on student evaluations of their instructors would be called a 2×2 ("two by two") factorial ANOVA because there are two factors, each with two levels.

Comprehension Check 9.2

An investigator wants to study the effects of behavior therapy (therapy vs. no therapy), intelligence (low, average, and high), and disorder type (affective disorder, psychosexual disorder, substance use disorder, and personality disorder) on social adjustment. How would one "label" this ANOVA design?

(Answer on p. 298.)

Most factorial ANOVA designs are **fully crossed.** That is, the researcher studies all possible combinations of the levels of the two or more factors. Factorial designs that do not include some of the possible combinations are called **nested designs.**

fully crossed designs *Factorial ANOVA designs in which all possible combinations of the levels of the factors are examined.*
nested designs *Factorial ANOVA designs in which some of the combinations of levels of the factors are not examined.*

Table 9.1 illustrates three fully crossed 3×2 factorial designs. In each of these designs, rows represent the levels of factor A (a_1, a_2, and a_3) and columns represent the levels of factor B (b_1, b_2). Each cell represents one of the combinations of levels of factors A and B. Notice the notation used throughout Table 9.1 to represent row means ($\overline{X}_{a_1}$, $\overline{X}_{a_2}$, and $\overline{X}_{a_3}$), column means $\overline{X}_{b_1}$ and $\overline{X}_{b_2}$), cell means ($\overline{X}_{a_1b_1}$, $\overline{X}_{a_1b_2}$, etc.) and the grand mean ($\overline{X}_G$).

The simplest form of factorial ANOVA, called the **completely randomized factorial ANOVA,** is represented in Table 9.1a. The critical feature of this design is that each cell is occupied by a different, independent sample. That is, each subject (s_1, s_2, etc.) is exposed to one and only one treatment combination. Both factors in this design are referred to as **between-subjects factors.**

completely randomized factorial ANOVA *A fully crossed ANOVA in which each treatment combination (cell) is represented by a different, independent sample.*
between-subjects factors *Factors whose levels are represented by independent samples.*

Another type of factorial ANOVA, called the **randomized-block factorial ANOVA,** is represented in Table 9.1b. This factorial ANOVA is also fully crossed, but each treatment combination (cell) is now represented by the same cases (in a repeated-measures procedure) or matched cases (in a matched-samples procedure). Both factors in the randomized-block factorial design are referred to as **within-subjects factors.** Randomized-block factorial ANOVAs offer greater power to identify treatment effects than is available from the completely randomized factorial ANOVA, but repeated measures and matched samples are not practical in every research situation.

randomized-block factorial ANOVA *A fully crossed ANOVA in which each treatment combination (cell) is represented by the same sample (repeated measures) or matched samples.*
within-subjects factors *Factors whose levels are represented by dependent samples—repeated measures or matched samples.*

TABLE 9.1

Three forms of the 3 × 2 factorial ANOVA. Table 9.1a depicts the completely randomized factorial ANOVA. Table 9.1b is the randomized-block factorial ANOVA. Table 9.1c is a split-plot factorial ANOVA.

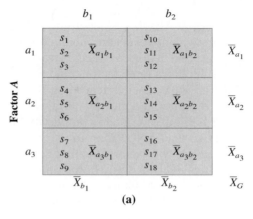

Factor B

		b_1		b_2		
Factor A	a_1	s_1 s_2 s_3	$\overline{X}_{a_1b_1}$	s_{10} s_{11} s_{12}	$\overline{X}_{a_1b_2}$	$\overline{X}_{a_1}$
	a_2	s_4 s_5 s_6	$\overline{X}_{a_2b_1}$	s_{13} s_{14} s_{15}	$\overline{X}_{a_2b_2}$	$\overline{X}_{a_2}$
	a_3	s_7 s_8 s_9	$\overline{X}_{a_3b_1}$	s_{16} s_{17} s_{18}	$\overline{X}_{a_3b_2}$	$\overline{X}_{a_3}$
		$\overline{X}_{b_1}$		$\overline{X}_{b_2}$		$\overline{X}_G$

(a)

Factor *B*

		b_1		b_2		
Factor *A*	a_1	s_1 s_2 s_3	$\overline{X}_{a_1b_1}$	s_1 s_2 s_3	$\overline{X}_{a_1b_2}$	$\overline{X}_{a_1}$
	a_2	s_1 s_2 s_3	$\overline{X}_{a_2b_1}$	s_1 s_2 s_3	$\overline{X}_{a_2b_2}$	$\overline{X}_{a_2}$
	a_3	s_1 s_2 s_3	$\overline{X}_{a_3b_1}$	s_1 s_2 s_3	$\overline{X}_{a_3b_2}$	$\overline{X}_{a_3}$
		$\overline{X}_{b_1}$		$\overline{X}_{b_2}$		$\overline{X}_G$

(b)

Factor B

		b_1		b_2		
Factor *A*	a_1	s_1 s_2 s_3	$\overline{X}_{a_1b_1}$	s_1 s_2 s_3	$\overline{X}_{a_1b_2}$	$\overline{X}_{a_1}$
	a_2	s_4 s_5 s_6	$\overline{X}_{a_2b_1}$	s_4 s_5 s_6	$\overline{X}_{a_2b_2}$	$\overline{X}_{a_2}$
	a_3	s_7 s_8 s_9	$\overline{X}_{a_3b_1}$	s_7 s_8 s_9	$\overline{X}_{a_3b_2}$	$\overline{X}_{a_3}$
		$\overline{X}_{b_1}$		$\overline{X}_{b_2}$		$\overline{X}_G$

(c)

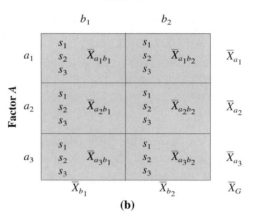

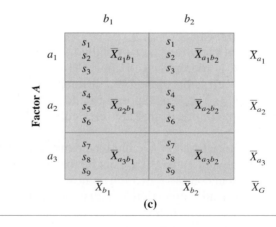

The **split-plot factorial ANOVA,** shown in Table 9.1c, is a hybrid. Here, one factor (A) is a between-subjects factor, where each level is represented by different, independent samples. Another factor (B) is a within-subjects factor, where each level is represented by the same cases (using a repeated-measures procedure) or matched cases (using a matched-samples procedure).

split-plot factorial ANOVA *A fully crossed ANOVA that includes one or more between-subjects factors and one or more within-subjects factors.*

COMPREHENSION CHECK 9.3

A researcher wants to investigate the effects of two teaching methods on the academic achievement of male and female students. How would one assign subjects to cells in this design so as to produce completely randomized, randomized-block, and split-plot designs?
(Answer on p. 298.)

This just begins to describe the possibilities. There are **fixed effects models** and **random effects models.** In the former, the levels of each factor represent all levels of interest to the researcher. In the latter, the levels have been randomly sampled from some larger set. If some factors include all levels of interest and other factors include only a random sampling of the levels of interest, we have a **mixed effects model.**

fixed effects models *A factorial ANOVA in which all factors include all levels of interest to the researcher.*

random effects models *A factorial ANOVA in which the levels of all factors have been sampled randomly from some larger sets that are of interest to the researcher.*

mixed effects models *A factorial ANOVA in which the levels of some factors represent all levels of interest to the researcher, whereas the levels of other factors have been sampled randomly from some larger set that is of interest.*

But there's more! Factorial ANOVAs are handled differently depending on whether there are an equal or an unequal number of cases in each treatment combination. And, when the parametric assumptions of ANOVA aren't met (an interval- or ratio-scale dependent variable showing normal distributions and approximately equal variances in each cell), there are a variety of nonparametric versions of factorial ANOVA that relax these assumptions.

There are still more variations, but you get the idea. A limited treatment of factorial ANOVA must leave something out. In this chapter we will examine only the simplest factorial ANOVA, the two-factor, completely randomized, fixed effects factorial ANOVA, with equal sample sizes. Readers wanting information about more complex ANOVA designs should consult Keppel (1982),[1] Kirk (1968),[2] or Lindman (1974).[3]

9.2 Main Effects and Interaction Effects

A question may have occurred to you at this point. If one wants to study two or more independent variables, why not just perform two or more one-way ANOVAs, one for each independent variable of interest? The most compelling answer is that factorial ANOVA not only enables us to evaluate the main effect of each factor (which is what a series of one-way ANOVAs would do), but also lets us compare the various treatment combinations—the interaction effect. The capacity to evaluate interaction effects is unique to the factorial ANOVA.

[1]Keppel, G. (1982). *Design and analysis: A researcher's handbook.* Englewood Cliffs, NJ: Prentice-Hall.

[2]Kirk, R. E. (1968). *Experimental design: Procedures for the behavioral sciences.* Belmont, CA: Brooks/Cole.

[3]Lindman, H. R. (1974). *Analysis of variance in complex experimental designs.* San Francisco: W. H. Freeman.

line graphs *Plots of the cell means obtained from factorial ANOVA designs.*

Line graphs like those shown in Figure 9.1 are useful in better understanding main and interaction effects. Line graphs are simply plots of the cell means obtained in factorial research designs. The ordinate represents the dependent variable, the abscissa represents levels of factor *A*, and each of the lines shows one of the levels of factor *B*. Finally, the points in the line graph represent the means of each of the combinations of levels of the factors (cells).

A factor *A* main effect is indicated when the average elevation of the points above one level of factor *A* differs substantially from the average elevation of the points above another level of factor *A*. Look at Figure 9.1a. The average number of absences is clearly lower in classes with restrictive attendance policies (a_1) than in classes with nonrestrictive attendance policies (a_2). Figure 9.1c, in contrast, shows no factor *A* main effect. The average levels of intrinsic scholastic motivation are equal under conditions of no reward (a_1) and reward (a_2).

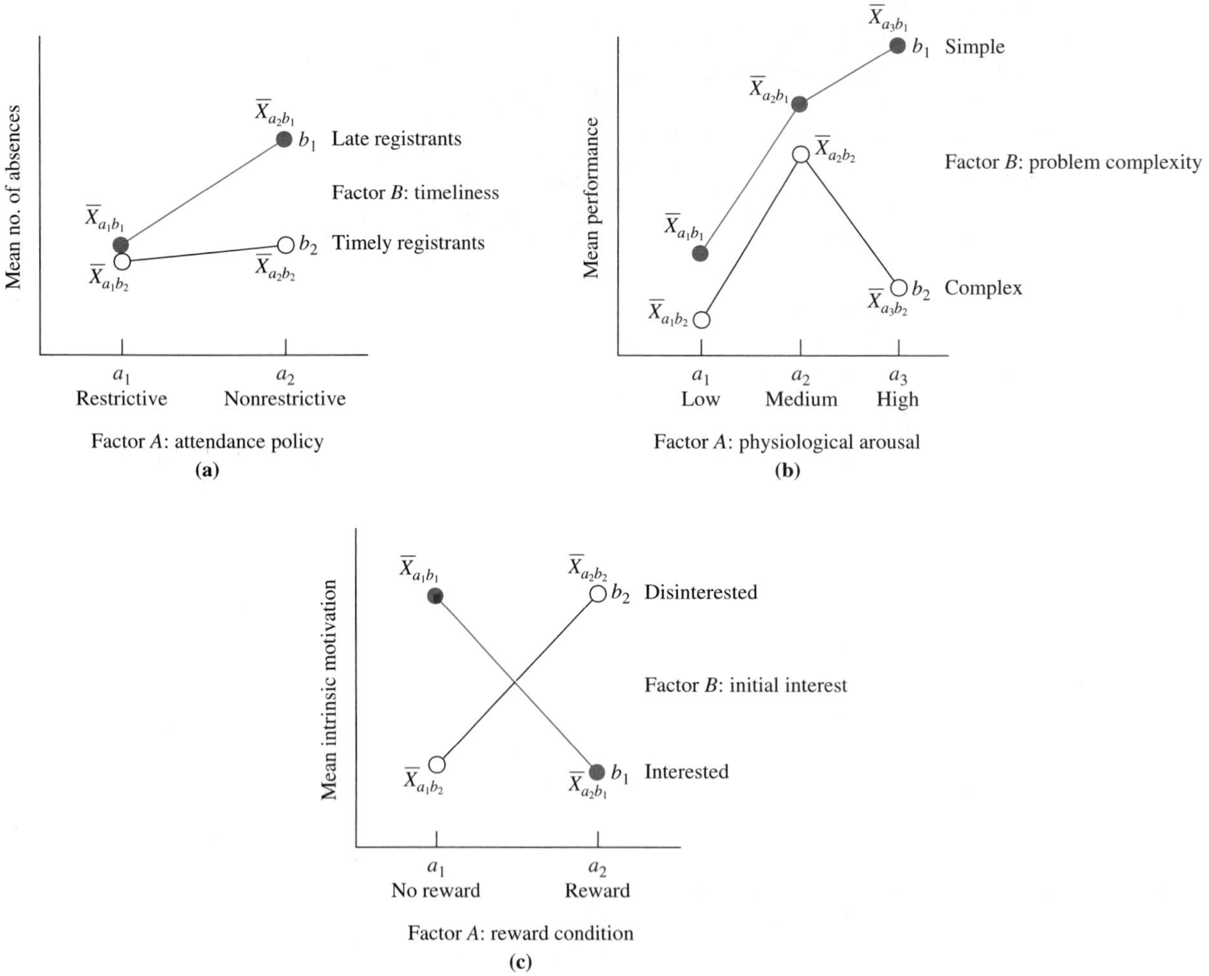

FIGURE 9.1

Line graphs are useful in identifying main and interaction effects. (a) and (b) show main effects of factors *A* and *B* as well as ordinal interaction effects. (c) shows no main effects, but depicts a disordinal interaction effect.

A factor B main effect is indicated when the average elevation of points forming one level of factor B (one line in the graph) differs substantially from the average elevation of points forming another level of factor B (another line in the graph). Figure 9.1a illustrates a factor B main effect. The average level of the points representing late registrants (b_1) is substantially higher than the average level of the points representing timely registrants (b_2). In contrast, Figure 9.1c shows no factor B main effect. The average level of points representing interested students (b_1) does not differ from the average level of points representing disinterested students (b_2).

An interaction effect is indicated any time the lines of a line graph are nonparallel. Figure 9.1c shows a **disordinal interaction effect,** one in which the lines cross. In a disordinal interaction effect, the effect of factor A is reversed depending on the level of factor B, and vice versa. Children who are initially interested in school (b_1) show greater intrinsic scholastic motivation under conditions of no monetary reward (a_1) than when they are paid for earning good grades (a_2). In an opposite pattern, children who are initially disinterested in school (b_2) show greater intrinsic scholastic motivation under conditions of reward (a_2) than under conditions of no reward (a_1).

disordinal interaction effect *An interaction effect represented in a line graph by crossing lines. The effect of one factor is reversed depending on the level of the other factor.*

Figure 9.1a depicts an **ordinal interaction effect,** where the lines are nonparallel but do not cross. Here, the attendance of late registrants (b_1) is better in classes where there are restrictions on absenteeism (a_1) than in classes where there are no restrictions on absences (a_2). In contrast, timely registrants (b_2) attend class regularly whether absences are restricted (a_1) or not (a_2).

ordinal interaction effect *An interaction effect represented in a line graph by diverging lines that do not cross. The effect of one factor is influenced by the level of the other factor, but is not reversed.*

Comprehension Check 9.4

Describe the main and interaction effects shown in Figure 9.1b. Draw your own line graphs depicting 2 × 2 factorial ANOVAs in which: (a) there is a factor A main effect only; (b) there is a factor B main effect only; (c) there are factor A and factor B main effects only; and (d) there are factor A and factor B main effects and an $A \times B$ interaction effect.

(Answer on p. 298.)

Example 9.1 at the end of this chapter provides a concrete example of the completely randomized factorial ANOVA and related statistical procedures. You may wish to refer to this example as you read the chapter.

9.3 Partitioning the Variance in a Factorial Design

Recall from Chapter 8 that the variability of data in a completely randomized one-way ANOVA can be broken down (or "partitioned") into two components. First, within-group variability is the variability seen from one score to the next within any given group, and is represented by SS_{Within} and MS_{Within}. This within-group variability is the consequence of individual differences and measurement error. Second, between-group variability is the variability seen from one group mean to the next, and is represented by $SS_{Between}$ and $MS_{Between}$. Between-group variability is the consequence of individual differences, measurement error, *and treatment effects.* The strength of the treatment effect can therefore be measured by the ratio:

$$F = \frac{\text{between-group variance}}{\text{within-group variance}}$$

The variability of data obtained in a factorial design can also be partitioned into several sources. F tests are then used to compare these sources of variability in testing the main effects of each factor as well as the interaction effect.

Comprehension Check 9.5

Explain why treatment effects cannot affect within-group variability. Explain why treatment effects do affect between-group variability.

(Answer on p. 299.)

Within-Group Sum of Squares

Look back at Table 9.1a. Subjects within any given cell of the completely randomized factorial design are all exposed to the same treatment combination. It follows that any variability in scores seen within cells cannot be due to treatment effects, but must be due only to individual differences and measurement error. This variability is reflected in the within-group sum of squares (SS_{Within}), computed according to Equation 9.1.

Equation 9.1

$$SS_{Within} = \Sigma(X_{a_1b_1} - \overline{X}_{a_1b_1})^2 + \Sigma(X_{a_1b_2} - \overline{X}_{a_1b_2})^2 + \cdots + \Sigma(X_k - \overline{X}_k)^2$$

where

$X_{a_1b_1}$ to X_k = the individual scores
$\overline{X}_{a_1b_1}$ to $\overline{X}_k$ = the cell means
k = the number of cells

In words, the within-group sum of squares (SS_{Within}) is computed by: (1) subtracting from each score in each cell ($X_{a_1b_1}$, $X_{a_1b_2}$, etc.) that cell's mean ($\overline{X}_{a_1b_1}$, $\overline{X}_{a_1b_2}$, etc.); (2) squaring these differences; (3) summing the values obtained in step 2 for each cell; and (4) summing the values obtained in step 3 across the cells.

Comprehension Check 9.6

The data provided below were collected from 12 companies in a completely randomized factorial study of the effects of management style (directive vs. participative) and organizational financial strength (weak vs. strong) on employee morale (measured on a 1–10 scale). Use Equation 9.1 to compute SS_{Within} and explain what this value represents.

(cont.)

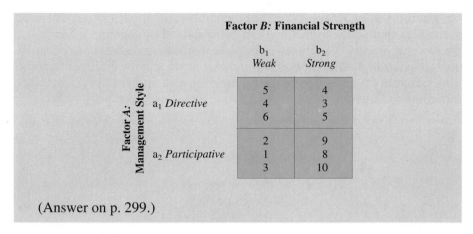

		Factor *B:* Financial Strength	
		b_1 *Weak*	b_2 *Strong*
Factor *A:* Management Style	a_1 *Directive*	5 4 6	4 3 5
	a_2 *Participative*	2 1 3	9 8 10

(Answer on p. 299.)

Between-Group Sum of Squares

Between-group variability is also present in the factorial ANOVA, seen as variability from one cell mean to the next. As was true with one-way ANOVA, between-group variability is the result of individual differences, measurement error, *and the different treatments received by cases in different cells*—treatment effects. This between-group variability is measured by the between-group sum of squares ($SS_{Between}$), computed according to Equation 9.2.

Equation 9.2

$$SS_{Between} = (\overline{X}_{a_1b_1} - \overline{X}_G)^2 N_{a_1b_1} + (\overline{X}_{a_1b_2} - \overline{X}_G)^2 N_{a_1b_2} + \cdots + (\overline{X}_k - \overline{X}_G)^2 N_k$$

where

$\overline{X}_{a_1b_1}$ to $\overline{X}_k$ = the cell means
$\overline{X}_G$ = the grand mean
$N_{a_1b_1}$ to N_k = the sample sizes in each cell
k = the number of cells

In words, the between-group sum of squares ($SS_{Between}$) is computed by: (1) subtracting the grand mean ($\overline{X}_G$) from each cell mean ($\overline{X}_{a_1b_1}$, $\overline{X}_{a_1b_2}$, etc.); (2) squaring these differences; (3) multiplying each value obtained in step 2 by that cell's corresponding size ($N_{a_1b_1}$, $N_{a_1b_2}$, etc.); and (4) summing the values obtained in step 3.

COMPREHENSION CHECK 9.7

Use Equation 9.2 to compute $SS_{Between}$ for the data given in Comprehension Check 9.6. Explain what this value represents.
(Answer on p. 299.)

Some of the between-group variability represented by $SS_{Between}$ is a result of different cells being exposed to different levels of factor *A* (rows). this is the factor *A* treatment effect. Some is due to different cells being exposed to different levels of factor *B* (columns). This is the factor *B* treatment effect. And some of the between-group variability seen from one cell mean to the next is due to different cells being exposed to different combinations of levels of factors *A* and *B*. This is the $A \times B$ interaction effect.

factor A sum of squares (SS_A) *Based on the sum of squared deviations of row means around the grand mean, SS_A reflects variability due to individual differences, measurement error, and the factor* A *treatment effect.*

Factor A Sum of Squares. The amount of variability from one cell mean to the next that is due to factor A can be evaluated by looking at how much the row means vary. Variability from one row mean to the next can be attributed to individual differences, measurement error, and the effect of factor A. This variability is measured by the **factor A sum of squares** (SS_A), computed according to Equation 9.3.

Equation 9.3

$$SS_A = (\overline{X}_{a_1} - \overline{X}_G)^2 N_{a_1} + (\overline{X}_{a_2} - \overline{X}_G)^2 N_{a_2} + \cdots$$

where

$\overline{X}_{a_1}, \overline{X}_{a_2}$, etc. = the row means
$\overline{X}_G$ = the grand mean
N_{a_1}, N_{a_2}, etc. = the sample sizes in each row

In words, the factor A sum of squares (SS_A) is computed by: (1) subtracting the grand mean ($\overline{X}_G$) from each row mean ($\overline{X}_{a_1}, \overline{X}_{a_2}$, etc.); (2) squaring each of these differences; (3) multiplying each of the squared differences obtained in step 2 by the number of cases in its corresponding row (N_{a_1}, N_{a_2}, etc.); and (4) summing the values obtained in step 3.

Comprehension Check 9.8

Use Equation 9.3 to compute SS_A for the data given in Comprehension Check 9.6 and explain what this value represents.
(Answer on p. 299.)

factor B sum of squares (SS_B) *Based on the sum of squared deviations of column means around the grand mean, SS_B reflects variability due to individual differences, measurement error, and the factor* B *treatment effect.*

Factor B Sum of Squares. The amount of variability from one cell mean to the next that is due to factor B can be evaluated by looking at how much the column means vary. Variability from one column mean to the next can be attributed to individual differences, measurement error, and the effect of factor B. This variability is measured by the **factor B sum of squares** (SS_B), is computed according to Equation 9.4.

Equation 9.4

$$SS_B = (\overline{X}_{b_1} - \overline{X}_G)^2 N_{b_1} + (\overline{X}_{b_2} - \overline{X}_G)^2 N_{b_2} + \cdots$$

where

$\overline{X}_{b_1}, \overline{X}_{b_2}$, etc. = the column means
$\overline{X}_G$ = the grand mean
N_{b_1}, N_{b_2}, etc. = the sample sizes in each column

In words, the factor B sum of squares (SS_B) is computed by: (1) subtracting the grand mean ($\overline{X}_G$) from each column mean ($\overline{X}_{b_1}, \overline{X}_{b_2}$, etc.); (2) squaring each of these differences; (3) multiplying each of the squared differences obtained in step 2 by the number of cases in its corresponding column (N_{b_1}, N_{b_2}, etc.); and (4) summing the values obtained in step 3.

Comprehension Check 9.9

Use Equation 9.4 to compute SS_B for the data given in Comprehension Check 9.6 and explain what this value represents.
(Answer on p. 299.)

Interaction Sum of Squares. Some of the variability from one cell mean to the next ($SS_{Between}$) is due to different cells being exposed to different levels of factor *A* (SS_A). An additional source of the variability from one cell mean to the next is due to different cells being exposed to different levels of factor *B* (SS_B). And the third source of variability from one cell mean to the next is due to different cells being exposed to different combinations of the levels of factors A and B, measured by the **interaction sum of squares** (SS_{AB}).

interaction sum of squares (SS_{AB}) SS_{AB} *reflects variability of cell means resulting from individual differences, measurement error, and exposure of different cells to different combinations of levels of factors* A *and* B.

The fact that the overall or total between-group variability ($SS_{Between}$) is produced by factor A effects (SS_A), factor B effects (SS_B), and interaction effects (SS_{AB}) means that we can compute SS_{AB} most easily by subtraction, as shown in Equation 9.5.

Equation 9.5

$$SS_{AB} = SS_{Between} - SS_A - SS_B$$

In words, the interaction sum of squares (SS_{AB}) is computed by subtracting SS_A and SS_B from $SS_{Between}$.

COMPREHENSION CHECK 9.10

Use Equation 9.5 to compute SS_{AB} for the data given in Comprehension Check 9.6 and explain what this value represents. (Answer on p. 299.)

Total Sum of Squares. We have now covered all of the sources of variability in the completely randomized factorial ANOVA. SS_{Within} measures variability due to individual differences and measurement error. $SS_{Between}$ measures variability due to individual differences, measurement error, and three kinds of treatment effects: SS_A, SS_B, and SS_{AB}. SS_A measures variability due to individual differences, measurement error, and factor *A* treatment effect. SS_B measures variability due to individual differences, measurement error, and factor *B* treatment effect. And SS_{AB} measures variability due to individual differences, measurement error, and the interaction treatment effect.

The sum total of these sources of variability is reflected in the total sum of squares (SS_{Total}). Although SS_{Total} is not used directly in the calculations of the completely randomized factorial ANOVA, it provides a useful check on the computational accuracy of the other sums of squares. Check to see that SS_{Total}, computed according to Equation 9.6, is equal to $SS_{Within} + SS_{Between}$ and also that it is equal to $SS_{Within} + SS_A + SS_B + SS_{AB}$.

Equation 9.6

$$SS_{Total} = \Sigma(X - \overline{X}_G)^2$$

where

X = all individual scores
$\overline{X}_G$ = the grand mean

In words, we compute the total sum of squares (SS_{Total}) by: (1) subtracting the grand mean ($\overline{X}_G$) from each score in the data table (X); (2) squaring each of these differences; and (3) summing these squared values.

COMPREHENSION CHECK 9.11

Use Equation 9.6 to compute SS_{Total} for the data presented in Comprehension Check 9.6 and explain what this value represents. (Answer on p. 299.)

Degrees of Freedom in Factorial ANOVA

Recall that the problem with sums of squares is that they reflect not only data variability, but also how many values are varying. We learned in Chapter 8 that the solution to this problem is to divide sums of squares by their corresponding degrees-of-freedom (df) values to obtain mean squares. Degrees of freedom for the two-way completely randomized factorial ANOVA are

$$df_{Between} = (A - 1) + (B - 1) + (A - 1)(B - 1)$$

$$df_A = A - 1$$

$$df_B = B - 1$$

$$df_{AB} = (A - 1)(B - 1)$$

$$df_{Within} = N - (A)(B) = N - k$$

$$df_{Total} = N - 1$$

where

A = the number of levels of factor A (rows)

B = the number of levels of factor B (columns)

N = the total number of cases in the design

k = the number of cells in the design

COMPREHENSION CHECK 9.12

Compute the number of degrees of freedom for the data presented in Comprehension Check 9.6.

(Answer on pp. 299–300.)

factor A mean squares (MS_A) *The measure of row mean variance used as the numerator of the F test for the factor A main effect.*

Mean Squares in Factorial Anova

The **factor A mean squares** (MS_A) is computed according to Equation 9.7.

Equation 9.7

$$MS_A = \frac{SS_A}{df_A}$$

where

$df_A = A - 1$ (where A = number of rows)

In words, the factor A mean squares (MS_A) is computed by dividing SS_A by df_A and measures the variance of the row means. The greater the factor A treatment effect, the greater will be the differences among row means and the larger MS_A will become.

COMPREHENSION CHECK 9.13

Use Equation 9.7 to compute MS_A for the data presented in Comprehension Check 9.6.

(Answer on p. 300.)

The **Factor *B* mean squares** (MS_B) is computed according to Equation 9.8.

Equation 9.8

$$MS_B = \frac{SS_B}{df_B}$$

where

$df_B = B - 1$ (where B = number of columns)

In words, the factor *B* mean squares (MS_B) is computed by dividing SS_B by df_B and measures the variance of the column means. The greater the factor *B* treatment effect, the greater will be the differences among the column means, and the larger MS_B will become.

factor *B* mean squares (MS_B) *The measure of column mean variance used as the numerator of the* F *test for the factor* B *main effect.*

COMPREHENSION CHECK 9.14

Use Equation 9.8 to compute MS_B for the data presented in Comprehension Check 9.6.
(Answer on p. 300.)

interaction mean squares (MS_{AB}) *The measure of cell mean variance used as the numerator of the* F *test for the* A × B *interaction effect.*

The **interaction mean squares** (MS_{AB}) is computed according to Equation 9.9.

Equation 9.9

$$MS_{AB} = \frac{SS_{AB}}{df_{AB}}$$

where

$df_{AB} = (A - 1)(B - 1)$ (where A = number of rows
B = number of columns)

In words, the interaction mean squares (MS_{AB}) is computed by dividing SS_{AB} by df_{AB} and measures the variance of the cell means that is attributable to the different treatment combinations to which the cells are exposed. The stronger the interaction treatment effect, the larger MS_{AB} will become.

COMPREHENSION CHECK 9.15

Use Equation 9.9 to compute MS_{AB} for the data presented in Comprehension Check 9.6.
(Answer on p. 300.)

The mean squares within groups (MS_{Within}) is computed according to Equation 9.10.

Equation 9.10

$$MS_{Within} = \frac{SS_{Within}}{df_{Within}}$$

where

$df_{Within} = N - (A)(B) = N - k$ (where N = number of cases
A = number of rows
B = number of columns
k = number of cells)

In words, the mean squares within groups (MS_{Within}) is computed by dividing SS_{Within} by df_{Within} and measures within-cell variability resulting from individual differences and measurement error. This is a measure of data variability that is not affected by any treatment effect.

COMPREHENSION CHECK 9.16

> Use Equation 9.10 to compute MS_{Within} for the data presented in Comprehension Check 9.6.
> (Answer on p. 300.)

9.4 *F* TESTS IN THE COMPLETELY RANDOMIZED FACTORIAL ANOVA

The factorial ANOVA provides separate *F* tests for each main effect and for the interaction effect. Each of these *F* tests compares a source of between-group variance (MS_A, MS_B, and MS_{AB}) against within-group variance (MS_{Within}) so as to evaluate the strength of the factor *A*, factor *B*, and $A \times B$ interaction treatment effects.

COMPREHENSION CHECK 9.17

> Before you read further, can you guess which MS ratios measure factor *A*, factor *B*, and the $A \times B$ interaction effects?
> (Answer on p. 300.)

The Factor A Main Effect

The *F* test for the main effect of factor *A* is computed according to Equation 9.11.

Equation 9.11

$$F_A = \frac{MS_A}{MS_{Within}}$$

MS_A measures variance due to individual differences, measurement error, and factor *A* (row) treatment effect. MS_{Within} measures variance due just to individual differences and measurement error. Thus the ratio $F_A = MS_A/MS_{Within}$ reflects the strength of the factor *A* treatment effect (and the size of the differences among the row means).

COMPREHENSION CHECK 9.18

> Use Equation 9.11 to compute F_A for the data presented in Comprehension Check 9.6.
> (Answer on p. 300.)

The Factor B Main Effect

The *F* test for the main effect of factor *B* is computed according to Equation 9.12.

$$F_B = \frac{MS_B}{MS_{Within}}$$

Equation 9.12

MS_B measures variance due to individual differences, measurement error, and factor B (column) treatment effect. MS_{Within} measures variance due just to individual differences and measurement error. Thus, the ratio $F_B = MS_B/MS_{Within}$ reflects the strength of the factor B treatment effect (and the size of the differences among the column means).

COMPREHENSION CHECK 9.19

Use Equation 9.12 to compute F_B for the data presented in Comprehension Check 9.6.
(Answer on p. 300.)

The Interaction Effect

The F test for the interaction effect is computed according to Equation 9.13.

$$F_{AB} = \frac{MS_{AB}}{MS_{Within}}$$

Equation 9.13

MS_{AB} measures variance due to individual differences, measurement error, and the various combinations of levels of factors A and B (cells). MS_{Within} measures variance due just to individual differences and measurement error. Thus the ratio $F_{AB} = MS_{AB}/MS_{Within}$ reflects the strength of the interaction treatment effect (and the size of the differences among the cell means).

COMPREHENSION CHECK 9.20

Use Equation 9.13 to compute F_{AB} for the data presented in Comprehension Check 9.6.
(Answer on p. 300.)

The Factorial ANOVA Summary Table

The many calculations of any ANOVA require some kind of organization. This is particularly true for the factorial ANOVA and is provided by the ANOVA summary table. Table 9.2 presents the format of the ANOVA summary table for the completely randomized factorial design. Although the table usually presents the results of one's calculations, Table 9.2 summarizes the equations used in computing the completely randomized factorial ANOVA.

COMPREHENSION CHECK 9.21

Organize the results of your calculations from Comprehension Checks 9.6 to 9.20 into an ANOVA summary table.
(Answer on p. 300.)

TABLE 9.2

The ANOVA summary table for the completely randomized factorial ANOVA provides a standardized format within which the results of the ANOVA are presented. The equations of the completely randomized factorial ANOVA are summarized in this table.

Source	SS	df	MS	F
Between	$(\overline{X}_{a_1b_1} - \overline{X}_G)^2 N_{a_1b_1} +$ $(\overline{X}_{a_1b_2} - \overline{X}_G)^2 N_{a_1b_2} + \cdots +$ $(\overline{X}_k - \overline{X}_G)^2 N_k$	$(A - 1) + (B - 1) +$ $(A - 1)(B - 1)$		
A	$(\overline{X}_{a_1} - \overline{X}_G)^2 N_{a_1} +$ $(\overline{X}_{a_2} - \overline{X}_G)^2 N_{a_2} + \cdots$	$(A - 1)$	$\frac{SS_A}{df_A}$	$\frac{MS_A}{MS_{Within}}$
B	$(\overline{X}_{b_1} - \overline{X}_G)^2 N_{b_1} +$ $(\overline{X}_{b_2} - \overline{X}_G)^2 N_{b_2} + \cdots$	$(B - 1)$	$\frac{SS_B}{df_B}$	$\frac{MS_B}{MS_{Within}}$
$A \times B$	$SS_{Between} - SS_A - SS_B$	$(A - 1)(B - 1)$	$\frac{SS_{AB}}{df_{AB}}$	$\frac{MS_{AB}}{MS_{Within}}$
Within	$\Sigma(X_{a_1b_1} - \overline{X}_{a_1b_1})^2 +$ $\Sigma(X_{a_1b_2} - \overline{X}_{a_1b_2})^2 + \cdots +$ $\Sigma(X_k - \overline{X}_k)^2$	$N - (A)(B) = N - k$	$\frac{SS_{Within}}{df_{Within}}$	
Total	$\Sigma(X - \overline{X}_G)^2$	$N - 1$		

9.5 LOGIC OF THE *F* TESTS IN FACTORIAL ANOVA

In earlier chapters we divided significance testing into four logical steps: (1) formulating the null and alternative hypotheses; (2) computing the test statistic; (3) comparing the test statistic against the sampling distribution of that test statistic; and (4) choosing between the null and alternative hypotheses. The *F* tests of the factorial ANOVA can also be viewed from this conceptual perspective.

two-way interaction *An interaction effect involving two factors. The effect of factor* A *depends on the level of factor* B.
three-way interaction *An interaction effect involving three factors. The interaction between two factors depends on the level of the third factor.*
higher-order interaction *Any interaction effect involving three or more factors.*

The Null and Alternative Hypotheses

Any factorial ANOVA includes at least three significance tests. In the simplest factorial ANOVA, with two factors, there are tests of the main effects of factors *A* and *B* and a test of the interaction effect. Factorial ANOVAs that include more than two factors produce more significance tests. In a three-way ANOVA, for instance, there are main-effects tests for factors *A, B,* and *C.* There are also several **two-way interaction** tests: $A \times B$, $A \times C$, and $B \times C$. And there is a **three-way interaction** test: $A \times B \times C$, where we determine if the interaction between two factors is itself dependent on the level of a third factor. With more factors there are even more of these **higher-order interaction** effects.

COMPREHENSION CHECK 9.22

Name all of the *F* tests available from a four-way factorial ANOVA. Describe in general terms what a four-way interaction would indicate.
(Answer on p. 301.)

To keep this discussion manageable, we are focusing on the two-factor ANOVA. Each *F* test of this factorial ANOVA has its own null and alternative hypothesis. The null hypothesis (H_0) for the main effect of factor *A* attributes differences among row means to sampling error. According to H_0, these means differ by no more than would be likely if the samples represented by the rows were drawn from a population of identically treated cases. The alternative hypothesis (H_1) for the factor *A* main effect suggests that the differences among row means are too large to be a likely result of sampling error. According to H_1, samples drawn from a population of identically treated cases would be unlikely to differ by the amount seen. Therefore, it is more likely that samples (rows) represent populations that differ on the dependent variable being analyzed.

The null and alternative hypotheses for the main effect of factor B follow the same pattern. H_0 explains differences among column means as the likely result of sampling error. H_1 asserts that these column differences are too large to be a result of sampling error alone. It is more likely that the samples (columns) represent populations that differ on the dependent variable.

Finally, the null hypothesis for the interaction effect attributes differences among cell means (treatment combinations) to sampling error. The alternative hypothesis concludes instead that the cell means differ because the samples (cells) represent populations that differ on the dependent variable under examination.

COMPREHENSION CHECK 9.23

Give the null and alternative hypotheses for each of the F tests of the two-way ANOVA begun in Comprehension Check 9.6.

(Answer on p. 301.)

The Test Statistic

The F ratio is the test statistic in the factorial ANOVA. Separate F tests are performed to evaluate differences among row means (F_A), differences among column means (F_B), and differences among cell means (F_{AB}). Each of these F tests provides a measure of the degree to which the means being compared differ by more than one would expect on the basis of sampling error alone.

The Sampling Distribution of F

The probability that any given value of F would occur in a set of samples drawn from a population of identically treated cases is determined from the sampling distribution of F. Critical values that mark the .05 and .01 critical regions of this sampling distribution are given in the table of critical values of F (Table 6 in Appendix B).

Critical values of F_A are found by entering this table with df_A (for $df_{Numerator}$ in the table) and df_{Within} (for $df_{Denominator}$ in the table). Critical values of F_B are found by entering the table with df_B (for $df_{Numerator}$) and df_{Within} (for $df_{Denominator}$). And critical values of F_{AB} are found by entering the table with df_{AB} (for $df_{Numerator}$) and df_{Within} (for $df_{Denominator}$).

Choosing Between the Null and Alternative Hypotheses

If an obtained value of F meets or exceeds the listed critical value at the chosen level of significance, it follows that an F of that size, and the difference among means that it represents, would be unlikely to occur in samples drawn from a population of identically treated cases. We reject H_0, accept H_1, and conclude that the samples probably represent populations that differ on the dependent variable under examination. On the other hand, if the obtained value of F is smaller than the listed critical value, we know that the means that produced this F ratio do not differ by more than would be expected on the basis of sampling error. We conclude that H_0 offers a reasonable explanation for differences among the means.

COMPREHENSION CHECK 9.24

> Evaluate the significance of the F ratios computed in Comprehension Checks 9.18 to 9.20.
> (Answer on p. 301.)

9.6 INTERPRETING FACTORIAL ANOVAS

When none of the F tests of the factorial ANOVA is statistically significant, interpretation is straightforward: None of the differences is large enough to be the likely result of anything more than sampling error. There are no reliable treatment effects of any sort. When one or more F tests is significant, however, several issues of interpretation arise. First, the presence of a significant interaction effect precludes any simple interpretation of main effects. An interaction effect, by definition, means that the effect of one factor, the main effect, is conditional upon the levels of the other factor(s). Second, a significant F tells us that a reliable difference exists *somewhere* among the means evaluated by that F test, but it does not tell us *which* means differ significantly. Additional analyses are necessary to tease out the source(s) of significance. Finally, a significant F in factorial ANOVA points to the presence of a reliable treatment effect but does not provide a directly interpretable measure of the strength of that effect. The F statistic is influenced not only by the strength of the treatment effect, but also by the number of factors, the number of levels within each factor, and the number of cases exposed to each treatment combination.

Significant Main Effects

In the absence of an interaction effect, main effects are easy to interpret. A factor A main effect indicates that there is a significant difference somewhere among the row means; the factor A treatment effect is reliable. A factor B main effect indicates that there is a significant difference somewhere among the column means; the factor B treatment effect is reliable. But when one or more main effects is accompanied by an interaction effect, interpretation becomes more complicated.

COMPREHENSION CHECK 9.25

> There is a significant main effect of financial strength (factor B) in the data presented in Comprehension Check 9.6. What does this main effect tell you? Why must one qualify statements about the effect of financial strength on employee morale?
> (Answer on p. 301.)

Significant Interaction Effects

Given a factor A main effect and an $A \times B$ interaction effect, for instance, can we any longer say simply that factor A affects the dependent variable? No. The interaction effect tells us that factor A may affect the dependent variable at one level of factor B, but not at another. Or factor A may have very different effects on the dependent variable at different levels of factor B. In the presence of an $A \times B$ interaction effect it is too simple to say only that factor A affects the dependent variable. The presence of an interaction effect has a similar influence on our ability to interpret a main effect of factor B. The interaction effect tells us that the effect of factor B is conditional on the level of factor A. In sum, interaction effects prevent us from making simple, unconditional statements about the main effects of the factors in a factorial ANOVA.

Perhaps some examples will make this clearer. Look back at Figure 9.1a. Suppose that there is a main effect of factor A, with restrictive attendance policies (a_1) producing fewer absences than nonrestrictive attendance policies (a_2). Can we say simply that restricting the number of allowed absences reduces absenteeism? No; it's not that simple. The interaction effect reveals that restricting absences reduces the absenteeism of late registrants (b_1), but timely registrants (b_2) are largely unaffected. Suppose that there is a main effect of factor B in Figure 9.1a, with late registrants (b_1) showing more absences as a group than timely registrants (b_2). Can we say that "late registrants show significantly more absences than timely registrants"? No; the interaction effect shows that things are more complicated than this. Late registrants are absent more often in classes that do not restrict absences (a_2), but not in classes with restrictive attendance policies (a_1).

As another example, consider the situation depicted in Figure 9.1b. Suppose that there is a main effect of factor A—physiological arousal level—with significantly higher performance in the medium-arousal (a_2) and high-arousal (a_3) conditions than in the low-arousal (a_1) condition. Is it accurate to say that as arousal increases from low to medium to high levels, problem-solving performance first improves and then levels off? No. At the highest level of arousal, performance actually declines for difficult tasks (b_2), but continues to improve for simple tasks (b_1).

When there are both significant interaction effects and main effects, interaction effects should be given greater consideration in interpreting the results of the factorial ANOVA. Interaction effects require that main effects be described in conditional terms.

Comprehension Check 9.26

Interpret the significant interaction between management style (factor A) and financial strength (factor B) in the data presented in Comprehension Check 9.6.

(Answer on p. 301.)

Post-Hoc Data Snooping

Part of interpreting the results of the factorial ANOVA involves finding the source(s) of significant F tests. A significant F test tells us that, at the very least, the largest between-group difference contributing to that F ratio is statistically significant. Determining which other differences are significant requires the use of post-hoc comparisons. The Tukey HSD ("honestly significant difference") procedure, introduced in Chapter 8, is often used for post-hoc comparisons of cell means in the factorial ANOVA. Another post-hoc comparison procedure, the Scheffé test, is more useful in comparing row or column means to identify the source(s) of significant main effects.

Tukey's HSD. Equation 8.15 (Chapter 8) is used in computing Tukey's HSD following a significant factorial ANOVA. In this application, the value of k in Equation 8.15 is set equal to the number of cells in the factorial design. The difference between two cell means is significant at the chosen level of significance if that absolute difference meets or exceeds HSD.

COMPREHENSION CHECK 9.27

Use Equation 8.15 to compute Tukey's HSD for the data presented in Comprehension Check 9.6. Identify cell means that differ at the .01 level of significance.

(Answer on pp. 301–302.)

Scheffé test *A post-hoc comparison procedure that allows means to be combined prior to comparison.*

Scheffé Test. The **Scheffé test** is another post-hoc comparison procedure. Since it is less powerful than the Tukey HSD test in pairwise comparisons, the Tukey procedure is recommended if the aim is to compare any two cell means. Even so, the Scheffé test has one advantage over the Tukey procedure. The Scheffé test can be used in comparing combinations of means. This makes the Scheffé test very useful in exploring the source(s) of significant main effects in factorial ANOVA.

The presence of a significant factor A main effect tells us that, at the very least, the two levels of factor A (rows) that differ the most are significantly different. If there are only two levels of factor A, and thus only two row means, there is no need for further exploration to find the source of the significant F_A test. However, if there are three or more levels of factor A, we may wish to determine if any of the other differences between row means are significant. This is where the Scheffé test comes in. Comparing any two row means is really a matter of comparing: (1) the combination of cell means that form one row; and (2) the combination of cell means that form the other row. The Scheffé test is appropriate to this application because it provides a way of combining the cell means prior to the comparison.

In a similar manner, the source of a significant factor B main effect is obvious if there are only two levels of this factor. When there are three or more levels of factor B, though, the Scheffé test can be used to combine cell means associated with the columns being compared.

COMPREHENSION CHECK 9.28

Why is there no real point in a post-hoc exploration of the significant factor B main effect found in the data presented in Comprehension Check 9.6?

(Answer on p. 302.)

We begin the Scheffé test by computing the value C, the "comparison," according to Equation 9.14.

Equation 9.14

$$C = w_1\overline{X}_1 + w_2\overline{X}_2 + \cdots + w_k\overline{X}_k$$

where

w_1 to w_k = the weights applied to each of k means
$\overline{X}_1$ to $\overline{X}_k$ = k means
k = the number of means in the analysis

In this equation, the weights w_1 through w_k may take on any values as long as the sum of the weights is 0. Thus, some of the means must receive positive weights and some must receive negative weights. Means that are to be combined are all given weights of the same sign (positive or negative) and size. Means that are not to be included in a given comparison are given weights of 0.

An example will be helpful in clarifying the computation of C. Return to Figure 9.1b, where there are three levels of factor A. Suppose that we wish to compare $\overline{X}_{a_1}$ to $\overline{X}_{a_2}$. Using Equation 9.14, we can compute C in any of the following ways:

$$C = .5(\overline{X}_{a_1b_1})+.5(\overline{X}_{a_1b_2})-.5(\overline{X}_{a_2b_1})-.5(\overline{X}_{a_2b_2})+0(\overline{X}_{a_3b_1})+0(\overline{X}_{a_3b_2})$$

or

$$C = -1(\overline{X}_{a_1b_1})-1(\overline{X}_{a_1b_2})+1(\overline{X}_{a_2b_1})+1(\overline{X}_{a_2b_2})+0(\overline{X}_{a_3b_1})+0(\overline{X}_{a_3b_2})$$

or

$$C = 3(\overline{X}_{a_1b_1})+3(\overline{X}_{a_1b_2})-3(\overline{X}_{a_2b_1})-3(\overline{X}_{a_2b_2})+0(\overline{X}_{a_3b_1})+0(\overline{X}_{a_3b_2})$$

Notice that in all of these expressions, means that are to be combined receive weights of the same sign and magnitude. Also notice that the weights of means being compared have opposite signs. Means that are not being compared are given weights of 0. Finally, notice that the weights sum to zero. The value C simply measures the difference between the means being compared.

Comprehension Check 9.29

Use Equation 9.14 to compute the value of C needed to compare $\overline{X}_{b_1}$ and $\overline{X}_{b_2}$ for the data presented in Comprehension Check 9.6.
(Answer on p. 302.)

Once C is computed, it is evaluated for statistical significance using the t statistic computed according to Equation 9.15.

Equation 9.15

$$t = \frac{C}{\sqrt{\text{MS}_{\text{Within}}\left(\frac{w_1^2}{N_1}+\frac{w_2^2}{N_2}+\cdots+\frac{w_k^2}{N_k}\right)}}$$

where

C	= the comparison value (Equation 9.14)
$\text{MS}_{\text{Within}}$	= $\text{MS}_{\text{Within}}$ from the significant ANOVA
w_1 to w_k	= the weights applied to the k means in computing C
k	= the number of means in the analysis
N_1 to N_k	= the sample sizes in cells 1 to k

In words, we compute t by: (1) squaring each weight (w) used in computing C and dividing each squared weight by the number of cases corresponding to that weight's cell mean (N_1 to N_k); (2) summing the values computed in step 1; (3) multiplying the result of step 2 by $\text{MS}_{\text{Within}}$ from the ANOVA; (4) finding the square root of the result of step 3; (5) dividing the value of C (Equation 9.14) by the result of step 4.

COMPREHENSION CHECK 9.30

Use Equation 9.15 to compute the test statistic t in the Scheffé post-hoc comparison of $\overline{X}_{b_1}$ and $\overline{X}_{b_2}$ from Comprehension Check 9.6.
(Answer on p. 302.)

The value of t obtained using Equation 9.15 is statistically significant if it meets or exceeds the critical value of t computed according to Equation 9.16.

Equation 9.16

$$t_{\text{Critical}} = \sqrt{(k - 1)F_{(\alpha,\, \text{df}_{\text{Between}},\, \text{df}_{\text{Within}})}}$$

where

k = the number of means in the analysis
$F_{(\alpha,\, \text{df}_{\text{Between}},\, \text{df}_{\text{Within}})}$ = the critical value of F for the chosen significance level (α), and $\text{df}_{\text{Between}}$ and $\text{df}_{\text{Within}}$ of the significant ANOVA

In words, the critical value of t (t_{Critical}) in the Scheffé test is computed by: (1) finding in Table 6 of Appendix B the critical value of F at the desired level of significance for $\text{df}_{\text{Between}}$ (for $\text{df}_{\text{Numerator}}$) and $\text{df}_{\text{Within}}$ (for $\text{df}_{\text{Denominator}}$); (2) multiplying this critical value of F by one less than the number of cells in the factorial design ($k - 1$); and (3) finding the square root of the result of step 2.

COMPREHENSION CHECK 9.31

Use Equation 9.16 to evaluate the statistical significance (.05 level) of the t statistic computed in Comprehension Check 9.30.
(Answer on p. 302.)

Like the Tukey HSD procedure, the Scheffé test protects against Type I errors in a series of comparisons by setting the Type I error rate at the chosen level of significance for the entire set of all possible comparisons. Although this provides good protection from Type I errors, it is achieved by raising the Type II error rate. As a result, it is not unusual to find no significant Scheffé comparisons even when the F test is significant.

Strength of Association: Omega-Square

Omega-square (ω^2) is used to measure the strength of association between independent and dependent variables in a variety of significant difference tests. This statistic was introduced in Chapter 7, where it was used in conjunction with the t test. In Chapter 8, ω^2 was used with the one-way ANOVA to measure strength of association. ω^2 is also useful in the context of factorial ANOVA to provide a standardized measure of the strength of main and interaction treatment effects.

Equations 9.17 to 9.19 describe the computation of ω^2 for factor A and factor B main effects and the $A \times B$ interaction effect:

Equation 9.17

$$\omega_A^2 = \frac{\text{SS}_A - (\text{df}_A)\text{MS}_{\text{Within}}}{\text{SS}_{\text{Total}} + \text{MS}_{\text{Within}}}$$

$$\omega_B^2 = \frac{SS_B - (df_B)MS_{Within}}{SS_{Total} + MS_{Within}}$$

Equation 9.18

$$\omega_{AB}^2 = \frac{SS_{AB} - (df_{AB})MS_{Within}}{SS_{Total} + MS_{Within}}$$

Equation 9.19

In words, we compute ω^2 by: (1) multiplying MS_{Within} by the degrees of freedom associated with the numerator of the F test for the treatment effect being evaluated (that is, df_A for the factor A main effect, df_B for the factor B main effect, or df_{AB} for the interaction effect); (2) subtracting the result of step 1 from the sum of squares associated with the numerator of the F test for the treatment effect being evaluated (that is, SS_A for the factor A main effect, SS_B for the factor B main effect, or SS_{AB} for the interaction effect); (3) summing $SS_{Total} + MS_{Within}$; and (4) dividing the result of step 2 by the result of step 3.

COMPREHENSION CHECK 9.32

Use Equations 9.17 to 9.19 to compute ω_A^2, ω_B^2, and ω_{AB}^2 for the data presented in Comprehension Check 9.6.

(Answer on p. 302.)

EXAMPLE 9.1

Completely Randomized Factorial ANOVA

We met Dr. Jerry Atric in the last chapter (Example 8.1). Chief Psychologist and Custodian at the Home for Retired Statisticians, Dr. Atric is responsible for maintaining decorum at the home. His problem is that several of the retired statisticians have starting shouting obscenities at passing neighbors. Dr. Atric learned from a pilot study (Example 8.1) that fining the offending residents of the home for each offense with lost computer time is generally effective in reducing the frequency of these outbursts. However, the fines don't seem to work equally well on everyone. Dr. Atric has noticed that long-time statistics teachers seem particularly recalcitrant, even in the face of fines. In order to evaluate this impression more systematically, Dr. Atric has decided to conduct another experiment in which both level of fine and teaching tenure (years spent teaching statistics) are examined in a factorial study.

The ANOVA

In this 3 × 2 completely randomized factorial design, factor A is fines, represented by three levels: no fine, 10 minutes, and 20 minutes of lost computer time. Factor B is teaching tenure, represented by two levels: short-term (under 15 years) and long-term (15 or more years). Six residents of the home were randomly assigned to each of the 6 treatment combinations of this design and Dr. Atric recorded the number of obscene outbursts from each subject during the week following initiation of the fines. These data, along with cell means, row means, column means, and the grand mean, are presented in the data table that follows. Cell means are next plotted in the line graph.

Factor *B*: Teaching Tenure

Factor *A*: Fine	b_1 *Short-Term*		b_2 *Long-Term*		
a_1 *No Fine*	13, 14, 12, 17, 15, 13	$\overline{X}_{a_1b_1} = 14.0$	14, 15, 13, 18, 16, 14	$\overline{X}_{a_1b_2} = 15.0$	$\overline{X}_{a_1} = 14.5$
a_2 *10 min*	7, 8, 6, 11, 9, 7	$\overline{X}_{a_2b_1} = 8.0$	17, 18, 16, 21, 19, 17	$\overline{X}_{a_2b_2} = 18.0$	$\overline{X}_{a_2} = 13.0$
a_3 *20 min*	2, 3, 1, 6, 4, 2	$\overline{X}_{a_3b_1} = 3.0$	20, 21, 19, 24, 22, 20	$\overline{X}_{a_3b_2} = 21.0$	$\overline{X}_{a_3} = 12.0$
		$\overline{X}_{b_1} = 8.33$		$\overline{X}_{b_2} = 18.0$	$\overline{X}_G = 13.17$

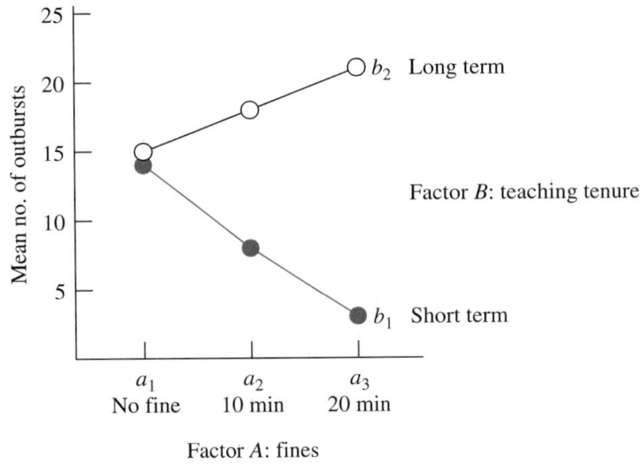

The line graph suggests a relatively weak factor *A* main effect, a stronger factor *B* main effect, and an interaction effect. The statistical significance of these effects is evaluated below using the completely randomized factorial ANOVA.

Null and Alternative Hypotheses

H_0: Differences among row means (factor *A*—fines), column means (factor *B*—teaching tenure), and cell means ($A \times B$ interaction), are small enough to be a likely consequence of sampling error. Samples drawn from a population of identically treated cases commonly differ by the amounts seen here.

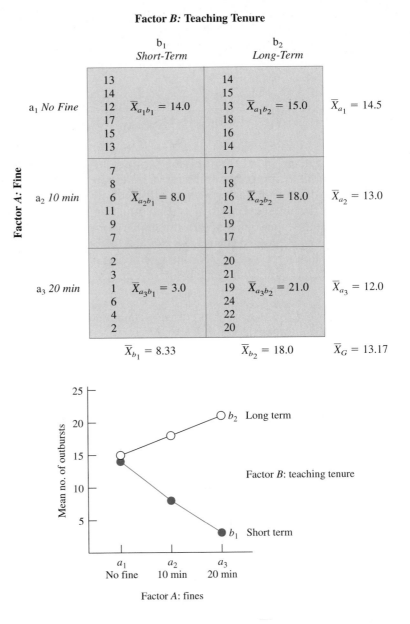

H_1: Differences among row, column, and cell means are too large to be a likely result of sampling error alone. Samples drawn from a population of identically treated cases very seldom differ by the amounts seen here. Therefore, these samples probably represent populations that differ on the dependent variable.

Test Statistic

The F tests of the completely randomized factorial ANOVA are computed below according to Equations 9.1 to 9.9.

According to Equation 9.1,

$$\begin{aligned} SS_{Within} &= \Sigma(X_{a_1b_1}) - \overline{X}_{a_1b_1})^2 + \Sigma(X_{a_1b_2} - \overline{X}_{a_1b_2})^2 + \cdots + \\ &\quad \Sigma(X_{a_3b_2} - \overline{X}_{a_3b_2})^2 \\ &= (13 - 14.0)^2 + (14 - 14.0)^2 + \cdots + (13 - 14.0)^2 + \\ &\quad (14 - 15.0)^2 + (15 - 15.0)^2 + \cdots + (14 - 15.0)^2 + \\ &\quad \cdots + (20 - 21.0)^2 + (21 - 20.0)^2 + \cdots + (20 - 21.0)^2 \\ &= 96.00 \end{aligned}$$

According to Equation 9.2,

$$\begin{aligned} SS_{Between} &= (\overline{X}_{a_1b_1} - \overline{X}_G)^2 N_{a_1b_1} + (\overline{X}_{a_1b_2} - \overline{X}_G)^2 N_{a_1b_2} + \cdots + \\ &\quad (\overline{X}_{a_3b_2} - \overline{X}_G)^2 N_{a_3b_2} \\ &= (14.0 - 13.17)^2 6 + (15.0 - 13.17)^2 6 + \cdots + (21.0 - 13.17)^2 6 \\ &= 1313.00 \end{aligned}$$

According to Equation 9.3,

$$\begin{aligned} SS_A &= (\overline{X}_{a_1} - \overline{X}_G)^2 N_{a_1} + (\overline{X}_{a_2} - \overline{X}_G)^2 N_{a_2} + (\overline{X}_{a_3} - \overline{X}_G)^2 N_{a_3} \\ &= (14.5 - 13.17)^2 12 + (13.0 - 13.17)^2 12 + (12.0 - 13.17)^2 12 \\ &= 38.00 \end{aligned}$$

According to Equation 9.4,

$$\begin{aligned} SS_B &= (\overline{X}_{b_1} - \overline{X}_G)^2 N_{b_1} + (\overline{X}_{b_2} - \overline{X}_G)^2 N_{b_2} \\ &= (8.33 - 13.17)^2 18 + (18.00 - 13.17)^2 18 \\ &= 841.00 \end{aligned}$$

According to Equation 9.5,

$$\begin{aligned} SS_{AB} &= SS_{Between} - SS_A - SS_B \\ &= 1313.00 - 38.00 - 841.00 \\ &= 434.00 \end{aligned}$$

According to Equation 9.6,

$$\begin{aligned} SS_{Total} &= \Sigma(X - \overline{X}_G)^2 \\ &= (13 - 13.17)^2 + (14 - 13.17)^2 + \cdots + (20 - 13.17)^2 \\ &= 1409.00 \end{aligned}$$

(Notice that $SS_{Total} = SS_{Within} + SS_A + SS_B + SS_{AB}$

$= SS_{Within} + SS_{Between}$)

According to Equation 9.7,

$$\begin{aligned} MS_A &= \frac{SS_A}{df_A} \\ &= \frac{38.00}{3 - 1} \\ &= 19.00 \end{aligned}$$

According to Equation 9.8,

$$\begin{aligned} MS_B &= \frac{SS_B}{df_B} \\ &= \frac{841.00}{2 - 1} \\ &= 841 \end{aligned}$$

According to Equation 9.9,

$$\begin{aligned} MS_{AB} &= \frac{SS_{AB}}{df_{AB}} \\ &= \frac{434.00}{(3 - 1)(2 - 1)} \\ &= 217.00 \end{aligned}$$

According to Equation 9.10,

$$\begin{aligned} MS_{Within} &= \frac{SS_{Within}}{df_{Within}} \\ &= \frac{96.00}{36 - (3)(2)} \\ &= 3.20 \end{aligned}$$

According to Equation 9.11,

$$F_A = \frac{MS_A}{MS_{Within}}$$

$$= \frac{19.00}{3.20}$$

$$= 5.94$$

According to Equation 9.12,

$$F_B = \frac{MS_B}{MS_{Within}}$$

$$= \frac{841.00}{3.20}$$

$$= 262.81$$

According to Equation 9.13,

$$F_{AB} = \frac{MS_{AB}}{MS_{Within}}$$

$$= \frac{217.00}{3.20}$$

$$= 67.81$$

These results are summarized in the ANOVA summary table that follows.

Source	**SS**	**df**	**MS**	***F***
Between	1,313.00	5		
A	38.00	2	19.00	5.94
B	841.00	1	841.00	262.81
$A \times B$	434.00	2	217.00	67.81
Within	96.00	30	3.20	
Total	1,409.00	35		

The Sampling Distribution of F

Finally, we compare each of the obtained *F* ratios to the sampling distribution of *F*. Critical values of *F* are listed in Table 7 in Appendix B. The critical value of *F* for each *F* test is found by entering this table using $df_{Within} = 30$ (for $df_{Denominator}$ in the table) and $df_A = 2$, $df_B = 1$, and $df_{AB} = 2$ (for $df_{Numerator}$) for the F_A, F_B, and F_{AB} tests, respectively. Critical values of *F* that mark the .01 critical region are 5.39 (for F_A), 7.56 (for F_B), and 5.39 (for F_{AB}).

Choosing Between H_0 *and* H_1

All of the obtained *F* ratios meet or exceed these critical values of *F*. We can conclude that *F* ratios as large as those observed, and the differences among sample means that they reflect, are unlikely to result from sampling error alone. We reject all null hypotheses and conclude that the samples in this analysis probably differ because they represent populations that differ.

In interpreting these results, it is helpful to look again at the line graph. The significant factor A (fines) main effect indicates that, ignoring teaching tenure (factor B), obscene outbursts decline in frequency as fines are increased. The significant factor B (teaching tenure) main effect indicates that, ignoring fine levels (factor A), long-term statistics teachers exhibit more frequent outbursts than do short-term teachers. Finally, and most interestingly, the significant $A \times B$ interaction effect indicates that the effect of fines depends on teaching tenure. It is apparent from the line graph that fines reduce the frequency of obscene outbursts among short-term statistics teachers. For long-term teachers, though, obscene outbursts increase as fines increase. It appears that fining long-term statistics teachers just makes them mad! Fines may be useful with some of the retirees (the short-term teachers), but will be counterproductive with others (the long-term teachers).

Post-Hoc Comparisons

The significant F ratios obtained in this completely randomized factorial ANOVA indicate the presence of significant differences among the sample means. Post-hoc comparisons are used here to identify some of the sources of these significant F ratios.

The Tukey HSD Test: The Tukey HSD test is used to perform pairwise comparisons of cell means in factorial designs. *Which* means are to be compared in any given analysis should be guided both by one's interests and by the pattern of results suggested by the line graph. In this analysis, we might be interested in knowing if, among short-term teachers, increasing fines from 10 to 20 minutes produces a significant decline in the frequency of obscene outbursts. After all, there's no reason to use stronger fines than necessary.

The observed difference between these means is

$$\overline{X}_{a_2b_1} - \overline{X}_{a_3b_1} = 8.0 - 3.0 = 5.0$$

Next, we compute Tukey's HSD according to Equation 8.15:

$$\begin{aligned} \text{HSD} &= q_{(\alpha,\ \text{df}_{\text{Within}},\ k)} \sqrt{\frac{\text{MS}_{\text{Within}}}{n}} \\ &= q_{(.01,\ 30,\ 6)} \sqrt{\frac{3.20}{6}} \\ &= 5.24 \sqrt{\frac{3.20}{6}} \\ &= 3.83 \end{aligned}$$

Since the observed difference (5.0) exceeds Tukey's HSD (3.83), we can conclude that 20-minute fines are significantly more effective than 10-minute fines in reducing the frequency of obscene outbursts in this group of retirees.

The Scheffé Test: The Scheffé post-hoc comparison procedure is used to compare combinations of means. This makes the Scheffé test useful in exploring main effects in factorial ANOVA. In the present example, there is little point in comparing the two column means. The significant F_B ratio tells us everything there is to know about the factor B main effect: The two column means differ significantly. However, the factor A main effect is open to exploration. Which of the row means differ significantly? The significant F_A ratio tells us that the greatest row mean difference must be significant, but what about the other differences? This question can be answered using the Scheffé test. To illustrate this procedure, we will compare behavior under the no-fine (a_1) and 10-minute-fine (a_2) conditions.

First, the comparison (C) is computed according to Equation 9.14. Cell means to be combined are given weights (w) of equal size and sign. Cell means to be contrasted are given weights of opposite signs. Cell means not included in the comparison are given weights of 0. Finally, weights must sum to 0.

$$C = w_1(\overline{X}_1) + w_2(\overline{X}_2) + \cdots + w_k(\overline{X}_k)$$

$$= .5(\overline{X}_{a_1b_1}) + .5(\overline{X}_{a_1b_2}) - .5(\overline{X}_{a_2b_1}) - .5(\overline{X}_{a_2b_2}) + 0(\overline{X}_{a_3b_1}) + 0(\overline{X}_{a_3b_2})$$

$$= .5(14.0) + .5(15.0) - .5(8.0) - .5(18.0) + 0(3.0) + 0(21.0)$$

$$= 1.5$$

Next, Equation 9.15 is used to compute the test statistic t.

$$t = \frac{C}{\sqrt{\text{MS}_{\text{Within}}[(w_1^2/n_1) + (w_2^2/n_2) + (w_3^2/n_3) + (w_4^2/n_4) + (w_5^2/n_5) + (w_6^2/n_6)]}}$$

$$= \frac{1.5}{\sqrt{3.20[(.5^2/6) + (.5^2/6) + (-.5^2/6) + (-.5^2/6) + (0^2/6) + (0^2/6)]}}$$

$$= 2.05$$

Equation 9.16 is used to compute t_{Critical}.

$$t_{\text{Critical}} = \sqrt{(k-1)F_{(\alpha,\ \text{df}_{\text{Between}},\ \text{df}_{\text{Within}})}}$$

$$= \sqrt{(6-1)F_{(.01,\ 5,\ 30)}}$$

$$= \sqrt{(6-1)3.70}$$

$$= 4.30$$

The obtained value of $t = 2.05$ falls short of $t_{\text{Critical}} = 4.30$. We conclude that the difference between the row means representing the no-fine and 10-minute-fine conditions is nonsignificant. The even smaller difference between row means for 10- and 20-minute fines ($\overline{X}_{a_2} - \overline{X}_{a_3} = 1.0$) must therefore also be nonsignificant. Only the largest row mean difference ($\overline{X}_{a_1} - \overline{X}_{a_3} = 2.5$) can be assumed to be statistically significant.

Strength of Association: Omega-Square

It is helpful in evaluating the practical significance of a statistically significant treatment effect to have a measure of the strength of association between the independent and dependent variables. Omega-square (ω^2) is computed below for the A and B main effects and the $A \times B$ interaction effect, using Equations 9.17 to 9.19:

According to Equation 9.17,

$$\omega_A^2 = \frac{SS_A - (df_A)MS_{Within}}{SS_{Total} + MS_{Within}}$$

$$= \frac{38.0 - (2)3.2}{1409.0 + 3.2}$$

$$= .02$$

According to Equation 9.18,

$$\omega_B^2 = \frac{SS_B - (df_B)MS_{Within}}{SS_{Total} + MS_{Within}}$$

$$= \frac{841.0 - (1)3.2}{1409.0 + 3.2}$$

$$= .59$$

According to Equation 9.19,

$$\omega_{AB}^2 = \frac{SS_{AB} - (df_{AB})MS_{Within}}{SS_{Total} + MS_{Within}}$$

$$= \frac{434.0 - (2)3.2}{1409.0 + 3.2}$$

$$= .30$$

In interpreting these ω^2 values, remember that ω^2 ranges from 0, when there is no association between the independent and dependent variables, to 1, when the association is perfect. We see that the factor B main effect is the strongest of the three ($\omega_B^2 = .59$). The factor A main effect, though statistically significant, is very weak and unimportant ($\omega_A^2 = .02$). Finally, the interaction effect is of moderate strength ($\omega_{AB}^2 = .30$).

SUMMARY

Factorial ANOVA is a significant difference testing procedure that is used to examine the effects of two or more independent variables, called factors, within a single analysis. The factorial ANOVA evaluates the statistical significance of differences between row means (due to the main effect of factor A), column means (due to the main effect of factor B), and cell means (due to the interaction of factors A and B). It is this ability to evaluate interaction effects that is the factorial ANOVA's greatest asset.

The factorial ANOVA provides separate F tests for each main effect and the interaction effect. Each F test compares the variability of group means (row means, column means, or cell means) against the variability of scores seen within groups. Variability of scores within groups reflects individual differences and measurement error. Variability of means reflects individual differences, measurement error, *and treatment effects.* Thus, each F test measures its corresponding treatment effect by showing how much more variability has occurred in group means than can be attributed to individual differences and measurement error alone.

By comparing the F tests obtained in factorial ANOVA against the sampling distribution of F, we can determine the probability that each F, and the differences among means it represents, would have occurred in samples drawn from a population of identically treated cases.

In interpreting the results of a factorial ANOVA, we look first for a significant interaction effect. If the interaction effect is significant, no simple statements can be made about main effects, because the effect of one factor is conditional on the other factor. Interpretation of the factorial ANOVA also involves using post-hoc comparisons to identify the source(s) of the significant F ratio(s). Both the Tukey HSD and Scheffé tests are used for this purpose. Finally, a significant F test in factorial ANOVA tells us only that there is a reliable effect. This may or may not be large enough to be important from a practical perspective. The statistic omega-square (ω^2) provides a standardized measure of effect strength that is useful in evaluating practical significance.

Review Exercises

9.1. Identify the independent and dependent variables in each of the following research designs.

(a) A motivation psychologist wants to evaluate the effects of failure on the achievement motivation of male and female college students.

(b) A sociologist wants to know if gang loyalty is related to the age and income levels of gang members.

(c) A teacher wants to see if students taught using two different teaching methods show differences in achievement at each of four tests throughout the semester.

9.2. Identify main and interaction effects in each of the following graphs.

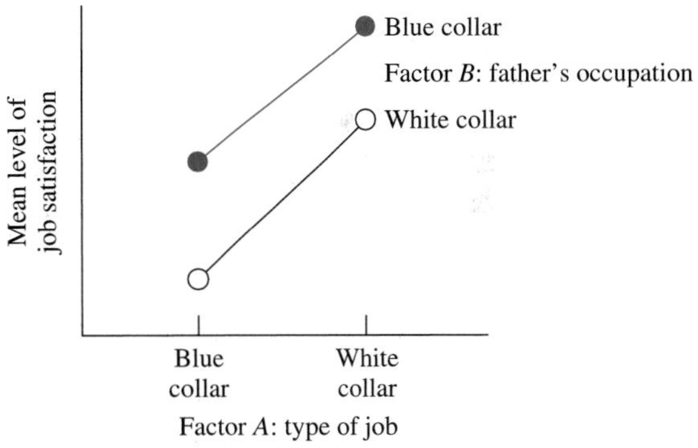

(b)

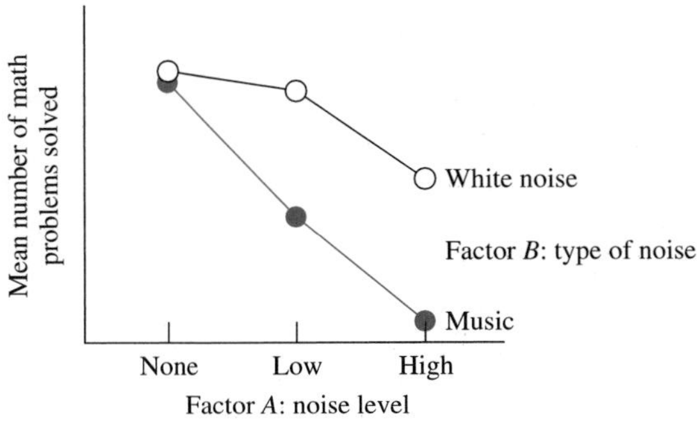

(a)

9.3. Shown on p. 297 are statistics test scores that have been collected from traditional and nontraditional students who received either televised or classroom instruction. Draw a line graph based on these data, and summarize the results of this research.

Factor A: Type of Instruction	Factor B: Type of Student — Traditional	Factor B: Type of Student — Nontraditional
Televised	65	78
	70	72
	75	80
	78	85
Classroom	90	88
	92	86
	94	87
	94	90

9.4. Use a completely randomized factorial ANOVA to evaluate main and interaction effects for the data provided in Review Exercise 9.3. Present your results in the form of an ANOVA summary table.

9.5. Use the Scheffé post-hoc comparison procedure to evaluate differences between the row means. Aside from its instructional value, explain why this post-hoc comparison is unnecessary.

9.6. Use the Tukey HSD post-hoc comparison procedure to explore differences among cell means.

9.7. Compute and interpret ω^2 values for main and interaction effects.

Answers to Comprehension Checks

9.1. **(a)** Factor *A:* biofeedback (no treatment vs. treatment)
Factor *B:* headache type (stress-related vs. hormone-related)
Dependent variable: pain

(b) Factor *A:* gender of instructor (male vs. female)
Factor *B:* gender of student (male vs. female)
Dependent variable: evaluation ratings

(c) Factor *A:* type of therapy (behavior vs. psychodynamic)
Factor *B:* intelligence (levels not specified)
Dependent variable: depression

9.2. This is a "three-way" or "2 × 3 × 4" factorial ANOVA.

9.3. In the completely randomized factorial design, four separate groups would be used, each assigned to one of the cells of the 2 × 2 design. A randomized-block factorial design involving repeated measures would be impossible, because it is impossible for any given subject to serve first as a male and then as a female. Still, a matched-samples procedure could be used, where subjects in the four treatment conditions are matched on one or more variables other than gender. In a split-plot factorial design, if the within-subjects factor is teaching method, one could use either a repeated-measures or a matched-samples procedure. If the within-subjects factor is gender, only a matched-samples procedure is possible.

9.4. A factor *A* main effect is indicated by the difference in the average elevations of points over a_1 vs. a_2 and a_3. A factor *B* main effect is shown by the difference in average elevations of points forming line b_1 and line b_2. The nonparallel lines indicate an interaction effect. Because these lines do not cross, this is an ordinal interaction.

There are many possible configurations that would produce the specified combinations of main and interaction effects. Some possibilities follow.

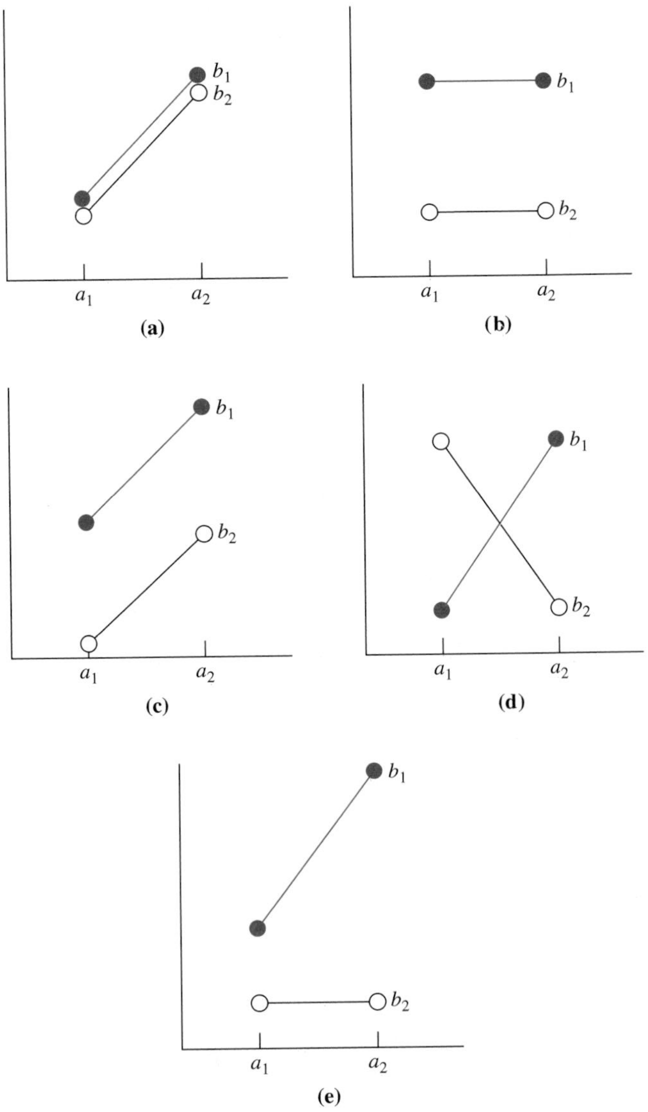

9.5. Treatment effects cannot affect within-group variability, because all cases within any given group have been treated the same. Treatment effects do affect between-group variability, because different groups receive different treatments.

9.6. Cell, row, and column means and the grand mean are given below.

Factor *B*: Financial Strength

Factor *A*: Management Style	b_1 *Weak*	b_2 *Strong*	
a_1 *Directive*	5, 4, 6 $\quad \overline{X}_{a_1b_1} = 5.0$	4, 3, 5 $\quad \overline{X}_{a_1b_2} = 4.0$	$\overline{X}_{a_1} = 4.5$
a_2 *Participative*	2, 1, 3 $\quad \overline{X}_{a_2b_1} = 2.0$	9, 8, 10 $\quad \overline{X}_{a_2b_2} = 9.0$	$\overline{X}_{a_2} = 5.5$
	$\overline{X}_{b_1} = 3.5$	$\overline{X}_{b_2} = 6.5$	$\overline{X}_G = 5.0$

SS_{Within} is computed according to Equation 9.1.

$$SS_{\text{Within}} = \Sigma(X_{a_1b_1} - \overline{X}_{a_1b_1})^2 + \Sigma(X_{a_1b_2} - \overline{X}_{a_1b_2})^2$$

$$+ \Sigma(X_{a_2b_1} - \overline{X}_{a_2b_1})^2 \Sigma(X_{a_2b_2} - \overline{X}_{a_2b_2})^2$$

$$= (5 - 5.0)^2 + (4 - 5.0)^2 + (6 - 5.0)^2 +$$

$$(2 - 2.0)^2 + (1 - 2.0)^2 + (3 - 2.0)^2 +$$

$$(4 - 4.0)^2 + (3 - 4.0)^2 + (5 - 4.0)^2 +$$

$$(9 - 9.0)^2 + (8 - 9.0)^2 + (10 - 9.0)^2$$

$$= 8.00$$

This value represents the amount of data variability that is produced by individual differences and measurement error.

9.7. Equation 9.2 is used to compute SS_{Between}.

$$SS_{\text{Between}} = (\overline{X}_{a_1b_1} - \overline{X}_G)^2 N_{a_1b_1} + (\overline{X}_{a_1b_2} - \overline{X}_G)^2 N_{a_1b_2} +$$

$$(\overline{X}_{a_2b_1} - \overline{X}_G)^2 N_{a_2b_1} + (\overline{X}_{a_2b_2} - \overline{X}_G)^2 N_{a_2b_2}$$

$$= (5.0 - 5.0)^2 3 + (2.0 - 5.0)^2 3 + (4.0 - 5.0)^2 3 +$$

$$(9.0 - 5.0)^2 3$$

$$= 78.00$$

This value represents the amount of data variability that is produced by individual differences, measurement error, *and* the combined effects of factor *A*, factor *B*, and the various combinations of levels of factors *A* and *B*—the $A \times B$ interaction effect.

9.8. Equation 9.3 is used to compute SS_A.

$$SS_A = (\overline{X}_{a_1} - \overline{X}_G)^2 N_{a_1} + (\overline{X}_{a_2} - \overline{X}_G)^2 N_{a_2}$$

$$= (4.5 - 5.0)^2 6 + (5.5 - 5.0)^2 6$$

$$= 3.00$$

This value represents the amount of data variability that is produced by individual differences, measurement error, and the effect of factor *A*.

9.9. Equation 9.4 is used to compute SS_B.

$$SS_B = (\overline{X}_{b_1} - \overline{X}_G)^2 N_{b_1} + (\overline{X}_{b_2} - \overline{X}_G)^2 N_{b_2}$$

$$= (3.5 - 5.0)^2 6 + (6.5 - 5.0)^2 6$$

$$= 27.00$$

This value represents the amount of data variability that is produced by individual differences, measurement error, and the effect of factor *B*.

9.10. Equation 9.5 is used to compute SS_{AB}.

$$SS_{AB} = SS_{\text{Between}} - SS_A - SS_B$$

$$= 78.00 - 3.00 - 27.00$$

$$= 48.00$$

This value represents the amount of data variability that is produced by individual differences, measurement error, and the $A \times B$ interaction treatment effect.

9.11. Equation 9.6 is used to compute SS_{Total}.

$$SS_{\text{Total}} = \Sigma(X - \overline{X}_G)^2$$

$$= (5 - 5.0)^2 + (4 - 5.0)^2 + \cdots + (10 - 5.0)^2$$

$$= 86.00$$

This value represents the total amount of variability in the data: $SS_{\text{Total}} = SS_{\text{Between}} + SS_{\text{Within}} = SS_A + SS_B + SS_{AB} + SS_{\text{Within}}$.

9.12. Degrees of freedom for the completely randomized factorial ANOVA are

$$df_{\text{Between}} = (A - 1) + (B - 1) + (A - 1)(B - 1)$$

$$= (2 - 1) + (2 - 1) + (2 - 1)(2 - 1)$$

$$= 3$$

$$df_A = A - 1$$

$$= 2 - 1$$

$$= 1$$

$$df_B = B - 1$$
$$= 2 - 1$$
$$= 1$$

$$df_{AB} = (A - 1)(B - 1)$$
$$= (2 - 1)(2 - 1)$$
$$= 1$$

$$df_{\text{Within}} = N - (A)(B) = N - k$$
$$= 12 - (2)(2) = 12 - 4$$
$$= 8$$

$$df_{\text{Total}} = N - 1$$
$$= 12 - 1$$
$$= 11$$

9.13. Equation 9.7 is used to compute MS_A.

$$MS_A = \frac{SS_A}{df_A}$$
$$= \frac{3.0}{1}$$
$$= 3.0$$

9.14. Equation 9.8 is used to compute MS_B.

$$MS_B = \frac{SS_B}{df_B}$$
$$= \frac{27.0}{1}$$
$$= 27.0$$

9.15. Equation 9.9 is used to compute MS_{AB}.

$$MS_{AB} = \frac{SS_{AB}}{df_{AB}}$$
$$= \frac{48.0}{1}$$
$$= 48.0$$

9.16. Equation 9.10 is used to compute MS_{Within}.

$$MS_{\text{Within}} = \frac{SS_{\text{Within}}}{df_{\text{Within}}}$$
$$= \frac{8.0}{8}$$
$$= 1.0$$

9.17. $F_A = \dfrac{MS_A}{MS_{\text{Within}}}$

$$F_B = \frac{MS_B}{MS_{\text{Within}}}$$

$$F_{AB} = \frac{MS_{AB}}{MS_{\text{Within}}}$$

9.18. F_A is computed according to Equation 9.11.

$$F_A = \frac{MS_A}{MS_{\text{Within}}}$$
$$= \frac{3.0}{1.0}$$
$$= 3.0$$

9.19. F_B is computed according to Equation 9.12.

$$F_B = \frac{MS_B}{MS_{\text{Within}}}$$
$$= \frac{27.0}{1.0}$$
$$= 27.0$$

9.20. F_{AB} is computed according to Equation 9.13.

$$F_{AB} = \frac{MS_{AB}}{MS_{\text{Within}}}$$
$$= \frac{48.0}{1.0}$$
$$= 48.0$$

9.21.

Source	SS	df	MS	F
Between groups	78.0	3		
A	3.0	1	3.0	3.0
B	27.0	1	27.0	27.0
$A \times B$	48.0	1	48.0	48.0
Within groups	8.0	8	1.0	
Total	86.0	11		

9.22. F tests available from a four-way ANOVA would be as follows:

Main effects: A, B, C, D

Two-way interactions: $A \times B, A \times C, A \times D, B \times C, B \times D, C \times D$

Three-way interactions: $A \times B \times C, A \times B \times D, A \times C \times D, B \times C \times D$

Four-way interaction: A × B × C × D

A four-way interaction can be practically impossible to interpret in specific terms. In general, a four-way interaction indicates that a three-way interaction is dependent on the level of some fourth factor.

9.23. For the factor A main effect:

H_0: The difference between the row means is small enough to be the likely consequence of sampling error. Two samples drawn from a population of identically treated cases would likely differ by as much as is seen here.

H_1: The difference between the row means is too large to be the likely consequence of sampling error alone. Two samples drawn from a population of identically treated cases would be unlikely to differ by this much. Therefore, the two rows probably represent populations that differ on the dependent variable.

For the factor B main effect:

H_0: The difference between the column means is small enough to be the likely consequence of sampling error. Two samples drawn from a population of identically treated cases would likely differ by as much as is seen here.

H_1: The difference between the column means is too large to be the likely consequence of sampling error alone. Two samples drawn from a population of identically treated cases would be unlikely to differ by this much. Therefore, the two columns probably represent populations that differ on the dependent variable.

For the $A \times B$ interaction effect:

H_0: The differences among the cell means are small enough to be the likely consequence of sampling error. Four samples drawn from a population of identically treated cases would likely differ by as much as is seen here.

H_1: The differences among the cell means are too large to be the likely consequence of sampling error alone. Four samples drawn from a population of identically treated cases would be unlikely to differ by this much. Therefore, the four cells probably represent populations that differ on the dependent variable.

9.24. Critical values of F are listed in Table 6, Appendix B. The critical values of F for $df_A = 1$ (for $df_{Numerator}$ in the table) and $df_{Within} = 8$ (for $df_{Denominator}$ in the table) are 5.32 (for the .05 level of significance) and 11.26 (for the .01 level of significance). The obtained value of $F_A = 3.0$. This is nonsignificant.

Critical values of F for $df_B = 1$ (for $df_{Numerator}$) and $df_{Within} = 8$ (for $df_{Denominator}$) are 5.32 (.05 level) and 11.26 (.01 level). The obtained $F_B = 27.0$ is therefore significant at the .01 level.

Critical values of F for $df_{AB} = 1$ (for $df_{Numerator}$) and df_{Within} (for $df_{Denominator}$) are 5.32 (.05 level) and 11.26 (.01 level). The obtained $F_{AB} = 48.0$ is therefore significant at the .01 level.

9.25. A line graph helps greatly in interpreting the results of a factorial ANOVA. The line graph below depicts the cell means for the data presented in Comprehension Check 9.6.

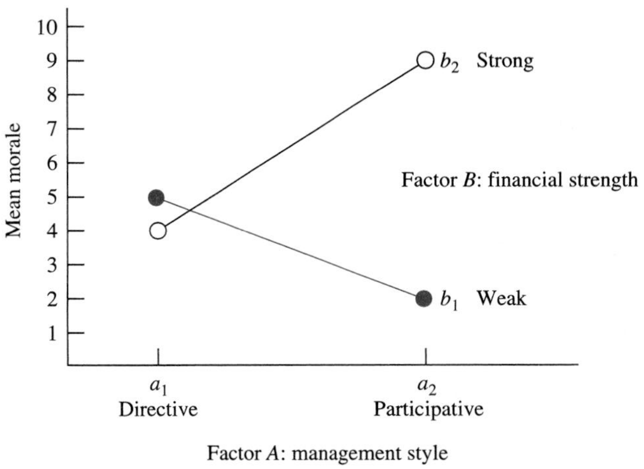

The factor B (financial strength) main effect must be interpreted cautiously, because there is a significant interaction effect. It means that, *if we ignore management style,* employee morale is better in financially strong organizations than in financially weak organizations. However, we *have* information about management style that shows that financial strength affects employee morale only in organizations that practice participative management styles. Where management style is directive, morale is essentially unaffected by the organization's financial strength.

9.26. The interaction effect shown in the line graph above indicates that when an organization is financially weak, employee morale will be low to moderate regardless of management style. In financially strong organizations, though, morale is boosted substantially by a participative management style and is depressed by a directive style.

9.27. Tukey's HSD is computed according to Equation 8.15 (where k = the number of cells in the factorial ANOVA).

$$\text{HSD} = q_{(\alpha, df_{Within}, k)} \sqrt{\frac{MS_{Within}}{n}}$$

$$= q_{(.01, 8, 4)} \sqrt{\frac{1.00}{3}}$$

$$= 6.20\sqrt{\frac{1.00}{3}}$$

$$= 3.58$$

Pairs of cell means that differ by this much or more are significantly different:

$\overline{X}_{a_1b_1} - \overline{X}_{a_1b_2} = 5 - 4 = 1.0$ (nonsignificant)

$\overline{X}_{a_2b_1} - \overline{X}_{a_2b_2} = 2 - 9 = -7.0$ (significant)

$\overline{X}_{a_1b_1} - \overline{X}_{a_2b_1} = 5 - 2 = 3.0$ (nonsignificant)

$\overline{X}_{a_1b_2} - \overline{X}_{a_2b_2} = 4 - 9 = -5.0$ (significant)

9.28. The significant F_B ratio tells us that there is a difference somewhere among the column means. There are only two column means, so these two must be the source of the significant F.

9.29. Equation 9.14 is used to compute C for the Scheffé post-hoc comparison.

$$C = w_1\overline{X}_1 + w_2\overline{X}_2 + \cdots + w_k\overline{X}_k$$

$$= .5(\overline{X}_{a_1b_1}) + .5(\overline{X}_{a_2b_1}) - .5(\overline{X}_{a_1b_2}) - .5(\overline{X}_{a_2b_2})$$

$$= .5(5) + .5(2) - .5(4) - .5(9)$$

$$= -3.0$$

9.30. Equation 9.15 is used to compute the test statistic t in the Scheffé post-hoc comparison.

$$t = \frac{C}{\sqrt{\text{MS}_{\text{Within}}[(w_1^2/n_1) + (w_2^2/n_2) + (w_3^2/n_3) + (w_4^2/n_4)]}}$$

$$= \frac{-3.0}{\sqrt{1.0[(.5^2/3) + (.5^2/3) + (-.5^2/3) + (-.5^2/3)]}}$$

$$= -5.20$$

9.31. Equation 9.16 is used to compute the critical value of t in the Scheffé post-hoc comparison.

$$t_{\text{Critical}} = \sqrt{(k - 1)F_{(\alpha,\ \text{df}_{\text{Between}},\ \text{df}_{\text{Within}})}}$$

$$= \sqrt{(4 - 1)F_{(.01,\ 3,\ 8)}}$$

$$= \sqrt{(4 - 1)7.59}$$

$$= 4.77$$

The obtained value of $t = -5.20$ exceeds this critical value. The Scheffé post-hoc comparison indicates that the difference between the column means is significant.

9.32. Equations 9.17 to 9.19 are used to compute ω^2 values for the factorial ANOVA.

$$\omega_A^2 = \frac{\text{SS}_A - (\text{df}_A)\text{MS}_{\text{Within}}}{\text{SS}_{\text{Total}} + \text{MS}_{\text{Within}}}$$

$$= \frac{3.0 - (1)1.0}{86.0 + 1.0}$$

$$= .02$$

$$\omega_B^2 = \frac{\text{SS}_B - (\text{df}_B)\text{MS}_{\text{Within}}}{\text{SS}_{\text{Total}} + \text{MS}_{\text{Within}}}$$

$$= \frac{27.0 - (1)(1.0)}{86.0 + 1.0}$$

$$= .30$$

$$\omega_{AB}^2 = \frac{\text{SS}_{AB} - (\text{df}_{AB})\text{MS}_{\text{Within}}}{\text{SS}_{\text{Total}} + \text{MS}_{\text{Within}}}$$

$$= \frac{48.0 - (1)1.0}{86.0 + 1.0}$$

$$= .54$$

These ω^2 values show an almost nonexistent factor A (financial strength) main effect, and moderate effect strengths for factor B (management style), and the $A \times B$ interaction effect.

CORRELATION

10

Chapter Outline

Is there a reliable relationship between Scholastic Aptitude Test (SAT) scores and college grade-point averages (GPA)? Are scores on statistics tests related to the order in which students complete and return their tests? Does religious preference show any systematic relationship to political preference?

correlation *The study of relationships between variables.*

All of these questions focus on relationships between variables. This is the domain of **correlation.** All correlational procedures measure the strength of relationship between variables, the degree to which the variables are "linked" or "go together."

In this chapter we will study three different correlational statistics. The Pearson product-moment correlation is useful in examining relationships between two normally distributed interval or ratio scale variables. The Spearman rank-order correlation is a nonparametric statistic used to evaluate the strength of relationship between ordinal scale variables. Another nonparametric statistic, chi-square, is used in combination with Cramer's *V* to explore relationships between nominal scale variables.

COMPREHENSION CHECK 10.1

> What do all correlational procedures have in common? How do the Pearson, Spearman, and χ^2 procedures differ?
> (Answer on p. 338.)

10.1 THE PEARSON PRODUCT-MOMENT CORRELATION

Pearson product-moment correlation (r_P) *A correlational statistic that measures the strength of linear relationship between two normally distributed interval or ratio scale variables.*

Of the three correlational procedures presented in this chapter, the **Pearson product-moment correlation** (r_P) is by far the most widely used. Therefore it is to this statistic that we will turn first. The general features of the Pearson correlation are described first, followed by an example of this statistical procedure in Example 10.1.

The Pearson correlation measures the strength of the relationship between two variables by assessing the degree to which scores on those variables "agree." That is, to what extent do cases that score high on *X* score equally high (or equally low) on *Y*, and to what degree do cases that score low on *X* score equally low (or equally high) on *Y?*

Data for the Pearson Correlation

The Pearson correlation examines the strength of the relationship between two variables, *X* and *Y*, measured for *N* cases. Each case provides one score on the variable *X* and one score on the variable *Y*. It is assumed that both variables are approximately normally distributed and are measured at the interval or ratio scale. (See Note 1) For example, if we recorded shoe size (*X*) and feetal anxiety (*Y*) for 10 psychopodiatric patients, we would have data suitable to a Pearson correlation analysis. Table 10.1 presents these data for $N = 10$ cases. There are two scores for each case in this table: shoe size (*X*) and feetal anxiety (*Y*). The Pearson correlation will measure the degree to which scores "agree" on these variables. Do cases with above-average shoe sizes have equally above-average (or below-average) feetal anxiety? Do cases with below-average shoe sizes have equally below-average (or above-average) feetal anxiety?

Table 10.1

Shoe sizes (*X*) and feetal anxiety scores (*Y*) for 10 psychopodiatric patients

Case	(*X*) Shoe Size	(*Y*) Feetal Anxiety
1	14	85
2	13	100
3	11	85
4	10	75
5	9	60
6	12	75
7	8	80
8	12	95
9	8	50
10	11	60

Comprehension Check 10.2

Describe the types of data that are suitable for analysis by the Pearson product-moment correlation. What does the Pearson correlation tell us about those data?

(Answer on p. 338.)

The Scatterplot

It is a good idea to begin the correlational analysis by constructing a **scatterplot.** This is a graph of the data, which depicts many important aspects of the relationship between *X* and *Y*. The data on shoe size (*X*) and feetal anxiety (*Y*) presented in Table 10.1 have been graphed in the scatterplot shown in Figure 10.1.

scatterplot *A graph of the data in a correlational analysis, which depicts the relationship between* X *and* Y.

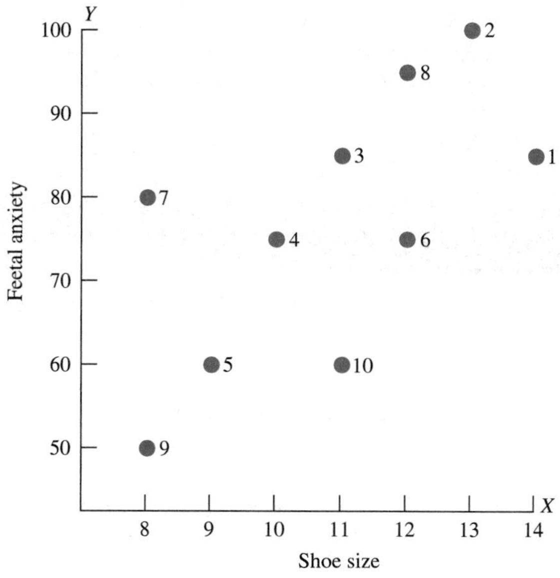

Figure 10.1

A scatterplot depicting the positive correlation between shoe size (*X*) and feetal anxiety (*Y*). Data are given in Table 10.1.

Each axis of the scatterplot represents one of the variables, with scores on X represented along the abscissa and scores on Y represented along the ordinate. Each case is represented in the scatterplot by a point. In Figure 10.1, each point is accompanied by a case identification number. This is done here for instructional purposes. Scatterplots normally do not include case identifications. The location of each point is determined by using that case's scores on the X and Y variables as coordinates. Thus, case 1 has a shoe size of 14 ($X = 14$) and a feetal anxiety score of 85 ($Y = 85$). To locate case 1 in the scatterplot, we find the score of 14 on the abscissa, 85 on the ordinate, and mark a point in the scatterplot at the intersection of these two values. Each of the other cases is located in a similar manner.

COMPREHENSION CHECK 10.3

Construct a scatterplot for the following data.

Case	*X*	*Y*
1	1	1
2	4	4
3	2	3
4	3	5
5	5	5

(Answer on p. 338.)

Let us consider next how one "reads" the scatterplot. What do these graphs tell us about the relationship between X and Y? What should we look for in a scatterplot?

Direction of the Relationship. For one thing, the scatterplot indicates the "direction" of the relationship, either positive or negative. Figure 10.1 depicts a **positive correlation** between X and Y. We can see from the graph that as shoe size (X) increases, feetal anxiety (Y) also increases. There is direct agreement between cases' scores on the two variables. The points forming the scatterplot slope upward from left to right across the scatterplot. Other examples of positive correlations are Scholastic Aptitude Test (SAT) scores and college grade-point average (GPA), height and weight, and population density and crime rate.

positive correlation *A correlation in which there is direct agreement between the locations of cases on* X *and* Y*. As scores on* X *increase, scores on* Y *also increase.*

Many other variables are **negatively correlated.** Here again the variables move together, but now they move in opposite directions. Table 10.2 shows scores on wind speed (X) and spitting distance (Y) from this year's Windy City Expectoration Jubilee. At this year's fete, 10 hardy souls competed to see how far each could spit into the wind. These data are graphed in Figure 10.2. Notice in Figure 10.2 that the points slope downward from left to right across the scatterplot. This scatterplot depicts a negative correlation. In a negative correlation, the data show inverse agreement: low wind speeds are associated with high spitting distances; high wind speeds are associated with low spitting distances.

negative correlation *A correlation in which there is inverse agreement between the locations of cases on* X *and* Y*. As scores on* X *increase, scores on* Y *decrease.*

COMPREHENSION CHECK 10.4

Think of your own examples of positive and negative correlations and draw scatterplots that depict the general nature of these correlations. Explain what is meant when a correlation is "positive" and "negative."

(Answer on pp. 338–339.)

TABLE 10.2

Wind speeds (X) and spitting distances (Y) for 10 contestants in this year's Windy City Expectoration Jubilee

Contestant	X Wind Speed (mph)	Y Spitting Distance (yards)
1	7.5	3.5
2	15.0	2.5
3	10.0	2.0
4	20.0	2.5
5	25.0	1.0
6	11.0	4.0
7	12.0	3.0
8	25.0	0!!
9	18.0	1.5
10	5.0	5.0

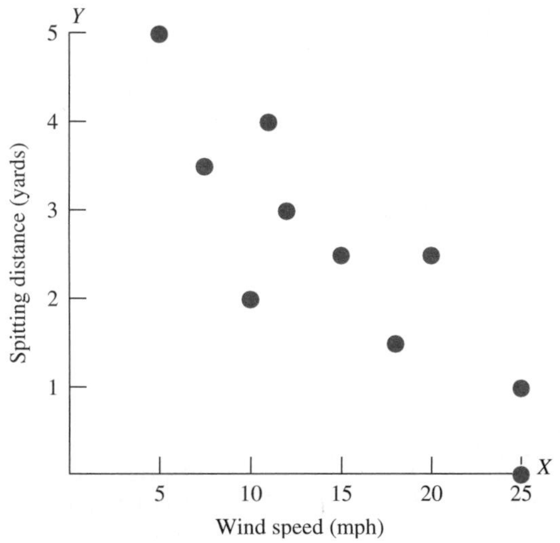

FIGURE 10.2

A scatterplot depicting the negative correlation between wind speed (X) and spitting distance (Y). Data are given in Table 10.2.

Strength of the Relationship. The scatterplot also provides information about the strength of the relationship between two variables. Look back at Figures 10.1 and 10.2. In addition to depicting relationships that differ in direction, these scatterplots also show relationships of different strength. Strength of relationship is represented in a scatterplot by the amount of scattering or dispersion of the points. Imagine straight lines fitted through the points in Figures 10.1 and 10.2. Do you see that the points in Figure 10.1 are more scattered around this imaginary line than are the points in Figure 10.2? This tells us that the correlation between shoe size and feetal anxiety (Figure 10.1) is weaker than the correlation between wind speed and spitting distance (Figure 10.2).

The strongest possible relationship, called a *perfect* relationship, is indicated by a scatterplot in which all the points fall along a straight line. Perfect correlations can be either positive or negative. In both instances the points of the scatterplot form a line. The only difference is in the direction of the line's slope. As we will see in the next chapter, perfect relationships are so called because they enable us to predict with perfect accuracy a case's score on one variable if we know that case's score on the other variable.

FIGURE 10.3

Three scatterplots depicting correlations of varying strengths. (a) shows a perfect correlation. (b) shows a moderate correlation. (c) shows no correlation.

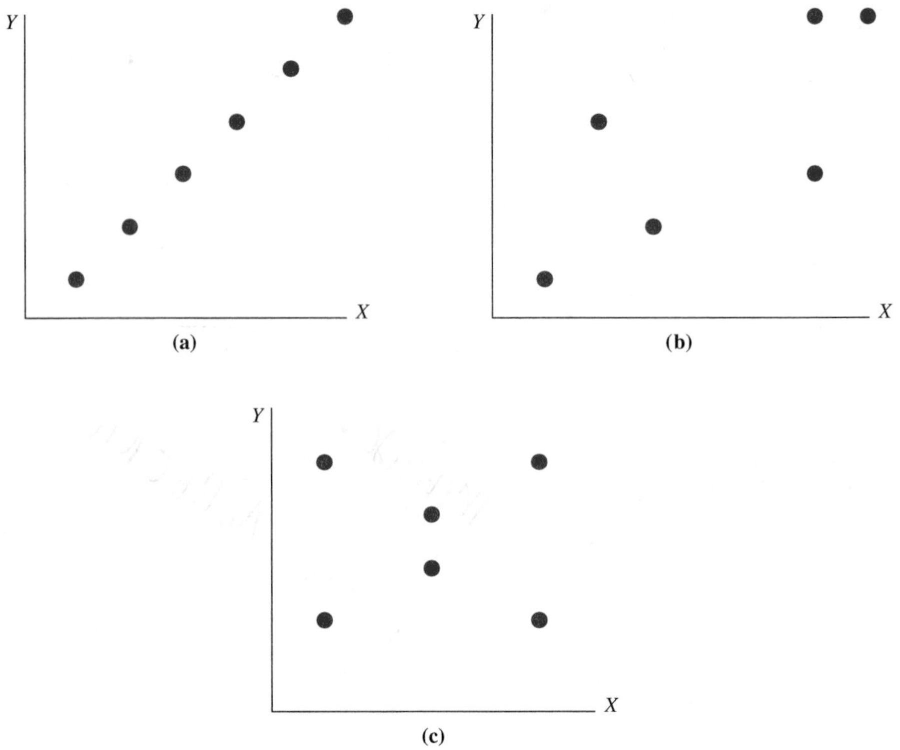

Figure 10.3 presents scatterplots showing correlations of various strengths. In Figure 10.3a the points are in perfect alignment and we have a perfect correlation. In Figure 10.3b there is more scattering and the correlation is weaker. Finally, in Figure 10.3c it is impossible to determine where a line could be best fitted through the points. One fit is as good (or bad) as the next. This scatterplot represents the absence of any correlation between *X* and *Y*.

COMPREHENSION CHECK 10.5

Draw scatterplots showing: (a) a weak negative correlation; (b) a strong positive correlation; and (c) no correlation.
(Answer on p. 339.)

There are two exceptions to the rule that scatterplots that form straight lines represent perfect correlations. If the line is either perfectly vertical, as in Figure 10.4a, or perfectly horizontal, as in Figure 10.4b, the scatterplot indicates a correlation of zero. A moment's reflection will reveal how a straight-line scatterplot can signal a zero correlation. When we say that two variables are correlated, we mean that their values go together or *covary*. In order for two variables to go together or covary, each must "go" or vary. In Figure 10.4a, the vertical scatterplot shows that scores vary on *Y*, but not on *X*. In Figure 10.4b, the horizontal scatterplot shows that scores vary on *X*, but they do not vary on *Y*. In both instances, because scores show no variance on one variable, the correlation becomes zero.

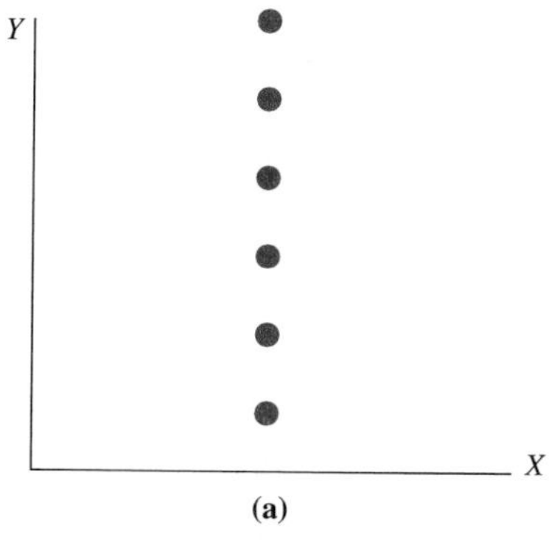

FIGURE 10.4

Two scatterplots depicting zero correlations. In (a) there is no variance in scores on X. In (b) there is no variance in scores on Y.

COMPREHENSION CHECK 10.6

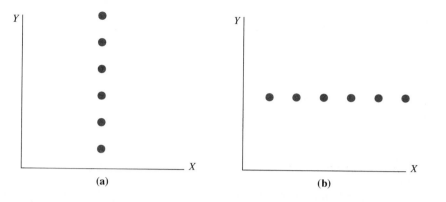

Using the notion that the correlation measures the degree to which cases are located in the same place on variables X and Y, explain why perfectly vertical or horizontal scatterplots indicate zero correlation. (Answer on p. 339.)

Linearity. The Pearson correlation measures the strength of only the **linear relationship** between two variables. Many other, **nonlinear relationships** may exist between X and Y that are not measured by r_P. The scatterplot is especially useful in identifying those nonlinear relationships to which r_P is insensitive.

linear relationship *In a scatterplot, a linear relationship between X and Y is one that can best be described by a straight line.*

nonlinear relationship *In a scatterplot, a nonlinear relationship between X and Y is one that can best be described by some type of curve.*

Linear relationships are indicated by scatterplots in which the points are best fitted by a straight line. Nonlinear relationships show up as scatterplots that are best fitted with curves. Figure 10.5a depicts the relationship between the number of hours spent studying statistics (X) and scores on a statistics exam (Y). The points in this scatterplot are better described by a curve than by a line. As study time increases, so do test scores, but there appears to be a

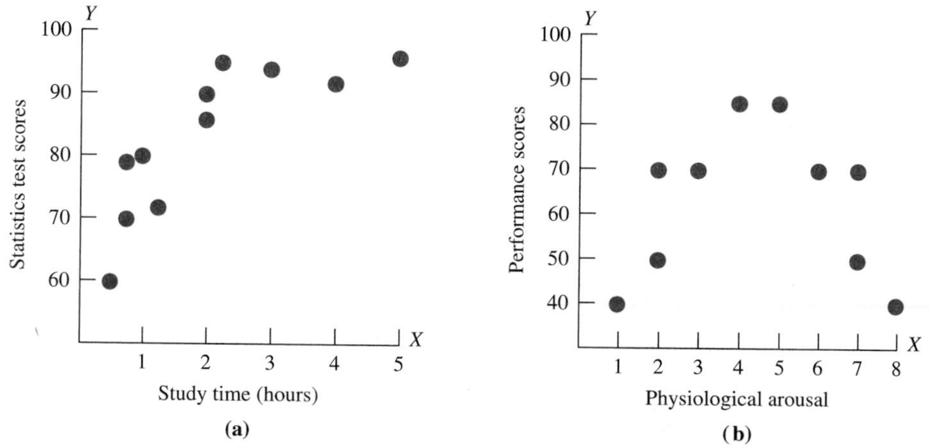

FIGURE 10.5

Two scatterplots depicting nonlinear relationships. (a) shows the nonlinear monotonic relationship between study time (in hours) and statistics test scores. (b) shows the inverted-U shaped relationship between physiological arousal and task performance.

point of diminishing returns. The relationship between study time and test scores seen in Figure 10.5a, therefore, is nonlinear, and the Pearson correlation would not be entirely appropriate as a measure of relationship strength. Figure 10.5b depicts the well-known inverted-U shaped relationship between physiological arousal level (X) and task performance (Y). This is another nonlinear relationship that would be very poorly measured with the Pearson correlation. Although nonlinear relationships can be identified mathematically, a scatterplot provides a far more expedient method of accomplishing this.

COMPREHENSION CHECK 10.7

Think of your own example of a nonlinear relationship and represent this relationship in a scatterplot.
(Answer on p. 339.)

homoscedasticity *Correlational data show homoscedasticity to the degree that the relationship is of approximately equal strength throughout the entire range of both variables.*

heteroscedasticity *Correlational data show heteroscedasticity to the degree that the relationship is of different strengths along different ranges of the variables.*

Homoscedasticity. Correlational data show **homoscedasticity** to the degree that the strength of the relationship between X and Y is approximately equal across the full range of both variables. Homoscedasticity is represented in a scatterplot by approximately equal dispersion of points around the entire length of an imaginary line fitted through the points. **Heteroscedasticity** is the opposite of this, where the relationship between X and Y shows greater strength in some locations of the scatterplot than in other locations. Figure 10.6 compares scatterplots depicting homoscedasticity (Figure 10.6a) and heteroscedasticity (Figure 10.6b). In Figure 10.6a the points are evenly dispersed along the entire length of an imaginary line fitted through them. This suggests approximately equal relationship strength throughout the entire range of the variables. In Figure 10.6b the points cluster tightly in one place and are very dispersed in another. Relationship strength varies considerably depending on where in the range of variables one looks. Heteroscedasticity is a kind of correlational equivalent to an interaction effect in a factorial ANOVA: The strength of the correlation is conditional upon which range of the variables—low values or high values—one is dealing with.

COMPREHENSION CHECK 10.8

Explain why heteroscedastic relationships are more complicated than homoscedastic relationships.
(Answer on p. 339.)

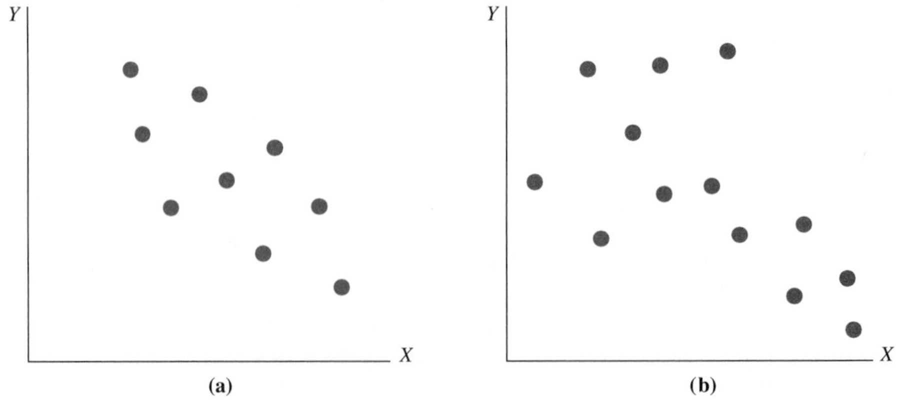

FIGURE 10.6

Two scatterplots showing homoscedasticity (a) and heteroscedasticity (b).

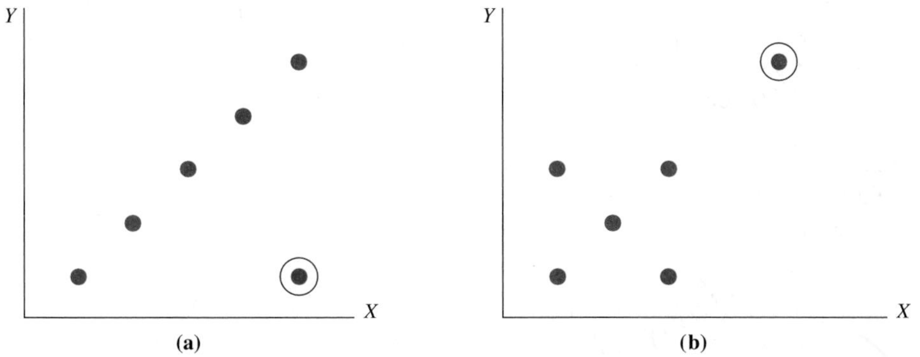

FIGURE 10.7

Two scatterplots depicting outliers (circled). In (a) the outlier attenuates an otherwise perfect correlation. In (b), the outlier inflates an otherwise zero correlation.

The Presence of Outliers. Figure 10.7 presents two scatterplots that contain outliers. In the context of correlational analysis, an **outlier** is a case that is different from the majority of other cases in its combined or conjoint values on *X* and *Y*. Although an outlier may show scores on *X* and *Y* that are each well within the normal ranges for those variables, the *pair* of scores makes the outlier quite unusual. This makes the scatterplot, which depicts cases by their conjoint scores on *X* and *Y*, especially useful in identifying outliers.

outlier *A case in a correlational analysis whose conjoint values on* X *and* Y *mark it as different from the majority of cases.*

There are several good reasons to search for outliers. For one thing, outliers may indicate data-entry errors. Instead of recording an IQ score as 100, for instance, it may have been recorded as 10. In addition, statements made about the correlation between *X* and *Y* based on the rest of the cases do not apply to outliers. Outliers are exceptions to the rule and can make for an interesting study once they are identified. Finally, as we will explore more fully in the next section, outliers exert a disproportionate effect on the size of the computed correlation in much the same way that extreme scores distort the mean of a distribution.

COMPREHENSION CHECK 10.9

What is an outlier, and why do we want to know if there are outliers in a correlational analysis?
(Answer on p. 339.)

10.2 COMPUTING THE PEARSON CORRELATION

The scatterplot provides insights into the relationship between *X* and *Y* that cannot be obtained as easily from any other source. Even so, the information that the scatterplot conveys is rather general. Information about relationship strength, in particular, is too vague. We can see from a scatterplot that variables *X* and *Y* have a "weak," "moderate," or "strong" relationship, but we often need greater precision than this. That is where the Pearson correlation comes in. The Pearson correlation is computed according to Equation 10.1.(See Note 2)

Equation 10.1

$$r_P = \frac{\Sigma z_X z_Y}{N}$$

where

r_P = the Pearson product-moment correlation
z_X = the z scores on variable X
z_Y = the z scores on variable Y
N = the total number of cases in the analysis

In words, r_P is computed by: (1) converting variables X and Y to z-score form; (2) multiplying corresponding values of z_X and z_Y, (called the "cross-products"); (3) summing these cross-products; and (4) dividing this sum by N, the number of cases.

COMPREHENSION CHECK 10.10

Use Equation 10.1 to compute r_P for the data given in Comprehension Check 10.3.
(Answer on p. 339.)

To understand how r_P measures the relationship between X and Y, first remember that z_X tells us the location of a case's score on the X variable, expressed as the number of standard deviations the score falls from the mean. Negative z scores fall below the average, z scores of zero are exactly average, and positive z scores are located above the average. Similarly, z_Y locates each case's score on the Y variable.

Now, suppose that every case that has scored high on X has scored equally high on Y, and every case that has scored low on X has scored equally low on Y. There is perfect direct agreement between the locations of scores on X and Y. For example:

Case	z_X	z_Y
1	−1.42	−1.42
2	− .71	− .71
3	0	0
4	+ .71	+ .71
5	+1.42	+1.42

You can see that each case has scored in exactly the same location on both the X and Y variables. Now let's see what happens when we compute r_P for these data using Equation 10.1. In computing the numerator of Equation 10.1, we find that every cross-product of z_X and z_Y is either positive or zero, and the sum of the cross-products of z_X and z_Y ($\Sigma z_X z_Y$) is equal to N:

$$(-1.42 \times -1.42) + (-.71 \times -.71) + (0 \times 0) + (.71 \times .71) + (1.42 \times 1.42) = 5$$

When we divide the sum of the cross-products by $N = 5$ ($r_P = \Sigma z_X z_Y/N$), we get $r_P = +1$. A correlation of $+1$ means that each case has scored at exactly the same location on both X and Y. There is perfect direct agreement between the locations of the scores on variables X and Y.

Suppose instead that every case that scored high on X scored equally *low* on Y, and every case that scored low on X scored equally *high* on Y. There is now perfect inverse agreement between the locations of cases on X and Y. For example:

Case	z_X	z_Y
1	−1.42	+1.42
2	− .71	+ .71
3	0	0
4	+ .71	− .71
5	+1.42	−1.42

Let us again compute r_P for these data using Equation 10.1. In computing the numerator of Equation 10.1, we find that every cross-product of z_X and z_Y is either negative or zero, and the sum of these cross-products of z_X and z_Y ($\Sigma z_X z_Y$) is equal to $-N$:

$$(-1.42 \times 1.42) + (-.71 \times .71) + (0 \times 0) + (.71 \times -.71) + (1.42 \times -1.42) = -5$$

When we divide the sum of the cross-products by $N = 5$ ($r_P = \Sigma z_X z_Y / N$), we get $r_P = -1$. A correlation of -1 points again to perfect agreement between the locations of scores on X and Y, but now the agreement is inverse: High scores on X are associated with equally low scores on Y; and low scores on X are associated with equally high scores on Y.

Let us consider one final situation, in which there is no consistent relationship between locations of scores on X and Y:

Case	z_X	z_Y
1	−1.12	+1.12
2	−1.12	−1.12
3	0	0
4	+1.12	−1.12
5	+1.12	+1.12

Now some of the cross-products of z_X and z_Y are negative, some are positive, and some are zero, and the sum of the cross-products of z_X and z_Y ($\Sigma z_X z_Y$) is equal to 0:

$$(-1.12 \times 1.12) + (-1.12 \times -1.12) + (0 \times 0) + (1.12 \times -1.12) + (1.12 \times 1.12) = 0$$

Dividing this sum of cross-products by $N = 5$ ($r_P = \Sigma z_X z_Y / N$) gives $r_P = 0$. A correlation of 0 points to the absence of any consistent agreement between the locations of scores on X and Y.

In general, as cases show increasing direct agreement in their locations on variables X and Y, the cross-products of z_X and z_Y become more strongly positive, up to $+N$. As cases show increasing inverse agreement in their locations on variables X and Y, the cross-products of z_X and z_Y become more strongly negative, up to $-N$. In computing r_P, we sum the cross-products of z_X and z_Y and divide by N, thereby computing the mean of the cross-products. (Whenever we add several values and divide this sum by the number of values, we are computing a mean.) The Pearson correlation, then, is a mean. It is the mean of the cross-products of z_X and z_Y. Since the cross-products of z_X and z_Y represent the amount of agreement between the locations of cases on X and Y, r_P represents the average level of agreement between the locations of cases on variables X and Y.

COMPREHENSION CHECK 10.11

Two sets of cross-products of z_X and z_Y are provided below. Which set reflects a positive correlation? Which set reflects a negative correlation? Which set reflects the stronger correlation?

z_X	z_Y	$z_X z_Y$
−1.56	−1.42	2.22
− .89	.71	− .63
− .22	− .71	.16
.45	1.42	.64
1.12	.71	.80
1.12	− .71	− .80

z_X	z_Y	$z_X z_Y$
−1.37	1.09	−1.49
− .62	.16	− .10
.13	.16	.02
.87	− .78	.68
1.62	−1.71	−2.77
− .62	1.09	− .68

(Answer on pp. 339–340.)

Interpreting r_P

The Pearson correlation tells us two things about the relationship between *X* and *Y*. First, the direction of the relationship (positive or negative) is given by the sign r_P (+ or −).

Second, the strength of the relationship is reflected in the absolute value of r_P. We saw in the preceding examples that r_P ranges from −1 (a perfect negative correlation) to 0 (no correlation) to +1 (a perfect positive correlation). As we will see in the next chapter, the squared correlation (r_P^2) provides an even more useful measure of relationship strength. Briefly, r_P^2 indicates the proportion of variance in *Y* that is explained by variation in *X* (or vice versa). Ranging from 0 to 1, r_P^2 is interpreted much like the statistic omega-square (ω^2) that we used in previous chapters to measure the strength of treatment effects in significant difference tests.

COMPREHENSION CHECK 10.12

What two things does r_P tell us about the relationship between *X* and *Y*? (Answer on p. 340.)

There is more to know, though, about interpreting r_P. We will see next that high values of r_P do not always indicate strong relationships between *X* and *Y*, and low values of r_P do not always reflect weak relationships.

Restricted Variance. We learned from Figure 10.4 that if either *X* or *Y* shows no variance, there can be no correlation between *X* and *Y*. It is also true that even *restricting* the variance of *X* and/or *Y* will tend to reduce the size of the correlation between the variables. To get an accurate picture of the correlation between *X* and *Y*, both variables must be free to vary fully.

Figure 10.8 depicts again the correlation between shoe size and feetal anxiety. The correlation computed using all the data points is $r_P = .66$. Now consider what happens to this correlation if we limit our examination to only those cases with shoe sizes of 12 or larger and feetal anxiety scores of 75 or higher. This situation is depicted in the inset scatterplot of Figure 10.8: The correlation that was so obvious in the full data set has completely disappeared. The scatterplot shows that the correlation is weakened by restricting the range of the variables. This impression is verified by the value of r_P com-

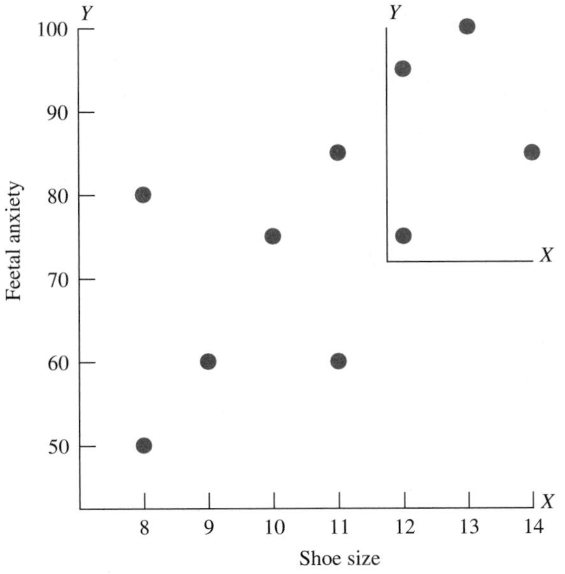

FIGURE 10.8

A scatterplot depicting the correlation between shoe size (X) and feetal anxiety (Y). Using the full range of variables, the correlation is quite strong. Restricting the range on X and Y severely attenuates the correlation.

puted for the inset scatterplot: $r_P = .12$. Variables that are strongly related can produce misleadingly low correlations if either or both of the variables are not free to vary fully.

You may wonder how often this is a problem. Quite often, actually. Consider, for instance, a personnel psychologist who wants to see if sales volume is correlated with achievement motivation. The psychologist rounds up several sales people, tests their motivation, and correlates these scores with sales volume records. Right? Wrong. Although sales volume and motivation are probably correlated, the psychologist approaching the problem from this angle is unlikely to see much of that correlation. By limiting the study to current employees, the psychologist is unintentionally restricting the range of the variables. We can assume that employees with low sales volume figures have already resigned or been terminated. Therefore, the sample consists of only those folks with relatively high sales volume figures. Since sales volume is not free to vary fully, we can expect that the correlation between sales volume and motivation will be attenuated.

COMPREHENSION CHECK 10.13

Think of another example in which a particular sample would likely restrict the range of variables studied in a correlation. Why does restricting the range reduce the correlation?

(Answer on p. 340.)

Nonlinearity. We learned earlier that the Pearson correlation measures only the linear relationship between two variables. The Pearson correlation is insensitive to nonlinear relationships. Consequently, variables that are strongly related in a nonlinear manner may easily produce a very low Pearson correlation. Let's verify this principle with some numbers.

Figure 10.5 gave two examples of nonlinear relationships. Look first at Figure 10.5b, which represents the inverted-U shaped relationship between physiological arousal and task performance. The correlation depicted in this scatterplot is $r_P = 0$! Does this mean that physiological arousal and task performance are unrelated? Not at all. They just do not show the *linear* relationship to which the Pearson correlation is sensitive.

Although the Pearson correlation is insensitive to nonlinear relationships, it is the most widely used measure of correlation in the social and behavioral sciences. Most of the relationships that we study contain at least some linear component to which r_P is sensitive. Look at Figure 10.5a, which represents the relationship between the number of hours spent studying and subsequent scores on a statistics test. Even though this relationship is somewhat nonlinear, there is still a strong linear component, as reflected in the computed Pearson correlation: $r_P = .77$.

COMPREHENSION CHECK 10.14

What is meant when it is said that a nonlinear relationship has a linear *component*?

(Answer on p. 340.)

Outliers. Figure 10.7 provided two examples of scatterplots containing outliers. It was suggested that outliers like these exert a disproportionate effect on computed correlations. Let's see. In Figure 10.7a, data that would produce a perfect correlation without the outlier show a correlation of only $r_P = .54$ when the outlier is included in the analysis. In Figure 10.7b, the scatterplot shows no correlation between the variables until the outlier is introduced. With this one case added, r_P jumps to .65.

Outliers exert a disproportionate effect on the value of r_P because: (1) r_P is the mean of the cross-products of z_X and z_Y; (2) an outlier produces a cross-product that is extreme; and (3) the mean is affected disproportionately by extreme scores.

COMPREHENSION CHECK 10.15

In the data below there is one outlier. Plot these scores in a scatterplot to identify that case. Now compute the cross-products of z_X and z_Y and describe how the outlier's cross-product differs from those of the other cases.

Case	z_X	z_Y
1	− .94	−1.57
2	− .27	− .66
3	.40	.24
4	1.74	.85
5	− .94	1.15

(Answer on p. 340.)

The Statistical Significance of r_P

The Pearson correlation describes the strength of the linear relationship between *X* and *Y in the sample at hand.* The problem with samples, though, is sampling error. A sample may or may not give an accurate picture of the state of affairs in the population from which that sample was drawn. In the case of correlation, our problem is this: When we find a correlation between X and Y in a sample, can we conclude that X and Y are *really* correlated? Maybe the sample correlation is just a fluke, found in this sample but in few or no others drawn from the same population. How can we determine that a correlation found in one sample would likely be found in other samples drawn from the same population? This, of course, brings us back to the issue of statistical significance. We will see that testing the statistical significance of r_P involves the same logic that we encountered in significant difference testing. This makes perfect sense if one remembers that a significant difference between groups points to a significant relationship (correlation) between the variable that defines group membership (the independent variable) and the dependent variable.

COMPREHENSION CHECK 10.16

When we test the statistical significance of a correlation, what are we trying to find out? What does it mean when a correlation is statistically significant? What does it mean when a correlation is not statistically significant?

(Answer on p. 340.)

The Null and Alternative Hypotheses. When X and Y are found to be correlated in a sample, there are two possible explanations, the null and alternative hypotheses. The null hypothesis (H_0) attributes the observed correlation to sampling error. A correlation of the observed size is small enough that it would be relatively common among samples drawn from a population in which X and Y are completely uncorrelated. The alternative hypothesis (H_1) explains the sample correlation differently. According to H_1, the observed correlation is too large to attribute reasonably to sampling error. A correlation of the size observed would be quite unlikely in samples drawn from a population in which X and Y are uncorrelated. It is more likely that X and Y are correlated in the sample because they are correlated in the population from which the sample was drawn.

COMPREHENSION CHECK 10.17

How does the null hypothesis explain a sample correlation? How does the alternative hypothesis explain a sample correlation?

(Answer on p. 340.)

The Test Statistic. When we studied tests of significant differences, test statistics were defined as values computed from sample data that vary as a function of the *size of the difference* being tested for significance. In the context of tests of the significance of correlations, a test statistic can be defined similarly as a value computed from sample data that varies as a function of the *strength of the relationship* being tested for significance. The most obvious test statistic for the Pearson correlation is r_P itself. Consistent with our definition, r_P does indeed vary in value as a function of the size of the linear relationship between X and Y. (See Note 3)

COMPREHENSION CHECK 10.18

The test statistic in a significant difference test reflects the size of the difference being tested for significance. The test statistic in a correlation reflects the strength of the relationship being tested for significance. In what sense are these really the same thing?

(Answer on p. 340.)

The Sampling Distribution of r_P. Once we have obtained a sample value of r_P, we want to determine the probability that a population in which X and Y are uncorrelated could have produced such a sample. This is accomplished by comparing our obtained r_P against the sampling distribution of r_P. Let us consider this sampling distribution.

Imagine a population in which X and Y are uncorrelated. Now imagine drawing all possible samples of size N from that population and computing r_P for each sample. From one sample to the next, the value of r_P would be expected to vary because of sampling error. The single most common value would be 0, because the samples are coming from a population in which X and Y are uncorrelated. Even so, one would expect to see quite a few small positive and small negative values of r_P. Sampling error would even give us some larger values of r_P, though very large values would be quite rare. If we plotted the frequency of occurrence of the r_P values obtained from one sample to the next, they would form the **sampling distribution of r_P**. The general shape of this sampling distribution is shown in Figure 10.9.

sampling distribution of r_P *The theoretical distribution of values of* r_P *obtained from all possible samples of size* N *drawn from a population in which there is no correlation between* X *and* Y.

It should come as no surprise by now to find that the exact shape of the sampling distribution of r_P varies depending on sample size (N). With small samples, the sampling distribution of r_P is relatively flat, and large values of r_P occur fairly frequently. As sample sizes increase, though, the sampling distribution of r_P becomes more and more normal in shape, and large values of r_P occur less and less frequently.

COMPREHENSION CHECK 10.19

In which of the sampling distributions depicted in Figure 10.9 would $r_P = .70$ be most likely to be statistically significant?

(Answer on p. 340.)

FIGURE 10.9

The sampling distribution of the Pearson correlation (r_P) varies according to sample size. As sample sizes increase, the distribution approaches normal. Lower sample sizes are associated with elevated tails. The single most frequently occurring value of r_P is 0.

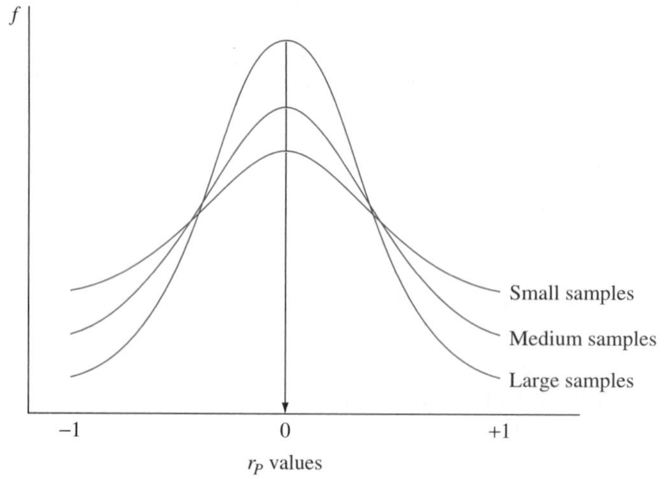

The sampling distribution of r_P is described in Table 8 of Appendix B, "Critical values of the Pearson product-moment correlation." This table lists absolute values of r_P that mark off the upper and lower critical regions of the sampling distribution. The table is entered using $df = N - 2$, where N = the number of cases.(See Note 4) Table 8 provides for both one-tail and two-tail tests of the significance of r_P. One-tail significance tests are used when the direction of the correlation (positive or negative) has been predicted in advance. Two-tail tests are used when the direction has not been predicted.

Choosing Between the Null and Alternative Hypotheses. If an obtained value of r_P meets or exceeds the critical value, we know that it is a value that seldom occurs in samples drawn from a population in which X and Y are uncorrelated. It follows that the sample that yielded this r_P probably did not come from such a population, but rather from a population in which X and Y *are* correlated. We reject H_0 and accept H_1. On the other hand, if an obtained value of r_P falls short of the critical value, we know that it is a value that occurs quite frequently in samples drawn from a population in which X and Y are uncorrelated. We conclude that the X and Y are uncorrelated in the population and that the sample r_P can reasonably be attributed to sampling error. We have accepted H_0 as a reasonable explanation of the observed r_P.

COMPREHENSION CHECK 10.20

If one does not know in advance if a correlation will be positive or negative, should one use a one-tail or a two-tail significance test in evaluating the correlation?
(Answer on p. 340.)

As an example, suppose we have computed a correlation of $r_P = -.60$ using data from 10 cases. For $df = N - 2 = 10 - 2 = 8$, Table 8 lists one-tail critical values of r_P of .5494 (.05 level of significance), .6319 (.025 level of significance), .7155 (.01 level of significance), and so on. The obtained $r_P = -.60$ exceeds only the first of these critical values (remember that we use absolute values of r_P in assessing significance). Thus, we know the probability is less than .05 ($p < .05$) that a population in which X and Y are uncorrelated would produce a sample in which r_P is as large as $-.60$. This is a pretty low probability. It is more likely, then, that the variables *are* correlated in the population from which the sample was drawn. We reject H_0 and accept H_1.

COMPREHENSION CHECK 10.21

For a sample of $N = 90$, what value of r_P would be required for the correlation to be considered significant at the .01 level (one-tail)?
(Answer on p. 340.)

EXAMPLE 10.1

The Pearson Product-Moment Correlation

Statistical prognosticators at Double Cross/Double Shield Insurance have noticed that claims for in-patient treatment of serious psychopodiatric disorders tend to go hand in hand with caps on mental health coverage. Policy holders whose policies strictly limit coverage for psychopodiatric disorders seem to spend fewer days in the hospital than do patients whose policies provide more generous coverage. Suspicious that psychopodiatrists may be basing treatment more on insurance coverage than on patient need, statisticians at Double Cross decide to take a closer look.

They have decided to use the Pearson correlation to explore the relationship between insurance coverage in thousands of dollars (X) and duration of hospitalization in days (Y). Data for the analysis are presented below for 10 policy holders in both raw-score and z-score form.

	X		Y	
Client	*Insurance Cap*	z_X	*Hospitalization*	z_Y
1	$ 40	−.29	14	−.72
2	$ 80	.77	20	−.32
3	$ 20	−.82	15	−.66
4	$ 0	−1.35	10	−.99
5	$100	1.29	38	.88
6	$ 60	.24	21	−.25
7	$ 80	.77	40	1.02
8	$100	1.29	50	1.69
9	$ 20	−.82	35	.68
10	$ 10	−1.08	5	−1.33

These data are graphed below in a scatterplot. We can draw the following conclusions from the scatterplot. There is a positive relationship between insurance coverage and duration of in-patient treatment in this sample: As insurance coverage increases, so does the length of hospitalization. This is as was suspected. The scatterplot shows that the relationship is primarily linear, is of moderate strength, and is homoscedastic. There are no obvious outliers. All in all, the data appear to be suitable to a Pearson correlation.

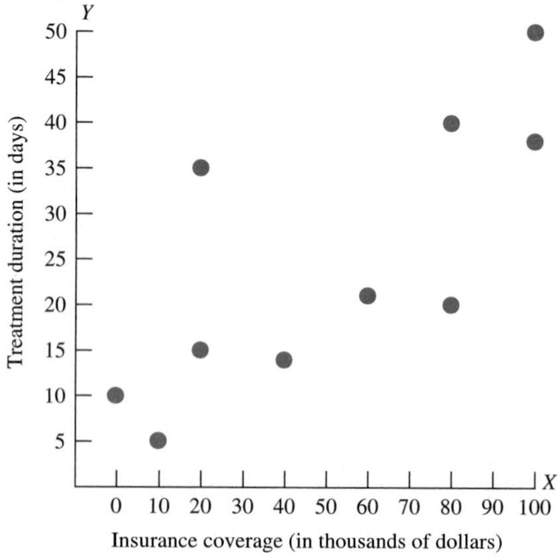

The Pearson correlation is computed according to Equation 10.1:

$$r_P = \frac{\Sigma z_X z_Y}{N}$$

$$= \frac{(-.29 \times -.72) + (.77 \times -.32) + \cdots + (-1.08 \times -1.33)}{10}$$

$$= .75$$

Null and Alternative Hypotheses

H_0: The observed correlation is a consequence of sampling error. It is quite likely that a sample with a correlation of this size would be drawn from a population in which the variables are uncorrelated.

H_1: The observed correlation is too large to attribute to sampling error. It is unlikely that a sample with a correlation this large would be drawn from a population in which the variables are uncorrelated. It is more likely that the sample shows a correlation because the variables are correlated in the population.

Test Statistic

The Pearson correlation serves as its own test statistic. It varies in value as a function of the strength of the relationship being tested for significance.

The Sampling Distribution of r_P

In order to choose between H_0 and H_1, we compare the obtained value of $r_P = .75$ against the sampling distribution of r_P with df $= N - 2 = 10 - 2 = 8$. The general shape of this sampling distribution is shown below. Critical values of r_P are found in Table 8 in Appendix B, "Critical values of the Pearson correlation."

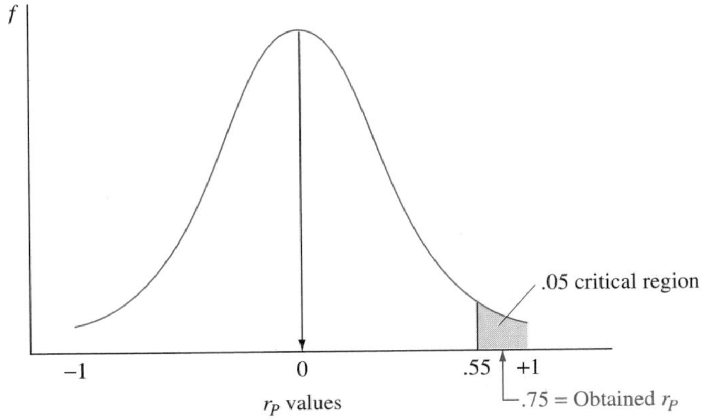

Choosing Between H_0 and H_1

We see that the obtained value of $r_P = .75$ falls within the .05 critical region. (A one-tail test is used because the direction of the relationship was predicted in advance of data collection.) It is unlikely that such a large correlation would occur in a sample drawn from a population in which the variables are uncorrelated. It is therefore more likely that the sample shows a correlation because the variables are correlated in the population. We reject the null hypothesis and conclude that the positive correlation between insurance coverage and duration of in-patient psychopodiatric treatment is statistically significant and reliable.

10.3 The Spearman Rank-Order Correlation

Spearman rank-order correlation r_S *A correlational statistic that measures the relationship between two ordinal scale variables.*

The **Spearman rank-order correlation** (r_S) is used to measure correlation between two ordinal scale variables. The general features of the Spearman correlation are described first, followed by an example of this procedure in Example 10.2.

Like the Pearson correlation, r_S varies from -1 to 0 to $+1$, with the sign and size of r_S interpreted in exactly the same manner as the Pearson correlation. When $r_S = +1$, there is perfect direct agreement between the rank-ordering of cases on variables *X* and *Y*: High ranks on *X* are matched by equally high ranks on *Y;* and low ranks on *X* are matched by equally low ranks on *Y.* When $r_S = -1$, there is perfect inverse agreement between the rank ordering of cases: High ranks on *X* are matched by equally low ranks on *Y;* and low ranks on *X* are matched by equally high ranks on *Y.* When $r_S = 0$, there is no consistent agreement between cases' ranks on *X* and *Y.*

Comprehension Check 10.22

How are the Pearson and Spearman correlations different? How are they similar?
(Answer on p. 340.)

Computing the Spearman Correlation

The first step in computing r_S is to rank-order the values of both *X* and *Y* if they are not already in this form. Scores on the two variables are ranked separately. It is convenient to rank scores in ascending order. Thus, the lowest score on each variable is ranked 1, the second lowest score on each variable is ranked 2, and so on. Tied scores each receive a rank equal to the average of their positions in an ordered array. Once scores are ranked, r_S is computed according to Equation 10.2.(See Note 5)

$$r_S = 1 - \frac{6\Sigma D^2}{N(N^2 - 1)}$$

Equation 10.2

where

r_S = the Spearman rank-order correlation
D = difference between corresponding ranks on X and Y
N = the number of cases in the analysis

In words, r_S is computed by: (1) computing the differences between corresponding ranks (D); (2) squaring these differences (D^2); (3) summing these squared differences; (4) multiplying the result of step 3 by 6; (5) subtracting 1 from N^2, where N is the number of cases; (6) multiplying the result of step 5 by N; (7) dividing the result of step 4 by the result of step 6; and (8) subtracting the result of step 7 from the number 1.

Comprehension Check 10.23

Use Equation 10.2 to compute r_S for the following data.

X	*Y*
38	19
35	10
40	24
30	17
30	10
33	13

(Answer on p. 340.)

The Spearman Correlation and Nonlinear Monotonic Relationships

When we rank-order scores on an interval or ratio scale variable, unequal differences between adjacent scores are made equal. For instance, reaction-time scores of .5, 1, and 2 seconds take on ranks of 1, 2, and 3. In their original form, the difference between reaction times of 1 and 2 seconds was twice as great as the difference between .5 and 1 second. Expressed as ranks, though, the numerical differences between adjacent scores are all equal.

This rescaling of variables that occurs when scores are rank-ordered changes the form of the relationship between the variables as well. Most importantly, nonlinear **monotonic relationships** are made linear by ranking the variables. You already know what a nonlinear relationship is: It is a relationship that is best described by a curve rather than a line. A monotonic relationship is one in which for each increase in X there is an increase in Y, or for each increase in X there is a decrease in Y. Look at Figure 10.5a again. This scatterplot depicts a nonlinear monotonic relationship. It is nonlinear because it curves. It is monotonic because for each increase in X (study time), there is an increase in Y (test scores). Figure 10.5b, though nonlinear, is *not* monotonic. Toward the left side of the scatterplot, an increase in X is accompanied by

monotonic relationship *A relationship between* X *and* Y *in which for every increase in* X *there is an increase in* Y, *or for every increase in* X *there is a decrease in* Y.

an increase in *Y*. Toward the right side of the scatterplot, however, an increase in *X* is accompanied by a decrease in *Y*.

Let's rank-order the variables depicted in Figure 10.5a and construct a new scatterplot with the rank-ordered variables. The data we need are given in Table 10.3, and the new scatterplot is shown in Figure 10.10. The nonlinear trend that was so clear in the original data has disappeared. By ranking the data, the nonlinear monotonic relationship has been made linear. The Spearman rank-order correlation computed on these ranks is $r_S = .88$. This is noticeably higher than the Pearson correlation computed on the original scores ($r_P = .77$) and better captures the true strength of the relationship between the variables.

TABLE 10.3

Study times in hours (*X*) and statistics test scores (*Y*) are presented in both original form and as rank orders. Notice that tied scores are assigned a rank equal to the average of the scores' positions in an ordered array.

X		*Y*	
Study Time (hours)	*Study Time Ranks*	*Test Scores*	*Test Score Ranks*
.50	1	59	1
.75	2.5	70	2
.75	2.5	78	4
1.00	4	80	5
1.25	5	72	3
2.00	6.5	90	7.5
2.00	6.5	85	6
2.25	8	94	11
3.25	9	93	9.5
4.00	10	90	7.5
5.00	11	93	9.5

FIGURE 10.10

Scatterplot showing the relationship between ranks on study time (in hours) and ranks on statistics test scores. Compare this scatterplot to Figure 10.5a, which plots the original scores. By ranking the data, a nonlinear monotonic relationship is made linear. Data are given in Table 10.3.

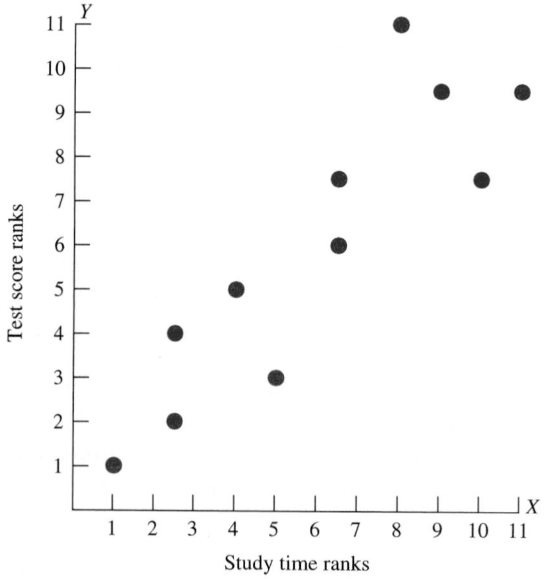

COMPREHENSION CHECK 10.24

Why does the Spearman rank-order correlation provide a better measure of nonlinear monotonic relationships than does the Pearson correlation?

(Answer on p. 340.)

The Statistical Significance of r_S

The meaning, logic, and mechanics of the significance test of r_S are identical to those of the Pearson correlation. Only the table of critical values changes slightly. For the Spearman rank-order correlation, use Table 9 of Appendix B, "Critical values of the Spearman rank-order correlation.(See Note 6) An obtained value of r_S is statistically significant if it meets or exceeds the table value for the selected sample size (N), level of significance (.05, .01, etc.), and one- or two-tail test.

EXAMPLE 10.2

The Spearman Rank-Order Correlation

Professor Yogi Zen, Chairperson of the Department of Phrenology at Rocky Bottom State University, has observed that the professional productivity of his faculty seems to be inversely related to their tendency to self-aggrandize. He wonders if it is generally true among university faculty that these two characteristics are negatively correlated. Lacking good measures of either self-aggrandizement or productivity, Professor Zen has decided to rank-order his sample of faculty on these variables and use the Spearman rank-order correlation to study the relationship between the two. His data are presented below. Shown along with ranks are values of D^2, the squared differences between corresponding ranks.

Faculty	Rank on Self-Aggrandizement	Rank on Productivity	D^2
1	2	9	49
2	1	8	49
3	3	7	16
4	7	2	25
5	5	4	1
6	4	6	4
7	9	3	36
8	10	5	25
9	6	1	25
10	8	10	4

The Spearman rank-order correlation is computed according to Equation 10.2.

$$r_S = 1 - \frac{6\Sigma D^2}{N(N^2 - 1)}$$

$$= 1 - \frac{6(49 + 49 + \cdots + 4)}{10(100 - 1)}$$

$$= -.42$$

Null and Alternative Hypotheses

H_0: The observed correlation can be attributed to sampling error. It is quite likely that a population in which there is no correlation between the variables would produce a sample showing a correlation of this size.

H_1: The observed correlation is too large to attribute to sampling error. It is unlikely that such a large correlation would be seen in a sample drawn from a population in which the variables are uncorrelated. It is more likely that the variables are correlated in the population.

Test Statistic

The Spearman rank-order correlation serves as its own test statistic. It varies in value as a function of the strength of the relationship being tested for significance.

The Sampling Distribution of r_S

In choosing between H_0 and H_1, we compare the obtained value of $r_S = -.42$ against the sampling distribution of r_S. The general shape of this sampling distribution is shown below. Critical values of r_S are found in Table 9 of Appendix B, "Critical values of the Spearman rank-order correlation."

Choosing Between H_0 and H_1

We see that the obtained value of $r_S = -.42$ falls outside the .05 critical region of the sampling distribution. The obtained r_S value is small enough to occur fairly often in samples drawn from a population in which the variables are unrelated. Thus, there is insufficient evidence to reject the null hypothesis. The negative correlation between self-aggrandizement and productivity seen in this sample is not sufficiently large to be considered reliable.

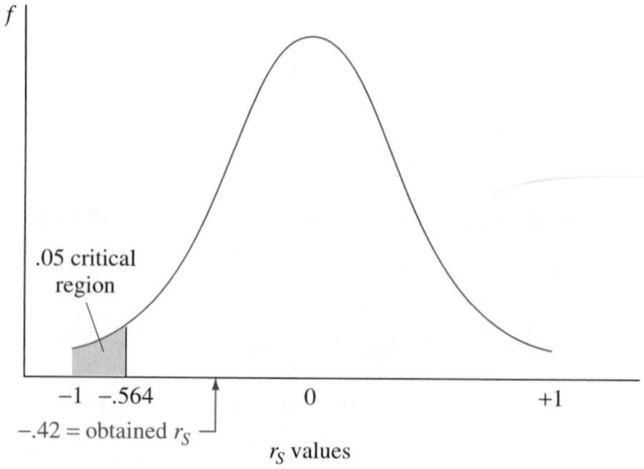

10.4 The Chi-Square Test of Association and Cramer's V Statistic

Two statistics familiar to you from previous chapters are used again to explore correlations between nominal scale variables. In the **chi-square test of association,** χ^2 is the test statistic used to evaluate the statistical significance of the relationship between two nominal variables. Cramer's *V* rescales χ^2 to a value falling between 0 and 1, making interpretation of the strength of the relationship more convenient. After considering the general characteristics of these statistics, study Example 10.3.

chi-square (χ^2) test of association *A test of the relationship between two nominal scale variables.*

The Contingency Table

The analysis of the relationship between two nominal scale variables begins by organizing the data into a contingency table. Table 10.4 provides an example of a contingency table constructed in studying the relationship between political inclination and automobile preference. Each cell in the contingency table represents one of the possible combinations of categories of the two nominal scale variables being investigated. Reported in each cell is the number of cases that fall into that combination of categories—the observed frequencies (f_o). It is assumed in the χ^2 test of association that each case appears in one and only one cell of the contingency table and that each case is completely independent of the others. Expected frequencies (f_e) are also recorded in parentheses in each of the cells of the contingency table. These values represent the number of cases that one would expect to find in each cell of the table *if the variables being investigated are not related.* Any difference between observed and expected frequencies, then, gives evidence that the variables *are* related. More will be said in the next section about computing expected frequencies. Also seen in Table 10.4 are row totals and column totals. These are simply the sums of the observed frequencies in rows and columns, respectively. Row percentages represent the percentage of the total sample (*N*) found in each row.

Comprehension Check 10.25

For each case listed below, there is an indication of gender (male or female) and color preference (red, green, or blue). Construct a con-

(cont.)

Table 10.4

A contingency table summarizing data for a χ^2 analysis of the relationship between political inclination and automobile preference

Political Inclination	Automobile Preference: *Foreign*	Automobile Preference: *Domestic*	**Row Totals**	**Row Percentages**
Liberal	18 (12.79)	7 (12.23)	25	55.6%
Conservative	5 (10.21)	15 (9.77)	29	44.4%
Column Totals	23	22	$N = 45$	

tingency table to organize these data. Include f_o values, row and column totals, and row percentages. Also see if you can figure out how to determine f_e values.

Case	Gender	Color Preference
1	M	Red
2	M	Blue
3	F	Green
4	F	Red
5	M	Blue
6	F	Red
7	F	Red
8	M	Red
9	M	Blue
10	M	Green
11	M	Blue
12	F	Red
13	F	Blue
14	M	Green
15	M	Blue
16	F	Green
17	F	Red
18	F	Red
19	M	Blue
20	M	Blue

(Answer on p. 341.)

Computing Chi-Square

Expected Frequencies. We begin the χ^2 analysis by computing expected frequencies (f_e) for each cell of the contingency table. Expected frequencies are computed in the χ^2 test of association just as they are in the χ^2 test for two independent samples (Chapter 7). The expected frequency for each cell of the contingency table is found by multiplying that cell's corresponding column total by the cell's corresponding row percentage, expressed as a proportion. The data presented in Table 10.4 illustrate this process. For the liberal–foreign cell, $f_e = .556 \times 23 = 12.79$; for the conservative–domestic cell, $f_e = .444 \times 22 = 9.77$; and so on.

Expected frequencies indicate how many cases one would expect to see in each cell of the contingency table if the variables were unrelated. Therefore, any differences between expected frequencies and observed frequencies suggest that there is a relationship between the variables. The greater the discrepancy between the observed and expected frequencies across all the cells of the contingency table, the stronger is the relationship between the variables. On the other hand, in the absence of any relationship between the variables, observed and expected frequencies will be identical.

COMPREHENSION CHECK 10.26

Compute f_e values for each cell in the contingency table you constructed in Comprehension Check 10.25. Is there any indication of a relationship between gender and color preference?

(Answer on p. 341.)

Chi-Square. In each cell of the contingency table in which f_e and f_o differ we have evidence for a relationship between the variables. What we need is a way of accumulating or combining the f_o vs. f_e differences that appear throughout the contingency table. The χ^2 statistic provides this numerical index of the discrepancy between f_o and f_e across all the cells of the contingency table. The χ^2 statistic is computed using Equation 7.7 from Chapter 7.

COMPREHENSION CHECK 10.27

Use Equation 7.7 to compute and interpret χ^2 for the data in Table 10.4. Also compute and interpret χ^2 for the contingency table you constructed in Comprehension Check 10.25.
(Answer on p. 341.)

The Statistical Significance of χ^2

The same logic that we have examined for the Pearson and Spearman correlations applies as well to the significance test of χ^2. The null hypothesis claims that there is no relationship between the variables in the population; the sample χ^2 is greater than 0 only because of sampling error. The alternative hypothesis attributes the greater-than-zero χ^2 to a real relationship between the variables in the population from which the sample was drawn.

The test statistic, of course, is χ^2. We have seen that χ^2 grows larger as the relationship between nominal scale variables grows stronger.

We determine the probability that an obtained value of χ^2 would have occurred in a sample drawn from a population in which the variables being studied are unrelated by comparing the obtained χ^2 value to the sampling distribution of χ^2. Although this sampling distribution of chi-square is familiar to you from previous encounters, it won't hurt to consider it again in the context of the χ^2 test of association.

Imagine a population in which nominal scale variables X and Y are unrelated. Imagine drawing all possible samples of size N from that population and computing χ^2 for each sample. Finally, imagine plotting the frequency of occurrence of the varying values of χ^2 that you would see from one sample to the next. This is the sampling distribution of χ^2. The lowest possible value of χ^2 would be 0, obtained in samples in which $f_o = f_e$ for every cell of the contingency table. Larger and larger values of χ^2 would occur less and less frequently. Table 3 of Appendix B, "Critical values of chi-square," lists critical values of χ^2 that mark several critical regions of the sampling distribution of χ^2. Table 3 is entered according to the selected level of significance and degrees of freedom. For the χ^2 test of association, degrees of freedom are computed as $\text{df} = (R - 1)(C - 1)$, where R = the number of rows of the contingency table and C = the number of columns of the contingency table. An obtained χ^2 is significant at the selected level of significance if it meets or exceeds the tabled critical value.

COMPREHENSION CHECK 10.28

Evaluate the statistical significance of the χ^2 values you computed in Comprehension Check 10.27. What do these significance tests tell you?
(Answer on p. 341.)

Small Expected Frequencies and χ^2

We have seen previously (Chapters 6 and 7) that the χ^2 statistic is inflated by low values of f_e. This is a problem again with the χ^2 test of association.

Picture a 3 × 2 contingency table (3 rows and 2 columns). Suppose that in one cell of the table $f_o = 5$ and $f_e = 1$. Without knowing anything else about the data, we know that the χ^2 will be significant. For df $= (R - 1)(C - 1) = (3 - 1)(2 - 1) = 2$, the critical value of χ^2 at the .01 level of significance is 9.21. The contribution to χ^2 of the one known cell of the contingency table is $(f_o - f_e)^2/f_e = (5 - 1)^2/1 = 16$. The outcome of the χ^2 test has been determined by a discrepancy of only four cases between observed and expected frequencies in only one cell of the table. If this makes you uncomfortable, good! It should.

Because χ^2 is so strongly affected by small expected frequencies, it is recommended that the χ^2 test of association be used only when all expected frequencies in a 2 × 2 contingency table are at least 5. For larger tables, at least 80% of the cells should contain expected frequencies of at least 5, and no cell should contain an expected frequency of less than 1. When expected frequencies are too small, it is sometimes possible to combine or eliminate categories to obtain expected frequencies that are sufficiently large. Of course, we may also add data from more cases. As a third alternative, useful only with 2 × 2 contingency tables, χ^2 can be computed using Yates's correction as presented in Chapter 7 (Equation 7.8).

COMPREHENSION CHECK 10.29

> Why do we avoid small expected frequencies when using χ^2? What can we do when our f_e values are too small?
> (Answer on p. 341.)

Cramer's V Statistic

Although χ^2 reflects the strength of association between nominal scale variables, its value is also affected by sample size. As sample size increases, f_o and f_e values increase and χ^2 increases as well. The lowest possible value of χ^2 is always 0 and always means that there is no relationship between the variables. The upper limit of χ^2, however, depends on how large the sample is. This makes χ^2 a very inconvenient measure of relationship strength. More useful is Cramer's *V* statistic, described in Chapter 7 (Equation 7.10).

When the variables are unrelated, χ^2 will equal 0 and Cramer's *V* will also equal 0. When the relationship between the variables is perfect, such that one can predict perfectly a case's category membership on one nominal variable by knowing its membership on the other variable, Cramer's *V* will equal 1.

COMPREHENSION CHECK 10.30

> Use Equation 7.10 to compute and interpret Cramer's *V* for the χ^2 values you computed in Comprehension Check 10.27.
> (Answer on p. 341.)

Interpreting Relationships Between Nominal Scale Variables

Unlike the other correlational statistics we have studied, neither χ^2 nor Cramer's *V* can take on negative values. This makes sense if you stop to think about it. A positive correlation means that scores on *X* and *Y* increase and decrease together. A negative correlation means that scores on one variable increase as scores on the other variable decrease. When dealing with nominal scale variables, though, the terms "increase" and "decrease" are meaningless. Membership in one category of a nominal scale variable is not "greater" or "lesser" than membership in a different category. Therefore, two nominal scale variables may be correlated, but it would make no sense to say that they are "positively" or "negatively" correlated.

How then *does* one interpret a significant χ^2? A statistically significant χ^2 tells us that there is a reliable relationship between the variables, and Cramer's *V* gives us a measure of the strength of that relationship. Can we stop there? No. Interpreting a significant relationship between nominal variables requires that one describe the nature of that relationship. In Table 10.4, for instance, not only are political inclination and automobile preference related, we can describe that relationship: Political liberals tend to prefer foreign automobiles, whereas political conservatives tend to prefer domestic automobiles.

In general, the analysis and interpretation of correlations involving nominal scale variables involves three components. First, we evaluate the significance (reliability) of the relationship with the χ^2 statistic. Second, we assess the strength of the relationship with Cramer's *V*. Third, we interpret the relationship by describing which categories of the first variable go with which categories of the second variable. When dealing with multicategory nominal scale variables and the large contingency tables that these variables produce, this last step can be most trying.

COMPREHENSION CHECK 10.31

Interpret the nature of the relationship between age and political inclination depicted in the contingency table below.

Political orientation	Age: *Young*	Age: *Old*
Liberal	$f_o = 15$	$f_o = 5$
Conservative	$f_o = 3$	$f_o = 10$

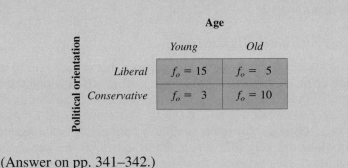

(Answer on pp. 341–342.)

EXAMPLE 10.3

The Chi-Square Test of Association and Cramer's *V*

Researchers at the marketing firm of Connum, Duppum, and Lie are curious to know if there is any relationship between age and cola preference. Knowing this will help them better target their advertisements to the appropriate audiences. They have gathered data pertaining to age and cola preference from a sample of $N = 67$ consumers as summarized in the contingency table that follows. Shown in this table are observed and expected frequencies (in parentheses), row and column totals, and row percentages.

		Preferred Cola				
		Burpee	*Same Ol' Sludge*	*Old Brown*	**Row Totals**	**Row Percentages**
Age	*12–20 years*	15 (6.48)	5 (10.08)	4 (7.56)	24	36%
	21–40 years	2 (4.50)	3 (7.00)	12 (5.25)	17	25%
	41 and older	1 (7.02)	20 (10.92)	5 (8.19)	26	39%
	Column Totals	18	28	21	$N = 67$	

Expected frequencies (f_e) that appear in each cell of the contingency table represent the number of cases that would be expected in that cell if there were no relationship between the variables. Each is obtained by multiplying a cell's corresponding column total by the cell's corresponding row percentage, expressed as a proportion.

The chi-square statistic is computed according to Equation 7.7.

$$\chi^2 = \Sigma\frac{(f_o - f_e)^2}{f_e}$$

$$= \frac{(15 - 6.48)^2}{6.48} + \frac{(5 - 10.08)^2}{10.08} + \cdots + \frac{(5 - 8.19)^2}{8.19}$$

$$= 41.75$$

The fact that this χ^2 value is greater than zero tells us that there is a relationship between age and cola preference in the sample. We must now evaluate this relationship for significance, assess its strength, and interpret the nature of the relationship.

Null and Alternative Hypotheses

H_0: The greater-than-zero χ^2 obtained from this sample can be attributed to sampling error. A sample drawn from a population in which the variables are unrelated would be likely to display a χ^2 value as large as this one.

H_1: The χ^2 obtained from this sample is unlikely to be the result of sampling error. It is unlikely that a population in which the variables are unrelated would produce a sample showing a χ^2 this large. It is more likely that the variables are related in the population.

Test Statistic

The χ^2 statistic serves as the test statistic in the test of association between nominal scale variables. Chi-square varies in value as a function of the strength of the relationship being tested for significance.

The Sampling Distribution of χ^2

In order to choose between H_0 and H_1, we compare the obtained value of $\chi^2 = 41.75$ against the sampling distribution of χ^2 for df $= (R - 1)\,(C - 1)$

$= (3 - 1)(3 - 1) = 4$. The general shape of this sampling distribution is shown below. Critical values of χ^2 are found in Table 3 of Appendix B, "Critical values of χ^2."

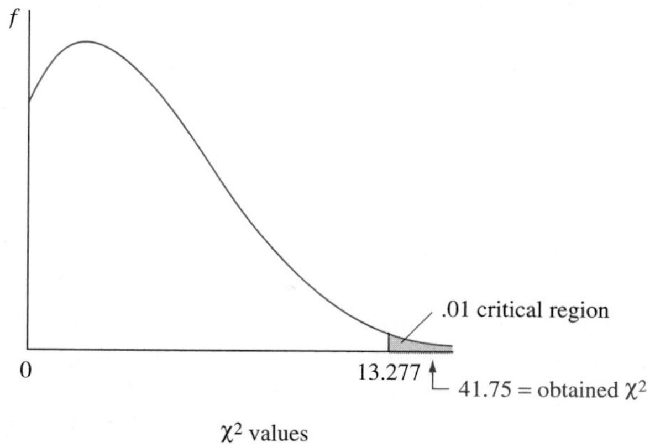

Choosing Between H_0 *and* H_1

The obtained value of $\chi^2 = 41.75$ falls well within the .01 critical region. It is unlikely that such a large χ^2 would be produced by a sample coming from a population in which the variables are unrelated. It is more likely, then, that the variables *are* related in the population. We reject the null hypothesis and declare the relationship between age and cola preference to be statistically significant.

Cramer's V

Next we assess the strength of the relationship using Cramer's *V*, computed according to Equation 7.10.

$$V = \sqrt{\frac{\chi^2}{N(n-1)}}$$

$$= \sqrt{\frac{41.75}{67(3-1)}}$$

$$= .56$$

Since V can range from 0 to 1, a value of $V = .56$ represents a moderately strong relationship.

Interpreting the Relationship

Finally, we must interpret the nature of the relationship between age and cola preference by looking at the pattern of observed frequencies in the contingency table. It appears that the youngest consumers prefer Burpee Cola, the oldest prefer Same Ol' Sludge, and those of intermediate age prefer Old Brown.

10.5 Correlation and Causation

Students who are beginning their study in the social and behavioral sciences are routinely warned against inferring causation from correlation: A correlation between variables does not necessarily mean that the variables are causally related. A classic illustration of this principle is the positive correlation between the amount of ice cream consumed and the number of drownings during the same time period. Although the two are correlated, eating ice cream certainly does not cause drowning, nor do drownings cause increased consumption of ice cream. Rather, the correlation is the result of a causal chain involving other variables: Warm weather causes people both to eat ice cream and go swimming, and it is the swimming that results in drownings. There are many other examples of correlations that do not support causal conclusions. Say a researcher found that smokers caught more colds in a year's time than nonsmokers. Does this correlation support the conclusion that smoking causes colds? Of course not. Maybe smokers make more trips to the store to buy tobacco, thereby exposing themselves to more cold viruses. Or perhaps stress causes people to smoke and also inhibits the action of the immune system, leading to colds. There are a multitude of possible explanations of the correlation, none of which involves a direct causal link between smoking and colds. The important point is that we cannot automatically conclude that two variables are causally linked just because they are correlated.

At the same time, it would be wrong to think that we can *never* draw causal conclusions from correlations. Clearly, if two variables are causally linked, they will be correlated. How, then, can we determine if a correlation does or does not support a causal conclusion?

Drawing causal conclusions depends not on how research data are analyzed, with correlations or other statistics, but on how the data are gathered. Causal connections are established by conducting experiments. Recall from Chapter 1 that in an experiment, one variable (the independent variable) is manipulated by the researcher, and a second variable (the dependent variable) is measured subsequent to this manipulation. If our manipulations of the independent variable are accompanied by subsequent variation in the dependent variable, we are justified in concluding that the two are causally linked. And what do we call it when two variables vary together? That's right, a correlation. In sum, when we have manipulated one variable (X), measured a second variable (Y) subsequent to that manipulation, and found a correlation between X and Y, we can conclude that X exerted a causal influence on Y.

Under what circumstances can we *not* draw causal conclusions from correlations? The short answer is, under any other circumstances. If the researcher has not *actively manipulated* the independent variable and/or if the dependent variable is not measured *subsequent* to that manipulation, a correlation cannot support a causal interpretation.

By tradition, most experiments aimed at establishing causal links between variables use significant difference tests in data analysis, not correlations. For example, one randomly selected group of depressed patients is administered a placebo and a second randomly selected group is given a daily dosage of 150 milligrams of an experimental drug. After a suitable period of time has elapsed, the two groups' levels of depression (the dependent variable) are measured in some fashion and are compared, perhaps with a t test. If the group means differ significantly, the difference can be causally attributed to the experimental drug. However, a correlation might just as easily have been used to establish this causal connection. If different patients were randomly assigned by the researcher to receive different drug dosages (X) and their levels of depression were subsequently measured (Y), a correlation between drug dosage and depression would indicate a causal connection between the drug and depression.

The key to drawing causal conclusions lies in how the data are collected, not in what statistical method is used to analyze those data. It is only through tradition that significant difference tests, rather than correlations, have become the standard method for analyzing data gathered in experiments.

> Explain when a correlation *can* and when it *cannot* be used to establish a causal connection between two variables.
> (Answer on p. 342.)

COMPREHENSION CHECK 10.32

10.6 STATISTICAL VS. PRACTICAL SIGNIFICANCE OF CORRELATIONS

The distinction between statistical and practical significance has been a recurring theme in earlier chapters. We have seen that small differences that are unimportant in any practical sense can be found to be statistically significant if samples are sufficiently large. Similarly, very small, unimportant correlations can be statistically significant if they are based on large enough sample sizes.

Very small values of Pearson's r_P, Spearman's r_S, and χ^2 will all yield statistical significance given sufficiently large sample sizes. Take a look at Table 8 of Appendix B, "Critical values of the Pearson product-moment correlation." Given a sample of size $N = 102$ (so that df $= 100$), a correlation as low as .1638 becomes statistically significant. Though statistically significant, there aren't many situations in which a relationship this weak would be thought of as important. Table 9 of Appendix B, "Critical values of the Spearman rank-order correlation," also shows that as N increases, the critical value of r_S decreases. As for the chi-square statistic, as N increases, the value of χ^2 itself increases, making it more likely that the χ^2 will meet or exceed the tabled critical value.

There is no substitute for common sense in evaluating the practical significance of correlations. Perhaps the most critical test of any correlation is this: To what degree does this correlation enhance our ability to accurately predict scores on one variable given scores on the other variable? It is to this extension of correlation that we will turn in the next chapter.

> Explain why even weak correlations (r_P, r_S, and χ^2) will achieve statistical significance when based on large samples.
> (Answer on p. 342.)

COMPREHENSION CHECK 10.33

SUMMARY

Three correlational procedures are described in this chapter: Pearson product-moment correlation, Spearman rank-order correlation, and the chi-square test of association. All correlations look at relationships between variables, but differ according to the kinds of data to which they are most suited.

Interpreting correlations is often facilitated by the use of graphs called scatterplots. Scatterplots can alert one to a variety of circumstances that can cause computed correlations to be misleading.

Although correlations do not always support causal conclusions concerning variables, causal connections will be reflected in correlations. In general, if one variable (X) is manipulated by an experimenter, a second variable (Y) is subsequently measured, and X and Y are found to be correlated, this correlation will support the conclusion that X has a causal effect on Y.

When sample sizes are large, even weak correlations will be found to be statistically significant. There is no substitute for common sense in interpreting the practical significance of a correlation.

NOTES

1. The Pearson correlation may also be used to assess the relationship between one interval or ratio scale variable and a second, dichotomously scored nominal scale variable (i.e., scores are all 0 or 1).This correlation is commonly called a point-biserial correlation, but it is computed using the Pearson formula given in Equation 10.1 or the computational formula given in Note 2 below. Alternatively, the point-biserial correlation may be computed more conveniently using the following computational formula:

$$r_{pb} = \frac{\overline{X}_0 - \overline{X}_1}{s_X}\sqrt{pq}$$

where

pb = the point-biserial correlation
$\overline{X}_0$ = the mean on the continuous variable X of cases scored 0 on the dichotomous variable Y
$\overline{X}_1$ = the mean on the continuous variable X of cases scored 1 on the dichotomous variable Y
s_X = the standard deviation of the continuous variable X for all cases
p = the proportion of cases scoring 0 on the dichotomous variable Y
q = the proportion of cases scoring 1 on the dichotomous variable Y

The statistical significance of the point-biserial is evaluated in exactly the same manner as the Pearson correlation.

2. The Pearson correlation may be computed more conveniently using the following computational formula:

$$r_P = \frac{N\Sigma XY - (\Sigma X)(\Sigma Y)}{\sqrt{[N\Sigma X^2 - (\Sigma X)^2][N\Sigma Y^2 - (\Sigma Y)^2]}}$$

where

N = the total number of cases in the analysis
X = scores on the variable X
Y = scores on the variable Y

3. The t statistic is often computed from r to serve as a test statistic for the significance of r with df = $N - 2$:

$$t = \frac{r\sqrt{N - 2}}{\sqrt{1 - r^2}}$$

where

r = the correlation being tested for significance
N = the total number of cases in the analysis

4. Notice in Table 8 in Appendix B that not all degrees of freedom values are listed. Values of df jump from 20 to 25, 25 to 30, and so on. If the correct degrees of freedom value for a particular situation is not listed in the table, the recommended practice is to use the next lower value that is listed. For instance, if $N = 48$ so that df $= N - 2 = 48 - 2 = 46$, one would use the next lower listed value: df = 45.
5. The Spearman rank-order correlation may also be computed by applying the Pearson product-moment correlation (Equation 10.1) directly to the ranks. When there are no tied ranks, these two computational approaches produce identical results. When there are ties, the value of r_S produced using Equation 10.2 will tend to be spuriously high, and it is actually preferable to use the Pearson correlation formula.
6. When N is large, critical values of r_P and r_S are identical. The t statistic may also be used in testing the significance of the Spearman rank-order correlation, substituting r_S for r in the equation given in Note 3.

Review Exercises

10.1. For each of the research problems described below, select the most appropriate correlational statistic.
(a) An industrial/organizational psychologist studying mid-level managers believes that the relationship between IQ and managerial performance is nonlinear. At lower IQ levels, even small increases in IQ translate into improved performance. At higher IQ levels, however, even large increases in IQ do not have much effect on performance. How can this relationship between IQ and performance be measured?
(b) How might a sociologist evaluate the relationship between geographical region and political preference?
(c) A social worker wants to measure the correlation between annual family income and scores on a test of parenting effectiveness. What statistic would be most useful?

10.2. Shown below are Graduate Record Examination (GRE) scores (X) and graduate grade-point averages (GPA) (Y) for 10 psychology graduate students. Construct a scatterplot and describe the relationship between these variables.

X *GRE*	*Y* *Graduate GPA*
1,020	3.74
940	3.25
1,120	3.94
1,070	3.94
1,280	3.76
1,070	3.71
1,150	3.81
990	3.67
1,240	3.53
1,100	3.67

10.3. Compute r_P between the GRE and graduate GPA scores given in Review Exercise 10.2 and interpret this statistic.

10.4. Listed below are IQ scores (X) and undergraduate grade-point averages (GPA) (Y) for 10 students. Compute r_P for: (a) all the cases; and (b) for just cases whose IQs are 110 or higher. Why is the second correlation lower than the first?

X *IQ*	*Y* *GPA*
90	2.0
90	3.0
100	2.5
100	3.0
100	3.5
110	3.0

(cont.)

X	*Y*
IQ	*GPA*
110	4.0
115	3.5
120	3.5
120	4.0

10.5. Shown below are scores on age (*X*) and income (*Y*). Identify the outlier and describe its effect on the correlation between age and income.

X	*Y*
Age	*Income*
21	$14,000
28	$38,000
32	$35,000
47	$27,000
55	$45,000
63	$56,000

10.6. Evaluate the statistical significance of the correlations you computed between: (a) GRE and graduate GPA (Review Exercise 10.3); (b) IQ and undergraduate GPA (Review Exercise 10.4); and (c) age and income (Review Exercise 10.5).

10.7. Use the data on GRE and graduate GPA in Review Exercise 10.2 to compute the Spearman rank-order correlation.

10.8. Evaluate the statistical significance of r_S computed in Review Exercise 10.7.

10.9. Shown below is a contingency table that summarizes data on marital status and academic major of 74 students. Use χ^2 to evaluate the statistical significance of the relationship between these variables.

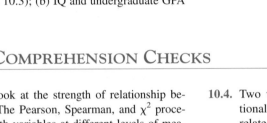

Marital Status

Major	*Single*	*Married*	*Divorced*
Sociology	8	6	12
Psychology	14	10	8
Social work	4	6	6

10.10. Use Cramer's *V* to measure the strength of the relationship between marital status and academic major (Review Exercise 10.9).

Answers to Comprehension Checks

10.1. All correlations look at the strength of relationship between variables. The Pearson, Spearman, and χ^2 procedures are used with variables at different levels of measurement: Pearson for interval or ratio, Spearman for ordinal, χ^2 for nominal.

10.2. The Pearson correlation requires scores on two variables from each of *N* cases. The variables are assumed to be normally distributed and measured at the interval or ratio scale. The Pearson correlation measures the strength of the linear relationship between the variables, that is, the degree to which cases' locations on *X* "agree," either directly or inversely, with their locations on *Y*.

10.3.

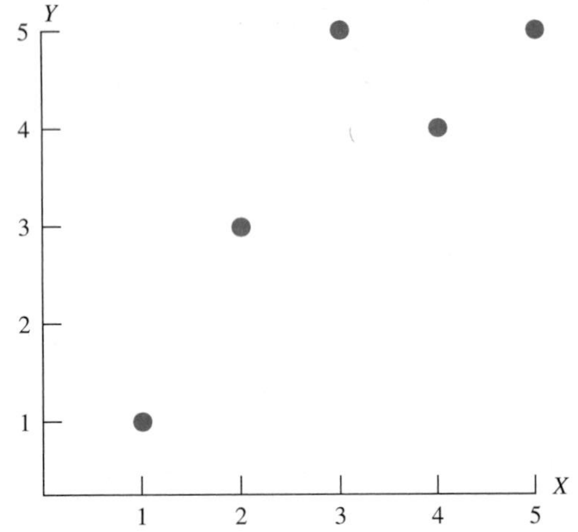

10.4. Two variables that are positively correlated are educational achievement and income level. Two negatively correlated variables are age and reaction time. A positive correlation means that low scores on *X* are associated with low scores on *Y* and high scores on *X* are associated with high scores on *Y*. A negative correlation means that low scores on *X* are associated with high scores on *Y* and high scores on *X* are associated with low scores on *Y*.

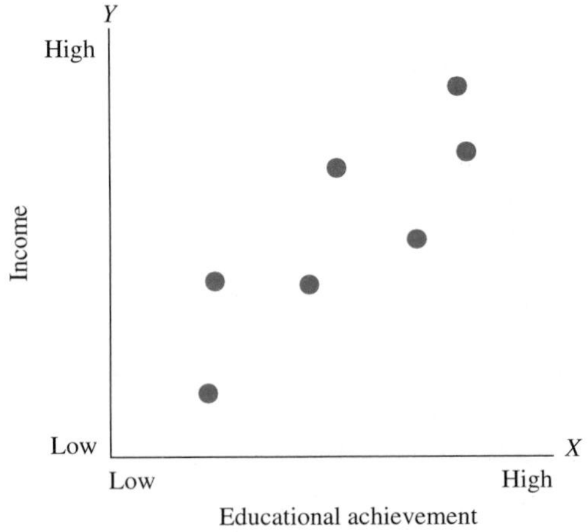

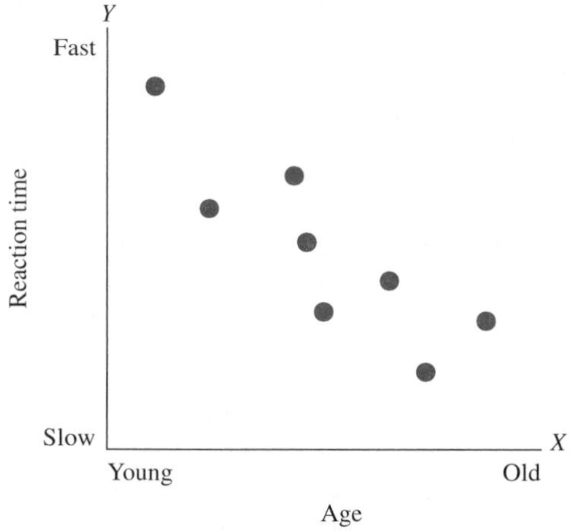

10.5.

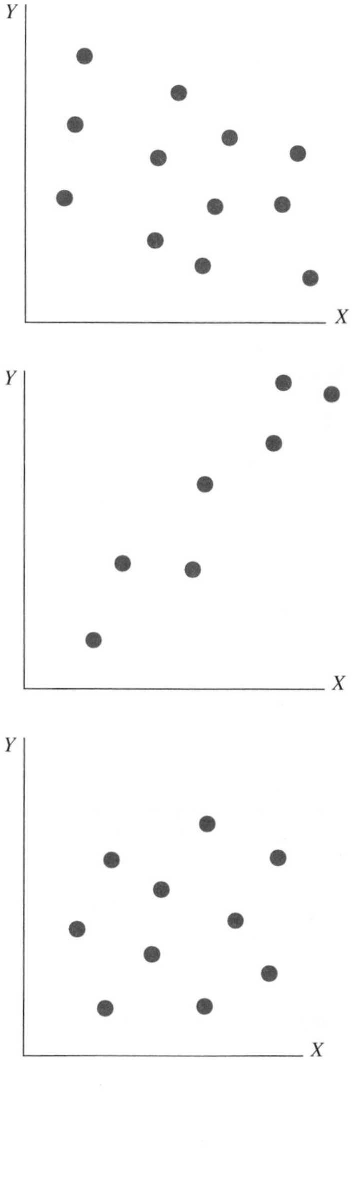

10.6. In vertical and horizontal scatterplots, the cases cannot show agreement in their locations on the two variables because cases are always located in one place on one variable and in different places on the other variable.

10.7. Two variables that show a nonlinear relationship are aspirin dosage and subsequent pain. As aspirin dosage increases, there is a diminishing return on pain reduction.

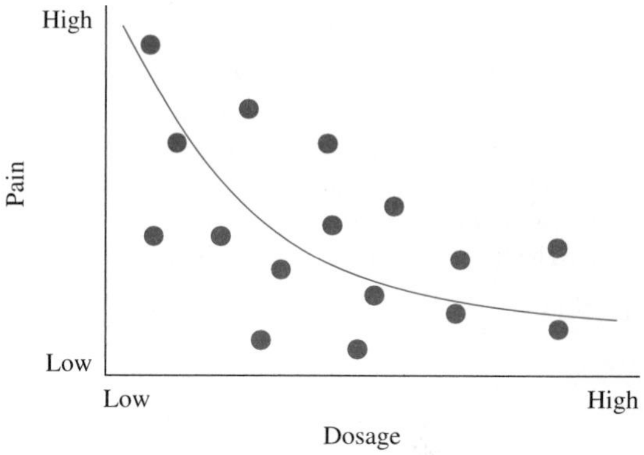

10.8. In a heteroscedastic relationship, any statement about the strength of the relationship must be qualified by specifying the range of variables being considered.

10.9. An outlier in a correlational analysis is a case whose conjoint values on X and Y make that case deviant from the majority. Outliers are important because (1) they sometimes indicate data entry errors; (2) they are "exceptions to the rule"; and (3) they exert a disproportionate effect on the computed correlation.

10.10. Equation 10.1 defines r_P as

$$r_P = \frac{\Sigma z_X z_Y}{N}$$

For the data given,

X	z_X	Y	z_Y
1	−1.42	1	−1.73
4	.71	4	.27
2	−.71	3	−.40
3	0	5	.93
5	1.42	5	.93

Therefore we compute r_P as

$$\frac{(-1.42 \times -1.73) + \cdots + (1.42 \times .93)}{5}$$

$$= .85$$

10.11. The first data set represents a positive correlation, as shown by the fact that most of the cross-products of z_X and z_Y are positive. The second set represents a negative correlation, as shown by the fact that most of the cross-products are negative. The second correlation is stronger, because these cross-products are more strongly negative than the first cross-products are positive.

10.12. The Pearson correlation indicates the direction and strength of the linear relationship.

10.13. One example would be the study of the correlation between age and mood in a retirement home. Restricting range reduces correlations because the correlation is a measure of how strongly two variables covary. If the variables are not free to vary fully, they cannot *co*vary fully.

10.14. Even in most nonlinear relationships, a line *can* be fitted through the points of the scatterplot, so these relationships have a linear component. They are nonlinear because a curve fits *better* than a line.

10.15. Outliers always show extreme cross-products of z_X and z_Y. The last case is the outlier, as shown by its negative cross-product. All the other cross-products are positive.

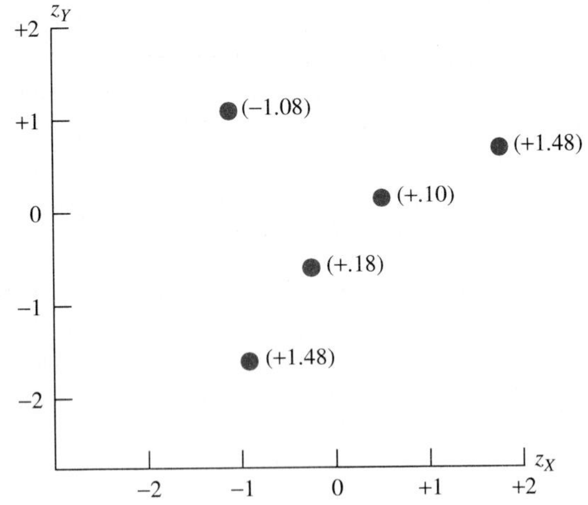

10.16. The significance test of a correlation determines the probability that a population in which the correlation is zero would produce a sample having a correlation of the observed size. A significant correlation is one that would be unlikely to occur if the population correlation was zero. Therefore, a significant correlation indicates that the population correlation is greater than zero (in absolute terms). It follows that a replication would probably produce another sample with an above-zero correlation. A nonsignificant sample correlation is one that would likely occur even in a population in which the correlation is zero.

10.17. The null hypothesis attributes the sample correlation to sampling error. The alternative hypothesis attributes the sample correlation to an above-zero correlation in the population.

10.18. When groups show a significant difference, it really means that there is a significant correlation between the independent variable that defines group membership and scores on the dependent variable.

10.19. A correlation of $r_P = .70$ would be most likely to be statistically significant in a sampling distribution based on large samples.

10.20. When the direction of the correlation is not predicted in advance of data collection, the two-tail significance test is most appropriate. This is because the researcher is interested in either positive or negative correlations.

10.21. For $N = 90$, $\text{df} = N - 2 = 88$. Since Table 8 in Appendix B does not list 88 degrees of freedom, we use the next smaller listing, df = 80. The critical value of r_P for the one-tail test at the .01 significance level is .2565.

10.22. The Pearson and Spearman correlations both measure agreement between cases' scores on *X* and *Y* on a scale of −1 to 0 to +1. The Pearson uses scores at the interval or ratio level, and the Spearman assesses agreement between cases' rank orders on the variables.

10.23. Equation 10.2 defines r_S as

$$r_S = 1 - \frac{6\Sigma D^2}{N(N^2 - 1)}$$

We begin by rank-ordering scores on *X* and *Y*, computing differences between corresponding ranks (*D*), and squaring those differences (D^2).

X	Rank on *X*	*Y*	Rank on *Y*	D^2
38	5	19	5	0
35	4	10	1.5	6.25
40	6	24	6	0
30	1.5	17	4	6.25
30	1.5	10	1.5	0
33	3	13	3	0

Then, we compute r_S as

$$1 - \frac{6(0 + 6.25 + 0 + \cdots + 0)}{6(36 - 1)}$$

$$= 1 - .36 = .64$$

10.24. The Spearman correlation provides a better measure of nonlinear monotonic relationships because it correlates ranks rather than original scores. When the variables are rank-ordered, the shape of the relationship is transformed from nonlinear monotonic to linear.

10.25.

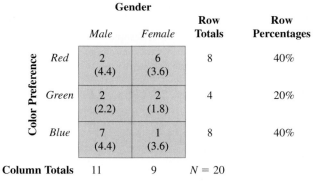

Color Preference	Gender: *Male*	*Female*	Row Totals	Row Percentages
Red	2 (4.4)	6 (3.6)	8	40%
Green	2 (2.2)	2 (1.8)	4	20%
Blue	7 (4.4)	1 (3.6)	8	40%
Column Totals	11	9	$N = 20$	

10.26. Expected frequencies are computed for each cell by multiplying each cell's corresponding column total by that cell's corresponding row percentage (proportion) as follows:

$$f_e \text{ (first cell)} = .40 \times 11 = 4.4$$

$$f_e \text{ (second cell)} = .40 \times 9 = 3.6$$

$$f_e \text{ (third cell)} = .20 \times 11 = 2.2$$

.
.
.

$$f_e \text{ (last cell)} = .40 \times 9 = 3.6$$

There are differences between f_o and f_e in every cell. Because f_e is the number of cases that we would expect if the variables were unrelated, these discrepancies give evidence for some relationship between the variables.

10.27. Equation 7.7 defines χ^2 as

$$\chi^2 = \Sigma\frac{(f_o - f_e)^2}{f_e}$$

For the data provided in Table 10.4, we compute χ^2 as

$$\chi^2 = \frac{(18 - 12.79)^2}{12.79} + \cdots + \frac{(15 - 9.77)^2}{9.77}$$
$$= 9.82$$

For the contingency table in Comprehension Check 10.25,

$$\chi^2 = \frac{(2 - 4.4)^2}{4.4} + \cdots + \frac{(1 - 3.6)^2}{3.6}$$
$$= 6.36$$

Both χ^2 values are greater than zero, indicating some relationship between the variables under consideration.

10.28. For the first χ^2, df $= (R - 1)(C - 1) = (2 - 1)(2 - 1) = 1$. The obtained value of $\chi^2 = 9.82$ exceeds the critical value of χ^2 at the .01 level of significance. The obtained χ^2 value has a probability of less than .01 of occurring in a sample drawn from a population in which the variables are unrelated. It is much more likely, then, that the sample χ^2 results from the variables being related in the population.

For the second χ^2, df $= (R - 1)(C - 1) = (3 - 1)(2 - 1) = 2$. The obtained value of $\chi^2 = 6.36$ exceeds the critical value of χ^2 at the .05 level of significance. This χ^2 value has a probability of less than .05 of occurring in a sample drawn from a population in which the variables are unrelated. It is much more likely, then, that the sample χ^2 results from the variables being related in the population.

10.29. Small expected frequencies have an inflating effect on χ^2. When f_e is small, a small difference between f_o and f_e can produce a significant χ^2. When faced with small f_e values, one can: (1) combine or eliminate some of the categories; (2) increase the sample size; or (3) for 2 × 2 contingency tables only, compute χ^2 using Yates's correction.

10.30. Equation 7.10 defines Cramer's V as

$$V = \sqrt{\frac{\chi^2}{N(n - 1)}}$$

For the first χ^2, $\chi^2 = 9.82$, $N = 45$, $n = 2$. Therefore we can compute V as

$$V = \sqrt{\frac{9.82}{45(2 - 1)}}$$
$$= .47$$

Because V can range from 0 to 1, $V = .47$ represents a moderately strong relationship.

For the second χ^2, $\chi^2 = 6.36$, $N = 20$, $n = 2$. Therefore we can compute V as

$$V = \sqrt{\frac{6.36}{20(2 - 1)}}$$
$$= .56$$

Because V can range from 0 to 1, $V = .56$ again represents a moderately strong relationship.

10.31. We interpret the relationship between nominal scale variables by examining the distribution of cases (observed frequencies) in the contingency table. It appears that the relationship between age and political inclination is such that younger people tend to be politically liberal, whereas older people tend to be politically conservative.

10.32. A correlation does indicate a causal relationship when it is computed between one variable (*X*) that has been manipulated in an experiment and a second variable (*Y*) that was subsequently measured. A correlation does not necessarily indicate a causal relationship if *X* has not been actively manipulated by the experimenter and/or if *Y* was not measured subsequent to the manipulation of *X*.

10.33. As sample sizes increase, critical values of r_P and r_S become smaller and smaller, meaning that even a small sample value can be identified as statistically significant. As sample sizes increase, sample values of χ^2 are increased, making it easier for the sample value to meet or exceed the table critical value of χ^2.

11 REGRESSION

Chapter Outline

A fundamental goal of science is to identify reliable relationships between variables. The chemist wants to know how the rate of a chemical reaction varies with heat. The meteorologist seeks to explain weather patterns in terms of pressure systems. The geologist tries to identify reliable relationships between geologic formations and the locations of oil deposits.

Social and behavioral scientists also seek to identify reliable relationships between variables. A sociologist examines the relationship between crime rate and cost of living. A social worker looks for a link between occupational stress and domestic violence. And a psychologist identifies a correlation between achievement motivation and performance in retail sales.

Once relationships between variables are established, scientists can pursue a second goal: prediction. Chemists try to predict chemical reactivity, meteorologists try to predict the weather, and geologists try to predict the locations of oil deposits. These predictions are all made possible by the previous discovery of regular trends and reliable relationships.

Prediction is also important in the social and behavioral sciences. Just as in the other sciences, our predictions are based on previously identified relationships between variables. The sociologist who discovers a significant correlation between crime rate and cost of living is positioned to predict the crime rate of any given locale, given its cost of living. The social worker who knows how occupational stress and domestic violence correlate is able to predict which families are most likely to experience violence, given information about stress. The psychologist who finds a significant correlation between achievement motivation and sales performance can predict the performance of applicants for a sales position, given their scores on a test of achievement motivation. In short, in any science, establishing that two variables are correlated sets the stage for predicting one variable from the other.

bivariate regression analysis *A statistical procedure that uses the correlation between two variables,* X *and* Y, *as the basis for predicting values on one variable from values on the second variable.*

Predicting one variable from another on the basis of the Pearson product-moment correlation between the two variables is known as **bivariate regression analysis.** Based as it is on the Pearson correlation, bivariate regression analysis is used appropriately with any data that meet the requirements of the Pearson correlation. Regression analysis is a tool that enables us to predict the future based on our observations of the past. You can think of regression analysis as statistical fortune telling.

The concepts and mechanics of bivariate regression analysis are discussed in this chapter. A complete example of this method is provided in Example 11.1 at the end of the chapter.

COMPREHENSION CHECK 11.1

List some examples of variables that are related but do *not* lend themselves to bivariate regression analysis.

(Answer on p. 366.)

11.1 THE SCATTERPLOT AND REGRESSION LINE

You learned in Chapter 10 that the scatterplot is useful in depicting the correlation between two variables. Since correlation is the necessary precondition for regression analysis, it should come as no surprise that the scatterplot can help us to understand regression.

Look at Figure 11.1a, a scatterplot that depicts the correlation between shoe size and feetal anxiety that we studied in Chapter 10.(See Note 1) Notice in particular the line that has been fitted through the scatterplot. You learned in Chapter 10 that the amount of scattering of points around this line reflects the strength of the correlation and that the slope of the line reflects the direction of the correlation. But we have never named this line, and it is time now to do that. The line is called the **regression line,** and it summarizes the linear relationship between X and Y.

regression line *A line fitted through the points of a scatterplot that summarizes and describes the relationship between the variables.*

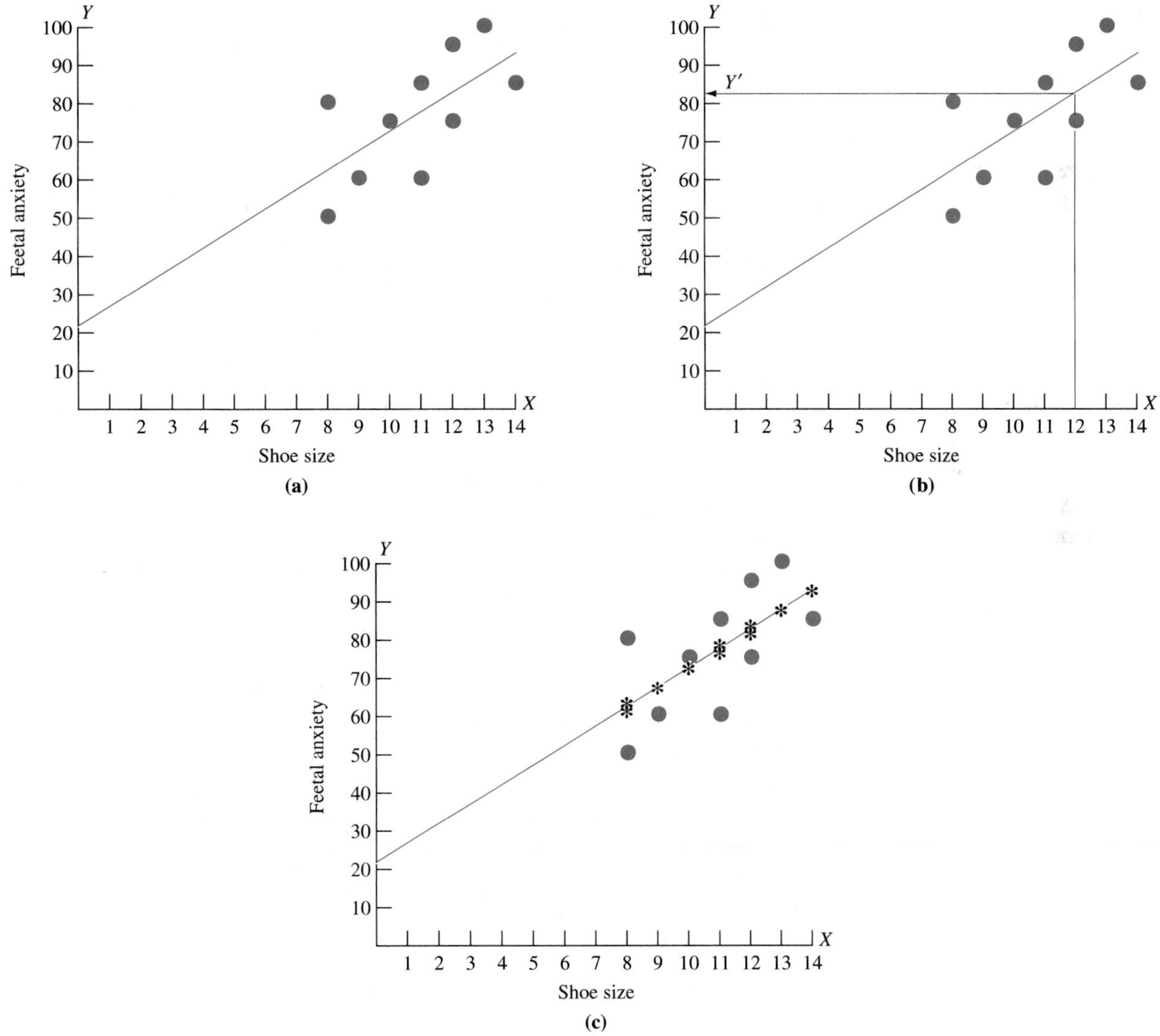

FIGURE 11.1

(a) shows the regression line for predicting feetal anxiety (Y) from shoe size (X). (b) shows how this line is used in predicting Y from X. (c) shows, as asterisks, predicted values of Y for each case. These points define the regression line.

The scatterplot and the correlation tell us that X and Y *are* related; the regression line tells us *how* they are related. The regression line summarizes and describes the relationship between X and Y in a way that enables us to predict Y from X.(See Note 2)

COMPREHENSION CHECK 11.2

Considering only the regression line in Figure 11.1a, try to describe the relationship between shoe size and feetal anxiety.
(Answer on p. 366.)

We'll consider later how the regression line is best fitted through a scatterplot; here let's just focus on how it is used in making predictions. Look at Figure 11.1b and suppose that we are trying to predict feetal anxiety for someone who wears a size 12 shoe. First, find the shoe size of 12 on the X axis. Next, draw a vertical line from this point up to the regression line. Finally, draw a horizontal line from the regression line to the Y axis. The value at which this line intersects the Y axis, about 83 in this example, is called Y' (pronounced "Y prime") and is the predicted value of Y when $X = 12$. We use the Y' symbol to distinguish between predicted and obtained values of Y: Y' values are predicted; Y refers to values that were actually obtained.

COMPREHENSION CHECK 11.3

Use Figure 11.1b to determine the predicted value of feetal anxiety for someone with a shoe size of 10.
(Answer on p. 366.)

The mechanics of using the regression line to predict Y from X are simple enough once the line has been fitted through the scatterplot. But it isn't always easy to see where the line should be placed. Fitting the regression line by eye is imprecise at best, especially when the correlation is low and the scatterplot points are very scattered. Identifying predicted values of Y by eye is also a rather sloppy process that is limited by the accuracy of one's diagram and the keenness of one's eyes. Fortunately, regression analysis is not normally accomplished with graphs, but with a mathematical equation that gives us the extra precision we are looking for.

COMPREHENSION CHECK 11.4

Shown below are scores of six statistics students on the first and final exams. Draw a scatterplot for these data. (Make a fairly large diagram—you will be using it again later.) Try to fit a regression line by eye. What two decisions must you make as you decide where the line should be placed?

X (first exam)	*Y* (final exam)
90	93
80	61
86	73
60	73
78	85
95	80

(Answer on p. 366.)

11.2 The Linear Regression Equation

The equation that defines the regression line, called the **least-squares linear regression equation,** is shown as Equation 11.1.(See Note 3)

Equation 11.1

$$Y' = a + b_Y X$$

where

Y' = the predicted values of Y
a = the regression constant (see Equation 11.3)
b_Y = the regression coefficient (see Equation 11.2)

least-squares linear regression equation *The equation that defines the regression line in a way that meets the least-squares criterion—minimizing the sum of the squared errors of prediction.*

In words, the predicted value of the variable Y (Y') for any given value of the variable X is computed by: (1) multiplying X by the regression coefficient (b_Y); and (2) adding the regression constant (a) to this product. The meaning and computation of the regression coefficient and regression constant are discussed below.

Equation 11.1 is called the *linear* regression equation because it defines the *line* that best fits the scatterplot. It is called the *least-squares* linear regression equation because the line that it describes is fitted so as to *minimize* the *squared* errors of prediction. In simple language, Equation 11.1 predicts Y from X based on the linear relationship between X and Y and does so in a way that minimizes prediction errors.

Comprehension Check 11.5

Why would the following data be poorly suited to regression analysis?

X	Y
1	1
4	3
5	1
2	3
3	5

(Answer on p. 367.)

You can see from Equation 11.1 that as X varies from one case to the next, Y' varies as well.(See Note 4) This is illustrated in Table 11.1, which lists shoe sizes (X), feetal anxiety scores (Y), and predicted feetal anxiety scores (Y') for the 10 cases depicted in Figure 11.1. As the value of X varies from one case to the next, Y' varies as well. Plot an asterisk in Figure 11.1c for each pair of X and Y' values listed in Table 11.1. You will see that these points form a line through the scatterplot. This is the regression line. And this is the sense in which we say that Equation 11.1 "defines the regression line" and "describes the relationship between X and Y." Given values of X, Equation 11.1 generates corresponding values of Y' that form the regression line.

TABLE 11.1

Shoe sizes (X), feetal anxiety scores (Y), and predicted feetal anxiety scores (Y') for 10 psychopodiatric patients

Shoe Size X	Feetal Anxiety Y	Predicted Feetal Anxiety Y'
14	85	92.93
13	100	87.79
11	85	77.53
10	75	72.39
9	60	67.26
12	75	82.66
8	80	62.13
12	95	82.66
8	50	62.13
11	60	77.53

COMPREHENSION CHECK 11.6

For the data presented in Comprehension Check 11.4, $a = 51.42$ and $b_Y = .32$. Use these values and Equation 11.1 to compute Y' for each of the 6 cases and plot these predicted values in your scatterplot. How close is this line to the one you place by eye in Comprehension Check 11.4?
(Answer on p. 367.)

Looking at Equation 11.1, you can see that the regression constant (a) and regression coefficient (b_Y) do all the work. Once values of a and b_Y have been determined, any desired value of X can be substituted into Equation 11.1 to determine the Y' that corresponds to that value of X. Let's look more closely at these two work horses of the regression equation.

The Regression Coefficient

Positioning the regression line in a scatterplot requires making two decisions, as illustrated in Figure 11.2. First, what slope should the regression line take (Figure 11.2a)? Should it slant upward, with a positive slope, or downward, with a negative slope? How steep a slope should the line take? Second, once the slope of the line has been determined, what altitude should the regression line take (Figure 11.2b)? Should it be located toward the top of the scatterplot, more toward the middle, or farther down?

regression coefficient (b_Y) *A component of the least-squares linear regression equation that determines the slope of the regression line. This value specifies the amount of change in Y′ for each 1-point increase in X.*

The slope of the regression line is set in the regression equation by b_Y, the **regression coefficient.** The regression coefficient sets the slope of the line by dictating how much change will occur in Y' for each 1-point change in X. If b_Y is positive, it indicates how much Y' will *increase* for each 1-point increase in X. If b_Y is negative, it indicates how much Y' will *decrease* for each 1-point increase in X. In Figure 11.1, for instance, Y' increases about 5.13 points for every 1-point increase in X. Therefore, $b_Y = 5.13$ in the regression equation that defines this line.

COMPREHENSION CHECK 11.7

Suppose that $b_Y = .10$ for the data presented in Comprehension Check 11.4. Use Equation 11.1 to recompute Y' for each case and plot these new predicted values in your scatterplot. What does lowering

(cont.)

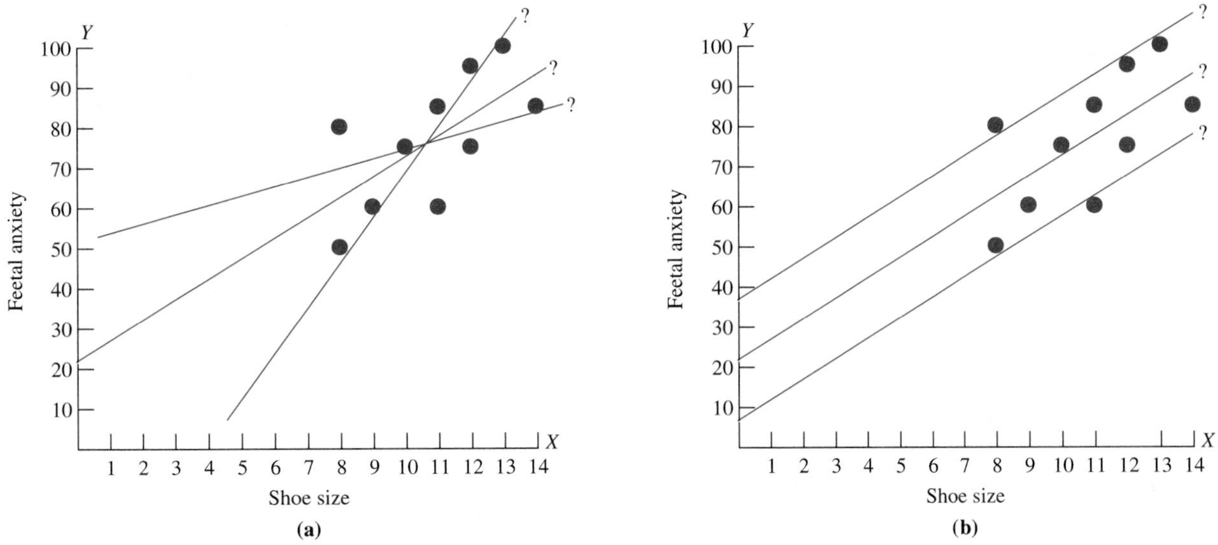

FIGURE 11.2

The position of the regression line is based on two decisions. One must decide on the correct slope (a) and the correct altitude (b).

b_Y do to the regression line? Suppose that $b_Y = .60$, recompute Y' values, and plot them. What does increasing b_Y do to the regression line?
(Answer on p. 367.)

The regression coefficient is computed according to Equation 11.2.

Equation 11.2

$$b_Y = r\left(\frac{s_Y}{s_X}\right)$$

where

b_Y = the regression coefficient
r = the correlation between X and Y
s_Y × the standard deviation of Y
s_X = the standard deviation of X

In words, we compute the regression coefficient (b_Y) by: (1) dividing the standard deviation of Y (s_Y) by the standard deviation of X (s_X); and (2) multiplying the resulting value by the Pearson correlation between X and Y (r).

COMPREHENSION CHECK 11.8

The regression coefficient for the data presented in Comprehension Check 11.4 is $b_Y = .32$. Confirm this by using Equation 11.2 to compute b_Y for yourself. What does this value tell you about predicting final exam scores from scores on the first exam?
(Answer on pp. 367–368.)

The Regression Constant

regression constant (a) *A component of the least-squares linear regression equation that determines the altitude of the regression line. This value specifies the value of Y′ when X = 0.*

Y intercept *Another name for the regression constant (a). This is the value of Y′ when X = 0, that is, the point at which the regression line crosses the Y axis.*

The altitude of the regression line is set in the regression equation by the value a, the **regression constant.** You can see from Equation 11.1 that as a increases, all values of Y' increase as well, thereby elevating the entire regression line. Conversely, as the value of a decreases, all Y' values decrease and the whole regression line is lowered. The regression constant is sometimes called the ***Y intercept*** because it fixes the value on the Y axis through which the regression line passes.(See Note 5)

In Figure 11.1, for instance, when $X = 0$, $Y' = 21.06$. Thus, $a = 21.06$ in the regression equation that defines this regression line.

COMPREHENSION CHECK 11.9

Suppose that $a = 40$ for the data presented in Comprehension Check 11.4. Use Equation 11.1 to recompute Y' values for each case and plot these new values in your scatterplot. What does lowering a do to the regression line? Suppose that $a = 70$ and recompute and plot Y' values. What does increasing a do to the regression line?

(Answer on p. 368.)

The regression constant is computed according to Equation 11.3.

Equation 11.3

$$a = \overline{Y} - b_Y\overline{X}$$

where

a = the regression constant
$\overline{Y}$ = the mean of Y
b_Y = the regression coefficient (see Equation 11.2)
$\overline{X}$ = the mean of X

In words, the regression constant (a) is computed by: (1) multiplying $\overline{X}$ by the regression coefficient (b_Y); and (2) subtracting this product from $\overline{Y}$.

COMPREHENSION CHECK 11.10

The regression constant for the data presented in Comprehension Check 11.4 is $a = 51.42$. Confirm this by using Equation 11.3 to compute a for yourself. What does this value tell you about predicting final exam scores from scores on the first exam?

(Answer on p. 368.)

11.3 MEASURING PREDICTIVE ACCURACY AND INACCURACY

The problem with regression analysis is that the predicted values of Y are usually wrong. Only when the correlation between X and Y is perfect will predicted and obtained values of Y match exactly, and perfect correlations are pretty rare in the social and behavioral sciences.

Look at Table 11.2, which lists again the data on shoe size and feetal anxiety that we've been following. In addition to shoe sizes (X), obtained feetal anxiety scores (Y), and predicted feetal anxiety scores (Y'), the last column of

TABLE 11.2

Shoes sizes (X), feetal anxiety scores (Y), predicted feetal anxiety (Y'), and residual scores ($Y - Y'$) for 10 psychopodiatric patients

Shoe Sizes X	Feetal Anxiety Y	Predicted Feetal Anxiety Y'	Residuals $Y - Y'$
14	85	92.93	−7.93
13	100	87.79	12.21
11	85	77.53	7.47
10	75	72.39	2.61
9	60	67.26	−7.26
12	75	82.66	−7.66
8	80	62.13	17.87
12	95	82.66	12.34
8	50	62.13	−12.13
11	60	77.53	−17.53

this table lists differences between Y and Y' values for each case. Known as **residual scores,** these $Y - Y'$ values indicate the size of the prediction error for each case. Notice that there is not one case in which the obtained and predicted values of Y match. In cases of overprediction ($Y < Y'$), the residual score is negative. In cases of underprediction ($Y > Y'$), the residual score is positive. When the predicted and obtained values match exactly ($Y' = Y$), the residual score is 0.

residual scores ($Y - Y'$) *The residual score for each case in the sample used to develop the regression equation is computed as the difference between the obtained and predicted values of Y. Residual scores quantify prediction error for each case.*

COMPREHENSION CHECK 11.11

Compute residual scores for the data presented in Comprehension Check 11.4. Identify errors of overprediction and underprediction.
(Answer on p. 368.)

The residual scores recorded in Table 11.2 illustrate three principles that are true in any regression analysis. First, predictions are more accurate for some cases than for others (unless $r = \pm 1.0$, in which case predictions are perfectly accurate for all cases). Predicted scores are very close to obtained scores for some of the cases; the discrepancy is much greater for other cases. Second, some predictions are too high and some are too low. Regression analysis produces errors of both overprediction and underprediction. Third, errors of overprediction and underprediction are balanced, as shown by the fact that the sum of the residual scores is 0:

$$\Sigma(Y - Y') = 0$$

This will always be true and provides a check on computational accuracy in regression analysis.

COMPREHENSION CHECK 11.12

Sum the residual scores you computed in Comprehension Check 11.11. What does their zero sum tell you?
(Answer on p. 368.)

You may wonder at this point: "Why bother? If predictions from regression analysis are going to be wrong more often than not, what point is there in making them?" The answer to this question is that predictions that are a little off may often be better than no predictions at all, especially if the errors are relatively small. Deciding whether or not to use a regression equation, then, requires that we be able to determine how much prediction error is likely to occur. Only once this is known can we make a rational decision to use or not use the regression equation.

Assessing predictive accuracy generally involves two stages. First, prediction errors occurring in the sample data used to develop the regression equation are used to estimate how much error would occur if the equation were used to make predictions for new cases. In other words, we use errors of *post*diction to estimate errors of *pre*diction. If this first-stage analysis indicates that prediction error is within acceptable limits, the predictive accuracy of the regression equation is further evaluated in a second stage called **cross-validation.** In a cross-validation study, the regression equation developed from the data of one sample is checked for accuracy by making predictions for a second cross-validation sample.

cross-validation *A method of checking predictive accuracy in which the regression equation developed using the data from one sample is used to make predictions for a second "cross-validation" sample.*

We will focus here on just the first stage of the process: how errors in the sample used to develop the regression equation are used to estimate future errors of prediction. This will require that you become familiar with the concepts of total variance, predicted variance, and residual variance.

Total Variance

total variance (s_Y^2) *The variance of the obtained values of* Y.

Total variance is nothing new to you. It is just the variance of the obtained values of Y (s_Y^2). For the data in Table 11.1, $s_Y^2 = 230.25$.

COMPREHENSION CHECK 11.13

What is the total variance (s_Y^2) for the data presented in Comprehension Check 11.4?
(Answer on p. 368.)

The whole point of correlation and regression is to try to explain this variance in Y, that is, to determine *why* Y varies. To the degree that X and Y are correlated so that we can predict Y from X, we can say that some of the variance in Y is "predicted" or "explained" by variability in X. However, some of the variance in Y is likely the result of other factors. This variance in Y is "unpredicted" or "unexplained" by X. The total variance of Y consists of the sum total of these two components: predicted variance and unpredicted variance.

Predicted Variance

predicted variance ($s_{Y'}^2$) *The variance of* Y′*—the predicted values of* Y. *Predicted variance is that portion of the total variance in* Y (s_Y^2) *that is explained or predicted by* X.

Predicted variance ($s_{Y'}^2$) can be thought of in a number of ways. First, and most simply, predicted variance is the variance of the predicted values of Y. This being the case, it can be computed by applying the usual variance formula to the Y' values as in Equation 11.4.

Equation 11.4

$$s_{Y'}^2 = \frac{\Sigma(Y' - \overline{Y'})^2}{N}$$

where

$s_{Y'}^2$ = the predicted variance
Y' = the predicted values of Y
$\overline{Y'}$ = the mean of the Y' values
N = the number of cases

In words, predicted variance ($s^2_{Y'}$) is computed by: (1) subtracting the mean of the Y' values ($\overline{Y'}$) from each Y' value; (2) squaring each of these differences; (3) summing these squares; and (4) dividing the result of step 3 by the number of cases (N).

COMPREHENSION CHECK 11.14

Use Equation 11.4 to compute predicted variance ($s^2_{Y'}$) for the data presented in Comprehension Check 11.4.
(Answer on p. 368.)

There is a second way of thinking about predicted variance. Values of Y' are predicted on the basis of the correlation between X and Y. It follows that $s^2_{Y'}$ represents variability in Y that occurs *because* of the relationship between X and Y. We sometimes call $s^2_{Y'}$ **explained variance,** because it measures the variability in Y that is explained by variability in X.

explained variance *A term that is synonymous with predicted variance.*

When the correlation between X and Y is perfect, Y' and Y will match perfectly for every case. There are no errors of prediction. In this situation, s^2_Y and $s^2_{Y'}$ will be exactly equal because Y and Y' values are the same. In most situations, though, the correlation is less than perfect. In these situations, $s^2_{Y'}$ will be less than s^2_Y. This is because only part of the total variability in Y is explained by X. Predicted variance represents only that portion of the total variance in Y that is linked to X. When there is no correlation between X and Y, none of the variability in Y is explained by X, so $s^2_{Y'} = 0$. To summarize, as the correlation between X and Y grows from 0 to ± 1.0, $s^2_{Y'}$ grows from 0 to equal s^2_Y.

For the data in Table 11.2, $s^2_{Y'} = 99.07$. Notice that this is less than $s^2_Y = 230.25$. Less variance is *predicted* than has *occurred* because the correlation between shoe size and feetal anxiety is less than perfect ($r = .66$). Thus, only some of the variability in feetal anxiety is explained by shoe size.

COMPREHENSION CHECK 11.15

For the data presented in Comprehension Check 11.4, $s^2_Y = 102.58$ and $s^2_{Y'} = 12.83$. Considered together, what do these two variances tell you about the predictive power of the regression equation?
(Answer on p. 368.)

Coefficient of Determination. One very useful measure of the predictive accuracy of a regression equation is based on a comparison of $s^2_{Y'}$ and s^2_Y. The ratio $s^2_{Y'}/s^2_Y$ is called the **coefficient of determination.** The coefficient of determination tells us the proportion of the total variance in Y that has been predicted by the variable X. Because predictive accuracy is ultimately determined by the strength of the correlation, we're not surprised to find that the coefficient of determination is equal to r^2. This is all summarized in Equation 11.5.

coefficient of determination *The proportion of variance in Y that is predicted or explained by X.*

Equation 11.5

$$r^2 = \frac{s^2_{Y'}}{s^2_Y}$$

where

r^2 = the coefficient of determination
$s^2_{Y'}$ = the predicted variance
s^2_Y = the total variance (variance of Y)

For the data on shoe size and feetal anxiety, $r^2 = .66^2 = .44$. Thus, about 44% of the variance in feetal anxiety is explained by shoe size.

COMPREHENSION CHECK 11.16

> Use Equation 11.5 to compute the coefficient of determination for the data presented in Comprehension Check 11.4. Interpret this value.
> (Answer on pp. 368–369.)

The coefficient of determination, r^2, is very much like the statistic omega-square (ω^2), the measure of association strength used in conjunction with t tests and analysis of variance. Omega-square measures the proportion of variance in the dependent variable that is explained by the independent variable. The coefficient of determination measures the proportion of variance in Y that is explained by X.

Coefficient of Determination and Predicted Variance. If you have 10 coins in total and the *proportion* of the coins that are nickels is .4, *how many* nickels do you have? The answer is found by multiplying the total number of coins by the proportion of coins that are nickels:

$$.4 \times 10 = 4$$

The coefficient of determination (r^2) is the proportion of the total variance (s_Y^2) that is predicted by X. It follows that we can compute predicted variance ($s_{Y'}^2$), just as we computed how many coins were nickels above, by using Equation 11.6.

Equation 11.6

$$s_{Y'}^2 = (r^2)s_Y^2$$

where

$s_{Y'}^2$ = the predicted variance
r = the correlation between X and Y
s_Y^2 = the total variance (variance of Y)

In words, predicted variance ($s_{Y'}^2$) is equal to the coefficient of determination (r^2) times the total variance (s_Y^2). For the data on shoe size and feetal anxiety, Equation 11.6 gives

$$\begin{aligned} s_{Y'}^2 &= (r^2)s_Y^2 \\ &= (.66^2)230.25 \\ &= (.44)230.25 \\ &= 101.31 \end{aligned}$$

Equation 11.6 is the most practical approach to computing $s_{Y'}^2$. Unlike Equation 11.4, Equation 11.6 gives $s_{Y'}^2$ without requiring that we compute all the Y' values. Because less computation is involved, Equation 11.6 introduces less rounding error and provides a more accurate indication of $s_{Y'}^2$.

COMPREHENSION CHECK 11.17

Use Equation 11.6 to compute $s^2_{Y'}$ for the data presented in Comprehension Check 11.4. Why does this value differ slightly from the value computed in Comprehension Check 11.14? Which value do you think is more accurate?

(Answer on p. 369.)

Residual Variance

residual variance ($s^2_{Y-Y'}$) *Residual variance can be defined in three ways: (1) it is the variance of the residual scores; (2) it is the average squared error of prediction; and (3) it is that portion of the total variance in* Y *that is not predicted in* X.

Residual variance ($s^2_{Y-Y'}$) can also be viewed from several perspectives. First, $s^2_{Y-Y'}$ is the variance of the residual scores. As such, it can be computed by applying the usual variance formula to the $Y - Y'$ values as shown in Equation 11.7.

Equation 11.7

$$s^2_{Y-Y'} = \frac{\Sigma[(Y - Y') - (\overline{Y - Y'})]^2}{N}$$

where

$s^2_{Y-Y'}$ = the residual variance
$Y - Y'$ = the residual scores
$\overline{Y - Y'}$ = the mean of the residual scores
N = the number of cases

In words, residual variance ($s^2_{Y-Y'}$) is computed by: (1) subtracting the mean of the residual scores ($\overline{Y - Y'}$) from each residual score ($Y - Y'$); (2) squaring these differences; (3) summing these squared values; and (4) dividing the result of step 3 by the number of cases (N).

COMPREHENSION CHECK 11.18

Use Equation 11.7 to compute $s^2_{Y-Y'}$ for the data presented in Comprehension Check 11.4.

(Answer on p. 369.)

Because the sum of the residual scores will always be 0, $\overline{Y - Y'}$ in Equation 11.7 will always be 0. We can therefore simplify this expression as shown in Equation 11.8.

Equation 11.8

$$s^2_{Y-Y'} = \frac{\Sigma(Y - Y')^2}{N}$$

where

$s^2_{Y-Y'}$ = the residual variance
$Y - Y'$ = the residual scores
N = the number of cases

In words, Equation 11.8 indicates that we can compute residual variance by: (1) squaring each residual score; (2) summing these squares; and (3) dividing this sum by N.

Equation 11.8 suggests another way of thinking about residual variance. In Equation 11.8 we are summing the squared residual scores and dividing by N. In other words, we are computing the mean of the squared residual scores. Residual scores are prediction errors, so it follows that the residual variance can be defined as the average (mean) squared error of prediction.

For the data on shoe size and feetal anxiety, $s^2_{Y-Y'} = 131.20$. This is the variance of the residual scores. It is also the average squared error of prediction in the sample data.

COMPREHENSION CHECK 11.19

Interpret the residual variance value you computed in Comprehension Check 11.18.
(Answer on p. 369.)

There is a third useful way of looking at residual variance. Residual variance is that portion of the total variance in Y that is not explained by X. In other words, $s^2_{Y-Y'}$ refers to the variability in Y that is left over (the "residue") after we remove from the total variance (s^2_Y) that part which was successfully predicted ($s^2_{Y'}$). This idea is captured in Equation 11.9.

Equation 11.9

$$s^2_{Y-Y'} = s^2_Y - s^2_{Y'}$$

where

$s^2_{Y-Y'}$ = the residual variance
s^2_Y = the total variance (variance in Y)
$s^2_{Y'}$ = the predicted variance

For the data on shoe size and feetal anxiety,

$$s^2_{Y-Y'} = s^2_Y - s^2_{Y'}$$

$$128.94 = 230.25 - 101.31$$

COMPREHENSION CHECK 11.20

Explain why the sum of $s^2_{Y'}$ and $s^2_{Y-Y'}$ must equal s^2_Y. Show that this is the case for the data presented in Comprehension Check 11.4.
(Answer on p. 369.)

Coefficient of Nondetermination. As the relationship between X and Y grows stronger, more and more of the variance in Y will be explained by X and the residual variance left unexplained will grow correspondingly smaller. Conversely, as the relationship between X and Y grows weaker, less of the variance in Y will be explained by X, and the residual variance will grow correspondingly larger.

coefficient of nondetermination $(1 - r^2)$ *The proportion of variance in Y that is not predicted or explained by X.*

This suggests another way of measuring predictive accuracy (or inaccuracy). The ratio $s^2_{Y-Y'}/s^2_Y$ is called the **coefficient of nondetermination.** The coefficient of nondetermination is the proportion of the total variance in Y that is *not* explained by X.

Because the variance in Y must either be predicted or not predicted, and since r^2 is the proportion that *is* predicted, it follows that $1 - r^2$ must be the proportion that is *not* predicted. This is all summarized in Equation 11.10.

Equation 11.10

$$1 - r^2 = \frac{s^2_{Y-Y'}}{s^2_Y}$$

where

$1 - r^2$ = the coefficient of nondetermination
$s^2_{Y-Y'}$ = the residual variance
s^2_Y = the total variance (variance in Y)

For the data on shoe size and feetal anxiety, $1 - r^2 = 1 - .44 = .56$. Thus, about 56% of the variance in feetal anxiety is not explained by shoe size.

COMPREHENSION CHECK 11.21

Use Equation 11.10 to compute the coefficient of nondetermination for the data presented in Comprehension Check 11.4. Interpret this value.

(Answer on p. 369.)

Coefficient of Nondetermination and Residual Variance. If you have 10 coins in total and the *proportion* of the coins that are *not* nickels is .6, *how many* coins do you have that are not nickels? The answer is found by multiplying the total number of coins by the proportion of coins that are not nickels:

$$.6 \times 10 = 6$$

The coefficient of nondetermination ($1 - r^2$) is the proportion of the total variance (s^2_Y) that is *not* predicted by X. It follows that we can compute unpredicted or residual variance ($s^2_{Y-Y'}$), just as we computed how many coins were not nickels above, as shown in Equation 11.11.

Equation 11.11

$$s^2_{Y-Y'} = (1 - r^2)s^2_Y$$

where

$s^2_{Y-Y'}$ = the residual variance
r = the correlation between X and Y
s^2_Y = the total variance (variance of Y)

In words, residual variance ($s^2_{Y-Y'}$) is equal to the coefficient of nondetermination ($1 - r^2$) times the total variance (s^2_Y). For the data on shoe size and feetal anxiety, Equation 11.11 gives

$$\begin{aligned} s^2_{Y-Y'} &= (1 - r^2)s^2_Y \\ &= (1 - .66^2)230.25 \\ &= (.56)230.25 \\ &= 128.94 \end{aligned}$$

Equation 11.11 is the most practical approach to computing $s^2_{Y-Y'}$. Unlike Equations 11.7 and 11.8, Equation 11.11 gives $s^2_{Y-Y'}$ without requiring that we compute all the $Y - Y'$ values. Because there is less computation involved,

Equation 11.11 introduces less rounding error and provides a more accurate indication of $s^2_{Y-Y'}$.

COMPREHENSION CHECK 11.22

> Use Equation 11.11 to compute $s^2_{Y-Y'}$ for the data presented in Comprehension Check 11.4. Why does this value differ slightly from the value computed in Comprehension Check 11.18? Which value do you think is more accurate?
> (Answer on p. 369.)

Standard Error of the Estimate

standard error of the estimate ($s_{Y-Y'}$) *Defined as the square root of the residual variance, it is approximately equal to the average absolute error of prediction.*

We defined the residual variance earlier as the average squared error of prediction. The problem with the residual variance as a measure of prediction error is that most of us are not used to thinking about *squared* errors. We think about errors in absolute terms. The **standard error of the estimate** ($s_{Y-Y'}$) accommodates this preference. The standard error of the estimate is computed according to Equation 11.12 as the square root of the residual variance. As such, it is approximately equal to the average absolute error of prediction.

Equation 11.12

$$s_{Y-Y'} = \sqrt{s^2_{Y-Y'}}$$

where

$s_{Y-Y'}$ = the standard error of the estimate
$s^2_{Y-Y'}$ = the residual variance

For the data on shoe size and feetal anxiety that we have been following,

$$\begin{aligned} s_{Y-Y'} &= \sqrt{s^2_{Y-Y'}} \\ &= \sqrt{128.94} \\ &= 11.36 \end{aligned}$$

The standard error of the estimate is one of the most important measures of error in regression analysis. When combined with a little common sense, the standard error of the estimate helps us to decide whether the errors from a regression equation are acceptable or not. For example, in predicting students' college grade-point averages, a standard error of the estimate of 2.0 would clearly be unacceptable. This is an *average* error of two whole letter grades. For some individuals we would expect to see even worse predictions. On the other hand, a standard error of the estimate of 2.0 in predicting the number of pounds lost in a weight-reduction program would probably be quite acceptable. Two pounds are unimportant; two grade points are *very* important!

COMPREHENSION CHECK 11.23

> Use Equation 11.12 to compute $s_{Y-Y'}$ for the data presented in Comprehension Check 11.4. What does this value tell you about the predictive capability of the regression equation?
> (Answer on p. 369.)

11.4 Two Regression Lines

In many situations there is one obvious predictor variable (*X*) and one obvious outcome or criterion variable (*Y*). For example, we might be interested in predicting grade-point average from SAT scores, but it wouldn't make much sense to predict SAT scores from grade-point average. Similarly, we might like to predict sales performance from achievement-motivation test scores, but it wouldn't be of much interest to predict achievement-motivation test scores from sales performance.

In other situations, though, the distinction between predictor and criterion variables isn't so clear. One would be as likely to want to predict cost of living from crime rate as crime rate from cost of living. Similarly, we might be as interested in predicting stress level from health as in predicting health from stress level.

If *X* and *Y* are correlated, we can predict *Y* from *X* or *X* from *Y*. However, the regression line (and equation) that predicts *Y* from *X* (called the **regression line *of Y on X*)** is different than the regression line (and equation) that predicts *X* from *Y* (called the **regression line *of X on Y*).**

regression line of *Y* on *X* *The regression line (or equation) that predicts values of* Y *from values of* X.

regression line of *X* on *Y* *The regression line (or equation) that predicts values of* X *from values of* Y.

The regression line of *Y* on *X* is positioned so as to minimize errors in predicting *Y*. The regression line of *X* on *Y* is positioned somewhat differently in order to minimize errors in predicting *X*. The different positions of the two regression lines is most apparent when $r = 0$.

Suppose you want to predict a case's score on *Y* and know that there is no relationship between *X* and *Y*. What is your best guess as to that case's score on *Y*? Assuming that variable *Y* is approximately normally distributed, $\overline{Y}$ would be the single most frequently occurring score, so $\overline{Y}$ would be your best prediction. This would be true regardless of the case's score on *X*, because *X* and *Y* are unrelated. Figure 11.3a shows the regression line of *Y* on

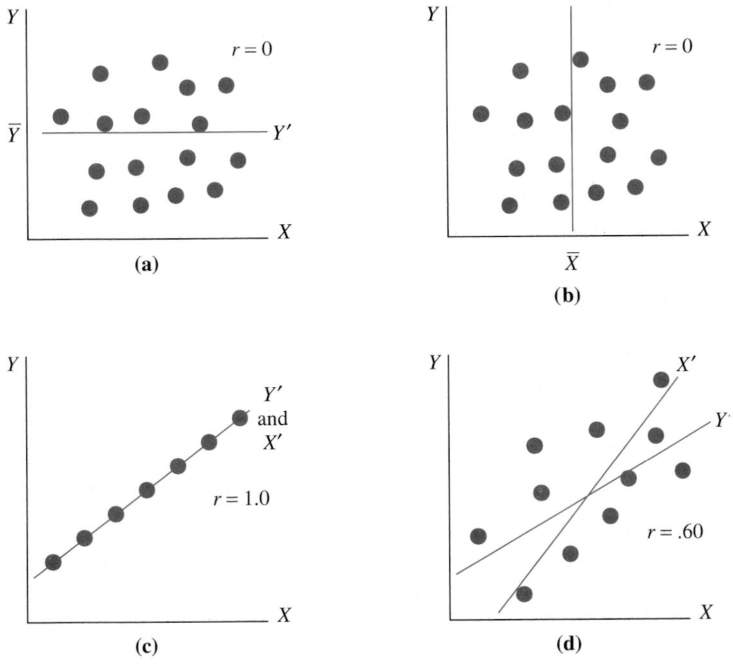

Figure 11.3

There are two regression lines: the regression line of *Y* on *X* and the regression line of *X* on *Y*. When $r = 0$, the regression line of *Y* on *X* is horizontal (a). When $r = 0$, the regression line of *X* on *Y* is vertical (b). When $r = 1$, both regression lines are the same (c). When the correlation is moderate, the regression lines diverge, but are not fully perpendicular (d).

X when $r = 0$. It is horizontal, indicating that no matter what the score on X is, $Y' = \overline{Y}$.

Suppose instead that you want to predict a case's score on X and know that X and Y are uncorrelated. What is your best guess as to the case's score on the X variable? Assuming that the distribution of X is approximately normal, the single most frequently occurring value of X would be $\overline{X}$. So $\overline{X}$ would be your best prediction. This would be true regardless of that case's score on Y, because X and Y are uncorrelated. The regression line of X on Y when $r = 0$ is shown in Figure 11.3b. This regression line is vertical, indicating that $X' = \overline{X}$ regardless of the score on Y.

Although the regression lines of Y on X and X on Y are different when $r = 0$, they are identical when $r = 1$. Figure 11.3c depicts a perfect positive correlation between X and Y. Only one line fits these points, and that one line can be used in predicting either Y from X or X from Y. Though not pictured, a perfect negative correlation is also fitted by only one regression line, and the same line is used in predicting either variable.

When the correlation between X and Y falls between 0 and ± 1, the regression lines fall between the two extreme positions considered above. The regression line of Y on X and the regression line of X on Y will no longer be perpendicular, but will still be separate. The lower the correlation, the closer to perpendicularity the lines will be. The higher the correlation, the less perpendicular the lines will be. Figure 11.3d depicts a moderate positive correlation between X and Y and shows the two regression lines. The regression line of Y on X meets the least-squares criterion described previously: It minimizes errors that occur in predicting Y from X and balances errors of overprediction and underprediction. The regression line of X on Y also meets the least-squares criterion: It minimizes the errors that occur in predicting X from Y and also balances errors of overprediction and underprediction.

Equations 11.1 to 11.3 provide the mathematics for predicting Y from X, and Equations 11.4 to 11.10 describe measures of predictive accuracy and inaccuracy for this regression equation. These same equations can be used in predicting X from Y: Just substitute X values wherever Y values appear, and substitute Y values wherever X values appear. Alternatively, one can simply relabel the X variable as Y and the Y variable as X and use Equations 11.1 to 11.10 in their original form.

COMPREHENSION CHECK 11.24

Position the regression line of X on Y in the scatterplot you drew in Comprehension Check 11.4. Why is it located differently than the regression line of Y on X (Comprehension Check 11.6)?
(Answer on pp. 369–370.)

EXAMPLE 11.1

Bivariate Regression Analysis

We watched in Example 10.1 as statisticians from Double Cross/Double Shield established that there is a significant positive correlation ($r = .75$) between psychopodiatric insurance coverage and the duration of in-patient treatment received by those suffering from serious psychopodiatric disorders. Policy holders with less coverage spent less time in the hospital; those with better coverage were hospitalized for longer periods of time.

Based on this relationship, it should be possible to use bivariate regression analysis to predict duration of hospitalization in days (Y) from insurance coverage in thousands of dollars (X). Data for this analysis are presented below, along with descriptive statistics for each variable.

X **Insurance cap**	Y **Hospitalization**
\$ 40	14
\$ 80	20
\$ 20	15
\$ 0	10
\$100	38
\$ 60	21
\$ 80	40
\$100	50
\$ 20	35
\$ 10	5
$\overline{X} = 51.00$	$\overline{Y} = 24.80$
$s_X^2 = 1289.00$	$s_Y^2 = 200.56$
$s_X = 35.90$	$s_Y = 14.16$

The Regression Equation

We begin the analysis by computing the components of the regression equation of Y on X. The regression coefficient (b_Y) is computed according to Equation 11.2:

$$\begin{aligned} b_Y &= r\left(\frac{s_Y}{s_X}\right) \\ &= .75\left(\frac{14.16}{35.90}\right) \\ &= .30 \end{aligned}$$

The regression coefficient sets the slope of the regression line. Because $b_Y = .30$, we know that each 1-point (\$1,000) increase in insurance coverage (X) presages an increase of .30 days of in-patient psychopodiatric treatment (Y').

The regression constant (a) is computed according to Equation 11.3.

$$\begin{aligned} a &= \overline{Y} - b_Y\overline{X} \\ &= 24.80 - .30(51.00) \\ &= 9.50 \end{aligned}$$

The regression constant determines the altitude of the regression line. Because $a = 9.50$, we know that the predicted length of hospitalization will be $Y' = 9.50$ days for a policy holder who has no coverage for psychopodiatric disorders ($X = 0$).

The regression coefficient and regression constant are used in the regression equation of Y on X (Equation 11.1) to predict Y for any given value of X.

The table that follows lists values of X, Y, and Y', and residual scores $(Y - Y')$ for each case.

X	Y	Y'	$Y - Y'$
40	14	21.50	−7.50
80	20	33.50	−13.50
20	15	15.50	−.50
0	10	9.50	.50
100	38	39.50	−1.50
60	21	27.50	−6.50
80	40	33.50	6.50
100	50	39.50	10.50
20	35	15.50	19.50
10	5	12.50	−7.50

These predicted values of Y define the regression line and are shown as asterisks in the scatterplot that follows.

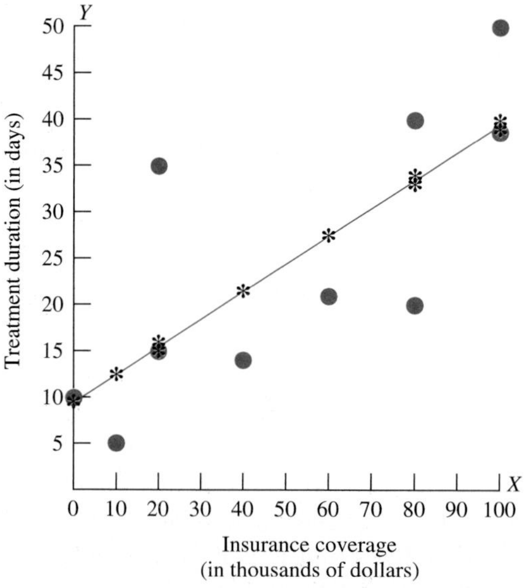

Notice first the slope of the regression line. It is positive, consistent with the positive correlation and positive regression coefficient. For every increase of 1 point ($1,000) on X, there is an increase of .30 points (days of treatment) in Y'. Now note the point at which the regression line meets the Y axis—the Y intercept. This is the value $a = 9.50$, which sets the altitude of the regression line.

Evaluating Predictive Accuracy

There are several measures of predictive accuracy and inaccuracy. Each measures errors of postdiction observed in the sample at hand in order to estimate errors of prediction that would occur were the regression equation to be used in making actual predictions.

Coefficient of Determination. Predictive accuracy is determined entirely by the strength of the correlation. The squared correlation ($r^2 = .75^2 = .56$) is called the coefficient of determination and indicates the proportion of the total variance in Y that is successfully predicted by X (Equation 11.5). We can see in this example that approximately 56% of the variability in treatment duration is explained by level of insurance coverage.

Coefficient of Nondetermination. The total variance in Y can be partitioned into two components: Some of the variance is predicted and some is not. The proportion that is predicted is given by the coefficient of determination, discussed above. The proportion that is not predicted is given by the coefficient of nondetermination: $1 - r^2 = 1 - .56 = .44$. Approximately 44% of the variance in treatment duration is not explained by level of insurance coverage.

Residual Variance. Residual variance ($s^2_{Y-Y'}$) can be defined as the variance of the residual scores. It can also be defined as the average squared error of prediction. The first definition suggests how this value can be computed; the second suggests how it can be most usefully interpreted. Residual variance is most easily computed according to Equation 11.11:

$$\begin{aligned} s^2_{Y-Y'} &= (1 - r^2)s^2_Y \\ &= (1 - .56)200.56 \\ &= 88.25 \end{aligned}$$

Therefore, the average *squared* error of prediction in these data is 88.25 days.

Standard Error of the Estimate. More useful than the residual variance as a measure of prediction error is the standard error of the estimate ($s_{Y-Y'}$). Defined and computed as the square root of the residual variance, the standard error of the estimate is most usefully thought of as approximately equal to the average absolute error of prediction. The standard error of the estimate is computed according to Equation 11.12:

$$\begin{aligned} s_{Y-Y'} &= \sqrt{s^2_{Y-Y'}} \\ &= \sqrt{88.25} \\ &= 9.39 \end{aligned}$$

Our regression equation is more accurate in its predictions for some policy holders than for others. The standard error of the estimate tells us that the approximate *average* error of prediction is 9.39 days. If the statisticians at Double Cross/Double Shield decide to use this equation in predicting the duration of in-patient psychopodiatric treatment from insurance coverage, they can expect prediction errors from one case to the next to average about 9.39 days.

Summary

Bivariate regression analysis uses the Pearson correlation between two variables as the basis for predicting values on one variable (Y) from values on a second variable (X). The correlation describes the strength of the linear relationship between the variables; the linear regression equation summarizes and describes that relationship in a way that enables one to predict one variable from the other.

The regression equation is useful to the extent that it makes accurate predictions. We can use the postdictive accuracy of the regression equation to assess its likely predictive accuracy.

The total variance of the criterion variable (s^2_Y) can be partitioned into two components. Some of the variance can be predicted using the regression equation and is called predicted variance ($s^2_{Y'}$). The remainder cannot be predicted and is called residual variance ($s^2_{Y-Y'}$). The ratio of predicted variance to total variance ($s^2_{Y'}/s^2_Y$) $= r^2$ is called the coefficient of determination and tells us the proportion of the total variance that is predicted. The ratio of residual variance to total variance ($s^2_{Y'}/s^2_Y$) $= 1 - r^2$ is called the coefficient of nondetermination and tells us the proportion of the total variance that is not predicted.

The standard error of the estimate ($s_{Y-Y'}$) is another useful statistic in the evaluation of the predictive adequacy of a regression equation. Computed as the square root of the residual variance, $s_{Y-Y'}$ is approximately equal to the average absolute error of prediction.

If two variables are correlated, either can be predicted from the other, but different regression equations are required. The regression equation of Y on X predicts Y from X in a manner that minimizes and balances errors in predicting Y. The regression equation of X on Y predicts X from Y in a manner that minimizes and balances errors in predicting X.

Notes

1. The axes of the scatterplots shown in Figure 11.1 include values of 0 for both variables even though the minimum observed score on X is 8 and the minimum observed score on Y is 50. This is done in order to include in these diagrams the point at which the regression line intersects the Y axis—the value of Y' when $X = 0$. It would *not* be good statistical practice to use the regression line in making predictions involving variable values beyond the observed range of the variables.
2. There are actually two regression lines, one to predict Y from X and another to predict X from Y. This distinction is discussed in the last section of the chapter.
3. When X and Y are expressed as standard (z) scores, Equation 11.1 can be simplified to

$$z_{Y'} = rz_X$$

where

$z_{Y'}$ = the predicted values of Y expressed in z-score form
r = the correlation between X and Y
z_X = the values of X expressed in z-score form

In the regression equation for standard scores the regression coefficient, b_Y, is equal to r. Because $b_Y = r(s_Y/s_X)$ and $s_X = s_Y = 1$, it follows that $b_Y = r$. The regression constant, a, is eliminated from the standard-score regression equation because it is equal to 0. The mean of the standard scores on variables X and Y are both 0, so $a = \overline{Y} - b_Y\overline{X} = 0 - r0 = 0$.

4. The linear regression equation generates different values of Y' for each different value of X only if X and Y are correlated. If the correlation is 0, $Y' = \overline{Y}$ for every value of X. This is because $b_Y = 0$ when $r = 0$:

$$\begin{aligned} b_Y &= r\left(\frac{s_Y}{s_X}\right) \qquad \text{(Equation 11.2)} \\ &= 0\left(\frac{s_Y}{s_X}\right) \\ &= 0 \end{aligned}$$

and when $b_Y = 0$, $a = \overline{Y}$:

$$\begin{aligned} a &= \overline{Y} - b_Y\overline{X} \qquad \text{(Equation 11.3)} \\ &= \overline{Y} - 0(\overline{X}) \\ &= \overline{Y} - 0 \\ &= \overline{Y} \end{aligned}$$

and when $b_Y = 0$ and $a = \overline{Y}$, $Y' = \overline{Y}$ for any value of X:

$$\begin{aligned} Y' &= a + b_YX \qquad \text{(Equation 11.1)} \\ &= \overline{Y} + 0(X) \\ &= \overline{Y} + 0 \\ &= \overline{Y} \end{aligned}$$

5. This is why $Y' = a$ when $X = 0$:

$$\begin{aligned} Y' &= a + b_YX \qquad \text{(Equation 11.1)} \\ &= a + b_Y0 \\ &= a + 0 \\ &= a \end{aligned}$$

Review Exercises

11.1. Listed below are undergraduate grade-point averages (GPA) (X) and graduate GPA (Y) for 10 sociology graduate students. Construct a scatterplot for X. What would you estimate the predicted graduate GPA to be for a student with an undergraduate GPA of 3.5?

X Undergraduate GPA	Y Graduate GPA
2.75	3.65
3.60	3.65
3.25	3.50
3.80	3.90
3.40	3.90
3.00	3.72
3.90	3.80
3.30	3.60
3.50	3.75
3.75	4.00

11.2. Use the least-squares linear regression equation to predict graduate GPA for each of the 10 cases listed in Review Exercise 11.1. Plot these predicted values in your scatterplot. Explain what a and b_Y accomplish in the regression equation.

11.3. Why would it be inappropriate to use the regression equation developed in Review Exercise 11.2 to predict graduate GPA for students with an undergraduate GPA below 2.75?

11.4. Compute residual scores ($Y - Y'$) for each case above and explain what these values tell you.

11.5. Compute the coefficient of determination for the preceding exercise and interpret this value.

11.6. Compute the coefficient of nondetermination for the preceding exercise and interpret this value.

11.7. Compute $s^2_{Y'}$ and $s^2_{Y-Y'}$ for the preceding exercise and interpret these values.

11.8. Compute $s_{Y-Y'}$ for the preceding exercise and interpret this value.

11.9. Use the regression equation of X (undergraduate GPA) on Y (graduate GPA) to plot the regression line of X on Y in the scatterplot you constructed in Review Exercise 11.1.

Answers to Comprehension Checks

11.1. The relationship between religious preference and political affiliation is an example of one that does not lend itself to regression analysis. These nominal scale variables cannot be correlated with the Pearson correlation and so are not appropriate to bivariate linear regression.

11.2. Within the observed ranges of the variables, as shoe size increases, feetal anxiety increases. The rate of increase appears to be roughly equal to between 5 and 6 feetal anxiety points for each increase of 1 shoe size.

11.3. Find size 10 on the X axis. Draw a vertical line up to the regression line. Draw a horizontal line from this point on the regression line to the Y axis. This is the predicted value of feetal anxiety: approximately 72.

11.4. The correct location of the regression line is shown to the right. Two decisions must be made in locating the line: (1) the slope of the line; and (2) the altitude of the line.

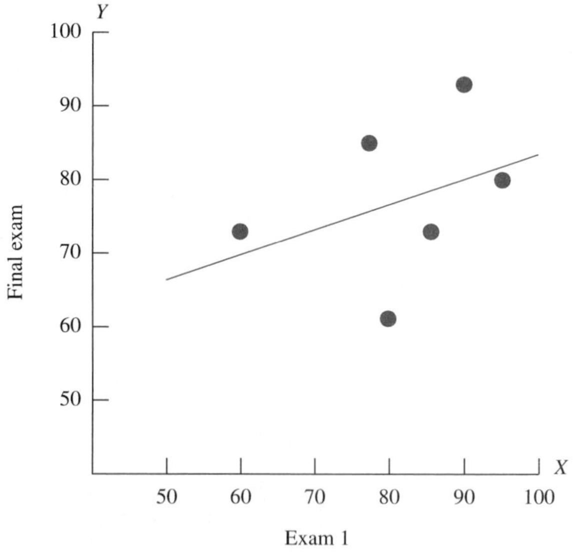

11.5. The relationship between X and Y is *nonlinear.* The linear regression equation defines a straight *line* that predicts Y from X.

11.6. Values of X, Y, and Y' are shown below.

X	Y	$Y' = a + b_Y X$
90	93	80.22 = 51.42 + .32(90)
80	61	77.02 = 51.42 + .32(80)
86	73	78.94 = 51.42 + .32(86)
60	73	70.62 = 51.42 + .32(60)
78	85	76.38 = 51.42 + .32(78)
95	80	81.82 = 51.42 + .32(95)

These predicted values are plotted below.

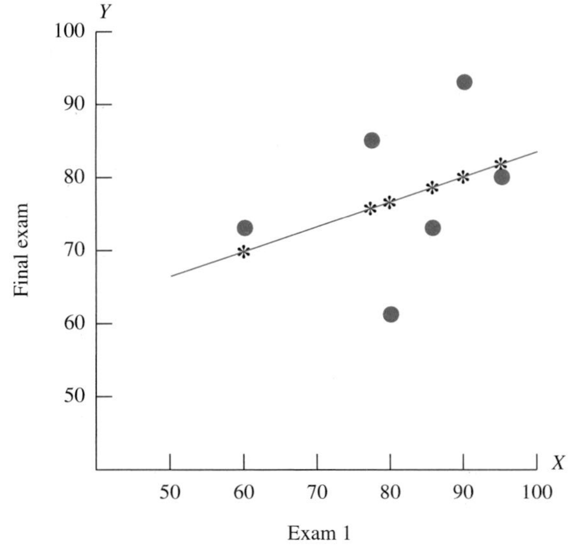

11.7. Values of Y' are computed below for $a = 51.42$ and $b_Y = .10$.

X	$Y' = a + b_Y X$
90	60.42 = 51.42 + .10(90)
80	59.42 = 51.42 + .10(80)
86	60.02 = 51.42 + .10(86)
60	57.42 = 51.42 + .10(60)
78	59.22 = 51.42 + .10(78)
95	60.92 = 51.42 + .10(95)

Values of Y' are computed below for $a = 51.42$ and $b_Y. = 60$.

X	$Y' = a + b_Y X$
90	105.42 = 51.42 + .60(90)
80	99.42 = 51.42 + .60(80)
86	103.02 = 51.42 + .60(86)
60	87.42 = 51.42 + .60(60)
78	98.22 = 51.42 + .60(78)
95	108.42 = 51.42 + .60(95)

Predicted values are plotted below along with the correct regression line. Lowering the regression coefficient (b_Y) lowers the overall altitude of the line somewhat and reduces its slope. Increasing the regression coefficient increases the overall altitude of the line somewhat and increases its slope.

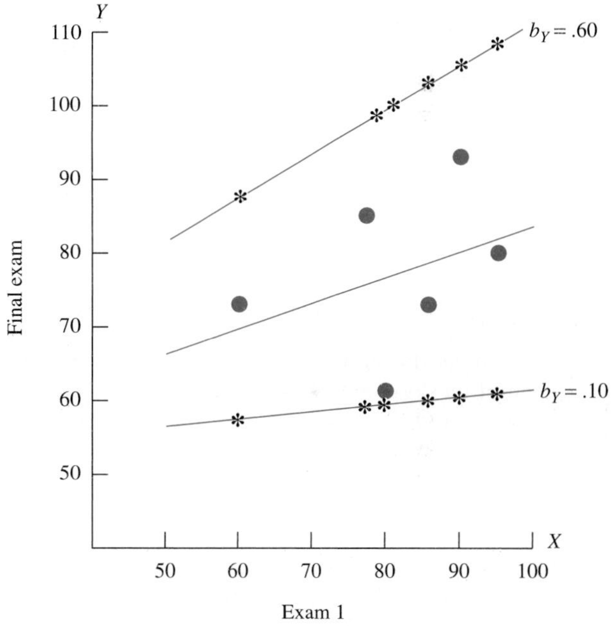

11.8. The regression coefficient (b_Y) is computed according to Equation 11.2.

$$b_Y = r\left(\frac{s_Y}{s_X}\right)$$

$$= .35\left(\frac{10.13}{11.19}\right)$$

$$= .32$$

This value indicates that for each 1-point increase in the first exam, the final exam is predicted to increase by about one-third point.

11.9. Values of Y' are computed below for $a = 40$ and $b_Y = .32$.

X	$Y' = a + b_YX$
90	68.80 = 40 + .32(90)
80	65.60 = 40 + .32(80)
86	67.52 = 40 + .32(86)
60	59.20 = 40 + .32(60)
78	64.96 = 40 + .32(78)
95	70.40 = 40 + .32(95)

Values of Y' are computed below for $a = 70$ and $b_Y = .32$.

X	$Y' = a + b_YX$
90	98.80 = 70 + .32(90)
80	95.60 = 70 + .32(80)
86	97.52 = 70 + .32(86)
60	89.20 = 70 + .32(60)
78	94.96 = 70 + .32(78)
95	100.40 = 70 + .32(95)

Predicted values are plotted below along with the correct regression line. Lowering the regression constant (a) has no effect on the slope of the regression line, but lowers its altitude. Increasing the regression constant also has no effect on slope, but raises the altitude of the regression line.

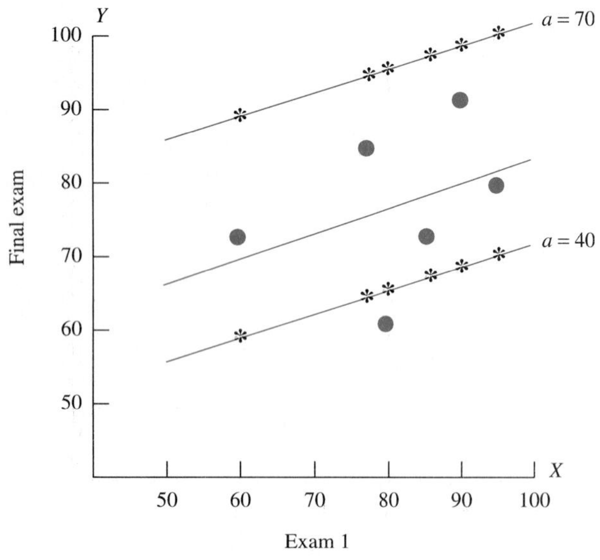

11.10. The regression constant (a) is computed according to Equation 11.4.

$$a = \overline{Y} - b_Y\overline{X}$$
$$= 77.50 - .32(81.50)$$
$$= 51.42$$

This value is the predicted final exam score when the score on the first test is 0.

11.11. Values of X, Y, Y', and $Y - Y'$ are shown below.

X	Y	Y'	$Y - Y'$
90	93	80.22	12.78
80	61	77.02	−16.02
86	73	78.94	−5.94
60	73	70.62	2.38
78	85	76.38	8.62
95	80	81.82	−1.82

Positive values are errors of underprediction; negative values are errors of overprediction.

11.12. The sum of the residual scores computed in Comprehension Check 11.11 is 0. This tells us that the overall amount of overprediction is balanced by the overall amount of underprediction.

11.13. The total variance (s_Y^2) is the variance of the obtained values of Y. For the data presented in Comprehension Check 11.4, this is

$$s_Y^2 = \frac{\Sigma(Y - \overline{Y})^2}{N}$$
$$= 102.58$$

11.14. Predicted variance ($s_{Y'}^2$) for the data presented in Comprehension Check 11.4 is computed according to Equation 11.4.

$$s_{Y'}^2 = \frac{\Sigma(Y' - \overline{Y'})^2}{N}$$
$$= \frac{(80.22 - 77.5)^2 + \cdots + (81.82 - 77.5)^2}{6}$$
$$= 12.83$$

11.15. Predicted variance ($s_{Y'}^2 = 12.83$) is only a small fraction of total variance ($s_Y^2 = 102.58$). This tells us that Y (final exam scores) is poorly explained by X (scores on the first exam).

11.16. The coefficient of determination for the data presented in Comprehension Check 11.4 is computed according to Equation 11.5.

$$r^2 = \frac{s^2_{Y'}}{s^2_Y}$$

$$.35^2 = \frac{12.83}{102.58}$$

$.123 = .125$ (the slight difference is a consequence of rounding error)

The coefficient of determination tells us that about 12% of the variance in final exam scores (*Y*) is predicted by scores on the first exam (*X*).

11.17. Predicted variance ($s^2_{Y'}$) for the data presented in Comprehension Check 11.4 is computed according to Equation 11.4.

$$s^2_{Y'} = (r^2)\, s^2_Y$$

$$= (.35^2)102.58$$

$$= 12.57$$

This value differs slightly from the one computed in Comprehension Check 11.14 ($s^2_{Y'} = 12.83$) because of differences in rounding error in the two computational methods. The value computed here is more accurate because it involves fewer computational steps—no Y' values are computed—and so less rounding error.

11.18. Residual variance ($s^2_{Y-Y'}$) for the data presented in Comprehension Check 11.4 is computed according to Equation 11.7.

$$s^2_{Y-Y'} = \frac{\Sigma[(Y - Y') - (\overline{Y - Y'})]^2}{N}$$

$$= \frac{(12.78 - 0)^2 + \cdots + (-1.82 - 0)^2}{6}$$

$$= 89.76$$

11.19. One interpretation of $s^2_{Y-Y'}$ is that it is the variance of the residual scores from the regression analysis. A second, more useful, way of looking at $s^2_{Y-Y'}$ is to view it as the average squared error of prediction. Thus, the average *squared* error in predicting final exam scores from first exam scores was about 90 points.

11.20. The sum of $s^2_{Y'}$ and $s^2_{Y-Y'}$ must always equal s^2_Y because total variance consists of only two components: that which is predicted and that which is not predicted. For the data presented in Comprehension Check 11.4,

$$s^2_Y = s^2_{Y'} + s^2_{Y-Y'}$$

$$102.58 = 12.57 + 89.76$$

$102.58 = 102.33$ (the slight difference is a consequence of rounding error)

11.21. The coefficient of nondetermination for the data presented in Comprehension Check 11.4 is computed according to Equation 11.10.

$$1 - r^2 = \frac{s^2_{Y-Y'}}{s^2_Y}$$

$$1 - .35^2 = \frac{89.76}{102.58}$$

$$.88 = .88$$

The coefficient of nondetermination tells us that about 88% of the variance in final exam scores (*Y*) is *not* predicted by first exam scores (*X*).

11.22. Residual variance ($s^2_{Y-Y'}$) for the data presented in Comprehension Check 11.4 is computed according to Equation 11.11.

$$s^2_{Y-Y'} = (1 - r^2)s^2_Y$$

$$= (1 - .35^2)102.58$$

$$= 90.01$$

This value differs slightly from the one computed in Comprehension Check 11.18 ($s^2_{Y-Y'} = 89.76$) because of differences in rounding error in the two computational methods. The value computed here is more accurate because it involves fewer computational steps—no $Y - Y'$ values are computed—and so less rounding error.

11.23. The standard error of the estimate ($s_{Y-Y'}$) for the data presented in Comprehension Check 11.4 is computed according to Equation 11.12.

$$s_{Y-Y'} = \sqrt{s^2_{Y-Y'}}$$

$$= \sqrt{90.01}$$

$$= 9.49$$

This tells us that the average absolute error made in predicting final exam scores from first exam scores is 9.49 points. This is a substantial error in an exam score.

11.24. The slope (b_X) and constant (a) of the regression equation of *X* on *Y* are computed below.

$$b_X = r\left(\frac{s_X}{s_Y}\right)$$

$$= .35\left(\frac{11.19}{10.13}\right)$$

$$= .39$$

$$a = \overline{X} - b_X\overline{Y}$$

$$= 81.50 - .39(77.50)$$

$$= 51.28$$

Values of X' are computed below for each case using the regression equation of X on Y:

X	Y	$X' = a + b_X Y$
90	93	87.55 = 51.28 + .39(93)
80	61	75.07 = 51.28 + .39(61)
86	73	79.75 = 51.28 + .39(73)
60	73	79.75 = 51.28 + .39(73)
78	85	84.43 = 51.28 + .39(85)
95	80	82.48 = 51.28 + .39(80)

These predicted X' values are plotted in the right column to show the regression line of X on Y. Also shown in this plot is the regression line of Y on X. The two lines are different because each seeks to minimize a different error. The regression line of X on Y minimizes errors in predicting X; the regression line of Y on X minimizes errors in predicting Y.

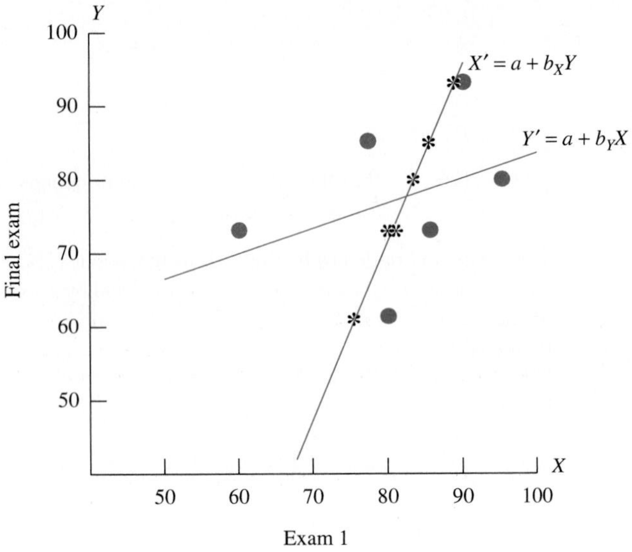

Choosing the Right Procedure

12

Chapter Outline

Omega-square, Wilcoxon T, dependent-samples t test, interval estimation, Kruskal-Wallis analysis of variance by ranks. . . . Dependent samples vs. independent samples, parametric statistics vs. nonparametric statistics, one-way analysis of variance vs. factorial analysis of variance. . . . Your first exposure to statistics may leave you feeling a little like you've got bees in your head!

Our tour through the statistical forest has covered a lot of territory, and you've looked at a lot of statistical trees. At any given point along the way you've probably felt more or less self-confident, but now that the journey is complete, do you remember which way you came? Do you remember which statistic does what and when?

This chapter should help. We'll fly over and map out the whole forest. You'll see where you've been and how you got there. When you've finished this chapter, you'll know how to find your way around the forest in the future.

12.1 What Is the Purpose of the Analysis?

The carpenter who selects a tool from the tool box does so with a plan in mind, a purpose. If the goal is to cut lumber, a saw is the tool of choice. If boards are to be smoothed, a plane may be selected. The social and behavioral scientist who selects a tool from the statistical tool box must also have a plan. You have to know the purpose of your analysis before you select a statistical tool.

You learned in Chapter 1 that statistical procedures can be divided into four basic categories on the basis of their intended purpose: (1) description; (2) evaluating differences; (3)examining relationships; and (4) making predictions. In choosing a statistic you must first determine your purpose. Once that is clear, other decisions follow, leading ultimately to the correct statistical procedure. Figures 12.1 to 12.4, which appear throughout this chapter, map out the statistical options. These decision trees outline the choices to be made as you move from purpose to procedure. Before we look at these maps, though, let's consider more closely the necessary first step: determining the purpose of the analysis.

Description

Some statistics are used to describe. Sometimes we seek to describe individual cases. Other times the goal is to describe a sample consisting of several cases. And occasionally our purpose is to describe an entire population on the basis of a sample drawn from that population. All of these purposes involve statistics in the first category—*description.*

Comprehension Check 12.1

Identify the individual, sample, and population descriptions from the following:

(a) We are 95% confident that the mean age at which American women bear their first child is between 18 and 26.

(b) The median age of a group of 20 residents of Rolling Meadows Retirement Home is 74.6.

(cont.)

(c) Bill falls at the 83rd percentile in his statistics class.

(Answer on p. 391.)

Evaluating Differences

Other statistics are used to evaluate differences. Significant difference tests assess differences between: (1) a sample and a population; (2) two samples; and (3) three or more samples. "Statistically significant" differences are reliable and replicable. Significant differences, though observed in sample data, most likely reflect differences in the corresponding populations as well. Significant difference tests belong to the second category of statistical procedures—*evaluating differences.*

COMPREHENSION CHECK 12.2

Identify the one-sample, two-sample, and multiple-sample significant difference tests from the descriptions that follow:

(a) Both male and female 4-year-olds show significantly higher heart rate when viewing *Teenage Mutant Ninja Turtles* than when viewing *Sesame Street,* but this effect is more pronounced for females than for males.
(b) Fifty migraine patients given sumatriptan show significantly faster recovery from migraine headache than do 50 patients receiving placebo.
(c) The mean IQ of students at Rocky Bottom State University is significantly lower than the mean IQ of college students nationwide.

(Answer on p. 391.)

Examining Relationships

Statistics in the third category are used to examine relationships between variables. These statistics measure the strength of correlations and also evaluate their statistical significance. Sample correlations that are statistically significant indicate the presence of similar correlations in the corresponding population. They are reliable and trustworthy. Procedures used to measure and evaluate correlations belong to the third category of statistical procedures—*examining relationships.*

COMPREHENSION CHECK 12.3

Which of the research questions posed below calls for a correlational analysis?

(a) Do males and females differ in verbal ability at ages 1, 5, 10, and 20 years?
(b) Is a sample of 50 Rocky Bottom State University students representative of the entire student body?
(c) Are intelligence and achievement motivation related?

(Answer on p. 391.)

Making Predictions

Once the relationship between two variables is established, it becomes possible to predict one variable from the other. Statistical procedures used in making predictions, and assessing the accuracy of these predictions, fall into the fourth category—*making predictions.*

COMPREHENSION CHECK 12.4

Which of the following research goals calls for the use of statistical prediction?

(a) A personnel psychologist wants to know if males and females differ in level of job satisfaction.
(b) A college admissions official wants to estimate college GPA based on high school GPA.
(c) A clinical psychologist wants to compare the effectiveness of behavior modification and psychoanalysis.

(Answer on p. 391.)

12.2 DESCRIPTION

Figure 12.1 outlines the decisions made in choosing an appropriate descriptive statistic. The first question to ask yourself is this: *Who or what do you want to describe?* An individual, a sample, or an entire population?

Individuals

Several statistics are used in describing individuals. Which one you use requires that you know the *level of measurement* of the variable of interest.

Nominal Scale. When cases are measured on a nominal scale variable, each individual case can be described by simply naming its *category membership.*

Ordinal Scale. When cases are measured on an ordinal scale variable, each case can be described by indicating its *rank order.*

Interval or Ratio Scale. Measurement on an interval or ratio scale variable opens up more variety in procedures for describing individuals. A case's *percentile rank* locates that case in the distribution by specifying the percentage of cases scoring at and below the case. Alternatively, a case's *z score* locates the case in the distribution by telling how many standard deviations the case falls above or below the mean. If we can assume that the data approximate a normal distribution, we can locate this z score in the *standard normal distribution* (Table 1 in Appendix B) to find the probability of observing scores above, scores below, or scores within any specified range of a case.

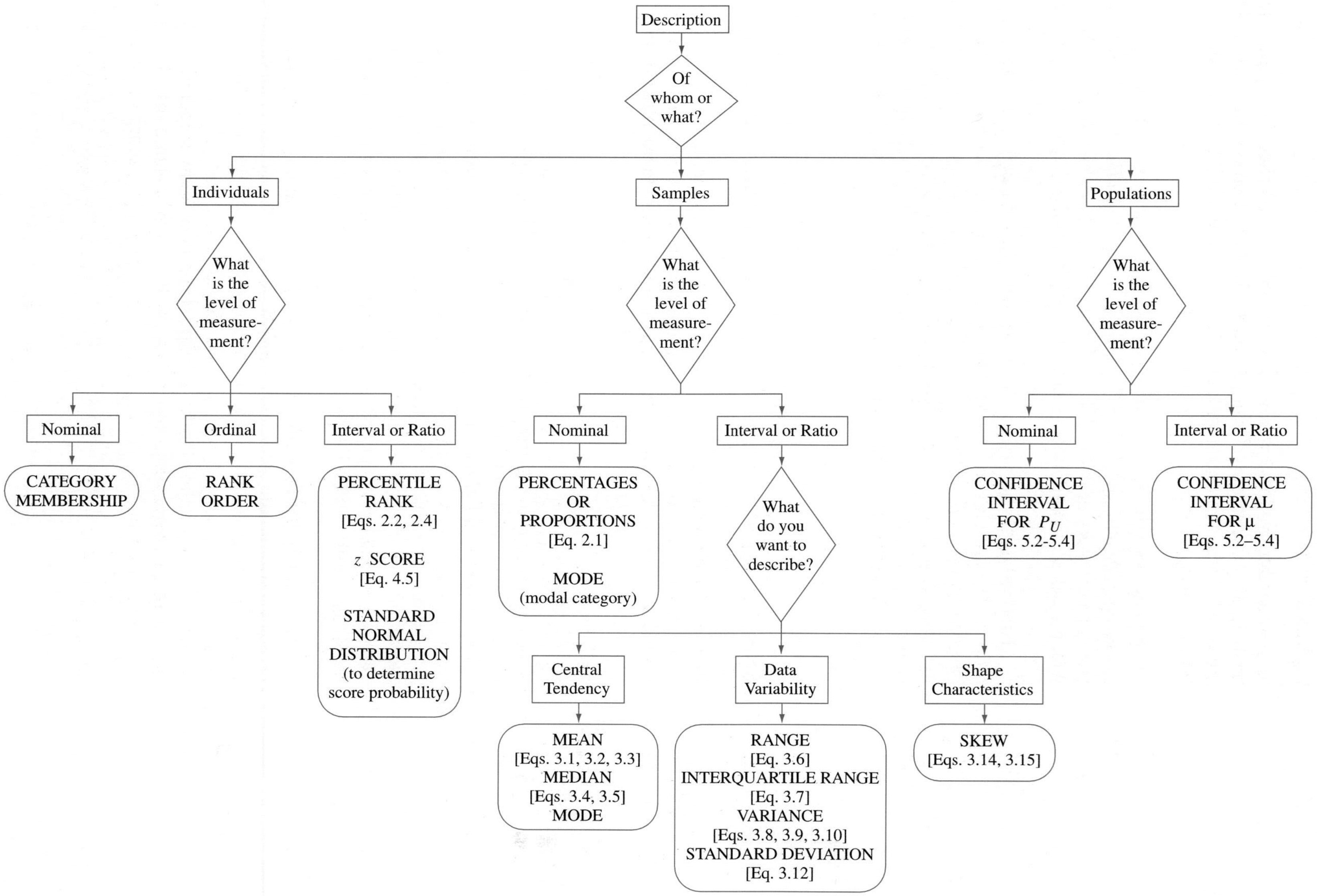

FIGURE 12.1
Decision tree for selecting descriptive statistics and procedures.

Samples

Sometimes we are less interested in describing individual cases than in describing the entire group or sample. Sample descriptive statistics are useful in these situations. Which statistic we use, though, depends again on the *level of measurement.*

Nominal Scale. When measured on a nominal scale variable, the sample can be described by specifying the *percentages or proportions* of cases that fall into each category of the variable. The *modal category,* that is, the category in which cases are found most frequently, represents the average or typical case.

Interval or Ratio Scale. When the sample is measured on an interval or ratio scale variable, several sample descriptive statistics are available, depending on *what one wants to describe. Central tendency,* the average or typical case, is reflected by the *mean,* the *median,* and the *mode.* Of these, the mean is used most often unless the data include extremely high or low outliers. In this case the median provides the more accurate indication of central tendency.

If *data variability* is the characteristic of interest, statistics such as the *range, interquartile range, variance,* and *standard deviation* are useful. Of these, the variance and standard deviation are used most often. The variance figures into the computation of other statistics, and the standard deviation is directly interpretable as roughly equal to the average absolute deviation of scores around the group mean.

When the *shape characteristics* of the sample distribution are of interest, statistics are available that measure *skew,* the lopsidedness of the distribution caused by outliers at one end of the distribution or the other.

Populations

If your purpose is to describe a whole population based on a sample from that population, the first step in selecting an appropriate statistical procedure is to determine the *level of measurement* of the descriptor variable.

Nominal Scale. If the sample is measured on a nominal scale variable, the *confidence interval for the population proportion* (p_U) provides a range of values having a known probability of capturing the proportion of cases in the population that possess the targeted characteristic.

Interval or Ratio Scale. If the sample is measured on an interval or ratio scale variable, the *confidence interval for* μ gives the range of values having a known probability of capturing the mean of the population (μ).

COMPREHENSION CHECK 12.5

Use Figure 12.1 to identify statistical procedures useful in addressing the research questions that follow.

(a) How variable were the scores on your last statistics test?

(b) Based on a sample of 100 male college students, how might one estimate the mean height of all male college students?

(cont.)

(c) How might one describe the relative performance of any single runner in a marathon without mentioning actual running time?

(d) The clinical practice of one therapist involves:

   80% marriage counseling

   15% depression

   3% anxiety disorders

   2% other disorders

   Based on this breakdown, how would you describe the average or typical client in this therapist's practice?

(e) How might one describe the test score of any given introductory psychology student so as to get a sense of "how good" it is?

(f) How might a statistics teacher describe the typical or average student in the class?

(g) What statistic would one use in describing a distribution of test scores distinguished by the presence of low-scoring outliers?

(h) Forty-two percent of the students enrolled in an introductory sociology class are male. Based on this sample, what percentage of the entire student body would you estimate is male?

(i) Each student in your class is either a freshman, sophomore, junior, or senior. If this is all you know about each student, how might you describe any one student from the class?

(Answer on p. 391.)

12.3 Evaluating Differences

Figure 12.2 outlines the decisions made in choosing an appropriate significant difference test, the second category of statistical procedures. The first question to be answered in choosing a significant difference test is this: *How many samples are involved?*

One-Sample Tests

One-sample tests are used to compare the characteristics of a sample against the characteristics of a much larger, often hypothetical, population. The purpose of this comparison is often to determine whether or not the sample can be considered representative of the population. Other times the sample has been treated in some unique way and the population is used as a kind of baseline or control group against which the effect of this treatment is evaluated. Different one-sample significant difference tests are used depending on the *level of measurement of the dependent variable.*

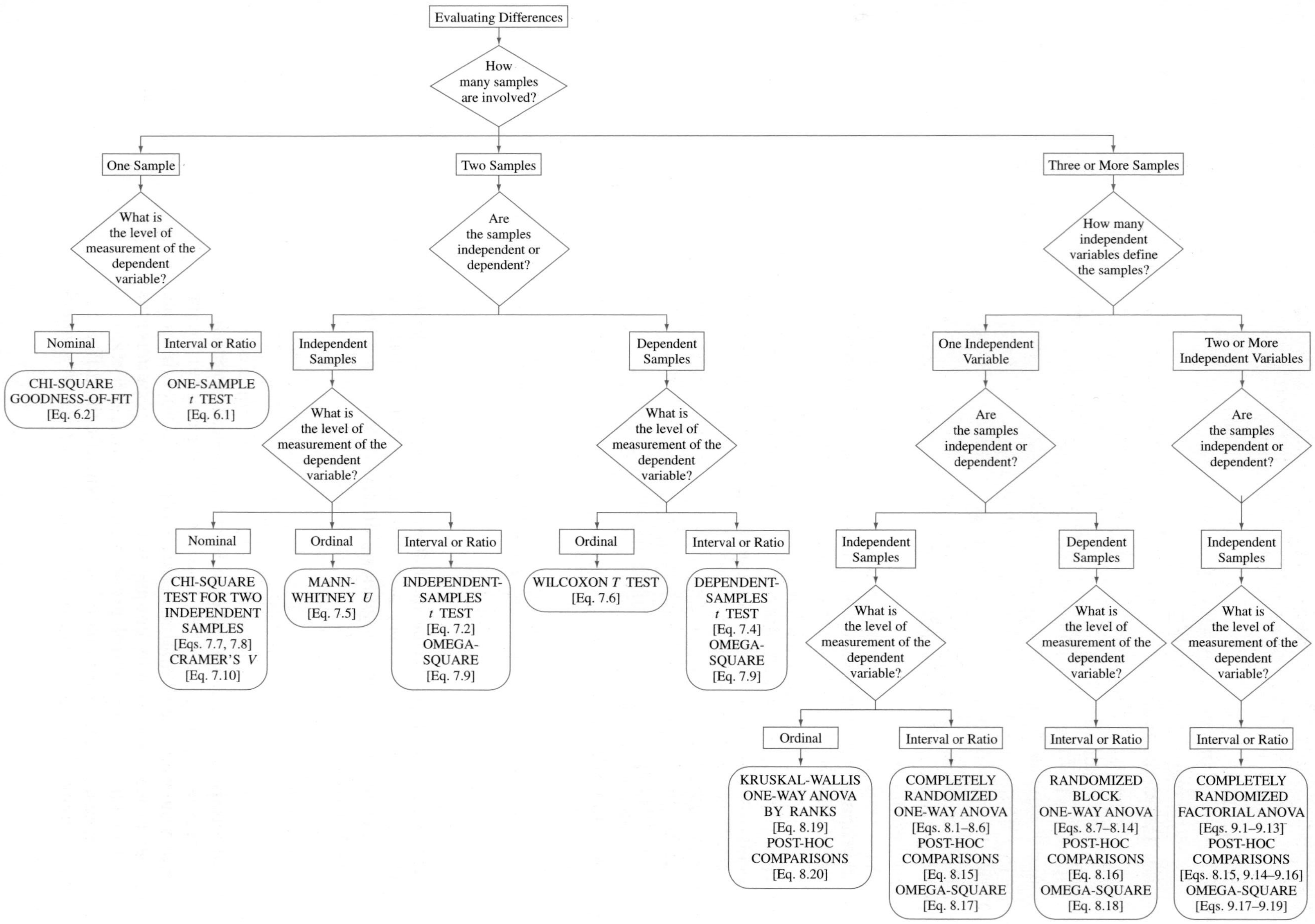

FIGURE 12.2

Decision tree for selecting statistics to evaluate differences.

Nominal Scale. A nominal-scale dependent variable calls for the *chi-square goodness-of-fit* test. This test uses the chi-square statistic to compare the sample frequencies in each category of the dependent variable against the frequencies that would be expected if the sample were distributed exactly like the population.

Interval or Ratio Scale. When the dependent variable is measured on an interval or ratio scale, sample and population means can be compared using the *one-sample t test.* The *t* statistic determines the likelihood that a $\overline{X} - \mu$ difference of a given size would occur in a sample drawn from the specified population.

Two-Sample Tests

There are several two-sample significant difference tests to choose from. In selecting one, you must first determine whether the two samples are *independent or dependent.*

Independent Samples. Samples are independent if each consists of different cases and the cases selected for inclusion in one sample are in no way influenced by the cases selected for inclusion in the other sample.

Depending on the *level of measurement of the dependent variable,* two independent samples can be compared using various different statistics. If the dependent variable is measured at the *nominal* level, the *chi-square test for two independent samples* compares the frequency distributions of the two samples. A significant chi-square statistic indicates that the distributions of the two samples differ by more than would be likely if the two samples were drawn from a population of identically treated cases. *Cramer's V* statistic can be used in conjunction with the chi-square test to measure the strength of association between the dependent variable and the independent variable that defines the groups.

If the dependent variable is measured on an *ordinal* scale, the *Mann-Whitney U* compares the rank orders of cases in the two independent samples. This comparison determines whether one sample scored reliably higher (or lower) than the other.

A dependent variable measured on an *interval or ratio* scale enables using the more powerful *independent-samples t test.* This procedure uses the *t* statistic to evaluate the probability that a $\overline{X}_1 - \overline{X}_2$ difference of the observed size would occur in two independent samples drawn from a population of identically treated cases. The *omega-square* statistic can be used in conjunction with the independent-samples *t* test to measure the strength of association between the dependent variable and the independent variable that defines the groups.

Dependent Samples. Samples are dependent if the composition of one sample *does* affect the composition of the other. Repeated-measures research designs, in which the same cases are measured twice, call for the use of dependent-samples procedures. Matched-samples designs do too, because the cases selected for inclusion in one sample are chosen specifically to be as similar as possible to cases in the other sample. All other things being equal, dependent-samples comparisons offer greater power than independent-samples comparisons.

When the dependent variable is measured on an *ordinal* scale, the *Wilcoxon T test* is used to compare the relative score levels of cases in the two dependent samples. An *interval- or ratio-scale* dependent variable enables using the more powerful *dependent-samples t test.* The *omega-square* statistic can be used in conjunction with the dependent-samples *t* test to measure the strength of association between the dependent variable and the independent variable that defines the two samples.

Three or More Samples

Differences between three or more samples are evaluated using some type of analysis of variance. Choosing the correct analysis requires that you first determine *how many independent variables define the samples.*

One Independent Variable. Sometimes several samples differ along one dimension or independent variable. Examples include comparisons of three different teaching methods, four different drug dosages, or several different racial groups.

If one independent variable defines the groups, *are the samples independent or dependent*? Samples are independent when they consist of different cases and the cases that comprise one sample in no way affect the composition of the other samples. Samples are dependent if the composition of one sample *does* affect the composition of the other samples. Repeated-measures and matched-samples research designs produce dependent samples.

If it is determined that the samples are independent, one next identifies the *level of measurement of the dependent variable.* Three or more independent samples measured on an *ordinal* scale can be compared using the *Kruskal-Wallis one-way analysis of variance by ranks.* This procedure will determine whether there are *any* statistically significant differences between the samples. *Post-hoc comparisons* (such as the Tukey HSD test) can be used to determine which between-group differences have produced the significant *H* statistic of the Kruskal-Wallis test.

Three or more independent samples measured at the *interval or ratio* level can be compared using the *completely randomized one-way analysis of variance.* This procedure assesses the significance of differences between sample means. *Post-hoc comparisons* (such as the Tukey HSD) are used to evaluate the significance of specific between-group differences following a significant *F* statistic in the ANOVA. The *omega-square* statistic can be used to measure strength of association between the dependent variable and the independent variable that defines the groups.

If the samples are dependent, the choice of significant difference tests depends again on the *level of measurement of the dependent variable.* If the dependent variable is measured on an *interval or ratio* scale, differences between the group means can be evaluated for significance using the *randomized-block one-way analysis of variance.* If the *F* test of this analysis is significant, *post-hoc comparisons* (such as the Tukey HSD) can identify which group means differ. The *omega-square* statistic can be used to measure the strength of association between the dependent variable and the independent variable that defines the groups.

Two or More Independent Variables. One-way analysis of variance procedures are used when the samples to be compared are defined by one independent variable. Factorial research designs, though, involve comparisons of groups defined by two or more independent variables. Most factorial designs are "fully crossed," such that all possible combinations of the levels of the two or more independent variables are represented, each by its own sample.

When the samples are defined by two or more independent variables, *are the samples independent or dependent*? If the cases comprising each sample are different and the composition of one sample in no way affects the composition of the other samples, the samples are independent. Given *independent samples,* and an *interval or ratio scale dependent variable,* the *completely randomized factorial analysis of variance* is the significant difference test to use. This procedure evaluates separately the statistical significance of each main effect (that is, the effect of each independent variable on the dependent variable), as well as the interaction effect (that is, the effect of the different treatment combinations on the dependent variable). *Post-hoc comparisons* (including both the Tukey HSD and Scheffé procedure) are used to identify the sources of significant main or interaction effects. The *omega-square* statistic provides a measure of the strength of each of the treatment effects.

COMPREHENSION CHECK 12.6

Use Figure 12.2 to identify statistical procedures useful in addressing the research questions that follow.

(a) Forty-six rats have been trained to run maze A and are rank-ordered on the basis of their performance after 10 trials. The same rats are then injected with an acetylcholine-enhancing drug, are given 10 trials in maze B, and are rank-ordered on performance. How might one compare performance under these two conditions?

(b) Fifty sixth-graders are divided into two equal groups. Group 1 works math problems in their classroom. Group 2 works the same problems outdoors. A record is kept of the number of problems answered correctly by each child. How might one compare performance under these two conditions?

(c) A statistics class includes 58% females and 42% males. In contrast, the university student body is 52% female and 48% male. On the basis of gender alone, can the statistics class be considered representative of the student body?

(d) How might one compare the average running speeds, measured in seconds, of runners in the first, second, third, and fourth quarters of a 1-mile race?

(e) How might one compare the racial composition of 40 public and 37 private universities?

(f) A psychologist counts the number of times 10 clients make eye contact with him during 15-minute interviews conducted both

(cont.)

before and after a series of assertiveness training sessions. How might the effectiveness of the training be evaluated?

(g) Three groups of bicycle racers take 0, 3, or 5 aspirin tablets, respectively, before a race. Order of finish is recorded for each rider. How might one compare the performance of these three groups?

(h) Two hundred psychology majors have missed an average of 3.7 classes this semester. University-wide, the average is 4.2 absences. Can psychology majors be considered representative of the student body in this respect?

(i) An industrial/organizational psychologist randomly selected 10 managers to attend a motivational seminar. Ten other managers were randomly assigned to a waiting-list control group. The managers were subsequently rank-ordered for overall effectiveness. How might these data be used in evaluating the effectiveness of the seminar?

(j) A sociologist has obtained cost-of-living data from 21 cities divided equally among the following geographical regions: New England, Middle Atlantic, and South Atlantic. How might these regions' cost of living be compared?

(k) What procedure might a sports psychologist use to evaluate the effects of mental practice on the free-throw performance (measured as number of baskets shot successfully in 20 trials) of male and female basketball players?

(Answer on pp. 391–392.)

12.4 Examining Relationships

The third category of statistical procedures are those that examine relationships between variables. When one seeks to determine if two variables "go together," are "correlated," or "if there is any relationship between variable *X* and variable *Y*," these are the statistics to turn to.

Figure 12.3 outlines the decisions required to choose the correct correlational procedure. In selecting a procedure from this category, first determine the *level of measurement* of the two variables.

Nominal Scales

When both variables are measured on nominal scales, use the *chi-square test of association.* This test evaluates the statistical significance of the relationship between two nominal scale variables. If the chi-square test is significant, the categories of the two nominal scale variables "go together" in a predictable manner. What the chi-square test does *not* provide is information about the strength of this relationship. This is where the *Cramer's V* statistic comes in. Cramer's *V* measures the strength of association between two nominal scale variables on a 0–1 scale.

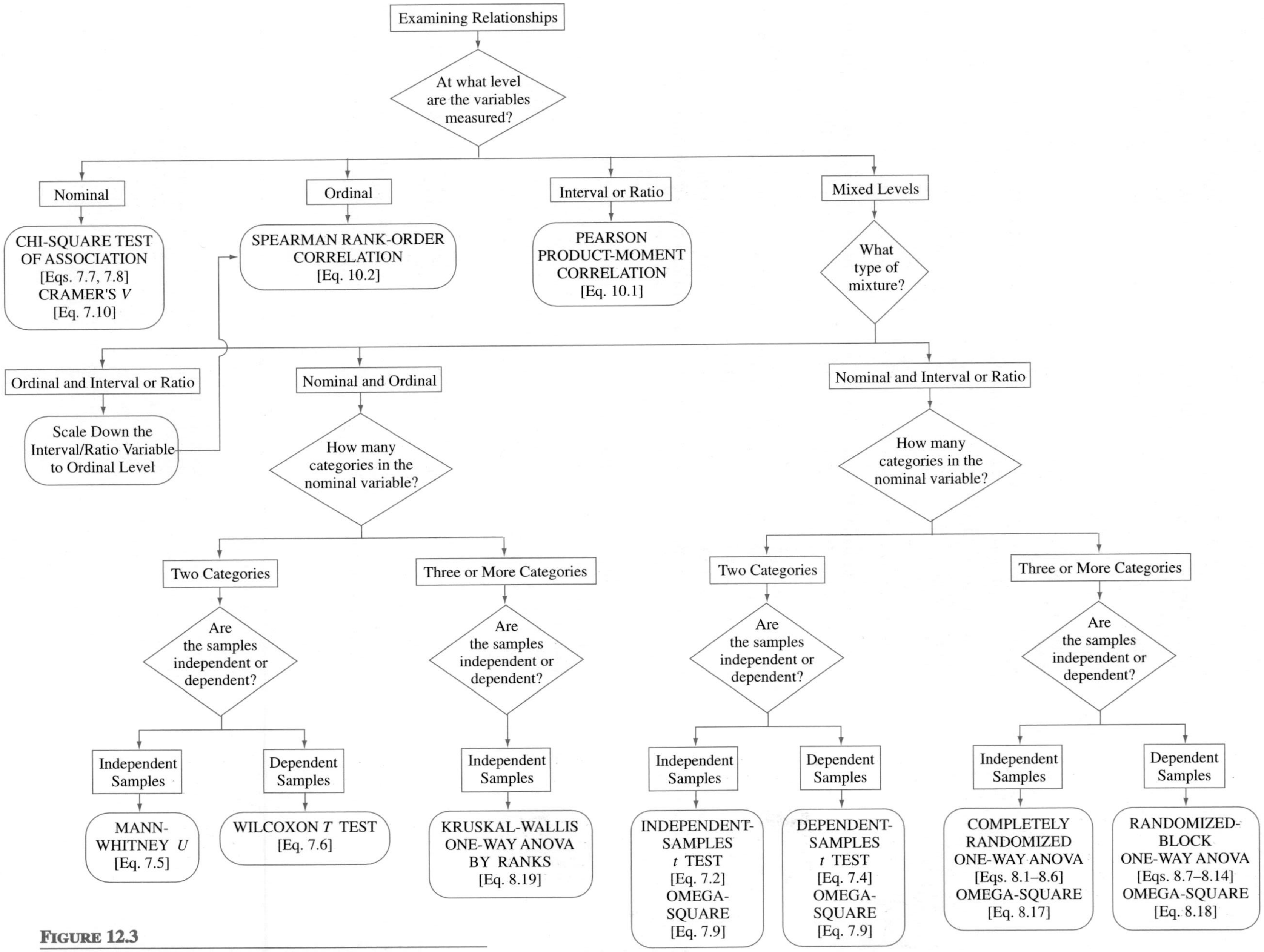

FIGURE 12.3
Decision tree for selecting statistics to evaluate relationships.

Ordinal Scales

If both variables in the analysis are measured on ordinal scales, the correlation between them is assessed using the *Spearman rank-order correlation.* Ranging from -1 to 0 to $+1$, this correlation indicates both the direction and strength of the relationship between variables. The Spearman rank-order correlation also provides a test of the statistical significance of the correlation.

Interval or Ratio Scales

If both variables in the analysis are measured on interval or ratio scales, the *Pearson product-moment correlation* is used to measure the strength of the linear relationship between the variables. The Pearson correlation also provides a test of the statistical significance of the relationship.

Mixed Levels of Measurement

What correlational statistic should be used if the two variables are measured at different levels? If depends on *what type of mixture* is involved.

Ordinal and Interval or Ratio Scales. If one variable is measured on an ordinal scale and the other is measured on an interval or ratio scale, the best procedure is to *scale down the interval or ratio scale variable to the ordinal level.* This is done by rank-ordering the cases based on their scores on the interval or ratio scale. This reduces the problem to one of relating two ordinal scale variables, a task that is well handled by the *Spearman correlation.*

Nominal and Ordinal Scales. If one variable is measured on a nominal scale and the other variable is ordinal, the relationship between the two variables can be evaluated by testing the significance of the difference between the categories of the nominal scale using the ordinal variable as the dependent variable. A significant difference between the categories indicates the presence of a relationship between the variables.

How many categories are there on the nominal scale variable? If there are *two categories,* represented by *independent samples,* use the *Mann-Whitney U* to compare the samples' rank-order scores. If the two categories of the nominal variable are represented by *dependent samples,* the *Wilcoxon T* is used instead to make the comparison.

If there are *three or more categories* on the nominal scale variable, represented by *independent samples,* the *Kruskal-Wallis one-way analysis of variance by ranks* is used to make the comparison.

Nominal and Interval or Ratio Scales. If one variable is measured on a nominal scale and the other variable is measured on an interval or ratio scale, the relationship between the two variables can be evaluated by testing the significance of the difference between the categories of the nominal scale using the interval or ratio variable as the dependent variable. If there are significant differences between the categories, one can conclude that there is a significant relationship between the variables. Moreover, one can use a measure of association strength to get a fix on the strength of this relationship.

How many nominal scale categories are there? Given *two categories* on the nominal variable, each represented by *independent* samples, the *independent-samples t test* is used to test the significance of the relationship, and *omega-square* provides a measure of the strength of the relationship. If the two categories of the nominal variable are represented by *dependent* samples, the *dependent-samples t test* is used to test the significance of the relationship, with *omega-square* again providing a measure of relationship strength.

When the nominal scale variable contains *three or more categories,* each represented by *independent samples,* the *completely randomized one-way analysis of variance* tests the significance of the relationship, and *omega-square* measures its strength. When the three or more categories are represented by *dependent samples,* the *randomized-block one-way analysis of variance* is used instead, again accompanied by *omega-square.*

COMPREHENSION CHECK 12.7

Use Figure 12.3 to identify statistical procedures useful in addressing the research questions that follow.

(a) A sports psychologist has kept records of the order of finish and racial status (white, African-American, Hispanic, Asian, other) status of 317 marathon runners. How can he determine if race and marathon performance are related?

(b) A personnel psychologist wants to know if there is a relationship between marital status (married vs. single) and job productivity, measured by supervisor rankings.

(c) A teacher has recorded the exam score of 27 students as well as the order in which they completed the exam. How can she determine if there is reliable relationship between time taken to complete the exam and performance on the exam?

(d) A marriage therapist videotaped counseling sessions with 21 couples. He has counted the number of times each spouse interrupts the other during these sessions. How can he assess the relationship between gender and the tendency to interrupt?

(e) A sociologist has data from 2,011 females on educational achievement (number of years of school completed) and family size (number of children). What statistic will measure the strength of the relationship between these two variables?

(f) Annual incomes are recorded for individuals in each of five racial groups. How can the relationship between race and income be measured?

(g) Twenty-three individuals have been rank-ordered for level of depression and level of aerobic fitness. How might one assess the relationship between mood and aerobic fitness from these data?

(h) On three separate occasions, 47 long-distance runners run 10-kilometer courses that are primarily uphill, primarily downhill, or primarily flat. Heart rate is measured in beats

(*cont.*)

per minute after each run. How might one evaluate the relationship between type of course and heart rate from these data?

(i) How might a sociologist assess the strength of the relationship between religious affiliation and political affiliation?

(j) With what statistic might one measure the association between gender and physical strength, measured as number of pounds each case can lift?

(Answer on pp. 392–393.)

12.5 Making Predictions

Once it is established that two variables are related, it becomes possible to predict one variable from the other. Figure 12.4 diagrams the decisions needed to select the correct procedure for making predictions. Translating relationships into predictions begins by figuring out *how the relationship was established.*

Pearson Product-Moment Correlation

The Pearson correlation provides the foundation for *bivariate linear regression,* in which scores on one interval or ratio scale variable are used to predict scores on a second interval or ratio scale variable.

Several *measures of predictive accuracy* are available to evaluate bivariate linear regression. The coefficient of determination gives the proportion of variance in one variable that is explained by the other. The coefficient of nondetermination gives the proportion of variance in one variable that is *not* ex-

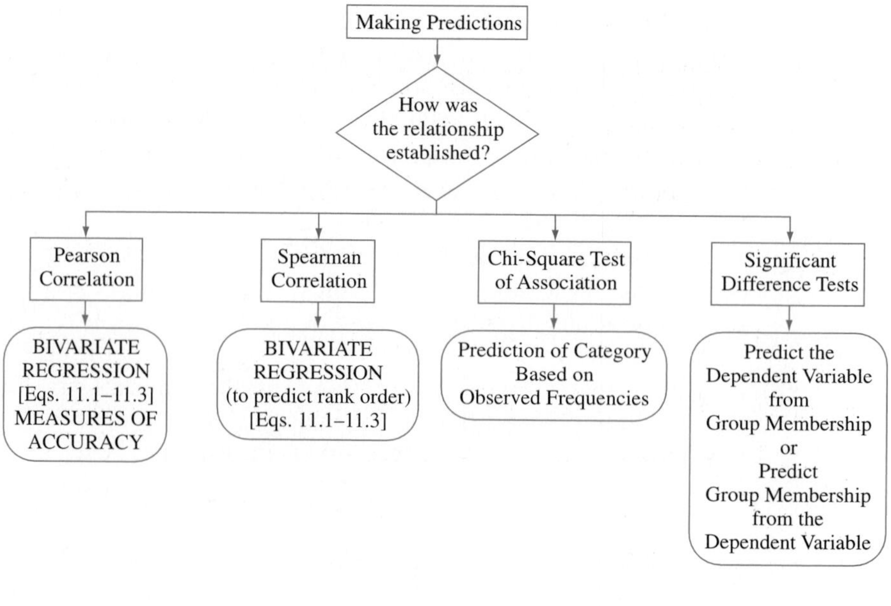

FIGURE 12.4

Decision tree for selecting statistics and procedures for making predictions.

plained by the other. Residual variance is the average squared error of prediction. The standard error of the estimate is roughly equal to the average absolute error of prediction.

Spearman Rank-Order Correlation

When both variables are expressed as rank orders, the Spearman correlation is used to measure the relationship. This correlation measures the strength of the monotonic relationship between the variables, but can be substituted in place of the Pearson r in the equations associated with *bivariate regression.* In this case, the regression equation predicts a case's rank order on one variable from its rank order on the other variable.

Chi-Square Test of Association

When the relationship between two nominal scale variables has been established using the chi-square test of association (and Cramer's V), it becomes possible to predict a case's category membership on one variable from its category membership on the other variable. We *predict category membership based on the observed frequencies* in the contingency table. This process will be illustrated with an example.

Table 12.1 is a contingency table that summarizes the relationship between gender (male vs. female) and arrests for violent crimes (violent criminals vs. all others) in the United States. You can see from the observed frequencies presented in this table that males commit 85% of the violent crimes in America:

$$\frac{\text{1,544,305 male violent criminals}}{\text{1,816,830 total violent criminals}} = 85\%$$

The observed frequencies show that females commit only 15% of the violent crimes:

$$\frac{\text{272,525 female violent criminals}}{\text{1,816,830 total violent criminals}} = 15\%$$

Gender and violent crime are clearly related: Males are far more likely than females to commit a violent crime.

Based on this relationship, we can predict a case's category membership on one variable from its category membership on the other variable. Suppose we know that someone is a violent criminal. The observed frequencies in

TABLE 12.1

Contingency table summarizing the statistically significant relationship between gender and violent crime

		Criminal Status		
		Violent Criminals	*All Others*	**Row Totals**
Gender	*Male*	1,544,305	123,955,695	125,500,500
	Female	272,525	125,227,475	125,500,000
Column totals		1,816,830	249,183,170	

Table 12.1 tell us that the probability that this person is a male is 85%, because 85% of all violent criminals are male.

Now suppose that we know that someone is male. The observed frequencies in Table 12.1 show that the probability that this male is a violent criminal is only about 1.24%, because only about 1.24% of all males are arrested for violent crimes:

$$\frac{1{,}544{,}305 \text{ male violent criminals}}{125{,}500{,}000 \text{ total males}} = 1.24\%$$

Relationships Based on Significant Differences

Correlational statistics are the most common way to assess relationships between variables, but they are not the only way. Significant difference tests also point to relationships. If two or more groups differ significantly, we know that the independent and dependent variables are related. It follows that if we know a case's independent variable group membership, we can make a rough prediction of that case's score on the dependent variable. Similarly, if we know the case's score on the dependent variable, we can predict the case's independent variable group membership.

Predicting the Dependent Variable from Group Membership. Suppose that two groups, A and B, are found to differ significantly on some ordinal, interval, or ratio scale dependent variable, with group A scores generally higher than group B scores. If you know that a given case is a member of group A, what would you predict about that case's score on the dependent variable? Your best bet would be that it is relatively high, probably falling near the mean of group A. If you know that a case is a member of group B, your best prediction for that case's score on the dependent variable is that it is relatively low, probably falling near the group B mean.

The same principle applies when there are three or more groups. Whenever there are significant between-group differences and we know a case's group membership, we can predict that that case's score on the dependent variable probably falls somewhere near the mean of its group.

If the scores of each group are normally distributed, we can use the standard normal distribution (Table 1 in Appendix B) to be even more specific: If a case is a member of group A, and group A scores are normally distributed, we know that there is a 34% probability that the case falls between the mean and 1 standard deviation above the mean; the probability is 68% that the case falls within 1 standard deviation on either side of the mean; the probability is 95% that the score falls within 1.96 standard deviations on either side of the mean; and so on.

Predicting Group Membership from the Dependent Variable. Let's continue to suppose that groups A and B differ significantly, with group A scoring generally higher than group B. If you have a case with a high score on the dependent variable, what is its most likely group membership? The case probably belongs to the group with the higher scores—group A. It also follows that if the case has a low score on the dependent variable, it most likely belongs to the low-scoring group—group B.

As before, if the distributions of scores within groups are normal, we can be more precise about predicting group membership. We can use the standard normal distribution (Table 1 in Appendix B) to determine the probability that any given score would be found in any given group by measuring that score's distance from each group mean.

COMPREHENSION CHECK 12.8

Use Figure 12.4 to identify statistical procedures useful in addressing the research questions that follow.

(a) A significant Spearman rank-order correlation between ranked sociability and ranked sales volume shows these two variables to be related. How might a personnel psychologist use this relationship to predict sales success from sociability?

(b) The contingency table that follows summarizes the relationship between gender and color preference. A chi-square analysis has found this relationship to be statistically significant. Given a male, what color preference would be most likely? Given a case that prefers red, what gender would be most likely?

		Gender		
		Male	*Female*	**Row Totals**
Color	*Red*	20	60	80
	Green	20	20	40
	Blue	70	10	80
Column totals		110	90	$N = 200$

(c) An independent-samples t test has confirmed that people blink their eyes at a significantly faster rate when lying ($\overline{X}_1 = 10.1$ blinks per minute; $\hat{s}_1 = 5.2$) than when telling the truth ($\overline{X}_2 = 6.4$ blinks per minute; $\hat{s}_2 = 4.3$). On the basis of this significant difference, would you predict that someone who blinks 7 times per minute is lying or telling the truth? What would you predict the blink rate would be for someone who is lying?

(d) The Pearson product-moment correlation between Graduate Record Examination (GRE) scores and graduate grade-point average (GPA) in psychology is about .3. Based on this correlation, how would one predict graduate GPA from GRE?

(Answer on p. 393.)

SUMMARY

The skillful application of statistical tools requires that one recognize the circumstances that call for each procedure. Description, evaluating differences, examining relationships, and making predictions are the four basic purposes to which statistics are applied. Identifying one's purpose is therefore the first step in choosing an appropriate procedure.

Descriptive statistics are used to describe individuals, samples, and populations. Choosing the right procedure from each of these subgroups requires knowing the level of measurement of the descriptor variable, as well as what it is that you want to describe.

Significant difference tests are used in evaluating differences. There are one-sample tests, two-sample tests, and tests for situations involving three or more samples. Selecting the correct significant difference test requires knowing the level of measurement of the dependent variable, whether the samples being compared are independent or dependent, and, in the case of multiple-sample comparisons, whether the samples differ on one or more than one independent variable.

A variety of correlational statistics are used to examine relationships between variables. Scale of measurement is again the crucial factor in selecting the right correlational procedure. Most standard measures of correlation require that both variables be measured at the same level. When the two variables are measured at different levels, significant difference tests and measures of association can be used to evaluate relationships. The logic is that if samples differ on some dependent variable, there is a relationship between that dependent variable and the independent variable(s) that defines the samples.

If two variables are related, one variable can be predicted from the other. Procedures used in making predictions vary depending on how the relationship between variables was established.

Review Exercises

For each of the research questions described below, identify the most likely statistical procedure.

12.1. Is there a significant difference between male and female scores on the verbal portion of the SAT?

12.2. Does a male's age (middle-aged vs. older) and facial hair (beard vs. no beard) affect ratings of his masculinity?

12.3. Having established that religious preference and political preference are related, how can we predict one from the other?

12.4. Do college graduates differ from high school graduates in the frequency with which they display each of 10 psychopathologies?

12.5. Do managers who undergo sensitivity training spend more time interacting with their subordinates after training than they did before training?

12.6. Three groups of Alzheimer's patients received either a placebo, 50 milligrams, or 100 milligrams of an experimental drug for 6 weeks before taking a memory test. How can differences among the groups be evaluated?

12.7. Male and female students in a speech class have been rank-ordered according to their levels of speech anxiety. How can it be determined if males and females differ in speech anxiety?

12.8. How might we best describe the political preference of an individual voter?

12.9. Based on a sample of 1,000 voters, how might we estimate the proportion of voters in the nation who prefer one presidential candidate over another?

12.10. How might we best describe the racial composition of a specific introductory sociology class?

12.11. How can graduate grade-point average be predicted from Graduate Record Examination scores?

12.12. How might we describe one student's level of academic achievement in a class of students who have been rank-ordered on this variable?

12.13. How might we describe the variability of GRE scores of applicants to a graduate psychology program?

12.14. Samples of alcoholics, cocaine addicts, and heroine addicts have been rank-ordered for trait anxiety. How can differences among these groups be evaluated?

12.15. Sexual attitudes of teenagers are evaluated before and again after a high school sex education class. How can attitude change be evaluated?

12.16. How can a researcher see if the racial composition of a sample of 100 students mirrors the racial distribution of the university?

12.17. How can a researcher determine if the average age of a sample of 100 students matches the average age of the entire student body?

12.18. Ten husbands and their wives are rank-ordered for assertiveness. How can it be determined whether the husbands or wives are more assertive?

12.19. Three groups of depressed patients have been formed by matching patients on age and initial levels of depression. The groups receive either 10 milligrams, 20 milligrams, or 40 milligrams of an experimental drug for 6 weeks and are then tested to measure their depression. How can differences among these groups be evaluated?

12.20. How might the typical or average weight be established for a group of participants in a weight-loss program?

12.21. How can we describe the weight of an individual who is enrolled in a weight-loss program?

12.22. How can we determine if undergraduate GPA and scores on a test of self-esteem are related?

12.23. Scores on a statistics test have been rank-ordered and the order in which students completed the test recorded. How can the relationship between these variables be measured?

12.24. How can one measure the degree of correspondence between a therapist's initial diagnoses of 50 clients and her final diagnoses?

12.25. How might we estimate the mean IQ of a population of junior high school students after testing only 50 students?

ANSWERS TO COMPREHENSION CHECKS

12.1. **(a)** Population
(b) Sample
(c) Individual

12.2. **(a)** Multiple-sample
(b) Two-sample
(c) One-sample

12.3. Scenario (c) calls for a correlational analysis. Scenario (a) is a factorial design calling for a significant difference test. Scenario (b) is a one-sample significant difference test.

12.4. Scenario (b) calls for statistical prediction. Scenarios (a) and (c) both call for two-sample significant difference tests.

12.5. For each research problem, the correct sequence of choices in Figure 12.1 is listed below.

(a) Purpose: Description
Of what or whom? Samples
What is the level of measurement? Interval or ratio
What do you want to describe? Data variability
RANGE, INTERQUARTILE RANGE, VARIANCE, STANDARD DEVIATION

(b) Purpose: Description
Of what or whom? Populations
What is the level of measurement? Interval or ratio
CONFIDENCE INTERVAL FOR THE POPULATION MEAN

(c) Purpose: Description
Of what or whom? Individuals
What is the level of measurement? Ordinal
RANK ORDER

(d) Purpose: Description
Of what or whom? Samples
What is the level of measurement? Nominal
MODAL CATEGORY

(e) Purpose: Description
Of what or whom? Individuals
What is the level of measurement? Interval or ratio
PERCENTILE RANK, *z* SCORE, STANDARD NORMAL DISTRIBUTION

(f) Purpose: Description
Of what or whom? Samples
What is the level of measurement? Interval or ratio
What do you want to describe? Central tendency
MEAN, MEDIAN, MODE

(g) Purpose: Description
Of what or whom? Samples
What is the level of measurement? Interval or ratio
What do you want to describe? Shape characteristics
SKEW

(h) Purpose: Description
Of what or whom? Populations
What is the level of measurement? Nominal
CONFIDENCE INTERVAL FOR POPULATION PROPORTION

(i) Purpose: Description
Of what or whom? Individuals
What is the level of measurement? Nominal
CATEGORY MEMBERSHIP

12.6. For each research problem, the correct sequence of choice points in Figure 12.2 is listed below.

(a) Purpose: Evaluating differences
How many samples are involved? Two samples
Are the samples independent or dependent?
Dependent samples
What is the level of measurement of the dependent variable? Ordinal
WILCOXON *T* TEST

(b) Purpose: Evaluating differences
How many samples are involved? Two samples
Are the samples independent or dependent?
Independent samples
What is the level of measurement of the dependent variable? Interval or ratio
INDEPENDENT-SAMPLES *t* TEST

(c) Purpose: Evaluating differences
How many samples are involved? One sample
What is the level of measurement of the dependent variable? Nominal
CHI-SQUARE GOODNESS-OF-FIT TEST

(d) Purpose: Evaluating differences
How many samples are involved? Three or more samples
How many independent variables define the samples? One independent variable
Are the samples independent or dependent? Dependent samples
What is the level of measurement of the dependent variable? Interval or ratio
RANDOMIZED-BLOCK ONE-WAY ANOVA

(e) Purpose: Evaluating differences
How many samples are involved? Two samples
Are the samples independent or dependent? Independent samples
What is the level of measurement of the dependent variable? Nominal
CHI-SQUARE TEST FOR TWO INDEPENDENT SAMPLES

(f) Purpose: Evaluating differences
How many samples are involved? Two samples
Are the samples independent or dependent? Dependent samples
What is the level of measurement of the dependent variable? Interval or ratio
DEPENDENT-SAMPLES *t* TEST

(g) Purpose: Evaluating differences
How many samples are involved? Three or more samples
How many independent variables define the samples? One independent variable
Are the samples independent or dependent? Independent samples
What is the level of measurement of the dependent variable? Ordinal
KRUSKAL-WALLIS ONE-WAY ANOVA BY RANKS

(h) Purpose: Evaluating differences
How many samples are involved? One sample
What is the level of measurement of the dependent variable? Interval or ratio
ONE-SAMPLE *t* TEST

(i) Purpose: Evaluating differences
How many samples are involved? Two samples
Are the samples independent or dependent? Independent samples
What is the level of measurement of the dependent variable? Ordinal
MANN-WHITNEY *U*

(j) Purpose: Evaluating differences
How many samples are involved? Three or more samples
Are the samples independent or dependent? Independent samples
What is the level of measurement of the dependent variable? Interval or ratio
COMPLETELY RANDOMIZED ONE-WAY ANOVA

(k) Purpose: Evaluating differences
How many samples are involved? Three or more samples
How many independent variables define the samples? Two or more independent variables
Are the samples independent or dependent? Independent samples
What is the level of measurement of the dependent variable? Interval or ratio
COMPLETELY RANDOMIZED FACTORIAL ANOVA

12.7. For each research problem, the correct sequence of choice points in Figure 12.3 is listed below.

(a) Purpose: Examining relationships
At what level are the variables measured? Mixed levels
What type of mixture? Nominal and ordinal
How many categories in the nominal variable? Three or more categories
Are the samples independent or dependent? Independent samples
KRUSKAL-WALLIS ONE-WAY ANOVA BY RANKS

(b) Purpose: Examining relationships
At what level are the variables measured? Mixed levels
What type of mixture? Nominal and ordinal
How many categories in the nominal variable? Two categories
Are the samples independent or dependent? Independent samples
MANN-WHITNEY *U*

(c) Purpose: Examining relationships
At what level are the variables measured? Mixed levels
What type of mixture? Ordinal and interval or ratio
Scale down the interval/ratio variable to ordinal level
SPEARMAN RANK-ORDER CORRELATION

(d) Purpose: Examining relationships
At what level are the variables measured? Mixed levels
What type of mixture? Nominal and interval or ratio
How many categories in the nominal variable? Two categories
Are the samples independent or dependent? Dependent samples
DEPENDENT-SAMPLES *t* TEST

(e) Purpose: Examining relationships
At what level are the variables measured? Interval or ratio

PEARSON PRODUCT-MOMENT CORRELATION

(f) Purpose: Examining relationships
At what level are the variables measured? Mixed levels
What type of mixture? Nominal and interval or ratio
How many categories in the nominal variable? Three or more categories
Are the samples independent or dependent? Independent samples
COMPLETELY RANDOMIZED ONE-WAY ANOVA

(g) Purpose: Examining relationships
At what level are the variables measured? Ordinal
SPEARMAN RANK-ORDER CORRELATION

(h) Purpose: Examining relationships
At what level are the variables measured? Mixed levels
What type of mixture? Nominal and interval or ratio
How many categories in the nominal variable? Three or more categories
Are the samples independent or dependent? Dependent samples
RANDOMIZED-BLOCK ONE-WAY ANOVA

(i) Purpose: Examining relationships
At what level are the variables measured? Nominal
CHI-SQUARE TEST OF ASSOCIATION

(j) Purpose: Examining relationships
At what level are the variables measured? Mixed levels
What type of mixture? Nominal and interval or ratio
How many categories in the nominal variable? Two categories
Are the samples independent or dependent? Independent samples
INDEPENDENT-SAMPLES *t* TEST

12.8. For each research problem, the correct sequence of choice points in Figure 12.4 is listed below.

(a) Purpose: Making predictions
How was the relationship established? Spearman correlation
BIVARIATE REGRESSION (to predict rank order)

(b) Purpose: Making predictions
How was the relationship established? Chi-square test of association
PREDICTION OF CATEGORY BASED ON OBSERVED FREQUENCIES

Given a male case: $p(\text{red}) = .18$; $p(\text{green}) = .18$; $p(\text{blue}) = .64$
Given a red preference: $p(\text{male}) = .25$; $p(\text{female}) = .75$

(c) Purpose: Making predictions
How was the relationship established? Significant difference test
PREDICT THE DEPENDENT VARIABLE FROM GROUP MEMBERSHIP
or
PREDICT GROUP MEMBERSHIP FROM THE DEPENDENT VARIABLE

A case with a score of 7 falls .42 standard deviations above the mean of truth-tellers and .60 standard deviations below the mean of liars. This case is most likely truthful.

The best estimate of the score of a liar would be the mean of the distribution of liars: 10.1.

(d) Purpose: Making predictions
How was the relationship established? Pearson correlation
BIVARIATE REGRESSION

Appendix A

An Introduction to Summation Notation

Can you imagine trying to tell someone how to play the first violin part of a Beethoven symphony using words alone? Impossible! How about the banjo version of "Oh Susannah"? Even that would be a tremendously difficult task. Communicating about music in words alone is almost impossible. Composers need special symbols—musical notation—to indicate which notes are to be played in which order, which notes are to be sharp or flat, and to set the rhythm and tempo of the piece. Musical notation makes it much easier to communicate about music.

Statistics is a lot like music in this regard. Just as composers use musical notation to tell musicians how to play a piece of music, statisticians use mathematical notation to describe how numbers are to be manipulated. You are already familiar with many of the symbols used in statistics, such as the + sign for addition, × for multiplication, and exponents that tell you to square numbers. But you are probably less familiar with other symbols used in statistics. The purpose of this appendix is to familiarize you with statistical notation.

A.1 Variables

Statistics can be defined as the study of data variability. The variables that we study in the social and behavioral sciences include ages of individuals, crime rates of cities, and numbers of errors made by rats in mazes. Statistical procedures help us to study this variability. With statistics we can get past data variability to describe whole groups. With statistics we can see if the variability seen from one group to the next is the consequence of different treatments received by those groups. With statistics we determine which variables vary together.

With so much time spent studying variables, it isn't surprising that we've developed symbols to make the job easier. Instead of listing every value of every variable every time we want to work with those variables, we use symbols to represent our variables. Instead of listing 180 IQ scores, we refer to the variable X. Instead of listing 76 cities' crime rates, we refer to the variable Y.

The uppercase letters X and Y are commonly used to represent variables, but you will find other symbols used to represent numbers. N stands for the number of cases in an analysis and k often stands for the number of different groups or samples one is studying. Sometimes we use Greek letters as symbols to represent numbers. μ, the lowercase Greek letter mu, is the symbol used to stand for a population mean. The symbol used to represent the standard deviation of a population is σ, the lowercase Greek letter sigma. χ^2, chi-square, is another statistic that is represented by a Greek letter, and there are many more symbols that you will encounter as you study statistics.

Variable Subscripts

Subscripts can be used in conjunction with letters and other symbols to specify more precisely *which* value of a variable one is referring to. For instance, X_3 is a reference to the third value of the variable X. $\overline{X}_2$ is the mean of the second group. The standard deviation of the first group is represented by s_1.

A.2 Summation Notation

summation notation *Mathematical notation common in statistics that uses the summation sign (Σ) in directing the summing of numbers.*

Summation notation is another type of notation that is used in statistics. Many statistical procedures require summing lists of numbers, and summation notation tells us which numbers to sum. Summation notation is in use any time you see the uppercase Greek letter sigma, Σ, the summation sign.

The summation sign directs one to sum the values that follow the Σ. For example, if X is the name of a variable consisting of the values 13, 32, 16, and 7, ΣX means: "Sum the values of the variable X."

$$X = 13 + 32 + 16 + 7 = 68$$

Or, if Y is the name of a variable consisting of the values 2, −4, 10, 6, and 0, ΣY means: "Sum the values of the variable Y."

$$\Sigma Y = 2 + -4 + 10 + 6 + 0 = 14$$

The Summation Index

summation index *Information listed above and below the summation sign (Σ) that specifies the starting and stopping points for the summation.*

Sometimes we need to be more specific in describing *which* values of the variable are to be summed. This specificity is obtained by adding a **summation index** to the summation sign. The summation index is found above and below the Σ and indicates which value the summing is to begin with (below the Σ), and which value the summing is to end with (above the Σ). Thus, $\sum_{i=1}^{N} X_i$ is read: "Sum the values of the variable X, *beginning with the first* (X_1) and *ending with the Nth* (the last—X_N). Suppose that X is a variable consisting of the values 4, 3, 10, and 5. Then $\sum_{i=1}^{N} X_i$ is read: "Sum the values of the variable X beginning with the first and ending with the last."

$$\sum_{i=1}^{N} X_i = 4 + 3 + 10 + 5 = 22$$

The notation $\sum_{i=2}^{N} X_i$ is read: "Sum the values of the variable X beginning with the second value and ending with the last."

$$\sum_{i=2}^{N} X_i = 3 + 10 + 5 = 18$$

The notation $\sum_{i=2}^{3} X_i$ is read: "Sum the values of the variable X beginning with the second value and ending with the third."

$$\sum_{i=2}^{3} X_i = 3 + 10 = 13$$

The expressions ΣX and $\sum_{i=1}^{N} X_i$ are equivalent. Both tell us to sum all the values of the variable X. Most often when we are summing the values of some variable, we will want to sum them all. To save time and ink, the summation index is often omitted.

A.3 Working with Parentheses and Brackets

We've covered the basics of summation notation. We'll turn now to slightly more complicated expressions involving parentheses and brackets.

When reading summation notation that includes parentheses and brackets, perform the operations specified in the innermost set of parentheses first, then move outside the parentheses and do what is directed there. In other words, work from the inside out.

In the spirit of learning by doing, consider each of the following examples of summation notation involving parentheses. For each, assume that $X = 1, 4, 2, 6$ and $Y = 2, 1, 0, 3$.

1. $(\Sigma X) + 1 = 14$
   Working inside the parentheses first:"Sum the values of the variable X." Next, moving outside the parentheses:"Add 1."
2. $\Sigma(X + 1) = 17$
   Working inside the parentheses first:"Add 1 to each value of the variable X." Next, moving outside the parentheses: "Sum these values."
3. $(\Sigma X)3 = 39$
   Working inside the parentheses first:"Sum the values of the variable X." Next, moving outside the parentheses: "Multiply this value by 3."
4. $(\Sigma X)^2 = 169$
   Working inside the parentheses first:"Sum the values of the variable X." Next, moving outside the parentheses:"Square this value."
5. $\Sigma X^2 = 57$
   This expression is a little tricky. Should we first add the values of X and then square the sum? Or should we first square the values of the variable X and sum these squared values? Compare this expression to the preceding one. There, we first added, then squared. Here we first square each value of the variable X and then sum these squared values.
6. $[\Sigma(X + 1)]^2 = 289$
   Working inside the innermost set of parentheses: "Add 1 to each value of the variable X." Next, moving outside these parentheses: "Sum these values." Finally, moving outside the brackets: "Square this value."

7. $[(\Sigma X) + 1]^2 = 196$
   Working inside the innermost set of parentheses:"Sum the values of the variable *X*." Next, moving outside the parentheses: "Add 1 to this sum." Finally, moving outside the brackets: "Square this value."
8. $\Sigma XY = 24$
   Multiply corresponding values of *X* and *Y* (i.e., the first value of *X* times the first value of *Y*, the second value of *X* times the second value of *Y*, etc.). Then sum these products.
9. $\Sigma(X + Y) = 19$
   Working inside the parentheses first: "Add corresponding values of *X* and *Y*." Next, moving outside the parentheses: "Add these values."
10. $\Sigma(X^2 + Y^2) = 71$
    Working inside the parentheses first: "Square each value of the variable *X*. Square each value of the variable *Y*. Add corresponding squares together." Next, moving outside the parentheses: "Add these values."

A.4 Working with Complex Summation Notation

More complex summation notation expressions are seen occasionally. Don't panic! These complex expressions are really just collections of simpler expressions. Take the raw score formula for the Pearson correlation (r) as an example:

$$r = \frac{\Sigma XY - \dfrac{(\Sigma X)(\Sigma Y)}{N}}{\sqrt{\left[\Sigma X^2 - \dfrac{(\Sigma X)^2}{N}\right]\left[\Sigma Y^2 - \dfrac{(\Sigma Y)^2}{N}\right]}}$$

This equation looks pretty awesome until you notice that it's built up of simpler expressions as labeled below:

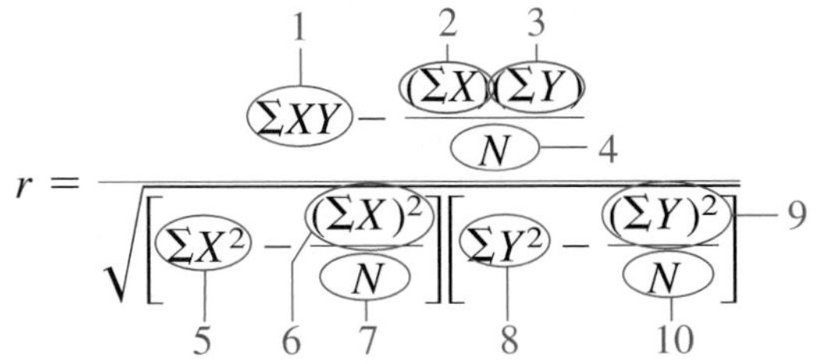

1. Multiply corresponding values of *X* and *Y* and add these values—24.
2. Sum the values of the variable *X*—13.
3. Sum the values of the variable *Y*—6.
4. *N* is the number of pairs of cases—4.
5. Square each value of *X* and sum these squared values—57.
6. Sum the values of the variable *X* and square this sum—169.
7. *N* is the number of pairs of scores—4.
8. Square each value of the variable *Y* and sum these squared values—14.
9. Sum the values of the variable *Y* and square this sum—36.
10. *N* is the number of pairs of scores—4.

Once the numerical values associated with each component of the expression are determined, the problem is reduced to one of simple arithmetic:

$$r = \frac{24 - \dfrac{(13)(6)}{4}}{\sqrt{\left(57 - \dfrac{169}{4}\right)\left(14 - \dfrac{36}{4}\right)}}$$
$$= .52$$

Appendix B

TABLES

TABLE 1: TABLE OF AREAS UNDER THE NORMAL CURVE

The table of areas under the normal curve indicates proportions of area under the normal curve located: (1) between any specified z score (column A) and the mean (column B); and (2) beyond any specified z score (column C).

To use this table, the data must be normally distributed, and raw scores must be transformed to z scores.

Although column A lists only positive z scores, the symmetric shape of the normal distribution means that negative z scores will have the same proportions of area as their positive counterparts.

TABLE 1 Table of areas under the normal curve

(A) z	(B) Area Between Mean and z	(C) Area Beyond z	(A) z	(B) Area Between Mean and z	(C) Area Beyond z	(A) z	(B) Area Between Mean and z	(C) Area Beyond z
0.00	.0000	.5000	0.50	.1915	.3085	1.00	.3413	.1587
0.01	.0040	.4960	0.51	.1950	.3050	1.01	.3438	.1562
0.02	.0080	.4920	0.52	.1985	.3015	1.02	.3461	.1539
0.03	.0120	.4880	0.53	.2019	.2981	1.03	.3485	.1515
0.04	.0160	.4840	0.54	.2054	.2946	1.04	.3508	.1492
0.05	.0199	.4801	0.55	.2088	.2912	1.05	.3531	.1469
0.06	.0239	.4761	0.56	.2123	.2877	1.06	.3554	.1446
0.07	.0279	.4721	0.57	.2157	.2843	1.07	.3577	.1423
0.08	.0319	.4681	0.58	.2190	.2810	1.08	.3599	.1401
0.09	.0359	.4641	0.59	.2224	.2776	1.09	.3621	.1379
0.10	.0398	.4602	0.60	.2257	.2743	1.10	.3643	.1357
0.11	.0438	.4562	0.61	.2291	.2709	1.11	.3665	.1335
0.12	.0478	.4522	0.62	.2324	.2676	1.12	.3686	.1314
0.13	.0517	.4483	0.63	.2357	.2643	1.13	.3708	.1292
0.14	.0557	.4443	0.64	.2389	.2611	1.14	.3729	.1271
0.15	.0596	.4404	0.65	.2422	.2578	1.15	.3749	.1251
0.16	.0636	.4364	0.66	.2454	.2546	1.16	.3770	.1230
0.17	.0675	.4325	0.67	.2486	.2514	1.17	.3790	.1210
0.18	.0714	.4286	0.68	.2517	.2483	1.18	.3810	.1190
0.19	.0753	.4247	0.69	.2549	.2451	1.19	.3830	.1170
0.20	.0793	.4207	0.70	.2580	.2420	1.20	.3849	.1151
0.21	.0832	.4168	0.71	.2611	.2389	1.21	.3869	.1131
0.22	.0871	.4129	0.72	.2642	.2358	1.22	.3888	.1112
0.23	.0910	.4090	0.73	.2673	.2327	1.23	.3907	.1093
0.24	.0948	.4052	0.74	.2704	.2296	1.24	.3925	.1075
0.25	.0987	.4013	0.75	.2734	.2266	1.25	.3944	.1056
0.26	.1026	.3974	0.76	.2764	.2236	1.26	.3962	.1038
0.27	.1064	.3936	0.77	.2794	.2206	1.27	.3980	.1020
0.28	.1103	.3897	0.78	.2823	.2177	1.28	.3997	.1003
0.29	.1141	.3859	0.79	.2852	.2148	1.29	.4015	.0985
0.30	.1179	.3821	0.80	.2881	.2119	1.30	.4032	.0968
0.31	.1217	.3783	0.81	.2910	.2090	1.31	.4049	.0951
0.32	.1255	.3745	0.82	.2939	.2061	1.32	.4066	.0934
0.33	.1293	.3707	0.83	.2967	.2033	1.33	.4082	.0918
0.34	.1331	.3669	0.84	.2995	.2005	1.34	.4099	.0901
0.35	.1368	.3632	0.85	.3023	.1977	1.35	.4115	.0885
0.36	.1406	.3594	0.86	.3051	.1949	1.36	.4131	.0869
0.37	.1443	.3557	0.87	.3078	.1922	1.37	.4147	.0853
0.38	.1480	.3520	0.88	.3106	.1894	1.38	.4162	.0838
0.39	.1517	.3483	0.89	.3133	.1867	1.39	.4177	.0823
0.40	.1554	.3446	0.90	.3159	.1841	1.40	.4192	.0808
0.41	.1591	.3409	0.91	.3186	.1814	1.41	.4207	.0793
0.42	.1628	.3372	0.92	.3212	.1788	1.42	.4222	.0778
0.43	.1664	.3336	0.93	.3238	.1762	1.43	.4236	.0764
0.44	.1700	.3300	0.94	.3264	.1736	1.44	.4251	.0749
0.45	.1736	.3264	0.95	.3289	.1711	1.45	.4265	.0735
0.46	.1772	.3228	0.96	.3315	.1685	1.46	.4279	.0721
0.47	.1808	.3192	0.97	.3340	.1660	1.47	.4292	.0708
0.48	.1844	.3156	0.98	.3365	.1635	1.48	.4306	.0694
0.49	.1879	.3121	0.99	.3389	.1611	1.49	.4319	.0681

TABLE 1 *(cont.)*

(A) z	(B) Area Between Mean and z	(C) Area Beyond z	(A) z	(B) Area Between Mean and z	(C) Area Beyond z	(A) z	(B) Area Between Mean and z	(C) Area Beyond z
1.50	.4332	.0668	2.00	.4772	.0228	2.50	.4938	.0062
1.51	.4345	.0655	2.01	.4778	.0222	2.51	.4940	.0060
1.52	.4357	.0643	2.02	.4783	.0217	2.52	.4941	.0059
1.53	.4370	.0630	2.03	.4788	.0212	2.53	.4943	.0057
1.54	.4382	.0618	2.04	.4793	.0207	2.54	.4945	.0055
1.55	.4394	.0606	2.05	.4798	.0202	2.55	.4946	.0054
1.56	.4406	.0594	2.06	.4803	.0197	2.56	.4948	.0052
1.57	.4418	.0582	2.07	.4808	.0192	2.57	.4949	.0051
1.58	.4429	.0571	2.08	.4812	.0188	2.58	.4951	.0049
1.59	.4441	.0559	2.09	.4817	.0183	2.59	.4952	.0048
1.60	.4452	.0548	2.10	.4821	.0179	2.60	.4953	.0047
1.61	.4463	.0537	2.11	.4826	.0174	2.61	.4955	.0045
1.62	.4474	.0526	2.12	.4830	.0170	2.62	.4956	.0044
1.63	.4484	.0516	2.13	.4834	.0166	2.63	.4957	.0043
1.64	.4495	.0505	2.14	.4838	.0162	2.64	.4959	.0041
1.65	.4505	.0495	2.15	.4842	.0158	2.65	.4960	.0040
1.66	.4515	.0485	2.16	.4846	.0154	2.66	.4961	.0039
1.67	.4525	.0475	2.17	.4850	.0150	2.67	.4962	.0038
1.68	.4535	.0465	2.18	.4854	.0146	2.68	.4963	.0037
1.69	.4545	.0455	2.19	.4857	.0143	2.69	.4964	.0036
1.70	.4554	.0446	2.20	.4861	.0139	2.70	.4965	.0035
1.71	.4564	.0436	2.21	.4864	.0136	2.71	.4966	.0034
1.72	.4573	.0427	2.22	.4868	.0132	2.72	.4967	.0033
1.73	.4582	.0418	2.23	.4871	.0129	2.73	.4968	.0032
1.74	.4591	.0409	2.24	.4875	.0125	2.74	.4969	.0031
1.75	.4599	.0401	2.25	.4878	.0122	2.75	.4970	.0030
1.76	.4608	.0392	2.26	.4881	.0119	2.76	.4971	.0029
1.77	.4616	.0384	2.27	.4884	.0116	2.77	.4972	.0028
1.78	.4625	.0375	2.28	.4887	.0113	2.78	.4973	.0027
1.79	.4633	.0367	2.29	.4890	.0110	2.79	.4974	.0026
1.80	.4641	.0359	2.30	.4893	.0107	2.80	.4974	.0026
1.81	.4649	.0351	2.31	.4896	.0104	2.81	.4975	.0025
1.82	.4656	.0344	2.32	.4898	.0102	2.82	.4976	.0024
1.83	.4664	.0336	2.33	.4901	.0099	2.83	.4977	.0023
1.84	.4671	.0329	2.34	.4904	.0096	2.84	.4977	.0023
1.85	.4678	.0322	2.35	.4906	.0094	2.85	.4978	.0022
1.86	.4686	.0314	2.36	.4909	.0091	2.86	.4979	.0021
1.87	.4693	.0307	2.37	.4911	.0089	2.87	.4979	.0021
1.88	.4699	.0301	2.38	.4913	.0087	2.88	.4980	.0020
1.89	.4706	.0294	2.39	.4916	.0084	2.89	.4981	.0019
1.90	.4713	.0287	2.40	.4918	.0082	2.90	.4981	.0019
1.91	.4719	.0281	2.41	.4920	.0080	2.91	.4982	.0018
1.92	.4726	.0274	2.42	.4922	.0078	2.92	.4982	.0018
1.93	.4732	.0268	2.43	.4925	.0075	2.93	.4983	.0017
1.94	.4738	.0262	2.44	.4927	.0073	2.94	.4984	.0016
1.95	.4744	.0256	2.45	.4929	.0071	2.95	.4984	.0016
1.96	.4750	.0250	2.46	.4931	.0069	2.96	.4985	.0015
1.97	.4756	.0244	2.47	.4932	.0068	2.97	.4985	.0015
1.98	.4761	.0239	2.48	.4934	.0066	2.98	.4986	.0014
1.99	.4767	.0233	2.49	.4936	.0064	2.99	.4986	.0014

TABLE 1 *(cont.)*

(A) z	(B) Area Between Mean and z	(C) Area Beyond z	(A) z	(B) Area Between Mean and z	(C) Area Beyond z	(A) z	(B) Area between mean and z	(C) Area beyond z
3.00	.4987	.0013	3.12	.4991	.0009	3.24	.4994	.0006
3.01	.4987	.0013	3.13	.4991	.0009	3.25	.4994	.0006
3.02	.4987	.0013	3.14	.4992	.0008	3.30	.4995	.0005
3.03	.4988	.0012	3.15	.4992	.0008	3.35	.4996	.0004
3.04	.4988	.0012	3.16	.4992	.0008	3.40	.4997	.0003
3.05	.4989	.0011	3.17	.4992	.0008	3.45	.4997	.0003
3.06	.4989	.0011	3.18	.4993	.0007	3.50	.4998	.0002
3.07	.4989	.0011	3.19	.4993	.0007	3.60	.4998	.0002
3.08	.4990	.0010	3.20	.4993	.0007	3.70	.4999	.0001
3.09	.4990	.0010	3.21	.4993	.0007	3.80	.4999	.0001
3.10	.4990	.0010	3.22	.4994	.0006	3.90	.49995	.00005
3.11	.4991	.0009	3.23	.4994	.0006	4.00	.49997	.00003

Source: From R. P. Runyon & A. Haber, *Fundamentals of behavioral statistics,* 6th ed. New York: McGraw-Hill, Table A (pp. 459-460), 1987. Reprinted with permission of McGraw-Hill.

TABLE 2: CRITICAL VALUES OF *t*

The table of critical values of *t* lists critical values of the *t* statistic that mark specified critical regions of the sampling distribution of *t*. An obtained value of *t* is statistically significant if it meets or exceeds the critical value of *t* listed in the table for the chosen level of significance and specified number of degrees of freedom (df).

TABLE 2 **Critical values of *t***

df	**Level of Significance for One-Tail Test (α)**					
	.10	*.05*	*.025*	*.01*	*.005*	*.0005*
	Level of Significance for Two-Tail Test (α)					
	.20	*.10*	*.05*	*.02*	*.01*	*.001*
1	3.078	6.314	12.706	31.821	63.657	636.619
2	1.886	2.920	4.303	6.965	9.925	31.598
3	1.638	2.353	3.182	4.541	5.841	12.941
4	1.533	2.132	2.776	3.747	4.604	8.610
5	1.476	2.015	2.571	3.365	4.032	6.859
6	1.440	1.943	2.447	3.143	3.707	5.959
7	1.415	1.895	2.365	2.998	3.499	5.405
8	1.397	1.860	2.306	2.896	3.355	5.041
9	1.383	1.833	2.262	2.821	3.250	4.781
10	1.372	1.812	2.228	2.764	3.169	4.587
11	1.363	1.796	2.201	2.718	3.106	4.437
12	1.356	1.782	2.179	2.681	3.055	4.318
13	1.350	1.771	2.160	2.650	3.012	4.221
14	1.345	1.761	2.145	2.624	2.977	4.140
15	1.341	1.753	2.131	2.602	2.947	4.073
16	1.337	1.746	2.120	2.583	2.921	4.015
17	1.333	1.740	2.110	2.567	2.898	3.965
18	1.330	1.734	2.101	2.552	2.878	3.922
19	1.328	1.729	2.093	2.539	2.861	3.883
20	1.325	1.725	2.086	2.528	2.845	3.850
21	1.323	1.721	2.080	2.518	2.831	3.819
22	1.321	1.717	2.074	2.508	2.819	3.792
23	1.319	1.714	2.069	2.500	2.807	3.767
24	1.318	1.711	2.064	2.492	2.797	3.745
25	1.316	1.708	2.060	2.485	2.787	3.725
26	1.315	1.706	2.056	2.479	2.779	3.707
27	1.314	1.703	2.052	2.473	2.771	3.690
28	1.313	1.701	2.048	2.467	2.763	3.674
29	1.311	1.699	2.045	2.462	2.756	3.659
30	1.310	1.697	2.042	2.457	2.750	3.646
40	1.303	1.684	2.021	2.423	2.704	3.551
60	1.296	1.671	2.000	2.390	2.660	3.460
120	1.289	1.658	1.980	2.358	2.617	3.373
∞	1.282	1.645	1.960	2.326	2.576	3.291

Source: Table 2 is taken from Table III of Fisher & Yates, *Statistical tables for biological, agricultural, and medical research,* published by Longman Group UK Ltd., 1974.

TABLE 3: CRITICAL VALUES OF χ^2

The table of critical values of χ^2 lists critical values of the χ^2 statistic that mark specified critical regions of the sampling distribution of χ^2. An obtained value of χ^2 is statistically significant if it meets or exceeds the critical value of χ^2 listed in the table for the chosen level of significance and specified number of degrees of freedom (df).

TABLE 3 **Critical values of χ^2**

	Level of Significance (α)			
df	*.10*	*.05*	*.02*	*.01*
1	2.706	3.841	5.412	6.635
2	4.605	5.991	7.824	9.210
3	6.251	7.815	9.837	11.341
4	7.779	9.488	11.668	13.277
5	9.236	11.070	13.388	15.086
6	10.645	12.592	15.033	16.812
7	12.017	14.067	16.622	18.475
8	13.362	15.507	18.168	20.090
9	14.684	16.919	19.679	21.666
10	15.987	18.307	21.161	23.209
11	17.275	19.675	22.618	24.725
12	18.549	21.026	24.054	26.217
13	19.812	22.362	25.472	27.688
14	21.064	23.685	26.873	29.141
15	22.307	24.996	28.259	30.578
16	23.542	26.296	29.633	32.000
17	24.769	27.587	30.995	33.409
18	25.989	28.869	32.346	34.805
19	27.204	30.144	33.687	36.191
20	28.412	31.410	35.020	37.566
21	29.615	32.671	36.343	38.932
22	30.813	33.924	37.659	40.289
23	32.007	35.172	38.968	41.638
24	33.196	36.415	40.270	42.980
25	34.382	37.652	41.566	44.314
26	35.563	38.885	42.856	45.642
27	36.741	40.113	44.140	46.963
28	37.916	41.337	45.419	48.278
29	39.087	42.557	46.693	49.588
30	40.256	43.773	47.962	50.892

Source: From R. P. Runyon & A. Haber, *Fundamentals of behavioral statistics,* 6th ed. New York: McGraw-Hill, Table B (p. 461), 1987. Reprinted with permission of McGraw-Hill.

TABLE 4: CRITICAL VALUES OF *U*

The table of critical values of *U* lists critical values of the Mann-Whitney *U* statistic. An obtained value of *U* is statistically significant at the chosen level of significance if it falls outside the upper and lower critical values listed for any given N_1 and N_2.

TABLE 4 Critical values of *U*

Critical Values for a One-Tail Test at .05 Significance Level or Two-Tail Test at .10 Significance Level

N_2 \ N_1	1	2	3	4	5	6	7	8	9	10	11	12	13	14	15	16	17	18	19	20
1	—	—	—	—	—	—	—	—	—	—	—	—	—	—	—	—	—	—	0 19	0 20
2	—	—	—	—	0 10	0 12	0 14	1 15	1 17	1 19	1 21	2 22	2 24	2 26	3 27	3 29	3 31	4 32	4 34	4 36
3	—	—	0 9	0 12	1 14	2 16	2 19	3 21	3 24	4 26	5 28	5 31	6 33	7 35	7 38	8 40	9 42	9 45	10 47	11 49
4	—	—	0 12	1 15	2 18	3 21	4 24	5 27	6 30	7 33	8 36	9 39	10 42	11 45	12 48	14 50	15 53	16 56	17 59	18 62
5	—	0 10	1 14	2 18	4 21	5 25	6 29	8 32	9 36	11 39	12 43	13 47	15 50	16 54	18 57	19 61	20 65	22 68	23 72	25 75
6	—	0 12	2 16	3 21	5 25	7 29	8 34	10 38	12 42	14 46	16 50	17 55	19 59	21 63	23 67	25 71	26 76	28 80	30 84	32 88
7	—	0 14	2 19	4 24	6 29	8 34	11 38	13 43	15 48	17 53	19 58	21 63	24 67	26 72	28 77	30 82	33 86	35 91	37 96	39 101
8	—	1 15	3 21	5 27	8 32	10 38	13 43	15 49	18 54	20 60	23 65	26 70	28 76	31 81	33 87	36 92	39 97	41 103	44 108	47 113
9	—	1 17	3 24	6 30	9 36	12 42	15 48	18 54	21 60	24 66	27 72	30 78	33 84	36 90	39 96	42 102	45 108	48 114	51 120	54 126
10	—	1 19	4 26	7 33	11 39	14 46	17 53	20 60	24 66	27 73	31 79	34 86	37 93	41 99	44 106	48 112	51 119	55 125	58 132	62 138
11	—	1 21	5 28	8 36	12 43	16 50	19 58	23 65	27 72	31 79	34 87	38 94	42 101	46 108	50 115	54 122	57 130	61 137	65 144	69 151
12	—	2 22	5 31	9 39	13 47	17 55	21 63	26 70	30 78	34 86	38 94	42 102	47 109	51 117	55 125	60 132	64 140	68 148	72 156	77 163
13	—	2 24	6 33	10 42	15 50	19 59	24 67	28 76	33 84	37 93	42 101	47 109	51 118	56 126	61 134	65 143	70 151	75 159	80 167	84 176
14	—	2 26	7 35	11 45	16 54	21 63	26 72	31 81	36 90	41 99	46 108	51 117	56 126	61 135	66 144	71 153	77 161	82 170	87 179	92 188
15	—	3 27	7 38	12 48	18 57	23 67	28 77	33 87	39 96	44 106	50 115	55 125	61 134	66 144	72 153	77 163	83 172	88 182	94 191	100 200
16	—	3 29	8 40	14 50	19 61	25 71	30 82	36 92	42 102	48 112	54 122	60 132	65 143	71 153	77 163	83 173	89 183	95 193	101 203	107 213
17	—	3 31	9 42	15 53	20 65	26 76	33 86	39 97	45 108	51 119	57 130	64 140	70 151	77 161	83 172	89 183	96 193	102 204	109 214	115 225
18	—	4 32	9 45	16 56	22 68	28 80	35 91	41 103	48 114	55 123	61 137	68 148	75 159	82 170	88 182	95 193	102 204	109 215	116 226	123 237
19	0 19	4 34	10 47	17 59	23 72	30 84	37 96	44 108	51 120	58 132	65 144	72 156	80 167	87 179	94 191	101 203	109 214	116 226	123 238	130 250
20	0 20	4 36	11 49	18 62	25 75	32 88	39 101	47 113	54 126	62 138	69 151	77 163	84 176	92 188	100 200	107 213	115 225	123 237	130 250	138 262

(Dashes in the body of the table indicate that no decision is possible at the stated level of significance.)

Critical Values for a One-Tail Test at .025 Significance Level or Two-Tail Test at .05 Significance Level

N_2 \ N_1	1	2	3	4	5	6	7	8	9	10	11	12	13	14	15	16	17	18	19	20
1	—	—	—	—	—	—	—	—	—	—	—	—	—	—	—	—	—	—	—	—
2	—	—	—	—	—	—	—	0 16	0 18	0 20	0 22	1 23	1 25	1 27	1 29	1 31	2 32	2 34	2 36	2 38
3	—	—	—	—	0 15	1 17	1 20	2 22	2 25	3 27	3 30	4 32	4 35	5 37	5 40	6 42	6 45	7 47	7 50	8 52
4	—	—	—	0 16	1 19	2 22	3 25	4 28	4 32	5 35	6 38	7 41	8 44	9 47	10 50	11 53	11 57	12 60	13 63	13 67
5	—	—	0 15	1 19	2 23	3 27	5 30	6 34	7 38	8 42	9 46	11 49	12 53	13 57	14 61	15 65	17 68	18 72	19 76	20 80
6	—	—	1 17	2 22	3 27	5 31	6 36	8 40	10 44	11 49	13 53	14 58	16 62	17 67	19 71	21 75	22 80	24 84	25 89	27 93
7	—	—	1 20	3 25	5 30	6 36	8 41	10 46	12 51	14 56	16 61	18 66	20 71	22 76	24 81	26 86	28 91	30 96	32 101	34 106
8	—	0 16	2 22	4 28	6 34	8 40	10 46	13 51	15 57	17 63	19 69	22 74	24 80	26 86	29 91	31 97	34 102	36 108	38 111	41 119
9	—	0 18	2 25	4 32	7 38	10 44	12 51	15 57	17 64	20 70	23 76	26 82	28 89	31 95	34 101	37 107	39 114	42 120	45 126	48 132
10	—	0 20	3 27	5 35	8 42	11 49	14 56	17 63	20 70	23 77	26 84	29 91	33 97	36 104	39 111	42 118	45 125	48 132	52 138	55 145
11	—	0 22	3 30	6 38	9 46	13 53	16 61	19 69	23 76	26 84	30 91	33 99	37 106	40 114	44 121	47 129	51 136	55 143	58 151	62 158
12	—	1 23	4 32	7 41	11 49	14 58	18 66	22 74	26 82	29 91	33 99	37 107	41 115	45 123	49 131	53 139	57 147	61 155	65 163	69 171
13	—	1 25	4 35	8 44	12 53	16 62	20 71	24 80	28 89	33 97	37 106	41 115	45 124	50 132	54 141	59 149	63 158	67 167	72 175	76 184
14	—	1 27	5 37	9 47	13 51	17 67	22 76	26 86	31 95	36 104	40 114	45 123	50 132	55 141	59 151	64 160	67 171	74 178	78 188	83 197
15	—	1 29	5 40	10 50	14 61	19 71	24 81	29 91	34 101	39 111	44 121	49 131	54 141	59 151	64 161	70 170	75 180	80 190	85 200	90 210
16	—	1 31	6 42	11 53	15 65	21 75	26 86	31 97	37 107	42 118	47 129	53 139	59 149	64 160	70 170	75 181	81 191	86 202	92 212	98 222
17	—	2 32	6 45	11 57	17 68	22 80	28 91	34 102	39 114	45 125	51 136	57 147	63 158	67 171	75 180	81 191	87 202	93 213	99 224	105 235
18	—	2 34	7 47	12 60	18 72	24 84	30 96	36 108	42 120	48 132	55 143	61 155	67 167	74 178	80 190	86 202	93 213	99 225	106 236	112 248
19	—	2 36	7 50	13 63	19 76	25 89	32 101	38 114	45 126	52 138	58 151	65 163	72 175	78 188	85 200	92 212	99 224	106 236	113 248	119 261
20	—	2 38	8 52	13 67	20 80	27 93	34 106	41 119	48 132	55 145	62 158	69 171	76 184	83 197	90 210	98 222	105 235	112 248	119 261	127 273

(Dashes in the body of the table indicate that no decision is possible at the stated level of significance.)

Critical Values for a One-Tail Test at .01 Significance Level or Two-Tail Test at .02 Significance Level

N_2 \ N_1	1	2	3	4	5	6	7	8	9	10	11	12	13	14	15	16	17	18	19	20
1	—	—	—	—	—	—	—	—	—	—	—	—	—	—	—	—	—	—	—	—
2	—	—	—	—	—	—	—	—	—	—	—	—	0 26	0 28	0 30	0 32	0 34	0 36	1 37	1 39
3	—	—	—	—	—	—	0 21	0 24	1 26	1 29	1 32	2 34	2 37	2 40	3 42	3 45	4 47	4 50	4 52	5 55
4	—	—	—	—	0 20	1 23	1 27	2 30	3 33	3 37	4 40	5 43	5 47	6 50	7 53	7 57	8 60	9 63	9 67	10 70
5	—	—	—	0 20	1 24	2 28	3 32	4 36	5 40	6 44	7 48	8 52	9 56	10 60	11 64	12 68	13 72	14 76	15 80	16 84
6	—	—	—	1 23	2 28	3 33	4 38	6 42	7 47	8 52	9 57	11 61	12 66	13 71	15 75	16 80	18 84	19 89	20 94	22 98
7	—	—	0 21	1 27	3 32	4 38	6 43	7 49	9 54	11 59	12 65	14 70	16 75	17 81	19 86	21 91	23 96	24 102	26 107	28 112
8	—	—	0 24	2 30	4 36	6 42	7 49	9 55	11 61	13 67	15 73	17 79	20 84	22 90	24 96	26 102	28 108	30 114	32 120	34 126
9	—	—	1 26	3 33	5 40	7 47	9 54	11 61	14 67	16 74	18 81	21 87	23 94	26 100	28 107	31 113	33 120	36 126	38 133	40 140
10	—	—	1 29	3 37	6 44	8 52	11 59	13 67	16 74	19 81	22 88	24 96	27 103	30 110	33 117	36 124	38 132	41 139	44 146	47 153
11	—	—	1 32	4 40	7 48	9 57	12 65	15 73	18 81	22 88	25 96	28 104	31 112	34 120	37 128	41 135	44 143	47 151	50 159	53 167
12	—	—	2 34	5 43	8 52	11 61	14 70	17 79	21 87	24 96	28 104	31 113	35 121	38 130	42 138	46 146	49 155	53 163	56 172	60 180
13	—	0 26	2 37	5 47	9 56	12 66	16 75	20 84	23 94	27 103	31 112	35 121	39 130	43 139	47 148	51 157	55 166	59 175	63 184	67 193
14	—	0 28	2 40	6 50	10 60	13 71	17 81	22 90	26 100	30 110	34 120	38 130	43 139	47 149	51 159	56 168	60 178	65 187	69 197	73 207
15	—	0 30	3 42	7 53	11 64	15 75	19 86	24 96	28 107	33 117	37 128	42 138	47 148	51 159	56 169	61 179	66 189	70 200	75 210	80 220
16	—	0 32	3 45	7 57	12 68	16 80	21 91	26 102	31 113	36 124	41 135	46 146	51 157	56 168	61 179	66 190	71 201	76 212	82 222	87 233
17	—	0 34	4 47	8 60	13 72	18 84	23 96	28 108	33 120	38 132	44 143	49 155	55 166	60 178	66 189	71 201	77 212	82 224	88 234	93 247
18	—	0 36	4 50	9 63	14 76	19 89	24 102	30 114	36 126	41 139	47 151	53 163	59 175	65 187	70 200	76 212	82 224	88 236	94 248	100 260
19	—	1 37	4 53	9 67	15 80	20 94	26 107	32 120	38 133	44 146	50 159	56 172	63 184	69 197	75 210	82 222	88 235	94 248	101 260	107 273
20	—	1 39	5 55	10 70	16 84	22 98	28 112	34 126	40 140	47 153	53 167	60 180	67 193	73 207	80 220	87 233	93 247	100 260	107 273	114 286

(Dashes in the body of the table indicate that no decision is possible at the stated level of significance.)

TABLE 4 *(cont.)*

Critical Values for a One-Tail Test at .005 Significance Level or Two-Tail Test at .01 Significance Level

N_2 \ N_1	1	2	3	4	5	6	7	8	9	10	11	12	13	14	15	16	17	18	19	20
1	—	—	—	—	—	—	—	—	—	—	—	—	—	—	—	—	—	—	—	—
2	—	—	—	—	—	—	—	—	—	—	—	—	—	—	—	—	—	—	0 / 38	0 / 40
3	—	—	—	—	—	—	—	—	0 / 27	0 / 30	0 / 33	1 / 35	1 / 38	1 / 41	2 / 43	2 / 46	2 / 49	2 / 52	3 / 54	3 / 57
4	—	—	—	—	—	0 / 24	0 / 28	1 / 31	1 / 35	2 / 38	2 / 42	3 / 45	3 / 49	4 / 52	5 / 55	5 / 59	6 / 62	6 / 66	7 / 69	8 / 72
5	—	—	—	—	0 / 25	1 / 29	1 / 34	2 / 38	3 / 42	4 / 46	5 / 50	6 / 54	7 / 58	7 / 63	8 / 67	9 / 71	10 / 75	11 / 79	12 / 83	13 / 87
6	—	—	—	0 / 24	1 / 29	2 / 34	3 / 39	4 / 44	5 / 49	6 / 54	7 / 59	9 / 63	10 / 68	11 / 73	12 / 78	13 / 83	15 / 87	16 / 92	17 / 97	18 / 102
7	—	—	—	0 / 28	1 / 34	3 / 39	4 / 45	6 / 50	7 / 56	9 / 61	10 / 67	12 / 72	13 / 78	15 / 83	16 / 89	18 / 94	19 / 100	21 / 105	22 / 111	24 / 116
8	—	—	—	1 / 31	2 / 38	4 / 44	6 / 50	7 / 57	9 / 63	11 / 69	13 / 75	15 / 81	17 / 87	18 / 94	20 / 100	22 / 106	24 / 112	26 / 118	28 / 124	30 / 130
9	—	—	0 / 27	1 / 35	3 / 42	5 / 49	7 / 56	9 / 63	11 / 70	13 / 77	16 / 83	18 / 90	20 / 97	22 / 104	24 / 111	27 / 117	29 / 124	31 / 131	33 / 138	36 / 144
10	—	—	0 / 30	2 / 38	4 / 46	6 / 54	9 / 61	11 / 69	13 / 77	16 / 84	18 / 92	21 / 99	24 / 106	26 / 114	29 / 121	31 / 129	34 / 136	37 / 143	39 / 151	42 / 158
11	—	—	0 / 33	2 / 42	5 / 50	7 / 59	10 / 67	13 / 75	16 / 83	18 / 92	21 / 100	24 / 108	27 / 116	30 / 124	33 / 132	36 / 140	39 / 148	42 / 156	45 / 164	48 / 172
12	—	—	1 / 35	3 / 45	6 / 54	9 / 63	12 / 72	15 / 81	18 / 90	21 / 99	24 / 108	27 / 117	31 / 125	34 / 134	37 / 143	41 / 151	44 / 160	47 / 169	51 / 177	54 / 186
13	—	—	1 / 38	3 / 49	7 / 58	10 / 68	13 / 78	17 / 87	20 / 97	24 / 106	27 / 116	31 / 125	34 / 125	38 / 144	42 / 153	45 / 163	49 / 172	53 / 181	56 / 191	60 / 200
14	—	—	1 / 41	4 / 52	7 / 63	11 / 73	15 / 83	18 / 94	22 / 104	26 / 114	30 / 124	34 / 134	38 / 144	42 / 154	46 / 164	50 / 174	54 / 184	58 / 194	63 / 203	67 / 213
15	—	—	2 / 43	5 / 55	8 / 67	12 / 78	16 / 89	20 / 100	24 / 111	29 / 121	33 / 132	37 / 143	42 / 153	46 / 164	51 / 174	55 / 185	60 / 195	64 / 206	69 / 216	73 / 227
16	—	—	2 / 46	5 / 59	9 / 71	13 / 83	18 / 94	22 / 106	27 / 117	31 / 129	36 / 140	41 / 151	45 / 163	50 / 174	55 / 185	60 / 196	65 / 207	70 / 218	74 / 230	79 / 241
17	—	—	2 / 49	6 / 62	10 / 75	15 / 87	19 / 100	24 / 112	29 / 124	34 / 148	39 / 148	44 / 160	49 / 172	54 / 184	60 / 195	65 / 207	70 / 219	75 / 231	81 / 242	86 / 254
18	—	—	2 / 52	6 / 66	11 / 79	16 / 92	21 / 105	26 / 118	31 / 131	37 / 143	42 / 156	47 / 169	53 / 181	58 / 194	64 / 206	70 / 218	75 / 231	81 / 243	87 / 255	92 / 268
19	—	0 / 38	3 / 54	7 / 69	12 / 83	17 / 97	22 / 111	28 / 124	33 / 138	39 / 151	45 / 164	51 / 177	56 / 191	63 / 203	69 / 216	74 / 230	81 / 242	87 / 255	93 / 268	99 / 281
20	—	0 / 40	3 / 57	8 / 72	13 / 87	18 / 102	24 / 116	30 / 130	36 / 144	42 / 158	48 / 172	54 / 186	60 / 200	67 / 213	73 / 227	79 / 241	86 / 254	92 / 268	99 / 281	105 / 295

(Dashes in the body of the table indicate that no decision is possible at the stated level of significance.)

Source: From R. P. Runyon & A. Haber, *Fundamentals of behavioral statistics,* 6th ed. New York: McGraw-Hill, Table I (pp. 473–476), 1987. Reprinted with permission of McGraw-Hill.

Table 5: Critical Values of T

The table of critical values of *T* lists critical values of the Wilcoxon *T* statistic. An obtained value of *T* is statistically significant at the chosen level of significance if it is less than or equal to the critical value listed in the table for the specified number of pairs (*N*).

Table 5 **Critical values of *T***

	Level of Significance for One-Tail Test (α)					Level of Significance for One-Tail Test (α)			
	.05	*.025*	*.01*	*.005*		*.05*	*.025*	*.01*	*.005*
	Level of Significance for Two-Tail test (α)					**Level of Significance for Two-Tail test (α)**			
N	*.10*	*.05*	*.02*	*.01*	*N*	*.10*	*.05*	*.02*	*.01*
5	0	—	—	—	28	130	116	101	91
6	2	0	—	—	29	140	126	110	100
7	3	2	0	—	30	151	137	120	109
8	5	3	1	0	31	163	147	130	118
9	8	5	3	1	32	175	159	140	128
10	10	8	5	3	33	187	170	151	138
11	13	10	7	5	34	200	182	162	148
12	17	13	9	7	35	213	195	173	159
13	21	17	12	9	36	227	208	185	171
14	25	21	15	12	37	241	221	198	182
15	30	25	19	15	38	256	235	211	194
16	35	29	23	19	39	271	249	224	207
17	41	34	27	23	40	286	264	238	220
18	47	40	32	27	41	302	279	252	233
19	53	46	37	32	42	319	294	266	247
20	60	52	43	37	43	336	310	281	261
21	67	58	49	42	44	353	327	296	276
22	75	65	55	48	45	371	343	312	291
23	83	73	62	54	46	389	361	328	307
24	91	81	69	61	47	407	378	345	322
25	100	89	76	68	48	426	396	362	339
26	110	98	84	75	49	446	415	379	355
27	119	107	92	83	50	466	434	397	373

Source: From R. P. Runyon & A. Haber, *Fundamentals of behavioral statistics,* 6th ed. New York: McGraw-Hill, Table J (p. 477), 1987. Reprinted with permission of McGraw-Hill.

TABLE 6: CRITICAL VALUES OF *F*

The table of critical values of *F* lists critical values of the *F* statistic that mark specified critical regions of the sampling distribution of *F*. An obtained value of *F* is statistically significant if it meets or exceeds the critical value of *F* listed in the table for the chosen level of significance and specified degrees of freedom. Critical values of *F* for the .05 level of significance are printed in light print; values for the .01 level of significance are printed in bold print.

TABLE 6 **Critical values of *F***

Degrees of Freedom for Numerator (columns); Degrees of Freedom for Denominator (rows)

Denominator df	α	1	2	3	4	5	6	7	8	9	10	11	12	14	16	20	24	30	40	50	75	100	200	500	∞
1	.05	161	200	216	225	230	234	237	239	241	242	243	244	245	246	248	249	250	251	252	253	253	254	254	254
	.01	**4052**	**4999**	**5403**	**5625**	**5764**	**5859**	**5928**	**5981**	**6022**	**6056**	**6082**	**6106**	**6142**	**6169**	**6208**	**6234**	**6258**	**6286**	**6302**	**6323**	**6334**	**6352**	**6361**	**6366**
2	.05	18.51	19.00	19.16	19.25	19.30	19.33	19.36	19.37	19.38	19.39	19.40	19.41	19.42	19.43	19.44	19.45	19.46	19.47	19.47	19.48	19.49	19.49	19.50	19.50
	.01	**98.49**	**99.01**	**99.17**	**99.25**	**99.30**	**99.33**	**99.34**	**99.36**	**99.38**	**99.40**	**99.41**	**99.42**	**99.43**	**99.44**	**99.45**	**99.46**	**99.47**	**99.48**	**99.48**	**99.49**	**99.49**	**99.49**	**99.50**	**99.50**
3	.05	10.13	9.55	9.28	9.12	9.01	8.94	8.88	8.84	8.81	8.78	8.76	8.74	8.71	8.69	8.66	8.64	8.62	8.60	8.58	8.57	8.56	8.54	8.54	8.53
	.01	**34.12**	**30.81**	**29.46**	**28.71**	**28.24**	**27.91**	**27.67**	**27.49**	**27.34**	**27.23**	**27.13**	**27.05**	**26.92**	**26.83**	**26.69**	**26.60**	**26.50**	**26.41**	**26.30**	**26.27**	**26.23**	**26.18**	**26.14**	**26.12**
4	.05	7.71	6.94	6.59	6.39	6.26	6.16	6.09	6.04	6.00	5.96	5.93	5.91	5.87	5.84	5.80	5.77	5.74	5.71	5.70	5.68	5.66	5.65	5.64	5.63
	.01	**21.20**	**18.00**	**16.69**	**15.98**	**15.52**	**15.21**	**14.98**	**14.80**	**14.66**	**14.54**	**14.45**	**14.37**	**14.24**	**14.15**	**14.02**	**13.93**	**13.83**	**13.74**	**13.69**	**13.61**	**13.57**	**13.52**	**13.48**	**13.46**
5	.05	6.61	5.79	5.41	5.19	5.05	4.95	4.88	4.82	4.78	4.74	4.70	4.68	4.64	4.60	4.56	4.53	4.50	4.46	4.44	4.42	4.40	4.38	4.37	4.36
	.01	**16.26**	**13.27**	**12.06**	**11.39**	**10.97**	**10.67**	**10.45**	**10.27**	**10.15**	**10.05**	**9.96**	**9.89**	**9.77**	**9.68**	**9.55**	**9.47**	**9.38**	**9.29**	**9.24**	**9.17**	**9.13**	**9.07**	**9.04**	**9.02**
6	.05	5.99	5.14	4.76	4.53	4.39	4.28	4.21	4.15	4.10	4.06	4.03	4.00	3.96	3.92	3.87	3.84	3.81	3.77	3.75	3.72	3.71	3.69	3.68	3.67
	.01	**13.74**	**10.92**	**9.78**	**9.15**	**8.75**	**8.47**	**8.26**	**8.10**	**7.98**	**7.87**	**7.79**	**7.72**	**7.60**	**7.52**	**7.39**	**7.31**	**7.23**	**7.14**	**7.09**	**7.02**	**6.99**	**6.94**	**6.90**	**6.88**
7	.05	5.59	4.74	4.35	4.12	3.97	3.87	3.79	3.73	3.68	3.63	3.60	3.57	3.52	3.49	3.44	3.41	3.38	3.34	3.32	3.29	3.28	3.25	3.24	3.23
	.01	**12.25**	**9.55**	**8.45**	**7.85**	**7.46**	**7.19**	**7.00**	**6.84**	**6.71**	**6.62**	**6.54**	**6.47**	**6.35**	**6.27**	**6.15**	**6.07**	**5.98**	**5.90**	**5.85**	**5.78**	**5.75**	**5.70**	**5.67**	**5.65**
8	.05	5.32	4.46	4.07	3.84	3.69	3.58	3.50	3.44	3.39	3.34	3.31	3.28	3.23	3.20	3.15	3.12	3.08	3.05	3.03	3.00	2.98	2.96	2.94	2.93
	.01	**11.26**	**8.65**	**7.59**	**7.01**	**6.63**	**6.37**	**6.19**	**6.03**	**5.91**	**5.82**	**5.74**	**5.67**	**5.56**	**5.48**	**5.36**	**5.28**	**5.20**	**5.11**	**5.06**	**5.00**	**4.96**	**4.91**	**4.88**	**4.86**
9	.05	5.12	4.26	3.86	3.63	3.48	3.37	3.29	3.23	3.18	3.13	3.10	3.07	3.02	2.98	2.93	2.90	2.86	2.82	2.80	2.77	2.76	2.73	2.72	2.71
	.01	**10.56**	**8.02**	**6.99**	**6.42**	**6.06**	**5.80**	**5.62**	**5.47**	**5.35**	**5.26**	**5.18**	**5.11**	**5.00**	**4.92**	**4.80**	**4.73**	**4.64**	**4.56**	**4.51**	**4.45**	**4.41**	**4.36**	**4.33**	**4.31**
10	.05	4.96	4.10	3.71	3.48	3.33	3.22	3.14	3.07	3.02	2.97	2.94	2.91	2.86	2.82	2.77	2.74	2.70	2.67	2.64	2.61	2.59	2.56	2.55	2.54
	.01	**10.04**	**7.56**	**6.55**	**5.99**	**5.64**	**5.39**	**5.21**	**5.06**	**4.95**	**4.85**	**4.78**	**4.71**	**4.60**	**4.52**	**4.41**	**4.33**	**4.25**	**4.17**	**4.12**	**4.05**	**4.01**	**3.96**	**3.93**	**3.91**
11	.05	4.84	3.98	3.59	3.36	3.20	3.09	3.01	2.95	2.90	2.86	2.82	2.79	2.74	2.70	2.65	2.61	2.57	2.53	2.50	2.47	2.45	2.42	2.41	2.40
	.01	**9.65**	**7.20**	**6.22**	**5.67**	**5.32**	**5.07**	**4.88**	**4.74**	**4.63**	**4.54**	**4.46**	**4.40**	**4.29**	**4.21**	**4.10**	**4.02**	**3.94**	**3.86**	**3.80**	**3.74**	**3.70**	**3.66**	**3.62**	**3.60**
12	.05	4.75	3.88	3.49	3.26	3.11	3.00	2.92	2.85	2.80	2.76	2.72	2.69	2.64	2.60	2.54	2.50	2.46	2.42	2.40	2.36	2.35	2.32	2.31	2.30
	.01	**9.33**	**6.93**	**5.95**	**5.41**	**5.06**	**4.82**	**4.65**	**4.50**	**4.39**	**4.30**	**4.22**	**4.16**	**4.05**	**3.98**	**3.86**	**3.78**	**3.70**	**3.61**	**3.56**	**3.49**	**3.46**	**3.41**	**3.38**	**3.36**
13	.05	4.67	3.80	3.41	3.18	3.02	2.92	2.84	2.77	2.72	2.67	2.63	2.60	2.55	2.51	2.46	2.42	2.38	2.34	2.32	2.28	2.26	2.24	2.22	2.21
	.01	**9.07**	**6.70**	**5.74**	**5.20**	**4.86**	**4.62**	**4.44**	**4.30**	**4.19**	**4.10**	**4.02**	**3.96**	**3.85**	**3.78**	**3.67**	**3.59**	**3.51**	**3.42**	**3.37**	**3.30**	**3.27**	**3.21**	**3.18**	**3.16**
14	.05	4.60	3.74	3.34	3.11	2.96	2.85	2.77	2.70	2.65	2.60	2.56	2.53	2.48	2.44	2.39	2.35	2.31	2.27	2.24	2.21	2.19	2.16	2.14	2.13
	.01	**8.86**	**6.51**	**5.56**	**5.03**	**4.69**	**4.46**	**4.28**	**4.14**	**4.03**	**3.94**	**3.86**	**3.80**	**3.70**	**3.62**	**3.51**	**3.43**	**3.34**	**3.26**	**3.21**	**3.14**	**3.11**	**3.06**	**3.02**	**3.00**
15	.05	4.54	3.68	3.29	3.06	2.90	2.79	2.70	2.64	2.59	2.55	2.51	2.48	2.43	2.39	2.33	2.29	2.25	2.21	2.18	2.15	2.12	2.10	2.08	2.07
	.01	**8.68**	**6.36**	**5.42**	**4.89**	**4.56**	**4.32**	**4.14**	**4.00**	**3.89**	**3.80**	**3.73**	**3.67**	**3.56**	**3.48**	**3.36**	**3.29**	**3.20**	**3.12**	**3.07**	**3.00**	**2.97**	**2.92**	**2.89**	**2.87**
16	.05	4.49	3.63	3.24	3.01	2.85	2.74	2.66	2.59	2.54	2.49	2.45	2.42	2.37	2.33	2.28	2.24	2.20	2.16	2.13	2.09	2.07	2.04	2.02	2.01
	.01	**8.53**	**6.23**	**5.29**	**4.77**	**4.44**	**4.20**	**4.03**	**3.89**	**3.78**	**3.69**	**3.61**	**3.55**	**3.45**	**3.37**	**3.25**	**3.18**	**3.10**	**3.01**	**2.96**	**2.89**	**2.86**	**2.80**	**2.77**	**2.75**

TABLE 6 (*cont.*)

Degrees of Freedom for Numerator (columns); Degrees of Freedom for Denominator (rows)

	α	1	2	3	4	5	6	7	8	9	10	11	12	14	16	20	24	30	40	50	75	100	200	500	∞
17	.05	4.45	3.59	3.20	2.96	2.81	2.70	2.62	2.55	2.50	2.45	2.41	2.38	2.33	2.29	2.23	2.19	2.15	2.11	2.08	2.04	2.02	1.99	1.97	1.96
	.01	**8.40**	**6.11**	**5.18**	**4.67**	**4.34**	**4.10**	**3.93**	**3.79**	**3.68**	**3.59**	**3.52**	**3.45**	**3.35**	**3.27**	**3.16**	**3.08**	**3.00**	**2.92**	**2.86**	**2.79**	**2.76**	**2.70**	**2.67**	**2.65**
18	.05	4.41	3.55	3.16	2.93	2.77	2.66	2.58	2.51	2.46	2.41	2.37	2.34	2.29	2.25	2.19	2.15	2.11	2.07	2.04	2.00	1.98	1.95	1.93	1.92
	.01	**8.28**	**6.01**	**5.09**	**4.58**	**4.25**	**4.01**	**3.85**	**3.71**	**3.60**	**3.51**	**3.44**	**3.37**	**3.27**	**3.19**	**3.07**	**3.00**	**2.91**	**2.83**	**2.78**	**2.71**	**2.68**	**2.62**	**2.59**	**2.57**
19	.05	4.38	3.52	3.13	2.90	2.74	2.63	2.55	2.48	2.43	2.38	2.34	2.31	2.26	2.21	2.15	2.11	2.07	2.02	2.00	1.96	1.94	1.91	1.90	1.88
	.01	**8.18**	**5.93**	**5.01**	**4.50**	**4.17**	**3.94**	**3.77**	**3.63**	**3.52**	**3.43**	**3.36**	**3.30**	**3.19**	**3.12**	**3.00**	**2.92**	**2.84**	**2.76**	**2.70**	**2.63**	**2.60**	**2.54**	**2.51**	**2.49**
20	.05	4.35	3.49	3.10	2.87	2.71	2.60	2.52	2.45	2.40	2.35	2.31	2.28	2.23	2.18	2.12	2.08	2.04	1.99	1.96	1.92	1.90	1.87	1.85	1.84
	.01	**8.10**	**5.85**	**4.94**	**4.43**	**4.10**	**3.87**	**3.71**	**3.56**	**3.45**	**3.37**	**3.30**	**3.23**	**3.13**	**3.05**	**2.94**	**2.86**	**2.77**	**2.69**	**2.63**	**2.56**	**2.53**	**2.47**	**2.44**	**2.42**
21	.05	4.32	3.47	3.07	2.84	2.68	2.57	2.49	2.42	2.37	2.32	2.28	2.25	2.20	2.15	2.09	2.05	2.00	1.96	1.93	1.80	1.87	1.84	1.82	1.81
	.01	**8.02**	**5.78**	**4.87**	**4.37**	**4.04**	**3.81**	**3.65**	**3.51**	**3.40**	**3.31**	**3.24**	**3.17**	**3.07**	**2.99**	**2.88**	**2.80**	**2.72**	**2.63**	**2.58**	**2.51**	**2.47**	**2.42**	**2.38**	**2.36**
22	.05	4.30	3.44	3.05	2.82	2.66	2.55	2.47	2.40	2.35	2.30	2.26	2.23	2.18	2.13	2.07	2.03	1.98	1.93	1.91	1.87	1.84	1.81	1.80	1.78
	.01	**7.94**	**5.72**	**4.82**	**4.31**	**3.99**	**3.76**	**3.59**	**3.45**	**3.35**	**3.26**	**3.18**	**3.12**	**3.02**	**2.94**	**2.83**	**2.75**	**2.67**	**2.58**	**2.53**	**2.46**	**2.42**	**2.37**	**2.33**	**2.31**
23	.05	4.28	3.42	3.03	2.80	2.64	2.53	2.45	2.38	2.32	2.28	2.24	2.20	2.14	2.10	2.04	2.00	1.96	1.91	1.88	1.84	1.82	1.79	1.77	1.76
	.01	**7.88**	**5.66**	**4.76**	**4.26**	**3.94**	**3.71**	**3.54**	**3.41**	**3.30**	**3.21**	**3.14**	**3.07**	**2.97**	**2.89**	**2.78**	**2.70**	**2.62**	**2.53**	**2.48**	**2.41**	**2.37**	**2.32**	**2.28**	**2.26**
24	.05	4.26	3.40	3.01	2.78	2.62	2.51	2.43	2.36	2.30	2.26	2.22	2.18	2.13	2.09	2.02	1.98	1.94	1.89	1.86	1.82	1.80	1.76	1.74	1.73
	.01	**7.82**	**5.61**	**4.72**	**4.22**	**3.90**	**3.67**	**3.50**	**3.36**	**3.25**	**3.17**	**3.09**	**3.03**	**2.93**	**2.85**	**2.74**	**2.66**	**2.58**	**2.49**	**2.44**	**2.36**	**2.33**	**2.27**	**2.23**	**2.21**
25	.05	4.24	3.38	2.99	2.76	2.60	2.49	2.41	2.34	2.28	2.24	2.20	2.16	2.11	2.06	2.00	1.96	1.92	1.87	1.84	1.80	1.77	1.74	1.72	1.71
	.01	**7.77**	**5.57**	**4.68**	**4.18**	**3.86**	**3.63**	**3.46**	**3.32**	**3.21**	**3.13**	**3.05**	**2.99**	**2.89**	**2.81**	**2.70**	**2.62**	**2.54**	**2.45**	**2.40**	**2.32**	**2.29**	**2.23**	**2.19**	**2.17**
26	.05	4.22	3.37	2.89	2.74	2.59	2.47	2.39	2.32	2.27	2.22	2.18	2.15	2.10	2.05	1.99	1.95	1.90	1.85	1.82	1.78	1.76	1.72	1.70	1.69
	.01	**7.72**	**5.53**	**4.64**	**4.14**	**3.82**	**3.59**	**3.42**	**3.29**	**3.17**	**3.09**	**3.02**	**2.96**	**2.86**	**2.77**	**2.66**	**2.58**	**2.50**	**2.41**	**2.36**	**2.28**	**2.25**	**2.19**	**2.15**	**2.13**
27	.05	4.21	3.35	2.96	2.73	2.57	2.46	2.37	2.30	2.25	2.20	2.16	2.13	2.08	2.03	1.97	1.93	1.88	1.84	1.80	1.76	1.74	1.71	1.68	1.67
	.01	**7.68**	**5.49**	**4.60**	**4.11**	**3.79**	**3.56**	**3.39**	**3.26**	**3.14**	**3.06**	**2.98**	**2.93**	**2.83**	**2.74**	**2.63**	**2.55**	**2.47**	**2.38**	**2.33**	**2.25**	**2.21**	**2.16**	**2.12**	**2.10**
28	.05	4.20	3.34	2.95	2.71	2.56	2.44	2.36	2.29	3.24	2.19	2.15	2.12	2.06	2.02	1.96	1.91	1.87	1.81	1.78	1.75	1.72	1.69	1.67	1.65
	.01	**7.64**	**5.45**	**4.57**	**4.07**	**3.76**	**3.53**	**3.36**	**3.23**	**3.11**	**3.03**	**2.95**	**2.90**	**2.80**	**2.71**	**2.60**	**2.52**	**2.44**	**2.35**	**2.30**	**2.22**	**2.18**	**2.13**	**2.09**	**2.06**
29	.05	4.18	3.33	2.93	2.70	2.54	2.43	2.35	2.28	2.22	2.18	2.14	2.10	2.05	2.00	1.94	1.90	1.85	1.80	1.77	1.73	1.71	1.68	1.65	1.64
	.01	**7.60**	**5.52**	**4.54**	**4.04**	**3.73**	**3.50**	**3.32**	**3.20**	**3.08**	**3.00**	**2.92**	**2.87**	**2.77**	**2.68**	**2.57**	**2.49**	**2.41**	**2.32**	**2.27**	**2.19**	**2.15**	**2.10**	**2.06**	**2.03**
30	.05	4.17	3.32	2.92	2.69	2.53	2.42	2.34	2.27	2.21	2.16	2.12	2.09	2.04	1.99	1.93	1.89	1.84	1.79	1.76	1.72	1.69	1.66	1.64	1.62
	.01	**7.56**	**5.39**	**4.51**	**4.02**	**3.70**	**3.47**	**3.30**	**3.17**	**3.06**	**2.98**	**2.90**	**2.84**	**2.74**	**2.66**	**2.55**	**2.47**	**2.38**	**2.29**	**2.24**	**2.16**	**2.13**	**2.07**	**2.03**	**2.01**
32	.05	4.15	3.30	2.90	2.67	2.51	2.40	2.32	2.25	2.19	2.14	2.10	2.07	2.02	1.97	1.91	1.86	1.82	1.76	1.74	1.69	1.67	1.64	1.61	1.59
	.01	**7.50**	**5.34**	**4.46**	**3.97**	**3.66**	**3.42**	**3.25**	**3.12**	**3.01**	**2.94**	**2.86**	**2.80**	**2.70**	**2.62**	**2.51**	**2.42**	**2.34**	**2.25**	**2.20**	**2.12**	**2.08**	**2.02**	**1.98**	**1.96**
34	.05	4.13	3.28	2.88	2.65	2.49	2.38	2.30	2.23	2.17	2.12	2.08	2.05	2.00	1.95	1.89	1.84	1.80	1.74	1.71	1.67	1.64	1.61	1.59	1.57
	.01	**7.44**	**5.29**	**4.42**	**3.93**	**3.61**	**3.38**	**3.21**	**3.08**	**2.97**	**2.89**	**2.82**	**2.76**	**2.66**	**2.58**	**2.47**	**2.38**	**2.30**	**2.21**	**2.15**	**2.08**	**2.04**	**1.98**	**1.94**	**1.91**

TABLE 6 (cont.)

Degrees of Freedom for Denominator	α	1	2	3	4	5	6	7	8	9	10	11	12	14	16	20	24	30	40	50	75	100	200	500	∞
											Degrees of Freedom for Numerator														
36	.05	4.11	3.26	2.86	2.63	2.48	2.36	2.28	2.21	2.15	2.10	2.06	2.03	1.89	1.93	1.87	1.82	1.78	1.72	1.69	1.65	1.62	1.59	1.56	1.55
	.01	**7.39**	**5.25**	**4.38**	**3.89**	**3.58**	**3.35**	**3.18**	**3.04**	**2.94**	**2.86**	**2.78**	**2.72**	**2.62**	**2.54**	**2.43**	**2.35**	**2.26**	**2.17**	**2.12**	**2.04**	**2.00**	**1.94**	**1.90**	**1.87**
38	.05	4.10	3.25	2.85	2.62	2.46	2.35	2.26	2.19	2.14	2.09	2.05	2.02	1.96	1.92	1.85	1.80	1.76	1.71	1.67	1.63	1.60	1.57	1.54	1.53
	.01	**7.35**	**5.21**	**4.34**	**3.86**	**3.54**	**3.32**	**3.15**	**3.02**	**2.91**	**2.82**	**2.75**	**2.69**	**2.59**	**2.51**	**2.40**	**2.32**	**2.22**	**2.14**	**2.08**	**2.00**	**1.97**	**1.90**	**1.86**	**1.84**
40	.05	4.08	3.23	2.84	2.61	2.45	2.34	2.25	2.18	2.12	2.07	2.04	2.00	1.95	1.90	1.84	1.79	1.74	1.69	1.66	1.61	1.59	1.55	1.53	1.51
	.01	**7.31**	**5.18**	**4.31**	**3.83**	**3.51**	**3.29**	**3.12**	**2.99**	**2.88**	**2.80**	**2.73**	**2.66**	**2.56**	**2.49**	**2.37**	**2.29**	**2.20**	**2.11**	**2.05**	**1.97**	**1.94**	**1.88**	**1.84**	**1.81**
42	.05	4.07	3.22	2.83	2.59	2.44	2.32	2.24	2.17	2.11	2.06	2.02	1.99	1.94	1.89	1.82	1.78	1.73	1.68	1.64	1.60	1.57	1.54	1.51	1.49
	.01	**7.27**	**5.15**	**4.29**	**3.80**	**3.49**	**3.26**	**3.10**	**2.96**	**2.86**	**2.77**	**2.70**	**2.64**	**2.54**	**2.46**	**2.35**	**2.26**	**2.17**	**2.08**	**2.02**	**1.94**	**1.91**	**1.85**	**1.80**	**1.78**
44	.05	4.06	3.21	2.82	2.58	2.43	2.31	2.23	2.16	2.10	2.05	2.01	1.98	1.92	1.88	1.81	1.76	1.72	1.66	1.63	1.58	1.56	1.52	1.50	1.48
	.01	**7.24**	**5.12**	**4.26**	**3.78**	**3.46**	**3.24**	**3.07**	**2.94**	**2.84**	**2.75**	**2.68**	**2.62**	**2.52**	**2.44**	**2.32**	**2.24**	**2.15**	**2.06**	**2.00**	**1.92**	**1.88**	**1.82**	**1.78**	**1.75**
46	.05	4.05	3.20	2.81	2.57	2.42	2.30	2.22	2.14	2.09	2.04	2.00	1.97	1.91	1.87	1.80	1.75	1.71	1.65	1.62	1.57	1.54	1.51	1.48	1.46
	.01	**7.21**	**5.10**	**4.24**	**3.76**	**3.44**	**3.22**	**3.05**	**2.92**	**2.82**	**2.73**	**2.66**	**2.60**	**2.50**	**2.42**	**2.30**	**2.22**	**2.13**	**2.04**	**1.98**	**1.90**	**1.86**	**1.80**	**1.76**	**1.72**
48	.05	4.04	3.19	2.80	2.56	2.41	2.30	2.21	2.14	2.08	2.03	1.99	1.96	1.90	1.86	1.79	1.74	1.70	1.64	1.61	1.56	1.53	1.50	1.47	1.45
	.01	**7.19**	**5.08**	**4.22**	**3.74**	**3.42**	**3.20**	**3.04**	**2.90**	**2.80**	**2.71**	**2.64**	**2.58**	**2.48**	**2.40**	**2.28**	**2.20**	**2.11**	**2.02**	**1.96**	**1.88**	**1.84**	**1.78**	**1.73**	**1.70**
50	.05	4.03	3.18	2.79	2.56	2.40	2.29	2.20	2.13	2.07	2.02	1.98	1.95	1.90	1.85	1.78	1.74	1.69	1.63	1.60	1.55	1.52	1.48	1.46	1.44
	.01	**7.17**	**5.06**	**4.20**	**3.72**	**3.41**	**3.18**	**3.02**	**2.88**	**2.78**	**2.70**	**2.62**	**2.56**	**2.46**	**2.39**	**2.26**	**2.18**	**2.10**	**2.00**	**1.94**	**1.86**	**1.82**	**1.76**	**1.71**	**1.68**
55	.05	4.02	3.17	2.78	2.54	2.38	2.27	2.18	2.11	2.05	2.00	1.97	1.93	1.88	1.83	1.76	1.72	1.67	1.61	1.58	1.52	1.50	1.46	1.43	1.41
	.01	**7.12**	**5.01**	**4.16**	**3.68**	**3.37**	**3.15**	**2.98**	**2.85**	**2.75**	**2.66**	**2.59**	**2.53**	**2.43**	**2.35**	**2.23**	**2.15**	**2.06**	**1.96**	**1.90**	**1.82**	**1.78**	**1.71**	**1.66**	**1.64**
60	.05	4.00	3.15	2.76	2.52	2.37	2.25	2.17	2.10	2.04	1.99	1.95	1.92	1.86	1.81	1.75	1.70	1.65	1.59	1.56	1.50	1.48	1.44	1.41	1.39
	.01	**7.08**	**4.98**	**4.13**	**3.65**	**3.34**	**3.12**	**2.95**	**2.82**	**2.72**	**2.63**	**2.56**	**2.50**	**2.40**	**2.32**	**2.20**	**2.12**	**2.03**	**1.93**	**1.87**	**1.79**	**1.74**	**1.68**	**1.63**	**1.60**
65	.05	3.99	3.14	2.75	2.51	2.36	2.24	2.15	2.08	2.02	1.98	1.94	1.90	1.85	1.80	1.73	1.68	1.63	1.57	1.54	1.49	1.46	1.42	1.39	1.37
	.01	**7.04**	**4.95**	**4.10**	**3.62**	**3.31**	**3.09**	**2.93**	**2.79**	**2.70**	**2.61**	**2.54**	**2.47**	**2.37**	**2.30**	**2.18**	**2.09**	**2.00**	**1.90**	**1.84**	**1.76**	**1.71**	**1.64**	**1.60**	**1.56**
70	.05	3.98	3.13	2.74	2.50	2.35	2.32	2.14	2.07	2.01	1.97	1.93	1.89	1.84	1.79	1.72	1.67	1.62	1.56	1.53	1.47	1.45	1.40	1.37	1.35
	.01	**7.01**	**4.92**	**4.08**	**3.60**	**3.29**	**3.07**	**2.91**	**2.77**	**2.67**	**2.59**	**2.51**	**2.45**	**2.35**	**2.28**	**2.15**	**2.07**	**1.98**	**1.88**	**1.82**	**1.74**	**1.69**	**1.62**	**1.56**	**1.53**
80	.05	3.96	3.11	2.72	2.48	2.33	2.21	2.12	2.05	1.99	1.95	1.91	1.88	1.82	1.77	1.70	1.65	1.60	1.54	1.51	1.45	1.42	1.38	1.35	1.32
	.01	**6.96**	**4.88**	**4.04**	**3.56**	**3.25**	**3.04**	**2.87**	**2.74**	**2.64**	**2.55**	**2.48**	**2.41**	**2.32**	**2.24**	**2.11**	**2.03**	**1.94**	**1.84**	**1.78**	**1.70**	**1.65**	**1.57**	**1.52**	**1.49**
100	.05	3.94	3.09	2.70	2.46	2.30	2.19	2.10	2.03	1.97	1.92	1.88	1.85	1.79	1.75	1.68	1.63	1.57	1.51	1.48	1.42	1.39	1.34	1.30	1.28
	.01	**6.90**	**4.82**	**3.98**	**3.51**	**3.20**	**2.99**	**2.82**	**2.69**	**2.59**	**2.51**	**2.43**	**2.36**	**2.26**	**2.19**	**2.06**	**1.98**	**1.89**	**1.79**	**1.73**	**1.64**	**1.59**	**1.51**	**1.46**	**1.43**
125	.05	3.92	3.07	2.68	2.44	2.29	2.17	2.08	2.01	1.95	1.90	1.86	1.83	1.77	1.72	1.65	1.60	1.55	1.49	1.45	1.39	1.36	1.31	1.27	1.25
	.01	**6.84**	**4.78**	**3.94**	**3.47**	**3.17**	**2.95**	**2.79**	**2.65**	**2.56**	**2.47**	**2.40**	**2.33**	**2.23**	**2.15**	**2.03**	**1.94**	**1.85**	**1.75**	**1.68**	**1.59**	**1.54**	**1.46**	**1.40**	**1.37**
150	.05	3.91	3.06	2.67	2.43	2.27	2.16	2.07	2.00	1.94	1.89	1.85	1.82	1.76	1.71	1.64	1.59	1.54	1.47	1.44	1.37	1.34	1.29	1.25	1.22
	.01	**6.81**	**4.75**	**3.91**	**3.44**	**3.13**	**2.92**	**2.76**	**2.62**	**2.53**	**2.44**	**2.37**	**2.30**	**2.20**	**2.12**	**2.00**	**1.91**	**1.83**	**1.72**	**1.66**	**1.56**	**1.51**	**1.43**	**1.37**	**1.33**

TABLE 6 *(cont.)*

Degrees of Freedom for Denominator		Degrees of Freedom for Numerator																						
	α	**1**	**2**	**3**	**4**	**5**	**6**	**7**	**8**	**9**	**10**	**11**	**12**	**14**	**16**	**20**	**24**	**30**	**40**	**50**	**75**	**100**	**200**	**500**	∞
200	.05	3.89	3.04	2.65	2.41	2.26	2.14	2.05	1.98	1.92	1.87	1.83	1.80	1.74	1.69	1.62	1.57	1.52	1.45	1.42	1.35	1.32	1.26	1.22	1.19
	.01	**6.76**	**4.71**	**3.88**	**3.41**	**3.11**	**2.90**	**2.73**	**2.60**	**2.50**	**2.41**	**2.34**	**2.28**	**2.17**	**2.09**	**1.97**	**1.88**	**1.79**	**1.69**	**1.62**	**1.53**	**1.48**	**1.39**	**1.33**	**1.28**
400	.05	3.86	3.02	2.62	2.39	2.23	2.12	2.03	1.96	1.90	1.85	1.81	1.78	1.72	1.67	1.60	1.54	1.49	1.42	1.38	1.32	1.28	1.22	1.16	1.13
	.01	**6.70**	**4.66**	**3.83**	**3.36**	**3.06**	**2.85**	**2.69**	**2.55**	**2.46**	**2.37**	**2.29**	**2.23**	**2.12**	**2.04**	**1.92**	**1.84**	**1.74**	**1.64**	**1.57**	**1.47**	**1.42**	**1.32**	**1.24**	**1.19**
1000	.05	3.85	3.00	2.61	2.38	2.22	2.10	2.02	1.95	1.89	1.84	1.80	1.76	1.70	1.65	1.58	1.53	1.47	1.41	1.36	1.30	1.26	1.19	1.13	1.08
	.01	**6.66**	**4.62**	**3.80**	**3.34**	**3.04**	**2.82**	**2.66**	**2.53**	**2.43**	**2.34**	**2.26**	**2.20**	**2.09**	**2.01**	**1.89**	**1.81**	**1.71**	**1.61**	**1.54**	**1.44**	**1.38**	**1.28**	**1.19**	**1.11**
∞	.05	3.84	2.99	2.60	2.37	2.21	2.09	2.01	1.94	1.88	1.83	1.79	1.75	1.69	1.64	1.57	1.52	1.46	1.40	1.35	1.28	1.24	1.17	1.11	1.00
	.01	**6.64**	**4.60**	**3.78**	**3.32**	**3.02**	**2.80**	**2.64**	**2.51**	**2.41**	**2.32**	**2.24**	**2.18**	**2.07**	**1.99**	**1.87**	**1.79**	**1.69**	**1.59**	**1.52**	**1.41**	**1.36**	**1.25**	**1.15**	**1.00**

Source: From R. P. Runyon & A. Haber, *Fundamentals of behavioral statistics,* 6th ed. New York: McGraw-Hill, Table D (pp. 463–465), 1987. Reprinted with permission of McGraw-Hill.

TABLE 7: PERCENTAGE POINTS OF THE STUDENTIZED RANGE STATISTIC

The table of percentage points of the Studentized range statistic provides values of q used in computing Tukey's HSD. The correct value of q is found by entering the table with k (the number of means in the experiment), error df (the degrees of freedom associated with the denominator of the significant F statistic), and the chosen significance level (α).

TABLE 7 **Percentage points of the Studentized range statistic**

		k = Number of Means									
Error *df*	α	**2**	**3**	**4**	**5**	**6**	**7**	**8**	**9**	**10**	**11**
5	.05	3.64	4.60	5.22	5.67	6.03	6.33	6.58	6.80	6.99	7.17
	.01	5.70	6.98	7.80	8.42	8.91	9.32	9.67	9.97	10.24	10.48
6	.05	3.46	4.34	4.90	5.30	5.63	5.90	6.12	6.32	6.49	6.65
	.01	5.24	6.33	7.03	7.56	7.97	8.32	8.61	8.87	9.10	9.30
7	.05	3.34	4.16	4.68	5.06	5.36	5.61	5.82	6.00	6.16	6.30
	.01	4.95	5.92	6.54	7.01	7.37	7.68	7.94	8.17	8.37	8.55
8	.05	3.26	4.04	4.53	4.89	5.17	5.40	5.60	5.77	5.92	6.05
	.01	4.75	5.64	6.20	6.62	6.96	7.24	7.47	7.68	7.86	8.03
9	.05	3.20	3.95	4.41	4.76	5.02	5.24	5.43	5.59	5.74	5.87
	.01	4.60	5.43	5.96	6.35	6.66	6.91	7.13	7.33	7.49	7.65
10	.05	3.15	3.88	4.33	4.65	4.91	5.12	5.30	5.46	5.60	5.72
	.01	4.48	5.27	5.77	6.14	6.43	6.67	6.87	7.05	7.21	7.36
11	.05	3.11	3.82	4.26	4.57	4.82	5.03	5.20	5.35	5.49	5.61
	.01	4.39	5.15	5.62	5.97	6.25	6.48	6.67	6.84	6.99	7.13
12	.05	3.08	3.77	4.20	4.51	4.75	4.95	5.12	5.27	5.39	5.51
	.01	4.32	5.05	5.50	5.84	6.10	6.32	6.51	6.67	6.81	6.94
13	.05	3.06	3.73	4.15	4.45	4.69	4.88	5.05	5.19	5.32	5.43
	.01	4.26	4.96	5.40	5.73	5.98	6.19	6.37	6.53	6.67	6.79
14	.05	3.03	3.70	4.11	4.41	4.64	4.83	4.99	5.13	5.25	5.36
	.01	4.21	4.89	5.32	5.63	5.88	6.08	6.26	6.41	6.54	6.66
15	.05	3.01	3.67	4.08	4.37	4.59	4.78	4.94	5.08	5.20	5.31
	.01	4.17	4.84	5.25	5.56	5.80	5.99	6.16	6.31	6.44	6.55
16	.05	3.00	3.65	4.05	4.33	4.56	4.74	4.90	5.03	5.15	5.26
	.01	4.13	4.79	5.19	5.49	5.72	5.92	6.08	6.22	6.35	6.46
17	.05	2.98	3.63	4.02	4.30	4.52	4.70	4.86	4.99	5.11	5.21
	.01	4.10	4.74	5.14	5.43	5.66	5.85	6.01	6.15	6.27	6.38
18	.05	2.97	3.61	4.00	4.28	4.49	4.67	4.82	4.96	5.07	5.17
	.01	4.07	4.70	5.09	5.38	5.60	5.79	5.94	6.08	6.20	6.31
19	.05	2.96	3.59	3.98	4.25	4.47	4.65	4.79	4.92	5.04	5.14
	.01	4.05	4.67	5.05	5.33	5.55	5.73	5.89	6.02	6.14	6.25
20	.05	2.95	3.58	3.96	4.23	4.45	4.62	4.77	4.90	5.01	5.11
	.01	4.02	4.64	5.02	5.29	5.51	5.69	5.84	5.97	6.09	6.19
24	.05	2.92	3.53	3.90	4.17	4.37	4.54	4.68	4.81	4.92	5.01
	.01	3.96	4.55	4.91	5.17	5.37	5.54	5.69	5.81	5.92	6.02

TABLE 7 *(cont.)*

		k = Number of Means									
Error df	**α**	**2**	**3**	**4**	**5**	**6**	**7**	**8**	**9**	**10**	**11**
30	.05	2.89	3.49	3.85	4.10	4.30	4.46	4.60	4.72	4.82	4.92
	.01	3.89	4.45	4.80	5.05	5.24	5.40	5.54	5.65	5.76	5.85
40	.05	2.86	3.44	3.79	4.04	4.23	4.39	4.52	4.63	4.73	4.82
	.01	3.82	4.37	4.70	4.93	5.11	5.26	5.39	5.50	5.60	5.69
60	.05	2.83	3.40	3.74	3.98	4.16	4.31	4.44	4.55	4.65	4.73
	.01	3.76	4.28	4.59	4.82	4.99	5.13	5.25	5.36	5.45	5.53
120	.05	2.80	3.36	3.68	3.92	4.10	4.24	4.36	4.47	4.56	4.64
	.01	3.70	4.20	4.50	4.71	4.87	5.01	5.12	5.21	5.30	5.37
∞	.05	2.77	3.31	3.63	3.86	4.03	4.17	4.29	4.39	4.47	4.55
	.01	3.64	4.12	4.40	4.60	4.76	4.88	4.99	5.08	5.16	5.23

Source: From R. P. Runyon & A. Haber, *Fundamentals of behavioral statistics,* 6th ed. New York: McGraw-Hill, Table 0 (p. 486), 1987. Reprinted with permission of McGraw-Hill.

TABLE 8: CRITICAL VALUES OF THE PEARSON PRODUCT-MOMENT CORRELATION

The table of critical values of the Pearson product-moment correlation lists critical values of *r* that mark specified critical regions of the sampling distribution of *r*. An obtained value of *r* is statistically significant if it meets or exceeds the critical value of *r* listed in the table for the chosen level of significance and specified degrees of freedom (df).

TABLE 8 **Critical values of the Pearson product-moment correlation**

	Level of Significance for a One-Tail Test (α)				
	.05	*.025*	*.01*	*.005*	*.0005*
	Level of Significance for a Two-Tail Test (α)				
df = $N - 2$	*.10*	*.05*	*.02*	*.01*	*.001*
1	.9877	.9969	.9995	.9999	1.0000
2	.9000	.9500	.9800	.9900	.9990
3	.8054	.8783	.9343	.9587	.9912
4	.7293	.8114	.8822	.9172	.9741
5	.6694	.7545	.8329	.8745	.9507
6	.6215	.7067	.7887	.8343	.9249
7	.5822	.6664	.7498	.7977	.8982
8	.5494	.6319	.7155	.7646	.8721
9	.5214	.6021	.6851	.7348	.8471
10	.4973	.5760	.6581	.7079	.8233
11	.4762	.5529	.6339	.6835	.8010
12	.4575	.5324	.6120	.6614	.7800
13	.4409	.5139	.5923	.6411	.7603
14	.4259	.4973	.5742	.6226	.7420
15	.4124	.4821	.5577	.6055	.7246
16	.4000	.4683	.5425	.5897	.7084
17	.3887	.4555	.5285	.5751	.6932
18	.3783	.4438	.5155	.5614	.6787
19	.3687	.4329	.5034	.5487	.6652
20	.3598	.4227	.4921	.5368	.6524
25	.3233	.3809	.4451	.4869	.5974
30	.2960	.3494	.4093	.4487	.5541
35	.2746	.3246	.3810	.4182	.5189
40	.2573	.3044	.3578	.3932	.4896
45	.2428	.2875	.3384	.3721	.4648
50	.2306	.2732	.3218	.3541	.4433
60	.2108	.2500	.2948	.3248	.4078
70	.1954	.2319	.2737	.3017	.3799
80	.1829	.2172	.2565	.2830	.3568
90	.1726	.2050	.2422	.2673	.3375
100	.1638	.1946	.2301	.2540	.3211

Source: Table 8 is taken from Table VII of Fisher & Yates, *Statistical tables for biological, agricultural and medical research,* published by Longman Group UK Ltd., 1974.

TABLE 9: VALUES OF THE SPEARMAN RANK-ORDER CORRELATION

The table of critical values of the Spearman rank-order correlation lists critical values of r_S that mark specified critical regions of the sampling distribution of r_S. An obtained value of r_S is statistically significant if it meets or exceeds the critical value of r_S listed in the table for the chosen level of significance and specified number of pairs (*N*).

TABLE 9 **Critical values of the Spearman rank-order correlation**

	Level of Significance for One-Tail Test (α)			
	.05	*.025*	*.01*	*.005*
	Level of Significance for Two-Tail Test (α)			
N	*.10*	*.05*	*.02*	*.01*
5	.900	1.000	1.000	—
6	.829	.886	.943	1.000
7	.714	.786	.893	.929
8	.643	.738	.833	.881
9	.600	.683	.783	.833
10	.564	.648	.746	.794
12	.506	.591	.712	.777
14	.456	.544	.645	.715
16	.425	.506	.601	.665
18	.399	.475	.564	.625
20	.377	.450	.534	.591
22	.359	.428	.508	.562
24	.343	.409	.485	.537
26	.329	.392	.465	.515
28	.317	.377	.448	.496
30	.306	.364	.432	.478

Source: From R. P. Runyon & A. Haber, *Fundamentals of behavioral statistics,* 6th ed. New York: McGraw-Hill, Table G (p. 470), 1987. Reprinted with permission of McGraw-Hill.

Appendix C

Answers to Review Exercises

Chapter 1

1.1. **(a)** Each family is a case; numbers of children are the data.
(b) Each executive is a case; blood pressures are the data.
(c) Each city is a case; population densities are the data.

1.2. Descriptive statistics describe only the data at hand—the sample; inferential statistics use sample data to go beyond the sample at hand to the population.

1.3. **(a)** Correlation
(b) Description
(c) Regression
(d) Significant difference test

1.4. The key word "significantly" means that this sample finding is probably true as well in the larger population represented by the sample.

1.5. The key word "significantly" means that the correlation observed in this sample would probably be seen as well in the larger population represented by the sample.

1.6. A variable is a trait, attribute, or characteristic that *varies* from one case to the next.

1.7. Stand on the scale and observe which number is directly under the red line in the observation window.

1.8. **(a)** Ordinal
(b) Ratio
(c) Nominal
(d) Interval

1.9. Because the variable of gender has not been actively manipulated, but only passively observed.

1.10. **(a)** Independent variable: caffeine dosage; dependent variable: number of math problems completed
(b) Independent variable: teaching method; dependent variable: statistics test scores

1.11. **(a)** Correlational
(b) Experimental

1.12. **(a)** Measured by subjective report; manipulated by difficulty level of tasks undertaken
(b) Measured by number of problems completed in a given amount of time; manipulated by number and level of distractors in the environment

1.13. Statistics are the tools we use to make sense of the data that are gathered in research.

Chapter 2

2.1.

X	f	%	f_c	$\%_c$
98	1	4.0	25	100.0
89	1	4.0	24	96.0
88	1	4.0	23	92.0
86	2	8.0	22	88.0
85	3	12.0	20	80.0
84	4	16.0	17	68.0
81	3	12.0	13	52.0
80	1	4.0	10	40.0
79	1	4.0	9	36.0
72	1	4.0	8	32.0
71	2	8.0	7	28.0
68	1	4.0	5	20.0
60	2	8.0	4	16.0
57	1	4.0	2	8.0
50	1	4.0	1	4.0

(% is computed according to Equation 2.1; $\%_c$ is computed according to Equation 2.2)

2.2. Percentage distributions provide the clearest comparison when sample sizes are very different.

2.3.

X (i = 5)	f	%	f_c	$\%_c$
96–100	1	4.0	25	100.0
91–95	0	0.0	24	96.0
86–90	4	16.0	24	96.0
81–85	10	40.0	20	80.0
76–80	2	8.0	10	40.0
71–75	3	12.0	8	32.0
66–70	1	4.0	5	20.0
61–65	0	0.0	4	16.0
56–60	3	12.0	4	16.0
51–55	0	0.0	1	4.0
46–50	1	4.0	1	4.0

(% is computed according to Equation 2.1; $\%_c$ is computed according to Equation 2.2)

X (i = 10)	f	%	f_c	$\%_c$
91–100	1	4.0	25	100.0
81–90	14	56.0	24	96.0
71–80	5	20.0	10	40.0
61–70	1	4.0	5	20.0
51–60	3	12.0	4	16.0
41–50	1	4.0	1	4.0

2.4. Midpoints are computed according to Equation 2.3.

X (i = 5)	m
96–100	98
91–95	93
86–90	88
81–85	83
76–80	78
71–75	73
66–70	68
61–65	63
56–60	58
51–55	53
46–50	48

X (i = 10)	m
91–100	95.5
81–90	85.5
71–80	75.5
61–70	65.5
51–60	55.5
41–50	45.5

2.5. The percentile rank for $X = 60$ is 16. The percentile rank for $X = 88$ is 92.

2.6. Percentile ranks are estimated for scores in grouped distributions using Equation 2.4. The estimated percentile rank for $X = 60$ is 15.4. The estimated percentile rank for $X = 88$ is 82.0.

2.7. The score marking the 20th percentile is 68. There is no listing for the 75th percentile, so we use the next higher percentile: The score marking the 80th percentile is 85.

2.8. Equation 2.5 is used to estimate scores marking specified percentiles in grouped distributions. The score marking the 20th percentile is approximately 70.50. The score marking the 75th percentile is approximately 84.88.

2.9.

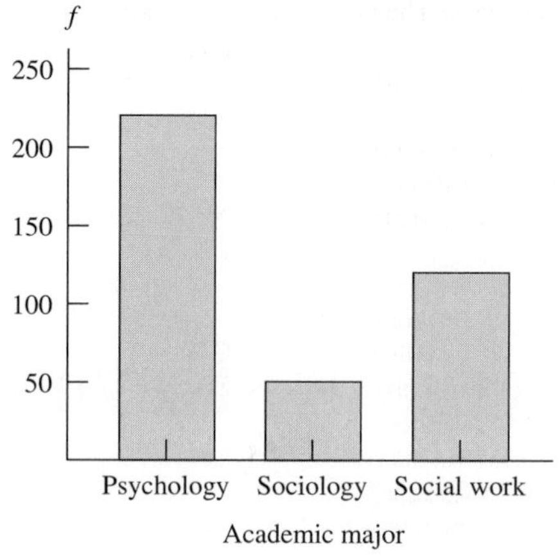

2.10.

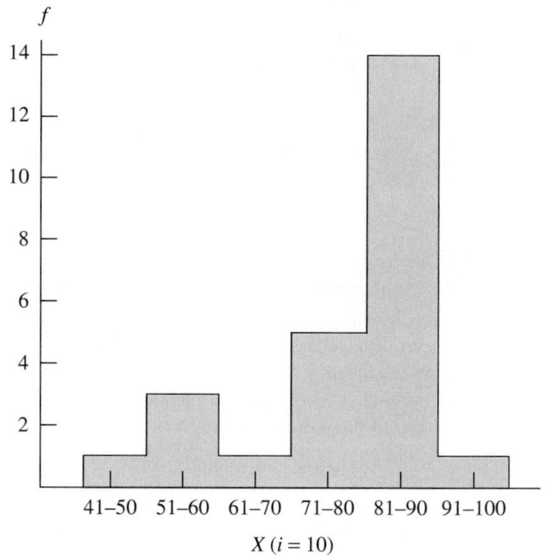

2.11.

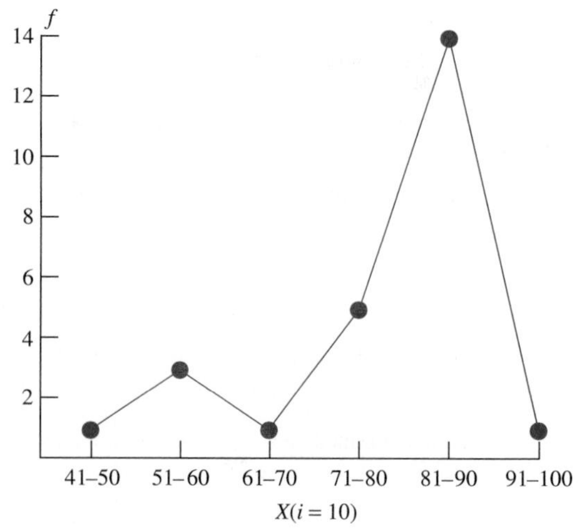

2.12. Central tendency: The typical or average score appears to be in the 80s.
Variability: Scores vary from a low in the 40s to a high in the 90s.
Skew: The scores are negatively skewed.
Kurtosis: The distribution seems a bit leptokurtic (peaked).
Modality characteristics: The distribution is essentially unimodal.

2.13. An extremely easy test would likely produce a distribution with mostly high scores and a few lower-scoring outliers—a negatively skewed distribution.

2.14. An extremely difficult test would likely produce a distribution with mostly low scores and a few high-scoring outliers—a positively skewed distribution.

2.15. **(a)** A bimodal grouped frequency distribution has been created by using unequal interval widths:

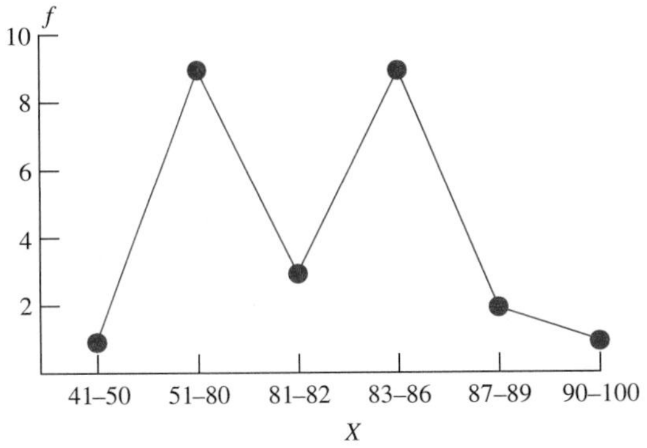

(b) Differences between numbers of students majoring in psychology, sociology, and social work have been minimized by using an excessively short ordinate.

(c)

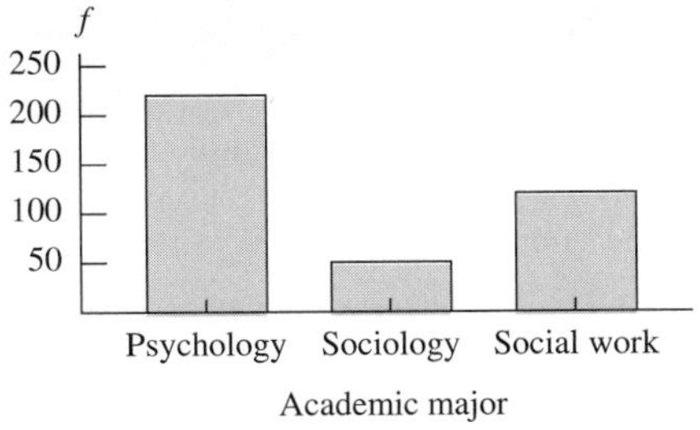

Chapter 3

3.1. The mean of a set of raw scores is computed according to Equation 3.1.

$$\overline{X} = 515$$

3.2. The mean of an ungrouped distribution is computed according to Equation 3.2.

$$\overline{X} = 515$$

3.3. The mean of a grouped distribution is estimated according to Equation 3.3.

$$\overline{X} = 26.31$$

3.4. This distribution is positively skewed and unimodal, with a modal class interval of 21–25. We can expect the mean of this distribution to be pulled excessively in the direction of the high outliers.

3.5. The median of a set of raw scores is computed according to Equation 3.4.

$$\text{Md} = 515$$

3.6. The median of an ungrouped frequency distribution is computed according to Equation 3.4.

$$\text{Md} = 515$$

3.7. The median of a grouped frequency distribution is estimated according to Equation 3.5.

$$\text{Md} = 25.5$$

3.8. The median provides a better indication than the mean of central tendency in a skewed distribution.

3.9. The mode is the most frequently occurring score(s) in the distribution. There are three modes in the set of 10 GRE scores: 500, 520, and 560.

3.10. The mode of an ungrouped frequency distribution is determined by identifying the score(s) that occur most frequently: 500, 520, and 560.

3.11. The mode of a grouped frequency distribution is estimated as the midpoint(s) of the most frequently occurring class interval(s): 23.

3.12. Central tendency of a multicategory nominal scale variable is indicated by the modal (most frequently occurring) category or categories: red.

3.13. The range is computed according to Equation 3.6.

$$\text{Range} = 150$$

3.14. In order to compute the interquartile range, we must first identify the scores marking the 75th and 25th percentiles:

X	f	f_c	$\%_c$
50	5	20	100
*40	6	15	75
30	4	9	45
*20	3	5	25
10	2	2	10

The interquartile range is computed according to Equation 3.7:

$$\text{IQR} = 20$$

3.15. The variance of a set of raw scores is computed according to Equation 3.8.

$$s^2 = 2{,}005.00$$

3.16. The variance of an ungrouped distribution is computed according to Equation 3.9.

$$s^2 = 2{,}005.00$$

3.17. The mean of the grouped distribution was estimated previously as $\overline{X} = 26.31$. The variance of a grouped distribution is estimated according to Equation 3.10.

$$s^2 = 42.80$$

3.18. The corrected sample variance is computed according to Equation 3.11.

$$\hat{s}^2 = 2{,}227.78$$

This value is somewhat larger than the sample variance computed previously ($s^2 = 2{,}005.00$).

3.19. The standard deviation is computed according to Equation 3.12.

$$s = 44.78$$

The corrected sample standard deviation is computed according to Equation 3.13.

$$\hat{s} = 47.20.$$

The corrected sample standard deviation is somewhat larger than the sample standard deviation.

3.20. The skew of the 10 GRE scores listed in Review Exercise 3.1 is computed according to Equation 3.14.

$$\text{Sk} = 0$$

The skew of the grouped distribution listed in Review Exercise 3.3 is also computed according to Equation 3.14 using mean (26.31) and median (25.50) estimated previously.

$$\text{Sk} = +.81$$

Chapter 4

4.1. 1.22 standard deviations fall between a score of 90 and the mean of 79. The score 1.5 standard deviations below the mean is 65.5.

4.2. **(a)** The proportion of area under the curve between 115 and 130 is .1359.
(b) The percentage of cases scoring between 115 and 130 is 13.59%.
(c) The probability of drawing a case at random that scores between 115 and 130 is .1359.

4.3. The probability of an event is computed according to Equation 4.1.

$$p = .17$$

4.4. 27.2 people comprise 20% of this population.

4.5. Probabilities of receiving each listed grade are computed according to Equation 4.1. The converse rule, described by Equation 4.2, is used to determine probabilities of *not* receiving each grade.

Grade	f	p**(grade)**	$p(\overline{\text{grade}})$
A	26	.13	.87
B	42	.20	.80
C	89	.43	.57
D	37	.18	.82
F	14	.07	.93

4.6. The addition rule, described by Equation 4.3, is used to determine these probabilities.
(a) .33
(b) .25
(c) .63

4.7. The multiplication rule, described by Equation 4.4, is used to determine these probabilities.
(a) .02
(b) .01
(c) .18

4.8. The multiplication rule, described by Equation 4.4, is used to determine this probability.

$$p = .00000003$$

4.9. Standard (z) scores are computed according to Equation 4.5.
(a) $z_{95} = 2.00$
(b) $z_{60} = -1.50$
(c) $z_{90} = 1.50$

4.10. Equation 4.5 is used to "work backwards" from z scores to raw scores.
(a) 63
(b) 91
(c) 75

4.11. Standard (z) scores are computed according to Equation 4.5. The mean of the distribution is $\overline{X} = 2.84$; the standard deviation is $s = 1.23$.

X	f	z
5	2	1.76
4	3	.94
3	8	.13
2	2	−.68
1	4	−1.50

The distribution of z scores is exactly the same shape as the distribution of raw scores.

4.12. The mean of any distribution of z scores will be 0. The standard deviation and variance will always be 1.

4.13. These scores are compared by converting them each to z scores according to Equation 4.5.

$z_A = 1.4$ Student A has the higher scholastic aptitude.

$z_B = .5$

4.14. **(a)** .3577
(b) .3577
(c) .6826
(d) .8364
(e) .0668
(f) .0401
(g) .5000
(h) .1359
(i) .0609

4.15. **(a)** .4082
(b) .2486
(c) .2981
(d) .3936
(e) .1193
(f) .1193
(g) .7486
(h) .7454

4.16. The score of 45 has an estimated percentile rank of 64.06.

4.17. **(a)** 45.39
(b) 45.39
(c) 97.61

4.18.

X	f	$\%_c$	z	Estimated Percentile Rank
5	4	100	1.85	96.78
4	6	88.57	.97	83.40
3	10	71.43	.10	53.98
2	12	42.86	−.78	21.77
1	3	8.57	−1.66	4.85

Actual and estimated percentile ranks differ because the estimates are based on the false assumption that the data are normally distributed.

Chapter 5

5.1. Sampling with replacement all possible samples of size $N = 2$ produces the samples listed below. Sample means are listed for each sample.

Ages $N = 2$	$\overline{X}$
10, 10	10
10, 30	20
10, 50	30
10, 70	40
10, 90	50
30, 30	30
30, 50	40
30, 70	50
30, 90	60
50, 50	50
50, 70	60
50, 90	70
70, 70	70
70, 90	80
90, 90	90

5.2.

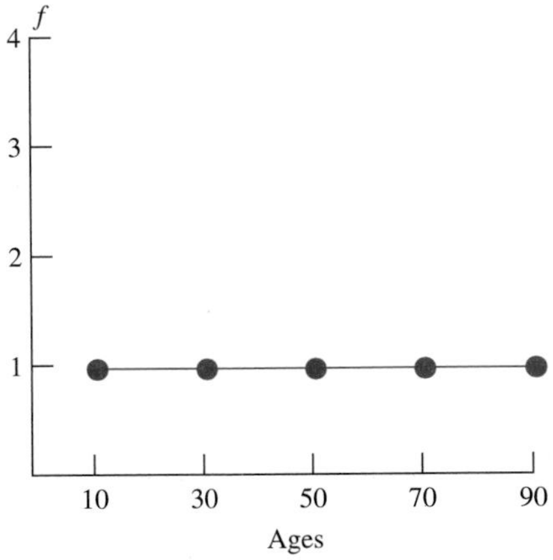

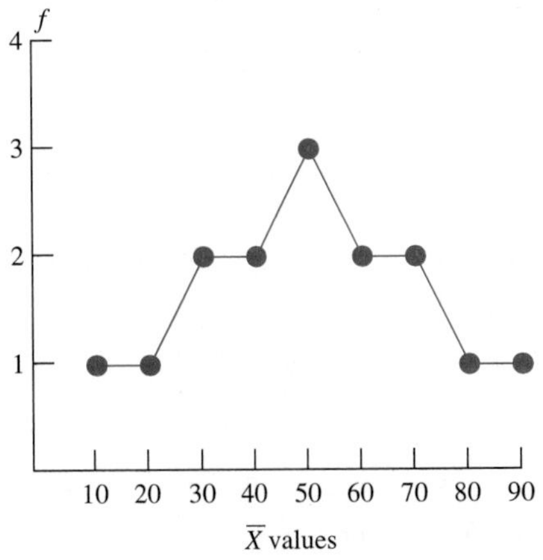

Although the population distribution is decidedly nonnormal, the sampling distribution of the mean is beginning to approximate a normal distribution even with a sample size as low as $N = 2$.

5.3. The mean of the population distribution is $\mu = 50$. The mean of the sampling distribution of the mean is also $\mu_{\overline{X}} = 50$.

5.4. The standard deviation of the sample means forming the sampling distribution of the mean is $s = 21.60$. This is close to, but not exactly the same as, the standard error of the mean computed according to Equation 5.1: $\sigma_{\overline{X}} = 20.00$. The central limit theorem tells us that Equation 5.1 is accurate only when sample sizes are $N \geq 50$.

5.5. Sampling with replacement all possible samples of size $N = 2$ produces the samples listed below. Sample proportions (means) are listed for each sample.

Samples $N = 2$	$p = \overline{X}$	Samples $N = 2$	$p = \overline{X}$
0, 0	0	1, 1	1
0, 1	.5	1, 1	1
0, 0	0	1, 0	.5
0, 1	.5	1, 1	1
1, 1	1	0, 0	0
1, 1	1	0, 1	.5
1, 0	.5	1, 1	1
	(cont.)		

5.6. The 90% confidence interval is computed according to Equation 5.2.

$$\overline{X} \pm 1.65\ \sigma_{\overline{X}}$$

$$100 \pm 1.65\ (2.12)$$

$$100 \pm 3.50$$

The 95% confidence interval is computed according to Equation 5.3.

$$\overline{X} \pm 1.96\ \sigma_{\overline{X}}$$

$$100 \pm 1.96\ (2.12)$$

$$100 \pm 4.16$$

The 99% confidence interval is computed according to Equation 5.4.

$$\overline{X} \pm 2.58\,\sigma_{\overline{X}}$$

$$100 \pm 2.58\,(2.12)$$

$$100 \pm 5.47$$

5.7. Seventy-five percent of the sample means in a normally distributed sampling distribution of the mean fall within $\pm 1.15\,\sigma_{\overline{X}}$ of the center of the distribution. Therefore, surrounding any one sample mean on each side by $1.15\,\sigma_{\overline{X}}$ will create a range of values that has a 75% probability of capturing $\mu_{\overline{X}} = \mu$. For the data at hand:

$$\overline{X} \pm 1.15\,\sigma_{\overline{X}} \quad \text{where} \quad \sigma_{\overline{X}} = \sigma/\sqrt{N}$$

$$100 \pm 1.15\,(2.12) \qquad = 15/\sqrt{50}$$

$$100 \pm 2.44 \qquad = 2.12$$

5.8. The 90% confidence interval is computed according to Equation 5.2.

$$\overline{X} \pm 1.65\,\sigma_{\overline{X}}$$

$$.8 \pm 1.65\,(.042)$$

$$.8 \pm .069$$

The 95% confidence interval is computed according to Equation 5.3.

$$\overline{X} \pm 1.96\,\sigma_{\overline{X}}$$

$$.8 \pm 1.96\,(.042)$$

$$.8 \pm .082$$

The 99% confidence interval is computed according to Equation 5.4.

$$\overline{X} \pm 2.58\,\sigma_{\overline{X}}$$

$$.8 \pm 2.58\,(.042)$$

$$.8 \pm .108$$

5.9. Eighty percent of the sample proportions (means) in a normally distributed sampling distribution of the proportion (mean) fall within $+1.28\,\sigma_{\overline{X}}$ of the center of the distribution. Therefore, surrounding any one sample proportion (mean) on each side by $1.28\,\sigma_{\overline{X}}$ will create a range of values that has an 80% probability of capturing the population proportion (mean). For the data at hand:

$$\overline{X} \pm 1.28\,\sigma_{\overline{X}} \quad \text{where} \quad \sigma_{\overline{X}} = \sigma/\sqrt{N}$$

$$.8 \pm 1.28\,(.042) \qquad = .42/\sqrt{100}$$

$$.8 \pm .054 \qquad = .042$$

5.10. As the level of confidence increases, the width of the confidence interval also increases. This is because as the level of confidence increases, so does the number of standard errors of the mean ($\sigma_{\overline{X}}$) that one must include on each side of the sample mean or proportion.

5.11. As data variability increases, the width of the confidence interval also increases. This is because as σ increases, so does the size of the standard error of the mean ($\sigma_{\overline{X}}$) that surrounds each side of the sample mean or proportion.

5.12. As sample size increases, the width of the confidence interval decreases. This is because as N increases, the size of the standard error of the mean ($\sigma_{\overline{X}}$) that surrounds each side of the sample mean or proportion also decreases.

5.13. The 95% confidence interval is defined by Equation 5.3 as

$$\overline{X} \pm 1.96\sigma_{\overline{X}}$$

Since the desired interval is to be 6 points wide, it would surround the mean on each side by 3 points:

$$\overline{X} \pm 3$$

It follows that these two expressions are equivalent:

$$\overline{X} \pm 1.96\,\sigma_{\overline{X}} = \overline{X} \pm 3$$

$$1.96\,\sigma_{\overline{X}} = 3$$

$$1.96\,\frac{\sigma}{\sqrt{N}} = 3$$

$$1.96\,\frac{12}{\sqrt{N}} = 3$$

$$\frac{12}{\sqrt{N}} = 1.53$$

$$1.53\,\sqrt{N} = 12$$

$$\sqrt{N} = 7.84$$

$$N = 61.51$$

5.14. The 99% confidence interval is defined by Equation 5.4 as

$$\overline{X} \pm 2.58\sigma_{\overline{X}}$$

The desired confidence interval is to surround the sample proportion (mean) on each side by .03 points:

$$\overline{X} \pm .03$$

It follows that these two expressions are equivalent:

$$\overline{X} \pm 2.58\sigma_{\overline{X}} = \overline{X} \pm .03$$

$$2.58\sigma_{\overline{X}} = .03$$

$$2.58\,\frac{\sigma}{\sqrt{N}} = .03$$

$$2.58\,\frac{.50}{\sqrt{N}} = .03$$

$$\frac{.50}{\sqrt{N}} = .01$$

$$.01\,\sqrt{N} = .5$$

$$\sqrt{N} = 50$$

$$N = 2{,}500$$

5.15. This size of this sample falls short of the 50 or more required by the central limit theorem. Also, we have no information about the population standard deviation and must estimate it from this relatively small sample. Under these circumstances, it makes sense to use values of t in computing the confidence interval. Equation 5.6 defines the 90% confidence interval as

$$\overline{X} \pm t_{(\text{df}=N-1;\ .10)}\hat{\sigma}_{\overline{X}} \quad \text{where} \quad \hat{\sigma}_{\overline{X}} = \frac{\hat{s}}{\sqrt{N}}$$

$$22.67 \pm 1.860\,\hat{\sigma}_{\overline{X}} \qquad = \frac{3.77}{\sqrt{9}}$$

$$22.67 \pm 1.860(1.26) \qquad = 1.26$$

$$22.67 \pm 2.34$$

5.16. If Republicans are scored 1 and Democrats are scored 0, the mean of the scores will equal the proportion of cases that are Republicans. Sample statistics follow.

$$p = \overline{X} = .60$$

$$\hat{s} = .52$$

$$N = 10$$

Given such a small sample, one should use values of t in computing the confidence interval. Equation 5.7 describes the 95% confidence interval:

$$\overline{X} \pm t_{(\text{df}=N-1;\ .05)}\hat{\sigma}_{\overline{X}} \quad \text{where} \quad \hat{\sigma}_{\overline{X}} = \frac{\hat{s}}{\sqrt{N}}$$

$$.60 \pm 2.262(.164) \qquad = \frac{.52}{\sqrt{10}}$$

$$.60 \pm .371 \qquad = .164$$

Chapter 6

6.1. Research question (c) is most appropriate to a one-sample test. Question (a) seeks to compare two samples. Question (b) involves comparing three samples. Only question (c) looks to compare one sample against a larger population.

6.2. **(a)** IV: gender (male vs. female)
DV: productivity
(b) IV: race (three groups)
DV: educational achievement
(c) IV: crime (sex offenders vs. all other criminals)
DV: age

6.3. A one-sample t test is most appropriate here. A two-tail test is used because a difference in either direction is of interest. Sample descriptive statistics follow.

$$\overline{X} = 23.0$$

$$\hat{s} = 5.25$$

$$N = 10$$

The one-sample t test is computed according to Equation 6.1:

$$t = \frac{\overline{X} - \mu}{\hat{\sigma}_{\overline{X}}}$$

$$= \frac{23.0 - 27}{1.66}$$

$$= -2.41$$

The critical value of t for a two-tail test at the .05 level of significance with df $= N - 1 = 9$ is 2.262. The obtained value exceeds this critical value, so the difference it represents is considered statistically significant. This sample is not representative of the specified population.

6.4. The one-sample t test is again appropriate for this comparison. The comparison is two-tailed because a difference in either direction is of interest. Sample descriptive statistics follow.

$$\overline{X} = 25.88$$

$$\hat{s} = 3.83$$

$$N = 8$$

The one-sample t test is computed according to Equation 6.1:

$$t = \frac{\overline{X} - \mu}{\hat{\sigma}_{\overline{X}}}$$

$$= \frac{25.88 - 28}{1.35}$$

$$= -1.57$$

The critical value of t for a two-tail test at the .05 level of significance with df $= N - 1 = 7$ is 2.365. The obtained value falls short of this value, so the difference it represents is not statistically significant.

6.5. The chi-square goodness-of-fit test can be used here. The first step in computing χ^2 is to find expected frequencies (f_e). These are frequencies that one would expect to see in the sample if it were distributed just like the population. To find these, we must first convert the listed population frequencies to percentages:

Population

Majors	%
Psychology	47.73%
Sociology	18.18%
Social work	34.09%

These percentages are used to find expected frequencies for each major in the sample:

Sample

Majors	f_o	f_e
Psychology	25	28.64
Sociology	15	10.91
Social work	20	20.45

The χ^2 test statistic is computed according to Equation 6.2:

$$\chi^2 = \Sigma\frac{(f_o - f_e)^2}{f_e}$$

$$= \frac{(25 - 28.64)^2}{28.64} + \ldots + \frac{(20 - 20.45)^2}{20.45}$$

$$= 2.01$$

The critical value of χ^2 at the .05 level of significance with $df = k - 1 = 2$ is 5.991. The obtained value falls short of this value, so the difference it represents is not statistically significant. The sample can be considered representative of the population.

6.6. The chi-square goodness-of-fit test can again be used here. The first step in computing χ^2 is to find expected frequencies (f_e). These are frequencies that one would expect to see in the sample if it were distributed just like the population. The population percentages provided are used to find expected frequencies in the sample:

Sample		
Scores	f_o	f_e
70–85	8	10.92
86–100	24	28.56
101–115	32	28.56
116–130	20	10.92

The χ^2 test statistic is computed according to Equation 6.2:

$$\chi^2 = \Sigma\frac{(f_o - f_e)^2}{f_e}$$

$$= \frac{(8 - 10.92)^2}{10.92} + \ldots + \frac{(20 - 10.92)^2}{10.92}$$

$$= 9.47$$

The critical value of χ^2 at the .05 level of significance with $df = k - 1 = 3$ is 7.815. The obtained value exceeds this value, so the difference it represents is considered statistically significant.

6.7. The smallest population percentage listed is 13%. This will produce the smallest expected frequency. Thirteen percent of how many cases will give us an expected frequency of 5? The answer is 39.

6.8. **(a)** The lower the level of significance, the greater is the likelihood of significance.
(b) A one-tail test is more likely to be significant than a two-tail test.
(c) The larger the sample, the more likely a difference is to be significant.
(d) The less variable the data, the more likely a difference is to be significant.

Chapter 7

7.1. Dependent-samples *t* test. This is a repeated-measures design that makes the samples dependent. There is no indication that the dependent variable fails to meet the parametric assumptions of the *t* test: interval or ratio scale of measurement; approximately equal population variances; and approximately normal population distributions.

7.2. Wilcoxon *T* test. This is a repeated-measures design that makes the samples dependent. The fact that the dependent variable is measured on an ordinal scale (rank-order data) calls attention to the need for the nonparametric Wilcoxon *T*.

7.3. Mann-Whitney *U*. This research question calls for the comparison of two independent samples. The fact that the dependent variable is measured on an ordinal scale (rank-order data) tells us that the Mann-Whitney *U* is appropriate.

7.4. Independent-samples *t* test. This research question is another comparison of independent samples. There is no indication that the parametric assumptions of the *t* test have been violated, which points us to the *t* test.

7.5. Chi-square test for two independent samples. This research question calls for the comparison of two entire distributions. The chi-square test for two independent samples is designed for this purpose.

7.6. Sample descriptive statistics follow.

Healthy	**Cardiac**
$\bar{X}_1 = 24.67$	$\bar{X}_2 = 32.33$
$\hat{s}_1^2 = 291.87$	$\hat{s}_2^2 = 135.47$
$N_1 = 6$	$N_2 = 6$

The standard error of the difference is computed according to Equation 7.1:

$$\hat{\sigma}_{\bar{X}_1 - \bar{X}_2} = \sqrt{\left[\frac{(N_1 - 1)\hat{s}_1^2 + (N_2 - 1)\hat{s}_2^2}{N_1 + N_2 - 2}\right]\left(\frac{N_1 + N_2}{N_1 N_2}\right)}$$

$$= 8.44$$

The independent-samples *t* test is computed according to Equation 7.2:

$$t_{\bar{X}_1 - \bar{X}_2} = \frac{(\bar{X}_1 - \bar{X}_2) - \mu_{\bar{X}_1 - \bar{X}_2}}{\hat{\sigma}_{\bar{X}_1 - \bar{X}_2}}$$

$$= -.91$$

This obtained value of *t* is evaluated for significance using a two-tail test because the direction of the difference was not specified in advance. For $df = N_1 + N_2 - 2 = 10$, the critical value of *t* for a two-tail test at the .05 level of significance is 2.228. The obtained value of *t* falls short of this critical value. We conclude that the difference is nonsignificant.

7.7. Sample descriptive statistics follow.

6 years	**10 years**
$\bar{X}_1 = 17.90$	$\bar{X}_2 = 26.70$
$\hat{s}_1^2 = 52.32$	$\hat{s}_2^2 = 99.34$
$N = 10$	

The standard error of the difference for a dependent-samples *t* test is computed according to Equation 7.3:

$$\hat{\sigma}_{\bar{D}} = \frac{\sqrt{\Sigma(D - \bar{D})^2 / (N - 1)}}{\sqrt{N}}$$

$$= 1.69$$

The dependent-samples t test is computed according to Equation 7.4:

$$t_{\overline{X}_1 - \overline{X}_2} = \frac{(\overline{X}_1 - \overline{X}_2) - \mu_{\overline{X}_1 - \overline{X}_2}}{\hat{\sigma}_{\overline{D}}}$$

$$= -5.20$$

This obtained value of t is evaluated for significance using a one-tail test because it has been hypothesized that the change in vocabulary test scores will be in the direction of improvement. For df $= N - 1 = 9$, the critical value of t for a one-tail test at the .0005 level of significance is 4.781. The obtained value of t exceeds this, so the obtained $\overline{X}_1 - \overline{X}_2$ difference can be considered statistically significant even at this very stringent significance level.

7.8. We begin by combining the data from the two groups and rank-ordering scores in ascending order.

Healthy		**Cardiac**	
Raw score	*Rank*	*Raw score*	*Rank*
20	5	40	9
42	10	48	11
11	2	30	7
15	3.5	15	3.5
50	12	25	6
10	1	36	8

The Mann-Whitney U statistic is computed according to Equation 7.5:

$$U = N_1N_2 + \frac{N_1(N_1 + 1)}{2} - R_1$$

$$= 23.5$$

This obtained value of U is evaluated for significance using a two-tail test because the direction of the difference was not hypothesized in advance. The critical boundary values of U for $N_1 = 6$ and $N_2 = 6$ at the .05 level of significance are 5 and 31. Because the obtained value of U falls within these boundaries, the difference is not considered statistically significant.

7.9. We begin by computing differences between corresponding scores (D). Next, these differences are ranked in ascending order, ignoring signs and any differences of 0. Signs are then reattached to ranks and the Wilcoxon T is computed according to Equation 7.6.

6 Years	**10 Years**	***D***	**Signed Ranks**
14	28	−14	−8
25	32	− 7	−6
10	15	− 5	−3.5
8	12	− 4	−2
16	30	−14	−8
22	28	− 6	−5
25	27	− 2	−1
21	38	−17	−10
28	42	−14	−8
10	15	− 5	−3.5

T = the smaller of: (1) the absolute sum of the positive ranks, or (2) the absolute sum of the negative ranks
= 0 (the sum of the positive ranks)

This obtained value of T is evaluated for significance using a one-tail test because the direction of the difference was hypothesized in advance. For $N = 10$, the critical value of T at the .005 significance level is 3. Any value less than this is significant, including the T obtained here.

7.10. Observed frequencies and expected frequencies (in parentheses) are shown in the contingency table that follows.

Grades	*Section 1*	*Section 2*	**Row Totals**	**Row %**
A	10 (9.36)	8 (8.64)	18	14.4%
B	13 (14.56)	15 (13.44)	28	22.4%
C	24 (26.52)	27 (24.48)	51	40.8%
D	15 (13.00)	10 (12.00)	25	20.0%
F	3 (1.56)	0 (1.44)	3	2.4%
Column Totals	65	60	$N = 125$	

At least 80% of the cells contain expected frequencies of 5 or larger, a condition for appropriate use of the chi-square test. The χ^2 statistic is computed according to Equation 7.8:

$$\chi^2 = \Sigma\frac{(f_o - f_e)^2}{f_e}$$

$$= 4.35$$

For df $= (R - 1)(C - 1) = 4$, the critical value of χ^2 for the .05 level of significance is 9.488. The obtained value falls short of this, and the difference is therefore not statistically significant.

7.11. Observed frequencies and expected frequencies (in parentheses) are shown in the contingency table that follows.

Political Affiliation	*Traditional*	*Nontraditional*	**Row Totals**	**Row %**
Republican	4 (5.58)	5 (3.43)	9	42.9%
Democrat	9 (7.42)	3 (4.57)	12	57.1%
Column Totals	13	8	$N = 21$	

Two cells of the contingency table contain expected frequencies of less than 5. Therefore, Yates's correction is used in computing the χ^2 statistic according to Equation 7.8:

$$\chi^{2'} = \sum \frac{[(|f_o - f_e|) - .5]^2}{f_e}$$

$$= .95$$

For df = $(R - 1)(C - 1) = 1$, the critical value of χ^2 for the .05 level of significance is 3.841. The obtained value of χ^2 falls short of this, so the difference is considered nonsignificant.

7.12. Omega-square is computed according to Equation 7.9. For the independent-samples t test of Review Exercise 7.6,

$$\omega^2 = \frac{t^2 - 1}{t^2 + df + 1}$$

$$= -.01$$

When the absolute value of $t < 1$, ω^2 will be negative, as it is here. Because interpretable values of ω^2 range only from 0 to 1, we set ω^2 equal to 0 here, indicating virtually no association between the independent variable (healthy vs. cardiac patient) and the dependent variable (depression).

For the dependent-samples t test of Review Exercise 7.7,

$$\omega^2 = \frac{t^2 - 1}{t^2 + \text{df} + 1}$$

$$= .70$$

Because ω^2 ranges from 0 to 1, $\omega^2 = .70$ reflects a substantial association between the independent variable (age) and the dependent variable (vocabulary).

7.13. Cramer's V is computed according to Equation 7.10. For the χ^2 test of Review Exercise 7.10,

$$V = \sqrt{\frac{\chi^2}{N(n - 1)}}$$

$$= .19$$

Because Cramer's V can range only from 0 to 1, $V = .19$ reflects a very weak association between the independent variable (section) and the dependent variable (grades).

For the χ^2 test of Review Exercise 7.11,

$$V = \sqrt{\frac{\chi^2}{N(n - 1)}}$$

$$= .32$$

This reflects a moderate association between the independent variable (traditional vs. nontraditional student) and the dependent variable (political preference).

Chapter 8

8.1. Tukey HSD procedure. The F statistic establishes that *some* of the means differ significantly; the Tukey HSD post-hoc comparison procedure determines *which* pairs of means differ.

8.2. The omega-square statistic. Omega-square provides a measure of the strength of the association between an independent variable (year in college) and the dependent variable (absenteeism). Ranging from 0 to 1, ω^2 provides an indication of the degree to which knowing a case's level on the independent variable enables predicting that case's score on the dependent variable (or vice versa).

8.3. Completely randomized one-way ANOVA. This research question involves a comparison of three independent samples on a dependent variable (productivity) that is measured on a ratio scale.

8.4. Randomized-block one-way ANOVA. This research question involves a repeated-measures comparison on an interval scale dependent variable.

8.5. Kruskal-Wallis one-way analysis of variance by ranks. This research question involves the comparison of three independent samples on a dependent variable measured on an ordinal scale.

8.6. The one-way ANOVA assumes that: (a) the dependent variable is measured on an interval or ratio scale; (b) the samples are drawn from populations that are normally distributed; and (c) the samples are drawn from populations showing approximately equal variances. Examination of these data show that the latter two assumptions are not met. None of the sample distributions is even approximately normal in shape, and the sample variances differ dramatically, ranging from 5.69 for the third to 254.11 for the second.

8.7. Sample descriptive statistics follow.

Freshmen	Sophomores	Juniors	Seniors
$\overline{X}_1 = 2.57$	$\overline{X}_2 = 2.50$	$\overline{X}_3 = 1.11$	$\overline{X}_4 = 1.00$
$N_1 = 7$	$N_2 = 8$	$N_3 = 9$	$N_4 = 9$

$\overline{X}_G = 1.73$
$N = 33$

The completely randomized ANOVA is computed using Equations 8.1 to 8.6. Results are summarized in the following ANOVA summary table.

Source	SS	df	MS	*F*
Between groups	17.94	3	5.98	8.42
Within groups	20.60	29	.71	
Total	38.55			

For 3 ("df numerator") and 29 ("df denominator") degrees of freedom, the critical value of F marking the .01 critical region is 4.54. The obtained F exceeds this critical value. We conclude that the samples differ significantly.

8.8. Post-hoc pairwise comparisons are performed following a significant completely randomized one-way ANOVA using Tukey's HSD. HSD is computed according to Equation 8.15:

$$\text{HSD} = q_{(\alpha,\, \text{df}_{\text{Within}},\, k)} \sqrt{\frac{\text{MS}_{\text{Within}}}{n}}$$

$$= q_{(.05,29,4)} \cdot \sqrt{\frac{.71}{7}}$$

$$= 3.90 \sqrt{\frac{.71}{7}}$$

$$= 1.24$$

Four pairwise differences meet or exceed this standard for significance: $\overline{X}_1 - \overline{X}_3 = 1.46, \overline{X}_2 - \overline{X}_3 = 1.39, \overline{X}_1 - \overline{X}_4 = 1.57$, and $\overline{X}_2 - \overline{X}_4 = 1.50$.

8.9. Omega-square for the completely randomized one-way ANOVA is computed according to Equation 8.17:

$$\omega^2 = \frac{SS_{Between} - (k - 1)MS_{Within}}{SS_{Total} + MS_{Within}}$$

$$= \frac{17.94 - (4 - 1).71}{38.55 + .71}$$

$$= .40$$

Because ω^2 ranges from 0 to 1, $\omega^2 = 40$ reflects a moderate association between the independent variable (year in school) and the dependent variable (absenteeism).

8.10. Sample descriptive statistics follow.

Quiet	Rock	Classical
$\overline{X}_1 = 8.10$	$\overline{X}_2 = 6.80$	$\overline{X}_3 = 8.10$

The randomized-block one-way ANOVA is computed according to Equations 8.7 to 8.14. Results are summarized in the following ANOVA summary table.

Source	SS	df	MS	F
Subjects	15.98	9	1.78	
Treatments	11.27	2	5.64	2.71
Residual	37.42	18	2.08	
Total	64.67			

For 2 ("df numerator") and 18 ("df denominator") degrees of freedom, the critical value of *F* marking the .05 critical region is 3.55. The obtained value of *F* fails to reach this critical value. We conclude that there are no significant differences among the conditions examined.

8.11. Tukey's HSD is computed for the randomized-block one-way ANOVA according to Equation 8.16:

$$HSD = q_{(\alpha,\, df_{Residual},\, k)} \sqrt{\frac{MS_{Residual}}{n}}$$

$$= q_{(.05,18,3)} \sqrt{\frac{2.08}{10}}$$

$$= 3.61 \sqrt{\frac{2.08}{10}}$$

$$= 1.65$$

None of the pairwise differences meets this standard for significance.

8.12. Omega-square for the randomized-block one-way ANOVA is computed according to Equation 8.18:

$$\omega^2 = \frac{SS_{Treatments} - (k - 1)MS_{Residual}}{SS_{Total} + MS_{Residual}}$$

$$= \frac{11.27 - (3 - 1)\,2.08}{64.67 + 2.08}$$

$$= .11$$

Since ω^2 ranges from 0 to 1, $\omega^2 = .11$ reflects a very weak association between the independent variable (working conditions) and the dependent variable (math performance).

8.13. These data are inappropriate for analysis using a parametric statistical procedure such as the completely randomized one-way ANOVA because the sample distributions all show a strong positive skew. This indicates that the populations these samples represent are probably also skewed. Parametric statistics assume that populations are normally distributed.

8.14. The Kruskal-Wallis one-way ANOVA by ranks analyzes rank-order data. We begin by combining the reaction-time scores from all three groups and ranking these scores in ascending order.

0 Glasses		2 Glasses		4 Glasses	
Raw	*Rank*	*Raw*	*Rank*	*Raw*	*Rank*
.1	2	.1	2	.1	2
.2	5.5	.4	12.5	.6	20.5
.2	5.5	.4	12.5	.6	20.5
.2	5.5	.4	12.5	.6	20.5
.2	5.5	.4	12.5	.6	20.5
.3	8.5	.5	16.5	.6	20.5
.3	8.5	.5	16.5	.7	25
.4	12.5	.6	20.5	.7	25
.4	12.5	.7	25	.9	27
Mean ranks:	7.33		14.50		20.17

The *H* test statistic in the Kruskal-Wallis one-way ANOVA by ranks is computed according to Equation 8.19:

$$H = \frac{12}{N(N + 1)}\left[\Sigma\frac{(\Sigma R)^2}{n}\right] - 3(N + 1)$$

$$= \frac{12}{27(27 + 1)}\left[\frac{(66)^2}{9} + \frac{(130.5)^2}{9} + \frac{(181.5)^2}{9}\right] - 3(27 + 1)$$

$$= 11.82$$

The *H* statistic is evaluated against the sampling distribution of χ^2. For $k - 1 = 2$ degrees of freedom, the critical value of χ^2 marking the .01 level of significance is 9.210. The obtained value of *H* exceeds this critical value, and we conclude that the samples differ significantly in their reaction times.

8.15. Tukey's HSD is computed for the Kruskal-Wallis one-way ANOVA by ranks according to Equation 8.20:

$$HSD = \frac{q_{(\alpha,\, k,\, \infty)}}{\sqrt{2}} \sqrt{\frac{N(N + 1)}{6(n)}}$$

$$= \frac{q_{(.05,3,\infty)}}{\sqrt{2}} \sqrt{\frac{27(27 + 1)}{6(9)}}$$

$$= \frac{3.31}{\sqrt{2}}\sqrt{\frac{27(27 + 1)}{6(9)}}$$

$$= 8.76$$

Tukey's HSD indicates the minimum difference between two samples' mean ranks that is considered statistically significant at the chosen level of significance. Using this standard, we conclude that reaction times differ significantly between the first and third groups.

Chapter 9

9.1. **(a)** DV: achievement motivation
IV_1: failure
IV_2: gender
(b) DV: gang loyalty
IV_1: age
IV_2: income level
(c) DV: academic achievement
IV_1: teaching method
IV_2: time (four tests)

9.2. The fact that the lines in the first diagram are not parallel indicates an interaction effect. There is also a main effect of factor *A* (noise level), shown by the declining math performance seen as one moves from no noise to low noise to high noise. Finally, a main effect of factor *B* (type of noise) is shown by the difference in average altitudes of the lines representing white noise and music. We can conclude from this bar graph that any type of noise, be it music or white noise, has a deleterious effect on performance in math, but the negative effect of musical noise occurs at lower volume levels than for white noise.

The fact that the lines in this second line graph are parallel indicates that there is no interaction effect. A main effect of factor *A* (type of job) is shown by the generally higher job satisfaction of white-collar workers than of blue-collar workers. A main effect of factor *B* (father's occupation) is shown by the generally higher levels of job satisfaction seen among workers whose fathers held blue-collar jobs.

9.3. Row, column, cell, and grand means are given below.

Factor A: Type of Instruction	Factor B: Type of Student b₁ *Traditional*	b₂ *Nontraditional*	
a₁ *televised*	72.00	78.75	$\overline{X}_{a_1} = 75.38$
a₂ *classroom*	92.50	87.75	$\overline{X}_{a_2} = 90.13$
	$\overline{X}_{b_1} = 82.25$	$\overline{X}_{b_2} = 83.25$	$\overline{X}_G = 82.75$

The line graph of cell means shows an $A \times B$ interaction effect as well as a factor *A* (type of instruction) main effect. There does not seem to be any main effect of factor *B* (type of student). Both traditional and nontraditional students do better in statistics when taught in the classroom than via television. However, this effect is somewhat stronger for traditional students than for nontraditional students.

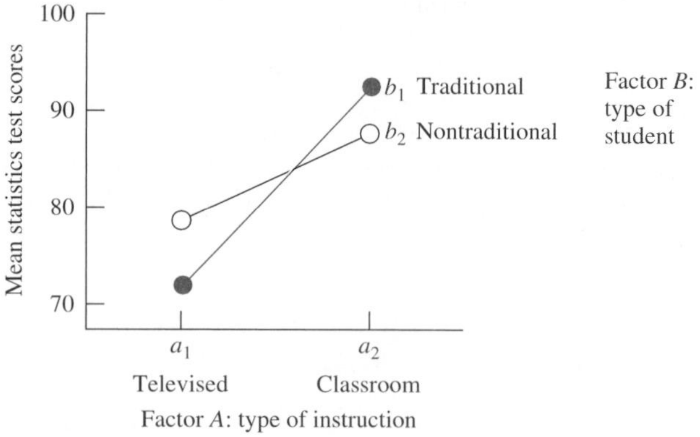

9.4. The completely randomized factorial ANOVA is computed according to Equations 9.1 to 9.9. Results are summarized in the following ANOVA summary table.

Source	SS	df	MS	*F*
Between	1,006.50	3		
A	870.25	1	870.25	51.07
B	4.00	1	4.00	.24
A × B	132.25	1	132.25	7.76
Within	204.50	12	17.04	
Total	1,211.00	15		

F_A is significant at the .01 level of significance. F_{AB} is significant at the .05 level of significance.

9.5. The comparison value, *C*, is computed according to Equation 9.14:

$$C = w_1\overline{X}_1 + w_2\overline{X}_2 + w_3\overline{X}_3 + w_4\overline{X}_4$$

$$= 1(72.00) + 1(78.75) - 1(92.50) - 1(87.75)$$

$$= -29.50$$

Equation 9.15 is used to compute the test statistic *t:*

$$t = \frac{C}{\sqrt{\text{MS}_{\text{Within}}[(w_1^2/N_1) + (w_2^2/N_2) + (w_3^2/N_3) + (w_4^2/N_4)]}}$$

$$= \frac{-29.50}{\sqrt{17.04(1^2/4) + (1^2/4) + (-1^2/4) + (-1^2/4)}}$$

$$= -7.15$$

Equation 9.16 is used to compute t_{Critical}:

$$t_{\text{Critical}} = \sqrt{(k - 1)F_{(\alpha,\, \text{df}_{\text{Between}},\, \text{df}_{\text{Within}})}}$$

$$= \sqrt{(4 - 1)F_{(.05,\, 3,\, 12)}}$$

$$= \sqrt{(4 - 1)3.49}$$

$$= 3.24$$

Because the obtained t exceeds t_{Critical}, we can conclude that the difference between row means is statistically significant. We knew this, though, from the significant F_A, making this post-hoc comparison unnecessary.

9.6. Tukey's HSD is computed according to Equation 8.15:

$$\text{HSD} = q_{(\alpha,\, \text{df}_{\text{Within}},\, k)}\sqrt{\frac{\text{MS}_{\text{Within}}}{n}}$$

$$= q_{(.05,12,4)}\sqrt{\frac{17.04}{4}}$$

$$= 4.20.\sqrt{\frac{17.04}{4}}$$

$$= 8.67$$

Based on an inspection of the line graph of the cell means in this analysis, perhaps the most interesting post-hoc comparisons involve assessing differences in performance between televised and classroom instruction. Among traditional students there is a statistically significant difference in favor of classroom instruction over televised instruction: 92.50 − 72 = 20.50 points. The same advantage of classroom instruction over televised instruction is seen among nontraditional students, but is somewhat less pronounced: 87.75 − 78.75 = 9.0 points.

9.7. Omega-square values are computed according to Equations 9.17 to 9.19:

$$\omega_A^2 = \frac{\text{SS}_A - (\text{df}_A)\text{MS}_{\text{Within}}}{\text{SS}_{\text{Total}} + \text{MS}_{\text{Within}}}$$

$$= \frac{870.25 - (1)17.04}{1{,}211.00 + 17.04}$$

$$= .69$$

$$\omega_B^2 = \frac{\text{SS}_B - (\text{df}_B)\text{MS}_{\text{Within}}}{\text{SS}_{\text{Total}} + \text{MS}_{\text{Within}}}$$

$$= \frac{4.00 - (1)17.04}{1{,}211.00 + 17.04}$$

= 0 (A negative value of ω^2 is uninterpretable, so when the computed value of ω^2 is negative, as it is here, it is set to 0)

$$\omega_{AB}^2 = \frac{\text{SS}_{AB} - (\text{df}_{AB})\text{MS}_{\text{Within}}}{\text{SS}_{\text{Total}} + \text{MS}_{\text{Within}}}$$

$$= \frac{138.25 - (1)17.04}{1{,}211.00 + 17.04}$$

$$= .10$$

Because ω^2 ranges from 0 to 1, we can see that the factor A main effect (type of instruction) is the most potent effect in the analysis. There is essentially no effect of factor B (type of student). Although the $A \times B$ interaction effect is statistically significant, the strength of the effect is quite weak.

Chapter 10

10.1. **(a)** The relationship between IQ and managerial performance that is described is nonlinear but monotonic. Of the three correlational statistics examined in this chapter, one, the Spearman rank-order correlation, is most appropriate to evaluating this type of relationship.

(b) Both geographic region and political preference are nominal scale variables. The χ^2 test of association and the Cramer's V statistic are suited to evaluating this type of relationship.

(c) The Pearson correlation is most suited to measuring the relationship between two interval or ratio scale variables such as family annual income and parenting effectiveness test scores.

10.2. The scatterplot shows that the relationship between GRE scores and graduate GPA is generally positive, of moderate strength, and possibly nonlinear but monotonic.

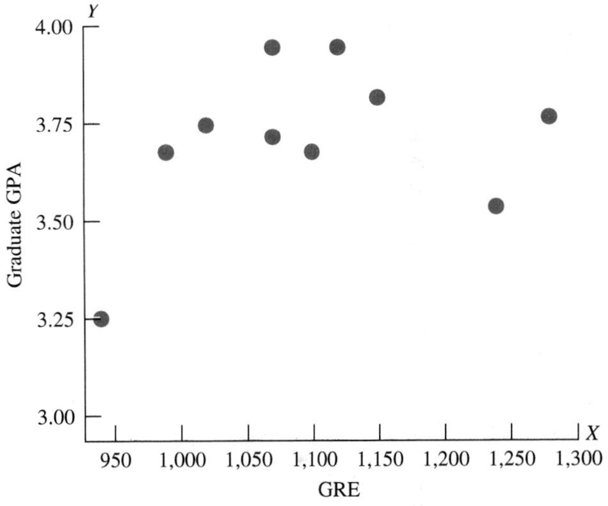

10.3. We begin by converting raw scores to z scores.

GRE	z_X	Grad. GPA	z_Y
1020	−.78	3.74	.21
940	−1.57	3.25	−2.37
1120	.22	3.94	1.26
1070	−.28	3.94	1.26
1280	1.81	3.76	.32
1070	−.28	3.71	.05
1150	.52	3.81	.58
990	−1.08	3.67	−.16
1240	1.41	3.53	−.89
1100	.02	3.67	−.16

Next, r_P is computed according to Equation 10.1:

$$r_P = \frac{\Sigma z_X z_Y}{N}$$

$$= \frac{(-.78 \times .21) + (-1.57 \times -2.37) + \ldots + (.02 \times -.16)}{10}$$

$$= .32$$

This tells us that there is a weak to moderate linear relationship between GRE scores and graduate GPA.

10.4. The Pearson correlation is computed according to Equation 10.1. For the entire data set, $r_P = .73$. For cases with IQs of 110 and higher, $r_P = .30$. By restricting the variance on the IQ variable, we have restricted the ability of the variables to covary and correlate. This is why the second correlation is lower than the first.

10.5. The outlier is the case with an age of 47 and income of $27,000. In a scatterplot of these data, this case is located noticeably away from the majority of other cases. Including the outlier in the correlation between age and income, $r_P = .78$. Excluding the outlier, $r_P = .89$. The outlier exerts a disproportionate attenuating effect on the size of the computed correlation.

10.6. **(a)** The critical value of r_P marking the .05 level of significance for df $= N - 2 = 8$ is .5494. (We use a one-tail test because one would expect a positive correlation between GRE and graduate GPA.) The obtained value of $r_P = .32$ falls short of this critical value and is considered statistically nonsignificant.

(b) The critical value of r_P marking the .01 level of significance for df $= N - 2 = 8$ is .7155. (We use a one-tail test because one would expect a positive correlation between IQ and undergraduate GPA.) The obtained value of $r_P = .73$ (using the full data set) exceeds this critical value and is considered statistically significant at the .01 level.

(c) The critical value of r_P marking the .05 level of significance for df $= N - 2 = 4$ is .7293. (We use a one-tail test because one would expect a positive correlation between age and income.) The obtained value of $r_P = .78$ (including data from the outlier) exceeds this critical value and is considered statistically significant at the .05 level.

10.7. We begin by ranking the cases on each variable.

GRE	GRE Rank	Grad. GPA	GPA Rank
1,020	3	3.74	6
940	1	3.25	1
1,120	7	3.94	9.5
1,070	4.5	3.94	9.5
1,280	10	3.76	7
1,070	4.5	3.71	5
1,150	8	3.81	8
990	2	3.67	3.5
1,240	9	3.53	2
1,100	6	3.67	3.5

Next, r_S is computed according to Equation 10.2:

$$r_S = 1 - \frac{6\Sigma D^2}{N(N^2 - 1)}$$

$$= 1 - \frac{6(-3^2 + 0^2 + \cdots + 2.5^2)}{10(10^2 - 1)}$$

$$= .35$$

The Spearman rank-order correlation, $r_S = .35$ computed for these data is approximately the same as the Pearson correlation computed previously, $r_P = .32$.

10.8. The critical value of r_S marking the .05 level of significance for $N = 10$ is .564. (We use a one-tail test because one would expect a positive correlation between GRE scores and graduate GPA.) The obtained value of $r_S = .35$ fails to reach this critical value, and we conclude that the relationship between GRE scores and graduate GPA is nonsignificant.

10.9. We first compute expected frequencies (f_e) for each cell of the contingency table. These are shown in parentheses.

Marital status

Major	*Single*	*Married*	*Divorced*	**Row Totals**	**Row %**
Sociology	8 (9.13)	6 (7.72)	12 (9.13)	26	35.1%
Psychology	14 (11.23)	10 (9.50)	8 (11.23)	32	43.2%
Social Work	4 (5.62)	6 (4.75)	6 (5.62)	16	21.6%
Column Totals	26	22	26	$N = 74$	

Next, χ^2 is computed according to Equation 7.7:

$$\chi^2 = \Sigma\frac{(f_o - f_e)^2}{f_e}$$

$$= \frac{(8 - 9.13)^2}{9.13} + \frac{(6 - 7.72)^2}{7.72} + \ldots + \frac{(6 - 5.62)^2}{5.62}$$

$$= 3.89$$

The critical value of χ^2 marking the .05 level of significance for df $= (R - 1)(C - 1) = (3 - 1)(3 - 1) = 4$ is 9.488. The obtained $\chi^2 = 3.89$ falls short of this critical value, and we conclude that there is no statistically significant relationship between marital status and academic major.

10.10. Cramer's V is computed according to Equation 7.10:

$$V = \sqrt{\frac{\chi^2}{N(n - 1)}}$$

$$= \sqrt{\frac{3.89}{74(3 - 1)}}$$

$$= .16$$

Since V can range from 0 to 1, $V = .16$ represents a weak relationship between the variables.

Chapter 11

11.1. The regression line for Y on X is placed so as to summarize the linear relationship between undergraduate GPA (X) and graduate GPA (Y). Using this regression line, we would estimate a graduate GPA of about 3.75 for a student whose undergraduate GPA is 3.5.

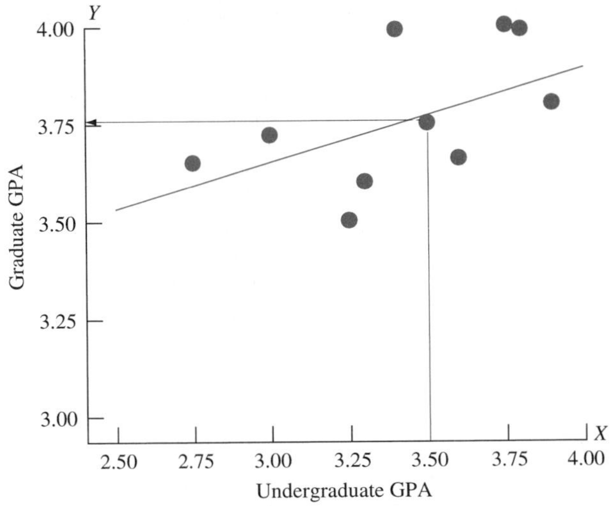

11.2. The regression coefficient (b_Y) is computed according to Equation 11.2:

$$b_Y = r\left(\frac{s_Y}{s_X}\right)$$

$$= .56\left(\frac{.15}{.35}\right)$$

$$= .24$$

The regression constant (a) is computed according to Equation 11.3:

$$a = \overline{Y} - b_Y\overline{X}$$

$$= 3.75 - .24(3.43)$$

$$= 2.93$$

The least-squares linear regression equation, Equation 11.1, is used to compute Y' values for each case. For example, for $X = 2.75$,

$$Y' = a + b_YX$$

$$= 2.93 + .24(2.75)$$

$$= 3.59$$

Similarly, for $X = 3.60$,

$$Y' = a + b_YX$$

$$= 2.93 + .24(3.60)$$

$$= 3.79$$

Predicted graduate GPAs are listed below for each of the 10 cases. (Also shown are residual scores ($Y - Y'$) for Review Exercise 11.4.)

X **Undergraduate GPA**	Y **Graduate GPA**	Y' **Predicted Graduate GPA**	$Y - Y'$ **Residuals**
2.75	3.65	3.59	.06
3.60	3.65	3.79	−.14
3.25	3.50	3.71	−.21
3.80	3.90	3.84	.06
3.40	3.95	3.75	.15
3.00	3.72	3.65	.07
3.90	3.80	3.87	−.07
3.30	3.60	3.72	−.12
3.50	3.75	3.77	−.02
3.75	4.00	3.83	.17

These predicted graduate GPAs are plotted with asterisks for each case in the following scatterplot.

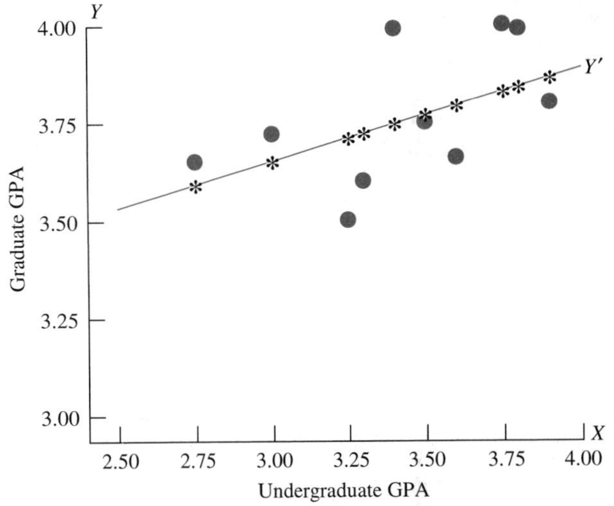

These predicted values follow the regression line of Y on X. The regression constant (a) sets the altitude of the regression line. It is the predicted value of Y when $X = 0$. The regression coefficient (b_Y) sets the slope of the regression line. It indicates how many points predicted graduate GPA (Y') will increase for each 1-point increase in undergraduate GPA (X).

11.3. It would be inappropriate to predict graduate GPA (Y) for students with undergraduate GPAs (X) below 2.75 because we don't know for sure what the relationship between X and Y looks like below $X = 2.75$.

11.4. Residual scores ($Y - Y'$) are listed in the table for Review Exercise 11.2. Each residual score indicates the amount and direction of the prediction error for each case in the analysis.

11.5. The coefficient of determination is computed according to Equation 11.5:

$$r^2 = \frac{s^2_{Y'}}{s^2_Y} = .31$$

This tells us that 31% of the variance in graduate GPA (Y) is predicted by undergraduate GPA (X).

11.6. The coefficient of nondetermination is computed according to Equation 11.10:

$$1 - r^2 = \frac{s^2_{Y-Y'}}{s^2_Y} = .69$$

This tells us that 69% of the variance in graduate GPA (Y) is not predicted by undergraduate GPA (X).

11.7. Predicted variance is most conveniently computed according to Equation 11.6:

$$s^2_{Y'} = (r^2)s^2_Y$$

$$= (.31).02$$

$$= .006$$

This is the variance of the predicted graduate GPAs (Y'). Residual variance is most conveniently computed according to Equation 11.11:

$$s^2_{Y-Y'} = (1 - r^2)s^2_Y$$

$$= (.69).02$$

$$= .014$$

This is the variance of the residual ($Y - Y'$) scores, as well as the average squared error of prediction.

11.8. The standard error of the estimate is computed according to Equation 11.12:

$$s_{Y-Y'} = \sqrt{s^2_{Y-Y'}}$$

$$= .12$$

This value is approximately equal to the average absolute error made in predicting graduate GPA (Y) from undergraduate GPA (X).

11.9. Equations 11.1 to 11.3 can be used to predict X from Y by relabeling undergraduate GPA as the Y variable and graduate GPA as the X variable. The regression line of X on Y is shown in the scatterplot that follows.

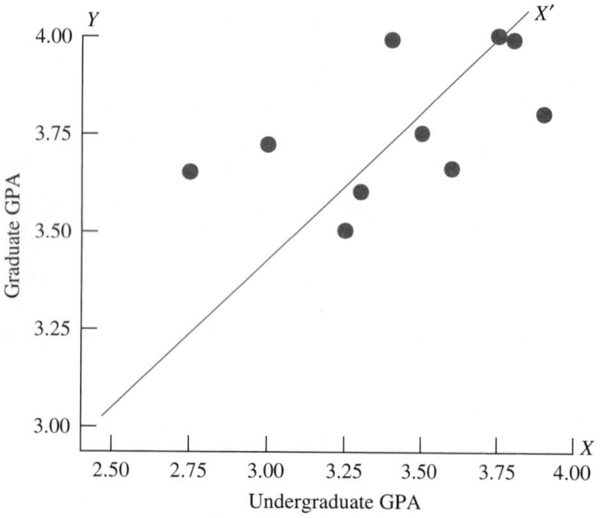

Chapter 12

12.1. Independent-samples t test
12.2. Completely randomized factorial analysis of variance
12.3. Prediction of category based on observed frequencies in the contingency table
12.4. Chi-square test for two independent samples
12.5. Dependent-samples t test
12.6. Completely randomized one-way analysis of variance
12.7. Mann-Whitney U
12.8. Specify category membership
12.9. Confidence interval for p_U
12.10. Specify percentages of proportions in each category and/or indicate modal category
12.11. Bivariate regression
12.12. Specify the case's rank order
12.13. Range, interquartile range, variance, and/or standard deviation
12.14. Kruskal-Wallis one-way analysis of variance by ranks
12.15. Dependent-samples t test
12.16. Chi-square goodness-of-fit test
12.17. One-sample t test
12.18. Wilcoxon T test
12.19. Randomized-block one-way analysis of variance
12.20. Mean, median, and/or mode
12.21. Percentile rank and/or z score
12.22. Pearson correlation
12.23. Spearman rank-order correlation
12.24. Chi-square test of association
12.25. Confidence interval for the population mean

Glossary

Abscissa The horizontal axis of a graph, used to represent scores or class intervals in data distributions and to represent the *X* variable in a scatterplot.

Addition rule A rule of probability that states that the probability of observing one or another of a set of mutually exclusive events is equal to the sum of the separate probabilities of those events.

Alternative hypothesis An explanation of an observed sample difference or correlation that attributes that sample result to the operation of more than sampling error.

Analysis of variance A family of procedures used to evaluate the significance of differences observed between two or more samples.

Analysis of variance summary table Used to summarize the results of ANOVA computations in a standard format.

Apparent limits The top and bottom scores included in each of the class intervals that form a grouped distribution.

Association strength Measures of association strength are statistics used in conjunction with significant-difference tests to measure the strength of association between the independent and dependent variables.

Bar graph A type of graph used with nominal scale data to depict frequency or percentage distributions. The altitude of the bars on the ordinate represents the frequency or percentage of cases in each nominal scale category.

Between-group factors Factors in an ANOVA whose levels are represented by independent samples.

Between-group variance Variability seen between the means of different treatment conditions.

Bimodal Refers to a distribution that shows two clear frequency peaks. A bimodal distribution suggests the presence of two distinct subgroups within the data set.

Bivariate regression analysis A statistical procedure that predicts one variable from a second based on the correlation between the two.

Case The unit of observation about which data are recorded.

Central limit theorem A theorem that describes the essential characteristics of the sampling distribution of the mean and related sampling distributions.

Central tendency Refers to the average or typical score in a distribution.

Chi-square goodness-of-fit test A nonparametric significance test that uses the χ^2 statistic to evaluate the difference between a sample distribution and a population distribution.

Chi-square test for two independent samples A nonparametric significance test that uses the χ^2 statistic to evaluate the difference between the distributions of two independent samples.

Chi-square test of association A test of the relationship between two nominal scale variables.

Class intervals Groups or ranges of adjacent scores used in grouped data distributions.

Coefficient of determination The proportion of variance in *Y* that is explained by *X* in regression analysis.

Coefficient of nondetermination The proportion of variance in *Y* that is not explained by *X* in regression analysis.

Completely randomized factorial analysis of variance A fully crossed factorial ANOVA in which each treatment combination is represented by an independent sample.

Completely randomized one-way analysis of variance A one-way ANOVA that compares two or more independent samples.

Confidence interval A range of values computed from sample data that has some known probability of capturing the population parameter being estimated.

Confidence interval for the population mean A range of values computed from sample data that has a known probability of capturing the population mean.

Confidence interval for the population proportion A range of values computed from sample data that has a known probability of capturing the population proportion.

Contingency table A table used to organize the data analyzed using the chi-square test for two independent samples and the chi-square test of association.

Converse rule A rule of probability stating that the probability that an event will not occur is equal to 1 minus the probability that the event will occur.

Corrected sample variance Computed from sample data, the corrected sample variance provides an estimate of the population variance.

Correlation A relationship between variables. A variety of statistics are used to measure the strength and statistical significance of correlations.

Correlational research Research in which two variables are passively measured in order to determine if the two vary together, that is, are correlated.

Cramer's *V* A measure of association strength used in conjunction with the χ^2 statistic.

Critical regions The extreme tail(s) of a sampling distribution. Statistics falling within the critical regions are considered unlikely to have occurred as a result of sampling error alone.

Critical values Values of a test statistic that mark the extreme tail(s) of a sampling distribution. Values exceeding the critical values are considered unlikely to have occurred as a result of sampling error alone.

Cross-validation Procedure used to check the predictive accuracy of a regression equation.

Data Numerical facts about cases. Data can represent qualitative characteristics of each case or can convey information about the quantity of some attribute possessed by each case.

Degrees of freedom Refers to the number of values that are free to vary once we have placed certain restrictions on the data. The specific shape of many sampling distributions depends on how many degrees of freedom there are in the situation.

Dependent variable The dependent variable is passively observed and measured in an experiment to see if it has been affected by the experimenter's manipulations of the independent variable.

Dependent-samples *t* test A parametric significance test that uses the *t* statistic to evaluate the difference between the means of two dependent samples.

Descriptive statistics Statistical procedures that serve to describe some characteristic of the cases represented by the data being analyzed.

Disordinal interaction effect An interaction effect represented in a line graph by crossed lines. The effect of one factor is reversed depending on the level of the other factor.

Empirical distribution A distribution of actual scores. Empirical distributions describe real data.

Experiment A type of research used to establish cause-and-effect relationships. One variable, the independent variable, is manipulated by the experimenter, and a second variable, the dependent variable, is measured subsequent to this manipulation.

Explained variance The variance of the predicted values in a regression analysis. Synonymous with predicted variance.

Ex-post-facto research A form of nonexperimental research involving comparisons of preexisting groups.

***F* statistic** The ratio of between-group variance to within-group variance used as the test statistic in ANOVA procedures.

Factor In the terminology of ANOVA, a factor is the same as an independent variable.

Factor *A* mean squares A measure of between-group variance due to factor *A* in a factorial ANOVA.

Factor *A* sum of squares A measure of between-group variability due to factor *A* in a factorial ANOVA.

Factor *B* mean squares A measure of between-group variance due to factor *B* in a factorial ANOVA.

Factor *B* sum of squares A measure of between-group variability due to factor *B* in a factorial ANOVA.

Factorial analysis of variance A family of ANOVA procedures that examines the separate and combined effects of two or more independent variables within the context of a single study.

Fixed effects models A factorial ANOVA in which all factors include all levels of interest to the researcher.

Frequency curve Similar to the frequency polygon, except that the lines connecting the points are replaced with a smooth curve.

Frequency polygon A type of graph used to depict distributions of ordinal, interval, and ratio scale data. The altitude of a point represents the frequency or percentage of each score or class interval. The points of the frequency polygon are connected with straight lines.

Fully crossed designs A factorial ANOVA design in which all possible combinations of the levels of the factors are examined.

Grouped data distribution Tables or graphs that indicate frequency, percentage, cumulative frequency, and/or cumulative percentage information for each of several class intervals in a data set.

***H* statistic** The test statistic in the Kruskal-Wallis one-way ANOVA by ranks.

Heteroscedasticity Refers to the degree to which the relationship between two continuous variables changes in strength across the range of the two variables.

Higher-order interaction Any interaction effect involving more than two factors.

Histogram A type of graph similar to a bar graph, except that there is no separation between the bars. Histograms are used to depict distributions of ordinal, interval, and ratio scale data.

Homoscedasticity Refers to the degree to which a relationship between two continuous variables is of approximately equal strength across the entire range of both variables.

Independent events Two or more events are independent if the occurrence of one event in no way affects the probability of the occurrence of the other event.

Independent variable In an experiment, the independent variable is actively manipulated by the experimenter to see if it has a causal effect on a second variable, the dependent variable.

Independent-samples t test A parametric significant difference test that uses the t statistic to evaluate the difference between the means of two independent samples.

Individual difference characteristics Refers to differences from one case to the next that introduce variability into the scores of identically treated cases.

Inferential statistics Statistical procedures that enable generalizing from sample data to the larger population.

Interaction effect When the effect of one factor in a factorial ANOVA is conditional upon the level of another factor.

Interaction mean squares A measure of between-group variance due to the interaction of factors in a factorial ANOVA.

Interaction sum of squares A measure of between-group variability due to the interaction of factors in a factorial ANOVA.

Interquartile range A measure of data variability equal to the difference between the scores at the 75th and 25th percentiles.

Interval estimation An inferential statistical procedure used to estimate population parameters from sample data through the construction of confidence intervals.

Interval scale Quantitative measurement that bases scores for each case on the number of fixed-size units of the attribute possessed by that case. The zero point is arbitrary; that is, 0 does not necessarily indicate the absence of the attribute.

Interval width Refers to the width of class intervals in a grouped data distribution. Interval width is equal to the difference between the upper limit and the lower limit of each interval, plus 1.

Kruskal-Wallis one-way analysis of variance by ranks A nonparametric alternative to the completely randomized one-way ANOVA used to analyze rank-order data.

Kurtosis Refers to the relative flatness or peakedness of a distribution.

Least-squares linear regression equation The equation that defines the regression line so as to minimize the sum of the squared errors of prediction.

Leptokurtic Refers to a distribution that is more peaked or steeper than a normal distribution.

Line graphs Plots of the cell means obtained from factorial ANOVA designs.

Linear relationship In a scatterplot, a linear relationship between X and Y is one that can best be described by a straight line.

Main effect The effect of any single factor in a factorial ANOVA.

Mann-Whitney U A nonparametric significance test that uses the U statistic to evaluate the difference in rank orders of two independent samples.

Matched-samples research design A research design in which the cases that comprise one sample are selected specifically so as to match the characteristics of cases comprising a second sample.

Mean The most common measure of central tendency. The mean is the arithmetic balancing point in the distribution.

Mean squares between groups A measure of between-group variance used in analysis of variance.

Mean squares within groups A measure of within-group variance used in analysis of variance.

Measurement The use of any rule to assign numbers to cases so as to represent the presence or absence or quantity of some attribute possessed by each case.

Measurement error Inaccuracy in measurement that introduces variability into the scores of identically treated cases.

Median A measure of central tendency above and below which an equal number of cases score. The middle score in a distribution.

Mesokurtic Refers to a distribution that is of moderate peakedness. A normal distribution is mesokurtic.

Midpoint The value falling exactly halfway between the upper and lower limits of a class interval in a grouped distribution.

Mixed effects models A factorial ANOVA in which the levels of some factors represent all levels of interest to the researcher, whereas the levels of other factors have been sampled randomly from the larger set that is of interest.

Mode A measure of central tendency defined as the most frequently occurring score(s), class interval(s), or nominal scale category or categories.

Monotonic relationship A relationship between two continuous variables in which the scatterplot shows either a straight line or a curve, excluding relationships in which the direction of the relationship reverses.

Multimodal Refers to a distribution that shows three or more clear frequency peaks. Multimodal distributions suggest the presence of multiple distinct subgroups within the data set.

Multiplication rule A rule of probability stating that the probability of observing a combination of two or more mutually exclusive, independent events is equal to the product of the separate probabilities of those events.

Mutually exclusive events Two or more events are mutually exclusive if only one of the events can occur on any single observation.

Negative correlation A correlation in which an increase in X is accompanied by a decrease in Y and vice versa.

Negative skew Refers to an asymmetrical distribution in which most scores are relatively high, with relatively few low-scoring outliers.

Nested designs A factorial ANOVA design in which some of the combinations of levels of the factors are not examined.

Nominal scale The level of measurement that involves determining for each case only the presence or absence of an attribute, not the quantity of the attribute.

Nonlinear relationship In a scatterplot, a nonlinear relationship is one that can best be described by a curve.

Nonparametric tests Significance tests that relax some of the assumptions associated with the parametric tests.

Normal distribution A theoretical distribution often approximated in nature. The normal distribution is bell-shaped and symmetrical, with specific percentages of cases falling between certain points.

Null hypothesis An explanation of an observed sample difference or correlation that attributes that sample result to sampling error.

Omega-square A measure of association strength used in conjunction with the t and F tests.

One-sample significant difference tests Procedures used to evaluate the significance of differences observed between a sample and a larger population.

One-sample *t* test A parametric significance test that uses the t statistic to evaluate the difference between a sample mean and a population mean.

One-tail significance test A one-tail significance test is used when the direction of the difference or correlation has been specified in advance of data collection.

One-way analysis of variance A family of significance tests used to evaluate the differences between two or more sample means.

Operational definitions Definitions of variables that specify the rules by which those variables are to be manipulated or measured.

Ordered array A set of scores arranged in either ascending or descending order.

Ordinal interaction effect An interaction effect represented in a line graph by diverging lines that do not cross. The effect of one factor is influenced by the level of the other factor, but is not reversed.

Ordinal scale The lowest level of measurement that still conveys quantitative information about cases. Ordinal measurement does not use a fixed-size unit of measure, so equal score differences do not necessarily reflect equal differences in the amount of the attribute being measured.

Ordinate The vertical axis of a graph, used to represent frequencies or percentages in data distributions and used to represent the Y variable in a scatterplot.

Outlier A case whose extreme score(s) mark it as unusual in the data distribution or scatterplot.

Parametric tests Significance tests that assume that the data being analyzed meet certain characteristics or parameters.

Pearson product-moment correlation A correlational statistic that measures the strength of linear relationship between two normally distributed interval or ratio scale variables.

Percentile Refers to the raw score corresponding to a specified percentile rank.

Percentile rank Refers to the percentage of cases in a data set that score at and below a given score or class interval. Synonymous with cumulative percentage.

Platykurtic Refers to a distribution that is flatter than a normal distribution.

Population The complete set of cases, often represented by the sample subset.

Positive correlation A correlation in which an increase in X is accompanied by an increase in Y and vice versa.

Positive skew Refers to an asymmetrical distribution in which most scores are relatively low, with relatively few high-scoring outliers.

Post-hoc comparisons Comparisons between samples that follow a significant ANOVA to identify the source(s) of the significant ANOVA.

Power Refers to the degree to which a significance test is resistant to Type II errors; the sensitivity of the test.

Predicted variance Synonymous with explained variance.

Probability The probability of an event is determined by that event's relative frequency of occurrence.

Qualitative data The data resulting from nominal level measurement. Indicates the qualities possessed by each case, but provides no quantitative information.

Quantitative data Numerical information resulting from ordinal, interval, or ratio scale measurement that conveys information about how much of some attribute each case possesses.

Quartiles The first quartile has a percentile rank of 25, the second quartile has a percentile rank of 50, and the third quartile has a percentile rank of 75.

Random effects models A factorial ANOVA in which the levels of all factors have been sampled randomly from some larger sets that are of interest to the researcher.

Randomized-block factorial analysis of variance A fully crossed ANOVA in which the treatment combinations are represented by dependent samples.

Randomized-block one-way analysis of variance A one-way ANOVA that compares two or more dependent samples.

Range A measure of data variability equal to the highest score minus the lowest score in the distribution.

Ratio scale Quantitative measurement that bases scores for each case on the number of fixed-size units of the attribute possessed by that case. The zero point is nonarbitrary; that is, 0 indicates the absence of the attribute.

Real limits Real limits extend beyond the upper and lower apparent limits of each class interval in a grouped distribution by one-half the unit of measure.

Rectangular distribution Refers to a distribution that has no noticeable frequency peak; all scores occur with approximately equal frequency.

Regression analysis An inferential statistical procedure used to predict one variable from another variable, based on the existence of a correlation between the two.

Regression coefficient A component of the regression equation that determines the slope of the regression line.

Regression constant A component of the regression equation that determines the altitude of the regression line. Synonymous with the term "*Y* intercept."

Regression line A line fitted through the points of a scatterplot that summarizes and describes the relationship between the variables.

Regression line of *X* on *Y* The regression line or equation used to predict *X* from *Y*.

Regression line of *Y* on *X* The regression line or equation used to predict *Y* from *X*.

Repeated-measures research design A research design in which the same cases are measured twice, before and after treatment.

Research design The plan for gathering data suitable to answering the research question at hand.

Residual scores Refers to differences between obtained and predicted values for each case in a regression analysis.

Residual sum of squares A measure of data variability due to measurement error and individual differences in the randomized block ANOVA.

Residual variance The variance of the residual scores in a regression analysis; the average squared error of prediction. Synonymous with unexplained variance.

Robustness Refers to the degree to which a statistical procedure is resistant to distortions when the data deviate from the parametric assumptions of the procedure.

Sample A group of cases that has been examined firsthand. A sample is a subset of a larger population, and samples are often examined because they are viewed as representative of larger populations.

Sampling distribution A theoretical distribution showing the frequency of occurrence of values of some statistic computed for all possible samples or sets of samples of some fixed size(s) sampled with replacement from a population.

Sampling distribution of χ^2 The theoretical distribution of values of the χ^2 statistic obtained when all possible samples or pairs of samples are drawn from a population and the χ^2 statistic is computed for each.

Sampling distribution of *F* The theoretical distribution of values of *F* obtained when all possible sets of samples are drawn from a population of identically treated cases and *F* is computed for each set.

Sampling distribution of r_P The theoretical distribution of values of r_P obtained from all possible samples of size *N* drawn from a population in which the variables are uncorrelated.

Sampling distribution of r_S The theoretical distribution of values of r_S obtained from all possible samples of size *N* drawn from a population in which the variables are uncorrelated.

Sampling distribution of *t* The theoretical distribution of values of the *t* statistic obtained when all possible samples or pairs of samples are drawn from a population and the *t* statistic is computed for each sample.

Sampling distribution of *T* The theoretical distribution of values of the Wilcoxon *T* statistic obtained when all possible dependent pairs of samples are drawn from a population of identically treated cases and the *T* statistic is computed for each pair.

Sampling distribution of the difference between means The theoretical distribution formed by drawing all possible pairs of samples from a population of identically treated cases, computing the difference between the means in each pair, and plotting the frequency of occurrence of these differences.

Sampling distribution of the mean A theoretical distribution showing the frequency of occurrence of values of the mean computed for all possible samples of size *N* sampled with replacement from a population.

Sampling distribution of the proportion A theoretical distribution showing the frequency of occurrence of values of the proportion computed for all possible samples of size *N* sampled with replacement from a population.

Sampling distribution of *U* The theoretical distribution of values of the Mann-Whitney *U* statistic obtained when all possible independent pairs of samples are drawn from a population of identically treated cases and *U* is computed for each pair.

Sampling error Refers to the random discrepancies that exist between the characteristics of a population and the characteristics of most samples drawn from that population.

Sampling with replacement A sampling procedure in which each case, once drawn for inclusion in a sample, is replaced into the population and becomes eligible for inclusion again in that same sample.

Sampling without replacement A sampling procedure in which each case, once drawn for inclusion in a sample, is not replaced into the population and therefore cannot be included more than once in any given sample.

Scatterplot A graph of the data in a correlational analysis that depicts the relationship between *X* and *Y*.

Scheffé test A post-hoc comparison procedure that enables comparing combinations of means.

Significance tests Inferential statistical procedures that determine which sample observations are strong enough to be considered replicable.

Significant difference tests A group of inferential statistical procedures that determine the likelihood that a difference seen in sample data is the result of chance fluctuations in the data.

Skew Refers to a deviation from normality in the shape of a distribution. Skewed distributions are lopsided.

Spearman rank-order correlation A correlational statistic that measures the relationship between two rank-order variables.

Split-plot factorial analysis of variance A fully crossed ANOVA that includes one or more within-subjects factors and one or more between-subjects factors.

Standard deviation A measure of data variability equal to the square root of the variance. Approximately equal to the average absolute deviation of scores around the mean.

Standard error of the difference The standard deviation of the sampling distribution of the difference between means.

Standard error of the estimate The square root of the residual variance; approximately equal to the average absolute error of prediction in regression analysis.

Standard error of the mean The standard deviation of the sampling distribution of the mean.

Standard normal distribution A normal distribution of standard (z) scores.

Standard scores A standard score, or z score, specifies the number of standard deviations between a score and the mean of the distribution.

Statistical significance A sample observation is statistically significant if the observation is probably true as well in the hypothetical population represented by that sample.

Statistics Procedures used to organize, condense, and analyze data. A statistic is also defined as a number computed from data that answers some question about those data.

Sum of squares A measure of data variability equal to the sum of squared deviations of scores around the mean.

Sum of squares between groups A measure of between-group variability based on the sum of squared deviations of sample means around the grand mean.

Sum of squares for subjects A measure of data variability due to individual differences in the randomized block ANOVA.

Sum of squares for treatments A measure of between-group variability in the randomized block ANOVA.

Sum of squares within groups A measure of within-group variability based on the sum of squared deviations of individual scores around the sample means.

Test statistic A number computed from data that varies in value as a function of the size of the difference or correlation being tested for significance.

Theoretical distribution An ideal, imaginary distribution of scores that exists only in theory, not in reality.

Three-way analysis of variance A factorial ANOVA that includes three factors.

Three-way interaction An interaction effect involving three factors.

Total sum of squares A measure of the total variability in the data, based on the sum of squared deviations of individual scores around the grand mean.

Total variance Refers to the variance of the obtained values of the criterion variable in regression analysis.

Treatment A term used loosely to refer to either: (1) an experimenter-administered manipulation or handling of a sample; or (2) some unique characteristic associated with a sample that is not under experimenter control.

Treatment effects Between-group differences on the dependent variable that are associated with the different treatments received by the different samples.

Tukey's HSD Tukey's "honestly significant difference" test is a post-hoc procedure used to perform pairwise comparisons of sample means.

Two-sample significant difference tests Procedures used to evaluate the significance of differences observed between two samples.

Two-tail significance test A two-tail significance test is used when the direction of the difference or correlation has not been specified in advance.

Two-way analysis of variance A factorial ANOVA that includes two factors.

Two-way interaction An interaction effect involving two factors.

Type I error A Type I error occurs when the null hypothesis is falsely rejected.

Type II error A Type II error occurs when we falsely fail to reject the null hypothesis.

Ungrouped cumulative frequency distribution A table or graph that indicates for each score in a data set the number of cases falling at that score and lower.

Ungrouped cumulative percentage distribution A table or graph that indicates for each score in a data set the percentage of cases falling at that score and lower. Cumulative percentages are also known as percentile ranks.

Ungrouped frequency distribution A table or graph that indicates the frequency of occurrence of each score in a data set.

Ungrouped percentage distribution A table or graph that indicates the percentage of cases in a data set receiving each score.

Unimodal Refers to a distribution that shows one clear frequency peak.

Variability Refers to the degree to which scores in a distribution are dispersed across a broad range.

Variable An attribute or characteristic that varies from one case to the next.

Variance A measure of data variability equal to the average squared deviation of scores around the mean.

Wilcoxon *T* test A nonparametric significance test that uses the Wilcoxon *T* statistic to evaluate the difference in rank orders of two dependent samples.

Within-group variance Refers to the variability of scores seen within each treatment condition.

Within-subjects factors Factors in an ANOVA whose levels are represented by dependent samples.

***X* axis** Synonymous with abscissa.

Yates's correction An adjustment used in computing the χ^2 statistic when a 2×2 contingency table contains expected frequencies less than 5.

***Y* axis** Synonymous with ordinate.

***Y* intercept** Synonymous with regression constant.

***z* score** Synonymous with standard score.

INDEX

W

X

Y

Z

Two Dependent Samples

Eq. 7.4 $$t_{\overline{X}_1-\overline{X}_2} = \frac{(\overline{X}_1 - \overline{X}_2) - \mu_{\overline{X}_1-\overline{X}_2}}{\hat{\sigma}_{\overline{D}}} \qquad \text{with df } = N-1$$

where $$\hat{\sigma}_{\overline{D}} = \frac{\sqrt{\Sigma(D-\overline{D})^2/(N-1)}}{\sqrt{N}}$$

Eq. 7.6 T = the smaller of: (1) the absolute sum of the positive ranks, or (2) the absolute sum of the negative ranks

Three or More Independent Samples

Eq. 8.1–8.6 Completely Randomized One-Way ANOVA

Source	SS	df	MS	F
Between Groups	$(\overline{X}_1 - \overline{X}_G)^2(N_1) +$ $(\overline{X}_2 - \overline{X}_G)^2(N_2) + \cdots +$ $(\overline{X}_k - \overline{X}_G)^2(N_k)$	$k - 1$	$\frac{SS_{\text{Between}}}{df_{\text{Between}}}$	$\frac{MS_{\text{Between}}}{MS_{\text{Within}}}$
Within Groups	$\sum_{i=1}^{N_1}(X_i - \overline{X}_1)^2 +$ $\sum_{i=1}^{N_2}(X_i - \overline{X}_2)^2 + \cdots +$ $\sum_{i=1}^{N_k}(X_i - \overline{X}_k)^2$	$N - k$	$\frac{SS_{\text{Within}}}{df_{\text{Within}}}$	
Total	$\sum_{i=1}^{N}(\overline{X}_i - \overline{X}_G)^2$			

Eq. 8.19 $$H = \frac{12}{N(N+1)}\left[\sum\frac{(\Sigma R_i)^2}{n_i}\right] - 3(N+1) \qquad \text{with df} = k-1$$